THE STATE OF
WORKING AMERICA

THE STATE OF
WORKING AMERICA
1996-97

LAWRENCE MISHEL

JARED BERNSTEIN

JOHN SCHMITT

ECONOMIC POLICY INSTITUTE

M. E. Sharpe
Armonk, New York
London, England

VISIT EPINET.ORG

The Economic Policy Institute's Web site
contains current analysis of issues addressed
in this book. There is also a section that
provides more comprehensive information
on some of the income, wage, and poverty
data series used in *The State of Working
America*. These data series are updated
with the latest information.

Recommended citation for this book is as follows:
Mishel, Lawrence, Jared Bernstein, and John Schmitt, *The State of Working America,
1996–1997*. Economic Policy Institute Series. Armonk: M. E. Sharpe, 1997.

ISBN: 0-7656-0023-4 (cloth)   0-7656-0024-2 (paper)

Printed in the United States of America

MV(c)   10   9   8   7   6   5   4   3   2   1
MV(p)   10   9   8   7   6   5   4   3

® GCIU

To my partner and wife, Sharon Simon.

L.M.

To my mother, Evelyn Bernstein, for her support and inspiration,
and to Kay, for her help throughout the writing of this book.

J.B.

To Sarah.

J.S.

Table of Contents

Acknowledgments

The preparation of this publication required the intensive work effort of many people on EPI's research staff. Jessica Burton and Miranda Martin diligently word processed the text and tables. Jorlie Cruz prepared all of the graphs and, along with David Hully, provided research assistance. David Webster and Yan Yuan did an enormous amount of excellent computer programming within a very short time-frame. The library staff, Terrel Hale and Rebecca Takacs, were a great help as well. Our colleagues provided much needed advice. In particular, Dean Baker, Max Sawicky, and Thea Lee helped with particular sections. Ruy Teixeira, Jeff Faux, Nan Gibson, and Edie Rasell provided useful comments on drafts. We are especially indebted to Edie Rasell for her work in constructing the income data series used for portions of Chapter 1.

It has been a pleasure to continue the partnership with Kim Arbogast and Patrick Watson in the development and production of this book. Pat reviewed every word we wrote and effectively edited, checked, made consistent, and substantially improved the text and presentation. Kim produced and designed the book. Nan Gibson, Elizabeth James, and Linda Ellis worked to provide a large audience. Maury Sullivan helped lay out the tables.

Many experts were helpful in providing data or their research papers for our use. We are particularly grateful to those who provided special tabulations: Dan Beller, Hank Farber, Peter Gottschalk, Richard Hinz, Allen Lerman, Jim Poterba, Andrew Samwick, Gene Steurle, and Edward Wolff. Others who provided data, advice, or their analysis include: Al Davis, Bruce Fallick, Ann Huff Stevens, Chinhui Juhn, Lynn Karoly, Lori Kletzer, Robert McIntyre, Bob McIntyre, Jack McNeil, Gordon Merman, Tom Nardone, Chuck Nelson, Marion Nichols, Anne Polivka, Larry Rosenblum, Shirley Smith, Carmen Devanos, Gary Sandefur, Wayne Shelley, and John Stinson.

We are grateful to the John D. & Catherine T. MacArthur Foundation and the Carnegie Corporation for providing support for the research and publication of this volume.

We also wish to thank the Russell Sage Foundation and the Rockefeller Foundation, which have supported our work on the relationship between wage inequality and technology. We also appreciate the support given by the Annie E. Casey Foundation, the John D. & Catherine T. MacArthur Foundation, the Carnegie Corporation, and the David and Lucille Packard Foundation for the development of the family income series we use in Chapter 1.

THE STATE OF
WORKING AMERICA

EXECUTIVE
SUMMARY

USING A WIDE VARIETY OF DATA ON FAMILY INCOMES, TAXES, WAGES, UNEM-
ployment, wealth, and poverty, *The State of Working America 1996-97* closely
examines the impact of the economy on the living standards of the American
people. The story we tell is one of great disparities.

As this book goes to press, the economy is in an expansion, but many of the
economic problems first evident in the 1980s continue to be felt. For example,
despite growth in both gross domestic product and employment between 1989
and 1995, median family income in 1995 was still $1,438 lower than it was in
1989, suggesting that overall growth does not, under current economic circumstances, lead to improved economic well-being for typical families. The 1980s'
trends toward greater income inequality and a tighter squeeze on the middle class
show clear signs of continuing in the 1990s.

The problem of deteriorating wages, which was primarily responsible for
the slow growth in incomes and widening inequality in the past, has not only
continued in the 1990s, but it has also pulled down new groups of workers. After more than a decade of wage growth for most women, the bottom two-thirds
of women in the workforce saw their wages decline between 1989 and 1995. In
the 1980s, families compensated for stagnant and declining male wages by working longer and sending more family members to work, a trend that appears to
have reached its maximum capacity. As a result, the incomes of middle-class
families have stagnated and fallen in the 1990s. At the same time, jobs have
become less secure and less likely to offer health and pension benefits. Middle-
class wealth (the value of tangible assets such as houses and cars, plus financial

3

assets, minus debts) has also fallen. These same factors have kept economically less-advantaged families in poverty despite an extended economic recovery.

American workers might be able to take some solace if their sacrifices now would eventually guarantee an improved standard of living for themselves or their children. Unfortunately, the country has little to show for the belt-tightening of the last 15 years: productivity growth and capital investment have been lackluster; only corporate profits and CEO pay are doing better than in the past.

To be sure, some bright spots have appeared. The unemployment rate in mid-1996 stands at 5.3%. Inflation hovers around 3.0% per year. Changes to the tax code in 1994 reversed some of the inequities built into the federal tax structure in the 1980s. The expansion of the earned income tax credit, in particular, was largely responsible for boosting the earnings of poor workers.

Nevertheless, the typical American family is worse off in the mid-1990s than it was at the end of the 1970s. The following is a summary of the economic realities that characterize the state of working America.

Family Incomes: Slow and Unequal Growth

Since 1979, the most important development regarding American incomes has been slow growth and increasing inequality. In the most recent period for which we have data, 1989-95, median family income fell by over $1,400, or 3.4%, despite a substantial rise in both 1994 and 1995. If the current economic recovery should end within the next two years or so, it is unlikely that the median family's income will have recovered its 1989 level. Meanwhile, the increase in income inequality has continued unabated in the first half of the 1990s.

This trend is disturbing for at least two reasons. First, although it is not surprising that incomes fell as unemployment rose between 1990 and 1992, the amount of the decline is greater than would be expected from a rise in the unemployment rate from 5.5% to 7.4%. Second, it is unique in the postwar period to have median family income fall during a recovery year, as it did in 1992-93 when unemployment fell, *average* incomes rose, and gross domestic product expanded.

Why have income trends continued to be negative in the 1990s? Along with overall slow growth, the primary reason is the continuing wage deterioration among middle- and low-wage earners, now joined by white-collar and even some groups of college-educated workers. Another key factor in understanding recent trends is the contribution of working wives.

In the 1980s, many families compensated for falling hourly compensation, which was particularly steep for male workers, by working more hours. Some families increased the number of family members in the paid workforce. In other families, the number of hours worked by members already in the labor force increased. In middle-income, married-couple families, for example, the average wife worked 314, or 35.8%, more hours in 1989 than in 1979. In the absence of increased hours and earnings by working wives, the incomes of the bottom 60% of married-couple families with children would have fallen in the 1980s. The 1990s, however, saw a notable slowdown in the growth (and, for some groups, even a decline) in hours and earnings of working wives in families with children. Wives' contributions were no longer able to offset the lower earnings of their husbands (whose wages continued to fall, except for the top 5% of earners). By 1994, all but the top 5% of married couples with children would have experienced flat or declining incomes in the absence of wives' work. Even with wives' contributions, the incomes of middle-class, married-couple families with children fell 0.7% between 1989 and 1994.

These trends toward slower and more uneven growth began in the 1980s. Upper-income groups experienced substantial income growth (for the top 1%, average income grew 87.5% between 1979 and 1989), while the bottom 40% of families experienced a decline. These developments produced a dramatic rise in the income gap between high- and low-income families, reversing uninterrupted progress in the postwar period toward lower inequality.

Younger families have been especially hard hit by overall slow family income growth and widening inequality. A cohort, or intergenerational, analysis of income growth shows that recent groups of young families have started out at lower incomes and obtained slower income gains as they approached middle age. One result of this trend has been to constrain income mobility, which had worked in the past to offset increasing income inequality.

Another major factor fueling growing inequality in the 1980s was the acceleration of capital-income growth due to high real interest rates and the stock market boom, both of which primarily benefited the richest families. The capital income of families in the top 1%, for example, doubled between 1979 and 1989.

The large increases in the capital incomes of the rich stem in large part from the increase in the rate of profit (the return to capital holdings). Profit rates continue to soar in the 1990s, and these gains have not led to increased investment in capital stock, nor have they been accompanied by increases in efficiency, as measured by productivity growth. Their main effect has been to increase the incomes of the richest families at the expense of the broad working class.

Taxes: A Further Cause of Worsening Inequality

Overall, taxes have increased little since 1973, with the total U.S. federal, state, and local tax burden (at about 30% of GDP) remaining one of the lightest among industrialized countries. Most of the increase since 1959 in the total tax burden (up 5.3 percentage points of GDP) has resulted from higher state and local taxes (up 3.3 percentage points of GDP). Federal taxes over the same period grew by less (2.0 percentage points). The effective federal tax rate for a middle-class family of four has changed little since 1980. In that year, such a family paid about 23.7% of its income in federal income tax and Social Security and Medicare contributions. By 1985, the contribution had increased slightly to 24.4%, a level maintained through 1995.

While average federal tax rates for most Americans have changed little since 1979, effective tax rates have changed substantially for those with the highest incomes. Between 1977 and 1985, for example, changes in tax laws reduced the tax bill for the wealthiest 1% of families by an average of $95,482 per family relative to what these families would have paid in the absence of those changes. Meanwhile, these same changes increased the tax payments of the bottom 80% of families by an average of $209 per family relative to what they would have paid without the new tax code. Progressive tax changes in 1986 and again in 1993 partially reversed some of these inequities. On net, however, the wealthiest 1% of families have seen their tax bill fall by $46,792 since 1977 relative to what it would have been without changes in the law.

The sharp reduction in the effective federal tax rates facing the richest 1% of taxpayers has contributed to the rise in income inequality since 1979. Nevertheless, since the typical family faces the same effective tax rates in the mid-1990s as in the late 1970s, changes in tax policy cannot account for the decline in living standards of the broad middle class. Most of the rise in inequality and fall in living standards, then, reflects what employers are putting into paychecks, not what the government is taking out.

Wages: Working Longer for Less

Since wages and salaries make up roughly three-fourths of total family income (more for the broad middle class), wage and salary trends are the primary determinant of the recent slow growth in income and the accompanying rise in income inequality. The real wages of the majority of workers fell between 1989 and 1995, with the bottom 80% of male earners and the bottom 60% of female earners suffering declines in their after-inflation wages. The typical male worker (half earn more, half earn less) saw a 6.3% drop in his hourly wage between

1989 and 1995, consistent with the pace of wage declines in the 1980s. The typical female worker experienced a 1.7% fall in hourly wages between 1989 and 1995, reversing some of the 5.7% increase during the 1980s for women at the median. The falling wages that the blue-collar, non-college-educated workforce experienced throughout the 1980s, then, have gone upscale toward the end of the 1980s and through the first half of the 1990s, spreading to higher-wage, white-collar men and to middle-wage women.

The worst declines in wages have been for entry-level jobs. The average hourly wage for high school graduates with one to five years of work experience, for example, fell almost 7% between 1989 and 1995. For male high school graduates, entry-level wages in 1995 were 27.3% below what they were in 1979; for females, wages in 1995 were 18.9% below their 1979 level. Young college graduates have not been spared. Male college graduates with one to five years' experience earned 9.5% less in 1995 than in 1989 (after a 10.7% decline in the 1980s). Their female counterparts were earning 7.7% less in 1995 than in 1989 (after an 11.2% increase in the 1980s).

Including fringe benefits in the preceding calculations does not significantly alter the picture of widespread wage decline, because growth since 1979 in average compensation (wages plus fringe benefits) has been only about 0.1% per year faster than average wage growth, making little difference even over 15 years. The 1980s and 1990s have also seen a decrease in the share of workers covered by employer health and pension benefits: the share of all private-sector workers with employer-provided health benefits fell from 79% in 1979 to 64% in 1993; the share with employer-provided pension coverage declined from 48% to 45% over the same period. Since those who lost benefits are generally less well-off than those who did not, it seems likely that a closer study of the changing distribution of fringe benefits would reveal another aspect of growing inequality over the last 15 years.

The tremendous increase in total compensation for corporate chief executive officers (CEOs) underscores the severity of the increase in wage inequality since the late 1970s. In 1978, for example, CEOs earned about 60 times the pay of the average worker. In 1989, their pay reached 122 times the average worker's earnings. By 1995, the ratio had increased to 173.

While economists continue to grapple with explanations for falling wages and widening wage inequality, a number of factors appear to account for most of the shifts in the wage structure. These include severe drops in the 1980s and 1990s in the value of the minimum wage and the number (and strength) of unionized workers; the decline in higher-wage manufacturing jobs and the corresponding expansion of low-wage, service-sector employment; the increasing globalization of the economy through immigration and trade; and the growth in contingent (temporary and part-time) and other nontraditional work arrangements.

Many policy makers have cited a technology-driven increase in demand for "educated" or "skilled" workers as the most important force behind wage inequality. The evidence suggests that the overall impact of technology on the wage and employment structure was no greater in the 1980s and 1990s than in the 1970s. Productivity growth, for example, was lackluster in the 1980s and 1990s, not what we would expect if technology were inducing a widespread restructuring of the economy. It is also difficult to reconcile the idea that technology is bidding up the wages of "more-skilled" and "more-educated" workers given the stagnation since 1989 in the wages of many college graduates and white-collar workers. Technology has been and continues to be an important force in shaping the economy, but no evidence exists that a "technology shock" during the 1980s and 1990s created a demand for "skill" that could not be satisfied by the ongoing expansion of the educational attainment of the workforce.

What does the future hold? The persistence of growing wage inequality in the first half of the 1990s and the expected continuation of the forces that have led to the recent growth in inequality suggest that more hard times lie ahead.

Jobs: Slow Growth and Greater Insecurity

The good news is that the average unemployment rate since the beginning of the business cycle in 1989 has been lower than during any cycle since 1967-73 and, by mid-1996, the unemployment rate stood below 5.5%. Unfortunately, job creation over the current business cycle has been well below rates for the postwar period, including the slow-growth 1980s. Fifteen years of poor job creation left 13.5 million workers (10.1% of the broad labor force) either unemployed, "underemployed," or working involuntarily in part-time jobs when they would prefer full-time employment. Furthermore, by a conservative estimate, almost 10% of those working are in "contingent" and "alternative" employment situations, which generally offer little or no job security, lower pay, and fewer benefits than comparable noncontingent or traditional work arrangements.

Job security, especially for men, is more precarious in the 1980s and 1990s than it was in the 1970s. For men, workers' attachment to their employers fell significantly between the 1980s and the 1970s, and those who switched jobs most frequently saw their inflation-adjusted incomes fall substantially. The poorer earnings performance of the frequent job changers suggests that workers were not switching jobs in order to take advantage of better opportunities with new employers. Furthermore, the share of men with 10 or more years at the same employer declined significantly between 1979 and 1993. Since the acquisition of job-specific skills is a key source of improved earnings opportunities for most workers (especially those without a college degree), the decline in the share of men with long job tenure has important implications for wage inequality and overall wage growth.

The story for women, at least with respect to job tenure, is more encouraging. The share of women with the same employer for 10 or more years increased strongly between 1979 and 1993. Nevertheless, by 1979 the share of women in long-tenure jobs was still substantially below the share of men in such jobs: for women age 35-44, for example, 25.2% had been with their employer 10 years or longer; for men of the same age the figure was 34.1%.

The rate of job loss for both men and women is higher in the 1990s than in the 1980s. Despite a 1.8 percentage-point decline in the male unemployment rate between the periods 1981-83 and 1991-93, more men reported losing a job in the previous three years in 1993 (15.0%) than in 1983 (14.5%). Over the same period, the female unemployment rate fell 2.3 percentage points, but the share of women who reported losing a job increased from 10.8% to 11.4%. "Downsizing," particularly of white-collar workers, was the most important factor contributing to the higher rate of job loss over the period. The increase in the number of downsized white-collar workers, however, does not mean that white-collar workers have suddenly become more vulnerable to job loss than are blue-collar workers. Despite a business-cycle-related decline in the job-loss rate for blue-collar workers, they are still much more likely than white-collar workers to be victims of job cutting.

The costs of job insecurity and job loss are high. On average, workers who reported losing a job in the previous three years made 15% less at their current job (if they had found one) than at the job from which they were laid off. About 25% of workers covered by their employers' health plans before they lost their jobs did not have coverage at their new jobs.

After steady increases during the 1980s in the share of workers holding multiple jobs or involuntarily working part time, both kinds of work arrangements have tapered off or declined in recent years. Workers holding more than one job for reasons of economic hardship grew rapidly in the 1980s, from 4.9% of total employment in 1979 to 6.2% in 1989. Between 1989 and 1995, however, the multiple-jobholding rate increased by only 0.2 percentage points. Meanwhile, the share of involuntary part-time workers, which grew steadily from 3.8% in 1979 to 5.5% in 1993, fell sharply, to 3.7% in 1995 (although it is not clear what portion of the decline might be due to a change in the government survey method used to measure work hours).

Wealth: The Rich Get Richer, The Rest Get Poorer

Stagnant and falling wages and incomes tell only part of the story of rising inequality. A family's ability to plan for the future and to cope with financial emergencies is strongly affected by its wealth (tangible assets such as a house and car plus financial assets such as stocks and bonds).

The distribution of wealth has historically been more unequal than the distribution of income and grew even more so during the economic recovery of 1983-89. In 1983, the richest 1% of families held 33.8% of all wealth; by 1989 their share had grown 5.2 percentage points to 39.0%. Meanwhile, the share of wealth held by the bottom 80% of families fell from 18.7% of the total to 16.3%. In the first part of the 1990s, the distribution of wealth became slightly more equal. The share of the top 1% of families fell to 37.2%, while the bottom 80% increased their share by 0.8%. From 1983 to 1992 (the most recent year for which we have complete data on the distribution of wealth), however, inequality increased.

Another worrying trend is the recent decline in total wealth per adult in the United States. Between 1989 and 1994, the value of tangible assets (the most widely held type of asset) has dropped nearly 2% each year. In contrast, the value of financial assets (held mostly by the wealthy) grew, though at only a 0.4% annual rate. Other measures also show a decline in the wealth owned by middle-class families. The net wealth of a middle-income family, for example, fell about 14.4% between 1984 and 1993. The decline in the wealth holdings of typical families has made an important contribution to the rise in economic insecurity in the early 1990s.

The stock market boom of the 1980s and 1990s has not enriched working families for the simple reason that the broad middle class does not own much stock. Less than one-third of households hold more than $2,000 in stock, and two-thirds of the value of all stock is owned by the wealthiest 10% of households. This concentrated ownership is as evident in pension and savings plans (where stock is held indirectly) as in the direct ownership of stock and mutual funds. In 1993, for example, only 15% of the bottom 80% of families (in terms of annual income) owned stocks or mutual funds; only 17% of the same families had an individual retirement account (IRA) or Keogh plan.

Poverty: Rates Remain High Despite Economic Expansion

As expected, the poverty rate increased in the recession of 1990-91. Unusually, however, poverty continued to rise through 1994 despite the economic recovery. The most recent poverty rate—13.8% in 1995—is 0.7 percentage points above the 1989 rate of 13.1%. Even with a growing economy between 1983 and 1989 and again between 1991 and 1995, poverty rates in the last 15 years have been high by historic standards, averaging 13.7% for the period 1979-89 and 14.1% for the period 1989-95.

Poverty rates for minorities and children are well above the national average. Almost one-third of blacks (29.3%) lived in poverty in 1995 (not too different from the 30.8% rate in 1989 and the 31.0% rate in 1979). More than one in five (20.8%) children were poor in 1994, up from the 20.0% rate in 1989 and the 16.4% rate in 1979. For minority children, poverty rates are especially high: 41.9% of black children and 40.0% of Hispanic children under 18 were poor in 1995. The poor also appear to be poorer now than at any time in the last 20 years: in 1994, the share of people in poverty whose incomes were below 50% of the poverty line (a pre-tax income of $7,785 for a family of four) was 38.1%.

Some argue that these rates are artificially high due to erroneous measurement. But a study by a nonpartisan panel of poverty experts shows that an updated measure of poverty would actually increase the number of poor by about 9 million persons (with most of the increase among the working poor). Regardless of the poverty definition used, poverty rates have been growing faster than economic conditions would predict.

The conventional wisdom typically defines the problem in terms of the supposedly counterproductive behavior of poor people themselves, implying that, with more effort, the poor could lift themselves up by their bootstraps. The implication is that the poor have failed to be lifted by the rising economic tide because of bad choices about family structure and lack of work effort. Recent trends in family structure and low-wage labor markets, however, contradict this analysis. The role of family structure (the shift to family types more vulnerable to poverty) has become increasingly *less* important since the 1970s. The shift to families headed by only one person, while fully explaining the increase in poverty over the 1970s, explains only half of the increase in poverty between 1979 and 1995, the rest stemming from other factors that led to poverty increases *within* each family type. Similarly, no evidence exists that welfare programs have created incentives that encourage people to live in poverty. In short, "behavioral" explanations are insufficient to explain the high and intractable poverty rates throughout the economic expansions of the 1980s and 1990s.

In fact, the problems analyzed throughout this book—heightened inequality of the income distribution, lessened progressivity of the tax system (with the exception of the recently expanded earned income tax credit), and, in particular, falling wages—all conspired to keep poverty rates historically high throughout the 1980s and into the 1990s. Moreover, the "safety net" (the social provision of assistance to those in poverty) grew less effective at providing relief to the poor.

Slight Variations Across Regions

Trends in the nation's 50 states and various regions, in broad terms, mirror those at the national level. Nevertheless, important regional differences exist in the trends for family income, employment, wages, and poverty. These different experiences underscore another dimension of inequality in the United States, one that flows from regional disparities in wage levels and job opportunities.

In general, over the 1980s most workers in the northeast did notably better on each indicator (e.g., median wages and incomes rose and poverty and unemployment fell) than did workers in the other regions. However, despite low unemployment, low-wage workers in some northeastern states (e.g., New York and Pennsylvania) lost ground. States in the West, particularly California, experienced relatively flat growth rates in terms of employment and median incomes, and wages for workers at the median and below declined.

During the 1990s, these trends in the Northeast and California have reversed. Between 1989 and 1995, incomes and employment contracted and poverty grew the most in these states (real median family income in the Northeast fell 1.7% per year). By the end of the period, indicators in these geographic areas stood well below their 1989 peak levels. Wage growth at the median was flat or negative in most areas of the country over this period; even average earnings, which include all workers from the poorest to the most wealthy and which typically expand in a recovery, did not increase between 1989 and 1994.

International Comparisons: Falling Behind in Wages, Productivity

While Americans still rank highest in the industrialized world in per capita income as measured by relative purchasing power, by many other indicators of economic well-being the United States is falling behind. American productivity and wage growth, wage and income inequality, and poverty rates, for example, all fail to meet Europe, Japan, and other industrialized economies. Even the much-touted American "jobs machine" is less impressive than its promoters claim.

U.S. productivity, defined as the value of total goods and services per worker, grew 1.1% per year between 1960 and 1994. Over the same period, productivity growth rates elsewhere were generally much higher: 4.5% in Japan, 2.7% in Germany, 2.8% in France, 2.0% in the United Kingdom, 3.5% in Italy, and 1.5% in Canada. Workers' wages mirrored these productivity trends. Compensation growth (wages plus benefits) per employee in the U.S. business sector grew at an annual rate of just 0.3% between 1979 and 1989 and 0.2% between 1989 and 1995. Meanwhile, the average growth rate in the other G-7 countries (those listed above) grew four times faster in 1979-89 (1.3%) and two times faster in 1989-95 (0.4%). Among production workers in manufacturing, relative wage performance was even more disappointing. Hourly compensation for these workers actually fell 0.6% per year between 1979 and 1989 and was unchanged between 1989 and 1994; manufacturing production workers in other advanced economies experienced an average increase of 1.5% per year in 1979-89 and 1.8% in 1989-94.

Relative to Europe, Japan, and other industrialized countries, the U.S. wage and income distribution is highly unequal and becoming more so. Data for the 1980s show that in the United States the annual earnings for high-income families (those with incomes higher than 90% of all families) were almost six times higher than for low-income families (those earning more than only 10% of all families). Among advanced industrialized countries, only Australia, Canada, and Italy came close, but there the ratio of high-income to low-income family earnings was significantly less, at about 4.0. Furthermore, while income inequality changed little during the 1980s in most comparable economies, it grew sharply in the United States, driven by a dramatic increase in the inequality of wages.

The United States also lags behind its competitors in its ability to pull its lowest-income members out of poverty. Prior to taxes and transfers, poverty (measured as 40% of median family income, adjusted for family size) is in fact higher in most other countries. The American rate in the mid-1980s, 19.9%, was lower than the rate for France, Germany, Sweden, and others. Yet after taxes and the transfer of government benefits, the U.S. rate of 13.3% was well above all other industrialized countries. Furthermore, over the course of the 1980s, as all countries suffered higher poverty rates, the American safety net became less effective at reducing poverty while other countries' systems of taxes and transfers expanded. Finally, U.S. poverty is the most persistent: in a three-year study tracking families in poverty, 14.4% of U.S. families were poor for the duration of the study, a higher percentage than in any other comparable country. (For Germany, the rate was 1.5%, for France, 1.6%.)

One area where U.S. economic performance has been praised is job creation. Between 1979 and 1989, the United States created more jobs (18.5 million net new jobs) than other comparable economies (Japan was second, with 6.5 million), but the rate of U.S. job creation was far less impressive. For instance, the rate of job creation for the United States, which takes into account its larger economy, was 18.7%—high, but less than Australia (26.5%) and Canada (20.1%), and not far ahead of double-digit performances in the Netherlands (13.5%) and Japan (12.0%). Between 1989 and 1994, the United States created almost 2 million net new jobs (less than Japan, with 3.4 million), but the rate of job creation was only 1.6%, below Australia (2.4%), Canada (6.1%), West Germany (2.5%), Japan (5.3%), and the Netherlands (5.9%). The United States is among the smallest spenders on job training and placement, a shortcoming that increases the likelihood that other countries will continue to outpace the United States in productivity and wage growth.

THE LIVING STANDARDS DEBATE

THE STATE OF WORKING AMERICA 1996-97 PRESENTS A COMPREHENSIVE statistical portrait of numerous dimensions of Americans' standard of living. By the mid-1990s, the overall economic environment facing American workers and their families had clearly improved. By 1995 the unemployment rate had fallen to the level of the previous business cycle peak in 1989, the result of steady job growth in the recovery following an initial phase of "jobless recovery." Moreover, the disturbing shift toward part-time work and multiple jobholding that was evident in the 1980s has not continued in the 1990s.

On the other hand, the financial condition of the typical worker continued the long-term deterioration that began in the late 1970s. The real wages of the majority of workers have fallen over the current business cycle, as they did in the last one (1979-89). As a result, income inequality between the richest Americans and the rest of the population is still on the rise.

The combination of falling wages and increased job loss that the blue-collar, non-college-educated workforce experienced in the 1980s has now spread upscale to higher-wage, white-collar men and to middle-wage women. Insecurity has been exacerbated by a decline in the net worth, or wealth, of middle-class families and by an erosion of good employer-provided health insurance or pension coverage. These trends indicate a disconnect between conventional measures of macroeconomic success and the actual living standards of the typical American. Our analysis suggests that wage deterioration and increased economic insecurity will continue in the near term, absent a major shift in government and management strategies.

The first part of this essay, which delineates the major income, wage, and other living-standard trends that have characterized the current business cycle from 1989 to 1995 (our latest data) and the prior business cycle from 1979 to 1989 finds that the typical American family is facing considerable economic pain. We then look at fundamental economic trends such as productivity, competitiveness, and capital accumulation (investment) in order to ask: has the economy's overall performance and efficiency been improving, or has it improved more rapidly in the 1980s and 1990s? This examination allows us to assess whether there has been some gain for all the pain. In other words, we seek to discover whether the process that is generating widespread wage deterioration, economic insecurity, and growing inequality can also be said to be generating a "better economy" or a "bigger economic pie." We find that there seems to be no overall gain or efficiency payoff associated with all of the evident pain. There is no evidence that the economic squeeze on families is part of some sacrifice that will improve economic conditions in a way that will benefit families in the future. The economic indicators that are setting records, however, are the overall profit rate, the return of all capital income (interest, profits) per dollar of assets, and the growth of executive compensation.

A different, competing view of the world states that the economy is primarily generating "good jobs" and that most families are faring well economically. If there is a problem, it is because a limited number of unskilled workers cannot keep up with the requirements of a new era of technological change and globalization or that demographic trends such as more female-headed families are generating inequality. In this view, economic forces are not creating any widespread stress on the living standards of working families.

The data compiled in this book do not support such an optimistic view. In the final sections of this essay we draw on the various chapters to examine a variety of "myths" about living standards.

Although this is an election year, including an election for president, we make no effort to assess living-standard trends by presidential or congressional period (nor have any earlier versions of this book). Given the cyclical nature of the economy, it is best to assess the economy's long-term performance by examining trends over the business cycle from peak to peak (comparing periods of relatively low unemployment) or by examining recoveries or downturns. Presidential years do not correspond to cyclical peaks or troughs and are, therefore, inappropriate time periods for economic analysis.

The Income and Wage Squeeze

The following sections describe the main features of the trends in jobs, incomes, and wages over the current business cycle from 1989 to 1995 and compare them to the trends over the 1979-89 business cycle.[1]

Employment Up, Unemployment Down

The relatively low 5.6% unemployment rate in 1995, comparable to that attained at the end of the last recovery in 1989, was achieved through steady employment growth in the current recovery following an initial phase characterized as the "jobless recovery." Involuntary part-time work and multiple jobholding are now no higher than they were at the start of the business cycle in 1989, although greater than they were in the late 1970s. Labor-force growth has been slow, however, primarily because there has been little growth in the proportion of the working-age population that wants to work.

Income Growth Slow and Unequal

Incomes typically fall in recessions and grow in recoveries, a process that leaves incomes higher at the end of the business cycle than at the beginning. In the 1979-89 cycle, the typical or median family's income grew slowly and by 1989 was only 4% higher than at the beginning of the cycle in 1979. Perhaps surprisingly, income problems have been even more severe in the 1990s. The current business cycle started with income declines from 1989 to 1993, the first such four-year stretch in the postwar period. Family incomes grew by $1,631 between 1993 and 1995, but the bottom 80% of families in 1995 still had incomes below their 1989 level, with the median family's income down 3.4%, or $1,438. If the current recovery should end within the next two years or so, it is unlikely that the median family's income will have recovered its 1989 level.

The 1980s have been rightly characterized as a period in which families "worked harder for less," meaning that it took more family members more hours at jobs that paid lower real wages to create modest growth in family income. In middle-income married-couple families with children, for instance, the average wife worked 314, or 35.8%, more hours in 1989 than in 1979. This increased work effort offset the 7% decline in the husbands' annual salary. Without an increase in the earnings of wives, the bottom 60% of married-couple families (with children) would have had lower income in 1989 than in 1979.

In the 1989-94 period, the wage deterioration among men was both more severe and more widespread. Families were no longer able to offset the lower earnings of husbands with more work or increased earnings from wives. As a result, the income of the bottom 60% of married-couple families lost ground over the 1989-94 period, driven by declines in husbands' wages that occurred across the bottom 95% of these families. Many families lost income because both wages and hours fell, while other families worked more but still lost ground.

Income growth in the 1989-95 period was as unequal as that of the 1980s. The combination of slow and unequal growth in the 1990s, however, meant higher poverty and falling incomes for the bottom 95% of families. There has been, therefore, a lack of correspondence between an economic expansion in the aggregate (more employment, more national income) and increased incomes for middle- and low-income families.

Widespread Wage Deterioration

Wage deterioration and growing wage inequality have continued from the 1980s into the 1989-95 period. For instance, wages have fallen among men, younger workers, and the 75% of the workforce without a four-year college degree in the 1990s as well as in the 1980s. For example, the wages of the average non-college-educated male fell 10.1% from 1979 to 1989 and another 7.2% between 1989 and 1995. The wages of a young male high school graduate dropped 21.8% in the 1980s and another 6.9% in the 1989-95 period. A young female high school graduate earned 18.9% less in 1995 than in 1979.

From the mid-1980s to the mid-1990s, however, even high-wage, white-collar, and college-educated men saw their wages fall or stagnate. Wage deterioration has been widespread over the 1989-95 period, as real wages declined among the bottom 80% of men. The erosion of women's wages also expanded in the 1990s: whereas real wages fell only among the bottom 20% of women in the 1980s, the bottom 60% of women experienced declining wages over the 1989-95 period. The erosion of employer-provided health insurance and pension coverage among employed men in both the 1980s and 1990s has put extra stress on families. In the 1989-93 period, health insurance coverage also began to decline among women workers.

The character of wage inequality has changed in the 1990s. In the 1980s there was a general widening of wages as high-wage earners fared better than middle-earners, and middle-earners fared better than low-earners. Since the mid- to late 1980s, however, wage inequality has taken another form: the vast majority have lost wages at the same pace while the highest wage earners are earning slightly more—that is, there has been a common, equivalent experience of wage decline affecting middle- and low-wage workers over the last 10 years. Nevertheless, the wage gap at the top of the wage scale—the gap between high-wage and middle-wage workers—has grown as quickly in the 1990s as in the 1980s among both men and women.

Another shift in the 1989-95 period is that education wage differentials—such as the well-known college–high school wage gap—have grown only modestly among men and much more slowly than in the 1980s. Consequently, a growing education wage gap has been a much less important, if not inconsequential, force in driving up overall wage inequality among both men and women in the 1990s.

Economic Insecurity on the Rise

Jobs are less secure than they used to be, and the consequence of job loss is more severe. Middle-income families have also seen their net wealth—their accumulated assets less their debt—decline in the early 1990s, leaving them with fewer resources to fall back on when a job loss occurs.

Each year over the 1991-93 period, 5% of the male workforce and 4% of the female workforce were permanently displaced from their jobs in a downsizing, facility closure, or permanent layoff. What is remarkable about these rates of displacement is that they occurred during an economic recovery and that they were higher than the rate of displacement during the depth of the early-1980s recession (the 1981-83 period) when unemployment was nearly 2% higher. White-collar workers, particularly middle managers, were significantly more likely to be displaced in the early 1990s than in the 1980s. The upscaling of displacement thus created insecurity for segments of the workforce that previously felt safe, and it required many of them to undergo the wrenching experience that was and still is relatively common among blue-collar workers.

Job loss due to downsizing, plant closings, or other reasons is often associated with a significant period of unemployment and a shift to a lower-paying job, frequently one with worse or no health care coverage. For instance, about a fourth of displaced workers who had health insurance in their old jobs were not covered in their new jobs. In today's labor market, this shift toward a "worse" job, not simply a spell of unemployment, fuels much of the anxiety and fear over job loss.

The erosion of the wealth holdings of middle-class families in the late 1980s and early 1990s has meant that many families have fewer personal resources to fall back on when paychecks are cut or disappear entirely. This wealth erosion further adds to economic insecurity. The recent decline in middle-class wealth also confirms that the benefits of the ongoing stock market boom have not accrued to typical working-class families. This should come as no surprise, since the 10% of families with the highest incomes own two-thirds of all stock, while the bottom 75% of households own less than 20%.

Explaining Wage Deterioration and Inequality

There is not one single cause of the recent growth of wage inequality and the deterioration of wages among non-college-educated workers since 1979. However, a number of factors, in total, seem to account for most of the shifts in the wage structure. All of these factors share a common characteristic: they reflect general deregulatory, laissez-faire shifts in the economy and forces that have weakened the bargaining power of workers, both union and nonunion and both blue collar and white collar. For instance, significant institutional shifts over the 1979-94 period, such as a severe drop in the value of the minimum wage and deunionization, explain one-third of the growing wage inequality among prime-age workers. The expansion of low-wage service-sector employment has perhaps contributed 20-30%. Similarly, the increasing globalization of the economy—immigration and trade—has created more wage inequality, explaining, in our judgment, from 15% to 25% of the total. Together, the combined effects of industry shifts and globalization (which overlap and are not cumulative) can conservatively account for another 25% to 40% of the growth of wage inequality. The weakening of labor-market institutions, the impact of globalization, and the shift to low-wage service industries can together account for two-thirds to three-fourths of the growth in wage inequality.

The high unemployment in the early 1980s and the high unemployment among non-college-educated workers throughout the 1979-94 period put further downward pressure on workers' wages and helped make possible radical shifts in the wage structure.

Last, in the 1990s there was a large jump in profitability that was not associated with faster growth or, in particular, faster productivity growth. If profitability had returned to rates comparable to those of earlier decades, there would have been significantly more room for compensation growth. There has been, therefore, a profit squeeze on wages in the 1990s.

All Pain, No Gain

For the vast American middle class and for low-income families, neither the 1979-89 nor the 1989-95 business cycle has brought increased prosperity. Circumstances would be worse if unemployment were high or rising and if another recession were under way. Nonetheless, American families are beset by a long-term erosion in wages, deteriorating job quality, and greater economic insecurity. To some, these are the unfortunate but unavoidable costs associated with a transition to a "new economy" or a new "global and technological age."

That there have been profound structural changes in the economy over the last two decades is beyond dispute. Whether we are making a transition to a new and better economy, however, is a matter worth examining. In the post-1979 period, economic policy has moved decisively toward creating a more laissez-faire, deregulated economy. Industries such as transportation (trucking, intercity buses, railroads, airlines) and communications have been deregulated. Management has actively pursued the weakening of union protections and the right to organize unions and to collectively bargain, goals accommodated by policy-making bodies. Social protections, such as safety, health, and environmental regulations, the minimum wage, government cash assistance (Aid to Families with Dependent Children, or AFDC), and the unemployment insurance system, have been weakened. Increased globalization, including greater international capital mobility and international trade, has also given greater scope to market forces and managerial discretion. Taxes on capital and the average and marginal tax rates for high-income families and business have been reduced. Plus, we have had the low inflationary environment preferred by investors, Wall Street, and the bond market. In sum, there has been a conscious, decided shift of national policy designed to unleash market forces and empower management decisionmakers.

The promise of all of these policies was to raise living standards and to generate more overall income growth. As with all policies and economic transformations, there were expected to be, and there have been, losers, as the large redistribution of income since 1979 attests. The question is, was there an overall improvement in the economy that would justify all of the social costs? In economists' terms, did the benefits outweigh the costs so that the winners could compensate the losers, at least potentially if not in practice? Or simply, was the gain worth the pain? Is there reason to believe we are making a transition to a *better* economy?

Our review of indicators suggests that the changes in the economy have been "all pain, no gain," that the factors causing the pain of greater dislocation, economic vulnerability, and falling wages do not seem to be making a better economy or generating a "payoff" that could potentially be redistributed to help the losers. Rather, there seems to be a large-scale redistribution of power, wealth, and income that has failed to lead to or be associated with improved economic efficiency, capital accumulation, or competitiveness.

Efficiency and Capital Accumulation

Greater economic growth can occur if there is either a faster growth in employment (or hours worked) or a faster growth in output per hour, otherwise called productivity growth. The unemployment rate in 1989 and in mid-1996 is comparable to that of 1979 (although more underemployment exists in mid-1996 than in the earlier periods), so the question of whether there was more growth boils down to whether productivity has grown faster in recent years. Or, equivalently, we can ask whether the economy is becoming more efficient or productive at a faster rate than has historically been the case.

Table A presents the trends in the two main indicators of productivity for the private nonfarm business sector. Clearly, productivity growth has been slower since 1973, and there is no evidence of any acceleration in the 1980s or 1990s. Throughout the 1979-95 period, productivity output per hour has been growing a steady 1% per year, while multifactor productivity growth (a measure of output growth due to a more efficient use of labor and capital together) has been miserably low. This is strong evidence, in terms of fundamental efficiency, that

TABLE A

Productivity Growth and Capital Accumulation, 1948-95

Year	Productivity*		Capital Accumulation	
	Output per Hour	Multifactor	Capital Services per Hour*	Equipment per Worker
Annual Growth**				
Pre-1973				
1948-73	n.a.	1.8%	2.8%	n.a.
1959-73	2.9%	1.9	2.9	3.7%
Post-1973				
1973-79	1.1%	0.3%	2.4%	4.2%
1979-89	1.0	0.0	2.4	2.8
1989-94	0.9***	0.2	1.4	2.3

*   Nonfarm business sector.
**   Log growth rate.
*** 1989-95.

Source: Authors' analysis.

the economy has not become better able to generate faster growth.

Two objections to this analysis are that productivity is mismeasured or understated (particularly in "services") and that the payoff is yet to come, as we learn to exploit microelectronic/computer technologies. Productivity may or may not be mismeasured, but the only relevant issue here is whether there has been a greater understatement of productivity growth in the 1980s or 1990s relative to the 1970s or earlier periods. No analysis has shown such a trend in mismeasurement. For instance, any errors in measuring service-sector productivity have been present for decades, and the service sector's *share* of output (or final demand) has not grown (although the service share of *employment* has grown), so any particular measurement error does not have growing importance.[2]

As to the other objection, it is not possible to know whether there is a payoff awaiting us in the future. Nevertheless, one expects that a large future payoff would have provided some initial, observable downpayment this far along in the process, but there is none anywhere in sight.

Another potential payoff might be large investments that build up our capital stock, thus providing a foundation for a larger economy in the near term and distant future. The two measures of capital accumulation in Table A do not indicate any acceleration of capital accumulation in the 1980s, and they suggest a deceleration in the 1990s. That is, the redistribution of income and wealth over the 1979-94 period and the high profitability in the 1990s have not been associated with the any exceptional growth in the capital stock.

Competitiveness

We are told that the U.S. economy is the most competitive it has been in years. Certainly, such a feat is a gain for the economy. Unfortunately, it is premature to claim victory over our competitiveness problems, especially if the goal is to compete successfully in global markets while maintaining a rising standard of living.

On one measure, the U.S. economy is faring better: it contributed 12.4% of the world's exports in 1994, up from 11.5% in 1979. Less noticed by observers is that the U.S. share of world imports is also at record highs, reaching a 16.5% share in 1994, up from 13.6% in 1979.[3] It should not be surprising, then, that the United States had a merchandise trade deficit equal to 2.4% of GDP in 1994 (it was 1.1% in 1979), an indication of a still existent competitiveness problem.[4]

Most disturbing is that the U.S. trade balance is in the red despite the fact that U.S. manufacturing workers are the only ones among the advanced countries to suffer real wage losses. In 1994, Japanese, Western European, and German manufacturing workers earned respectively 25%, 15%, and 60% higher hourly compensation (in dollars) than U.S. workers.[5] Moreover, the lowering of the dollar's value over the 1979-95 period contributes to a lower standard of living and should have helped to eliminate the trade deficit. That is, our trade position worsened despite falling wages and a lower dollar.

One area of improvement is that manufacturing-sector productivity grew faster in the 1980s and 1990s than in the 1970s. Manufacturing productivity grew 3.1% annually from 1959 to 1973 and then slowed to a 2.1% annual growth rate in the 1973-79 period. Manufacturing productivity recovered to a 2.7% annual growth rate in both the 1979-89 and 1989-94 periods, but that rate was in the mid-range of what other advanced countries achieved in either the 1980s or 1990s.[6] In sum, it is hard to find evidence that the United States has attained some competitive edge even though we achieved decent manufacturing productivity growth and reduced both wages and the value of the dollar.

More Schooling, Same Money

Last, we examine the growth in average hourly compensation, which includes both wages and benefits (health, pension, and payroll taxes). Given that no productivity acceleration took place, it should come as no surprise that hourly compensation in the private sector did not accelerate in the 1980s and 1990s relative to the 1970s (see **Table B**). In fact, compensation growth has been far slower since 1979, which means there would have been no improved gains in workers' pay even if wage inequality had not grown.

What has been overlooked is that compensation growth has been stagnant even though we have been steadily and rapidly upgrading the education levels of the workforce. Since 1973, for instance, there has been a 50% reduction in the share of workers who never attained a high school degree and a doubling of the share of workers with at least a four-year college degree, an increase to 25%. Table B illustrates the growth in education levels by tracking the average years of schooling in the workforce, which rose from 9.8 years in 1948 to 13.4 years in 1994. Between 1973 and 1994 the average years of education increased 1.6 years by one measure and 1.4 years by the other, significant growth in either case. Table B also presents a broader measure of labor skill, which reflects changes in the amount and economic value of experience and education levels. This skill index shows steady improvement over time and an acceleration in the 1980s and 1990s.

The growth in both schooling and labor quality outpaces that of hourly compensation in the 1979-94 period. In essence, all of the growth in average hourly compensation since 1973 can be attributed to more schooling. For instance, hourly

TABLE B

Hourly Compensation, Skill, and Education Growth, 1948-95

| Year | Real Hourly Compensation* (1992=100) | Average Years of School | | BLS Labor Skill Index* (1987=100) |
		Private Sector	Nonfarm Business**	
1948	n.a.	n.a.	9.8	91.0
1959	61.5	n.a.	10.5	94.7
1973	88.1	11.6	12.0	96.4
1979	95.4	12.3	12.5	96.5
1989	97.7	12.8	13.1	101.2
1994	98.4	13.2	13.4	105.0
1995	98.8	13.3	n.a.	n.a.
Annual Growth				
Pre-1973				
1948-73	n.a.	n.a.	0.8%	0.2%
1959-73	2.6%	n.a.	1.0	0.1
Post-1973				
1973-79	1.3%	0.9%	0.7%	0.0%
1979-89	0.2	0.4	0.5	0.5
1989-94	0.1	0.6	0.5	0.7
1989-95	0.2	0.6	n.a.	n.a.

*   Nonfarm business sector.
** Log growth rate.

Source: Authors' analysis.

compensation grew about 12% from 1973 to 1995. If one assumes (conservatively) that there is an 8% return to a year of schooling (workers with one more year of schooling earn 8% more than they would have otherwise), then adding one year to the average schooling level of the entire workforce should generate 8% higher compensation.[7] Over the 1973-95 period, greater schooling, in this scenario, generated either a 12.8% (1.6 years times 8%) or an 11.2% (1.4 years times 8%) growth in compensation, an amount equivalent to the actual growth. In contrast, hourly compensation grew much faster than the growth in schooling in the pre-1973 period. In effect, unlike the 1950s and 1960s, the last 20 years or so have seen no growth in the hourly compensation paid per year of schooling.

In effect, hourly compensation has risen since 1973 only because the workforce has more years of schooling. This situation is analogous to earning a higher annual wage because one works more hours at the same hourly wage— working harder at the same pay. While it is certainly a good thing to be able to work more hours, it would be a far better situation if annual wages grew primarily because of higher hourly wages (and one might even voluntarily reduce hours). Similarly with education, it would be far more preferable if hourly compensation grew beyond the growth created by more schooling, as was the case in the early postwar period.

Profitability

One economic indicator that *has* accelerated in recent years is profitability, before and after taxes. After plummeting in the 1970s, the rate of return on capital, or profitability, has steadily grown since the early 1980s, paralleling a boom in the stock market. By the 1994-95 period, profitability had grown to its highest level since 1959 (the earliest year for which data are available). This rise in profitability is not the consequence of an investment boom or a surge in productivity, since none occurred.[8]

There has also been a historic revolution in the pay levels of executives at the largest U.S. firms. The rapid growth of wages, benefits, bonuses, and other forms of compensation has greatly raised the pay of chief executive officers (CEOs) in the United States relative to the pay of average U.S. workers and even to the pay of CEOs in other countries. This fast growth of CEO pay started in the 1980s and has continued in the 1990s.[9]

Whatever process is generating this large growth in CEO pay and profits failed to lead to any improvements in the fundamentals of the U.S. economy or to widespread income gains. Higher profitability and CEO pay may be the only payoff or concrete sign of accomplishment from 16 years of transition to a more deregulated economy.

The Myths That Say "It's Not Really Happening"

These income, wage, employment, and wealth trends indicate that there are income problems facing a broad array of families, including upper-middle-income, middle-income, and lower-income families. This income squeeze has been ongoing since the late 1970s and has been generated primarily by the widespread deterioration of hourly wages that has occurred throughout the ups and downs of the business cycles of the 1980s and 1990s. In the late 1980s, the income squeeze moved upscale as white-collar workers, particularly men, saw their wages decline and their probability of job loss increase.

Spurred by an increased public consciousness of these trends, a flurry of reports and analyses has surfaced that denies or minimizes the income and wage problems discussed above. This section, therefore, draws on the findings reported in the various chapters to address some of the myths.

Myth: It's Mostly Demographics

Several types of demographic shifts (changes in population characteristics) have been invoked to explain or minimize current income problems.[10] The implicit claim is that, while the economy has been performing as well as ever for working families, current demographic trends (which are outside of our control) are problematic.

It is important to distinguish between factors that can explain why there is a *level* of inequality from ones that explain a *trend* toward growing inequality. This is easiest to illustrate with a discussion of changes in family composition, such as the decline in married-couple families and the rise in single-parent families. Since single-parent families have fewer earners, they tend to have lower incomes, leading to income disparities across families in any particular year. Whether *growth* in income inequality or *growth* in poverty can be attributed to single-parent, or female-headed, households depends primarily upon whether there has been a significant growth of these kinds of families in recent years. In fact, the shift toward single-parent or female-headed families was slower in the 1980s than in the 1970s, so this particular demographic shift is not a good candidate to explain the growth in either inequality or poverty that occurred in the 1980s but did not occur in the 1970s. Moreover, the shift toward single-parent households has been going on for decades, including periods in which inequality *lessened*. Therefore, the important forces creating inequality are the economic trends (such as changes in the wage structure) that previously produced greater equality but now create more inequality.

Another way to make this point is to note that the income problems in the post-1979 period have occurred within every type of family, married-couple and single-parent, so any explanation must go beyond shifts in family composition.

The growth of poverty in recent years has frequently been attributed to the growth in households headed by single women, who are more vulnerable to poverty because of their low incomes. The growth of female-headed households has often been equated to the growth of households headed by black women who have had children out of wedlock. However, poverty among black female-headed households did not contribute to higher poverty among female-headed households over the 1979-89 period and marginally lowered it in the 1990s. The information missing in many discussions is that the poverty among members of black female-headed households has been *declining* over the entire 1973-94 period. Consequently, the proportionate increase in more black families headed by single women (and the proportionate increase in the number of female-headed families that are black) has not fueled the growth in poverty among female-headed families. All of the growth of female-headed poverty is due to the greater likelihood that white female-headed households are poor.

Another demographic factor, the decline in family size, has been invoked to suggest that income declines have been less severe in terms of declining economic well-being than is indicated by conventional trends in family income. The argument is that if two families have the same income, then the smaller family is better off since there is more income per family member.

A shrinkage in family size is not an unambiguous indicator of improved economic well-being, since families may choose to have fewer children because they have reduced incomes. In any case, taking family size into account does not significantly alter an assessment of income trends: a family size–adjusted income measure shows the same stagnation in the 1980s and declines in the 1990s as the conventional measure (it actually shows a *greater* growth in inequality). Moreover, the size of the average family has been stable over the 1986-94 period, so this demographic shift has had no bearing on the income squeeze in the 1990s.

The increase in the number of wives entering the workforce is also said to lead to greater inequality because "like marry like," meaning that high-wage men are more likely to be married to high-wage women, thereby concentrating income at the top. The presence of working wives, however, has not led to more inequality in recent years, because the women in low- and middle-income families are more likely to work, a factor that actually helps to close the income gap. Moreover, the fastest growth in wives' work effort (hours worked per year) in the 1979-89 period was among the families in the bottom 60%, so increased work by wives actually dampened the growth of inequality. This pattern changed in the 1989-94 period when the increased work time of wives came disproportionately from the upper 60% of families. However, because the growth of work time by wives was small in the 1989-94 period, this factor contributed very little to the growth of inequality. Over the entire 1979-94 period, the impact of working wives was *equalizing*.

One major demographic factor that leads to greater income growth and lesser inequality is often ignored—the continued rise in education levels (detailed above in Table B). There has also been a more even distribution of educational attainment over the entire postwar period, including the 1980s and 1990s, a trend that lessens inequality.

When discussing demographic trends, it is misleading to focus on a few factors that lead to inequality while ignoring others, like education, that have an opposite (and, in the 1980s, larger) effect. A complete analysis of demographic trends since 1979 would show that they have not been a significant factor in creating slow or unequal income growth. An explanation of growing inequality of incomes and wages and the deterioration of wages for the majority must be found in the factors that determine the wages received rather than the character of the workers or families receiving those wages.

Myth: It's in the Benefits Package

It has been suggested that the rapid growth in benefits, or nonwage compensation, has offset the wage declines experienced by workers. The rapid growth in the costs of health insurance provided by employers lends some plausibility to this view, as does the fact that the value of benefits grew 1% annually from 1979 to 1994.[11]

The bottom line, however, is that hourly compensation (which includes fringe benefits), grew, on average, just slightly more than hourly wages, on average, over the 1979-94 period, 0.5% versus 0.4%. The reason that benefit growth had such little impact on compensation growth is that benefits, defined as health insurance, pensions, and payroll taxes, make up only 19% of the total compensation package, a share that has changed little in 15 years. Benefits have also increased less than is frequently thought: the costs of insuring workers for health care has risen rapidly, but so has the ability of employers to shift some of these costs onto workers or to create jobs with little or no health insurance. The average cost of health insurance per hour worked has been rising $.03 per year over the 1980s and 1990s (up $.45 over the entire 1979-94 period), hardly enough to offset the wage declines that took place—a $.75 drop for the median worker and a $2.04 drop for the median male worker.

These compensation data are averages for all workers and, therefore, do not directly address the growth of compensation for the typical or median worker. In fact, the non-college-educated workforce is less likely to be in an employer-provided health insurance or pension plan now than in 1979. That is, there has been a growth in inequality of both wages and benefits, and the growth of benefits for the typical or median worker has probably been less than the "average" growth.

Myth: Inflation Is Overstated, Growth Is Understated

Some analysts have claimed that wages and incomes are growing much faster than we think and that their growth only *seems* slow because the conventional measure of inflation overstates the growth of prices and thereby understates the growth in family incomes.[12] Given that the research in this area is far from complete, resting on just a few studies, the claim that inflation is significantly mismeasured must be considered unproven. However, whether inflation is mismeasured or not does not affect our conclusions that the *inequality* of incomes and wages has been growing rapidly since 1979. Nor does a mismeasured inflation negate the fact that income growth has been slower in the post-1973 period than in the earlier postwar period because, if anything, there were bigger problems with the measurement of inflation in the earlier period.

One reason for skepticism about the claim of mismeasured inflation is that a revised economic history based on the view that inflation has been less than the official measures yields several implausible scenarios (see Appendix C). If one accepts the current estimate of the poverty threshold ($15,570 for a family of four in 1995), then one would have to conclude that the equivalent threshold in 1960 was near what was actually the median household's income in that year, implying that nearly half of all households were living in poverty in 1960. That is, a long-standing mismeasurement of inflation implies that, when the original poverty threshold was set in the early 1960s, "poverty" was a condition that could describe half of American households. In fact, the widespread view in the early 1960s was that there were only "pockets of poverty."

Alternatively, if one accepts the poverty threshold originally set in the early 1960s and updates it to 1994 using a revised inflation measure, then a family of four would have needed only $8,750-$10,120 in 1994 to be nonpoor. With these lower poverty thresholds, the poverty rate in 1994 (the last year for which there are data) would have been measured somewhere between 6.9% and 8.3%, substantially lower than the official poverty rate of 14.5%.

Myth: It's in Your Stock Portfolio or Pension Plan

When public attention became focused on the disparity between a booming stock market and high profits, on the one hand, and faltering incomes and wages, on the other, an argument was made that workers are benefiting from the current economy through the increased value of their stockholdings, much of which is held in pension plans. That stock market gains have somehow offset wage declines is not credible, however, because the majority of households do not own any stock, either directly or indirectly through pension plans, and because half the workforce is not even covered by any employer-provided pension plan.[13]

In 1992, the latest year for which data are available, only 28.9% of households owned stock valued at $2,000 or more, including stock owned through mutual funds, savings plans (401(k)'s or IRAs), and defined-contribution pension plans or through direct ownership. Moreover, stock ownership is highly skewed: half of all the stock held by U.S. households is owned by the best-off 5%. In contrast (as noted above), the bottom three-fourths of households own less than 20% of all stock, with the bottom half owning less than 5%. There may be millions of people who own stock, but the gains from a stock market boom primarily benefit the best-off families, not the typical working family.

Myth: It's Unskilled and Disadvantaged Workers

The long-term squeeze on working families is downplayed, mostly inadvertently, when economists and journalists describe wage problems as affecting only low-skilled, unskilled, less-educated, or disadvantaged workers.[14] These terms are sometimes twisted a bit further in the popular press so that those experiencing declining wages are sometimes labeled "poorly educated," "undereducated," "miseducated," or "those who lack solid education or skills."

The overwhelming evidence is that declining wages are not limited to a small group of workers at "the bottom" no matter how defined. Among men, there have been declining wages since 1979 among the entire non-college-educated workforce, the three-fourths of the male workforce that includes those with junior college and high school degrees. Wages have been in decline for the bottom 90% of men, including white-collar and college-educated men, since the mid-1980s. Among women, wage growth was relatively widespread in the 1980s, but in the current business cycle from 1989 to 1995 wages have been stagnant or falling for the bottom 70% of women wage earners.

Therefore, the group experiencing wage problems can hardly be considered either small, at the bottom, or unskilled, especially when one considers that the U.S. workforce has more years of schooling than workers in other advanced countries.

Myth: We're a Mobile Society

Information on the income growth of individuals over time has been used to suggest that there has been no erosion of living standards. It is true that many individuals and families improve their economic standing over a decade or two, the result of wages growing as people grow in seniority, experience, and skills. That individuals' incomes grow over time has been the case for many decades.

Nevertheless, it is also true that workers and families are starting out in their twenties with *lower* wages and incomes and then experience *slower* income gains over the next few decades, with the result that they attain a lower living standard than the group that preceded them 10 years earlier, for instance. Given this process, it is possible that the typical income in a community, or country, can be steadily declining while most individuals (from a lower starting point) experience income gains. The measure of the economy's success, however, is whether the community's standard of living is greater.

It also has been pointed out that we are a "mobile" society in which individuals and families can improve their situations, rising from poor to middle class to rich. But there is no reason to believe that the existence of mobility negates the significance of *greater* inequality: to offset a growth in inequality requires that mobility *increase*. In fact, there was no more income mobility in the 1980s than in the 1970s. It is interesting to note as well that our reputation as a mobile society may not be well deserved: mobility is as great in Europe as in the United States.[15]

The Myths That Identify the Wrong Problem

Even where the basic facts of a long-term income squeeze and the growth of inequality are accepted, they are sometimes attributed to factors that have had either no role or a very limited role. This section examines some of these myths.

Myth: It's Big Government, High Taxes, Regulation, and Deficits

Some pundits have tried to blame recent income problems on higher taxes. The problem with this idea is that federal taxes, including all payroll, income, excise, and other taxes, do not take a larger share of incomes now than in the late 1970s. Income taxation has actually declined among the middle class, but payroll taxes, primarily for Social Security, have grown. The end result, however, is that the middle class is currently paying the same share of its income to the federal government that it did in 1977 or 1980. Also, there has not been any significant growth in state and local taxes that is squeezing families.[16]

The squeeze on middle-class incomes is driven by shifts in pre-tax incomes, primarily the fall in wages. It is not what the government is taking out of paychecks but what employers are putting in that has created the income squeeze.

What about the size of government? All of the measures of government's size over the 1979-94 period show that government has been shrinking. For instance, the size of the federal workforce (especially as a share of total employ-ment), the share of government taxes and spending in total income (or GDP), and the economic costs of regulation have all declined since 1979.[17] It is hard to see, therefore, how the "growth" of government could be associated with a de-terioration of wages and a growth in inequality that began around 1979. In fact, government grew proportionately bigger in the 1950s and 1960s, a time when incomes were growing faster than today.

How about the deficit? The productivity slowdown and the accompanying slower growth in *average* compensation and wages began about 1973, many years before the explosion of federal debt. Likewise, wage deterioration and growing inequality picked up after 1979 but large structural deficits (not related to the business cycle) did not occur until 1983. Nor could one say that the period of falling fiscal deficits from 1986 to 1995 has been a better one for the growth of workers' wages. Last, studies that analyze the impact of balancing the budget over seven years show that this will raise wages less than 0.5% by the end of the seven-year period, or less than 0.1% per year. These numbers suggest that defi-cits have had, at most, a small negative effect on *average* wages, and they pro-vide no reason to associate deficits with wage inequality.[18]

Myth: It's a Productivity Problem

Income problems have frequently been attributed to the fact that productivity since 1973 has grown more slowly than in the earlier postwar period. However, wage declines for large segments of the workforce took place only because there was *both* a productivity slowdown and a huge growth in wage inequality, with the latter being by far the most important factor.[19] It is true that most families would almost surely be better off today if productivity had grown by 2% rather than 1% since 1973. Nevertheless, even with slow productivity growth, there was still a 25% growth in output per hour over the 1973-95 period, an increase in the size of the economic pie that should have allowed all income groups to experi-ence real income gains.

Myth: It's a Skills or Technology Problem

The falling wages of unskilled workers and the growth in wage inequality are sometimes attributed to technological change and the notion that workers with-out skills are being left behind by the "new economy." Such a claim is inher-ently hard to test with data because "technology" is hard to quantify. Although reasonable people can disagree about whether technology has had little impact (our view) or a significant impact on wage inequality, it is unlikely that technol-

33

ogy is the predominant factor behind growing wage inequality.[20]

The basic portrait of wage shifts does not easily fit a technology/skill explanation. First, we have already noted that the groups experiencing wage losses are not a small group readily labeled "unskilled," since in the 1990s those for whom wages fell included the bottom 80% of men and the bottom 60% of women. Many of the workers affected have high school degrees, if not two-year or four-year college degrees. Nor can one see any bidding up of the wages of "more-skilled" or "more-educated" workers, since the wages of college graduates, especially men and *new* college graduates, have been falling.

Second, since the mid-1980s wage inequality has taken the form of the top tier of earners pulling away from both middle- and low-wage earners to an equal degree. The lowest-wage earners have been losing ground since the mid-1980s, but only as quickly as the middle-wage group, suggesting that the economic forces creating falling wages have been affecting "low-skill" and "middle-skill" earners equally. A technological explanation focused on the inadequate or outdated skills of low-wage workers cannot explain why wages for middle- and low-wage workers have moved in tandem over the last 10 years.

Third, many economists have pointed out that the technology story presumes that there has been a redeployment of skills in the workplace large enough to dramatically reduce the need for "unskilled" workers and increase the need for "skilled" workers. If so, why have we not seen a productivity boom based on this large-scale implementation of new technologies and the accompanying reorganization of work and workers?

Last, we have statistically examined whether the growth in the use of high-wage or college-educated workers and, equivalently, the shrinkage in the use of low-wage, non-college-educated workers has been greatest in the industries with the most technological change. While it is true that technologically progressive industries require more "skilled" workers, it is equally true that technological change had no greater impact, and maybe less, on the need for "skills" in the 1980s or 1990s than it did in the 1970s. There has been a continuous upgrading of the education levels of the workforce over the entire postwar period so that the growth in "skill levels" has generally met any technologically driven new need for skills. Our research shows nothing different about technology's impact on skill requirements in the 1980s and 1990s than in earlier periods and no evidence of a "technology shock," or an acceleration of technology's role. If there was no technology shock in the 1980s or 1990s, then technology cannot explain why wage inequality grew in the 1980s and 1990s but did not do so earlier (when technology's impact was similar).

Conclusion

Although employment and national income are growing and unemployment is falling, the incomes of the vast majority have not yet returned to their pre-recession, 1989 level. And if the current expansion should end within the next two years or so, it is unlikely that family incomes will be higher at the end of this business cycle than at the beginning. The primary problem is the broad-based erosion of wages and growing wage inequality that have continued as strongly in the 1990s as in the 1980s.

Policy discussions have increasingly, and usefully, characterized our options as whether we will follow a "high-wage" or a "low-wage" growth path. The panorama of indicators of economic performance and economic well-being that we present in this book suggests *that we have already taken the low-wage path*. No one in government or business has explicitly announced a program of lowering American wages and working conditions in order to become "competitive"; nevertheless, the cumulative impact of both government policy and business strategies has achieved a lowering of wages and the standard of living of most Americans.

Yet there is no evidence of our economy becoming more competitive or having improved in the fundamentals of capital accumulation or economic efficiency and productivity. In fact, the economic shift to a more deregulated economy over the 1979-94 period has been all pain and no gain. The economy is clearly in transition, but it is far from certain that it is headed to a better place. The fundamental economic problem we face is to generate adequate income growth for the majority based on jobs paying high hourly wages and benefits. Government policymakers and elected leaders must be judged on their ability to change the economic course of the country, to leave the low-wage for the high-wage path.

Endnotes

1. The information in this section is drawn from the chapters that follow, particularly Chapters 1, 3, 4, 5, 6.

2. The service share of final demand is computed from the *Economic Report of the President* (February 1996, Table B-7).

3. Shares of world exports and imports from OECD *Economic Outlook* (December 1995, Annex Table 46).

4. Computed from merchandise trade deficits as reported in *Economic Report of the President* (1996, p. 392) and GDP data on p. 280.

5. International comparisons of compensation levels and growth are reviewed in Chapter 8.

6. International comparisons of manufacturing productivity are drawn from the Bureau of Labor Statistics release USDL:95-342 (September 1995d) and U.S. data from BLS web site.

7. The 8% return to schooling was used by Krueger (1996).

8. Profitability trends are drawn from Baker (1996) and discussed further in Chapter 1.

9. CEO pay reviewed in Chapter 3.

10. This analysis draws on material in Chapters 1 and 6.

11. This analysis draws on material in Chapter 3.

12. This analysis draws on material in Appendix C.

13. This analysis draws on material in Chapter 5.

14. This analysis draws on material in Chapter 3.

15. This analysis draws on material in Chapter 1 and on Gottschalk (1996) and Gottschalk and Smeeding (1996).

16. This analysis draws on material in Chapter 2.

17. Data on the costs of regulation relative to GDP are presented in Bluestone, Mishel, and Rasell (1996). Measures of government's size are presented in Sawicky (1994).

18. The size of the structural deficit and the wage effect of balancing the budget are from the Congressional Budget Office (1996).

19. This analysis draws on material in Chapter 3.

20. This analysis draws on material in Chapter 3 and on Mishel and Bernstein (1996b).

DOCUMENTATION
AND METHODOLOGY

Documentation

The comprehensive portrait presented in this book of changes in incomes, taxes, wages, employment, wealth, poverty, and other indicators of economic performance and well-being relies almost exclusively on data in the tables and figures. Consequently, the documentation of our analysis is essentially the documentation of the tables and figures. For each, an abbreviated source notation appears at the bottom, and complete documentation is contained in the Table Notes and Figure Notes found at the back of the book. (In some circumstances, however, we incorporate data in the discussion that are not in a table or figure.) This system of documentation allows us to omit distracting footnotes and long citations within the text and tables. There is a different format for the Introduction, where the documentation is found in the Table Notes for the two tables and in endnotes following the text.

The abbreviated source notation at the bottom of each figure and table is intended to inform the reader of the general source of our data and to give due credit to the authors and agencies whose data we are presenting. We have three categories of designations for these abbreviated sources. In instances where we directly reproduce other people's work, we provide an "author-year" reference to the bibliography. Where we present our own computations based on other people's work, the source line reads "Authors' analysis of *author (year)*." In these instances we have made computations that do not appear in the original work and want to hold the original authors (or agencies) blameless for any errors. Our third category is simply "Authors' analysis," which indicates that the data presented are from our original analysis of microdata (such as much of the wage analysis) or our computations from published (usually government) data. We use this source notation when presenting descriptive trends from government income, employment, or other data, since we have made judgments about the appropriate time periods or other matters for the analysis that the source agencies have not made.

Time Periods

Economic indicators fluctuate considerably with short-term swings in the business cycle. For example, incomes tend to fall in recessions and rise during expansions. Therefore, economists usually compare business-cycle peaks with other peaks and compare troughs with other troughs so as not to mix apples and oranges. In this book, we examine changes between business-cycle peaks. The initial year for many tables is 1947, with intermediate years of 1967, 1973, 1979, and 1989, all of which were business-cycle peaks (at least in terms of having low unemployment). We also present data for the latest year for which data are available (usually 1994 or 1995) to show the changes over the current business cycle. Some information was available only for nonpeak years, and we included these data when we considered it important.

Growth Rates and Rounding

Since business cycles differ in length, we usually present the annual growth rates in each period rather than the total growth. We also present compound annual growth rates rather than simple annual rates. Compound annual growth rates are just like compound interest on a bank loan: the rate is compounded continuously rather than yearly. In some circumstances, as noted in the tables, we have used log annual growth rates. This is done to permit decompositions.

While annual growth rates may seem small, over time they can amount to large changes. For example, the median incomes of families headed by persons age 24 and below fell 2.4% per year between 1979 and 1989; over the full period, however, incomes declined a considerable 21.7%.

In presenting the data we round the numbers, usually to one decimal place, but we use unrounded data to compute growth rates, percentage shares, and so on. Therefore, it is not always possible to exactly replicate our calculations by using the data in the table. In some circumstances, this leads to an appearance of errors in the tables. For instance, we frequently present shares of the population (or families) at different points in time and compute changes in these shares. Because our computations are based on the "unrounded" data, the change in shares presented in a table may not match the difference in the actual shares.

Adjusting for Inflation

In most popular discussions, the Consumer Price Index for All Urban Consumers (CPI-U), often called simply the consumer price index, is used to adjust dollar values for inflation. However, some analysts hold that the CPI-U overstated inflation in the late 1970s and early 1980s by measuring housing costs inappropriately. The methodology for the CPI-U from 1983 onward was revised to address these objections. Not all agree that it should have been revised. We chose not to use the CPI-U so as to avoid any impression that this report overstates the decline in wages and understates the growth in family incomes over the last few decades.

Instead of the CPI-U, we adjusted dollar values for inflation using the CPI-U-X1 index, which uses the new methodology for housing inflation over the entire 1967-93 period. The CPI-U-X1, however, is based on small-sample, experimental indices for the 1970s, and there is some slight variation in methods over the entire period. Nevertheless, use of the CPI-U-X1 has become standard. Because it is not available for years before 1967, we extrapolate the CPI-U-X1 back to earlier years based on inflation as measured by the CPI-U.

Some economists have argued that the CPI (both the CPI-U and the CPI-U-X1) overstates the growth of inflation. We are skeptical that this is the case, and we continue to use the CPI-U-X1. See Appendix C, "The Measurement of Inflation," by Dean Baker for a discussion of this issue.

In our analysis of poverty in Chapter 6, however, we generally use the CPI-U rather than the CPI-U-X1 since Chapter 6 draws heavily from Census Bureau publications that use the CPI-U. Moreover, the net effect of all of the criticisms of the measurement of poverty is that current methods *understate* poverty. Switching to the CPI-U-X1 without incorporating other revisions (i.e., revising the actual poverty standard) would lead to an even greater understatement and would be a very selective intervention to improve the poverty measurement. (A fuller discussion of these issues appears in Chapter 6.)

Household Heads

We often categorize families by the age or the race/ethnic group of the "household head," that is, the person in whose name the home is owned or rented. If the home is owned jointly by a married couple, either spouse may be designated the household head. Every family has a single household head.

Hispanics

Unless specified otherwise, we follow the Census Bureau's designation of Hispanic persons. That is, Hispanics are included in racial counts (e.g., with blacks and whites) as well as in a separate category. For instance, in government analyses a white person of Hispanic origin is included both in counts of whites *and* in counts of Hispanics. In some tables (primarily in Chapter 3 on wages) we remove Hispanic persons from other racial (white or black) categories; using this technique, the person described above would appear only in counts of Hispanics.

CHAPTER 1

FAMILY INCOME
Slow Growth, Rising Inequality

FAMILY INCOME IS THE BEST SINGLE INDICATOR OF HOW AMERICANS ARE doing economically. In this regard, understanding the dynamics of family-income growth is central to the theme of this book. This chapter examines how the economy, through the production of jobs, wages, and returns on investment, has generated slow growth and increasing inequality in family incomes.

The median family has fared poorly in the 1990s: for the first time in the post-war period, family income fell four years in a row, declining each year from 1989 to 1993. The initial decline was attributable to the recession that began in 1990, but the median continued to fall as the recovery got under way in 1992. Median family income finally responded to overall growth between 1993 and 1994, when it grew $902 (1995 dollars), but the median family was still over $1,400 less well off in 1995 than it was at the peak of the last business cycle, in 1989.

This trend is disturbing for several reasons. First, although it is not surprising that incomes fell as unemployment rose between 1990 and 1992, the amount of the decline is greater than would be expected from a rise in the unemployment rate from 5.5% to 7.4%. Second, it is unique in the postwar period to have median family income fall during a recovery year, as it did in 1992-93 as unemployment fell, average incomes rose, and gross domestic product expanded. The $1,438 fall in median family income from 1989 to 1995 represents a 3.4% decline. Unfortunately, it is unlikely that family incomes will return to their pre-recession level for at least three or four more years, and probably not before another economic downturn.

The 1989-94 period has also seen an unabated expansion in the growth of income inequality, a trend that began in earnest in the late 1970s. While incomes fell (or rose more slowly) for all family types and for families throughout the income distribution, the pattern of decline did not slow the growth of inequality. Those at the lower end of the income scale lost ground at an even more rapid pace than in the previous decade, while only the richest 5% of families continued to experience income growth, though at a slower rate. Thus, between 1989 and 1994 incomes fell for the bottom 95% of families and, at the end of the period, the gap between those at the top and the bottom of the income ladder had reached a postwar high.

Why have income trends continued to be so negative in the 1990s? Along with overall slow growth, the primary reason is the continuing wage deterioration among middle- and low-wage earners, now joined by white-collar and even some groups of college-educated workers. Another key factor in understanding recent income trends is the contribution of working wives.

In the 1980s, many families compensated for falling hourly compensation, which was particularly steep for male workers, by working more hours (either through more family members working or through longer hours by those employed). This strategy—working longer for less—is most notable among families with children, in part because these families tend to have more potential workers than do families headed by one person. In fact, in the absence of increased hours and earnings by working wives in married-couple families with children in the 1980s, the incomes of the bottom 60% of families would have fallen.

In the 1990s, however, there was a slowdown in the growth (for some, even a decline) of hours and earnings among working wives in families with children, particularly among low- and middle-income women. Unlike the prior decade, wives' contributions were no longer able to offset the lower earnings of husbands, whose wages continued to fall, for all but the top 5%. By 1994, all but the top 5% would have experienced flat or declining incomes in the absence of wives' work. And even with wives' contributions, middle-class incomes fell.

The slowdown in wives' hours and earnings also affected inequality growth. In the 1980s, the fastest growth in wives' work effort was among the bottom 60%, and their contributions to their families' incomes counteracted, to an extent, the sharp growth of income among the richest married-couple families. The net effect was equalizing. But since hours and earnings losses were most concentrated among this same middle- and low-income group of wives in the 1990s, their earnings had little impact on the growth of inequality over this period. Over the full period, 1979-94, however, wives' contributions were equalizing.

As noted above, these negative trends toward slower and more uneven growth accelerated over the 1980s. Over this period, upper-income groups, particularly the upper 1%, experienced significant income growth, while the bottom 40% of families experienced a decline. These opposite movements resulted in a dramatic rise in the income gap between high- and low-income families, thus reversing the entire postwar progress in lessening inequality. For example, while the average income of families in the top 1% grew 87.5% from 1979 to 1989, that of families in the lowest fifth fell by 2.4%. The growth of the richest families slowed in the 1990s (the top 5% grew by 7.1%), while the losses to the bottom fifth accelerated (down 8.9%).

Not only have incomes grown slowly, they have declined for younger families. A cohort, or intergenerational, analysis of income growth shows that recent groups of young families have started out at lower incomes and obtained slower income gains as they approached middle age. Consequently, families headed by someone entering their prime earning years after 1974 may not achieve the same incomes in middle age as did the preceding generation. One result of this trend has been to constrain the growth of income mobility as a factor with the potential to offset increasing income inequality.

Another major factor fueling growing inequality in the 1980s was the acceleration of capital-income growth due to high real interest rates and the stock market boom, both of which primarily benefited the richest families. For example, the capital income of families in the top 1% doubled between 1979 and 1989. In contrast, hourly wages and fringe benefits, which provide support for most families, grew more slowly than inflation. Inequality among wage earners also rose as real wages rose among high-income groups but fell among the broad middle class and lower-income groups.

The large increases in the capital incomes of the rich stem in large part from the increase in the rate of profit, or the return to capital holdings. Profit rates continue to soar in the 1990s, but (as discussed in the Introduction) these gains have not led to increased investment in capital stock, nor have they been accompanied by increases in efficiency, as measured by productivity growth. Their main effect has been to increase the incomes of the richest families at the expense of the broad working class.

In the first few sections of this chapter we examine the changes in the level of income in recent years relative to other periods since 1947. This analysis focuses on changes in median family income for families overall as well as for families differentiated by the age or race/ethnicity of the household head and by family type (families with children, married-couples families, single-parent families, and so on). In the final sections we turn to the growth of inequality and its causes.

Median Income Grows Slowly in 1980s, Declines in 1989-95

Income growth over the last two business cycles—1979-89 and 1989-95—was slow and the gains were unequally distributed. **Tables 1.1** and **1.2** show changes in family income, adjusted for changes in consumer prices, in various cyclical peak (or low-unemployment) years since World War II. (These Census data exclude the impact of the sharp increase in capital incomes over the 1980s; we adjust for this omission below.) As explained in the section on documentation and methodology, examining income changes from business-cycle peak to business-cycle peak eliminates the distortion caused by the fact that incomes fall significantly in a recession and then recover in the subsequent upswing (**Figure 1A**).

Family income increased substantially in the two decades immediately following World War II (1947-67). During that time, median family income in-

TABLE 1.1

Median Family Income,* 1947-95
(1995 Dollars)

Year	Median Family Income*
1947	$19,088
1967	33,305
1973	38,910
1979	40,339
1989	42,049
1995	40,611
Total Increases	
1947-67	$14,218
1967-73	5,605
1973-79	1,428
1979-89	1,710
1989-95	-1,438

* Income includes all wage and salary, self-employment, pension, interest, rent, government cash assistance, and other money income.

Source: Authors' analysis of U.S. Bureau of the Census (1996) and unpublished Census data.

TABLE 1.2

Annual Growth of Median Family Income, 1947-95
(1995 Dollars)

Period	Median Family Income Growth		Adjusted for Family Size
	Percent	Dollars	Percent
1947-67	2.8%	$711	n.a.
1967-73	2.6	934	2.8%
1973-79	0.6	238	0.5
1979-89	0.4	171	0.5
1989-95	-0.6	-240	-0.5

Source: Authors' analysis of U.S. Bureau of the Census (1996) and unpublished Census data.

FIGURE 1A

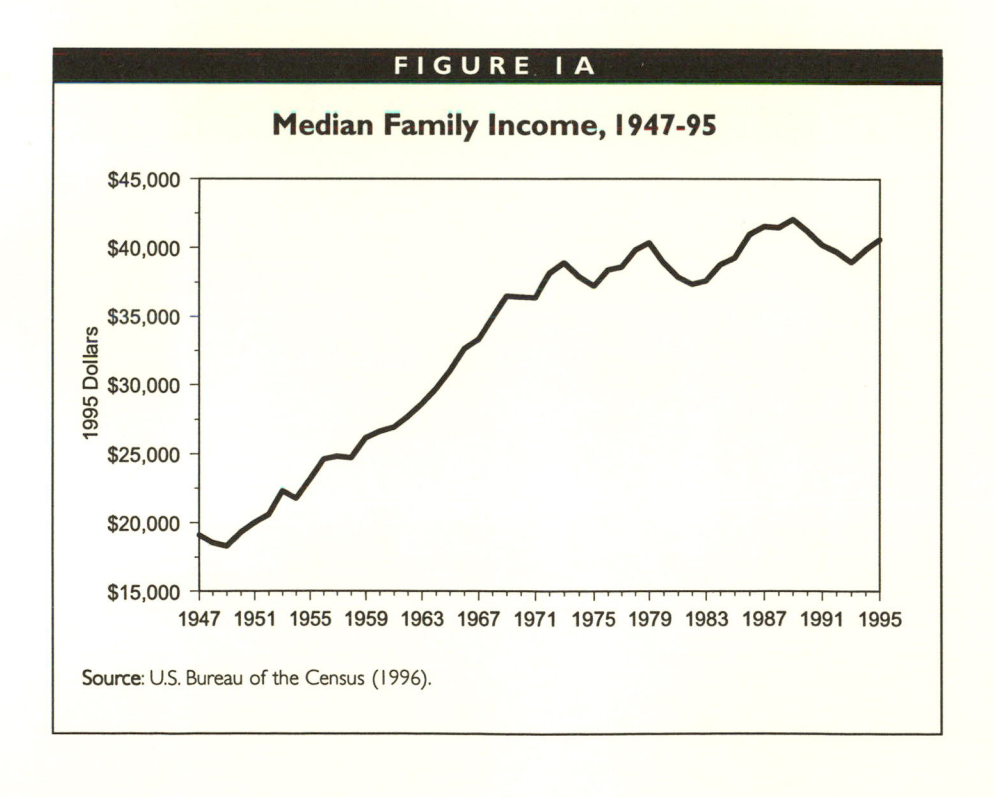

Median Family Income, 1947-95

Source: U.S. Bureau of the Census (1996).

creased by $14,218, for an annual rate of growth of 2.8% (Table 1.2). Family incomes continued to grow into the early 1970s, but since 1973 have risen slowly. In 1989, the median family's income was $1,710 greater than it was in 1979, translating into growth of just 0.4% per year from 1979 to 1989, or only two-thirds of the sluggish 0.6% annual growth of the 1973-79 period and only one-seventh the rate of the postwar years prior to 1973 (see **Figure 1B**). In fact, the $1,710 income growth over the 10 years after 1979 equals the amount that incomes rose every 20 months in the 1967-73 period.

The recession that began in 1990 and ended in 1991 (or in 1992 in terms of the unemployment trough) significantly reduced incomes through 1993 (see Figure 1A). Despite income growth from 1993 to 1995, the median family income in 1995 was 3.4%, or $1,438, below its 1989 level. The 1989-95 income loss was $272 below the income growth for the entire 1979-89 period (Table 1.1). The 1989-95 income decline appears to reflect more than the unemployment accompanying a normal business-cycle downturn. First, it is large, considering the less-than-average recessionary increase in unemployment, up 2.1% (from 5.3% to 7.4%). Second, the income decline reflects several ongoing and new structural shifts in

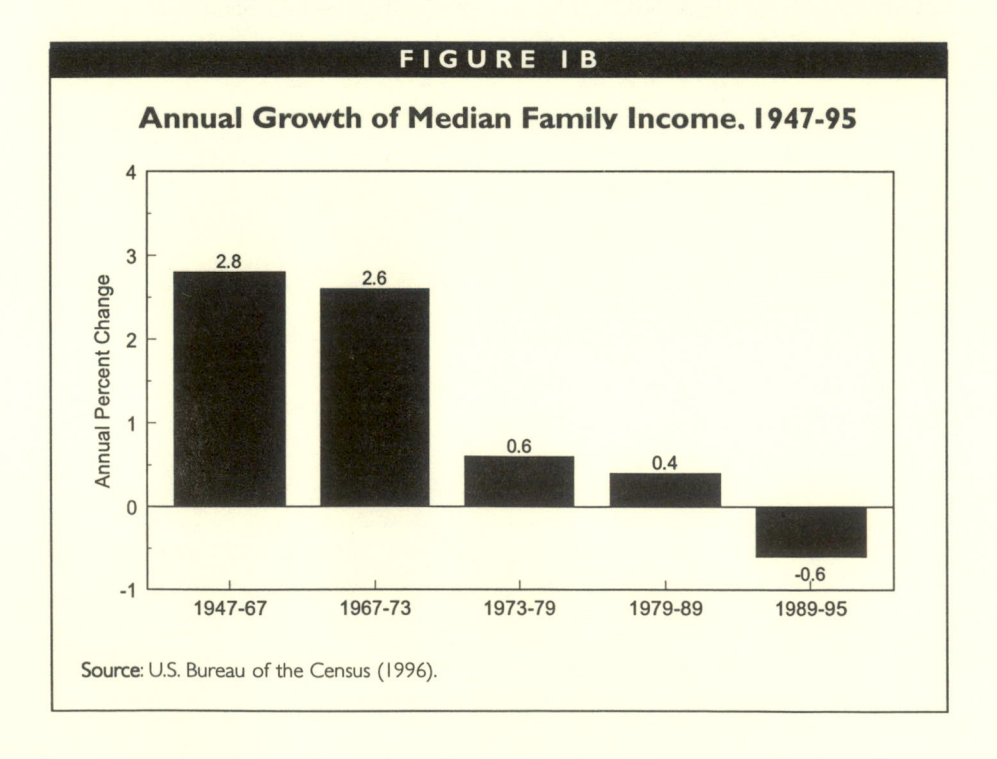

FIGURE 1B

Annual Growth of Median Family Income, 1947-95

Source: U.S. Bureau of the Census (1996).

income growth, such as the falloff in wages among white-collar and college-educated workers that preceded the recession (see Chapter 3), continuing reductions
in blue-collar wages, and a slowdown in labor-force growth (see Chapter 4).

The fact that the median income has yet to return to its pre-recessionary peak
is historically unique. Typically, job growth, falling unemployment, and increasing productivity—all of which occurred in the recovery that began in 1991—
would have helped to return the median family income to its previous level. As
we show below, however, increasing income inequality and continued earnings
declines have eroded the incomes of all but the top 5% of families.

It is common practice also to examine measures of family income growth
that adjust for changes in family size, since the same total family income shared
by fewer family members can be interpreted as improved economic well-being
for each family member. However, trends in incomes adjusted for family size
can be misleading, since the recent decline in the average family's size is partially due to lower incomes; that is, some families feel they cannot afford as many
children as they could have if incomes had continued to rise at early postwar
rates. Yet a family deciding to have fewer children or a person putting off starting a family because incomes are down appears "better off" in size-adjusted
family-income measures. It also seems selective to adjust family incomes for
changes in family size and not adjust for other demographic trends such as more
hours of work and the resulting loss of leisure.

Nevertheless, even when income growth is adjusted for the shift toward
smaller families (as in Table 1.2), the income growth from 1979 to 1989 is only
slightly more than the "unadjusted" measure (0.5% versus 0.4%). In fact, the
trends in size-adjusted income never diverge more than 0.2% from the unadjusted measure in any period, suggesting that the shrinking size of families has
only marginally offset the slow growth of median family income since 1973.

Young Families Hurt Most

Table 1.3 shows that the income declines have been greatest among the youngest
families. The average income of families headed by someone under age 25 declined at an annual rate of 2.4% from 1979 to 1989 and 1.8% from 1989 to 1995.
These young families in 1994 had $6,148 less income to spend in real dollars than
their 1967 counterparts had when they were starting out. This pattern of income
loss has meant that the income gap between the median income of these youngest
families and those of older persons has expanded since 1979.

TABLE 1.3

Median Family Income by Age of Householder, 1947-95
(1995 Dollars)

Year	Under 25	25-34	35-44	45-54	55-64	Over 65
1947	$14,768	$18,458	$20,738	$21,663	$20,165	$11,512
1967	24,535	33,986	38,789	40,623	33,763	16,491
1973	25,876	39,411	46,195	49,152	41,267	20,748
1979	26,796	39,764	47,190	52,104	45,133	23,317
1989	20,972	37,944	49,410	56,660	46,264	28,370
1995	18,756	36,020	46,527	55,029	45,264	28,301
Annual Growth Rate						
1947-67	2.6%	3.1%	3.2%	3.2%	2.6%	1.8%
1967-73	0.9	2.5	3.0	3.2	3.4	3.9
1973-79	0.6	0.1	0.4	1.0	1.5	2.0
1979-89	-2.4	-0.5	0.5	0.8	0.2	2.0
1989-95	-1.8	-0.9	-1.0	-0.5	-0.4	0.0

Source: Authors' analysis of U.S. Bureau of the Census (1996) and unpublished Census data.

Families headed by someone between the ages of 25 and 34 have also fared poorly relative to earlier years. The incomes of this type of family eroded 0.5% per year from 1979 to 1989 and 0.9% per year from 1989 to 1995, in stark contrast to their 3.1% and 2.5% annual growth rates between 1947-67 and 1967-73. Many families in this age group are likely to be bringing up young children and trying to buy a home of their own; their income problems thus represent income problems for the nation's children. Families with household heads age 25 to 34 in 1995 had incomes $3,744 less than their counterparts had in 1979. The deterioration of incomes for these young families is one of the most significant income developments over the last two decades.

The incomes of the 35-44 and 45-54 age groups grew modestly—0.5% and 0.8% per year—between 1979 and 1989, compared to growth of about 3.0% per year between 1947 and 1973. Incomes of families headed by someone over 65 increased at a 2.0% pace from 1979 to 1989, only half as fast as in the 1967-73 period. From 1989 to 1995, families headed by individuals in all age ranges experienced income losses, though these losses were smaller among older families.

Income Growth Among Racial/Ethnic Groups

Sluggish income growth has affected all racial groups, as **Table 1.4** illustrates. White families, who fared the best from 1947 to 1973, experienced on average very modest 0.6% annual growth in real income from 1979 to 1989. Black families, whose 1994 median income was 40% lower than that of whites, experienced slower income growth than whites in the 1973-79 period (0.3% versus 0.8%) and in the 1979-89 period (0.4% versus 0.5%). The median income of families of Hispanic origin declined slightly (0.1% per year) between 1979 and 1989.

The ratio of black to white median family income fell from 1967 to 1979 and then remained fairly constant, declining slightly by the end of the 1980s. Interestingly, in the 1989-95 period, the income of the median black family rose, while that of the median white family fell. These countervailing trends led to an

---

TABLE 1.4

Median Family Income by Race/Ethnic Group, 1947-95
(1995 Dollars)

Year	White	Black*	Hispanic**	Ratio to White Family Income of: Black	Hispanic
1947	$19,881	$10,164	n.a.	51.1%	n.a.
1967	34,569	20,467	n.a.	59.2	n.a.
1973	40,667	23,470	$28,139	57.7	69.2%
1979	42,093	23,836	29,180	56.6	69.3
1989	44,214	24,838	28,816	56.2	65.2
1995	42,646	25,970	24,570	60.9	57.6
Annual Growth Rate					
1947-67	2.8%	3.6%	n.a.		
1967-73	2.8	2.3	n.a.		
1973-79	0.6	0.3	0.6%		
1979-89	0.5	0.4	-0.1		
1989-95	-0.6	0.7	-2.6		

*   Prior to 1967, data for blacks include all nonwhites.
** Persons of Hispanic origin may be of any race.

Source: Authors' analysis of U.S. Bureau of the Census (1996) and unpublished Census data.

increase in the black/white ratio. (Chapter 6 reveals similar relative gains by blacks in poverty rates.) Though Hispanic family incomes are higher than those for blacks, they fell sharply in the 1990s, leading to an increased white/Hispanic gap. Over the 20-year period 1973-94, the ratio of Hispanic to white median income fell from 69.2% to 57.6%.

As noted, incomes fell for white and Hispanic families in the 1990s, though the annual loss for whites was 1.8% less than that of Hispanics, who lost $4,246 in the 1989-95 period. The median black family gained $1,132 over the period.

Only Married Couples Gain

The only type of family that experienced income growth over the 1980s was married couples with a wife in the paid labor force (**Table 1.5**). Incomes among married couples where the wife was not employed and among single-parent families, whether headed by a man or a woman, declined from 1979 to 1989. This was a dramatic turnaround for female-headed families, since their incomes grew 1.4% per year in the 1973-79 period. (The effect of this income decline on poverty rates is explored in Chapter 6.)

This pattern of income growth suggests that it was only among families with two adult earners that incomes grew in the 1979-89 period. The data in Table 1.5 also show sizable growth in the importance of working wives. In 1979, there were more married couples without a wife in the labor force than those with a wife in the labor force (41.9% versus 40.6% of all families). By 1995, married couples with two earners (assuming the husband worked) made up 47.0% of all families, while one-earner married couples were proportionately fewer in number, 30.0% of the total.

While this shift toward two-earner families has been a major factor in recent income growth, this shift appears to be attenuating, since the rate at which wives (and women in general) have been joining the labor force has slowed in recent years. For example, among married-couple families, wives joined the paid labor force at an annual rate of 1.3% in the 1970s, 0.8% in the 1980s, and 0.6% in the 1989-95 period. Furthermore, as we show below, the hours of work of wives in families with children fell or grew more slowly in the 1990s relative to the 1980s.

Married-couple families, although still predominant—representing 77.0% of all families in 1995—make up a smaller share of families than they did in the 1950s and 1960s. There has been a continuing rise in the importance of female-headed

TABLE 1.5

Median Family Income by Family Type, 1947-95
(1995 Dollars)

Year	Total	Married Couples Wife in Paid Labor Force	Wife Not in Paid Labor Force	Single Male- Headed	Female- Headed	All Families
1947	$19,579	n.a.	n.a.	$18,490	$13,678	$19,088
1967	35,438	41,799	31,954	28,608	18,028	33,305
1973	42,065	49,197	36,867	34,684	18,717	38,910
1979	44,132	51,200	36,465	34,615	20,347	40,339
1989	47,376	55,633	35,331	34,225	20,208	42,049
1995	47,062	55,823	32,375	30,352	19,691	40,611
Annual Growth Rate						
1947-67	3.0%	n.a.	n.a.	2.2%	1.4%	2.8%
1967-73	2.9	2.8%	2.4%	3.3	0.6	2.6
1973-79	0.8	0.7	-0.2	-0.0	1.4	0.6
1979-89	0.7	0.8	-0.3	-0.1	-0.1	0.4
1989-95	-0.1	0.1	-1.4	-2.0	-0.4	-0.6
Share of Families						
1951*	86.7%	19.8%	66.9%	3.0%	9.9%	100.0%
1967	86.4	31.6	54.8	2.4	10.6	100.0
1973	85.0	35.4	49.7	2.6	12.4	100.0
1979	82.5	40.6	41.9	2.9	14.6	100.0
1989	79.2	45.7	33.5	4.4	16.5	100.0
1995	77.0	47.0	30.0	5.0	18.0	100.0

*Earliest year available.

Source: Authors' analysis of U.S. Bureau of the Census (1996) and unpublished Census data.

families; in 1995 they represented 18.0% of the total. Although this phenomenon has been the focus of increased attention in recent years, the share of female-headed families grew much faster in the 1967-79 period than in the period since 1979. Note also that the median incomes of these female-headed families actually grew over the 1967-79 period, when their share of the population of families was increasing. This pattern suggests that income trends *within* demographic groups were a more important source of income loss than the often-cited shift to lower income families. Below, we examine the impact of demographics in greater detail. (Chapter

6 looks closely at this issue in the context of poverty.)

All family types lost income over the 1989-95 period, with the steepest losses experienced by single-headed families. Families with working wives were apparently somewhat insulated from the forces driving down incomes, as their incomes rose slightly (0.1% per year).

Growing Inequality of Family Income

The vast majority of American families have experienced either modest income growth or an actual erosion in their living standards in recent years, while the small minority of upper-income families had substantial income growth. The result has been an increase in inequality such that the gap between the incomes of the well-off and those of everyone else is larger now than at any point in the postwar period. The rich have gotten richer, low-income and even poor families are more numerous and are poorer than they have been in decades, and the middle has been "squeezed." This section examines the income trends of families at different income levels and the dramatic growth of income inequality in the 1980s and 1990s.

Table 1.6 presents information on the share of all family income received by families at different points in the income distribution. Families have been divided into fifths, or "quintiles," of the population, and the highest income group has been further divided into the top 5% and the next 15%. The 20% of families with the lowest incomes are considered the "lowest fifth," the next best-off 20% of families are the "second fifth," and so forth. The table also shows the trend in the "Gini ratio," a standard measure of inequality wherein higher numbers reveal greater inequality. Because the Census Bureau raised the "top-codes" (i.e., the highest income levels it would record) in 1994, income shares beyond that year are less comparable to those of prior years. Estimates suggest that, in the 1989-95 period, perhaps half of the increase in inequality at the top of the income scale is due to this change.

The upper 20% received 46.5% of all income in 1995. The top 5% received more of total income, 20.0%, than the families in the bottom 40%, who received just 14.5%. In fact, the 1994 share of total income in each of the three lowest-income fifths (i.e, the bottom 60% of families) was smaller than in 1947. As we will see in a later chapter providing international comparisons (Chapter 8), income in the United States is distributed far more unequally than in other industrialized countries.

The 1980s was a period of sharply increasing income inequality, reversing

TABLE 1.6

Shares of Family Income Going to Various Income Groups and to Top 5%, 1947-95

Year	Lowest Fifth	Second Fifth	Middle Fifth	Fourth Fifth	Top Fifth	Breakdown of Top Fifth		Gini Ratios
						Bottom 15%	Top 5%	
1947	5.0%	11.9%	17.0%	23.1%	43.0%	25.5%	17.5%	0.376
1967	5.4	12.2	17.5	23.5	41.4	25.0	16.4	0.358
1973	5.5	11.9	17.5	24.0	41.1	25.6	15.5	0.356
1979	5.2	11.6	17.5	24.1	41.7	25.9	15.8	0.365
1989	4.6	10.6	16.5	23.7	44.6	26.7	17.9	0.401
1995*	4.4	10.1	15.8	23.2	46.5	26.5	20.0	0.426
Point Change								
1947-67	0.4	0.3	0.5	0.4	-1.6	-0.5	-1.1	-0.018
1967-73	0.1	-0.3	0.0	0.5	-0.3	0.6	-0.9	-0.002
1973-79	-0.3	-0.3	0.0	0.1	0.6	0.3	0.3	0.009
1979-89	-0.6	-1.0	-1.0	-0.4	2.9	0.8	2.1	0.036
1989-95	-0.2	-0.5	-0.7	-0.5	1.9	-0.2	2.1	0.020

* These shares allow the top-code to increase and thus reveal greater inequality.

Source: Authors' analysis of unpublished Census data.

the trend toward less inequality over the postwar period into the 1970s. Between 1979 and 1989, the bottom 80% lost income share and only the top 20% gained. Moreover, the 1989 income share of the upper fifth, 44.6%, was far greater than the share it received during the entire postwar period and even higher than the 43% received in 1947. Even among the rich, the growth in income was skewed to the top: between 1979 and 1989, the highest 5% saw their income share rise 2.1 percentage points (from 15.8% to 17.9%), accounting for the bulk of the 2.9 percentage-point total rise in the income share of the upper fifth. The Gini ratio grew four times faster in the 1980s than in the 1970s, reflecting the acceleration of inequality over the decade.

The increase in inequality continued unabated over the 1989-95 period. For example, the share received by the top 5% grew from 17.9% in 1989 to 20.0%

in 1995 (recall that perhaps half of this increase is due to lifting the top-code). Comparing the bottom two rows of the table reveals that the rate of share loss among the bottom 80% was about half that of the 1980s. Since these two rows compare a ten-year to a five-year period, it appears that inequality grew at about the same annualized rate in both periods. The Gini ratio also continued to increase at a similar rate in the 1990s as in the 1980s. The top fifth, and in particular the top 5%, continued to gain at the expense of everyone else.

The increase in the income gap between upper- and lower-income groups is illustrated in **Figure 1C**, which shows the ratio of the average incomes of families in the top 5% to the average income of those in the bottom 20% from 1947 to 1994. The gap between the top and the bottom incomes fell from 1947 to 1979 but grew to a historic high of 18.2 by 1995, reversing three decades of lessening inequality.

Another way of viewing this recent surge in income inequality is to compare the "income cutoff" (the income of the best-off family in each group) of

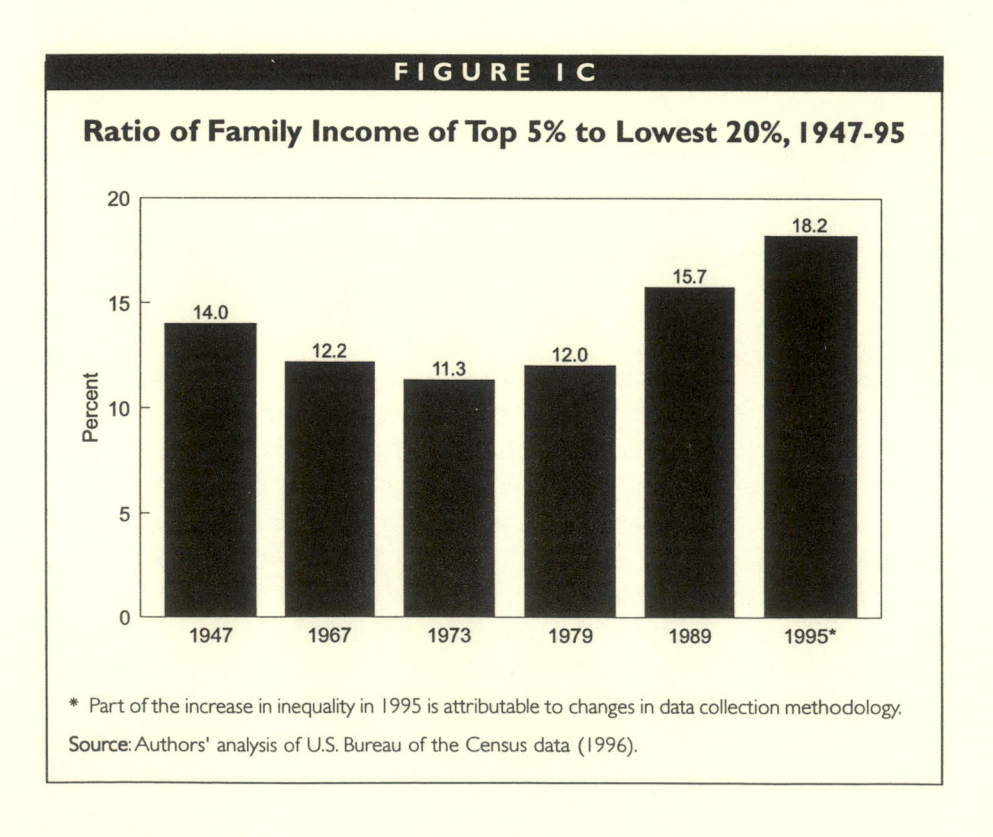

FIGURE 1C

Ratio of Family Income of Top 5% to Lowest 20%, 1947-95

* Part of the increase in inequality in 1995 is attributable to changes in data collection methodology.

Source: Authors' analysis of U.S. Bureau of the Census data (1996).

families by income group, as in **Table 1.7**. By focusing on this measure, we are able to discuss income gains and losses for complete groupings of families (e.g., the bottom 40%). Over the early postwar period, from 1947 to 1973, there was strong and even income growth across the income spectrum. From 1947 to 1967, for instance, the growth in the top value in each fifth ranged from the 2.5% annual pace obtained by the top 5% to the 2.9% annual pace obtained by those in the second fifth. Because incomes grew slightly faster for lower- and middle-income families than upper-income families (the top 5%) from 1947 through 1967, there was a general decline in income inequality, as shown by the falling Gini ratio in the previous table.

The pattern of income growth since 1973 has been far more uneven and far slower than in the earlier period. From 1973 to 1979 the fastest income growth was the 1.1% annual growth among the top 5% of families, which, though modest, was twice the 0.5% annual income growth among the first and second fifths.

TABLE 1.7

Real Family Income Growth by Income Group, 1947-95, Upper Limit of Each Group
(1995 Dollars)

Year	Lowest Fifth	Second Fifth	Middle Fifth	Fourth Fifth	Top 5%	Average
1947	$9,975	$16,096	$21,827	$30,971	$50,834	$22,331
1967	17,251	28,318	37,974	52,060	83,648	37,865
1973	19,634	32,398	45,203	62,164	96,913	43,983
1979	20,183	33,287	47,141	64,889	103,484	45,959
1989	19,668	34,413	50,145	73,189	121,629	51,012
1995	19,070	32,985	48,985	72,260	123,656	51,353
Annual Growth Rate						
1947-67	2.8%	2.9%	2.8%	2.6%	2.5%	2.7%
1967-73	2.2	2.3	2.9	3.0	2.5	2.5
1973-79	0.5	0.5	0.7	0.7	1.1	0.7
1979-89	-0.3	0.3	0.6	1.2	1.6	1.0
1989-95	-0.5	-0.7	-0.4	-0.2	0.3	0.1

Source: Authors' analysis of unpublished Census data.

Income cutoffs continued to grow slowly in the 1979-89 period, but the pattern of growth was even more unequal. The families with the lowest incomes actually lost ground from 1979 to 1989 (incomes fell 0.3% annually), while the top 5% accelerated to a 1.6% annual rate. In the most recent period, 1989-95, growth was flat on average, but inequality continued to grow. The bottom 40% of families lost 0.5% and 0.7% per year, while the top 5% gained 0.3%.

Figure 1D reveals the unequal annual growth of average incomes over the full postwar period. The top panel, covering the years 1947-73, shows strong and even growth. The bottom panel reveals the highly unequal nature of growth in the 1973-94 period.

A More Comprehensive Perspective on Income Inequality, 1979-94

The Census data shown up to this point are very useful in income analysis due to their established reliability and generally consistent definitions over time. These data are limited, however, in that Census income components are "capped" (amounts over a certain level are not reported), certain components are underreported (e.g., interest and transfer incomes), and realized capital gains are not included. Income capping and the omission of capital gains are particularly germane to the analysis of inequality, since these omissions will lead to a downward bias of the incomes of the top 5%. And to the extent that the income "caps" are more binding and that realized capital gains become larger over time, growth rates of the wealthiest families will be artificially dampened. At the other end of the income spectrum, the underreporting of transfer income such as welfare benefits will artificially depress the incomes of low-income families.

We have therefore used the Census data as a base and corrected for missing and underreported data. An appendix provides a detailed description of the techniques used to make these additions to the Census data. The techniques involve the use of various methods designed to take data from one source and append it to another. In this regard, the results are sensitive to assumptions embedded in the methods, but we are confident that the direction and magnitude of the income changes found with this comprehensive data reflect actual developments. Furthermore, by correcting these potential biases, we are able to examine trends in the top 1% of families. In cases where we were unable to reliably append the Census data (as for the top 1% families in 1994, due to the limits of available data), we do not report results.

FIGURE 1D

Family Income, Average Annual Change

1947-73

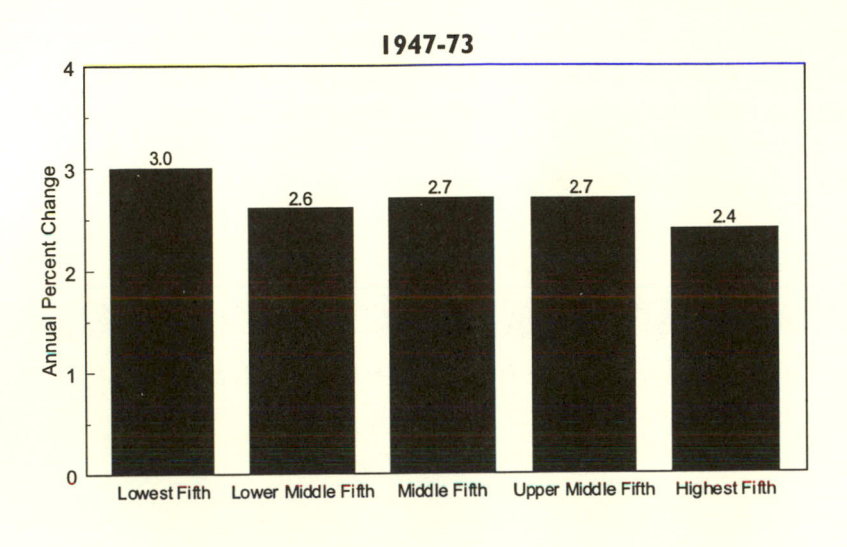

1973-94

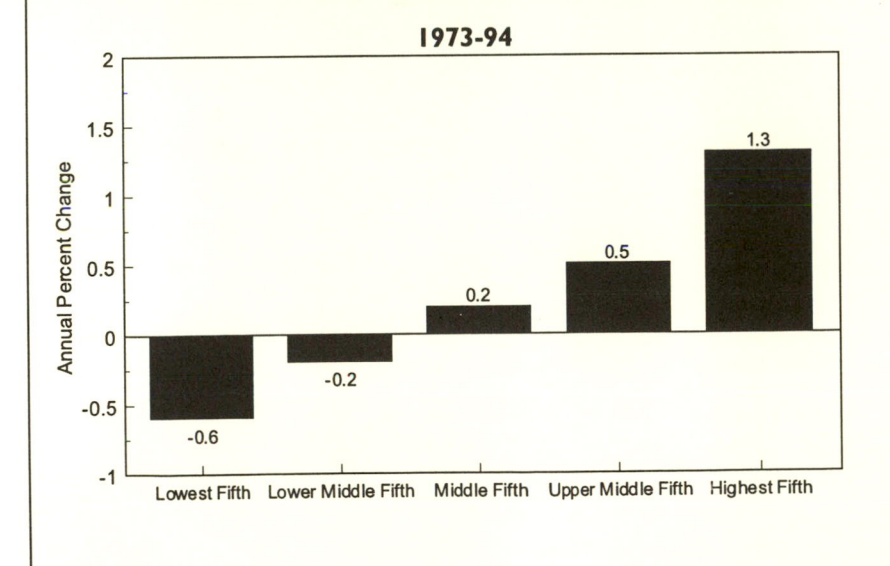

Source: Authors' analysis of U.S. Bureau of the Census (various years).

Table 1.8 uses the comprehensive data to examine the changes in average income for all families and for families with children in the 1979-94 period. (Unlike the following tables, this table excludes one-person families.) Over the 1980s, inequality widened among each type of family, as incomes were flat or falling for families in the bottom 40%, rising slowly for families in the middle fifth (4.0% overall), and growing quickly for families in the top 10%. The top 5% made particularly impressive gains: their incomes grew an average of 50%. As shown below, this strong growth is in large part due to increased income from capital, such as realized capital gains.

TABLE 1.8

Changes in Family Income by Family Type, 1979-94*

| | | Families with Children | | | |
| | | | Married Couples | | |
Income Group	All Families	All	All	Husband Works	Both Work
1979-89					
Average	7.7	3.1	6.8	1.5	6.7
Lowest Quintile	-7.5	-15.7	-4.6	-14.5	-5.1
Second Quintile	0.0	-5.8	0.1	-9.2	0.4
Middle Quintile	4.0	0.5	4.6	-2.0	4.8
Fourth Quintile	9.7	6.1	8.7	4.2	8.6
Top 80-90%	13.6	9.5	11.4	7.5	11.2
Top 90-95%	16.1	11.4	13.0	5.1	12.8
Top 5%	50.9	44.0	47.9	55.0	47.6
1989-94					
Average	-3.6	-2.4	0.5	-5.9	1.3
Lowest Quintile	-8.2	-10.0	-7.0	-13.2	-4.6
Second Quintile	-6.9	-7.5	-3.4	-11.7	-2.6
Middle Quintile	-5.1	-4.4	-1.1	-8.9	-0.4
Fourth Quintile	-3.0	-1.5	0.9	-4.6	1.5
Top 80-90%	-1.6	0.7	2.9	0.9	3.3
Top 90-95%	3.4	6.4	14.8	6.0	17.1
Top 5%	5.3	11.5	16.0	6.6	17.2

* Single individuals excluded.

Source: Authors' analysis.

The last two columns reveal the growth advantage in the 1980s to married couples with children where both the husband and wife worked. Average growth was significantly higher for those families where both worked (6.7% versus 1.5%), and second and third fifth staved off income decline due to wives' earnings. Below, we examine in detail the importance of working wives' contributions to income growth and inequality.

In the 1989-94 period, income decline was widespread. Average growth was negative overall (-3.6%), and only families in the top 10% gained. Again, the importance of both parents working is evident, as this group experienced the smallest losses (e.g., -4.6% in the bottom fifth versus -13.2% in families where the wife did not work) and the largest gains.

Table 1.9 examines changes among the various income groups for all families, including those families with one member (such families are excluded from all the previous tables). Between 1979 and 1989, average income grew 13.6% but incomes declined for the average family in the bottom 40%, with a sharper decline among the poorest group. While all families above the 80th percentile saw relatively rapid average income growth, those in the top 1% saw by far the most dramatic growth. Their average income grew from $279,122 to $523,449 (1994 dollars), an increase of 87.5%.

In the 1989-94 period, income decline continued (at a faster rate) for the lowest fifth. Other groups, whose incomes rose in the previous decade, experienced falling incomes in the 1990s. For example, the average income of the middle fifth fell 6.1% after rising moderately over the 1980s. The cumulative effect of the trends over the full period thus left the average family in the middle group over $1,500 worse off than in 1979. Even the first half of the top fifth (those in the 80th to 90th percentile) lost ground, as their average income fell by slightly more than 2%. Only the top 10% saw their average incomes increase in 1989-94. The full period—1979-94—thus left the average family in the top 5% more than $90,000 better off.

In light of the large increases in the incomes of those in the top fifth of families, **Table 1.10** takes a closer look at the two main components of growth at the top: labor and capital income (the next section examines the impact of these developments on national income). In the 1980s capital income doubled for the top 1% and top 5%, and the large differences in both the levels and growth of average capital incomes among the top fifth of families suggests that this income source was an important factor in the increase of income inequality over the 1980s. The growth in labor income was also strong among the top fifth, and growth over the 1980s was again disproportionately weighted toward the top 1%.

TABLE 1.9

Income Growth by Fifth and Among Top Fifth, 1979-94*
(1994 Dollars)

	Average Family Income			Percent Change	
	1979	1989	1994	1979-89	1989-94
Average	$45,464	$51,664	$50,960	13.6%	-1.4%
Lowest Quintile	10,088	9,741	8,875	-3.4	-8.9
Second Quintile	24,527	24,224	22,151	-1.2	-8.6
Middle Quintile	38,254	39,031	36,641	2.0	-6.1
Fourth Quintile	53,775	57,914	55,792	7.7	-3.7
Top 80-90%	72,210	81,055	79,386	12.2	-2.1
Top 90-95%	91,816	105,674	107,504	15.1	1.7
Top 95-99%	138,301	171,465	n.a.	24.0	n.a.
Top 1%	279,122	523,449	n.a.	87.5	n.a.
Top 5%	166,465	241,862	259,093	45.3	7.1

* Includes single-person families.

Source: Authors' analysis.

Between 1989 and 1994, capital incomes fell for each group within the top fifth (no data are available for the top 1% over this period). Falling interest rates and lower capital gains led to decreases of at least 14% in each group. Nevertheless, wage gains among the top 5% were enough to increase their average income by 7.1%. Furthermore, as the next table shows, despite their losses, families in the top fifth actually increased their share of total income in 1994, reflecting that their income decline was less than that of less well-off families.

The rapid growth of the incomes of those at the top of the income scale relative to the rest of the population over the 1979-89 period led to a substantial increase in the share of total income accruing to the rich (**Table 1.11**). By 1989, the upper 20% of families received close to half (49.3%) of all income, increasing their share of income by 5.0 percentage points since 1979. Within the upper fifth, however, the increase in shares went almost exclusively to the top 5%. The families in the 90th to 95th percentiles saw their share increase marginally, while that of the families in the first half of the top fifth lost 0.2 points. The unbal-

TABLE 1.10

Sources of Income Growth of Top Fifth, 1979-94
(1994 Dollars)

Income Group	Labor	Capital Income	Total*
Top 1%			
1979	$162,230	$106,072	$279,122
1989	294,634	215,048	523,449
1994	n.a.	n.a.	n.a.
Changes			
1979-89	81.6%	102.7%	87.5%
1989-94	n.a.	n.a.	n.a.
Top 5%			
1979	125,530	32,859	166,465
1989	163,354	67,941	241,862
1994	198,322	51,090	259,093
Changes			
1979-89	30.1	106.8	45.3
1989-94	21.4	24.8	7.1
Next 5%			
1979	78,764	7,350	91,816
1989	85,749	13,034	105,674
1994	86,513	11,189	107,504
Changes			
1979-89	8.9	77.3	15.1
1989-94	0.9	-14.2	1.7
Next 10%			
1979	62,656	4,698	72,210
1989	67,510	7,783	81,055
1994	67,718	5,521	79,389
Changes			
1979-89	7.7	65.7	12.2
1989-94	0.3	-29.1	-2.1

* Total income includes transfer and other income not shown.

Source: Authors' analysis.

TABLE 1.11

Change in Family Income Shares, 1979-94

Income Group	1979	1989	1994	Share Changes 1979-89	Share Changes 1989-94	Maximum Income 1989 (1994$)
Lowest Quintile	4.4	3.8	3.5	-0.7	-0.3	$17,296
Second Quintile	10.8	9.4	8.7	-1.4	-0.7	31,469
Middle Quintile	16.8	15.1	14.4	-1.7	-0.7	47,717
Fourth Quintile	23.7	22.5	21.9	-1.2	-0.5	70,974
Top Quintile	44.2	49.3	51.5	5.0	2.2	n.a.
Top 80-90%	15.9	15.7	15.6	-0.2	-0.1	94,477
Top 90-95%	10.1	10.2	10.5	0.1	0.3	121,312
Top 95-99%	12.2	13.3	n.a.	1.1	n.a.	220,918
Top 1%	6.1	10.1	n.a.	4.0	n.a.	n.a.
Top 5%	18.3	23.4	25.4	5.1	2.0	

Source: Authors' analysis.

anced income growth of the 1980s thus caused the bottom 90% of the population to lose income share to the upper 10%. Reflecting their spectacular income growth, the upper 1% of families increased their share of income from 6.1% in 1979 to 10.1% in 1989.

This pattern of unequal growth continued into the 1990s, as the top 10% received a yet larger share at the expense of the bottom 90%. By the end of the period, the 25.4% share of income going to the top 5% was only slightly below the 26.6% share going to the bottom 60%. Comparing these findings to those in Table 1.6 reveals that a more complete accounting of income sources shows both faster growth and higher levels of inequality in each period.

Some economists express doubts about analyses of income because the incomes of families fluctuate from year to year in response to special circumstances—a layoff, a one-time sale of an asset, and so on. As a result, a family's income may partially reflect transient events and not indicate its economic well-being over the long term. In this view, consumption levels of families provide a better measure of inequality, since families typically gear their consumption to their expected incomes over the long term.

Table 1.12, which presents the trend in the distribution of consumption, permits a view of this final dimension of growing inequality. Two measures of consumption inequality are reported: the ratio of consumption levels at different percentiles and the "mean log deviation," or MLD. Like the Gini ratio above, the MLD is a measure of inequality where larger values imply a more unequal distribution. Over the 1970s, the distance between levels of consumption of families at the top and the middle of the distribution grew slightly, from 1.87 to 1.90. A countervailing trend (decreasing inequality) occurred among families at the 50th percentile relative to those at the 10th, but these changes were small (the MLD grew slightly).

The 1980s, however, saw a large increase in consumption inequality, mirroring the trend in income inequality shown above. As the ratios show, the top pulled away from the middle (the 90/50 ratio grew from 1.90 to 2.13), and the middle pulled away from the bottom (the 50/10 ratio grew from 2.01 to 2.31). Reflecting this increased dispersion of consumption, the MLD grew from 0.143 to 0.189. Unlike the income data, these consumption data suggest a slight contraction of inequality since 1989. Whether this contraction reflects a true shift in trend is yet to be determined, but even with it, consumption inequality remains at a historically high level.

Other dimensions of the recent growth in inequality are examined in later chapters. Chapter 2 examines the effect of changes in tax levels and the distri-

---

TABLE 1.12

Distribution of Real Consumption Expenditure, 1972-93

Year	Ratio of Consumption Between Different Percentiles*			Mean Log Deviation of Consumption
	90th/10th	90th/50th	50th/10th	
1972/73	3.89	1.87	2.08	0.142
1980/81	3.82	1.90	2.01	0.143
1989	4.92	2.13	2.31	0.189
1993	4.61	2.11	2.18	0.180

* Ratios reflect adjustment for family size using equivalency scales.

Source: Authors' analysis of U.S. Deparment of Labor (1995).

bution of the tax burden on after-tax income inequality and growth. Chapter 3 examines and explains trends in wage levels and inequality. Chapter 5 looks at growing wealth inequality, and Chapter 6 examines the growth in poverty. We now turn to some explanations for the growth in income inequality.

Greater Capital Incomes, Lower Labor Incomes

The fortunes of individual families depend heavily on the sources of their incomes: labor income, capital income, or government assistance. For instance, one significant reason for the unequal growth in family incomes in the 1979-89 period was an increase in the share of personal total income that was in the form of capital incomes (such as rent, dividends, interest payments, capital gains) and a smaller share earned as wages and salaries. Since most families receive little or no capital income, this shift had a substantial impact on income distribution.

Table 1.13 presents data that show the sources of income for families in each income group in 1989. The top fifth received a larger share of its income (13.8%) from financial assets (capital) compared to the other 80% of the population. For instance, the top 1% received 41.0% of its income from financial assets. The other income groups in the upper 10% received from 12% to 19% of their income from capital. In contrast, the bottom 80% of families relied on capital income for less than 8% of their income in 1989.

Those without access to capital income depend either on wages (the broad middle) or on government transfers (the bottom) as their primary source of income. As a result, the cutback in government cash assistance primarily affects the income prospects of the lowest 40% of the population, but particularly the bottom fifth (see Chapter 6). For instance, roughly 40% of the income of families in the bottom fifth is drawn from government cash assistance programs (e.g., AFDC, Unemployment Insurance, Social Security, SSI). The income prospects of families in the 20th to 99th percentile, on the other hand, depend primarily on the level and distribution of wages and salaries.

The shift in the composition of personal income toward greater capital income is shown in **Table 1.14**. Over the 1979-89 period, capital income's share of market-based income (personal income less government transfers) shifted sharply upward, from 16.3% to 21.1%. This shift toward capital income was partly reversed over the 1989-95 period as interest rates and interest income fell. In 1995, however, capital income's share of 19.6% was still significantly above its 1979 value. Correspondingly, the share of labor income, including wages and

TABLE 1.13

Source of Family Income for
Each Family Income Group, 1989

Income Group	Labor	Capital*	Government Transfer	Other	Total
All	75.3	12.9	6.7	5.1	100.0
Bottom Four-Fifths					
First	46.3	4.6	39.9	9.1	100.0
Second	69.6	7.7	14.3	8.4	100.0
Middle	79.1	8.0	6.7	6.2	100.0
Fourth	83.4	8.0	3.9	4.7	100.0
Top Fifth	80.0	13.8	2.0	4.2	100.0
81-90%	83.6	9.6	2.4	4.3	100.0
91-95%	81.8	12.3	1.9	4.0	100.0
96-99%	74.3	19.4	1.6	4.6	100.0
Top 1%	57.6	41.0	0.4	1.1	100.0

* Includes rent, dividend, interest income, and realized capital gains.

Source: Authors' analysis.

all nonwage compensation (benefits), was lower in 1995 than in 1979, 71.5% versus 74.2%, despite an increase over the 1989-95 period.

This shift away from labor income and toward capital income is unique in the postwar period and is partly responsible for the recent surge in inequality. Since the rich are the owners of income-producing property, the fact that the assets they own have commanded an increasing share of total income automatically leads to income growth that is concentrated at the top. This is especially the case since there was also growth in the inequality of the distribution of capital incomes among families.

It is difficult to interpret changes in proprietor's income (presented in Table 1.14) because it is a mixture of both labor and capital income. That is, the income that an owner of a business (or farmer) receives results from his or her work effort (labor income) and his or her ownership (capital income) of the business or farm. To the extent that the shrinkage of proprietor's income results from a shuffle of people out of the proprietary sector (e.g., leaving farming) and into wage and salary employment, there will be a corresponding increase in labor's

TABLE 1.14

Shares of Market-Based Personal Income by Type, 1959-95

Income Type*	1959	1967	1973	1979	1989	1995
Total Capital Income	14.3%	15.6%	14.6%	16.3%	21.1%	19.6%
Rent	4.9	4.0	2.7	1.5	1.3	2.3
Dividends	3.4	3.6	2.7	2.7	3.2	4.0
Interest	6.1	8.0	9.2	12.0	16.6	13.3
Total Labor Income	72.2%	73.2%	74.3%	74.2%	70.5%	71.5%
Wages & Salaries	69.4	69.7	69.5	67.5	63.8	63.6
Fringe Benefits	2.8	3.5	4.8	6.7	6.7	7.9
Propriertor's Income*	13.5%	11.2%	11.1%	9.5%	8.5%	8.9%
Total Market-Based Personal Income**	100.0%	100.0%	100.0%	100.0%	100.0%	100.0%

*   Business and farm owners' income.
** Total of listed income types.

Source: Authors' analysis.

share of income (e.g., as farm income is replaced by wage income). This shift out of proprietor's income thus helps to explain a rising labor share in some periods. However, labor's share of income fell from 1979 to 1989 despite an erosion of the share of proprietor's income from 9.5% to 8.5%.

This analysis of personal income understates the shift toward capital income in the 1979-89 period because the data do not include the growth of capital gains, the profit made when capital assets are sold. Capital gains primarily accrue to the highest-income families since they control most of the wealth (see Chapter 5). Income from capital gains grew strongly in the 1980s, and thus the share of capital income would have grown more strongly in the 1979-89 period than is shown in Table 1.14. The decline in capital gains in the post-1989 period, however, suggests a larger decline in capital income's share than shown in the table.

From the point of view of national income (incomes generated by the corporate, proprietor, and government sectors), there does not appear to be as large a shift away from labor income toward capital income **(Table 1.15)**. For instance, labor's share of national income fell from 73.2% in 1979 to 72.3% in 1989 and then grew to 72.9% in 1994. A closer look at the underlying data, however, sug-

TABLE 1.15

Shares of Income by Type and Sector, 1959-94

Sector/Income Type	1959	1973	1979	1989	1994
National Income (All Sectors)					
Labor	68.5%	72.2%	73.2%	72.3%	72.9%
Capital	19.2	17.7	18.2	19.8	18.9
Proprietor Profit	12.3	10.1	8.6	7.9	8.2
Total	100.0	100.0	100.0	100.0	100.0
(a) Corporate and Business Sector					
Labor	44.3%	48.0%	50.3%	48.6%	48.5%
Capital	18.9	16.7	16.7	17.7	17.5
Total	63.2	64.6	67.0	66.2	66.0
(b) Proprietor's Sector					
Labor	9.0%	5.2%	4.7%	4.3%	4.3%
Capital	0.3	1.0	1.4	2.2	1.4
Proprietor Profit	12.3	10.1	8.6	7.9	8.2
Total	21.6	16.2	14.7	14.4	13.9
(c) Government/Nonprofit Sector					
Labor	15.2%	19.1%	18.3%	19.4%	20.1%
Capital	0.0	0.0	0.0	0.0	0.0
Total	15.2	19.1	18.3	19.4	20.1
Addendum					
Shares of Corporate-Sector Income*					
Labor	79.2%	82.6%	83.9%	82.4%	82.0%
Capital	20.8	17.4	16.1	17.6	18.0
Total	100.0	100.0	100.0	100.0	100.0

*   Does not include sole proprietorships, partnerships, and other private noncorporate businesses. The corporate sector, which includes both financial and nonfinancial corporations, accounted for 58% of national income and 71.6% of private-sector income in 1989.

Source: Authors' analysis.

gests a significant shift away from labor income. First, note that labor's share of national income had steadily risen from 1959 to 1979. One reason for the expanding share of labor income was the steady expansion of the government/nonprofit sector. When the government/nonprofit sector grows, there is a tendency for labor's share of income to grow because this sector generates *only* labor income and no capital income. For example, the growth of the government/nonprofit sector from 18.3% to 19.4% of national income between 1979 and 1989 necessarily added

1.1 percentage points to labor's share of national income (other things remaining equal). Labor's share of national income also grows as the proprietary sector (farm and nonfarm unincorporated businesses) shrinks, as it did from 1959 to 1979, because labor's share of income in that sector is relatively low (about one-third in 1979). When resources shift from a sector with a low labor share of income, such as the proprietor's sector, to sectors with a higher labor share (all of the other sectors), the share of labor income in the economy necessarily rises. Thus, the changing composition of income across organizational sectors (expanding government, shrinking proprietors) provides momentum for an increase in labor's share of national income and has done so for the entire postwar period.

Why, then, did labor's share of national income not continue to rise over the 1979-94 period, as it had earlier? Given the continued, albeit slow, expansion of the government/nonprofit sector, one would have expected a continued expansion of labor's share of national income. In fact, the rebound of labor's share from 1989 to 1994 matches the growth in the government/nonprofit sector and, therefore, does not represent a reversal of the 1979-89 trends. The failure of labor's share to grow stems primarily from the unique decline in labor's share of the corporate and business sector between 1979 and 1994, reversing the tendency toward more labor income from the 1960s to the 1970s. This is most clearly seen in the bottom panel of Table 1.15, which shows the division of incomes in the corporate sector—labor's share fell from 83.9% in 1979 to 82.4% in 1989 and then to 82.0% in 1994. These data suggest that there has been a shift away from labor income in the private sector (both corporate and proprietor), which does not show up in national income because of the growth of the labor-intensive government/nonprofit sector.

How important is the shift in the shares of labor and capital income? Between 1979 and 1994, labor's share in the corporate sector fell 1.9 percentage points. A return to the 1979 labor share would require hourly compensation to be 2.3% greater (83.9 divided by 82.0, less 1), a compensation growth equal to that typically achieved over five years. This calculation illustrates that seemingly small changes in income shares can have nontrivial implications for wage growth.

An examination of factor (labor or capital) income shares, however, cannot determine whether there has been a redistribution of income from labor to capital, or vice versa. This type of analysis assumes that if factor shares remain constant then there has been no redistribution. Such an analysis is too simple for several reasons. First, in contrast to most topics in economics, such an analysis makes no comparison of actual outcomes relative to what one might expect given a model of what drives factor income shares. This means we need to look at the current period relative to earlier periods and examine variables that affect income shares. Several trends suggest that, "other things being equal," capital's share might have been expected to decline and labor's share to rise. One reason for this expectation is that there has been a rapid growth in education levels and labor quality that would tend to raise labor's share. The primary trend, however, that would tend to lessen capital's share (and increase labor's share) is the rapid decline in the capital-output ratio since the early 1980s (see **Figure 1E**). This fall in the ratio of the capital stock to private-sector output implies that capital's role in production has lessened, suggesting that capital's income share would fall in tandem.

Rather than fall, the share of capital income has risen because there has been a rapid growth in the return to capital, before- and after-tax, starting in the late 1980s and continuing steadily through 1995 (**Table 1.16** and **Figure 1F**). That is, the amount of before-tax profit received per dollar of assets (i.e., the capital stock) has grown to its highest levels since the mid-1960s, while the after-tax return on capital is as high or higher than in any year since 1959 (the earliest year for which a measure is available). The relationship between the return to capital and capital's share of income is illustrated in the box on the following page.

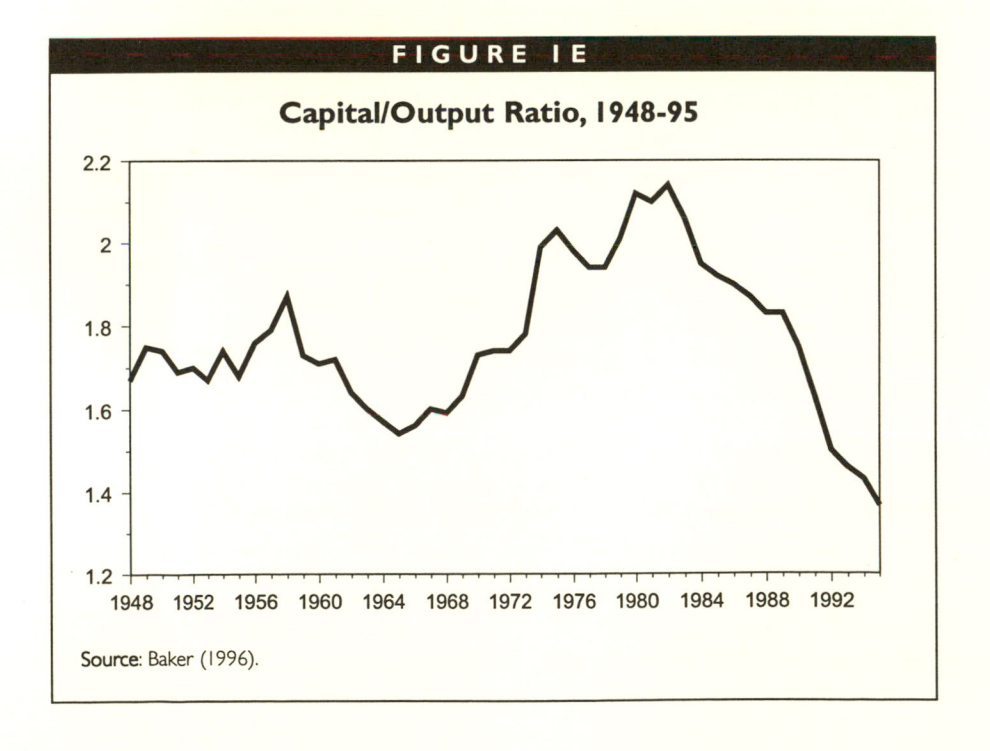

FIGURE 1E

Capital/Output Ratio, 1948-95

Source: Baker (1996).

TABLE 1.16

Profit Rates at Business Cycle Peaks, 1959-95

	1959	1973	1979	1989	1995
Profit Rate*					
Before-Tax	10.4%	7.6%	7.7%	7.5%	10.8%
After-Tax	5.6	4.7	5.1	5.1	7.0
Capital-Output Ratio	1.73	1.78	2.01	1.83	1.39

* Profit rate is the ratio of all capital income (profits, rent, and interest) to the capital stock.

Source: Update and Baker(1996).

RISING PROFIT RATES, CONSTANT PROFIT SHARE

There has been some confusion as to the difference between a rise in the *profit rate*, or return to capital (which has occurred in the last 15 years), and a rise in *capital's share of income*, which has grown much less. The following exercise is designed to show how these two rates differ and how each can rise or fall at its own pace.

Income is the sum of the returns to capital and labor. It can be expressed in the following equation:

$$(K * r) + (W * L) = Y$$

where K is the capital stock, r is the rate of return on capital (the profit rate), W is the average hourly wage, L is the number of labor hours, and Y is income.

Capital's share of income can be calculated by dividing capital income, K * r, by total income, Y. If the capital share remains constant, then the quantity (K * r)/Y doesn't change (nor does the labor share, (W * L)/Y). Capital's share, (K * r)/Y, can also be written as (K/Y) * r, where the quantity K/Y is equal to the ratio of the capital stock to total income. If K/Y falls,

as it has over the last 10 years, then r can rise, even if capital's share remains constant.

For example, if K = $2,000, r = .05, and Y = $1,000, then the capital share of income would be 10%:

$$(K * r)/Y = (\$2,000 * .05)/\$1,000 = \$100/\$1,000 = .10$$

If the capital stock fell to $1,000 (so that K´= $1,000), the profit rate rose to 10% (so that r´ = .10), and income remained unchanged (Y´ = $1,000), the capital share would still be 10%:

$$(K´ * r´)/Y´ = (\$1,000 * .10)/\$1,000 = \$100/\$1,000 = .10$$

In this example, the profit rate doubles, but the capital share of income remains the same because the capital stock has fallen 50%. Over the last 15 years, actual experience has fallen along these lines, i.e., the rise in the profit rate has been roughly proportional to the fall in the capital-to-output ratio, so there has been relatively little change in the capital share of income.

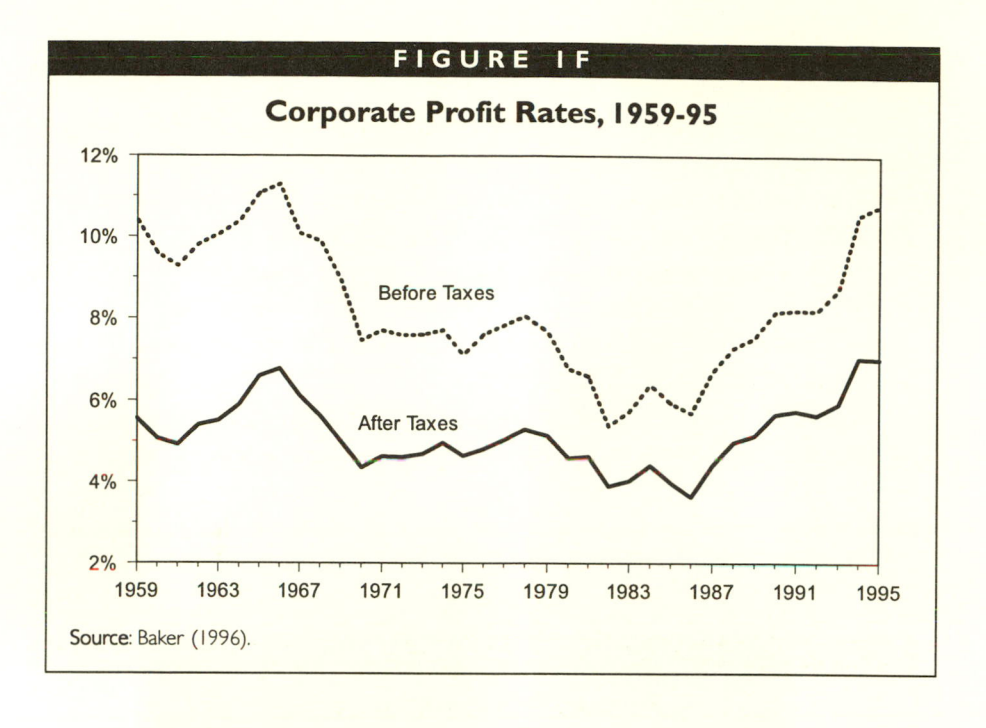

FIGURE 1F

Corporate Profit Rates, 1959-95

Before Taxes

After Taxes

Source: Baker (1996).

As discussed in the Introduction, this large increase in profitability does not correspond to a growth in efficiency, as measured by the ongoing growth of productivity in the economy. That is, this higher profitability is not a payoff for enhanced private-sector efficiency. Rather, higher profitability in the current context implies a larger flow of income to owners of capital out of the same steady stream of income (productivity) that the economy has been generating for several decades.

This growth in profitability has left less room for wage growth, or it might be considered the consequence of businesses successfully being able to restrain (or impose) slow wage growth as sales and profits grew in recent years. If the return to capital in 1994 and 1995 (10.66%) had been at the average of the cyclical peaks from 1959 to 1979 (8.37%), then hourly compensation would have been 3.6% higher. This is a nontrivial loss, comparable in size to the lost wages of the typical worker due to factors such as the shift to services, globalization, deunionization, or any of the other prominent causes of growing wage inequality discussed in Chapter 3.

The Impact of Demographic Changes on Income

It is often suggested that changes in the demographic composition of American families have been a major cause of the income problems documented above. While it is unquestionably the case that the increased share of economically vulnerable families has put downward pressure on income growth, this process is a dynamic one that has not been constant over time. In addition, some demographic factors, such as the increase in educational attainment, have led to increased family income. It is important, then, to look at the net effect of demographic shifts in different time periods.

Figure 1G shows the trend in average income for families (in this case, one-member families are not included). The figure presents both the actual average and the average that would have occurred if family composition did not change after 1967. The difference between the lines shows the cumulative effect of

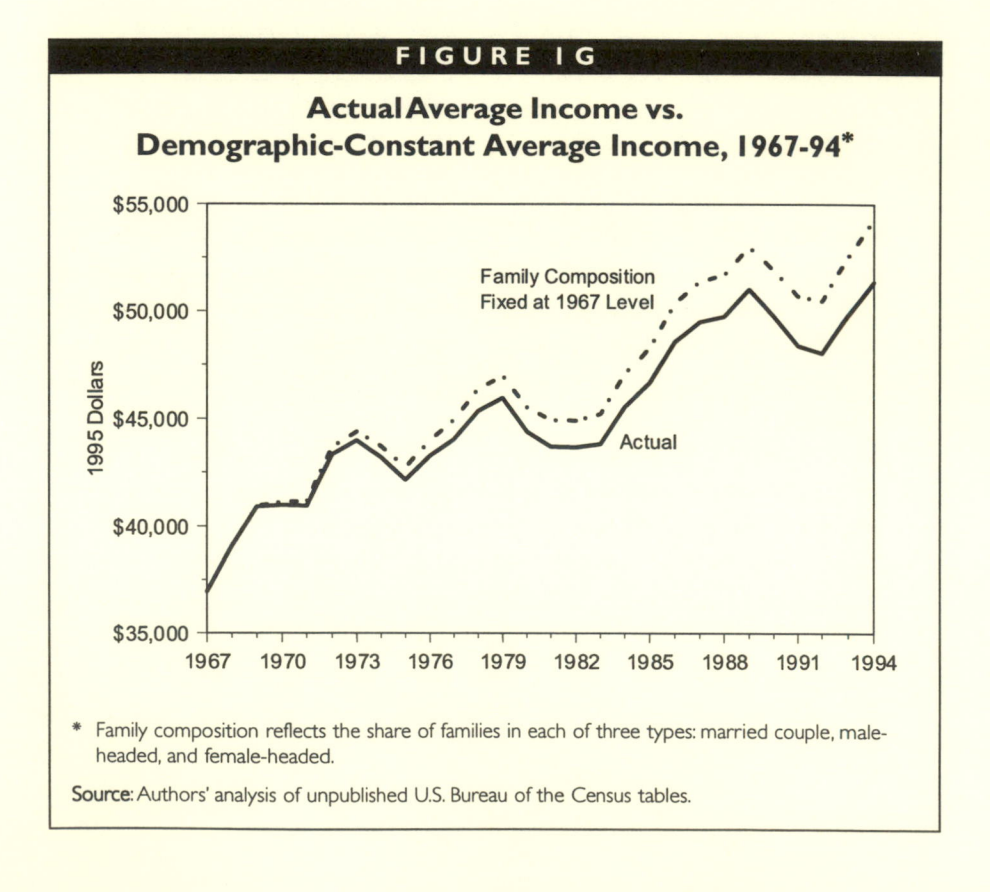

FIGURE 1G

Actual Average Income vs. Demographic-Constant Average Income, 1967-94*

Family Composition Fixed at 1967 Level

Actual

* Family composition reflects the share of families in each of three types: married couple, male-headed, and female-headed.

Source: Authors' analysis of unpublished U.S. Bureau of the Census tables.

changes in the composition of families. This simple "fixed-weight" analysis divides the population of families into three types: families headed by a married couple and families headed by either a single male or female. Over time, the income of married-couple families has gone up relative to that of families with a single head of household. Since this trend has been accompanied by a long-term shift from married-couple to single-headed families, we would expect the trend in mean income with family composition fixed in 1967 to lie above the actual trend.

As **Table 1.17** shows, by 1989 mean family income was $51,012; in the absence of family type changes, mean income would have been $53,003. Thus, the shift to families with slower income growth (or larger losses) reduced mean income by $1,990 in 1989. While this information reveals that changes in family composition had the expected negative impact on average family income in the 1980s, the most relevant question is whether this type of demographic change

TABLE 1.17

Growth in Household Income,
Actual and Fixed Demographic Weights, 1967-95

| Year | Average Family Income | | |
	Actual	Holding Family Type Constant*	Difference
1967	$37,866	$37,866	$0
1973	43,983	44,390	-407
1979	45,959	46,985	-1,026
1989	51,012	53,003	-1,990
1995	51,353	54,319	-2,966
Annualized Percent Change			
1967-73	2.53%	2.68%	-0.16
1973-79	0.74	0.95	-0.22
1979-89	1.05	1.21	-0.16
1989-95	0.11	0.41	-0.30

* These values represent what the average income would have been if the composition of family types had remained as in 1967.

Source: Authors' analysis of unpublished Census tables.

can be held responsible in large part for the increases in income stagnation and inequality in the 1980s.

The second panel in the table shows, in fact, that the impact of family-composition changes on mean income growth was greater in the 1970s than in the 1980s. During the earlier decade, the shift to single-headed families slowed the growth of mean income by 0.22 percentage points per year, while in the later period the effect of the shift was to slow growth by 0.16 points per year. In fact, this 0.16 point difference in the 1980s is the same-sized difference that prevailed in the 1967-73 period, when income growth among all family types was positive (see Table 1.5). The fact that family composition changes had a lesser effect over the period when income problems worsened for most family types (Table 1.5) suggests that income changes *within* each family type were more important than composition shifts *between* family types.

As seen earlier, the median income of each family type declined in the 1989-95 period. Among the three family types examined in Table 1.17, the only family type to experience *mean*, or average, income growth was married-couple families. Since the mean income of single-headed families fell in real terms, and the shift to these less-well-off family types continued apace, compositional changes had a strong effect on mean income growth over this period. In fact, instead of falling slightly, in the absence of family composition changes mean income would have grown in the 1989-95 period.

Table 1.17 presents a limited view of the impact of demographic change in that it controls only for shifts in three family types. **Table 1.18** extends this type of analysis by fixing a wider range of demographic factors in the base period, including age, race, and education. Once again, we see that demographic changes were favorable in the 1980s relative to the 1970s. Changes in the age structure, for example, lowered average income in the 1970s but actually increased the household median by $354 in the 1980s, due primarily to baby boomers entering their prime earning years. Race and household type (married couple, nonmarried couple, and unrelated individuals) are once again seen to decrease median income, but less so than in the 1970s. Finally, educational attainment had an expected positive effect, though slightly less in the later period. In fact, once education is included, the full effect of demographic change was income enhancing in the 1980s. (A similar finding of the poverty-reducing effect of educational upgrading is shown in Table 6.18.)

Finally, we examine the impact of family composition changes on the growth of income inequality in the period 1959-93 (**Table 1.19**). This table decomposes, or breaks down, the annual growth of the Gini ratio into the portion due to fam-

TABLE 1.18

Detailed Effects of Demographic Changes
on Median Household Income, 1970s and 1980s

Median Household Income, 1989 (1995 dollars): $35,527

Variable	1970s	1980s
Age	-$678	$354
Race	-135	-103
Household Type	-2,548	-1,417
Education	1,875	1,824

Source: U.S. Bureau of the Census (1992).

TABLE 1.19

Growth in Income Inequality as Measured
by the Gini Ratio, 1969-93

		Annual Growth Due to:		Percent of Change Due to:	
Period	Annual Growth in Gini Ratio (X100)	Family Composition Changes*	Other Causes	Family Composition Changes	Other Causes
1959-69	-0.460	0.050	-0.510	-10.9%	110.9%
1969-79	0.120	0.110	0.010	91.7	8.3
1979-93	0.386	0.100	0.286	25.9	74.1

* Change in annual growth rate due to shift from married-couple to male- or female-headed households.

Source: Authors' analysis of Karoly and Burtless (1995) and Burtless (1995).

ily composition changes (i.e., the shift from married-couple to male- and female-headed households and to one-person families) and to other causes, including the growth of inequality within family types. (As explained above, a growing Gini ratio means higher inequality.) As expected, family composition changes led to higher levels of income inequality throughout the period. For example, between 1969 and 1979, composition changes led to a 0.110 annual increase in the Gini ratio (these changes have been multiplied by 100 for presentation purposes). Increases in inequality within family types ("other causes") played a small role over this period. Since the total annual increase in the Gini was 0.120, family composition changes were the driving factor in increased income inequality, explaining 91.7% of the change. In the most recent period (1979-93), however, the Gini grew more than three times as fast as in the earlier period; yet the family composition effect fell slightly. At the same time, the contribution of other factors grew significantly, accounting for about three-quarters of the increase. Thus, demographic factors explained only 25.9% of the increase over the 1979-93 period, and inequality growth within demographic groups drove the increase. Again, demographic explanations are seen to be least applicable to the period over which inequality grew the most.

The Shrinking Middle Class?

Another dimension of income growth is the proportion of the population that has low, middle, and high incomes. Two factors determine the distribution of the population at various income levels—the rate of growth of average income and changes in income equality. As average income grows (holding inequality constant), there will be a greater proportion of the population at higher income levels. However, if inequality grows such that the low-income population receives an unusually low proportion of the income growth and the high income population obtains an unusually large proportion, then a rise in average income is unlikely to translate into a general upward movement of the population to higher income levels. Thus, as seen in Table 1.9, it is possible for incomes to grow on average while segments of the population suffer income declines.

Table 1.20 shows the proportion of families, households, and persons with low, middle, and high incomes in 1967, 1979, 1989, and 1995. For households and families, the definition of middle income has been arbitrarily set as a range from $15,000 to $50,000. Among persons, middle income has been set at 50% to 200% of median family (size-adjusted) income.

Over the 1967-89 period, the proportion of families with middle incomes declined as more families attained incomes beyond $50,000. The shift upward was much smaller over the 1979-89 period than in the 1967-79 period (4.2% versus 13.9%). The 1980s also saw a shifting of 0.6% of families out of the middle-income and into the low-income category. Family income losses since 1989 have led to a downward shift in income, as seen by the 1.6% shift out of the top group of families into the bottom group.

TABLE 1.20

Distribution of Persons, Households, and Families
by Income Level, 1967-95
(1995 Dollars)

Income Level	Percent of Persons by Income Levels				Percentage-Point Change		
	1967	1979	1989	1995	1969-79	1979-89	1989-95
Families (Income)							
Under $15,000	16.3%	13.0%	13.5%	14.0%	-3.3	0.5	0.5
$15,000 to $50,000	60.9	51.0	46.4	47.0	-9.9	-4.6	0.6
Over $50,000	22.8	36.0	40.1	39.0	13.2	4.1	-1.1
Total	100.0	100.0	100.0	100.0			
Households (Income)							
Under $15,000	24.0%	21.0%	20.2%	21.0%	-3.0	-0.8	0.8
$15,000 to $50,000	56.2	49.7	46.8	47.0	-6.5	-2.9	0.2
Over $50,000	19.8	29.3	33.0	31.9	9.5	3.7	-1.1
Total	100.0	100.0	100.0	100.0			
Persons (Income Relative to Median)*							
Less than 50%	17.9%	20.0%	22.1%	22.2%	2.1	2.1	0.1
50% to 200%	71.2	68.0	63.3	62.0	-3.2	-4.7	-1.3
More than 200%	10.9	11.9	14.7	15.9	1.0	2.8	1.2
Total	100.0	100.0	100.0	100.0			

* Each person assigned his or her family's per capita (size-adjusted) income. Figures in first column refer to 1969.

Source: U.S. Bureau of the Census (1996) and unpublished tables from John McNeil.

Among households, including single persons in addition to families, there was again a shift toward the top income group in both earlier periods, though the shift decelerated over the 1980s. As with families, the most recent period saw an exclusively downward shift, as a 1.1% share of households fell from the top and middle to the lowest group. Thus, the 1979-94 period saw a growth in the share of both households and families in the lowest and highest income groups and a decline in middle-income families.

The third panel of Table 1.20 examines the incomes of people—single and in families—according to the per capita incomes of their families (size-adjusted), with a single person given their individual income. In this analysis, the income of persons is measured relative to the median, which, unlike the above, is not a fixed "breakpoint" but shifts with the trend in the median. In this regard, this panel reveals more the distribution of relative income (i.e., the distance between persons in the income distribution) than changes in the absolute income levels, as in the earlier panels. The analysis shows a consistent shift out of middle incomes since 1969 (the earliest data point for this series), but the shift is into the lower- as well as into the higher-income group. The shift upward is stronger in the 1980s than in the 1970s (2.8% versus 1.0%), as those families at the top of the income scale pulled farther away from the pack. Over the most recent period, 1989-95, the share of families closest to the median has continued to shrink, with the larger share (1.2% out of 1.3%) shifting upward.

Table 1.21 continues this relative income analysis of persons from Table 1.20, but it categorizes families and persons by the education level of their household head and is limited to people in their prime earning years (25-64). Over the full 1969-94 period, the proportion of families headed by a high school graduate (or a high school dropout) who had either a middle-class or high relative income shrank, especially since 1979. Note in particular the large growth among the lowest relative income group (less than half the median). For example, between 1969 and 1989 this group grew by 16.6 percentage points for families headed by someone with less than a high school education and by 8.1 points for families with high-school-educated heads of household. Even among the "some college" category there has been a general shift to a smaller middle-income population and to a greater low-income population. (There was a 0.6 point increase in the percentage of high-income families in the 1979-89 period, which was fully reversed in 1989-95.) The families with college graduates as their household heads were shifting downward in relative income from 1969 to 1979 but upward after 1979. These changes in the income levels of families and persons by the educational attainment of the household head reflect the trends in wages for the various educational groups: college graduates' wages fell in the 1970s (because of a surplus in the supply of such workers), but grew modestly in the 1980s, and wages fell among the non-college-educated workforce between 1979 and 1995. (See Chapter 3 for an analysis of these trends.) The fact that even some college workers have lost ground since the late 1980s is reflected by the slight 0.2 increase in the share with low relative incomes over the 1989-94 period.

TABLE 1.21

Distribution of Prime-Age Adults
by Relative Income Level,* 1969-95

Family Income Relative to Median	Percent of Persons at Relative Income Levels				Percentage-Point Change		
	1969	1979	1989	1995	1969-79	1979-89	1989-95
Less Than High School							
Less than 50%	21.8%	28.9%	38.4%	42.7%	7.1	9.5	4.3
50% to 200%	71.3	65.5	57.1	53.8	-5.8	-8.4	-3.3
More than 200%	6.7	5.6	4.5	3.5	-1.1	-1.1	-1.0
Total	100.0	100.0	100.0	100.0			
High School Graduate							
Less than 50%	7.6%	11.0%	15.7%	17.2%	3.4	4.7	1.5
50% to 200%	77.7	75.6	71.3	70.0	-2.1	-4.3	-1.3
More than 200%	14.5	13.4	12.9	12.8	-1.1	-0.5	-0.1
Total	100.0	100.0	100.0	100.0			
Some College							
Less than 50%	5.9%	8.6%	10.3%	12.1%	2.7	1.7	1.8
50% to 200%	70.9	71.8	69.6	68.5	0.9	-2.2	-1.1
More than 200%	22.8	19.6	20.2	19.4	-3.2	0.6	-0.8
Total	100.0	100.0	100.0	100.0			
College Graduate							
Less than 50%	3.9%	5.1%	4.6%	4.8%	1.2	-0.5	0.2
50% to 200%	58.6	61.1	55.0	53.1	2.5	-6.1	-1.9
More than 200%	37.2	33.8	40.4	42.1	-3.4	6.6	1.7
Total	100.0	100.0	100.0	100.0			

* Persons from 25 to 64 years old, based on per capita (size-adjusted) family income.

Source: Unpublished tabulations by John McNeil.

Increased Work by Wives Cushions
Income Fall in 1980s, Less So in 1990s

Family-earnings growth has not only been slow and unequal, it has also come increasingly from greater work effort—from a rise in the number of earners per family and in the average weeks and weekly hours worked per earner.

In the 1980s, the primary source of the increased work effort was women, including many with children. As will be detailed in Chapter 3, this increased work effort has occurred simultaneously with a fall in real wages for men and for some groups of women over the decade. The result has been increases in annual earnings primarily through more work rather than through higher hourly wages. As we show below, in the 1990s (i.e., 1989-94), hours of work—as well as earnings—fell for low-wage women, neutralizing their contribution as a source of family income growth.

This trend is troublesome for several reasons. As the 1990s results will show, depending on increased work effort as the primary source of income growth is self-limiting, because it can only go on until all adult (or even teen) family members are full-time, full-year workers. The slowdown in the growth in women's labor-force participation in recent years may even, in fact, signal the near exhaustion of this type of income growth (see Chapter 4). Moreover, there are significant costs and problems associated with this type of growth, one of the most significant being the lack of adequate, affordable child care.

The problem is not that more women or mothers are working but that they are doing so because it is the only way to maintain family incomes in the face of lower real wages. Increased work elicited through falling real wages is a sign of poor performance of the economy. In addition, families are clearly worse off if, to obtain higher incomes, they must work more hours rather than rely on regular pay increases.

Married-couple families (77.7% of all families in 1994, Table 1.5) are most able to increase income through greater work effort because they have two potential adult workers. Single-parent families and individuals, however, can only increase work effort by having the adult work more weekly hours and/or more weeks in a year. It is for this reason that we focus first on the greater work hours of married couples with children.

Figure 1H, which graphs the median percent of total family income contributed by wives' earnings for all families with working wives, shows the growing importance of wives' earnings since 1970. The median percent contribution of working wives grew from around 26% of family income in 1979 to 32% in 1992. Note that all of the growth in this series occurred after 1980, when family income growth was slowest.

The income growth in total and by type of income among married-couple families with children is shown in **Table 1.22**. (The tables in this section use the comprehensive income data set discussed earlier.) Among the bottom two-fifths incomes were either stagnant or falling from 1979 to 1989, while the middle fifth achieved modest growth (4.2% over 10 years, or 0.4% annually). In contrast, the best-off married couples with children had far faster income growth: 12.9% in the 80th to 95th percentile and 49.1% among the top 5%. In the 1990s,

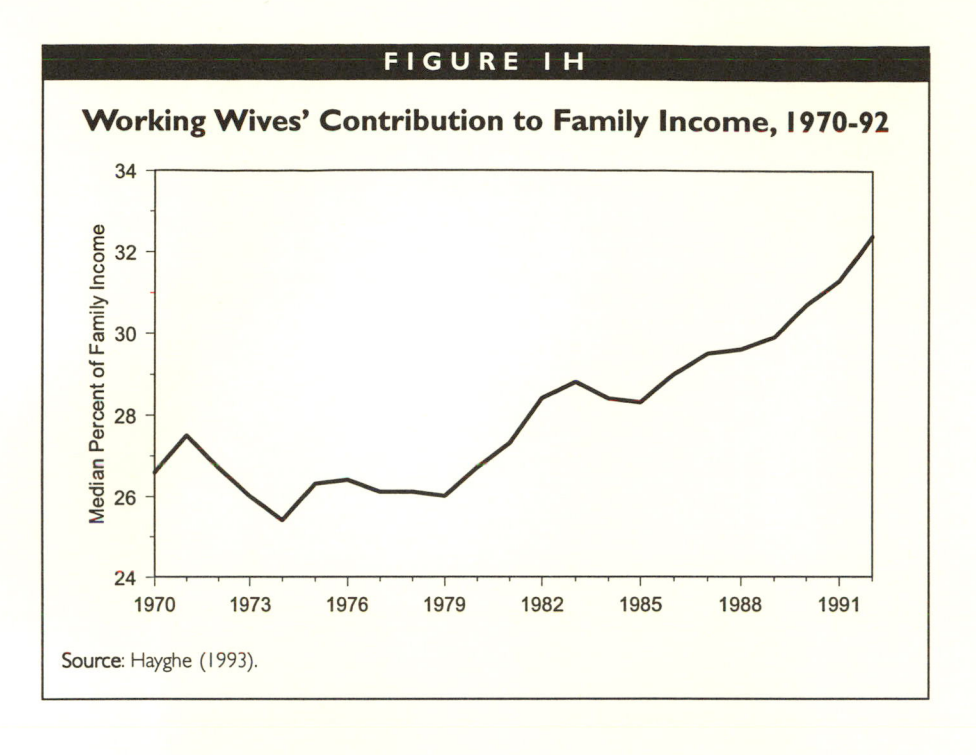

FIGURE 1H

Working Wives' Contribution to Family Income, 1970-92

Source: Hayghe (1993).

average income growth among these families slowed, but the uneven nature of growth persisted, as families in the bottom 60% lost ground (with an accelerated decline among the bottom 40%), while those at the top continued to gain.

The data in Table 1.22 also show the dollar changes in average incomes for each group by three sources: earnings of husbands, earnings of wives, and all other income, including transfers, capital incomes, and children's earnings. Over the 1980s, husbands' earnings fell among the bottom 60%, and other incomes were negative for all but the top 5%, but the earnings of wives grew in each income fifth. It is apparent that the rapid income growth among the top 5% was the result of a growth in both husbands' and wives' earnings, as well as that of other income (particularly capital sources, see Table 1.10). The falling incomes in the bottom two-fifths resulted from the fact that the higher earnings of wives failed to offset the fall in husbands' earnings, particularly in the lowest fifth.

In the 1989-94 period, there was a widespread decline in husbands' earnings for all but the top 5% of families with children. In addition, wives' earnings stagnated in the bottom 40% and grew more slowly in the third and fourth quintiles. Thus, whereas wives in all income quintiles were able to offset their

TABLE 1.22

Changes in Incomes of Married-Couple Families with Children, 1979-94

(1994 Dollars)

Family Income	Lowest Fifth	Second Fifth	Middle Fifth	Fourth Fifth	80 to 95%	Top 5%	Average
1979	19,099	35,313	46,476	59,686	83,038	175,751	53,358
1989	18,164	35,168	48,419	64,846	93,735	262,064	60,483
1994	16,604	33,905	48,093	65,753	100,929	308,213	63,421
Percent Change							
1979-89	-4.9	-0.4	4.2	8.6	12.9	49.1	13.4
1989-94	-8.6	-3.6	-0.7	1.4	7.7	17.6	4.9
Dollar Change by Source							
1979-89							
Total	-936	-145	1,943	5,160	10,697	86,314	7,125
Wives' Earnings	937	2,392	3,809	5,043	7,683	14,936	4,336
Husbands' Earnings	-1,638	-2,564	-1,717	282	4,060	53,972	2,180
Other Income	-234	26	-149	-165	-1,046	17,406	609
1989-94							
Total	-1,560	-1,264	-326	907	7,194	46,149	2,938
Wives' Earnings	37	171	1,226	1,725	7,078	6,969	2,042
Husbands' Earnings	-1,650	-1,524	-1,783	-459	-2,235	40,381	600
Other Income	54	89	231	-358	2,351	-1,200	296

Source: Authors' analysis.

husbands' losses in the 1980s, this was no longer the case for the bottom 60% in the 1990s. Though the average earnings of wives grew in the 1989-94 period, only among the top 60-95th percentile families were wives able to significantly offset the loss in the husbands' average earnings. In fact, the annualized 1989-94 rate of pay increases of both husbands and wives in the top fifth matched their rates of increase in the 1980s.

Table 1.23 presents the growth in annual hours worked by husbands and wives in families with children. These results show that it was more work, rather than higher hourly wages, that fueled income growth over the 1980s (the data include the growth in hours of wives who were already working along with the added hours of wives who joined the workforce over the period). The drop in husbands' an-

TABLE 1.23

Husbands' and Wives' Hours of Work, 1979-94

	Lowest Fifth	Second Fifth	Middle Fifth	Fourth Fifth	80 to 95%	Top5%	Average
Husbands' Hours							
1979	1,678	2,074	2,155	2,226	2,300	2,490	2,096
1989	1,706	2,138	2,212	2,274	2,364	2,554	2,148
1994	1,607	2,145	2,257	2,340	2,387	2,615	2,159
Change 1979-89							
Percent	1.7	3.1	2.6	2.2	2.8	2.5	2.5
Hours	28	65	56	48	65	63	52
Change 1989-94							
Percent	-5.8	0.3	2.1	2.9	1.0	2.4	0.5
Hours	-100	7	45	66	23	62	10
Wives' Hours							
1979	478	733	876	1,086	1,164	828	851
1989	653	1,009	1,190	1,332	1,407	1,146	1,105
1994	634	1,062	1,290	1,419	1,605	929	1,168
Change 1979-89							
Percent	36.5	37.8	35.8	22.7	20.9	38.4	29.9
Hours	175	277	314	247	243	318	255
Change 1989-94							
Percent	-2.9	5.3	8.5	6.5	14.1	-19.0	5.7
Hours	-19	53	101	86	198	-217	63

Source: Authors' analysis.

nual earnings from 1979 to 1989, shown in the previous table, occurred despite the fact that husbands were working more, not fewer, hours. In 1989, the average husband (including some not employed) in the second to top fifths worked at least full time and year-round (2,080 hours, or 40 hours for 52 weeks).

Wives' hours grew a great deal over the 1980s, about 30% on average, with above-average growth among wives in the bottom 60% and in the top 5%. The addition of 255 hours to the average family's labor supply added more than six weeks of paid work to the family's income.

For those in the bottom 60% of families with children, husbands' annual earnings fell in the 1980s because of the erosion of their hourly wages: they fell 8.0% for husbands in the middle fifth and 12.5% for husbands in the lowest fifth **(Table 1.24)**. Hourly wages grew only for husbands in the best-off fifth of families, by a moderate 4.2% for those in the top 80-95th percentile and by 40.1% for those in the top 5%. Despite these gains at the top, the majority of husbands in these families lost ground over the 1980s due to falling hourly wages, even with their increased work effort.

It is useful to note the degree to which an increase in wives' hours is neces-

TABLE 1.24

Change in the Hourly Wages of Husbands and Wives,*
1979-94
(1994 Dollars)

	Lowest Fifth	Second Fifth	Middle Fifth	Fourth Fifth	80 to 95%	Top5%	Average
Husbands' Hourly Wage							
1979	8.12	13.15	16.43	19.31	24.65	49.64	18.39
1989	7.02	11.55	15.23	19.03	25.70	69.54	18.95
1994	6.43	10.81	14.14	18.30	24.52	83.35	19.08
Percent Change							
1979-89	-13.5	-12.1	-7.3	-1.5	4.2	40.1	3.1
1989-94	-8.4	-6.5	-7.2	-3.8	-4.6	19.8	0.7
Wives' Hourly Wage							
1979	5.07	6.94	8.39	10.03	12.23	16.43	9.37
1989	5.15	7.41	9.38	11.96	15.58	24.91	11.13
1994	5.36	7.20	9.60	12.45	18.07	38.23	12.26
Percent Change							
1979-89	1.6	6.7	11.8	19.2	27.4	51.6	18.8
1989-94	4.1	-2.8	2.3	4.1	16.0	53.5	10.1

* In married-couple families with children.

Source: Authors' analysis.

sary to offset the fall in the wages of husbands, given that men earn significantly higher hourly wages. For example, the $1.20 drop in the hourly wage of husbands in the middle fifth from 1979 to 1989 (working 2,212 annual hours) created an annual loss of $2,654. Replacing this income would require a wife in the middle fifth (earning $9.38 hourly) to work 283 additional hours annually, or more than seven extra full-time weeks.

Over the 1989-94 period, husbands' hours of work fell in the bottom quintile, while wives' hours fell in the bottom fifth and grew slightly in the second fifth. It seems that the strategy of increasing hours of work to counteract wage decline was no longer viable for these families, and their incomes fell at a much faster rate than they had in the earlier decade. Whether these families unsuccessfully sought more work or simply decided to work less is unclear. It is clear, however, that their declining hours left them economically worse off. Hours of wives in the top 60% of families increased more slowly than in the prior period, and those of the wealthiest wives actually decreased. On average, wives' hours grew at an annual rate of 2.6% in the 1980s; the comparable rate for the 1990s was 1.1%.

Wage decline for husbands (Table 1.24) accelerated and was more widespread in the 1990s; only husbands in the top 5% saw an increase. The average hourly earnings of wives grew 10.1% over the period, with those in the lowest fifth and highest fifth increasing their rate of wage growth. Wives in the second fifth actually lost ground and, given their small increase in hours, were unable to contribute to family income growth as they had in the 1980s.

Table 1.25 and **Figure 1I** bring together the information from the prior tables to identify the role of increased earnings and hours worked by wives on family income growth in the 1980s and 1990s. The first panel focuses on the 1980s, and the bottom panel examines the 1989-94 period.

In the 1980s, without the increase in the earnings of wives, the lowest 40% of families would have experienced significantly greater losses than those that actually occurred. For example, while the average income of married-couple families with children in the second fifth fell slightly (0.4%) from 1979-89, the decline would have been 7.2% if wives' earnings had not increased and 6.2% if their hours had not increased. In addition, the average income of the middle fifth, which grew 4.2% over the decade, would have fallen, and the gains to the upper 40% would have been notably smaller (the top 5% is an exception due to the strong growth of husbands' wages).

As prior tables have shown, both increases in wives' hours and wages made positive contributions to family income growth in the 1980s. When we isolate the effects of these two factors, we find that, with the exception of those in the

TABLE 1.25

Role of Higher Wives' Earnings and Hours on Family Income Growth, 1979-94
(Married Couples with Children)

1979-89	Lowest Fifth	Second Fifth	Middle Fifth	Fourth Fifth	80 to 95%	Top 5%	Average
Change in Family Income							
Percent	-4.9	-0.4	4.2	8.6	12.9	49.1	13.4
Dollars	-936	-145	1,943	5,160	10,697	86,314	7,125
Change in Family Income Without Higher Wives' Earnings							
Percent	-9.8	-7.2	-4.0	0.2	3.6	40.6	5.2
Dollars	-1,872	-2,537	-1,867	117	3,014	71,378	2,791
Change in Family Income Without Higher Wives' Hours							
Percent	-9.6	-6.2	-2.2	3.7	8.3	44.6	8.0
Dollars	-1,835	-2,195	-1,000	2,212	6,915	78,400	4,291
Effect on Family Income of Change in:							
Wives' Earnings and Hours							
Percent	4.9	6.8	8.2	8.4	9.3	8.5	8.1
Dollars	937	2,392	3,809	5,043	7,683	14,936	4,334
Wives' Hours							
Percent	4.7	5.8	6.3	4.9	4.6	4.5	5.3
Dollars	899	2,050	2,943	2,949	3,783	7,914	2,833
Wives' Hourly Wage							
Percent	0.2	1.0	1.9	3.5	4.7	4.0	2.8
Dollars	38	343	867	2,094	3,901	7,022	1,501

(continued)

TABLE 1.25 (cont.)

Role of Higher Wives' Earnings and Hours on Family Income Growth, 1979-94 (Married Couples with Children)

1989-94	Lowest Fifth	Second Fifth	Middle Fifth	Fourth Fifth	80 to 95%	Top 5%	Average
Change in Family Income							
Percent	-8.6	-3.6	-0.7	1.4	7.7	17.6	4.9
Dollars	-1,560	-1,264	-326	907	7,194	46,149	2,938
Family Income Change Without Higher Wives' Earnings							
Percent	-8.8	-4.1	-3.2	-1.3	0.1	15.0	1.5
Dollars	-1,597	-1,435	-1,552	-817	116	39,180	895
Family Income Change Without Higher Wives' Hours							
Percent	-8.0	-4.7	-2.7	-0.3	3.9	20.8	3.6
Dollars	-1,458	-1,648	-1,294	-165	3,617	54,453	2,163
Effect on Family Income of Change in:							
Wives' Earnings and Hours							
Percent	0.2	0.5	2.5	2.7	7.6	2.7	3.4
Dollars	37	171	1,226	1,725	7,078	6,969	2,043
Wives' Hours							
Percent	-0.6	1.1	2.0	1.7	3.8	-3.2	1.3
Dollars	-102	384	968	1,072	3,577	-8,304	775
Wives' Hourly Wage							
Percent	0.8	-0.6	0.5	1.0	3.7	5.8	2.1
Dollars	139	-213	258	652	3,501	15,273	1,268

Source: Authors' analysis.

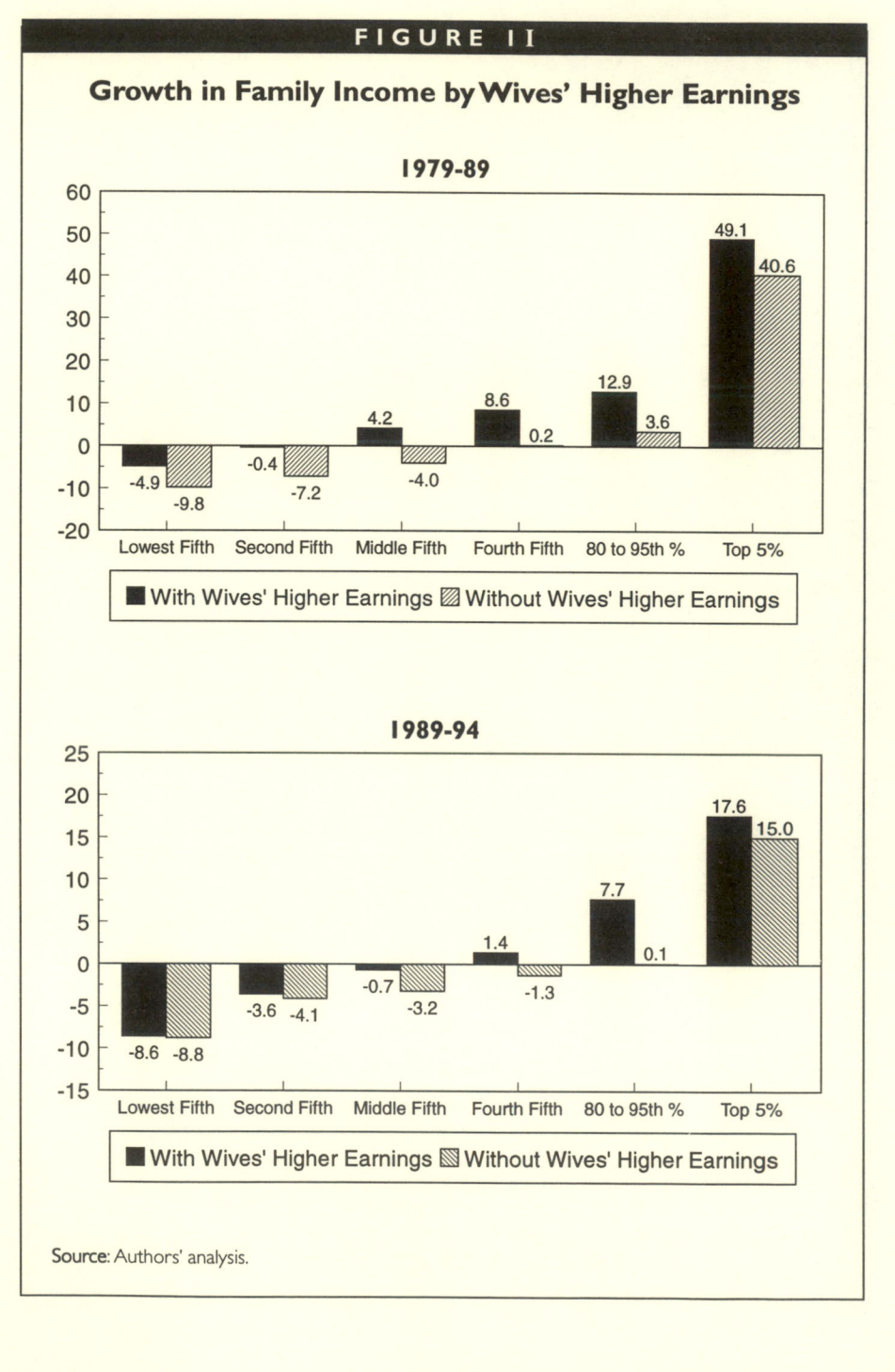

FIGURE 11

Growth in Family Income by Wives' Higher Earnings

1979-89

Lowest Fifth: -4.9 (With), -9.8 (Without)
Second Fifth: -0.4 (With), -7.2 (Without)
Middle Fifth: 4.2 (With), -4.0 (Without)
Fourth Fifth: 8.6 (With), 0.2 (Without)
80 to 95th %: 12.9 (With), 3.6 (Without)
Top 5%: 49.1 (With), 40.6 (Without)

■ With Wives' Higher Earnings ▨ Without Wives' Higher Earnings

1989-94

Lowest Fifth: -8.6 (With), -8.8 (Without)
Second Fifth: -3.6 (With), -4.1 (Without)
Middle Fifth: -0.7 (With), -3.2 (Without)
Fourth Fifth: 1.4 (With), -1.3 (Without)
80 to 95th %: 7.7 (With), 0.1 (Without)
Top 5%: 17.6 (With), 15.0 (Without)

■ With Wives' Higher Earnings ▨ Without Wives' Higher Earnings

Source: Authors' analysis.

top fifth, increases in wives' hours were the most important factor driving wives' contributions to family income. For example, in the bottom fifth, wage increases added 0.2% out of the 4.9% added to family income; in the second fifth, the wage contribution was 1.0% out of 6.8%. In the top fifth, wage and hour contributions are roughly equal.

The role of wives' earnings and hours was quite different in the 1990s relative to the earlier decade, particularly among lower-income families. Over this period, wives' contributions to their families' incomes in the lowest two-fifths were negligible; that is, their earnings or hours fell over the period. Thus, without any decline in hours, the average family with children in the bottom fifth would have lost $1,458 in 1989-94 instead of its actual loss of $1,560. In the second fifth, hours increased slightly but the wives' average wage fell, leading to a slightly positive effect (0.5%) on family income. Elsewhere throughout the distribution, wives' hours and earnings were positive contributors to family income, though generally at a slower rate than over the 1980s (note the effect of declining hours in the top 5%, which was offset by a sharp increase—5.8%—in the effect of wives' average wages).

Have the growing earnings of wives contributed to the growth of income inequality? The notion that the growth of "two-earner" families has contributed to growing inequality is intuitively plausible if one thinks that there has been a growth of high-wage employed women marrying high-wage men. It is true, in fact, that wives in higher-income families earn more than those in other families and that their hourly wages have grown the quickest (Table 1.24). However, the fastest growth in work hours has been among the wives in the bottom three-fifths (Table 1.23), and, at least over the 1980s, the effect of wives' hours on family income growth has been fairly even, while wage growth has been somewhat lower in the lowest two-fifths (Table 1.24). The data discussed so far, however, only indirectly relate to whether the pattern of growth of wives' earnings led to greater inequality and do not address whether inequality would be higher or lower without any earnings from wives. The following two tables address this omission.

The data in **Table 1.26** allow a direct examination of the effect of wives' earnings on income inequality from 1979 to 1994 and on the growth of inequality over that period. For example, in 1979, the availability of wives' earnings led to a more equal distribution of income, since without wives' earnings the lowest fifth would have had a 6.5% share of total income instead of the 7.2% share it had with wives' earnings. Overall in 1979, wives' earnings increased the income shares of the bottom four-fifths and decreased the share of income of the top fifth by 2.1 percentage points. In 1989, the availability of wives' earn-

TABLE 1.26

Effect of Wives' Earnings on Income Shares Among Married Couples with Children, 1979-94

	Lowest Fifth	Second Fifth	Middle Fifth	Fourth Fifth	80 to 95%	Top 5%	Average
Family Income Shares, 1979							
Actual	7.2	13.2	17.4	22.4	23.3	16.5	100.0
Without Wives' Earnings	6.5	12.5	16.9	22.1	23.8	18.2	100.0
Effect of Wives' Earnings	0.7	0.7	0.5	0.3	-0.4	-1.7	-0.0
Family Income Shares, 1989							
Actual	6.0	11.7	16.0	21.4	23.3	21.6	100.0
Without Wives' Earnings	5.2	10.6	15.1	20.8	23.5	24.8	100.0
Effect of Wives' Earnings	0.8	1.1	0.8	0.7	-0.3	-3.1	-0.0
Family Income Shares, 1994							
Actual	5.2	10.7	15.2	20.7	23.9	24.3	100.0
Without Wives' Earnings	4.4	9.8	14.2	19.8	23.5	28.2	100.0
Effect of Wives' Earnings	0.8	0.9	0.9	0.9	0.4	-3.9	0.0
Change in Income Shares, 1979-89							
Actual	-1.2	-1.5	-1.5	-0.9	-0.1	5.2	0.0
Without Wives' Earnings	-1.3	-1.9	-1.8	-1.3	-0.2	6.6	0.0
Effect of Wives' Earnings	0.2	0.4	0.3	0.4	0.1	-1.4	0.0
Change in Income Shares, 1989-94							
Actual	-0.8	-1.0	-0.8	-0.7	-0.1	2.6	0.0
Without Wives' Earnings	-0.8	-0.8	-0.9	-0.9	0.0	3.4	0.0
Effect of Wives' Earnings	0.0	-0.2	0.1	0.2	0.6	-0.8	0.0

Source: Authors' analysis.

ings had an even larger effect on raising the income shares of the lowest 80% of families and on lessening the income share of the top fifth, which fell by 3.4 points, with the largest share decline in the top 5%. In 1994, it was only the top 5% that would have gained income share had wives not worked.

The bottom panel reveals that between 1979 and 1989 the income shares of the bottom 95% of families with children fell, with the largest declines among the bottom 60%. In the absence of wives' earnings, however, income shares would have been 0.2 points lower in the bottom fifth and about 0.4 points lower in the middle three-fifths. This pattern shows that the shifts in wives' hours and wages were equalizing over the 1979-89 period.

In the latter period—1989-94—the top 20% gained income share, with fairly uniform losses among the bottom 80% of families. Note, however, that wives' earnings had no effect in the bottom fifth. Thus, the outcome of the slowdown in wives' earnings and hours, particularly among lower-income families, had little impact on inequality in the 1990s. Over the entire period (1979-94), how-ever, the equalizing effects of wives' contributions to family income in the 1980s dominated the neutral effects of the 1990s.

The above analysis, while revealing the generally equalizing nature of wives' contribution to family income, imposes a perhaps unrealistic "counterfactual"— family income without wives' earnings. **Table 1.27** presents a related type of analysis that does not depend on this assumption. Here, the squared coefficient of variation (CV)—a measure of inequality where larger numbers mean more

TABLE 1.27

Changes in Income Inequality of Married-Couple Families with Children, 1979-94

		Due to:		
	Total Growth of Squared CV	**Husbands' Earnings and Other Income**	**Wives' Earnings**	**Correlation of Wives' Earnings and Other Income**
1979-89	0.495	0.566	-0.112	0.041
1989-94	0.102	0.046	-0.009	0.065

Source: Authors' analysis.

inequality—is decomposed into its various components. These components are held constant in a base year, and thus these calculations assume that, for example, wives' earnings did not change from one period to the next (as opposed to the assumption that wives had no earnings). The components of the CV are husbands' earnings and other income, wives' earnings, and the correlation between wives' earnings and other income (this factor measures the extent to which increases in wives' earnings occurred simultaneously with increases in other income sources, including husbands' earnings and unearned income).

The first row reveals that the CV for married couples with children grew 0.495 from 1979-89. This growth was fully explained by the disequalizing changes in income sources other than wives' earnings (husbands' earnings and unearned income, such as realized capital gains, which grew a great deal over this period). Here again, wives' earnings are seen to be equalizing, as they led to a 0.112 point decrease in the CV over this period. The fact that high-earning wives were located in families with significant increases in other incomes drove the increase in the final component of the CV. The CV continued to increase in the 1990s, though more slowly than in the earlier period. The fact that wives' earnings were only slightly equalizing is attributable to the relative decline in the earnings and hours of less-well-off wives.

The growth in work hours in the 1979-89 period took place on average in all families and not just in married-couple families with children (to whom all of the data previously presented applied). In **Table 1.28,** we pool the hours of family work effort across the family and take the average for each fifth (these data are from a slightly different source from the previous tables; see table note). For the three family types in the table, family work effort increased for each income group over the 1980s, with the largest increases among the least well-off. Among all families, for example, those in the bottom fifth worked an average of 97 hours more in 1989 than in 1979, a 9.6% increase. The increase for the top group was 2.4%, though the potential increase among these families was constrained by their very high levels of work. Even unrelated individuals, who by definition cannot increase family work hours by sending more workers into the labor force, saw relatively large increases in their labor supply.

Hours of work fell for most families in the 1989-94 period; the average for all families declined by 1.2%. Of the family types we examine, only married couples with children were able to increase their average labor supply, and these increases took place only among the middle three-fifths of families. Even with these declines, family work hours have generally increased for all income groups since 1979.

TABLE 1.28

Changes in Family Hours Worked by Family Type, 1979-94

	Bottom	Second	Middle	Fourth	Top	Average
All						
1979	999	2,107	2,913	3,436	4,156	2722
1989	1,096	2,243	3,049	3,619	4,255	2852
1994	1,064	2,099	3,021	3,698	4,206	2818
Percent Change						
1979-89	9.6	6.5	4.6	5.3	2.4	4.8
1989-94	-2.9	-6.4	-0.9	2.2	-1.1	-1.2
Married Couples with Children						
1979	2,186	2,943	3,232	3,700	4,288	3270
1989	2,395	3,268	3,609	3,918	4,294	3497
1994	2,296	3,344	3,762	4,051	4,292	3549
Percent Change						
1979-89	9.5	11.1	11.7	5.9	0.1	6.9
1989-94	-4.1	2.3	4.3	3.4	-0.1	1.5
Unrelated Individuals						
1979	649	1,387	1,822	2,034	2,170	1612
1989	759	1,603	1,944	2,091	2,246	1729
1994	671	1,572	1,889	2,104	2,265	1700
Percent Change						
1979-89	17.0	15.6	6.7	2.8	3.5	7.2
1989-94	-11.6	-2.0	-2.8	0.6	0.8	-1.7

Source: Authors' analysis.

We conclude that in the 1980s families worked longer for less. In the case of married-couple families with children, husbands' earnings declines were offset by wives' increases in both hours and earnings. Since the relative increases were greater among lower-income families, the effect of wives' contributions was to lower family income inequality. In the 1990s, families had to contend with wage decline that was more widespread (i.e., wives' wages fell or grew more slowly) and with decreases in hours of work. Together, these factors neutralized the ability of working wives to counteract both increasing inequality and wage erosion experienced by husbands in nearly all families.

Because greater earnings from wives can contribute to greater income growth for married-couple families but not for single-parent families or individuals, it is possible that greater wives' earnings may have contributed to growing inequality among all families. For instance, if increased wives' earnings raised the incomes of married couples, as they did, and increased work effort did not raise the incomes of single-parent families or of individuals to the same degree, then overall income inequality would grow.

Falling Behind the Earlier Generations

Until this point we have exclusively focused on cross-section comparisons, such as comparing the incomes of high-income, older, or married-couple families in one year to those of another. Although these comparisons accurately portray changes in various dimensions of the income distribution over time, they do not trace the incomes of particular families or individuals. For instance, consider comparisons of income growth by income fifth over a 10-year period. A person or family may be in the middle fifth in the first year but in a higher or lower fifth 10 years later. Thus, a comparison of middle-income families over time actually compares one set of families in the first year to a different set of families in the later year.

It is especially important to note that the incomes of individuals and families generally follow a life-cycle pattern. Typically, a person, after completing schooling, starts earning income in a relatively low-paying entry-level job, sees fast income growth as job changes, accumulated experience, and seniority occur over the next two decades, and obtains slower income growth in his or her later working years. As **Figure 1J** shows, young families (headed by a person in his or her twenties) in 1994 had much lower incomes than families headed by a middle-aged person (in his or her forties or fifties). It also shows that incomes grow relatively rapidly as the household head proceeds through his or her thirties and forties, and that income growth slackens and then declines as the household head approaches retirement years.

Viewed this way, the income growth of families as a whole over a 10-year period depends both on how high incomes are for young families when they start out and on how fast incomes grow as families progress through their life-cycle pattern. In fact, the slow growth of median family incomes in recent years is most accurately portrayed as young families starting off with lower incomes than

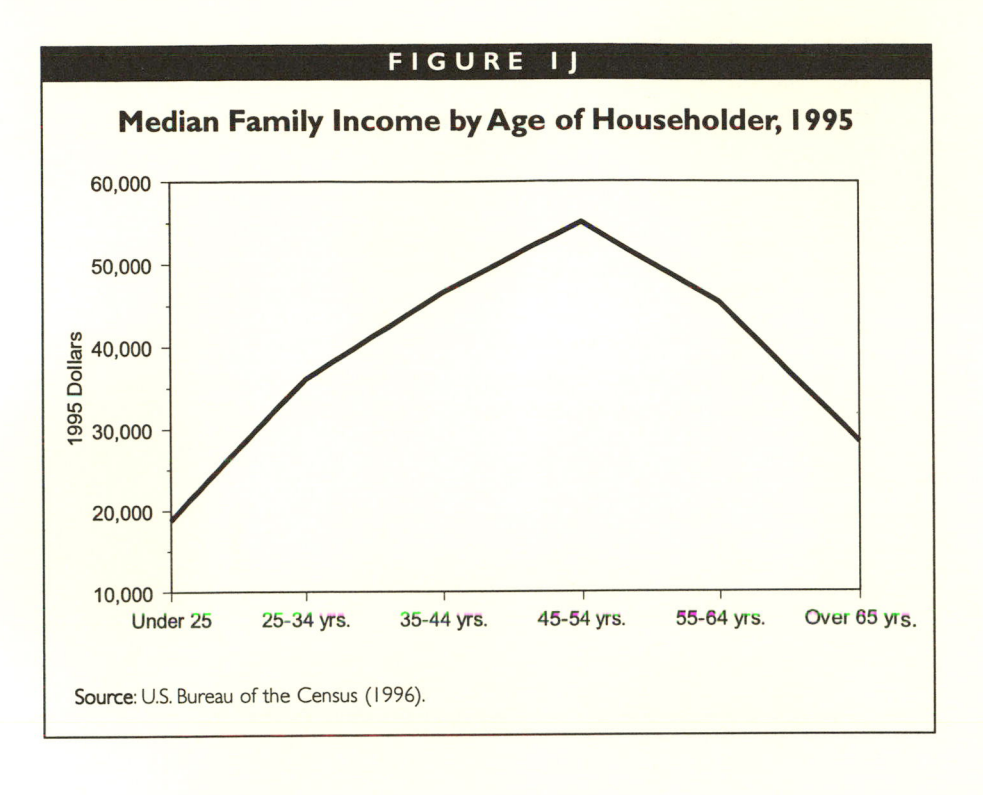

Median Family Income by Age of Householder, 1995

Source: U.S. Bureau of the Census (1996).

their predecessors while other families proceed to higher incomes at a historically slow pace.

No data are available that can trace the income growth of particular people or families over their full life cycles (though below we present data that follow the same persons over time). However, it is possible to examine the income trajectories of "birth cohorts" (a group of people born in the same years) over time, as in **Table 1.29**. The first column shows the median income, in 1995 dollars, of males age 25-34 in the years 1954 through 1994. The second column tracks the median income of 35- to 44-year-olds over these periods. We focus exclusively on males' median incomes, since trends in female income are confounded by large changes in labor supply over this period.

This type of table allows two related types of analyses. By comparing the income levels down each column, we can compare levels across cohorts, such as the different income levels experienced by 25- to 34-year-olds, at different points in time. Thus, reading down column 1 shows that the median income of young males age 25-34 was about 30% lower in 1994 than in 1974. We can also

TABLE 1.29

Median Income by Male 10-Year Birth Cohorts, 1954-94
(1995 Dollars)

Year	Ages 25-34	Ages 35-44	Ages 45-54
Males			
1954	$19,255	$21,289	$20,027
1964	$26,238	$29,748	$27,803
1974	$33,848	$40,686	$39,660
1984	$27,684	$37,589	$37,624
1994	$23,842	$32,386	$36,843
Percent Change			
1954-64	36.3%	39.7%	38.8%
1964-74	29.0	36.8	42.6
1974-84	-18.2	-7.6	-5.1
1984-94	-13.9	-13.8	-2.1

Source: Authors' analysis of unpublished tabulations by U.S. Bureau of the Census.

track a particular cohort's progress through time by reading "down the diagonal." For example, the median income of males age 25-34 was $19,255 in 1954. Ten years later, in 1964, when members of this cohort were ages 35-44, their median income was $29,748; and 10 years after that, when they were 45-54, this cohort's median income was $39,660.

We saw earlier (Table 1.3) that young persons starting out have been doing so from lower income levels in recent years. Table 1.29 corroborates this, as we see that 25- to 34-year-old males have started out with successively lower incomes in 10-year intervals since 1974 (note that this analysis does not follow our usual peak-to-peak comparisons). Similarly, the median incomes of males age 35-54 also fell over the past 20 years.

Perhaps more interesting, in this context, are the changes that occurred within cohorts. For example, note that the median income of men in the cohort that started out in 1964 grew from $26,238 to $40,686 in 1974, an increase of more than 60%. The next male cohort, beginning in 1974, started out higher, at $33,848, but grew less: its median income 10 years later was $37,589, an increase of 11%

(part of this decline is attributable to the fact that 1984 represents the beginning of a recovery). The next cohort started out lower (again, partly due to the business cycle), at $27,684, and its income grew 17%, to $32,386, 10 years later, a much smaller increase than that of the first cohort. Furthermore, only the cohort that began in 1954 experienced an increase from age 35-44 to age 45-54 (in fact, the cohort beginning in 1944 also gained in this context—from $21,289 to $27,803—but we cannot track them from their beginning). The other two cohorts that can be tracked through these age ranges—the cohorts beginning in 1964 and 1974—lost ground as they moved from the second into the third age group.

In sum, we find that each cohort continues to experience the expected age-income profile revealed in Figure 1J. Yet over the last 20 years, each successive cohort has been worse off than the preceding cohort at the same age. This break in upward income mobility across cohorts raises the issue of whether the most recent cohorts (those age 25-34 in 1984 and 1994) will ever achieve incomes equal to those of the earlier postwar cohorts. Given continued slow income growth and falling real wages (see Chapter 3), it is very possible that the recent (and some future) cohorts will have lifetime incomes inferior to those of their parents' generations.

Income Mobility

In this section, we examine a related aspect of the dynamic changes in economic well-being: how much income mobility exists in our economy? If a family is in the lowest fifth in one period, how likely is it to move up to a higher fifth over time? Is this likelihood fixed, or does it tend to fluctuate? These are the questions addressed below.

In order to address these mobility issues we use longitudinal data, or data that follow the same persons over time. Each person is assigned to an income fifth at the beginning and end of the relevant periods of observation based on his or her family's income (three-year incomes are used to "smooth out" temporary movements; we also exclude families headed by someone 62 or over to avoid income changes due to retirement). We create different income cutoffs for each period, meaning that the 20th percentile upper limit in 1979 will be different than that of 1989. This approach to income mobility examines a family's *relative*, as opposed to absolute, position in the income distribution. Thus, a family could improve its relative position (move from a lower to a higher fifth) but be less well-off in terms of its absolute income.

Table 1.30 presents a "transition matrix" for the period 1968-91. Going across each row in the table, the numbers reveal the percent of persons who either stayed in the same fifth or "transitioned" to a higher or lower one. For example, the first entry shows that 46.7% of persons in the bottom fifth in 1968 were also in the bottom fifth in 1991. At the other end of the income scale, 42.0% of those who started in the top fifth stayed there. The percent of "stayers" (those who did not transition out of the fifth they started out in) are shown in bold.

Note that large transitions are uncommon. Only 2.7% of those who began the period in the first fifth ended up in the top fifth, while only 6.7% fell from the top fifth to the lowest fifth. Those transitions that do occur are most likely to be a move up or down to the neighboring fifth. For example, among the middle three-fifths, about two-thirds of the transitions were to neighboring quintiles.

Though Table 1.30 does not reveal a great deal of income mobility, the data do show that mobility exists and that families can and do move up and down as their relative fortunes change. How does this realization connect with the large increases in cross-sectional inequality that we focused on throughout this chapter? In fact, if cross-sectional income inequality is higher in 1989 than in 1979, as we have shown, then, unless mobility has increased, families will grow further apart as time progresses. That is, if the rate of mobility is unchanged over time, increasing inequality will not be offset by changes in mobility. In order to

TABLE 1.30

Income Mobility, 1968-91

1968 Income Group	1991 Income Group					
	First Fifth	Second Fifth	Middle Fifth	Fourth Fifth	Top Fifth	Total
First Fifth	**46.7**	24.5	17.3	8.7	2.7	100.0
Second Fifth	23.6	**26.2**	26.4	14.3	9.6	100.0
Middle Fifth	13.6	21.8	**20.2**	26.2	18.2	100.0
Fourth Fifth	9.2	16.7	20.4	**26.2**	27.6	100.0
Top Fifth	6.7	10.8	16.1	24.5	**42.0**	100.0

Source: Unpublished tabulations of the PSID by Peter Gottschalk.

determine whether the rate of mobility has changed, we must compare two transition matrices covering periods of equal length.

Table 1.31 provides such a comparison. It presents two transition matrices, one for the 1970s and the other for the 1980s. These tables again show relative stability (the largest shares of persons are "stayers," located along the diagonal). For example, both ten-year periods reveal that about 85% of persons in families stayed in the first or second fifths. But more important in this context is the fact that mobility has not increased. The shares of both "stayers" and those who made transitions are very similar in both periods. For example, 61.5% remained in the lowest fifth over the 1970s, and 61.0% remained there in the 1980s. The shares who remained in the middle were almost identical (29.6% versus 29.5%), and only a slightly larger share remained in the top fifth in the 1980s. There is no evidence here of an increase in mobility to offset increased inequality.

TABLE 1.31

Income Mobility over the 1970s and 1980s

1969 Income Group	1979 Income Group					
	First Fifth	Second Fifth	Middle Fifth	Fourth Fifth	Top Fifth	Total
First Fifth	**61.5**	24.0	8.7	4.4	1.5	100.0
Second Fifth	22.7	**31.3**	27.5	12.9	5.6	100.0
Middle Fifth	9.6	22.5	**29.6**	26.1	12.2	100.0
Fourth Fifth	3.3	17.3	22.4	**31.6**	25.4	100.0
Top Fifth	2.9	5.0	11.9	25.1	**55.2**	100.0

1979 Income Group	1989 Income Group					
	First Fifth	Second Fifth	Middle Fifth	Fourth Fifth	Top Fifth	Total
First Fifth	**61.0**	23.8	9.5	4.6	1.1	100.0
Second Fifth	22.9	**33.2**	27.7	13.5	2.7	100.0
Middle Fifth	8.3	25.2	**29.5**	25.7	11.4	100.0
Fourth Fifth	4.6	13.0	23.0	**33.2**	26.2	100.0
Top Fifth	2.7	4.9	10.8	22.8	**58.8**	100.0

Source: Unpublished tabulations of the PSID by Peter Gottschalk.

Conclusion

The most important development regarding contemporary income trends is the slow and unequal growth that continues unabated. Over the 1979-89 period, rapid income growth among upper-income families (87.5% for the top 1%) and stagnant or falling incomes for the bottom 60% of families led to sharp increases in inequality. At the same time, the income of the median family grew more slowly (0.4% per year) than over any other postwar business cycle.

Since 1989, median family incomes have fallen for all family types, and the 1994 median is $2,168 below its 1989 level. While we predict that 1995 data will reveal an increase in this key indicator (as did the 1994 data), it is unlikely that the median will rise to its pre-recession level before the next economic downturn. In fact, our analysis of an important source of family income growth in the 1980s—the contributions of working wives—shows that this source was insufficient to counteract the negative hours and earnings trends in the 1990s that beset the bottom 80% of married-couple families with children. The continuation of labor-market problems, examined in detail in the following chapters, leads us to conclude that most families will continue to experience the same sluggish income growth that characterized the 1980s.

The remainder of the book elaborates on the themes established in this chapter. In the next chapter we focus on changes in the level and distribution of taxes in order to examine the extent to which the U.S. tax system has exacerbated or ameliorated the slow and unequal income growth of the 1980s and 1990s. The third and fourth chapters examine the labor-market trends (wages and employment) that are at the heart of the growth in inequality and sluggish income growth. Chapters 5 and 6 broaden the income analysis by examining trends in wealth and poverty. Chapter 7 examines the impact of wage and income trends from a regional perspective, and Chapter 8 compares trends in the United States to those in other advanced countries.

CHAPTER 2

TAXES
A Further Cause
of Rising Inequality

THE ANALYSIS IN CHAPTER 1 REVEALED THAT THE PRE-TAX INCOMES OF MOST families have stagnated, while the incomes of wealthy families have grown significantly. This chapter broadens the analysis by examining the role of the tax system in these developments.

Three main conclusions arise from this analysis. First, tax changes in the 1980s and 1990s have substantially reduced the taxes paid by the wealthiest 1% of families, while leaving the tax burden on the bottom four-fifths of families almost unchanged. For example, differences in tax laws between 1977 and 1996 lowered the federal tax payments of the top 1% of families by an average of $46,792 (or 18.5% of their average initial tax liability). Over the same period, the bottom four-fifths of families saw their average tax payments fall by just $115 (or 2.5%).

Second, the federal tax changes that contributed to widening income inequality over the full period can be broken into two distinct phases: an early phase, between 1977 and 1985, when the top 1% of families received large tax cuts (an average of $95,482 per family) and the bottom four-fifths saw their average tax burden increase by $209; and a later phase, marked by tax law changes in 1986 and 1993, in which the top 1% lost some but not all of the tax reductions from the earlier period and the bottom four-fifths saw small declines in their tax burden relative to 1977 levels.

The third, and perhaps most important, conclusion is that the widening inequality and the falling standards of living documented in Chapter 1 are, for the most part, independent of any of the changes in the tax structure made during the 1980s and 1990s. The economic problems facing the majority of Americans are, overwhelmingly, a product of their *before*-tax and not their *after*-tax incomes. As mentioned above, the tax burden on the bottom four-fifths of the population is projected to change little between 1977 and 1996. Thus, for this large group, changes in pre-tax income are the key determinants of their economic well-being. Even for the wealthiest 1% of families, whose tax burden was projected to fall dramatically between 1977 and 1996, 88% of the income gains they experienced over the period were due to changes in pre-tax, not post-tax, income.

The Tax Burden: Still Light Overall

Compared to other advanced industrialized countries, the overall U.S. tax burden is light and has increased little in the last 30 years. **Table 2.1** shows the total tax burden in the United States as a percent of gross domestic product (GDP) from 1959 to 1994, broken out by federal and state/local contributions. The overall burden gradually edged up during the postwar period, but it has held relatively constant since 1973, at between 29% and 31% of GDP. However, the state and local burden has grown by 3.3% of GDP over the full period, while the federal burden has grown by only 2.0%. As we show below, the effect of shifting the tax burden to state and local governments is to widen post-tax income inequality.

Table 2.2 puts the U.S. tax burden in an international context by showing government revenues as a percent of GDP for the Organization for Economic Cooperation and Development (OECD) countries (the group of advanced in-

---

TABLE 2.1

Federal vs. State and Local Tax Burdens, 1959-94

Revenue as Percent of Gross Domestic Product

	Federal	State & Local	Total
1959	17.9%	7.5%	25.4%
1967	18.3	8.9	27.2
1973	19.1	10.5	29.6
1979	20.0	9.8	29.8
1989	19.8	10.3	30.2
1994	19.9	10.8	30.7

Source: Authors' analysis of BEA's NIPA data.

---

dustrial countries). In 1993, (the latest year of available data), the United States had the fourth-lowest burden. The percentage point changes in the last column show that, since 1965, every other country except the United Kingdom has had a greater increase in the ratio of tax revenues to GDP than has the United States.

TABLE 2.2

Tax Revenues in OECD Countries, 1965-93, as a Percent of GDP*
(Ranked by 1993 Share)

	1965	1979	1989	1993	Percentage- Point Change 1965-93
Denmark	29.9%	44.5%	50.7%	49.9%	20.0
Sweden	35.0	49.0	55.5	49.9	14.9
Netherlands	32.7	44.3	44.9	48.0	15.3
Italy	25.5	26.6	37.9	47.8	22.3
Finland	30.3	36.7	43.4	45.7	15.4
Belgium	31.2	45.5	44.8	45.7	14.5
Norway	33.3	45.7	46	45.7	12.4
Luxembourg	30.6	45.3	42.2	44.6	14.0
France	34.5	40.2	43.7	43.9	9.4
Austria	34.7	41.0	41.0	43.6	8.9
Greece	22.0	30.1	34.6	41.2	19.2
Germany	31.6	37.8	38.2	39.0	7.4
Ireland	24.7	29.6	35.4	36.3	11.6
New Zealand	24.7	32.7	38.7	35.7	11.0
Canada	25.9	30.6	35.1	35.6	9.7
Spain	14.7	23.3	34.6	35.1	20.4
United Kingdom	30.4	32.6	36.2	33.6	3.2
Switzerland	20.7	31.1	31.7	33.2	12.5
Portugal	18.4	26.0	30.8	31.4	13.0
United States	25.8	28.8	29.7	29.7	3.9
Japan	18.3	24.4	30.7	29.1	10.8
Australia	23.2	27.5	30.6	28.7	5.5
Turkey	10.6	15.7	18.7	23.5	12.9

* Social Security included. United States numbers differ from those in Table 2.1 because the data come from different sources.

Source: OECD (1995).

Despite Progressive Changes, an Increase in Regressivity

Despite the relative stability of the total U.S. tax burden over time, the tax code has undergone frequent changes that have affected the *distribution* of the tax burden. Since the late 1970s, these changes have combined with changes in pretax income to enrich the highest-income families—primarily the top 1%—at the expense of almost everyone else.

In order to incorporate the effect of the most recent round of major tax changes, this section includes an analysis of the Congressional Budget Office's (CBO) projections of the impact of the Omnibus Budget Reconciliation Act of 1993 (OBRA93). These projections generally refer to the distribution of taxes and incomes in 1996 based on projected income levels and tax law in that year. Given the nature of tax law, the tax rate projections are likely to provide an accurate estimate of the distribution of tax burdens. Predicting the distribution of pre-tax incomes, however, is more difficult, so the analysis focuses on changes in tax rates by income class and not on changes in pre-tax income. (Since the years chosen for the federal tax analysis in this section are dictated by the timing of important tax legislation and the availability of data from the Congressional Budget Office, years other than the standard "peak" years, i.e., of low unemployment, appear in some of the tables that follow.)

After-tax family income inequality has increased since 1977, despite recent shifts toward a more progressive tax system (where those with higher incomes pay a larger share of their incomes in taxes). **Table 2.3** looks at the changes in income after all federal taxes between 1977 and 1992, the most recent year for which CBO has conducted analyses using actual, rather than projected, family income data. The average after-tax income of the top fifth of families grew 28.1% from 1977 to 1989, but the most dramatic growth occurred among the wealthiest families: the average income of the top 1% of the income distribution grew 102.2% after taxes during 1977-89. This increase exceeds the growth in pre-tax income (78.0%) by 24.2 percentage points, suggesting that reduced taxation substantially boosted the after-tax incomes of the wealthiest 1% of families in the 1977-89 period.

By contrast, the income of the average family in the bottom four-fifths of the income distribution fell by 1.8% before federal taxes and 2.2% after taxes in the 1977-89 period (Table 2.3). A closer look reveals that it was the poorest families who bore the brunt of these declines: pre- and post-tax income for the

TABLE 2.3

Average After-Tax Family Income Growth, 1977-92*
(1995 Dollars)

Income Group	After-Tax Income				Percent Change in After-Tax Income		Percent Change in Pre-Tax Income	
	1977	1985	1989	1992	77-89	89-92	77-89	89-92
Bottom Four-Fifths	$24,521	$23,502	$23,976	$22,588	-2.2%	-5.8%	-1.8%	-6.5%
First	9,228	7,987	8,264	7,376	-10.4	-10.8	-10.4	-12.1
Second	20,514	18,247	18,452	17,100	-10.1	-7.3	-9.8	-8.3
Third	30,185	28,229	28,623	26,980	-5.2	-5.7	-5.3	-5.9
Fourth	39,716	39,503	40,603	38,923	2.2	-4.1	2.4	-4.2
Top Fifth	$69,026	$82,828	$88,419	$84,966	28.1%	-3.9%	25.4%	-4.0%
81-90%	49,598	53,035	54,268	52,572	9.4	-3.1	9.7	-2.8
91-95%	62,153	67,813	70,877	66,506	14.0	-6.2	14.6	-5.6
96-99%	85,618	100,202	106,515	103,697	24.4	-2.6	22.3	-1.5
Top 1%	220,300	387,059	445,521	428,854	102.2	-3.7	78.0	-2.3
All	$33,617	$35,155	$36,566	$34,650	8.8%	-5.2%	8.6%	-3.8%

* Federal taxes only.

Source: Authors' analysis of CBO data.

bottom fifth both fell 10.4%. The second fifth saw its pre- and post-tax income slide by nearly the same amount.

The data for 1989-92, which compare the experience of a trough, or high-unemployment, year (1992) with that of a peak year (1989), not surprisingly, reveal widespread declines in both pre- and after-tax incomes. As in 1977-89, the after-tax income of the bottom four-fifths fell, but more rapidly than in the earlier period (-5.8% in just three years compared to -2.2% in the preceding 12 years). Unlike the 1977-89 period, however, the after-tax incomes of the top fifth also declined, reflecting in part the significant impact that the early-1990s recession had on the pre-tax incomes of white-collar workers. (We saw in Chapter 1, though, that white-collar workers recovered faster in 1992-94 from the ill effects of the recession than did other workers.)

Table 2.4 shows that between 1977 and 1989 the after-tax income shares of the bottom 90% of the income distribution fell, while the shares going to the top 10% grew. By 1989, the top 20% of families held almost 50% of total after-tax income, up from 43.9% in 1977 and 44.7% in 1980. Most of the gain to the upper fifth was generated by those in the top 1%, who gained 5.0 percentage points in their share of after-tax income over the 1977-89 period, with most of the shift (60%) occurring in the period between 1980 and 1985.

Over the 1989-92 period, a small, ambiguous shift toward after-tax income equality took place. The wealthiest 1% of families lost a 0.6 percentage-point share of total after-tax income, to the benefit of the rest of families in the top fifth and the some of the families in the middle. At the same time, however, the bottom two-fifths of families also saw their income shares decline, albeit by a smaller amount.

TABLE 2.4

Shares of After-Tax Income for All Families, 1977-92*

Income Group	1977	1980	1985	1989	1992	Percentage-Point Changes 1977-89	1989-92
Bottom Four-Fifths	56.1%	55.3%	51.3%	50.6%	50.9%	-5.5	0.3
First	5.7	5.4	4.4	4.3	4.1	-1.4	-0.2
Second	11.5	11.3	10.0	10.0	9.9	-1.5	-0.1
Third	16.3	16.1	15.1	15.0	15.2	-1.3	0.2
Fourth	22.6	22.5	21.8	21.3	21.6	-1.3	0.4
Top Fifth	43.9%	44.7%	48.7%	49.4%	49.1%	5.5	-0.3
81-90%	15.5	15.2	15.2	15.0	15.0	-0.6	0.1
91-95%	9.8	9.9	10.0	9.8	10.0	-0.0	0.2
96-99%	11.3	11.2	12.1	12.4	12.4	1.0	0.1
Top 1%	7.3	8.4	11.4	12.3	11.7	5.0	-0.6
All	100.0%	100.0%	100.0%	100.0%	100.0%	0.0	0.0

*   Federal taxes only.

Source: Authors' analysis of CBO data.

Table 2.5 extends the analysis of after-tax income through 1996, using projections of the 1996 family income distribution made by CBO in 1995. (The data for 1977 and 1989 are identical to those used in the preceding two tables.) The data summarized in the table can be used to identify the role of shifts in the tax structure on the growth of after-tax income inequality. Specifically, the table decomposes (i.e., breaks down into their component parts) the changes in after-tax income shares since 1977 into those due to pre-tax income shifts (discussed in Chapter 1) and those attributable to federal tax policy shifts.

TABLE 2.5

The Effects of Tax and Income Changes on After-Tax Income Shares, 1977-96(p)*

| | | | Change in Shares Due to: | | | |
| Income Group | Change in After-Tax Shares | | Pre-Tax Income Shifts | | Change in Tax Progressivity | |
	(1) 1977-89	(2) 1989-96(p)	(3) 1977-89	(4) 1989-96(p)	(5) 1977-89	(6) 1989-96(p)
Bottom Four-Fifths	-5.2%	-0.0%	-4.6%	-0.9%	-0.6%	0.9%
First	-1.3	0.1	-1.1	-0.3	-0.2	0.2
Second	-1.8	0.3	-1.6	0.0	-0.2	0.3
Third	-0.6	-0.5	-0.5	-0.6	-0.0	0.2
Fourth	-1.4	0.3	-1.3	0.0	-0.1	0.2
Top Fifth	5.2%	0.0%	4.6%	0.9%	0.6%	-0.9%
81-90%	-0.5	-0.2	-0.4	-0.2	-0.1	0.0
91-95%	0.0	0.1	0.1	0.1	-0.1	0.0
96-99%	1.1	0.2	1.1	0.2	0.0	-0.1
Top 1%	4.6	-0.1	3.8	0.8	0.7	-0.9
All	0.0%	0.0%	0.0%	0.0%	0.0%	0.0%

* Based on a recalculation of the underlying data in Tables 1.11 and 2.4 that forces the sum of the shares to be exactly 100%, which is not the case in the original data due to the inclusion of families with zero or negative income solely in the "All" category. Federal taxes only; (p) indicates CBO projections of 1996 income levels under 1996 tax law.

Source: Authors' analysis of CBO data.

Column 1 shows that the bottom 90% of families had a lower after-tax income share in 1989 than in 1977 (as noted in Table 2.4). The bottom 80% of families lost a 5.2% share of total after-tax income during the 1977-89 period, and 4.6 of these points were due to a relative loss of pre-tax income. By contrast, only 0.6 points of the 5.2 percentage-point drop were due to shifts in the distribution of the tax burden. Thus, shifts in the tax burden, though significant, were clearly not the primary mechanism of the overall redistribution of income from 1977 to 1989. Over the same period, the top 1% of families captured a 4.6 point larger share of the after-tax income, but again most of this improvement (3.8 points) was due to changes in pre-tax income share and much less (0.7 points) to changes in the tax structure.

Column 2 demonstrates that the after-tax income share for the bottom four-fifths of the population is not expected to change over the 1989-96 period. This stability is the result of two countervailing forces. The share of pre-tax income for the bottom four-fifths is projected to fall by 0.9 percentage points, indicating a further growth of pre-tax income inequality. The greater tax progressivity built into OBRA93, however, will fully offset these declines in the share of pre-tax income.

The full extent of the OBRA93 tax changes on expected tax rates and liabilities is shown in **Table 2.6** (which uses projected 1996 income levels). Unlike the above tables, this table shows the impact of OBRA93 once it is fully phased in (by 1998). The progressivity of the tax changes is evidenced by the decrease of rates and liabilities at the bottom of the income scale and the increase at the top. The poorest 20% of families are projected to pay 28.6% less in taxes under a fully phased-in OBRA93 than they would have in the absence of the change in tax law. Conversely, the average liability of the wealthiest taxpayers rises by 18.6%, from $177,045 to $209,925. On average, the bottom 80% of families pays less taxes as a result of the change (-2.6%), while the top fifth, on average, pays about 6.5% more.

In summary, the vast majority of the growth in income inequality is attributable to shifts in pre-tax income that occurred before taxation. Although the federal tax system exacerbated this trend toward greater inequality between 1977 and 1989, changes in the tax system since 1989, particularly OBRA93, are expected to partly reverse this long-term trend toward more regressive taxation. However, as we show below, given their vast income growth and the failure of even OBRA93 to tax them at past rates, the richest families continue to enjoy a lower federal tax liability than they would have had if the 1977 tax system were in place in 1996.

TABLE 2.6

Effect of 1993 Tax Law* on 1996 Tax Liabilities and Rates
(1995 Dollars)

Income Group	Effective Tax Rates			Tax Liabilities		
	Pre	After	Percentage-Point Change	Pre	After	Percent Change
Bottom Four-Fifths	15.9%	15.5%	-0.4%	$4,625	$4,504	-2.6%
First	7.0	5.0	-2.0	589	421	-28.6
Second	15.0	14.9	-0.1	3,142	3,121	-0.7
Third	19.3	19.5	0.2	6,659	6,728	1.0
Fourth	22.1	22.3	0.2	11,376	11,479	0.9
Top Fifth	26.2%	27.9%	1.7%	$31,478	$33,520	6.5%
81-90%	24.6	24.9	0.3	17,682	17,898	1.2
91-95%	25.9	26.3	0.4	24,093	24,465	1.5
96-99%	26.8	27.7	0.9	39,437	40,762	3.4
Top 1%	28.0	33.2	5.2	177,045	209,925	18.6
All	22.8%	23.75%	0.9%	$10,662	$11,083	3.9%

* OBRA93; federal taxes only.

Source: Authors' analysis of CBO projections. Table compares tax liabilities for CBO's projected 1996 pre-tax income distribution under pre- and post-OBRA93 tax law.

The Diminished Progressivity of Federal Tax Rates

Even though most of the income shifting between 1977 and 1989 occurred before taxes, regressive changes in federal taxes did contribute to the increased inequality of after-tax family incomes over the period. **Table 2.7** and **Figure 2A** present the effective federal tax rates (i.e., the ratio of taxes paid to pre-tax income) by family income group. The average effective tax rate for all families changed little between 1977 and 1989, falling one-tenth of a percentage point, but it is expected to have grown by 1.1 percentage points by the end of the 1989-96 period. A closer look at the table, however, reveals that the small decline in the overall effective federal tax rate in 1977-89 was the result of a steep drop

TABLE 2.7

Effective Federal Tax Rates, 1977-96(p)*

Income Group	1977	1980	1985	1989	1992	1996(p)	Percentage-Point Change 1977-89	1989-96(p)
Bottom Four-Fifths	16.3%	16.5%	16.7%	16.6%	16.0%	15.6%	0.3	-1.0
First	9.3	8.1	10.3	9.3	8.0	5.0	0.0	-4.3
Second	15.4	15.6	15.7	15.6	14.7	14.9	0.2	-0.7
Third	19.5	19.8	19.1	19.3	19.2	19.7	-0.2	-0.4
Fourth	21.9	22.9	21.7	22.0	21.9	22.6	0.1	0.6
Top Fifth	27.3%	27.5%	24.2%	25.6%	26.2%	28.1%	-1.7	2.5
81-90%	23.9	25.2	23.5	24.1	24.5	25.2	0.2	1.1
91-95%	25.3	26.4	24.3	25.6	26.0	26.7	0.3	1.1
96-99%	26.9	28.0	24.3	26.2	26.6	27.7	-0.7	1.5
Top 1%	35.6	31.8	24.9	26.8	27.8	32.7	-8.8	5.9
All	22.8%	23.3%	21.8%	22.7%	22.7%	23.8%	-0.1	1.1

*(p) indicates CBO projections of 1996 income levels under 1996 tax law.

Source: Authors' analysis of CBO data.

(8.8 percentage points) in the effective rate for the top 1% of families, combined with very small changes, both up and down, in the rates applicable to the other 99% of families. A similar pattern holds in 1989-96. The 1.1-percentage-point increase in overall effective federal tax rates reflects a 5.9-percentage-point rise for the top 1% of families and smaller changes, in both directions, for the rest of families. Changes in the earned-income tax credit (EITC) for low-wage workers, for example, helped drop the effective rate for the bottom fifth of families by 4.3 percentage points in 1989-96.

A basic conceptual problem, however, leads the numbers in Table 2.7 to systematically understate the deterioration in tax progressivity over the 1977-89 period and to overstate the improvements in tax progressivity in 1989-96. Tables 2.3-2.7 are based on effective tax rates calculated from the income distribution and corresponding tax law for each year. Thus, the effective tax rate for the top

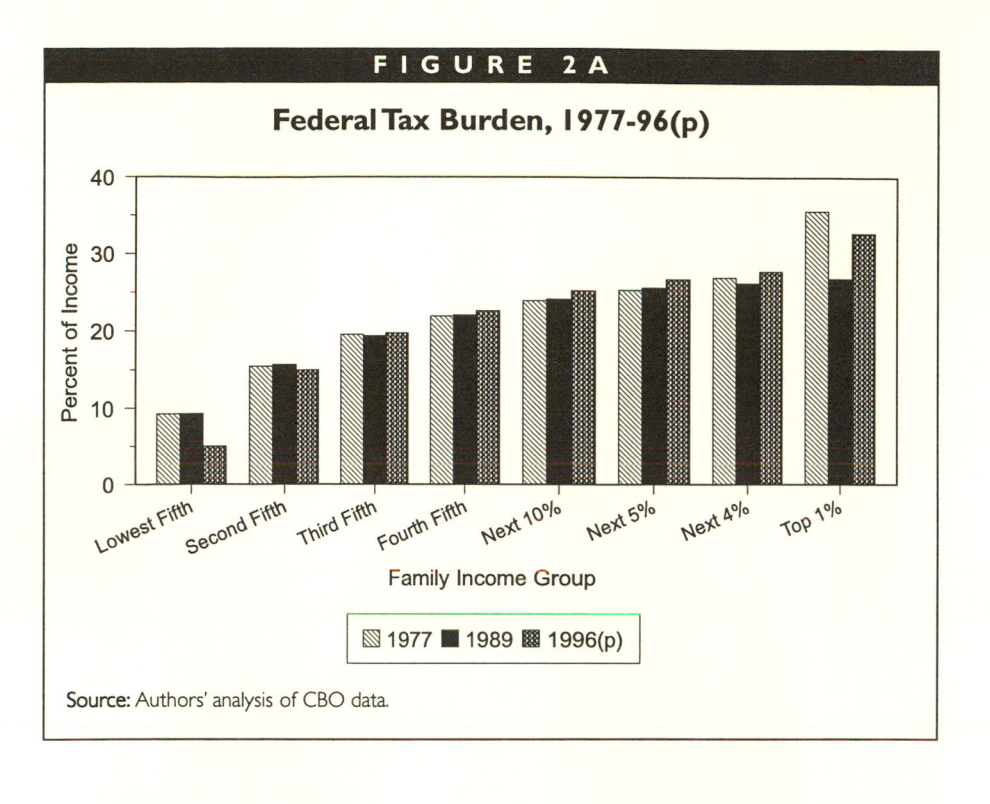

FIGURE 2A

Federal Tax Burden, 1977-96(p)

Family Income Group

☒ 1977 ■ 1989 ▧ 1996(p)

Source: Authors' analysis of CBO data.

1% of families in 1977 (35.6%; see Table 2.7) is determined by taking the total tax payments for the group in 1977 as a percentage of the total income for the group in the same year. The effective tax rate for the top 1% in 1996 (32.7%) is also calculated using the projected income and taxes paid in 1996. The change in the effective tax rate, then, is just the difference in the two (-2.9 percentage points). But the *pre*-tax incomes for the top 1% grew substantially over the 1977-96 period. These higher real incomes would have been treated differently in earlier years, when tax law included more tax brackets, particularly for high incomes. A better comparison of the tax changes over the period, then, would ask: what would a family with a given income in 1996 have paid in taxes if the 1977 tax law were applied to its (inflation-adjusted) 1996 income?

Table 2.8 presents the conclusions of such an analysis. For the bottom 95% of families, the recalculation makes little difference to their effective tax rates (compare with Table 2.7). But for the top 5%, and especially the top 1% of families—those who experienced the largest pre-tax income gains and those affected by the additional, higher tax brackets in 1977—the impact is substantial. A family in the top 1% of the 1996 income distribution would have paid

TABLE 2.8

Estimated Effective Federal Tax Rates on 1996 Income Under Prevailing Tax Law, 1977-96(p)*

(1995 Dollars)

Income Group	1977	1985	1989	1992	1996(p)	Percentage-Point Change 1977-89	1989-96(p)
Bottom Four-Fifths	16.0%	16.7%	16.4%	16.0%	15.6%	0.5	-0.9
First	9.0	10.2	9.2	8.0	5.0	0.2	-4.2
Second	14.2	15.7	15.5	14.7	14.9	1.3	-0.6
Third	18.8	19.1	19.2	19.2	19.7	0.4	0.5
Fourth	21.8	21.7	21.8	21.9	22.6	0.0	0.8
Top Fifth	26.3%	24.0%	25.0%	25.5%	26.5%	-1.3	1.5
81-95%	24.9	23.8	24.6	25.1	25.8	-0.3	1.2
96-99%	28.1	24.3	26.2	26.6	27.7	-1.9	1.5
Top 1%	40.1	25.0	26.7	27.8	32.7	-13.4	6.0
All	18.0%	18.1%	18.1%	17.9%	17.7%	0.1	-0.4

* (p) indicates CBO projections of 1996 income levels.

Source: McIntyre et al. (1996). Effective rates for 1977-92 calculated using inflation-adjusted 1996 income levels. Table 2.7, in contrast, uses the tax code and income levels for each year.

40.1% of its income in taxes under the 1977 tax law (versus the 35.6% actually paid by the top 1% of families in 1977). Thus, this alternative calculation shows an even steeper decline between 1977 and 1989 in the effective tax rates for the top 1% (-13.4%) than shown in Table 2.7 (-8.8%).

Most of the preceding tables have grouped families into fifths and examined how these groups have been affected by changes in tax policy over time. **Table 2.9** and **Figure 2B** use U.S. Treasury Department data that depart from this approach in order to illustrate how federal income and payroll tax changes have affected a family of four with a single earner. In both Table 2.9 and Figure 2B, the "middle-income" family earns the median family income for a family of four with one worker; the "low-income" family earns half the median; and the

TABLE 2.9

Effective Federal Tax Rate*
for a Family of Four with One Earner, 1977-95

Income Level**	1977	1980	1985	1989	1992	1995***	Percentage-Point Change 1977-89	Percentage-Point Change 1989-95
Low	15.3%	18.3%	20.7%	20.3%	19.9%	17.5%	5.0	-2.8
Middle	20.7	23.7	24.4	24.5	24.5	24.5	3.6	0.1
High	21.6	24.8	25.3	24.1	25.5	25.6	2.6	1.4

* Average rate for combined federal income, employee plus employer Social Security, and Medicare taxes.
** Low income is one-half median income for a family of four; middle is median income; high is twice median income.
*** Estimated; assumes tax law enacted as of April 1995.

Source: U.S. Department of Treasury (1995).

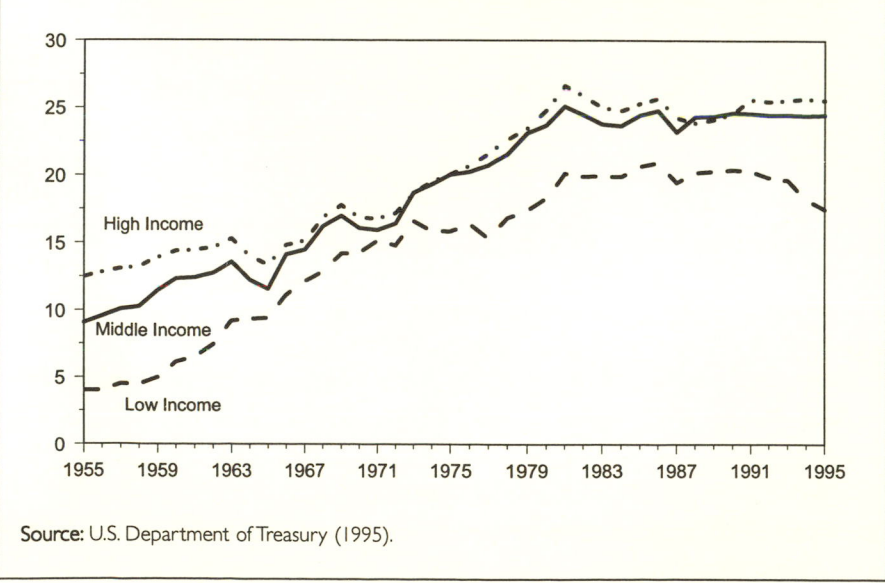

FIGURE 2B

Effective Federal Tax Rate for a Family of Four, 1955-95

Source: U.S. Department of Treasury (1995).

"high-income" family twice the median. The most striking features of Figure 2B are the steady rise in the effective federal tax rates in 1955-80 and the subsequent flattening out of the federal rates thereafter (confirming the pattern observed in the CBO data above). Table 2.9 also makes clear that, as the result of the expansion of the EITC, the effective tax rate for a "low-income" family of four fell 2.8 percentage points in 1989-95.

What Federal Tax Changes Mean in Dollars

The next step in our analysis is to examine the effect of changes in the tax system on the levels of after-tax income of each income class. The dollar effect of any change in a group's tax rate on the group's actual, after-tax income depends on both the size of the change in the tax rate and on the group's level of income. **Table 2.10** shows the average projected pre-tax family income in 1996 for each income group (column 1) in constant 1995 dollars. Columns 2 through 5 show the changes in the average amount of taxes paid by each income group due to federal tax changes enacted in different periods between 1977 and 1996 (projected), holding incomes constant at their projected 1996 levels. (The effective tax rates, as in Table 2.8, are calculated using projected 1996 income and applying the tax code in place in each of the earlier periods.) The final two columns show the cumulative effect of changes in the tax code in 1977-96 on 1996 federal tax payments.

The table shows that shifts in federal tax policy in 1977-85 were highly regressive, cutting the taxes for the average family in the top 5% by $5,592 and in the top 1% by $95,482. Since 1985, the tax system has been moving to reverse these regressive changes. Tax changes after 1985 caused the tax bill of the top 1% to rise by $10,750 in the late 1980s, and changes after 1989 are expected to increase the tax bill for the top group by an additional $37,940. The effective rate on the top 1%, however, is not expected to return to its 1977 level by 1996: the wealthiest families can still expect to pay $46,792 (18.5%) less in taxes in 1996 than they would have paid under the 1977 system.

The poorest fifth of families benefited from tax changes in the late 1980s and early 1990s (the Tax Reform Act of 1986 and OBRA93). By the end of the period, tax changes led to a $337 cut in their tax bill, or a 44.4% reduction over their liability under 1977 rates. Families in the middle three-fifths ended the 1977-96 period paying, on average, between $150 and $400 (3.7-4.9%) more in taxes than at the beginning of the period.

TABLE 2.10

Effect of Federal Tax Changes
on Family Tax Payments, 1977-96(p)
(1995 Dollars)

Income Group	Average 1996(p) Income Before Federal Taxes	The Effect of Federal Tax Changes, 1977-96(p), on the Amount of Tax Payments, Assuming 1996(p) Income Levels				Difference in Taxes, 1977-96(p)	
		1977-85	1985-89	1989-92	1992-96(p)	Dollars	Percent
Bottom Four-Fifths	$28,835	$209	-$72	$-137	-$115	-$115	-2.5%
First	8,413	101	-84	-101	-252	-337	-44.4
Second	20,950	314	-42	-168	42	147	4.9
Third	34,501	104	35	0	173	311	4.8
Fourth	51,476	-51	51	51	360	412	3.7
Top Fifth	$120,400	-$2,817	$1,282	$614	$1,192	$271	0.9%
81-95%	79,136	-870	633	396	554	712	3.6
96-99%	147,155	-5,592	2,796	589	1,619	-589	-1.4
Top 1%	632,330	-95,482	10,750	6,956	30,984	-46,792	-18.5
All	$47,148	$53	$6	-$131	-$58	-$130	-1.5

*(p) indicates CBO projections of 1996 income levels under the 1996 tax law.

Source: Authors' analysis of data from CBO and McIntyre et al. (1996).

The Causes of Changes
in the Federal Tax Burden

To show the source of the progressive and regressive changes in the federal tax system, **Table 2.11** decomposes the federal effective rates into their components: the personal income tax, payroll taxes, the corporate income tax, and the excise tax. Personal and corporate income taxes are progressive; the effective rates go up consistently as income rises. Excise and payroll tax rates are regressive, but, as regards the latter, the distribution of Social Security benefits may be a mitigating factor (as discussed below).

TABLE 2.11

Effective Tax Rates for Selected Federal Taxes, 1977-96(p)*

Group	Personal Income Tax		Payroll Tax		Corporate Income Tax		Excise Tax	
	1977	1996(p)	1977	1996(p)	1977	1996(p)	1977	1996(p)
Bottom Four-Fifths	4.7%	2.5%	7.1%	9.5%	2.7%	1.8%	1.9%	1.8%
First	-0.6	-6.9	5.1	7.7	1.9	1.3	2.9	3.0
Second	3.4	1.7	7.5	9.6	2.7	1.8	1.8	1.8
Third	6.9	6.1	8.1	10.2	3.0	2.0	1.5	1.4
Fourth	9.6	8.8	7.8	10.5	3.2	2.2	1.3	1.1
Top Fifth	16.1%	16.4%	5.3%	7.7%	5.0%	3.3%	0.9%	0.7%
81-90%	12.0	11.4	7.4	10.5	3.4	2.4	1.1	0.9
91-95%	13.9	13.3	6.5	9.9	3.9	2.7	1.0	0.8
96-99%	16.6	16.3	4.4	7.6	5.1	3.3	0.8	0.5
Top 1%	25.2	24.4	1.3	3.1	8.8	5.0	0.3	0.3
All	11.1%	11.2%	6.5%	8.9%	3.9%	2.7%	1.3%	1.1%

*(p) indicates CBO projections of 1996 income distribution under 1996 tax law.

Note: While rates fall for each group within the top fifth, the overall rate grows slightly. This results from a combination of small within-group rate changes and a large upward shift in pre-tax income shares toward the most heavily taxed, highest income group.

Source: Authors' analysis of CBO data.

Between 1977 and 1989, personal income tax rates fell slightly for the bottom 99% of families and substantially for the top 1% (see **Figure 2C**). After 1989, primarily as a result of OBRA93, personal income tax rates rose for the wealthiest 1% of families (though they did not return to their 1977 levels); fell for the bottom fifth; and were largely unchanged for the rest of families. Although the average personal income tax for the richest 1% of families is projected to fall from 25.2% to 24.4% over the full period, the effective rate for the bottom fifth is expected to fall even more steeply, from -0.6% to -6.9%, indicating that the tax system actually transfers money to this group through the EITC. Overall, these changes lead to a slightly higher income tax burden for the top fifth, which increases from 16.1% to 16.4%, and a lower burden for the bottom four-fifths, which falls from 4.7% to 2.5%.

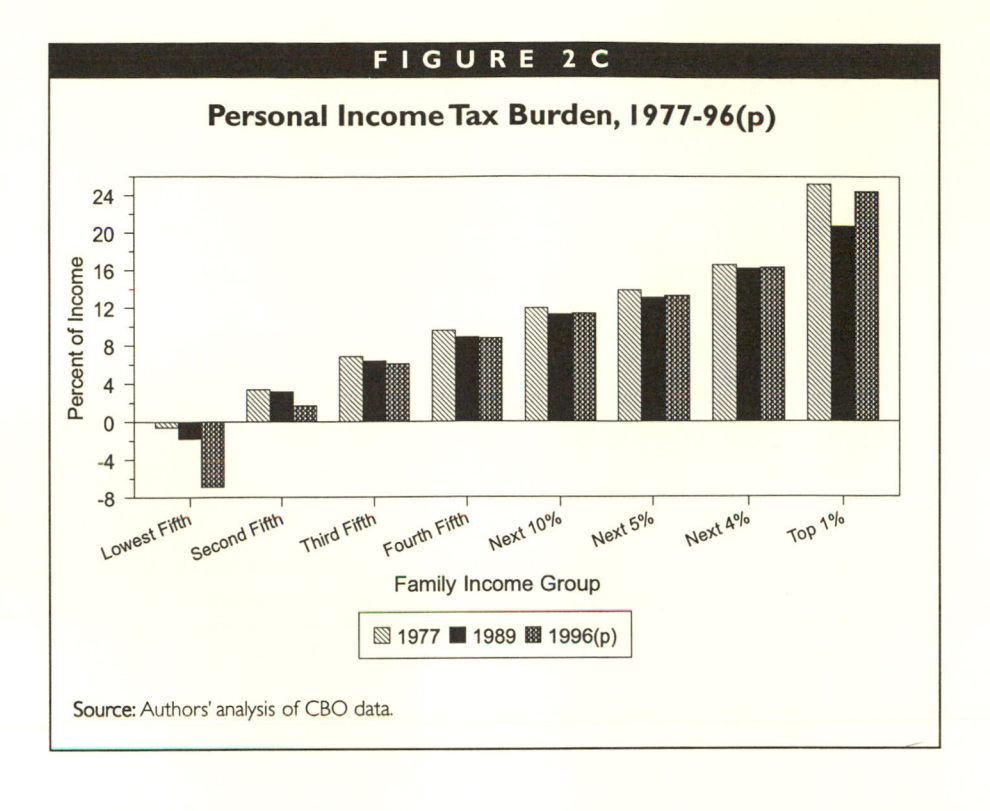

FIGURE 2C

Personal Income Tax Burden, 1977-96(p)

Family Income Group

Lowest Fifth · Second Fifth · Third Fifth · Fourth Fifth · Next 10% · Next 5% · Next 4% · Top 1%

Legend: 1977 ■ 1989 ▩ 1996(p)

Source: Authors' analysis of CBO data.

Between 1977 and 1996, the overall payroll tax rate is projected to rise from 6.5% to 8.9% (Table 2.11 and **Figure 2D**). While the payroll tax is expected to rise for all groups, the bottom 99% will see the largest increases in rates. Payroll taxes have a smaller impact on the wealthiest families, in part because the rich earn much of their income from investments (Chapter 1), which are not subject to payroll taxes, and in part because payroll taxes are capped: in 1996 they applied only to the first $60,875 (1995 dollars) of earnings. The payroll tax is by far the largest federal tax paid by the bottom 80% of the income distribution in 1996.

In this analysis, the tax incidence (i.e., those who ultimately bear the burden of the tax) of the payroll tax falls totally on employees: the employer portion is shifted to employees in the form of lower wages. While this is a common and valid assumption of payroll tax incidence, it does not speak to the total redistributive effects of the Social Security system, which incorporate both the taxation and benefit structure. Since retirement benefits are redistributed progressively (less wealthy retirees receive more benefits than they contributed over their lifetime,

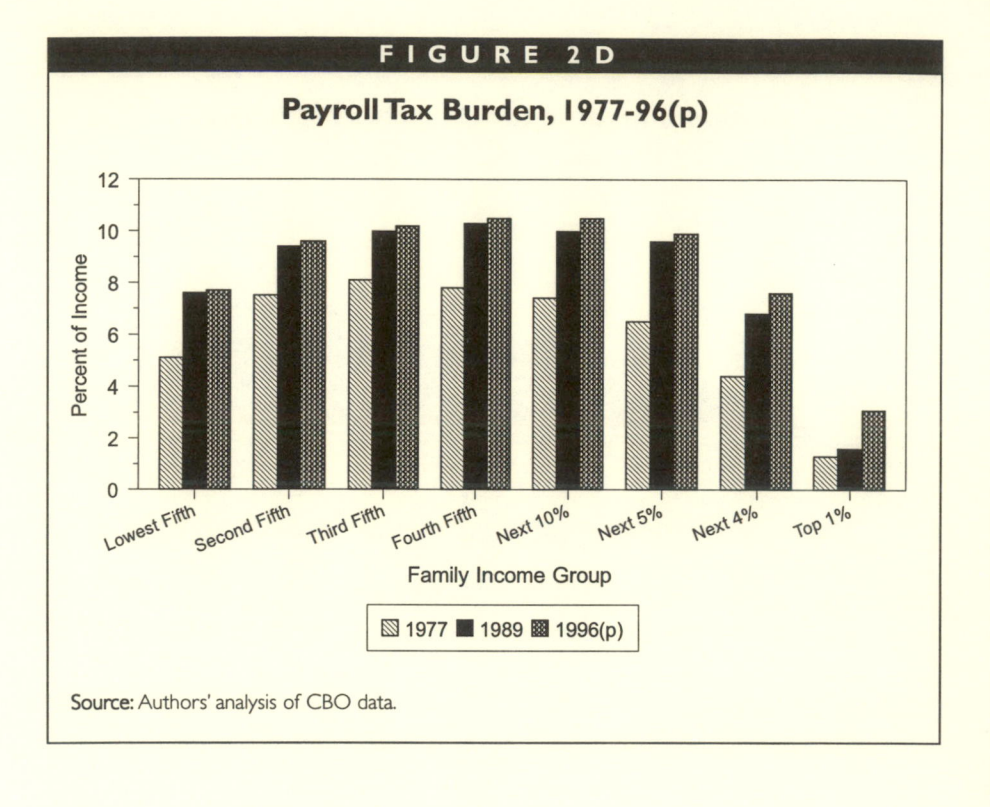

FIGURE 2D

Payroll Tax Burden, 1977-96(p)

Family Income Group

1977 1989 1996(p)

Source: Authors' analysis of CBO data.

while the most wealthy receive fewer benefits than they put in), the benefit structure counteracts the regressive nature of the tax evident in Table 2.11.

However, the age structure of the population is changing so that the number of beneficiaries is rising faster than the number of workers. Some analysts have argued that demographic phenomena will strain the social insurance system's ability to maintain its progressive benefit structure. (For example, the retirement age is already scheduled to rise to 67; researchers have found that the burden of this change is heaviest at the lower end of the income distribution.) Without this redistributive component, the burden of the tax falls on wage earners in the present, while its regressive nature is not mitigated for future generations. Therefore, the rise in payroll taxes is considered a regressive change.

Corporate income taxes, which have a progressive structure, have declined considerably. For example, the average effective rate for the richest fifth of families falls from 5.0% in 1977 to 3.3% in 1996 (Table 2.11 and **Figure 2E**). Since corporations are owned by households through shares of stock, households also bear the burden of corporate taxes. In this analysis, it is assumed that half of

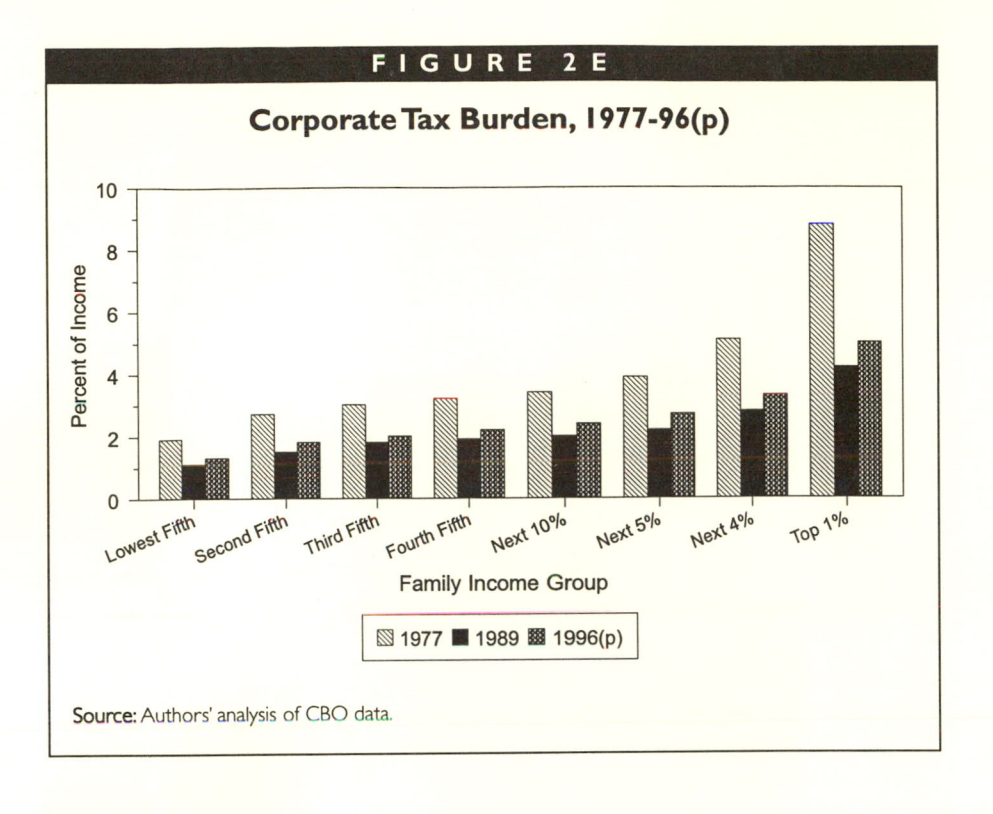

FIGURE 2E

Corporate Tax Burden, 1977-96(p)

Family Income Group

1977 1989 1996(p)

Source: Authors' analysis of CBO data.

corporate taxes are borne by stockholders in the form of lower dividends and slower stock appreciation and half are paid by consumers in the form of higher prices.

Excise taxes have fallen slightly since 1977, while maintaining their regressive structure. These taxes—levied on alcohol, gasoline, cigarettes—are the most regressive federal taxes (Table 2.11 and **Figure 2F**). In 1996, the poorest families are projected to pay 3.0% of their income in excise taxes, while the richest fifth, which spend smaller proportions of their incomes on goods subject to excise taxes, pay 0.3%.

We have already seen (Tables 2.7 and 2.8) the net effect of the changes in these four categories during the period 1977-96. **Table 2.12** and Figures 2C-2F make clear which components of the federal tax structure produced these outcomes. The total effective tax rate on all families is projected to rise by 1.1 percentage points over the period. The two factors contributing to this increase are the 2.4-point rise in payroll tax rates and a much smaller 0.1 rise in personal income tax rates. Declines in the corporate income tax (1.2 points) and in fed-

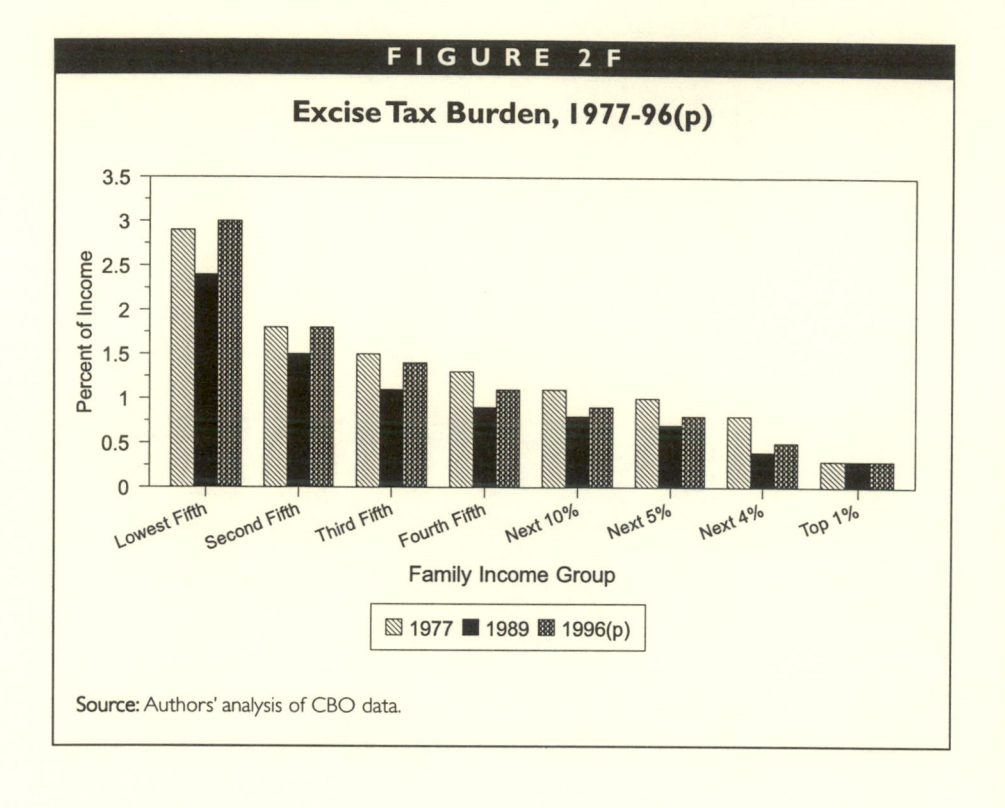

FIGURE 2F

Excise Tax Burden, 1977-96(p)

Family Income Group

1977 ■ 1989 ▦ 1996(p)

Source: Authors' analysis of CBO data.

eral excise tax rates (0.2 points) counteracted some, but not all, of the increases in payroll and income taxes. From the standpoint of tax progressivity, most of these developments were regressive. The regressive payroll tax increased, while the progressive corporate income tax decreased.

During 1977-96, the effective federal tax rate for the wealthiest 1% of families is expected to fall by 2.8 percentage points as the result of declines in the personal income tax (-0.8 percentage points) and corporate income tax (-3.8 points) and an increase in payroll taxes (1.8 points), with no change in the federal excise tax burden. For the bottom four-fifths of families, the average effective federal tax rate is projected to fall by 0.8 percentage points. For this group, personal income taxes are expected to drop 2.2 points (mostly because of a 6.3 point fall for the bottom fifth, which benefits from the EITC); corporate income tax effective rates should fall 0.9 points; and federal excise taxes are projected to fall 0.1 point. The effective rate on payroll taxes for the bottom four-fifths, however, is expected to rise by 2.4 points.

TABLE 2.12

Changes in Effective Federal Taxes, 1977-96(p)*

Income Group	Percentage-Point Change, 1977-96(p)				
	Personal Income Tax	Payroll Tax	Corporate Income Tax	Excise Tax	Total
Bottom Four-Fifths	-2.2%	2.4%	-0.9%	-0.1%	-0.8%
First	-6.3	2.6	-0.6	0.1	-4.2
Second	-1.7	2.1	-0.9	0.0	-0.5
Third	-0.8	2.1	-1.0	-0.1	0.2
Fourth	-0.8	2.7	-1.0	-0.2	0.7
Top Fifth	0.3	2.4%	-1.7%	-0.2%	0.8%
81-90%	-0.6	3.1	-1.0	-0.2	1.3
91-95%	-0.6	3.4	-1.2	-0.2	1.4
96-99%	-0.3	3.2	-1.8	-0.3	0.8
Top 1%	-0.8	1.8	-3.8	0.0	-2.8
All	0.1%	2.4%	-1.2%	-0.2%	1.1%

*(p) indicates CBO projections of 1996 income levels under 1996 tax law.

Source: Authors' analysis of CBO data.

Changes in Corporate Taxation: The Shift to Untaxed Profits

Although corporate rates have dropped, this decline does not necessarily lead to lower corporate tax liability, since the lower rates could be applied to greater absolute profits (i.e., an expanded tax base). In fact, this was a goal of the 1986 tax reform. However, contrary to the goal of the reform, corporate tax revenue declined through the period because of the growth of *untaxed* corporate income, that is, income from which certain expenses, like interest payments, have been deducted.

Between 1979 and 1994, total corporate profits as a percent of GDP were unchanged at 6.7% (**Table 2.13**), yet taxed profits fell significantly over this same period, from 7.6% to 5.4%. This phenomenon of relatively flat total profits

TABLE 2.13

Taxed and Untaxed Corporate Profits, 1967-94
(Nonfinancial Corporations Only)

	As Percent of GDP in:					
	1967	1973	1979	1986	1989	1994
Pre-Tax Profits						
Taxed Profits	8.1%	7.1%	7.6%	3.4%	4.4%	5.4%
Untaxed Profits	1.3	0.4	-0.9	3.2	2.7	1.3
Net Interest	1.1	1.6	1.8	2.2	2.7	1.4
Depreciation Allowances	0.4	0.3	-1.0	0.7	0.4	0.1
Other Deductions	-0.2	-1.4	-1.6	0.3	-0.3	-0.2
Total	9.4	7.6	6.7	6.6	7.1	6.7
After-Tax Profits	6.0	4.7	4.0	4.9	5.3	4.8
Taxable Profits Only	4.8	4.2	4.9	1.7	2.5	3.5
Corporate Profits Taxes*	3.3	2.9	2.7	1.7	1.8	1.9

* Federal, state, and local combined.

Source: Authors' analysis of BEA data.

and falling taxed profits is due to the rise in untaxed corporate profits, which rose from -0.9% of GDP in 1979 to 1.3% in 1994 (Table 2.13 and **Figure 2G**). Over the full period (1967-94), taxed corporate profits have been cut significantly, from 8.1% of GDP to 5.4%.

There are two main reasons for the shift from taxed to untaxed profits: increased indebtedness (along with higher real interest rates) and a more favorable tax treatment of depreciation. Since the late 1970s, corporations have increasingly raised money by selling bonds (i.e., they have borrowed) rather than by selling stocks. As a result, corporations have been paying out more and more of their gross profits as interest payments (on bonds) rather than as dividend payments (on stocks). This trend is reflected in Table 2.13 in the steady increase in net interest payments between 1967 and 1989, from 1.1% of GDP in 1967 to 2.7% in 1989. This trend reversed between 1989 and 1994, likely due to falling interest rates and a shift toward equity financing.

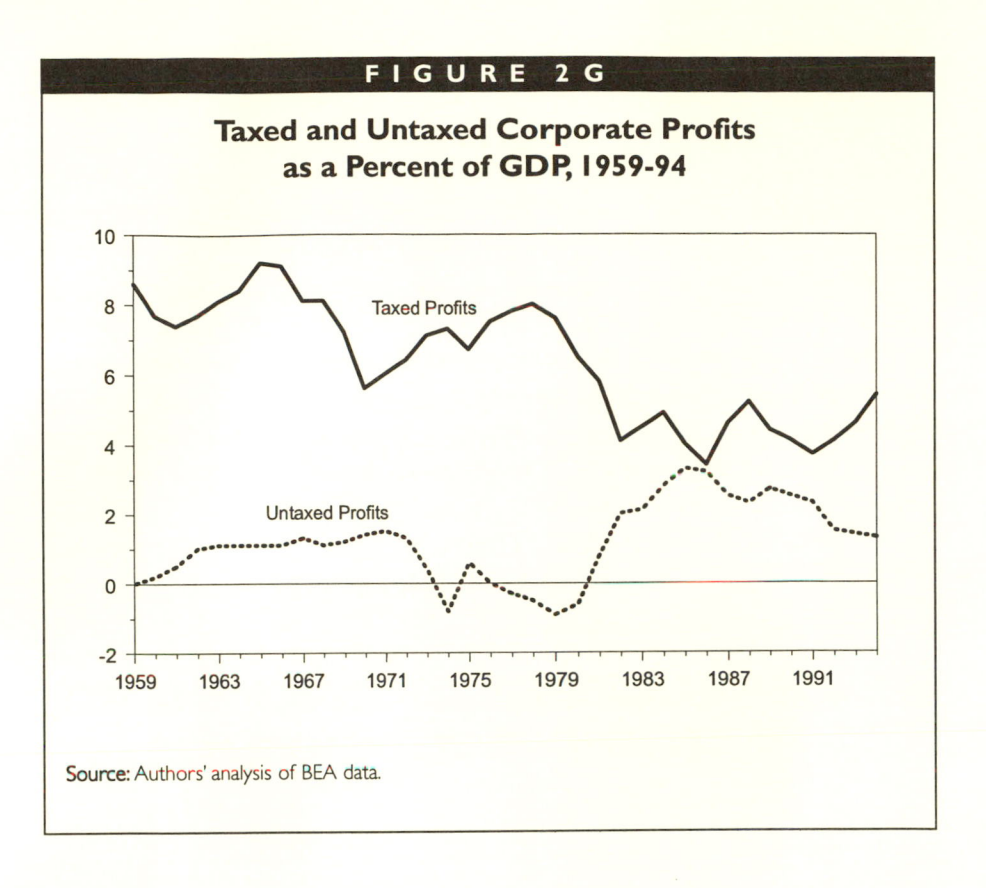

FIGURE 2G

Taxed and Untaxed Corporate Profits as a Percent of GDP, 1959-94

Source: Authors' analysis of BEA data.

Since interest payments are treated more favorably than dividends by the federal tax system (they are considered an expense for nonfinancial corporations and deducted from taxable profits), and since interest rates were high relative to inflation in the 1980s, the corporate emphasis on debt over equity has lowered the corporate tax burden. Corporate liability is lowered, then, as corporations deduct interest payments from their tax base.

The second reason for lower corporate taxes is the federal tax system's relatively favorable treatment of capital depreciation. With the introduction of the accelerated cost recovery system in 1981, corporations were able to take tax deductions on purchases of new equipment and other investments sooner. Since this accelerated depreciation allowed them to defer some of their taxes for several years, it amounted to an interest-free loan. This tax break grew over the mid-1980s, when untaxed profits due to depreciation allowances went from -1.0% of GDP in 1979 to 0.7% in 1986 (Table 2.13). Since 1986, Congress has taken back part of this tax cut, reducing untaxed profits in this category to 0.1% of GDP in 1994.

These shifts have led to a growing gap between actual and taxable corporate profits, which has in turn led to a sharp decrease in corporate profits taxes (Table 2.13). As a share of GDP, taxes on corporate profits have been cut almost in half over the period, from 3.3% in 1967 to 1.9% in 1994.

Table 2.14 shows the results of these changes on corporate taxes as a share of profits. Since 1977, corporate taxes have declined from 39.1% of actual profits (defined as the sum of taxable profits, net interest, and the difference between allowable depreciation and true depreciation) to 28.1% in 1994. Moreover, the 1994 effective tax rate, 28.1%, is about 60% of what corporate taxes were in 1959 (Table 2.14 and **Figure 2H**). The beneficiaries of this fall in corporate tax liability relative to true economic profits are by and large those who own and lend to corporations: the wealthy.

TABLE 2.14

Corporate Profits Tax Rates, 1959-94
(Nonfinancial Corporations Only)

Year	Corporate Taxes* as a Percent of	
	Taxable Profits	Actual Profits
1959	47.5%	47.5%
1967	41.2	35.6
1973	40.8	38.4
1977	37.8	39.1
1979	35.6	40.4
1986	49.9	25.7
1989	41.7	25.7
1992	35.3	25.7
1994	34.9	28.1

* Federal, state, and local combined.

Source: Authors' analysis of BEA data.

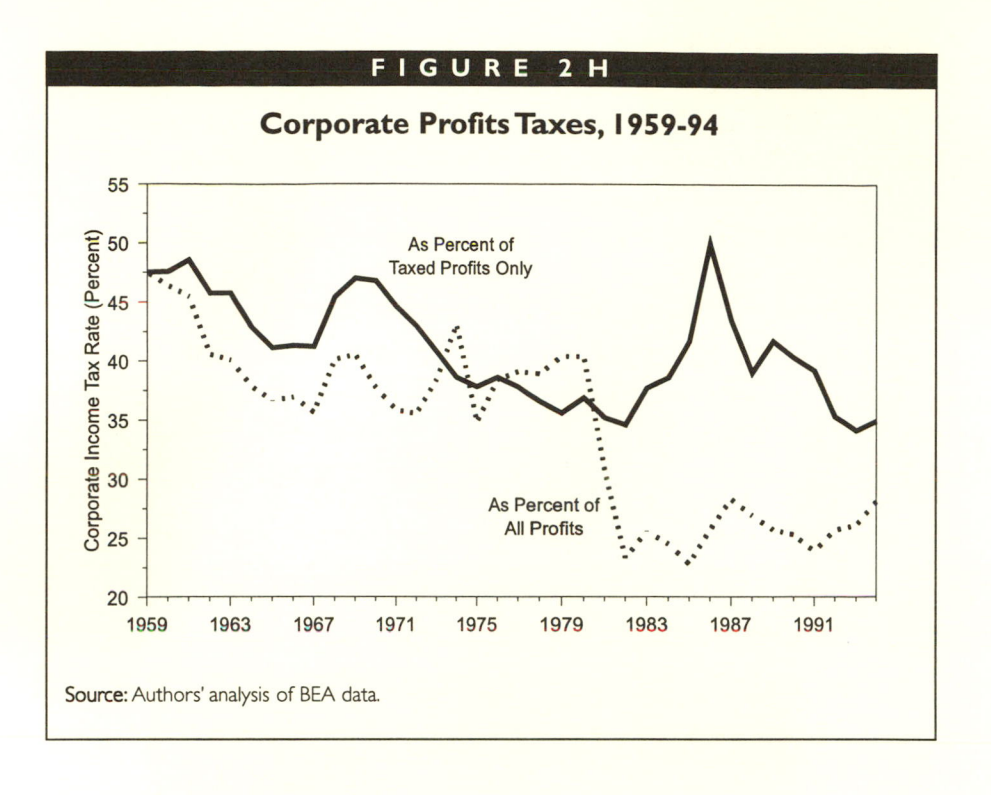

FIGURE 2H

Corporate Profits Taxes, 1959-94

Source: Authors' analysis of BEA data.

The Shift to State and Local Taxes

As noted in the beginning of this chapter, the proportion of total tax receipts contributed by state and local taxpayers has grown over time, relative to the federal tax burden (see Table 2.1). **Figure 2I**, which presents total tax receipts as a percentage of GDP, by different components, makes this point graphically. The figure shows that, starting in the postwar period, the growth of tax receipts has been led by state and local taxes (as well as federal payroll taxes, which were discussed above), while the federal income tax shows a relatively flat trend. Since state and local taxes are less progressive than federal taxes, the distribution of the overall tax burden is considerably, and increasingly, less progressive than the distribution of federal taxes alone.

State and local governments rely for their revenues predominantly on regressive taxes, such as sales taxes and property taxes (here regressivity is sensitive to incidence assumptions, discussed below), and on nontax sources of income such as fines and fees (regressive when they apply to consumption). **Table 2.15** gives the effective rates for state and local taxes by family income group

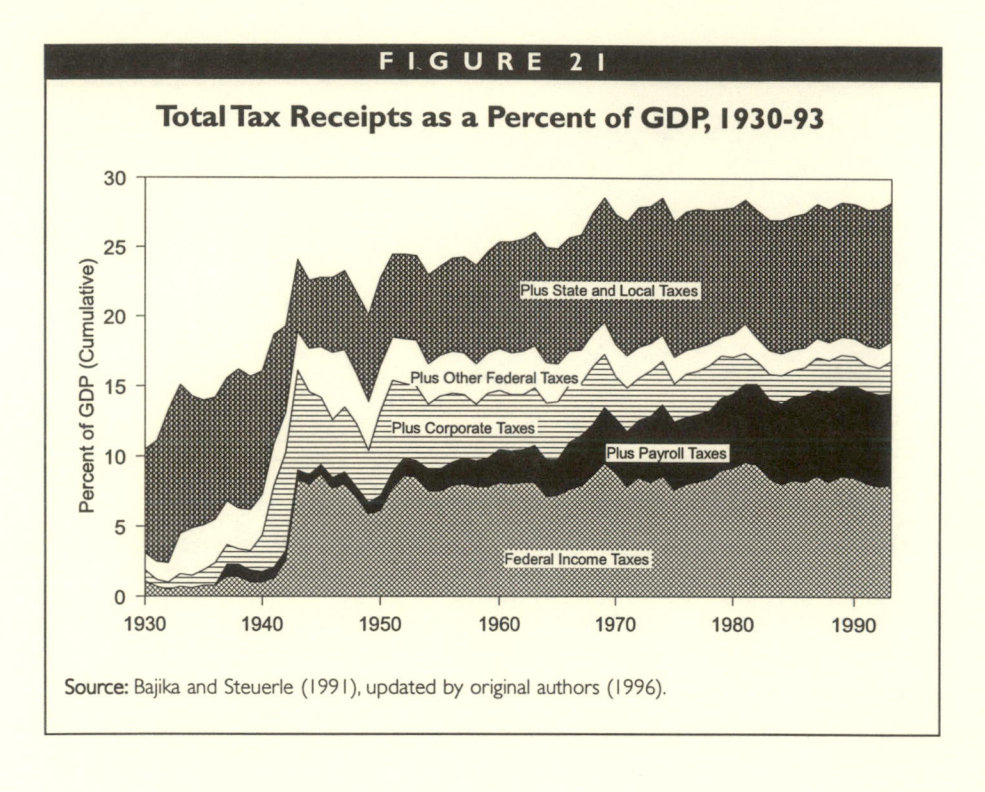

FIGURE 21

Total Tax Receipts as a Percent of GDP, 1930-93

Plus State and Local Taxes

Plus Other Federal Taxes

Plus Corporate Taxes

Plus Payroll Taxes

Federal Income Taxes

Source: Bajika and Steuerle (1991), updated by original authors (1996).

for a family of four (the findings are for 1991, the most recent data available). The regressive structure of the state and local burden is shown in the table's final column: the proportion of income that a family of four paid in state and local taxes fell as its income increased.

However, as with federal income and corporate taxes, state and local income and corporate taxes are progressive. Table 2.15 shows that the average family at the bottom of the income distribution paid 0.7% of its income in state and local personal income taxes, while the wealthiest 1% of families paid 4.6%. The state corporate tax is flat throughout most of the distribution, then slightly progressive at the top.

Conversely, property, sales, and excise taxes are regressive: the percentage of income that is taxed falls as income increases. This burden was exacerbated in 1986 when federal deductibility of state sales taxes was removed. In 1991, the poorest families in the average state paid 5.7% of their income in sales taxes and 1.9% in excise taxes. This proportion fell as income increased, until the wealthiest families paid a combined 1.3%.

The calculation of property tax incidence is particularly sensitive to the as-

TABLE 2.15

Total State and Local Taxes in 1991 (Effective Rates) as Shares of Income for Families of Four

Income Group	Personal Income Tax	Corporate Income Tax	Property Tax	Sales Tax	Excise Tax	Total Tax	Total After Federal Deductions
Bottom Four-Fifths	2.1%	0.1%	3.8%	4.0%	1.1%	11.1%	10.6%
First	0.7	0.1	5.4	5.7	1.9	13.8	13.8
Second	2.0	0.1	3.7	4.0	1.1	10.9	10.7
Third	2.6	0.1	3.2	3.3	0.8	10.0	9.5
Fourth	3.0	0.1	2.9	2.9	0.7	9.5	8.4
Top Fifth	3.7%	0.1%	2.6%	2.2%	0.4%	9.0%	7.5%
81-95%	3.5	0.1	2.7	2.4	0.5	9.2	7.7
96-99%	4.1	0.2	2.3	1.8	0.3	8.7	6.9
Top 1%	4.6	0.4	1.3	1.2	0.1	7.6	6.0
All	2.4%	0.1%	3.6%	3.6%	1.0%	10.6%	10.0%

Source: Authors' calculations based on McIntyre et al. (1991).

sumptions upon which the analysis is based. To the degree that owners of land and structures are able to shift the property tax burden onto tenants, the tax is regressive. Conversely, since ownership of land and capital generally rises with income, the property tax is progressive to the extent that those owners are unable to shift the tax forward onto property users.

The property tax column in Table 2.15 assumes that homeowners bear the full burden of their property taxes. For residential renters, half of the property tax is allocated to renters and half to owners. These two assumptions lead to the regressive structure reflected in the table, since poorer homeowners and renters devote a larger proportion of income to housing than do the wealthy. The property tax liability on business is assumed to be that part of state property tax revenue not accounted for by residential renters and homeowners.

The shift to state and local governments' revenues, as seen in Figure 2I, is of particular concern from a distributional perspective, since state and local taxes are more regressive than federal taxes. In spite of increases in social insurance taxes, in 1994, 52.6% of federal revenues still came from progressive taxes (personal, corporate, and estate), while only 20.9% of state/local revenues were raised progressively (**Table 2.16** and **Figures 2J** and **2K**). (Payroll taxes at the state level are not strictly comparable to those at the federal level, since these state contributions are mostly for pension funds for state and local employees. As such, they are more like personal assets than federal payroll taxes, which are distributed under a pay-as-you-go system. In this regard, they are less regressive than federal payroll taxes.) Over three-quarters (76.0%) of state/local revenues are raised from regressive taxes, compared with less than half (46.0%) of federal revenues.

Table 2.17 shows the percent of GDP taxed by progressive and regressive taxes, together with nontax revenues, at peaks of business cycles since 1959. While progressive taxes have varied slightly since 1959, regressive taxes have increased their share of GDP substantially—from 12.3% in 1959 to 17.4% in 1993—as the result of increases at both the federal and state/local levels. Nontax revenues have risen but remain low, at only 0.6% of GDP in 1993.

TABLE 2.16

Types of Federal vs. State & Local Taxes, as a Percent of Revenue at Each Level, 1994

Type of Tax	Federal	State & Local
Progressive	52.6%	20.9%
Personal Income Tax	39.5	16.7
Corporate Income Tax	11.9	4.1
Estate/Gift Taxes	1.1	0.0
Regressive	46.0%	76.0%
Excise/Customs/Sales/Other*	5.4	39.4
Contributions for Social Insurance	40.6	9.3
Property	0.0	27.3
Nontaxes**	1.5%	3.1%
Total	100.0%	100.0%

*   Other taxes include vehicle licenses, severance taxes, etc.
** Fines, certain fees, rents, royalties, tuition, hospital fees, etc.

Source: Authors' analysis of NIPA data.

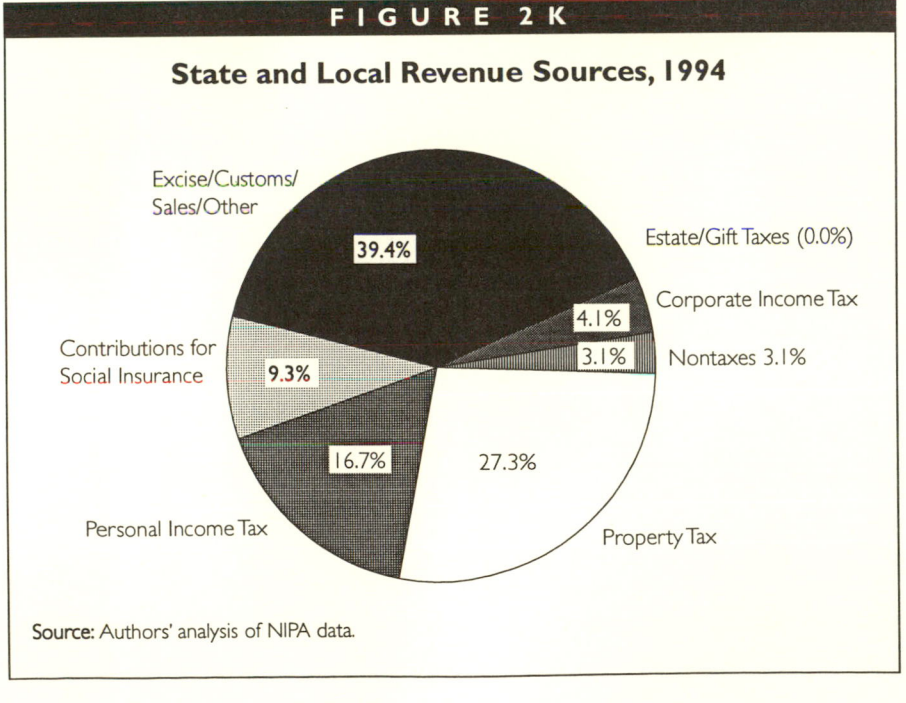

FIGURE 2J

Federal Revenue Sources, 1994

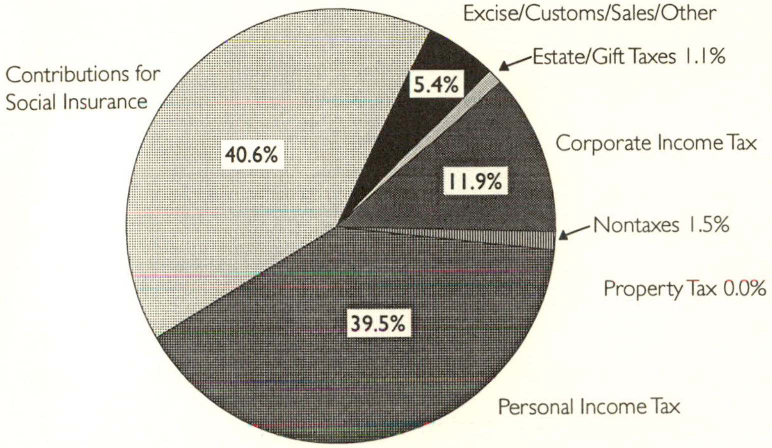

- Excise/Customs/Sales/Other — 5.4%
- Estate/Gift Taxes 1.1%
- Contributions for Social Insurance — 40.6%
- Corporate Income Tax — 11.9%
- Nontaxes 1.5%
- Property Tax 0.0%
- Personal Income Tax — 39.5%

Source: Authors' analysis of NIPA data.

FIGURE 2K

State and Local Revenue Sources, 1994

- Excise/Customs/Sales/Other — 39.4%
- Estate/Gift Taxes (0.0%)
- Corporate Income Tax — 4.1%
- Nontaxes 3.1%
- Contributions for Social Insurance — 9.3%
- Personal Income Tax — 16.7%
- Property Tax — 27.3%

Source: Authors' analysis of NIPA data.

TABLE 2.17

Types of Taxes as a Percent of GDP, 1959-93

Type of Tax	1959	1967	1973	1979	1989	1994
Progressive*	13.0%	12.7%	13.2%	13.9%	13.0%	12.7%
Federal	12.3	11.7	11.4	11.9	10.6	10.4
State & Local	0.7	1.0	1.8	2.0	2.3	2.3
Regressive**	12.3%	14.2%	16.1%	15.5%	16.7%	17.3%
Federal	5.5	6.5	7.6	7.9	9.0	9.1
State & Local	6.8	7.7	8.5	7.6	7.8	8.2
Nontaxes***	0.2%	0.3%	0.3%	0.3%	0.5%	0.6%
Federal	0.1	0.2	0.1	0.2	0.2	0.3
State & Local	0.1	0.1	0.1	0.2	0.3	0.3

*   Personal and corporate income taxes; estate and gift taxes.
**   Customs, excise, sales, and other taxes; property taxes; contributions for social insurance. Other taxes include vehicle licenses, severance taxes, etc.
*** Fines, certain fees, rents, royalties, tuition, hospital fees, etc.

Source: Authors' analysis of NIPA data.

Conclusion

The growth of income inequality documented in Chapter 1 has not been amelio-rated by either federal or state taxes. The federal personal income tax remains a progressive tax structure, but regressive changes in the personal income tax in 1977-89 and the increasing reliance on taxation from other, more regressive sources have limited the ability of the tax system to curb the rise in income inequality since the late 1970s. In fact, between 1977 and 1989, the tax system shifted to the advantage of the wealthiest 1% of families, who received large tax cuts at the expense of the poor and middle class. To some extent, tax changes since 1986 have reversed this trend, particularly regarding income taxes. How-ever, the tax system has still done little to counteract the steep increase in *pre-tax* income inequality, since it generates most revenues from regressive sources. The long-term rise in untaxed corporate profits and a shift to greater depen-dence on regressive state and local taxes have contributed to the increase in regressivity and after-tax income inequality.

CHAPTER 3

WAGES

Working Longer for Less

WAGE TRENDS HAVE BEEN THE PRIMARY DETERMINANT OF THE SLOW GROWTH in income and the greater income inequality experienced in recent years. This should not be surprising, since wages and salaries make up roughly three-fourths of total family income; the proportion is even higher among the broad middle class. This chapter examines what has happened to the wage structure and why wages continue to deteriorate for most workers.

The widespread deterioration of wages that began in the 1980s has continued over the current business cycle from 1989 to 1995. Wage inequality has continued in the most recent period as well, but its character is now different—it has grown at the "top" but not at the "bottom." That is, in the 1980s there was increasing divergence between the wages of high-wage and middle-wage workers and between middle-wage and low-wage workers. Since the late 1980s, however, top earners have continued to fare better than middle-wage earners, but middle-wage earners have lost ground at the same pace as low-wage earners.

The deterioration of wages over the 1989-95 period has been broad, encompassing the bottom 80% of men and the bottom 60% of women. The decline in the median wage of women workers in the 1990s represents a reversal from the 1980s, when the median woman's wage grew modestly at 0.5% per year.

Many high-wage workers, particularly men, have failed to see real wage improvements in the 1989-95 period. Male white-collar wages, including those for managers and technical workers, have declined, and the wages of male college graduates have stagnated and remain lower than their level of the mid-1980s or early 1970s. The wages of new college graduates have declined sharply among both men (-9.5%) and women (-7.7%) over the 1989-95 period, indicating that each years' graduating class is accepting more poorly paying jobs.

The deterioration of wages among non-college-educated workers, who make up 75% of the workforce, has continued in the 1990s at a somewhat faster pace than in the 1980s. Moreover, the wages earned by new high school graduates has continued to decline in the 1989-95 period, as it did in the 1979-89 period. For instance, the entry-level wages of high school graduates in 1995 were 27.3% and 18.9% less for young men and women respectively than in 1979.

These wage declines have not been offset by any growth in nonwage compensation or benefits. Employer costs for health care have risen modestly, but they have been offset in part by declining pension costs. As a result, growth in average hourly compensation over the 1979-94 period was just marginally higher than that of hourly wages, 0.5% versus 0.4% per year.

What is driving this widespread erosion of wages? Not poor productivity performance: productivity has been growing about 1% per year since 1979, and positive productivity cannot explain falling real wages. Growth in benefits, particularly health benefits, is not responsible, since the trend in compensation (wages and benefits) has paralleled that of wages.

There is no "smoking gun," or single factor, that can explain all or even most of the shift in the wage structure. However, a number of factors, in total, seem to account for most of the shifts. Significant institutional shifts, such as a severe drop in the value of the minimum wage and deunionization, explain one-third of the growing wage inequality among prime-age workers, and the expansion of low-wage service-sector employment has perhaps contributed 20%. Similarly, the increasing globalization of the economy—immigration and trade— has created more wage inequality, explaining, in our judgment, from 15% to 25% of the total. Together, the combined effects of industry shifts and globalization (which overlap and are not cumulative) can conservatively account for another 25-35% of the growth of wage inequality.

We reject the notion that the growth of wage inequality reflects primarily a technology-driven increase in demand for "educated" or "skilled" workers. There is evidence that the overall impact of technology on the wage and employment structure was no greater in the 1980s or 1990s than in the 1970s. Moreover, skill demand and technology have little relationship to the growth of within-group wage inequality (i.e., inequality among workers with similar levels of experience and education), which was responsible for a significant part of the overall growth of wage inequality in the 1980s. Technology has been and continues to be an important force, but there was no "technology shock" in the 1980s or 1990s, and no ensuing demand for "skill," that could not be satisfied by the continuing expansion of the educational attainment of the workforce.

It is also difficult to see a "bidding up" of the wages of "more-skilled" and "more-educated" workers when the wages of many college graduates and white-collar workers, especially men, have fallen each year since the mid-1980s and have been stagnant over the 1989-95 period. Moreover, it is misleading to label as "less educated" or "less skilled" a group constituting three-fourths of the workforce (and whose educational status ranges from high school dropouts to holders of associate-college degrees).

What does the future hold? The persistence of growing wage inequality in the first half of the 1990s and the expected continuation of most of the forces that led to the recent growth of inequality suggest that wage inequality will continue to grow, although perhaps more slowly. Offsetting trends, such as a rapid expansion of college graduates in the workforce or a surge in productivity growth, do not seem to be materializing.

More Hours and Stagnant Wages

To understand changes in wage trends it is important to distinguish between trends in annual, weekly, and hourly wages. Trends in annual wages, for instance, are driven by changes in both hourly wages and the amount of time spent working (weeks worked per year and hours worked per week). Likewise, weekly wage trends reflect changes in hourly pay and weekly hours. In this chapter we focus on the hourly pay levels of the workforce and its subgroups. We do this to be able to distinguish changes in earnings resulting from more (or less) work rather than more (or less) pay. Also, the hourly wage can be said to represent the "true" price of labor (exclusive of benefits, which we analyze separately). Chapter 4 addresses employment, unemployment, underemployment, and other issues related to changes in work time and opportunities.

Table 3.1 illustrates the importance of distinguishing between annual, weekly, and hourly wage trends. The annual wage and salary of the average worker in inflation-adjusted terms grew 0.4% annually between 1989 and 1994. However, much of this growth was due to longer working hours. For instance, the average worker worked 1,740 hours in 1994, 26 more—the equivalent of half an hour more each week—than the 1,714 hours worked in 1989. Correspondingly, that 0.4% yearly growth in annual wages was driven by a 0.3% yearly growth in annual hours and a minimal 0.1% yearly growth in real hourly wages. Any wage analysis that focuses on annual wages would miss the fact that most

TABLE 3.1

Trends in Average Wages and Average Hours, 1967-94
(1995 Dollars)

Year	Productivity per Hour (1992=100)	Wage Levels			Hours Worked		
		Annual Wages	Weekly Wages	Hourly Wages	Annual Hours	Weeks per Year	Hours per Week
1967	69.2	$19,511	$459.59	$11.96	1,633	42.4	38.4
1973	80.7	22,694	536.01	14.22	1,598	42.3	37.7
1979	86.4	22,862	534.92	14.11	1,620	42.7	37.9
1983	89.9	22,334	519.45	13.88	1,609	43.0	37.4
1989	95.8	24,600	552.42	14.35	1,714	44.5	38.5
1994	100.7	25,070	558.96	14.40	1,740	44.9	38.8
*Annual Growth Rate**							
1967-73	2.6%	2.5%	2.6%	2.9%	-0.4%	-0.0%	-0.3%
1973-79	1.1	0.1	-0.0	-0.1	0.2	0.2	0.1
1983-89	1.1	1.6	1.0	0.6	1.1	0.6	0.5
1979-89	1.0	0.7	0.3	0.2	0.6	0.4	0.2
1989-94	1.0	0.4	0.2	0.1	0.3	0.1	0.2

* Log growth rates.

Source: Authors' analysis of CPS data and Murphy and Welch (1989). For detailed information on table sources, see Table Notes.

---

of the growth from 1989 to 1994 was due to more work rather than higher hourly wages.

The 1979-89 period was also characterized by growing hours of work (up 94, from 1,620 to 1,714), while the real hourly wage was stagnant—growing $.24 over 10 years, or 0.2% annually. The 0.6% yearly growth in hours worked was driven by the increase in the average work year to 44.5 weeks from 42.7 weeks, a 0.4% annual growth, and a slight increase in the hours of the average workweek, to 38.5 hours. In the 1973-79 period, when hourly wages were essentially flat (falling 0.1% annually) and annual hours grew slowly (0.2% annually), the annual wage grew only 0.1% annually. In contrast, real hourly wages rose 2.9% annually between 1967 and 1973, while annual hours declined 0.4%. Thus, the post-1973 trend of greater work effort coupled with modestly rising or falling wages replaced a trend of strong real annual wage growth based on higher real hourly wages and reduced work time. Data for earlier years are not available.

Productivity growth over the last two decades has been less than that of the pre-1973 economy (Table 3.1), but these lower numbers are not sufficient to explain the modest growth in real wages. After all, hourly productivity actually *increased* by 1.1% or 1.0% over the last three business cycles, 1973-79, 1979-89, 1989-94.

Since 1979, few groups in the labor force have been able to enjoy even the modest growth in the "average wage" because of the large and continuing growth of wage inequality: high-wage workers received real wage gains while the remainder of the wage structure fell. Understanding and explaining this growth in wage inequality is a major focus of this chapter.

Contrasting Compensation and Wage Growth

There has been increased attention to the fact that "wages" do not make up the total pay package received by workers. It is possible that nonwage payments, sometimes referred to as "fringe benefits," have been growing rapidly, thereby driving total compensation to grow far faster than wages. Though widely believed, this characterization of the growth of workers' pay—disappointing wage growth but fast fringe-benefit and significant compensation growth—is incorrect. This section examines the growth of compensation using the only two available data series and finds that hourly compensation has grown slightly faster than wages since 1979 or 1989. This pattern implies that the widely available measures of wage growth for particular groups of workers are appropriate proxies for compensation growth.

Table 3.2 and **Figure 3A** examine the wage and compensation data that are developed as a major part of the Commerce Department's effort—the National Income and Product Accounts (NIPA)—to measure gross domestic product (GDP), the size of the national economy. Compensation levels exceed wage levels because they include employer payments for health insurance, pensions, and payroll taxes, primarily payments toward Social Security and unemployment insurance.

It is true that benefits have grown faster, if not far faster, than wages. For instance, over the 1979-94 period benefits grew 1.0% annually while wages grew only 0.4% annually. Yet, total compensation (wages and benefits) grew at relatively same rate as wages, 0.5% versus 0.4% per year. This apparent con-

TABLE 3.2

Growth of Average Hourly Wages, Benefits, and Compensation, 1959-94
(1995 Dollars)

Year	Wages & Salaries	Benefits*	Total Compensation	Benefit Share of Compensation
Hourly Pay**				
1959	$9.86	$0.94	$10.79	8.7%
1967	12.26	1.47	13.73	10.7
1973	14.52	2.34	16.86	13.9
1979	14.96	3.13	18.09	17.3
1989	15.81	3.48	19.29	18.1
1994	15.89	3.67	19.56	18.8
Annual Dollar Change				
1959-73	$0.33	$0.10	$0.43	
1973-79	0.07	0.13	0.20	
1979-89	0.08	0.04	0.12	
1989-94	0.02	0.04	0.05	
1979-94	0.06	0.04	0.10	
Annual Percent Change				
1959-73	2.8%	6.4%	3.2%	
1973-79	0.5	2.3	1.2	
1979-89	0.6	1.3	0.6	
1989-94	0.1	0.6	0.3	
1979-94	0.4	1.0	0.5	

*   Includes payroll taxes, health, pension, and other nonwage benefits.
**   Deflated by Personal Consumption Expenditure (PCE) Index for all items, except health, which is deflated by PCE Health Index.

Source: Authors' analysis of BEA NIPA data.

tradition is readily explained: nonwage compensation in 1979 totaled just 17.3% of total compensation. Thus, even a fast growth of a small part of compensation (benefits) did not lead to a growth in total compensation much greater than in wages.

Another way of assessing the limited role of benefits growth is to note that a 1% annual growth over the 1979-94 period translated to a $.04 per year growth, up $.54 from $3.13 in 1979 to $3.67 in 1994.

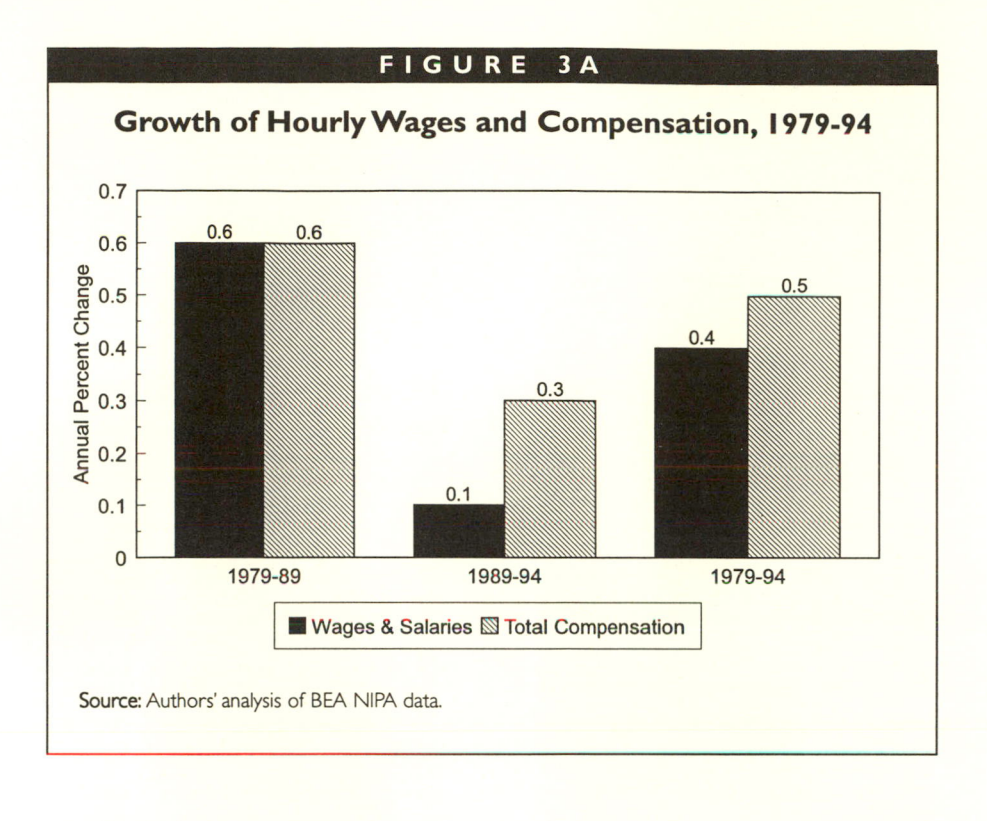

FIGURE 3A

Growth of Hourly Wages and Compensation, 1979-94

Source: Authors' analysis of BEA NIPA data.

The relationship between average compensation and average wage growth has not differed much in recent decades. Even in the period with the most rapid growth of benefits relative to wages (1959-73), compensation still grew only slightly faster than wages because benefits were such a smaller share of compensation—8.7% in 1959. In the 1979-89 period, compensation and wages actually grew at the same 0.6% annual rate. In the most recent period, 1989-94, compensation grew 0.2% faster than wages, but both wages and compensation grew more slowly than in the 1979-89 period. Over the entire 1979-94 period the growth of hourly compensation, 0.5% per year, was just 0.1% per year faster than wage growth of 0.4% per year. Over the most recent 15-year period, then, the difference between compensation and wage growth has been trivial.

Why is it that some analysts have presumed that fringe-benefit growth in recent years has balanced declining wages, thus leaving overall compensation to grow at its historical rate? This reasoning seems plausible, since health care costs have been rising rapidly and since most people assume that fringe benefits make up a large share of total compensation, perhaps as high as 40-45%.

However, the data presented in Table 3.2 show that benefits are not as important in the overall compensation package as is commonly believed, nor did compensation increase rapidly in recent years. Part of the confusion about the role of fringe benefits is definitional. In surveys of employers by trade associations and by the Bureau of Labor Statistics, fringe benefits are broadly defined (following standard corporate accounting procedures) to include paid leave (holidays and vacations), supplemental pay (overtime and shift premiums), and payroll taxes (the employer portion of Social Security and unemployment taxes). Under this broad definition, benefits do make up about 28% of total compensation costs. However, wage-related items that are received by workers in their regular paychecks, such as paid leave and supplemental pay, are defined as wages by workers when they report their wages in government surveys.

Thus, although studies of labor-market trends should examine both wage and benefit trends, those that focus on wage trends alone (usually because of a lack of benefit data) are not misleading. That is, taking account of payroll taxes or pension and insurance costs (including both health and life insurance), given their small size and slow growth, would not substantively alter the picture emerging from analyses, such as this one, of the government wage data frequently used to track labor-market trends. It should be kept in mind that the erosion of wages is slightly larger than the erosion of overall compensation.

The data in **Table 3.3** take a different look at the role of benefit growth in driving total compensation growth. These data are drawn from the Bureau of Labor Statistics' Employment Cost Index (ECI) program, which provides the value of wages and employer-provided benefits for each year since 1987. These ECI data corroborate our earlier finding that benefits, defined as pension, insurance (health and life), and payroll taxes, make up an 18-20% share of total compensation that has not risen significantly since 1987. In fact, these ECI data are somewhat more pessimistic than those in Table 3.2, since they show a nontrivial 4.6% *decline* in compensation and a 3.3% *decline* in benefits from 1989 to 1995. These numbers vary from the ones presented earlier because they describe only the private sector (government employment is excluded), and the definition of "hours worked" is different. Nevertheless, neither source of data provides much support for the view that, although "wage growth" may be disappointing, increased benefits are making up the difference. We return to a discussion of benefit growth below when we examine the growth of specific benefits, such as health insurance and pensions.

TABLE 3.3

Growth in Private-Sector Average Hourly Wages, Benefits, and Compensation, 1987-95

(1995 Dollars)

Year[***]	Wages & Salaries	Benefits[*]	Total Compensation[**]	Benefit Share of Compensation
Hourly Pay				
1987	$15.01	$3.38	$18.39	18.4%
1988	14.74	3.42	18.16	18.9
1989	14.56	3.37	17.93	18.8
1990	14.43	3.39	17.83	19.0
1991	14.06	3.33	17.39	19.2
1992	14.23	3.41	17.64	19.3
1993	14.25	3.41	17.66	19.3
1994	14.12	3.47	17.59	19.7
1995	13.84	3.26	17.10	19.1
Change 1989-95				
Dollars	$-0.72	$-0.11	$-0.83	
Percent	-4.9%	-3.3%	-4.6%	

*   Includes payroll taxes, health, pension, and other nonwage benefits.
**   Deflated by CPI-U-X1, except health, which is deflated by CPI-U-X1 Health Index.
*** Data are for March.

Source: Authors' analysis of BLS ECI Levels data.

Low-Paid Occupations Fared Worse

We now turn to the growth or decline in wages of the various segments of the workforce since 1973. In general, the workers who experienced the greatest fall in real wages were those who initially had lower wages, were without a college degree, were in blue-collar or service occupations, or were in younger age brackets. In recent years, however, the real wages of white-collar and college-educated workers have also eroded.

The data in **Table 3.4** and **Figure 3B** show wage trends for the 80% of the workforce who are "production and nonsupervisory workers." This category includes factory workers, construction workers, and a wide variety of service-

TABLE 3.4

Hourly and Weekly Earnings of
Production and Nonsupervisory Workers, 1947-95*
(1995 Dollars)

Year	Real Average Hourly Earnings	Real Average Weekly Earnings
1947	$7.12	$287.04
1967	11.25	427.56
1973	12.72	469.44
1979	12.69	452.90
1989	11.87	410.79
1995	11.46	395.37
Annual Growth		
1947-67	2.3%	2.0%
1967-73	2.1	1.6
1973-79	0.0	-0.6
1979-89	-0.7	-1.0
1989-95	-0.6	-0.6

* Production and nonsupervisory workers account for more than 80% of wage and salary employment.

Source: Authors' analysis.

sector workers ranging from restaurant and clerical workers to nurses and teachers. Between 1979 and 1995, average hourly earnings for these workers fell $1.23, from $12.69 to $11.46, a decline of about 0.7% each year. In contrast, hourly earnings were flat in the 1973-79 period and grew 2.1-2.3% per year from 1947 to 1973.

Weekly earnings fell at a rate of 1.0% each year from 1979 until 1989 because of reductions in both weekly hours and hourly earnings. Real hourly and weekly earnings fell in tandem over the 1989-95 period, however, as weekly hours remained stable. The earnings of production and nonsupervisory workers in 1995 were $395.37 per week (in 1995 dollars), $32 less than what they were in 1967.

Table 3.5 presents post-1973 average wage trends by occupation for men and women; it uses a data source that has wage, but no benefit, information. The decline in hourly wages from 1989 to 1995 among men was evident in nearly

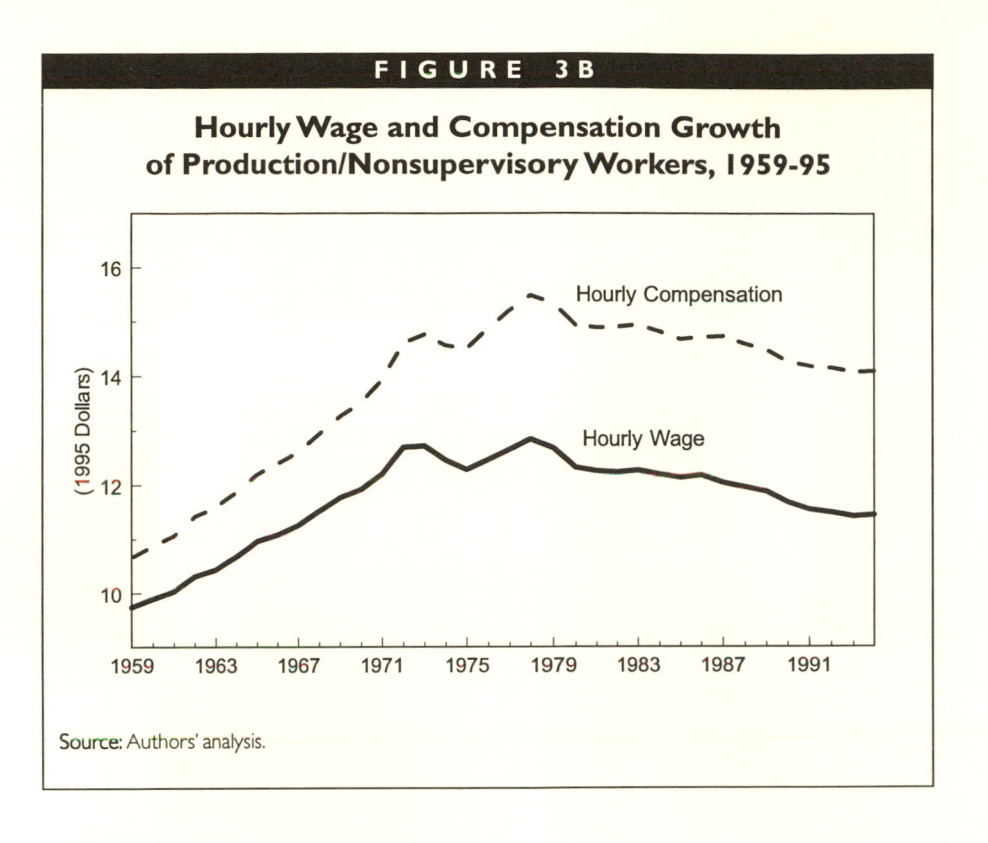

FIGURE 3B

Hourly Wage and Compensation Growth of Production/Nonsupervisory Workers, 1959-95

Source: Authors' analysis.

every occupation category, although greater among blue-collar (-7.1%) than white-collar (-1.4%) men. For blue-collar men, who made up 41.5% of male employment in 1995, these recent wage setbacks follow the deep real wage declines of the 1979-89 period. Men in the higher-paid white-collar occupations, on the other hand, enjoyed real wage growth in the 1980s, so their recent experiences represent a turnaround. White-collar men in 1995 earned slightly less, $18.05, than their counterparts did in 1973, $18.21.

Nearly three-fourths (74%) of women workers were white-collar workers in 1995, and their wage growth of 3.3% in the recent period from 1989 to 1995 was slow relative to the 9.2% growth in the prior decade, even after taking the different lengths of these time periods into account. The wages of women in blue-collar, service, and lower wage white-collar occupations (administrative, clerical, or sales) did not do well in either the 1980s or 1990s.

TABLE 3.5

Changes in Hourly Wages by Occupation, 1979-95
(1995 Dollars)

Occupation*	Percent of Employment 1995	Hourly Wage				Percent Change		
		1973	1979	1989	1995	1973-79	1979-89	1989-95
Males								
White Collar	45.4%	$18.21	$18.21	$18.31	$18.05	-0.0%	0.6%	-1.4%
Managers	13.1	20.17	20.28	21.71	21.36	0.5	7.1	-1.6
Professional	12.6	20.21	19.74	20.79	20.92	-2.3	5.3	0.6
Technical	3.3	17.18	16.94	17.41	16.97	-1.4	2.8	-2.5
Sales	10.0	15.82	16.03	15.00	14.44	1.3	-6.5	-3.7
Admin., Clerk	6.5	13.85	13.93	12.79	11.97	0.6	-8.2	-6.5
Service	10.5%	$11.41	$10.47	$9.54	$9.23	-8.2%	-8.9%	-3.2%
Protective	3.2	14.72	13.30	13.35	13.15	-9.7	0.4	-1.5
Other	7.3	9.78	9.17	7.89	7.49	-6.2	-13.9	-5.1
Blue Collar	41.5%	$13.73	$13.79	$12.51	$11.62	0.5%	-9.2%	-7.1%
Craft	18.7	15.70	15.40	14.18	13.33	-1.9	-7.9	-6.0
Operatives	8.6	12.30	12.74	11.65	10.65	3.5	-8.5	-8.6
Trans. Op.	7.5	12.92	13.20	11.74	11.03	2.2	-11.1	-6.0
Laborers	6.7	11.28	11.18	9.53	8.78	-0.9	-14.7	-7.9
Females								
White Collar	74.0%	$11.06	$10.89	$11.89	$12.28	-1.5%	9.2%	3.3%
Managers	12.9	12.73	12.49	14.47	14.80	-1.9	15.8	2.3
Professional	17.7	14.77	13.80	15.64	16.35	-6.6	13.3	4.6
Technical	4.0	11.65	12.18	13.04	12.87	4.6	7.1	-1.3
Sales	12.1	7.61	8.80	8.77	8.88	15.6	-0.3	1.2
Admin., Clerk	27.3	9.92	9.68	10.07	9.86	-2.4	4.0	-2.1
Service	15.6%	$7.21	$7.44	$6.96	$6.94	3.2%	-6.4%	-0.3%
Protective	0.7	n.a.	n.a.	n.a.	n.a.	n.a.	n.a.	n.a.
Other	14.9	7.16	7.39	6.81	6.76	3.2	-7.8	-0.8
Blue Collar	10.4%	$8.39	$8.91	$8.57	$8.36	6.3%	-3.9%	-2.4%
Craft	2.1	9.63	10.08	10.22	9.97	4.7	1.4	-2.4
Operatives	5.7	8.22	8.68	8.05	7.88	5.6	-7.2	-2.2
Trans. Op.	0.9	n.a.	n.a.	n.a.	n.a.	n.a.	n.a.	n.a.
Laborers	1.7	n.a.	n.a.	n.a.	n.a.	n.a.	n.a.	n.a.

* Data for private household and farming, forestry, and fishing occupations not shown and not included in wage calculations.

Source: Authors' analysis.

Wage Trends by Wage Level

For any given trend in average wages, there will be different outcomes for particular groups of workers if wage inequality rises, as it has in recent years. **Table 3.6** provides data on wage trends for workers at different points (or levels) in the wage distribution, thus allowing us to characterize wage growth for low-, middle-, and high-wage earners. The data, presented for the cyclical peak years 1973, 1979, and 1989 and for the most recent year for which we have data, 1995, show that the deterioration in real wages since 1979 was both broad and uneven. The breadth of recent wage problems is clear from the fact that real wages fell for the bottom 60% of wage earners over the 1979-89 period, while wages fell among the bottom 80% over the 1989-95

TABLE 3.6

Wages for All Workers by Wage Percentile, 1973-95
(1995 Dollars)

Year	\multicolumn{7}{c}{Wage by Percentile}
	10	20	40	50	60	80	90
Real Hourly Wage							
1973	$5.76	$6.96	$9.61	$11.02	$12.64	$16.79	$21.10
1979	6.10	6.96	9.62	10.88	12.60	17.37	21.33
1989	5.12	6.37	9.13	10.61	12.39	17.64	22.28
1995	5.06	6.19	8.70	10.13	11.98	17.30	22.35
Dollar Change							
1973-79	$0.34	$0.00	$0.00	$-0.14	$-0.04	$0.58	$0.23
1979-89	-0.98	-0.59	-0.48	-0.27	-0.21	0.27	0.95
1989-95	-0.06	-0.19	-0.43	-0.48	-0.41	-0.34	0.07
1979-95	-1.04	-0.77	-0.92	-0.75	-0.62	-0.08	1.02
Percent Change							
1973-79	5.8%	0.1%	0.0%	-1.3%	-0.3%	3.5%	1.1%
1979-89	-16.1	-8.5	-5.0	-2.4	-1.7	1.5	4.5
1989-95	-1.1	-2.9	-4.7	-4.6	-3.3	-1.9	0.3
1979-95	-17.0	-11.1	-9.5	-6.9	-4.9	-0.4	4.8

Source: Authors' analysis.

period. That is, only workers in the upper 20% of the wage scale obtained real wage growth.

The decline in wages was greater the lower the wage. Over the 1979-95 period, wages fell just 0.4% at the 80th percentile but were down 11.1% and 17.0% at the 20th and 10th percentiles respectively. The wage of the median worker, who earned more than half of the workforce but also less than half of the workforce, fell 2.4% from 1979 to 1989 and another 4.6% from 1989 to 1995.

This overall picture, however, masks somewhat different outcomes for men and women. Among men, wages have fallen more and at nearly all parts of the wage distribution (**Table 3.7** and **Figure 3C**). In the middle, the median male hourly wage fell 9.1% between 1979 and 1989 and another 6.3% between 1989 and 1995, for a total fall of 14.9%. Even high-wage men (those

TABLE 3.7

Wages for Male Workers by Wage Percentile, 1973-95
(1995 Dollars)

	Wage by Percentile						
Year	10	20	40	50	60	80	90
Real Hourly Wage							
1973	$6.80	$8.73	$11.79	$13.37	$15.15	$19.19	$24.45
1979	6.71	8.53	11.93	13.66	15.51	20.20	24.62
1989	5.86	7.34	10.67	12.41	14.61	19.80	24.80
1995	5.49	6.93	9.91	11.62	13.58	19.08	24.88
Dollar Change							
1973-79	$-0.09	$-0.20	$0.14	$0.29	$0.35	$1.01	$0.18
1979-89	-0.85	-1.19	-1.26	-1.25	-0.90	-0.40	0.17
1989-95	-0.37	-0.41	-0.76	-0.79	-1.03	-0.72	0.08
1979-95	-1.22	-1.59	-2.02	-2.04	-1.92	-1.12	0.25
Percent Change							
1973-79	-1.3%	-2.3%	1.2%	2.2%	2.3%	5.2%	0.7%
1979-89	-12.7	-13.9	-10.6	-9.1	-5.8	-2.0	0.7
1989-95	-6.4	-5.5	-7.1	-6.3	-7.0	-3.6	0.3
1979-95	-18.2	-18.7	-16.9	-14.9	-12.4	-5.5	1.0

Source: Authors' analysis.

FIGURE 3C

Hourly Wages for Men by Wage Percentile, 1973-95

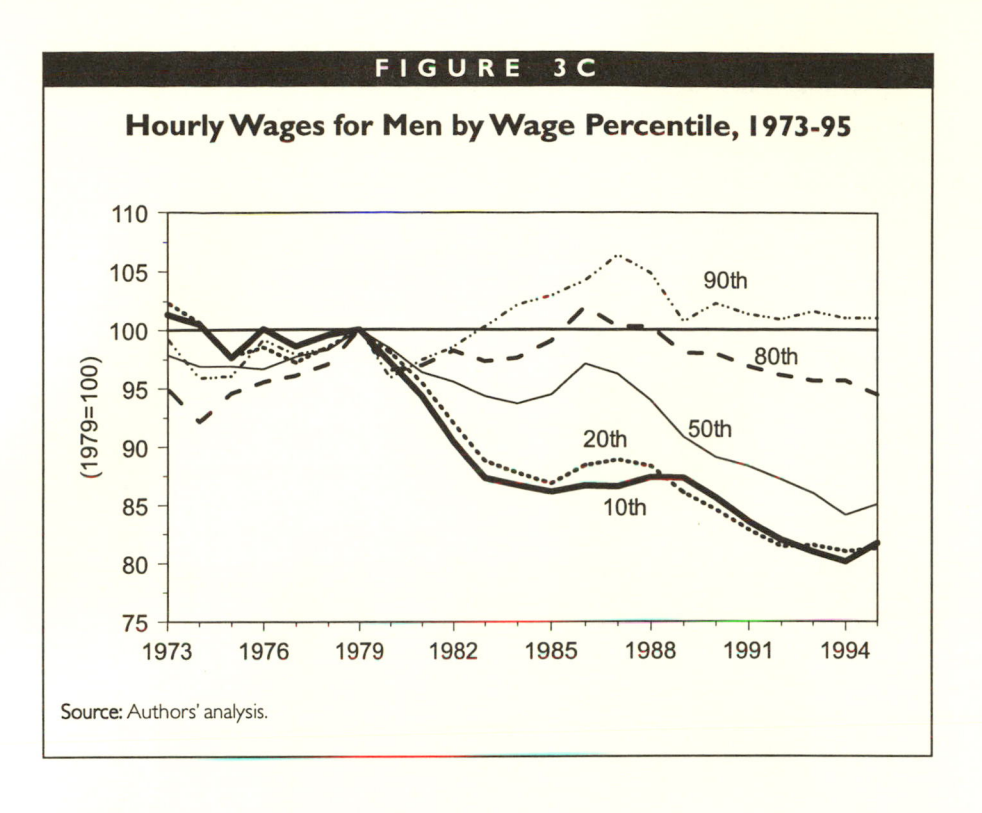

Source: Authors' analysis.

at the 80th percentile) experienced a decline in wages of 2.0% over the 1979-89 period, followed by a 3.6% drop after 1989. Wages among low-wage men fell the most—about 18%—from 1979 to 1995. These data thus show significant wage deterioration for nearly all men, with the bottom 60% suffering between a 12% and 18% wage reduction from 1979 to 1995. Since 1979, the median male hourly wage has fallen $2.04, or about 1% per year. Even the high-wage men at the 90th percentile who earned nearly $25 per hour have done well only in relative terms, since their wage was a marginal 1% higher in 1995 than in 1979.

The structure of male wage deterioration shifted in the 1980s and 1990s. In the 1980s, wages fell most the lower the wage, while in the 1990s there was an almost uniform wage decline among the bottom 60%. Thus, the wage spread between middle- and low-wage men did not grow in the 1990s, although the gap between high-wage men and middle- and low-wage men continued to grow.

The only significant wage growth between 1979 and 1995 appears to have been among higher-wage women (**Table 3.8** and **Figure 3D**). For instance, wages

TABLE 3.8

Wages for Female Workers by Wage Percentile, 1973-95
(1995 Dollars)

Year	Wage by Percentile						
	10	20	40	50	60	80	90
Real Hourly Wage							
1973	$4.80	$5.96	$7.49	$8.44	$9.50	$12.34	$15.26
1979	5.82	6.31	7.64	8.58	9.75	12.64	15.78
1989	4.76	5.87	7.80	9.07	10.36	14.63	18.36
1995	4.84	5.77	7.76	8.92	10.28	14.92	19.17
Dollar Change							
1973-79	$1.02	$0.35	$0.15	$0.14	$0.25	$0.30	$0.52
1979-89	-1.06	-0.44	0.16	0.49	0.61	1.98	2.58
1989-95	0.08	-0.10	-0.04	-0.15	-0.09	0.29	0.81
1979-95	-0.98	-0.53	0.12	0.34	0.52	2.28	3.39
Percent Change							
1973-79	21.3%	5.9%	2.0%	1.6%	2.7%	2.5%	3.4%
1979-89	-18.2	-7.0	2.1	5.7	6.2	15.7	16.3
1989-95	1.6	-1.6	-0.5	-1.7	-0.8	2.0	4.4
1979-95	-16.8	-8.5	1.6	4.0	5.3	18.0	21.5

Source: Authors' analysis.

grew 18.0% and 21.5% at the 80th and 90th percentiles between 1979 and 1995, but they declined among the lowest-wage women at the 20th percentile and below and grew modestly at the median, 4.0% over 16 years.

The surprising trend is the modest but pervasive decline in wages from the 20th to the 60th percentile among women in the 1989-95 period. Even high-wage women received only modest real wage gains after 1989. Thus, while women's wages were the bright spot of the 1980s, the wage trends for women have been far less favorable in the 1990s. One positive trend, however, is that wages for the lowest-wage women (the 10th percentile) stopped falling in the recent period, perhaps because of the rise in the minimum wage in the early 1990s.

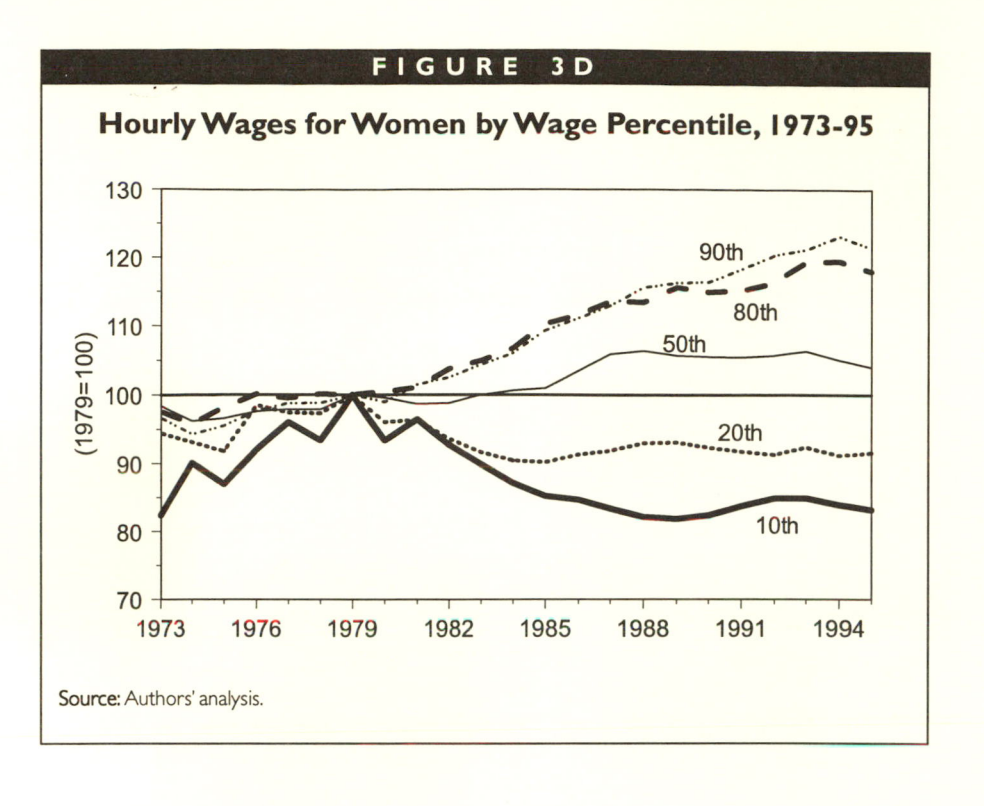

FIGURE 3D

Hourly Wages for Women by Wage Percentile, 1973-95

Source: Authors' analysis.

The Male-Female Wage Gap

From 1979 to 1989, the median hourly wage fell $1.25 for men and rose $0.49 for women (**Table 3.9**). These moves led to a growth in the hourly wage ratio between men and women by 10.6 percentage points, from 62.8% in 1979 to 73.1% in 1989, representing a sizable reduction in gender wage inequality. Even after this progress, however, women still earned more than one-fourth less than men in 1989.

This narrowing of the male/female wage gap in the 1980s was the result of both improvements in real hourly wages for women and real wage reductions for men. Table 3.9 provides an assessment of how much the narrowing of this male-female wage differential was due to rising real wages for women and how much to the real wage loss for men. If real wages among men had not fallen by 1989 but had remained at their 1979 level (at $13.66), the wage gap would have been 66.4%, a drop of just 3.6 rather than the actual 10.3 percentage points. Thus, falling real wages among men can explain 64.9% of the closing of the gender

TABLE 3.9

Changes in the Gender Wage Differential, 1973-95
(1995 Dollars)

Year	Median Hourly Wage			Women's Share of Employment
	Male	Female	Ratio	
1973	$13.37	$8.44	63.1%	38.5%
1979	13.66	8.58	62.8	41.7
1989	12.41	9.07	73.1	45.2
1995	11.62	8.92	76.7	46.1
1989 (alt.)*	13.66	9.07	66.4	
1995 (alt.)*	13.66	8.92	65.3	
Change				
1979-89	$-1.25	$0.49	10.3	
1989-95	-0.79	-0.15	3.6	

Contribution to Narrower Wage Gap of Changes in:**

Period	Male Wage Decline	Female Wage Growth	Total
1979-89	64.9%	35.1%	100.0%
1979-95	82.1	17.9	100.0

* Alternative scenario if male wages did not decline in real terms since 1979.
** The contribution of "female wage growth" is the growth of the gender differential assuming male real wages did not fall (the alternative scenario), relative to the actual change in the differential.

Source: Authors' analysis.

---

wage gap between 1979 and 1989; only 35.1% (3.6% divided by 10.3%) was due to women's rising real wages.

Since 1989, the wages for both the median-wage male and median-wage female have been *falling*. Therefore, any progress in lessening gender inequality could only result from women's wages falling more slowly, as has happened. In this manner, the gender wage ratio improved to 76.7%. Combining the entire 1979-95 period shows that male wage decline explains 82.1% of the closing of the gender wage gap.

The Expansion of Low-Wage Jobs

Another useful way of characterizing changes in the wage structure is to examine the trend in the proportion of workers earning low, middle, and high wages. These trends are presented in **Table 3.10** for all workers and for men and women. The workforce is divided into six wage groups based on multiples of the "poverty-wage level," or the hourly wage that a full-time, year-round worker must earn to sustain a family of four at the poverty threshold, which was $7.28 in 1995 (in 1994 dollars). Thus, workers are assigned to a wage group according to the degree to which they earned more (or less) than poverty-level wages.

Table 3.10 and **Figure 3E** show a significant expansion of workers earning far less than poverty-level wages since 1979. In 1979, only 4.2% of the workforce were "very low earners," with wages at least 25% below the poverty-level wage (labeled "0-75"). By 1989, 13.4% of the workforce earned such wages, a shift of 9.2% of the workforce into this low-wage group. An additional 1.0% became very low earners between 1989 and 1995. Likewise, in 1989, 28.5% of the workforce earned poverty-level wages (derived from adding the two lowest-paying categories together), a rise from 23.7% in 1979. The share of workers earning poverty-level wages rose to 29.7% in 1995. Thus, there was not only a sizable growth in the proportion of workers earning poverty-level wages over the 1973-95 period, but also a shift within this group to those earning very low wages.

Over the 1979-89 and 1989-95 periods, there was a general downward shift in the entire wage structure, with proportionately fewer workers in the middle- and high-wage groups in 1989 or 1995 than in, respectively, 1979 or 1989. The only exception is the modest expansion of the share of the workforce at the very highest earnings level (exceeding three times the poverty-level wage) and a slight growth of the workforce just above the poverty wage.

Among women, there was a larger shift to the "bottom" during the 1979-89 period—an additional 11.6% earned very low wages—and a larger shift upward—the two highest-wage groups grew by 6.6 percentage points. The shift downward among women appears to be an enlargement of the workforce earning very low wages, while the proportion earning poverty-level wages was stable, remaining at about 37.0%. In the 1989-95 period, the bottom of the wage structure was stable and the shift upward was smaller than in the 1980s. This mirrors the trends found in our earlier percentile analysis (Tables 3.6-3.8).

Among men, the overall changes in the wage structure between 1979 and 1995 meant proportionately fewer middle-wage workers and more low-wage

TABLE 3.10

Distribution of Total Employment
by Wage Level, 1973-1995

	Share of Employment by Wage Multiple of Poverty Wage*							
	Poverty-Level Wages:							
Year	0-75	75-100	Total**	100-125	125-200	200-300	300+	Total
Total								
1973	8.0%	15.6%	23.5%	13.3%	34.7%	19.9%	8.6%	100.0%
1979	4.2	19.4	23.7	15.3	31.4	21.0	8.7	100.0
1989	13.4	15.1	28.5	13.5	29.2	19.0	9.7	100.0
1995	14.4	15.3	29.7	14.6	27.7	18.0	10.0	100.0
Change								
1973-79	-3.7	3.9	0.1	2.0	-3.3	1.1	0.0	
1979-89	9.2	-4.3	4.9	-1.8	-2.2	-2.0	1.1	
1989-95	1.0	0.2	1.2	1.1	-1.5	-1.1	0.3	
Men								
1973	3.8%	9.0%	12.8%	9.7%	36.7%	27.9%	13.0%	100.0%
1979	2.4	11.0	13.4	11.3	32.1	29.6	13.6	100.0
1989	9.1	12.1	21.2	11.3	29.6	23.7	14.1	100.0
1995	10.6	12.7	23.3	13.2	28.6	21.5	13.5	100.0
Change								
1973-79	-1.5	2.1	0.6	1.6	-4.6	1.8	0.6	
1979-89	6.8	1.1	7.8	0.0	-2.5	-5.9	0.5	
1989-95	1.5	0.6	2.1	1.9	-1.1	-2.2	-0.6	
Women								
1973	14.0%	25.1%	39.1%	18.6%	31.7%	8.3%	2.3%	100.0%
1979	6.7	30.4	37.0	20.5	30.4	9.8	2.3	100.0
1989	18.2	18.6	36.8	16.0	28.6	13.8	4.7	100.0
1995	18.6	18.2	36.8	16.2	26.8	14.2	6.1	100.0
Change								
1973-79	-7.3	5.3	-2.1	1.9	-1.2	1.5	-0.0	
1979-89	11.6	-11.8	-0.3	-4.5	-1.8	4.1	2.5	
1989-95	0.4	-0.4	0.0	0.2	-1.9	0.3	1.4	

* The wage ranges are equivalent in 1994 dollars to: $5.46 and below (0-75), $5.47-$7.28 (75-100), $7.29-$9.10 (100-125), $9.11-$14.56 (125-200), $14.57-$21.84 (200-300), and $21.85 and above (300+).
** Combines lowest two categories.

Source: Authors' analysis.

FIGURE 3E

Share of Workers Earning Poverty-Level Wages, 1973-95

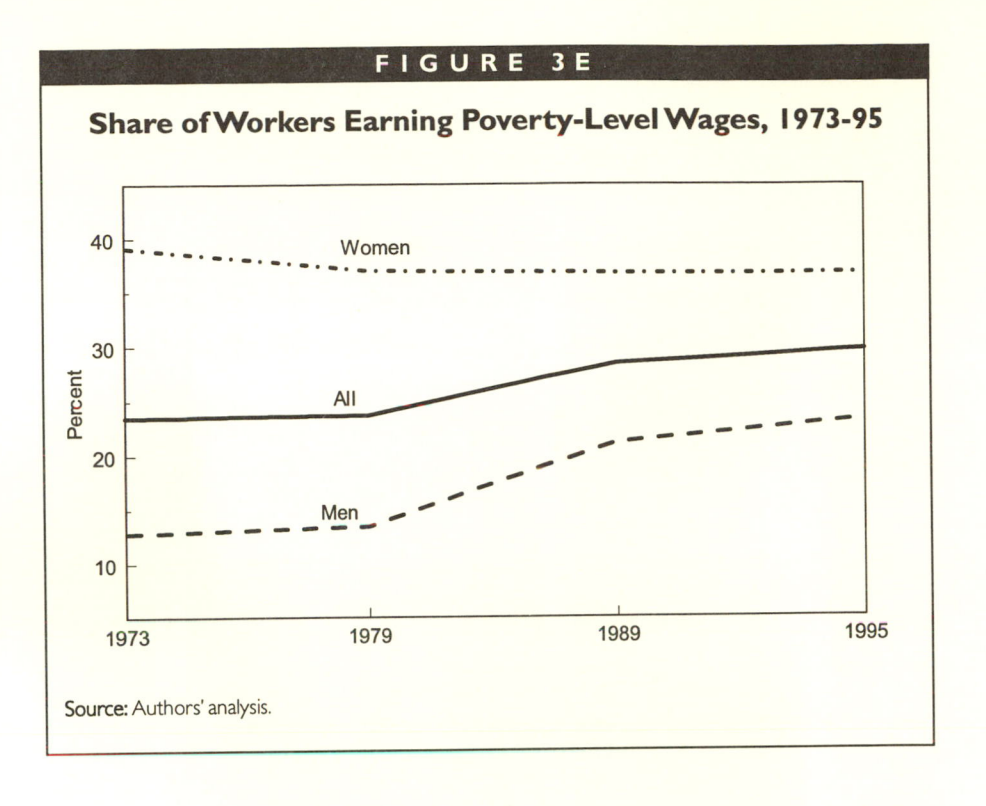

Source: Authors' analysis.

workers, with no growth of very high earners (up in the 1980s but reversed in the 1990s). For instance, there was an increased proportion of men earning less than the poverty-level wage—a 7.8% and then a 2.1% shift—and a shrinking proportion of men in the second- and third-highest wage groups.

Women are much more likely to earn low wages than men. In 1995, 36.8% of women earned poverty-level wages or less, significantly more than the share of men (23.3%). Women are also much less likely to earn very high wages. In 1995, only 6.1% of women, but 13.5% of men, earned at least three times the poverty-level wage.

Tables 3.11, **3.12**, and **3.13** (and **Figure 3F**) present an analysis similar to the one in Table 3.10 for white, black, and Hispanic employment. For instance, Table 3.11 shows that there was a modest shift downward in the wage structure for whites in the 1970s, followed by a larger downward shift in the 1979-89 period and again in the 1989-95 period. As with the total workforce, there was modest growth of high-wage employment among white men, at least until 1989, and a much larger shift to high-wage employment among white

TABLE 3.11

Distribution of White Employment
by Wage Level, 1973-95

| | Share of Employment by Wage Multiple of Poverty Wage* | | | | | | | |
| | Poverty-Level Wages: | | | | | | | |
Year	0-75	75-100	Total**	100-125	125-200	200-300	300+	Total
All Whites								
1973	6.9%	14.4%	21.3%	12.9%	35.0%	21.2%	9.5%	100.0%
1979	3.9	17.9	21.8	14.8	31.8	22.1	9.6	100.0
1989	11.9	13.8	25.6	13.1	29.8	20.5	11.0	100.0
1995	12.2	13.8	26.0	14.1	28.8	19.7	11.4	100.0
Change								
1973-79	-3.0	3.5	0.5	1.8	-3.2	0.9	0.0	
1979-89	8.0	-4.2	3.8	-1.6	-1.9	-1.7	1.4	
1989-95	0.3	0.0	0.3	1.0	-1.0	-0.8	0.4	
White Men								
1973	3.1%	7.6%	10.7%	8.9%	36.3%	29.6%	14.4%	100.0%
1979	2.0	9.4	11.4	10.3	32.0	31.3	15.0	100.0
1989	7.4	10.2	17.6	10.5	30.0	25.7	16.2	100.0
1995	8.2	10.6	18.7	12.3	29.7	23.6	15.7	100.0
Change								
1973-79	-1.1	1.8	0.7	1.3	-4.2	1.6	0.6	
1979-89	5.4	0.8	6.2	0.2	-2.0	-5.6	1.2	
1989-95	0.7	0.4	1.1	1.8	-0.3	-2.1	-0.5	
White Women								
1973	12.5%	24.5%	37.1%	18.9%	33.0%	8.7%	2.3%	100.0%
1979	6.3	29.2	35.6	20.7	31.4	10.0	2.3	100.0
1989	16.9	17.8	34.7	16.1	29.6	14.6	5.1	100.0
1995	16.6	17.3	33.9	16.2	27.9	15.3	6.7	100.0
Change								
1973-79	-6.2	4.7	-1.5	1.8	-1.6	1.3	0.0	
1979-89	10.6	-11.5	-0.9	-4.6	-1.8	4.6	2.7	
1989-95	-0.3	-0.5	-0.5	0.1	-1.7	0.8	1.6	

* The wage ranges are equivalent in 1994 dollars to: $5.46 and below (0-75), $5.47-$7.28 (75-100), $7.29-$9.10 (100-125), $9.11-$14.56 (125-200), $14.57-$21.84 (200-300), and $21.85 and above (300+).
** Combines lowest two categories.

Source: Authors' analysis.

TABLE 3.12

Distribution of Black Employment
by Wage Level, 1973-95

	Share of Employment by Wage Multiple of Poverty Wage*							
	Poverty-Level Wages:							
Year	0-75	75-100	Total**	100-125	125-200	200-300	300+	Total
All Blacks								
1973	14.8%	22.0%	36.8%	14.8%	32.9%	12.3%	3.2%	100.0%
1979	6.3	26.5	32.8	17.9	29.9	15.7	3.8	100.0
1989	19.1	19.4	38.5	15.7	27.0	14.4	4.3	100.0
1995	19.4	19.6	39.0	17.1	25.4	13.7	4.8	100.0
Change								
1973-79	-8.5	4.5	-4.0	3.0	-3.0	3.4	0.6	
1979-89	12.8	-7.1	5.7	-2.2	-2.9	-1.2	0.6	
1989-95	0.3	0.2	0.5	1.4	-1.7	-0.7	0.5	
Black Men								
1973	7.4%	17.4%	24.8%	13.9%	39.7%	17.6%	4.1%	100.0%
1979	4.3	19.1	23.4	16.2	32.9	21.8	5.7	100.0
1989	15.0	18.2	33.2	15.3	28.9	17.4	5.3	100.0
1995	15.2	18.6	33.8	17.6	27.0	16.3	5.3	100.0
Change								
1973-79	-3.2	1.8	-1.4	2.3	-6.8	4.2	1.6	
1979-89	10.7	-0.9	9.8	-0.9	-4.0	-4.4	-0.4	
1989-95	0.2	0.4	0.6	2.4	-1.9	-1.1	-0.0	
Black Women								
1973	23.3%	27.3%	50.7%	16.0%	25.0%	6.1%	2.2%	100.0%
1979	8.5	34.3	42.8	19.6	26.7	9.2	1.7	100.0
1989	23.1	20.5	43.6	16.1	25.3	11.6	3.5	100.0
1995	23.1	20.5	43.7	16.7	23.9	11.3	4.4	100.0
Change								
1973-79	-14.9	7.0	-7.9	3.7	1.6	3.0	-0.5	
1979-89	14.6	-13.8	0.8	-3.6	-1.4	2.4	1.7	
1989-95	0.1	-0.0	0.1	0.6	-1.3	-0.2	0.9	

* The wage ranges are equivalent in 1994 dollars to: $5.46 and below (0-75), $5.47-$7.28 (75-100), $7.29-$9.10 (100-125), $9.11-$14.56 (125-200), $14.57-$21.84 (200-300), and $21.85 and above (300+).
** Combines lowest two categories.

Source: Authors' analysis.

TABLE 3.13

Distribution of Hispanic Employment
by Wage Level, 1973-95

	Share of Employment by Wage Multiple of Poverty Wage*							
	Poverty-Level Wages:							
Year	0-75	75-100	Total**	100-125	125-200	200-300	300+	Total
All Hispanics								
1973	12.1%	22.2%	34.3%	16.8%	34.1%	11.5%	3.2%	100.0%
1979	5.3	28.2	33.5	18.0	29.8	14.8	3.8	100.0
1989	20.9	22.9	43.8	14.7	26.1	11.6	3.9	100.0
1995	26.1	22.0	48.1	16.0	22.0	9.9	4.0	100.0
Change								
1973-79	-6.8	5.9	-0.8	1.2	-4.3	3.3	0.6	
1979-89	15.5	-5.2	10.3	-3.4	-3.8	-3.2	0.0	
1989-95	5.3	-1.0	4.3	1.3	-4.0	-1.7	0.1	
Hispanic Men								
1973	8.8%	16.2%	25.0%	14.1%	40.6%	15.8%	4.4%	100.0%
1979	3.5	19.8	23.3	17.2	33.8	20.3	5.4	100.0
1989	17.4	21.6	39.0	14.3	27.7	14.1	4.9	100.0
1995	23.1	21.4	44.5	15.9	23.1	11.8	4.7	100.0
Change								
1973-79	-5.3	3.6	-1.7	3.1	-6.8	4.5	1.0	
1979-89	13.9	1.8	15.7	-2.8	-6.2	-6.2	-0.5	
1989-95	5.7	-0.2	5.5	1.5	-4.5	-2.3	-0.2	
Hispanic Women								
1973	17.8%	32.6%	50.4%	21.6%	22.7%	4.0%	1.2%	100.0%
1979	8.2	41.0	49.1	19.4	23.7	6.4	1.5	100.0
1989	26.0	24.9	50.9	15.2	23.8	7.9	2.3	100.0
1995	30.7	22.7	53.5	16.1	20.4	7.2	2.9	100.0
Change								
1973-79	-9.7	8.3	-1.3	-2.2	0.9	2.3	0.3	
1979-89	17.9	-16.1	1.8	-4.2	0.1	1.5	0.8	
1989-95	4.7	-2.1	2.6	0.9	-3.4	-0.7	0.6	

* The wage ranges are equivalent in 1994 dollars to: $5.46 and below (0-75), $5.47-$7.28 (75-100), $7.29-$9.10 (100-125), $9.11-$14.56 (125-200), $14.57-$21.84 (200-300), and $21.85 and above (300+).
** Combines lowest two categories.

Source: Authors' analysis.

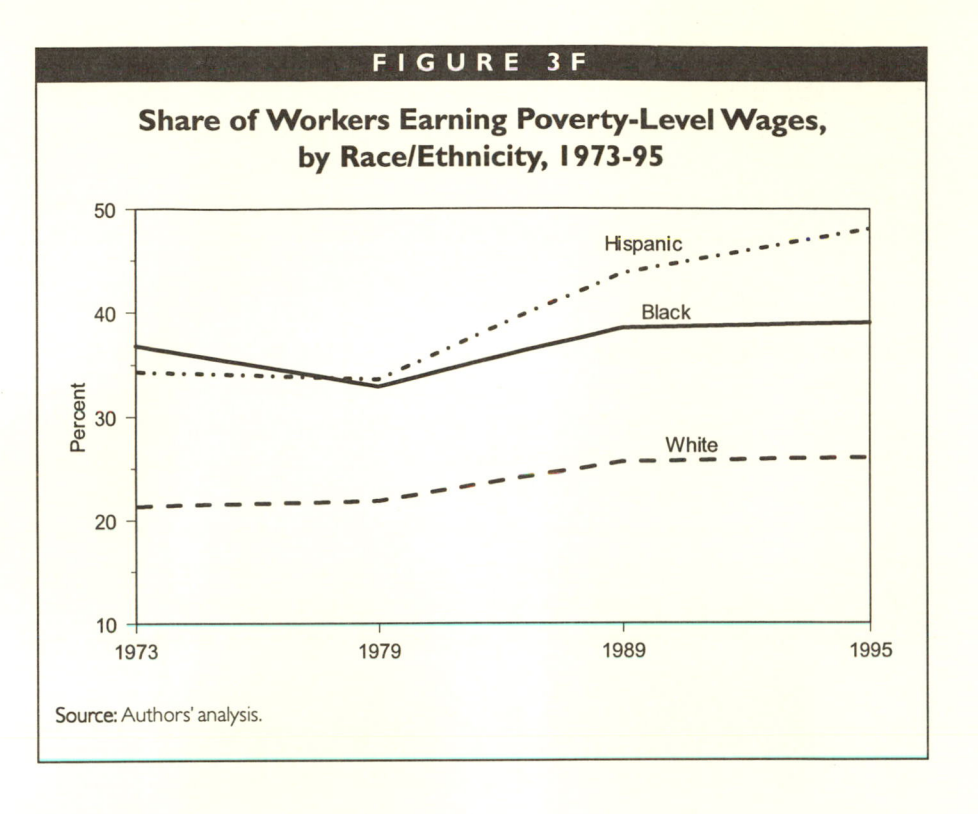

FIGURE 3F

Share of Workers Earning Poverty-Level Wages, by Race/Ethnicity, 1973-95

Source: Authors' analysis.

women. Over the entire period from 1973 to 1995, however, there was a signifi-cant shift toward proportionately fewer white men in the middle- and higher-wage groups and an equivalent growth of the share of men earning poverty-level wages, which grew from 10.7% in 1973 to 18.7% in 1995. Among white women, there was a simultaneous shift toward very low-wage work until 1989 and an expansion of women at the highest wage levels.

Among blacks (Table 3.12), there was a general downward shift out of better-paying employment into low-wage employment from 1979 to 1995, with modest growth of very high earners. By 1995, 39.0% of black workers (33.8% of black men and 43.7% of black women) were in jobs paying less than poverty-level wages. The post-1979 shift toward the very lowest-paying jobs (the "0-75" category)—an additional 10.9% of black men and 14.6% of black women—was much larger than among whites. However, the share of black women earning poverty-level wages has fallen considerably since 1973 (from 50.7% to 43.7%), while poverty wages became more commonplace among black men (up from 24.8% to 33.8%).

Since 1979, there has been a general downshifting of the Hispanic wage structure, for men and for men and women combined, with a very modest growth in the highest-wage jobs. Among Hispanic women, however, there was a large shift into the lowest-wage jobs between 1979 and 1995 (up 22.6 percentage points) but also some growth (1.4 percentage points) in employment paying three times the poverty-level wage.

Benefit Reduction

The data already reviewed show that real wages have declined for a wide array of workers over the last 16 years. We have also seen, in Tables 3.2 and 3.3, that total compensation, the real value of both wages and fringe benefits, rose only slightly faster than wages. Benefits did grow modestly, but since they make up a small (18-20%) share of compensation, their growth did not generate fast compensation growth. In this section we examine changes in benefits by type of benefit and examine changes in health and pension coverage for different groups of workers.

Table 3.14 provides a breakdown of growth in nonwage compensation, or benefits, using the two available data series (the "aggregates" were shown already in Tables 3.1 and 3.2). The NIPA data provide a long-term perspective. In the 1959-73 and 1973-79 periods, the inflation-adjusted value of benefits grew by $.10 and $.13 each year respectively, translating into annual growth rates of 6.4% and 2.3%. In contrast, the average value of benefits, including employer-provided health insurance, pension plans, and payroll taxes, grew just $.04 per year over the 1979-94 period. Benefit growth decelerated from its 1.3% pace in the 1979-89 period to a modest 0.6% annual pace from 1989 to 1994. The ECI data in the bottom panel of Table 3.14 confirm this slow 0.6% annual growth of benefits. In fact, the ECI data show an actual decline in benefits from $3.47 in 1994 to $3.26 in 1995.

How can it be that benefits grew so slowly when it is well known that health insurance costs have risen rapidly and there was a sizable hike in the payroll tax for Social Security in the 1980s? One reason is that health insurance costs are converted to "real" dollars by a health-costs price index and reflect the degree to which more health care was being bought. Even if health-costs were adjusted by a general "consumer" price index, however, the results would not change significantly (overall compensation growth would be 1.1% rather than 1.0% per year over the 1979-94 period). More important, health care costs have been con-

TABLE 3.14

Growth of Specific Fringe Benefits, 1959-95

(1995 Dollars)

Year	Voluntary Benefits			Payroll Taxes	Total Benefits and Nonwage Compensation
	Pension	Health*	Subtotal		
BEA NIPA**					
1959	$0.29	$0.24	$0.52	$0.41	$0.94
1967	0.42	0.34	0.76	0.71	1.47
1973	0.63	0.58	1.21	1.13	2.34
1979	0.85	0.88	1.74	1.39	3.13
1989	0.64	1.14	1.78	1.71	3.48
1994	0.68	1.28	1.96	1.71	3.67
Annual Dollar Change					
1959-73	$0.02	$0.02	$0.05	$0.05	$0.10
1973-79	0.04	0.05	0.09	0.04	0.13
1979-89	-0.02	0.03	0.00	0.03	0.04
1989-94	0.01	0.03	0.04	0.00	0.04
1979-94	-0.01	0.03	0.02	0.02	0.04
Annual Percent Change					
1959-73	5.7%	6.4%	6.0%	7.2%	6.4%
1973-79	5.0	7.0	6.0	3.5	2.3
1979-89	-2.9	2.6	0.2	2.0	1.3
1989-94	1.3	2.4	2.0	0.0	0.6
1979-94	-1.5	2.5	0.8	1.4	1.0
BLS ECI Levels***					
1987	$0.65	$1.21	$1.85	$1.53	$3.38
1989	0.52	1.28	1.80	1.57	3.37
1994	0.53	1.29	1.83	1.65	3.47
1995	0.52	1.15	1.67	1.59	3.26
Annual Percent Change					
1989-94	0.5%	0.2%	0.3%	0.9%	0.6%
1989-95	0.0	-1.7	-1.2	0.2	-0.6

*   Deflated by health-specific price index.
**   National Income and Product Accounts (NIPA).
*** Employment Cost Index (ECI) levels data for March of each year.

Source: Authors' analysis of BLS and BEA data.

tained because many workers (about a third of the workforce) receive no health insurance coverage from their employers and the share of workers covered has been falling (as discussed below). Thus, even rapid increases in health costs among a small group of workers with excellent health plans does not necessarily mean that health costs in the aggregate rose rapidly. Last, the efforts of employers to shift the costs of health care onto employees has probably helped to contain the growth of benefits paid by employers. Overall, health care costs per hour worked rose from $.88 in 1979 to $1.28 in 1994, a $.40 growth.

The drop in pension costs since 1979 has partially offset the rise in health care costs. In 1979, employers paid $.85 an hour for various pension and retirement schemes; by 1994 hourly pension costs were down to $.68. In the 1979-89 period this drop in pension costs nearly fully offset higher health costs, as reflected in the minimal rise in total "voluntary benefits" from $1.74 to $1.78.

Employers pay payroll taxes for their employees into a variety of social insurance programs: unemployment insurance, Medicare, Social Security, and workers compensation insurance. These costs grew 2% annually in the 1980s but did not grow at all in the post-1989 period. There was much more rapid growth of payroll taxes over the 1959-79 period, when such costs more than tripled, from $.41 to $1.39.

The data in Table 3.14 reflect "average" benefit costs. Given the rapid growth of wage inequality in recent years, it should not be surprising to find a growing inequality of benefits.

Tables 3.15 and **3.16** examine the decline in health and pension insurance coverage for different demographic groups between 1979 and 1993.

The share of workers covered by employer-provided (at least in part) health care plans dropped about 1 percentage point each year from 1979 to 1993, a total drop of 7 percentage points, from 71% to just 64% (Table 3.15). Unfortunately, there are no data available to show the degree to which the quality of coverage has improved or declined.

Health care coverage has declined more among men than women but similarly among both whites and blacks, with Hispanics suffering by far the largest drop. The drop in health care coverage by wage level repeats the pattern we already saw in wages—larger declines the lower the wage, a broad-based erosion, and some decline even for the highest wage group. This pattern is also reflected in the changes in coverage by education level.

Pension plan coverage (Table 3.16) has not declined as quickly as health care coverage: it dropped from 48% in 1979 to 45% in 1993. This decline is perhaps one of the reasons for the lessening of pension costs for employers over

TABLE 3.15

Change in Private-Sector Employer-Provided Health Insurance Coverage, 1979-93

| Group* | Health Insurance Coverage (%) | | | |
	1979	1988	1993	Change 1979-93
All Workers	71%	69%	64%	-7
Gender				
Men	76%	74%	68%	-8
Women	61	62	58	-5
Race				
White	72%	71%	66%	-6
Black	66	64	61	-5
Hispanic	63	56	47	-16
Education				
Less Than High School	63%	55%	45%	-18
High School Graduate	70	67	62	-8
Some College	72	68	63	-9
College	81	82	75	-6
More Than College	80	85	79	-1
Wage Fifth				
Lowest	40%	32%	27%	-8
Second	66	62	59	-7
Middle	79	76	71	-6
Fourth	87	83	80	-7
Top	90	90	87	-3

* Private-sector wage and salary workers age 18-64, with at least 20 weekly hours and 26 weeks of work.

Source: Department of Labor tabulations of CPS data.

the period. Lower pension coverage appears to be occurring only among men, whose coverage fell from 55% to 47% in this period. Women's pension coverage, on the other hand, actually rose, from 37% to 42%. Women workers, however, are still less likely than men to be covered by an employer's pension plan. Blacks and whites fared about equally poorly, experiencing a drop of 3 percentage points. Hispanics again were the hardest hit, with a decline of 6 percentage points in pension coverage from 1979 to 1993. Pension coverage fell among

TABLE 3.16

Change in Private-Sector Employer-Provided Pension Coverage, 1979-93

Group*	Pension Coverage (%)			
	1979	1988	1993	Change 1979-93
All Workers	48%	44%	45%	-3
Gender				
Men	55%	48%	47%	-8
Women	37	39	42	5
Race				
White	50%	47%	47%	-3
Black	45	39	42	-3
Hispanic	35	28	29	-6
Education				
Less Than High School	41%	31%	25%	-16
High School	49	44	44	-5
Some College	49	44	46	-3
College	56	54	55	-1
More Than College	60	58	59	-1
Wage Fifth				
Lowest	18%	14%	13%	-5
Second	35	33	34	-1
Middle	51	45	51	0
Fourth	68	59	61	-7
Top	76	69	72	-4

* Private-sector wage and salary workers age 18-24, with at least 20 weekly hours and 26 weeks of work.

Source: Department of Labor tabulations of CPS data.

college graduates and those with less than a college degree; it dropped off most among those at the lowest education levels. The pattern of decline in pension coverage by wage level shows coverage dropping most for the lowest and highest wage groups and some stability among the second and middle fifths. Perhaps most important, lower-wage workers are unlikely to have jobs with employer-provided pension plans, a situation in which more than half the workforce finds itself.

The decline in the quality of pension plans is portrayed in **Figure 3G**. Defined benefit plans guarantee a worker a fixed payment in retirement based on

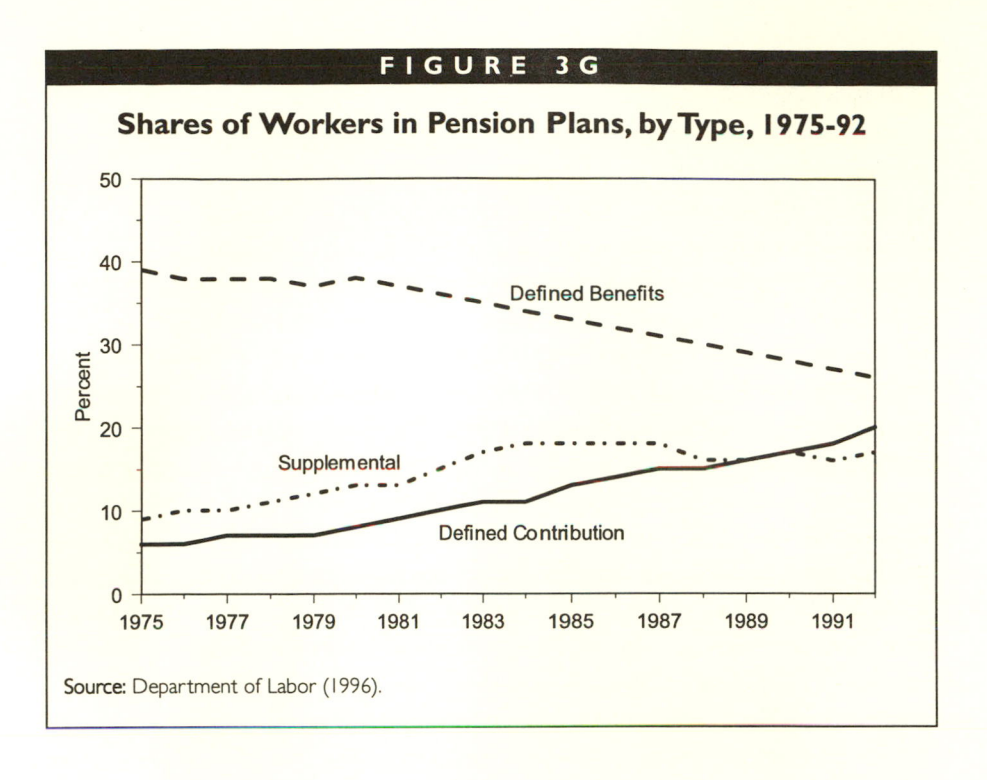

FIGURE 3G

Shares of Workers in Pension Plans, by Type, 1975-92

Source: Department of Labor (1996).

pre-retirement wages and years of service and are generally considered the best plans from a worker's perspective. Unfortunately, there has been a significant erosion in the share of the workforce covered by defined benefit plans. A larger share of workers are now covered by defined contribution plans, in which employers make contributions (to which employees sometimes can add) each year. With this type of plan, a worker's retirement income depends on his or her success in investing these funds, and investment risks are borne by the employee rather than the employer.

Dimensions of Inequality

In this section we shift the discussion from a presentation of wage and benefit trends overall, and for subgroups, to an examination of explanations for the pattern of recent wage growth. The items to be explained include stagnant average wages since 1973 and the dramatic growth in wage inequality in the 1980s and early 1990s. More specifically, it is important to understand both the average performance of wage growth and why particular groups fared well or poorly.

The data presented above have shown the stagnation of wages and overall compensation over the last 20 years. **Table 3.17** presents indicators of the variety of dimensions (excluding race and gender differentials) of the wage structure that have grown more unequal over the last 20 years. Any explanation of growing wage inequality must be able to explain the movement of these indicators. These inequality indicators are computed from our analysis of the Current Population Survey (CPS) Outgoing Rotation Group (ORG) data series. Whenever the trends being discussed are different in the other major data series (the March CPS), the difference will be noted in the discussion.

The top panel shows the trends in the 90/10 wage differential and its two components, the 90/50 and 50/10 wage differential (which are also shown in **Figures 3H** and **3I**), over the 1973-95 period. These differentials reflect the growth in overall wage inequality that we are attempting to explain. The 90/10 wage gap, for instance, shows the degree to which the 90th-percentile worker— a "high-wage" worker who makes more than 90% but less than 10% of the workforce—fared better than the low-wage worker at the 10th percentile. The growth in the 90/10 differential is frequently broken down into two components: the 90/50 wage gap shows how high earners fared relative to middle earners, and the 50/10 wage gap shows how middle earners fared relative to low earners.

Among men, there was a dramatic growth in wage inequality at the top and bottom in the 1979-89 period, which has continued, in terms of the 90/50 differential, as quickly through the 1989-95 period (Figure 3H). The character of this growing male wage inequality shifted in the most recent period. In the 1980s there was a growing separation between both the top and the middle and the middle and the bottom (seen in the 50/10 differential). However, in the 1989-95 period all of the growing wage inequality was generated by a divergence between the top and everyone else: the 90/50 differential grew but the 50/10 differential did not.

Among women, the wage inequality trends across time periods are sensitive to the "endpoints," or years selected for the analysis. The data on the 90/10 differential for women in Table 3.17 suggests a large decline in women's wage inequality in the 1970s and a larger growth in the 1980s. However, the year-by-year pattern, shown in Figure 3I, shows a large dip in wage inequality between 1978 and 1979 and an equal rise between 1979 and 1980. This "jumpiness" in the data reflects the movement of the 10th-percentile wage, which grew a lot in 1979 but then fell back to its 1978 level in 1980. A better descrip-

TABLE 3.17

Dimensions of Wage Inequality, 1973-95

Differential	Wage Differential				Change		
	1973	1979	1989	1995	1973-79	1979-89	1989-95
Total Wage Inequality							
90/10							
Men	128%	130%	144%	151%	2	14	7
Women	116	100	135	138	-16	35	3
90/50							
Men	60%	59%	69%	76%	-1	10	7
Women	59	61	71	77	2	10	6
50/10							
Men	68%	71%	75%	75%	3	4	0
Women	57	39	64	61	-18	26	-3
Between-Group Inequality							
*College/H.S.**							
Men	32.5%	27.3%	41.8%	44.1%	-5.2	14.5	2.3
Women	43.0	30.8	46.0	51.8	-12.2	15.2	5.8
*Middle/Young***							
Men	25.8%	25.2%	29.1%	29.5%	-0.6	3.9	0.4
Women	11.8	12.2	19.7	22.5	0.4	7.4	2.8
*Old/Middle***							
Men	4.2%	6.9%	10.6%	10.3%	2.6	3.8	-0.3
Women	-3.5	-1.6	1.8	3.7	2.0	3.4	1.9
Within-Group Inequality							
Men							
90/50	40.4%	41.1%	42.9%	46.1%	0.7	1.8	3.2
50/10	39.1	42.3	46.9	40.8	3.2	4.6	-6.1
Women							
90/50	38.6%	45.9%	45.5%	47.7%	7.3	-0.4	2.2
50/10	36.2	28.7	44.0	40.7	-7.5	15.3	-3.3

*   Estimated log differential between college-only and high school graduates, controlling for experience, marital status, race, and four regions.
** Estimated log differential where experience specified as a quartic with controls for education levels, marital status, race, and four regions. Young, middle, and old reflect workers with 5, 15, and 30 years' experience.

Source: Authors' analysis.

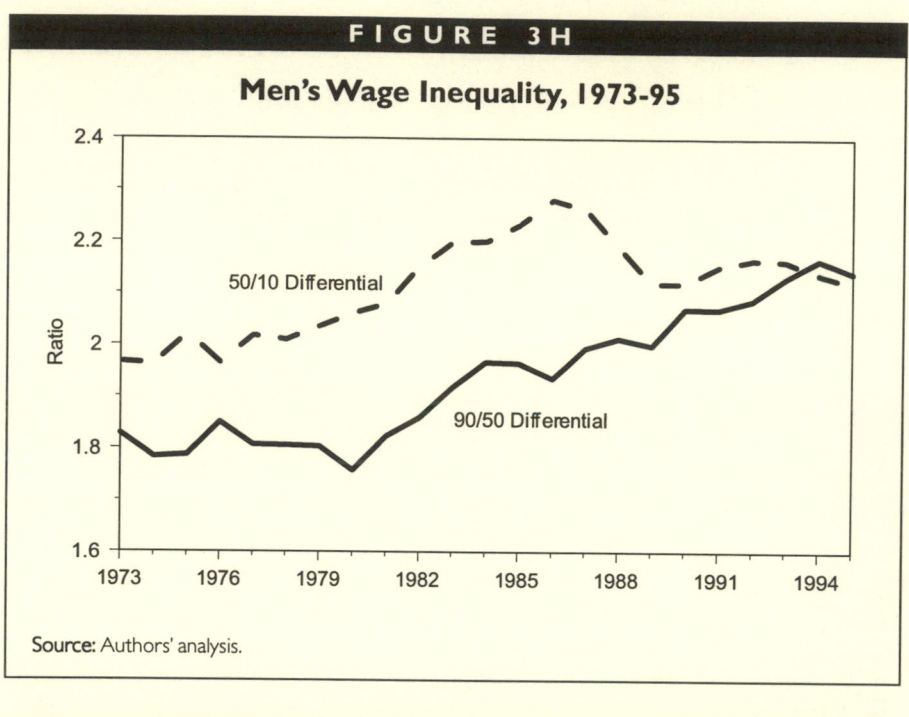

FIGURE 3H

Men's Wage Inequality, 1973-95

Source: Authors' analysis.

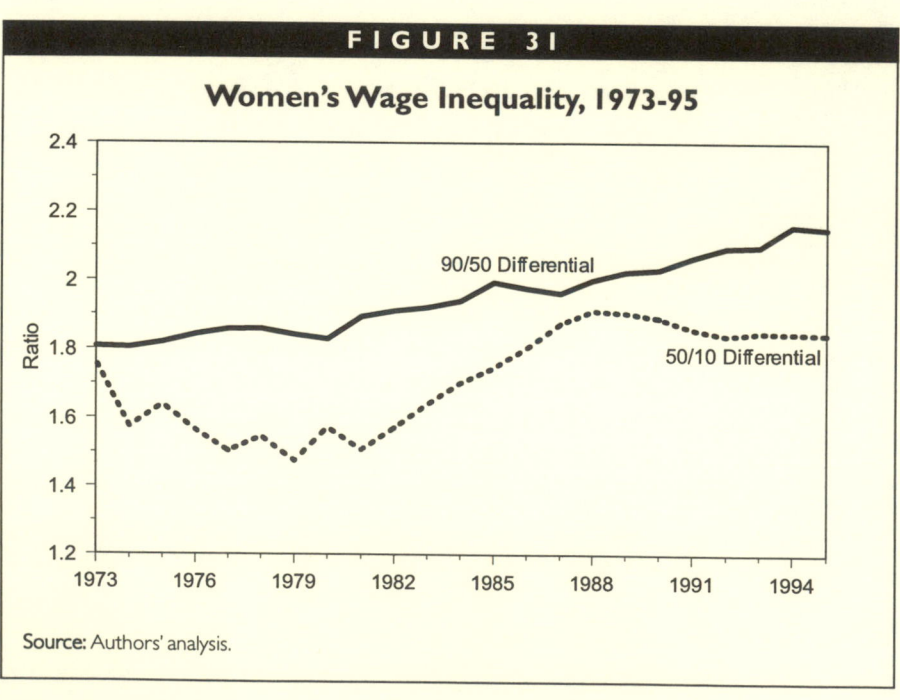

FIGURE 3I

Women's Wage Inequality, 1973-95

Source: Authors' analysis.

tion of the trends in women's wage inequality might be that wage inequality fell between 1973 and the late 1970s (1978-80) and then rose in the 1980s. Among women, the growth of the 90/50 differential was as strong as among men in both the 1980s and 1990s. There was, however, a stronger growth of inequality at the bottom (reflected in the 50/10 differential) among women in the 1980s and an actual decline in the 1990s.

Analysts have tended to "decompose," or break down, growing wage inequality into two types of inequality—"between-group" and "within-group." The former is illustrated in Table 3.17 in two ways: the growing wage differentials between groups of workers defined by their education levels and by their labor-market experience or age. The "college wage premium"—the wage gap between college and high school graduates—fell in the 1970s among both men and women but exploded in the 1980s. The growth of the college wage premium in the post-1989 period has differed between men and women. Among men there has been only modest growth in this education premium since 1989, which year-by-year trends (discussed below) show to be flat between 1990 and 1995. Among women, however, there has been a relatively steady growth of the college wage premium in the post-1989 period equivalent to that of the 1980s.

The growth of experience differentials, reflecting the wage gap between older and middle-age and younger workers, runs parallel to that of education differentials, although the changes are smaller. The wage gap between middle-age and younger workers grew in the 1980s and continued to grow after 1989 among women. Likewise, the wage gap between older and middle-age workers grew over the entire 1973-89 period and continued into the recent period among women.

Within-group wage inequality—wage dispersion among workers with comparable education and experience—has been a major dimension of growing wage inequality. The growth of within-group wage inequality, according to Table 3.17, has differed across time periods, the segment of the wage structure (the top versus the bottom), and gender. For instance, the growth of within-group wage inequality among men in the upper half of the wage structure (the 90/50 gap) has been growing over the entire 1973-95 period, but at an accelerated pace in the 1980s and again in the 1990s. In contrast, within-group wage inequality at the bottom among men grew similarly in the 1970s and the 1980s and then declined in the 1990s.

Within-group inequality grew the most at the bottom of the female wage structure in the 1980s, up 15.3 percentage points, but fell in both the 1970s and 1990s. Among higher-wage women the growth of within-group wage inequality was not a factor in the 1980s but has emerged as one in the 1990s.

Since growing or shrinking within-group wage inequality has been a significant factor in various periods, particularly the 1989-95 period, it is important to be able to explain and interpret these trends. Unfortunately, the interpretation of growing wage inequality among workers with similar "human capital" has not been the subject of much research. Some analysts suggest it reflects growing premiums for skills of workers that are not captured by traditional human-capital measures available in government surveys. Others suggest that changing "wage norms," employer practices, and institutions are responsible. We turn to these trends next.

What Explains Wage Trends?

The most commonly mentioned reason for recent wage problems is slow productivity growth (i.e., changes in output per hour worked) since 1973. As the data in Table 3.1 showed, productivity has been growing 1.0% annually over the entire 1973-95 period. This is a slower growth in productivity than occurred in the pre-1973 period, a time that was labeled "the productivity slowdown."

Slow productivity growth has been a major problem, but it provides only a partial explanation for average wage trends, since productivity has grown more than wages or compensation.

The relationship between hourly productivity and compensation growth is portrayed in **Figure 3J**, which shows the growth of each relative to 1973 (i.e., each is indexed so that 1973=100). As Figure 3J shows, there has been a 25% growth in productivity since 1973, enough to generate broadly shared growth in living standards and wages. Also, there is a gap between the growth of average compensation and productivity as well as between both median hourly compensation (for either men or all workers) and average compensation. The latter gap, between average and median compensation, is the larger gap and reflects growing wage inequality. Thus, the most important reason why median compensation (or wages) lags behind productivity is that growing inequality creates a "wedge" that prevents the typical worker from enjoying the "average" growth of national output or income.

There is much contention over the interpretation of the gap between average compensation and productivity. One explanation is that prices for national output have grown more slowly than prices for consumer purchases. Therefore, the same growth in nominal, or current-dollar, wages and output yields faster growth

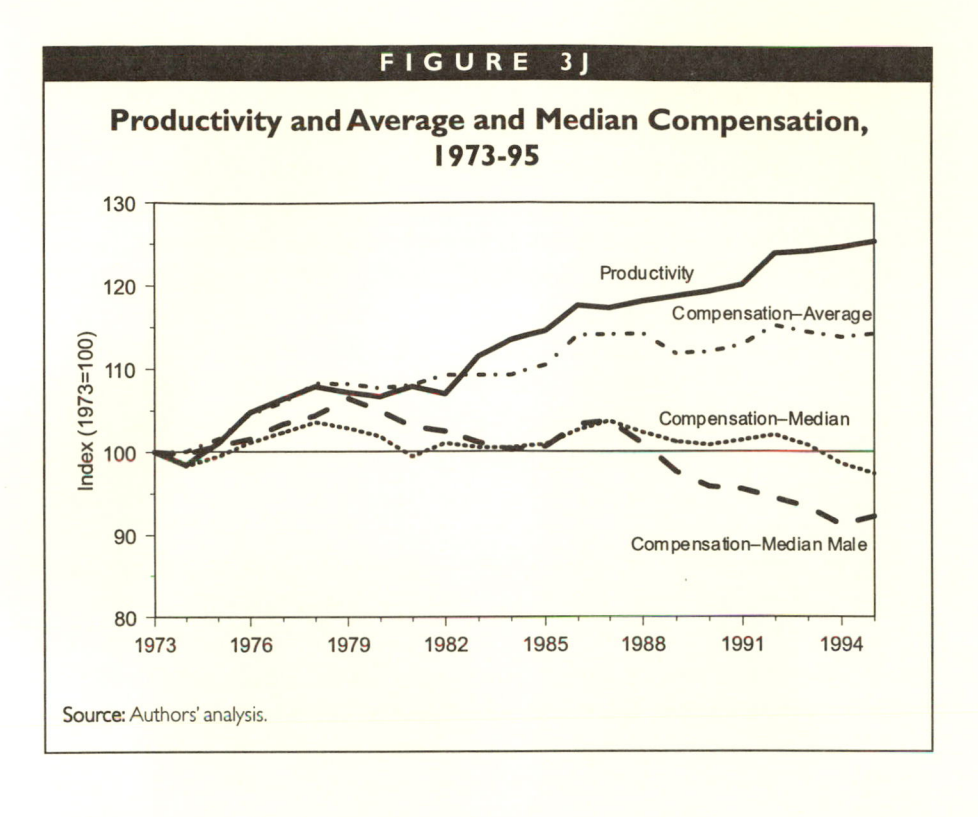

FIGURE 3J

Productivity and Average and Median Compensation, 1973-95

Source: Authors' analysis.

in real (inflation-adjusted) output (which is adjusted for changes in the prices of investment goods, exports, and consumer purchases) than in real wages (adjusted for changes in consumer purchases only). That is, workers have suffered a worsening "terms of trade," in which the prices of things they buy (i.e., consumer goods) have risen faster than the items they produce (consumer goods but also capital goods).

This "terms of trade" explanation is actually more of a description than an explanation. A growing gap between output and consumer prices has not been a persistent characteristic of our economy, and the emergence of this gap requires an exploration of what economic forces are driving it. Once the causes of the price gap are known (not simply "accounted for"), it can be interpreted. In the meantime, there are two ways to look at the divergence of compensation and productivity created by the "terms of trade" shift of prices. One is to note that, regardless of cause, the implication is that the "average" worker is not benefiting fully from productivity growth. Another is to note that the price divergence does not reflect a redistribution from labor to capital, that is, the gap between compensation and productivity growth reflects differences in price trends rather than a larger share of productivity growth going to capital incomes. These two viewpoints can be seen as either complements or substitutes.

This leaves open the question of whether wages are being squeezed by higher profits. In other words, has the growth in rates of profit meant that wages have grown less? As discussed in Chapter 1, there have been seemingly small changes in the shares of income going to labor and capital—called "factor income shares." This has been interpreted by some as evidence that there has been no labor-capital redistribution. However, a more complete examination would ask whether factor income shares have grown relative to what we expect given other changes in the economy. That is, one cannot tell whether stable shares imply no redistribution unless one specifies the "counterfactual"—what we expected them to be.

In fact, there are several reasons to have expected a *growth* in labor's share. One is that there has been rapid growth (relative to the pre-1979 period) in educational attainment. As labor quality grows there should be faster wage growth and a tendency for labor's share to rise. Second, since the early 1980s the growth of capital investment and accumulation has slowed relative to national output. That is, the capital-output ratio has been falling. With capital inputs falling in relation to output, one might expect capital's income share to fall. However, there has been a significant rise in profitability (capital income per dollar of assets), so that capital's share of income has remained relatively constant despite a fall in capital's contribution to output. Had there not been a surge in profitability, then capital's share would have fallen. As discussed in Chapter 1, had the growth in profitability been more modest, there could have been faster growth in hourly compensation.

Rising Education Wage Differentials

Changes in the economic returns to education affect the structure of wages by changing the wage gaps between different educational groups. The growth in "education wage differentials" has led to greater wage inequality in the 1980s and 1990s (see Table 3.17) and helps explain the relatively faster wage growth among high-wage workers. This section examines wage trends among workers at different levels of education and begins the discussion, carried on through the remainder of the chapter, of the causes of rising education wage differentials.

Table 3.18 presents the wage trends and employment shares (percentage of

TABLE 3.18

Change in Real Hourly Wage by Education, 1973-95
(1995 Dollars)

Year	Less Than High School	High School	Some College	College	Advanced Degree	Memo: Non-College Educated**
Hourly Wage						
1973	$10.65	$12.17	$13.45	$17.66	$21.52	$11.89
1979	10.59	11.86	12.92	16.55	20.34	11.80
1989	8.91	10.79	12.53	16.98	22.07	10.96
1995	8.16	10.46	11.64	17.26	22.81	10.39
Percent Change						
1973-79	-0.6%	-2.6%	-3.9%	-6.3%	-5.5%	-0.8%
1979-89	-15.9	-9.0	-3.1	2.6	8.5	-7.1
1989-95	-8.4	-3.0	-7.1	1.6	3.3	-5.2
1979-95	-23.0	-11.8	-9.9	4.3	12.1	-11.9
*Share of Employment**						
1973	28.5%	41.7%	15.1%	8.8%	3.6%	85.4%
1979	20.1	42.1	19.2	11.0%	5.0	81.3
1989	13.7	40.5	22.3	14.0%	6.9	76.5

*   Since the shares of those with one year of schooling beyond college are not shown, the presented shares do not sum to 100. There are no reliable data for 1995 using same definitions.
** Those with less than four years of college.

Source: Authors' analysis.

the workforce) for workers at various education levels over the 1973-95 period. It is common to point out that the wages of "more-educated" workers have grown faster than the wages of "less-educated" workers since 1979, with the real wages of "less-educated" workers falling sharply. This pattern of wage growth is sometimes described in terms of a rising differential, or "premium," between the wages of the college-educated and high-school-educated workforces (as shown earlier in Table 3.17).

The usual terminology of the "less educated" and "more educated" is misleading. Given that workers with some college education (from one to three years) also experienced falling real wages (down 9.9% from 1979 to 1995), it is apparent that the "less-educated" group with falling wages makes up more than three-fourths of the workforce. The last column of Table 3.18 shows the average non-college wage falling 11.9% over the 1979-95 period. Moreover, the "college-educated" group consists of two groups: one is those with just four years of college, who enjoyed a minimal 4.3% wage gain over the 1979-95 period, and the other is the more-educated ("advanced degree") but smaller (6.9% of the workforce in 1989) group that enjoyed 12.1% wage growth.

This increased differential between college-educated and other workers is frequently ascribed to a relative increase in employer demand for workers with greater skills and education. This interpretation follows from the fact that the wages of college-educated workers increased relative to others despite a sizable increase in their relative supply, from 11.0% of the workforce in 1979 to 14.0% in 1989. That is, given the increased supply of college-educated workers, the fact that their relative wages were bid up implies a strong growth in employer demand for more-educated workers, presumably reflecting technological and other workplace trends.

Yet an increased relative demand for educated workers is only a partial explanation, especially if ascribed to a benign process of technology or other factors leading to a higher value for education, thus bidding up the wages of more-educated workers. Note, for instance, that the primary reason for an increased wage gap between college-educated and other workers is the precipitous decline of wages among the non-college-educated workforce and not any strong growth of the college wage. Moreover, as discussed below, there are many important factors (that may not reflect changes in demand for skill), such as the shift to low-wage industries, deunionization, a falling minimum wage, and import competition, that can also lead to a wage gap between "more-" and "less-" educated workers. Below, we present direct evidence that technological change has not been the driving force behind growing wage inequality.

Tables 3.19 and **3.20** present trends in wage and employment shares for the various education groups for men and women. Among men, the wages of non-college-educated workers have been falling steadily since 1979: they fell 10.1% over the 1979-89 period and another 7.2% between 1989 and 1995. The decline in wages was sizable even among men with "some college"—13.4% from 1979 to 1995. The wage of the average high-school-educated male fell somewhat more, 16.7% from 1979 to 1995, while the wages of those without a high school degree fell 27.0%. In contrast, the wages of male college graduates did not rise at all over the 1989-95 period and rose just 0.6% from 1979 to 1989. Year-by-year data show male college wages peaked in the 1985-86 period.

TABLE 3.19

Change in Real Hourly Wage for Men by Education, 1973-95
(1995 Dollars)

| | | | | | | Memo: | |
| | Less Than High School | High School | Some College | College | Advanced Degree | Non-College Educated** | College-H.S. Wage Differential*** |
Year							
1973	$12.45	$14.65	$15.43	$20.32	$22.62	$14.00	32.5%
1979	12.22	14.25	15.14	19.43	22.15	13.89	27.3
1989	10.09	12.51	14.27	19.54	24.43	12.49	41.8
1995	8.92	11.87	13.11	19.55	25.28	11.59	44.4
Percent Change							
1973-79	-1.9%	-2.7%	-1.9%	-4.4%	-2.1%	-0.7%	
1979-89	-17.4	-12.2	-5.7	0.6	10.3	-10.1	
1989-95	-11.6	-5.1	-8.1	0.0	3.5	-7.2	
1979-95	-27.0	-16.7	-13.4	0.6	14.1	-16.5	
*Share of Employment**							
1973	30.6%	38.1%	15.6%	8.9%	4.5%	84.3%	
1979	22.3	38.6	18.8	11.5	6.1	79.7	
1989	15.9	38.7	21.0	14.2	7.8	75.5	

*   Since the shares of those with one year of schooling beyond college are not shown, the presented shares do not sum to 100. There are no reliable data for 1995 using same definitions.
**   Those with less than four years of college.
*** Estimated with controls for education, experience as a quartic, four regions, marital status, and race.

Source: Authors' analysis.

This pattern of stagnant wages for college men and declining wages for non-college-educated men has meant a rise in the relative wage or premium for male college graduates. As shown in the last column, the estimated college-high school wage premium grew from 27.3% in 1979 to 41.8% in 1989 and to 44.4% in 1995. As **Figure 3K** shows, however, there has been a flattening of the college-high school premium in the 1990s (seen in the estimated differentials using the two main wage data series—the CPS Outgoing Rotation Group (ORG) data and the March CPS series). Since there has not been an acceleration of the supply of college-educated men (as shown in a later section), this

TABLE 3.20

Change in Real Hourly Wage for Women
by Education, 1973-95
(1995 Dollars)

Year	Less Than High School	High School	Some College	College	Advanced Degree	Memo: Non-College Educated**	Memo: College-H.S. Wage Differential***
1973	$7.51	$9.26	$10.31	$13.70	$18.42	$8.92	43.0%
1979	7.84	9.28	10.16	12.42	16.19	9.19	30.8
1989	7.00	9.02	10.79	14.02	18.51	9.27	46.0
1995	6.99	8.95	10.20	14.84	19.54	9.05	51.8
Percent Change							
1973-79	4.5%	0.2%	-1.5%	-9.4%	-12.1%	3.0%	
1979-89	-10.7	-2.8	6.3	12.9	14.3	0.9	
1989-95	-0.3	-0.8	-5.5	5.9	5.5	-2.4	
1979-95	-10.9	-3.6	0.4	19.5	20.7	-1.5	
*Share of Employment**							
1973	25.6%	47.7%	14.4%	8.7%	2.3%	87.1%	
1979	17.2	46.7	19.6	10.4	3.5	83.6	
1989	11.2	42.6	23.9	13.8	5.8	77.8	

* Since the shares of those with one year of schooling beyond college are not shown, the presented shares do not sum to 100. There are no reliable data for 1995 using same definitions.
** Those with less than four years of college.
*** Estimated with controls for education, experience as a quartic, four regions, marital status, and race.

Source: Authors' analysis.

implies, within a conventional demand-supply framework, that there was a slowdown in the growth of relative demand for college workers.

A somewhat different pattern has prevailed among women (Table 3.20). In the 1979-89 period wages fell modestly (2.8%) among high-school-educated women but significantly among those without a high school degree (10.7%). Women with some college, unlike their male counterparts, saw wage gains in the 1980s (6.3%), but not as much as college-educated women (12.9%). This pattern of wage growth, however, still resulted in an equivalent growth of the

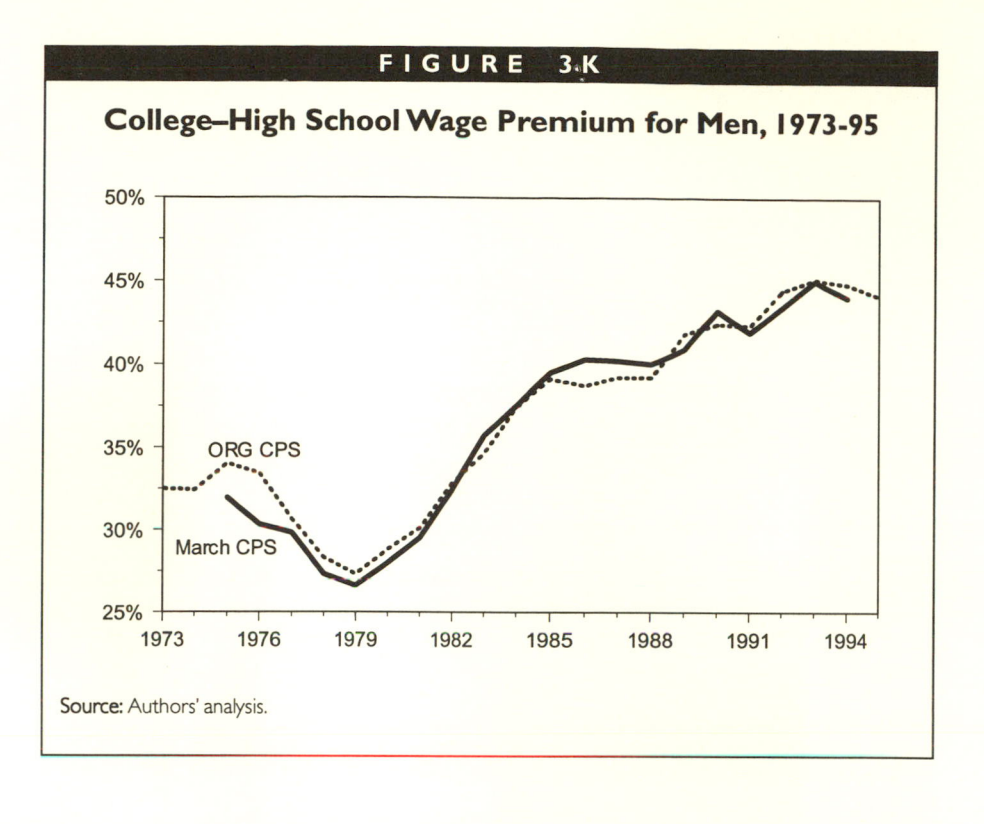

FIGURE 3.K

College–High School Wage Premium for Men, 1973-95

Source: Authors' analysis.

college-high school wage differential from 30.8% in 1979 to 46.0% in 1989. Thus, inequality grew as quickly among women as among men but the relative losers—non-college-educated women—saw stagnant, not declining, wages.

The pattern of wage growth among women shifted in the 1990s; wages were stagnant for those with or without a high school degree but fell among those with some college. In 1995, wages for women with less than a college degree were slightly lower (1.5%) than they were in 1979. Wages among college-educated women continued to grow strongly in the 1989-95 period. In contrast with men, the college-high school differential among women grew strongly in the 1990s (**Figure 3L**). Since there has been strong growth in the supply of college-educated women, this growing wage differential implies an accelerated growth of relative demand for these workers.

Even though the wages of college-educated women have grown rapidly since 1979, a female college graduate in 1995 still earned about what a male with only some college earned in 1989 ($14.27 versus $14.84) and about what a high-school-educated male earned in 1973 ($14.65).

FIGURE 3L

College–High School Wage Premium for Women, 1973-95

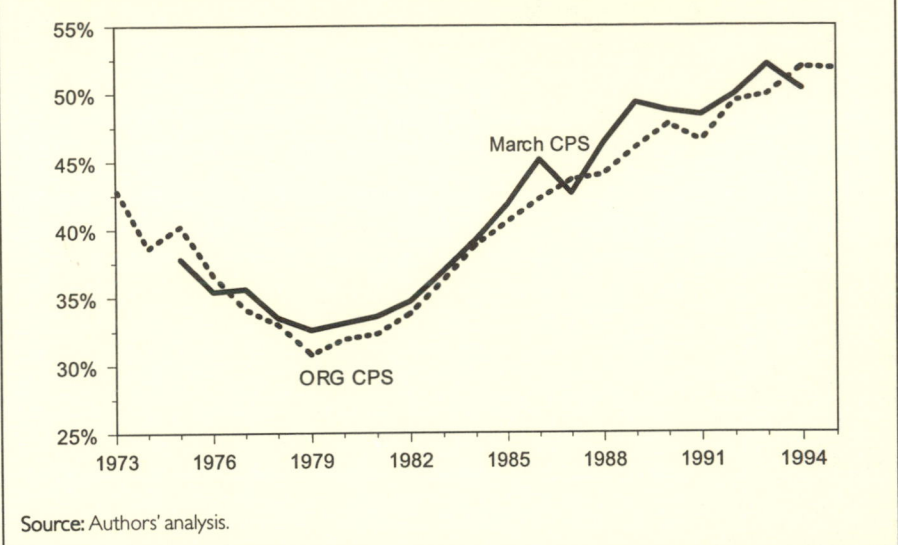

Source: Authors' analysis.

TABLE 3.21

Educational Attainment of Workforce, 1995

Highest Degree Attained	Percent of Workforce:		
	Men	Women	All
Less Than High School	12.7%	8.8%	10.8%
High School\GED	33.1	33.5	33.3
Some College	24.8	28.2	26.4
Assoc. College	3.5	4.6	4.0
College B.A.	17.3	17.4	17.3
Advanced Degree*	8.6	7.5	8.1
Total	100.0	100.0	100.0
Memo			
High School or Less	45.8%	42.3%	44.1%
Less Than College Degree	74.1	75.1	74.6
College Only	17.3	17.4	17.3
More Than College	8.6	7.5	8.1

* Includes law degrees, Ph.D.s, and similar degrees.

Source: Authors' analysis.

Table 3.21 shows a breakdown of the workforce in 1995 by the highest degree attained. Only about one-fourth (25.4%) of the workforce has at least a four-year college degree (17.3% have no more than a college degree and 8.1% also have a graduate or professional degree). Roughly two-thirds (70.5%) of the workforce has no more than a high school degree, with 10.8% never completing high school, 33.3% completing high school, and another 26.4% with some college but no degree beyond high school. An additional 4.0% hold associate degrees. These data reinforce our earlier discussion that the wage reductions experienced by the "less educated" (frequently defined by economists as those without a college degree) since 1979 have affected 75% of the workforce.

Young Workers Have Been Hurt Most

Since 1973, the wages of younger workers have been falling faster than the wages of older workers. As a result, there have been significant changes in the wage differentials between younger and older workers, as shown earlier in Table 3.17. Since the wages of both younger and non-college-educated workers have fallen most rapidly, it follows that the wages of workers who are both young and non-college educated have fallen dramatically. These adverse wage trends were strongest among men. **Table 3.22** presents trends in "entry-level" wages for high school and college graduates as reflected in the wages of workers with 1-5 years of experience. The entry-level hourly wage of a young, male high school graduate in 1989 was 21.8% less than that for the equivalent worker in 1979, a drop of $2.28 per hour, and another 6.9% less by 1995. The accumulated wage declines from 1979 forward left entry-level wages for male high school graduates 27.3% lower in 1995 than in 1979; among women, the entry-level high school wage fell 18.9% in this period. This dramatic decline in entry-level wages among high school graduates is shown in **Figure 3M**.

Entry-level wages among male college graduates were stagnant over the 1973-89 period and fell 9.5% from 1989 to 1995. Thus, new male college graduates earned $1.54 less per hour in 1995 than their counterparts did in 1973. This sharp decline in entry-level wages of college graduates also took place among women, where the wage fell 7.7% over the 1989-95 period. The fact that entry-level wages for college graduates remain higher than for high school graduates means that it still makes economic sense for individuals to complete college. Nevertheless, men who obtain a college degree will have a lower wage than that obtained by an earlier generation of male college gradu-

TABLE 3.22

Hourly Wages by Education and Experience, 1973-95
(1995 Dollars)

Education/	Hourly Wage				Percent Change			
Experience	1973	1979	1989	1995	1973-79	1979-89	1989-95	1979-95
High School								
Men								
1-5 yrs.	$10.54	$10.43	$8.15	$7.58	-1.0%	-21.8%	-6.9%	-27.3%
16-20	15.96	15.99	13.55	12.63	0.1	-15.2	-6.8	-21.0
31-35	16.92	17.20	15.52	14.41	1.6	-9.8	-7.2	-16.2
Women								
1-5 yrs.	$7.93	$7.92	$6.89	$6.42	-0.2%	-13.0%	-6.7%	-18.9
16-20	9.64	9.69	9.46	9.30	0.5	-2.4	-1.6	-4.0
31-35	10.03	9.90	9.97	9.92	-1.3	0.7	-0.6	0.1
College								
Men								
1-5 yrs.	$14.08	$14.04	$13.86	$12.54	-0.2%	-1.3%	-9.5%	-10.7%
16-20	24.85	22.58	21.54	21.99	-9.2	-4.6	2.1	-2.6
31-35	25.22	25.56	24.64	24.89	1.3	-3.6	1.0	-2.6
Women								
1-5 yrs.	$12.30	$11.24	$12.51	$11.55	-8.6%	11.2%	-7.7%	2.7%
16-20	15.62	13.44	14.77	16.31	-14.0	9.8	10.4	21.3
31-35	14.87	13.45	14.51	16.05	-9.6	7.9	10.6	19.4

Source: Authors' analysis.

ates. For instance, the wage of a college-educated male with 16-20 years' experience (in his late 30s) was $21.99 per hour in 1995, nearly $3.00 less than what an equivalent worker earned in 1973.

As already noted above, there is not only a growing inequality between groups of workers characterized by education or experience levels but also a growing inequality among workers with similar education and experience, a dimension of wage inequality referred to as "within-group" wage inequality. This growth in within-group wage inequality was shown earlier in Table 3.17. The analysis in **Table 3.23** goes a step further by presenting wage trends of high-, middle-, and low-wage workers among high school and college graduates. In other words, the data track the wages of the 90th-, 50th- (median), and 10th-percentile high-

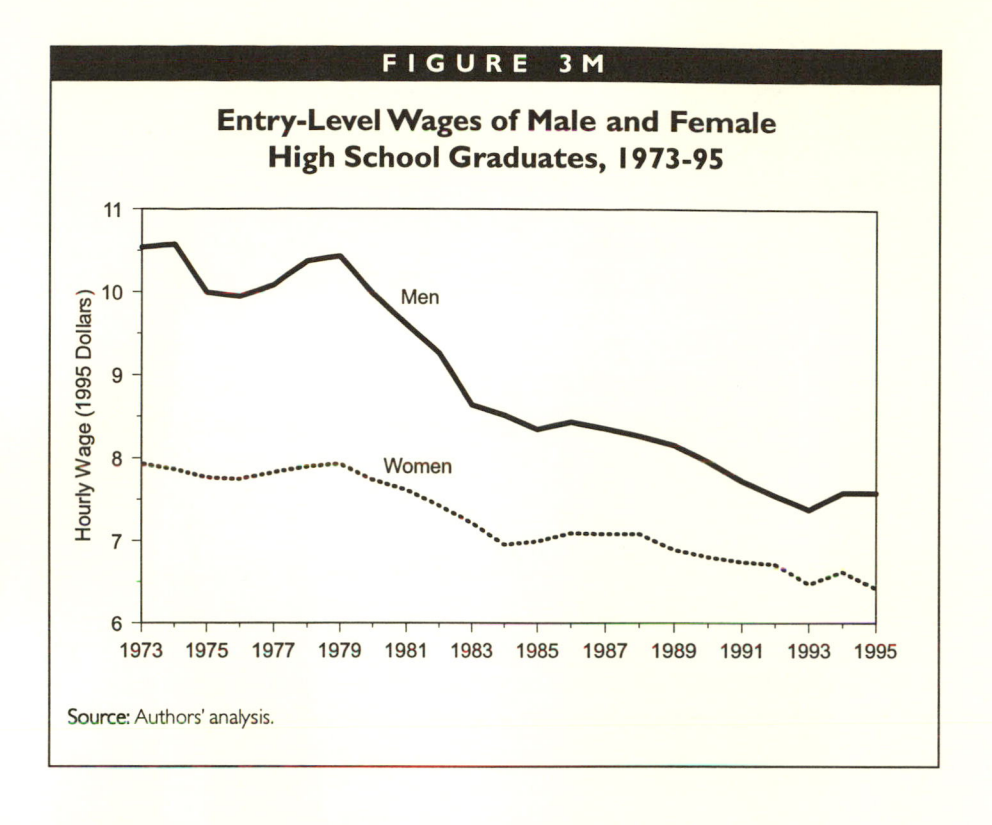

FIGURE 3M

Entry-Level Wages of Male and Female High School Graduates, 1973-95

Men

Women

Source: Authors' analysis.

school-educated and college-educated workers by gender.

Because of rising within-group inequality, the wage growth of the median, or "typical," worker in each group has been less than that of the "average" worker. For instance, the wage of the median male high school graduate fell 20.0% over the 1979-95 period, compared to the 16.7% wage drop of the "average" male high school graduate (Table 3.19). Similarly, the wage growth of male college graduates in the 1979-95 period was 0.6% at the average (Table 3.19), but down 1.0% at the median.

The growing disparity of wages within groups is amply demonstrated in Table 3.23. While the high (90th percentile) wage among female college graduates grew 27.6% from 1979 to 1995, the low (10th percentile) wage in this group rose just 0.9%, a 27 percentage-point divergence. Similarly, there was a large divergence between wage growth at the top of the college male wage ladder (5.7%) relative to the bottom (a 13.2% drop) over the 1979-95 period.

TABLE 3.23

Hourly Wages by Decile Within Education Groups, 1973-95
(1995 Dollars)

Education/ Gender Decile	Hourly Wage				Percent Change			
	1973	1979	1989	1995	1973-79	1979-89	1989-95	1979-95
High School								
Men								
10	$7.36	$6.83	$5.80	$5.73	-7.2%	-15.1%	-1.2%	-16.1%
50	13.49	13.21	11.32	10.57	-2.1	-14.3	-6.6	-20.0
90	22.09	21.80	20.23	19.03	-1.3	-7.2	-5.9	-12.7
Women								
10	$5.06	$5.83	$4.66	$4.78	15.2%	-20.0%	2.4%	-18.1%
50	8.38	8.24	8.05	7.81	-1.8	-2.3	-3.0	-5.2
90	13.93	14.23	14.60	14.45	2.1	2.6	-1.0	1.5
College								
Men								
10	$9.36	$9.01	$8.38	$7.82	-3.8%	-7.1%	-6.6%	-13.2%
50	17.52	16.98	17.36	16.81	-3.1	2.2	-3.2	-1.0
90	32.68	31.20	31.51	32.97	-4.5	1.0	4.7	5.7
Women								
10	$7.26	$6.48	$6.60	$6.54	-10.7%	1.9%	-0.9%	0.9%
50	12.42	11.25	12.76	13.20	-9.5	13.4	3.5	17.3
90	19.69	19.16	22.22	24.45	-2.7	16.0	10.0	27.6

Source: Authors' analysis.

Decomposing the Growth in Wage Inequality

The data presented so far illustrate the various dimensions of wage inequality. There has been a growing gap between workers by both education and experience (or age). This "between-group" inequality can also be characterized as a growth in education and experience differentials, as increases in the "returns to education and experience," or as a shift in the rewards or price of "skill." We have also seen that wage inequality has grown among workers with similar education and experience ("within group"), as illustrated by a growing wage gap among college graduates and high school graduates.

The question remains, however, as to how much the growth in overall wage inequality in particular time periods has been driven by changes in between-group versus within-group wage inequality. Plus, it is useful to know the role of the growth of between- and within-group inequality on growing wage inequality at the top (the 90/50 differential) versus the bottom (the 50/10 differential).

Unfortunately, there is no analysis available that completely "decomposes" the growth of wage inequality into the contribution of between- and within-group inequality over the 1973-95 period. Such an analysis would allow us to state, for instance, what percentage share of the growth of inequality is due to the growing returns to education, experience, and other factors, with the role of all contributing factors summing to 100%.

Tables 3.24 and **3.25** present a "partial" decomposition that isolates the impact of the growth of between-group inequality—changing education and experience differentials—on total wage inequality. This is done by imposing a series of counterfactuals. For instance, one can determine the wages of workers in 1995 as if the wage differentials by education and experience that prevailed in 1989 were also present in 1995. The difference between the counterfactual measures of inequality in 1995 relative to the actual measures of inequality (such as the 90/10 wage differential) captures the effect of the 1989-95 change in wage differentials on wage inequality in this period. This "effect of changing wage differentials" can then be compared to the actual growth of wage inequality to gauge its proportionate contribution.

The estimates in Tables 3.24 and 3.25 of the role of between-group inequality are an "upper-bound," meaning that the contribution may be less but is not greater than that presented. These are upper-bound estimates because there has been no direct quantification of the "other" components of wage inequality, which include the impact of changes in the distribution of "skills" (i.e., more college graduates or older workers) and within-group wage inequality. Because changes in the composition of the workforce may have an equalizing effect, it is possible that two forces for inequality, between- and within-group, can have "contributions" totaling more than 100%.

The partial decomposition of the growth of male wage inequality in Table 3.24 yields the following results:

- Overall wage inequality (the 90/10 differential) grew marginally (2.1 percentage points) in the earliest (1973-79) period, despite a shrinkage of inequality at the top (the 90/50 differential), because inequality at the bottom (the 50/10 differential) grew.

- The large growth of wage inequality in the 1979-89 period was from a widening at the top—the 90/50 differential grew 10.3 percentage points. The

TABLE 3.24

Decomposing the Change in
Overall Wage Inequality Among Men, 1973-95

Change Period	Change in Differential*			Percent of Overall Change		
	90-10	90-50	50-10	90-10	90-50	50-10
(a) 1973-79						
Overall	2.1	-1.4	3.5	100.0%	100.0%	100.0%
Returns to "Skill"**	-2.1	-0.4	-1.6	-100.0	30.5	-46.7
Other***	4.1	-1.0	5.1	200.0	69.5	146.7
(b) 1979-89						
Overall	14.3	10.3	4.0	100.0%	100.0%	100.0%
Returns to "Skill"**	8.7	5.4	3.3	61.0	52.7	82.5
Other***	5.6	4.9	0.7	39.0	47.3	17.5
(c) 1989-95						
Overall	6.9	6.9	0.0	100.0%	100.0%	100.0%
Returns to "Skill"**	1.5	1.2	0.3	21.7	16.9	n.a.
Other***	5.4	5.7	-0.3	78.3	83.1	n.a.
(d) 1973-95						
Overall	23.2	15.7	7.5	100.0%	100.0%	100.0%
Returns to "Skill"**	8.1	6.2	2.0	35.0	39.1	26.4
Other***	15.1	9.6	5.5	65.0	60.9	73.6

* In logs.
** Change in between-group inequality, i.e., change in returns to education and experience.
*** Changes in within-group inequality and change in levels of education and experience.

Source: Authors' analysis of Outgoing Rotation Group of CPS.

---

change in the returns to education and experience (between-group inequality) had more impact in the 1980s on the 90/50 than on the 50/10 differential. Education and experience differentials explain, at most, about half (52.7%) of the growth of the 90/50 differential during this period. The growth of between-group inequality could account for as much as 61% of the growth of the male 90/10 differential in the 1980s.

- The character of inequality growth shifted in the 1990s as widening between-group inequality became a less important determinant of the growth in the

TABLE 3.25

Decomposing the Change in
Overall Wage Inequality Among Women, 1973-95

Change Period	Change in Differential*			Percent of Overall Change		
	90-10	90-50	50-10	90-10	90-50	50-10
(a) 1973-79						
Overall	-16.0	1.8	-17.8	100.0%	100.0%	100.0%
Returns to "Skill"**	-6.5	-3.0	-3.5	40.8	-166.9	19.8
Other***	-9.5	4.8	-14.2	59.2	266.9	80.2
(b) 1979-89						
Overall	35.2	9.5	25.6	100.0%	100.0%	100.0%
Returns to "Skill"**	13.0	6.2	6.8	37.0	64.5	26.7
Other***	22.2	3.4	18.8	63.0	35.5	73.3
(c) 1989-95						
Overall	2.7	6.0	-3.3	100.0%	100.0%	100.0%
Returns to "Skill"**	2.8	2.0	0.8	104.9	34.0	-23.9
Other***	-0.1	4.0	-4.1	-4.9	66.0	123.9
(d) 1973-95						
Overall	21.9	17.3	4.6	100.0%	100.0%	100.0%
Returns to "Skill"**	9.3	5.2	4.1	42.6	30.0	90.2
Other***	12.6	12.1	0.4	57.4	70.0	9.8

* In logs.
** Change in between-group inequality, i.e., change in returns to education and experience.
*** Changes in within-group inequality and change in levels of education and experience.

Source: Authors' analysis of Outgoing Rotation Group of CPS.

90/10 differential; its role shrank, from an 8.7-percentage-point contribution over the 1979-89 period to a modest 1.5-point contribution in 1989-95. Also in the 1990s, the 50/10 wage differential did not grow among men, although the 90/50 differential grew as quickly in the 1990s as in the 1980s (6.9 and 10.3 percentage points respectively over the 1989-95 and 1979-89 periods). Only a small portion of the growth in the 90/50 differential in the 1990s, 1.2 of a 6.9-percentage-point growth, can be attributed to changes in the returns to education and experience. This result corresponds to the earlier discussion of the small growth of education and experience differentials among men in the 1990s (Table 3.17).

• When one looks over the entire 1973-95 period, the growth of between-group wage inequality can account for, at most, 35% of the total growth of wage inequality. This suggests that any explanation of growing male wage inequality over the long term must focus at least as much on explaining within-group as between-group inequality.

It is more difficult to identify the percentage contribution of between-group wage inequality to the growth of total women's wage inequality in specific time periods over the 1970s and 1980s because of the "jumpiness" of the data describing the 50/10 differential in the 1978-80 period (as discussed along with Table 3.17). The partial decomposition in Table 3.25, however, provides a reliable indicator of the effect of growing between-group inequality. It appears that the effect of between-group inequality fell more in the 1970s (down 6.5 percentage points) and grew more in the 1980s (up 13.0 percentage points) among women than among men. Nevertheless, the effect of growing between-group inequality over the entire 1973-89 period was comparable among men and women (about 6.5 percentage points), which amounts to less than a third of the growth of the 90/10 differential of 19.2 percentage points from 1973 to 1989.

In the 1989-95 period, the 50/10 differential declined and between-group inequality rose only slightly. In contrast, the 90/50 differential grew at the same pace as in the 1980s, but only a third of the growth could be attributed to changes in the returns to education and experience. Thus, as with men, the importance of between-group inequality in driving the continuing growth of the 90/50 differential has diminished in the 1990s. Over the entire 1973-95 period, between-group inequality can explain only 30% of the 17.3-percentage-point growth in the 90/50 differential but nearly all of the small 4.6-percentage-point growth in the 50/10 differential.

School Quality and Tests

One potential explanation for the poor performance of wages for the non-college-educated workforce is a deterioration in school quality. That is, if schools have worsened, then the lower wages of high school graduates might simply reflect that they are less knowledgeable. Several studies have rejected this explanation on the grounds that a significant growth in wage inequality and in education premiums has occurred in every age group. If "school deterioration" were the driving force behind wage inequality, then one would expect these wage developments to be limited to recent entrants to the workforce and not affect the graduates of the 1970s, 1960s, and 1950s. The data in Table 3.22, for instance, show that wages for high school men fell over the 1980s and 1990s not only among recent high school graduates but also for those who had graduated roughly 20 to 35 years earlier.

Another reason for skepticism is that there is not much evidence of a deterioration in school quality, although there is not much evidence of overall improvement either.

Table 3.26 shows that there was an equalizing of test scores over the period when wage inequality was expanding. For instance, the math and reading scores of the best test scorers—those at the 80th percentile—were flat over this period. In contrast, test scores grew among the rest of the student population and, in fact, grew the most among the bottom scorers at the 20th and 40th percentiles. Thus, to the degree that test scores reflect knowledge and cognitive abilities, the evidence suggests that "learning" and "school quality" trends should have been leading to better wages among some groups and a lessening of wage inequality.

TABLE 3.26

Test Scores by Percentile, 1975-90

Percentile	1978	1982	1986	1990
Mathematics				
20	270.1	270.0	276.5	277.3
40	291.8	289.9	293.2	296.2
60	310.3	307.3	308.7	313.0
80	330.3	326.6	328.3	331.6
	1975	**1980**	**1988**	**1990**
Reading				
20	249.7	251.4	260.3	257.6
40	277.0	276.8	282.4	281.2
60	298.6	297.8	301.4	301.4
80	322.2	320.6	322.9	325.4

Source: Greenberg (1993) analysis of National Assessment of Educational Progress (NAEP) test scores for 17-year-olds.

Moreover, test scores were stable or slightly higher in 1990 than in 1975 (for reading) or in 1978 (for mathematics), suggesting no deterioration in school quality among the high, middle, or low test scorers. Therefore, new workforce entrants have not seen lower wages because they have done more poorly in school.

The Shift to Low-Paying Industries

There was a large employment shift to low-wage sectors in the 1980s and 1990s. This shift is a consequence of trade deficits and deindustrialization as well as stagnant or falling productivity growth in service-sector industries. This section examines the significant erosion of wages and compensation for non-college-educated workers that results from an employment shift to low-paying industries. This "industry-shift" effect is not the consequence of some natural evolution from an agriculture to a manufacturing to a service economy. For one, a significant part of the shrinkage of manufacturing is trade related. More important, industry shifts would not provide a downward pressure on wages if service-sector wages were more closely aligned with manufacturing wages, as is the case in other countries. Moreover, since health coverage, vacations, and pensions are related to the specific job or sector in which a worker is employed, the sectoral distribution of employment matters more in the United States than in other countries. An alternative institutional arrangement found in other advanced countries sets health, pensions, vacation, and other benefits through legislation in a universal manner regardless of sector or firm. Therefore, the downward pressure of industry shifts can be said to be the consequence of institutional structures.

Trends in employment growth by major industry sector are presented in **Table 3.27**. The 18.1 million (net) jobs created between 1979 and 1989 involved a loss of roughly 1.2 million manufacturing and mining jobs and an increase of 19.3 million jobs in the service sector. The largest amount of job growth (14.2 million) was in the two lowest-paying service-sector industries—retail trade and services (business, personnel, and health). In fact, these two industries accounted for 79% of all the net new jobs over the 1979-89 period.

The shift toward low-paying industries has continued in the 1990s. In fact, almost as many jobs were lost in goods-producing industries from 1989 to 1995 as over the 1979-89 period. Low-wage retail jobs have played a smaller role in overall job creation, contributing 15.7% of the new jobs, but the services industry (primarily health and temporary services) became more important, supplying 67.6% of the net new jobs. Together, these low-wage industries accounted for 83.3% of all new jobs.

TABLE 3.27

Employment Growth by Sector, 1979-95

Industry Sector	Employment (000)			Job Growth (000)		Industry Share of Job Growth		Hourly Compensation 1993
	1979	1989	1995	1979-89	1989-95	1979-89	1989-95	(1993$)
Goods Producing	26,461	25,254	24,227	-1,207	-1,027	-6.7%	-11.8%	$20.22
Mining	958	692	579	-266	-113	-1.5	-1.3	n.a.
Construction	4,463	5,171	5,246	708	75	3.9	0.9	19.71
Manufacturing	21,040	19,391	18,403	-1649	-988	-9.1	-11.3	20.09
Durable Goods	12,760	11,394	10,595	-1366	-799	-7.6	-9.2	21.88
Nondurable Goods	8,280	7,997	7,808	-283	-189	-1.6	-2.2	17.75
Service Producing	63,363	82,642	92,380	19,279	9,738	106.7%	111.8%	$15.51
Trans., Comm., Util.	5,136	5,625	6,192	489	567	2.7	6.5	24.07
Wholesale	5,204	6,187	6,324	983	137	5.4	1.6	18.12
Retail	14,989	19,475	20,841	4,486	1,366	24.8	15.7	9.28
Fin., Ins., Real Est.	4,975	6,668	6,949	1,693	281	9.4	3.2	20.27
Services	17,112	26,907	32,796	9,795	5,889	54.2	67.6	16.34
Government	15,947	17,779	19,280	1,832	1,501	10.1	17.2	n.a.
Total	89,823	107,895	116,607	18,072	8,712	100.0%	100.0%	$16.70

Source: Authors' analysis.

The extent of the shift to low-wage industries in the 1980s is more evident in an analysis of changes in the shares of the workforce in various sectors (**Table 3.28**). Several high-wage sectors, such as construction, transportation, wholesale, communications, and government, increased employment in the 1980s or 1990s but ended up providing a smaller or similar share of overall employment over time. A lower share of employment in these high-wage sectors puts downward pressure on wages. Overall, the share of the workforce in low-paying services and in retail trade was 7.3 percentage points higher in 1989 than in 1979. The parallel trend was the 8.0-percentage-point drop in the share of the workforce in high-paying industries, such as manufacturing, construction, mining, government, transportation, communications, and utilities. In the 1990s, the only private-sector industry to significantly expand its employment share was services, which is the second-lowest-paying industry.

The effect on pay levels of the employment shift toward lower-paying sectors

TABLE 3.28

Changes in Employment Share by Sector, 1979-95

Industry Sector	Share of Employment			Change in Employment Share	
	1979	1989	1995	1979-89	1989-95
Goods Producing	29.5%	23.4%	20.8%	-6.1	-2.6
Mining	1.1	0.6	0.5	-0.4	-0.1
Construction	5.0	4.8	4.5	-0.2	-0.3
Manufacturing	23.4	18.0	15.8	-5.5	-2.2
Durable Goods	14.2	10.6	9.1	-3.6	-1.5
Nondurable Goods	9.2	7.4	6.7	-1.8	-0.7
Service Producing	70.5%	76.6%	79.2%	6.1	2.6
Trans., Comm., Util.	5.7	5.2	5.3	-0.5	0.1
Wholesale	5.8	5.7	5.4	-0.1	-0.3
Retail	16.7	18.0	17.9	1.4	-0.2
Fin., Ins., Real Est.	5.5	6.2	6.0	0.6	-0.2
Services	19.1	24.9	28.1	5.9	3.2
Government	17.8	16.5	16.5	-1.3	0.1
Total	100.0%	100.0%	100.0%	0.0	0.0

Source: Authors' analysis.

is illustrated in **Table 3.29**. The first panel shows the level of pay that would have prevailed in 1989 if the workforce were in the same occupations and industries as in 1980 (the earliest available year for this analysis) but worked at 1989 wage levels. The second row of this panel shows the actual pay levels in 1989. The difference between the pay levels in the first two rows thus reflects the change in the industrial and occupational composition of employment between 1980 and 1989. The percentage difference between the first two rows is thus a measure of the effect of changes in the composition of employment on wages, benefits, and compensation. Since there was a shift toward higher-paying *occupations* in this period, this comparison understates the adverse effect of the shift to lower-paying *industries* (which was partially offset by occupational changes).

TABLE 3.29

Effect of Structural Employment Shifts on Pay Levels, 1980-95
(1995 Dollars)

Period	Hourly Pay		
	Compensation	**Benefits**	**Wages**
1989 Pay Levels with Employment Composition of:			
1980	$18.17	$3.37	$14.81
1989	17.55	3.15	14.40
*Composition Effect, 1980-89**			
Dollars	-$0.62	-$0.22	-$0.40
Percent	-3.4%	-6.6%	-2.7%
1995 Pay Levels With Employment Composition of:			
1990	$17.45	$3.35	$14.09
1995	17.10	3.26	13.84
*Composition Effect, 1990-95**			
Dollars	-$0.35	-$0.09	-$0.25
Percent	-2.0%	-1.8%	-2.7%

* The effect of changes in the occupation and industry composition of employment. Pay levels at composition of 1980 and 1990 are data underlying the Employment Cost Index corrected for difference between household and employment surveys. Other pay levels have "current weights" and are ECI Levels data.

Source: Authors' analysis.

The change in the composition of employment from 1980 to 1989 led to a 2.7% fall in wages, a 6.6% fall in benefits (all nonwage compensation), and a 3.4% fall in total compensation. These results suggest that industry shifts depressed compensation growth by at least 0.3% each year over the 1980-89 period (3.4% over nine years).

This analysis is repeated in the second panel of Table 3.29 for the 1990-95 period. In the most recent years, the shifting pattern of employment depressed wages (down 2.7%) more than benefits (down 1.8%). Again, industry shifts depressed compensation by about 0.3% or 0.4% each year. Over the entire 1980-95 period, industry shifts depressed average compensation by more than 5%, amounting to a reduction of nearly a dollar per hour. Thus, the impact of industry shifts have been neither trivial nor "small."

Another way to illustrate the impact of the shifts in employment is to compare the growth in the Employment Cost Index, in which employment composition is fixed, to the growth in the actual change in hourly compensation. This difference over the 1987-95 period is shown in **Figure 3N**. The published in-

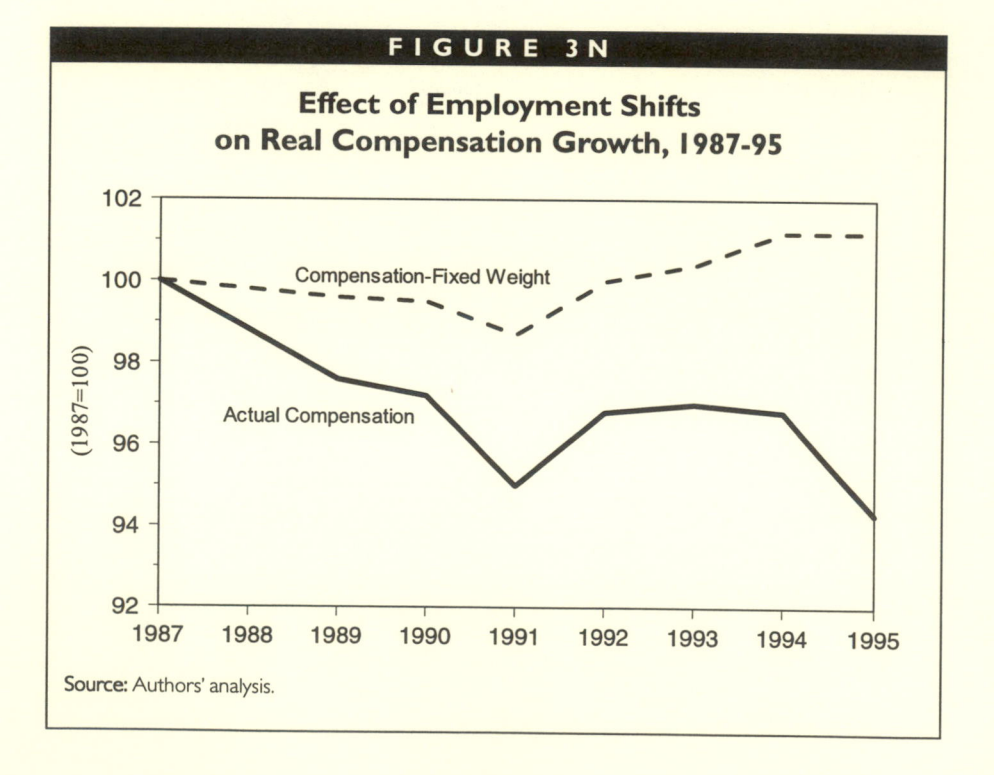

FIGURE 3N

Effect of Employment Shifts on Real Compensation Growth, 1987-95

Source: Authors' analysis.

dex, which holds the employment composition constant, suggests modest growth in real hourly compensation of 1.2% over the 1987-95 period. An index that allows employment to shift shows real compensation falling nearly 6% over the 1987-95 period and steadily diverging from the other index. Thus, the growth of the fixed-weight (employment composition held constant) index is misleading in terms of the actual growth of real hourly compensation precisely because composition shifts are large and negative.

Table 3.30 presents an analysis of the impact of the shift in the industry mix

TABLE 3.30

The Effect of Industry Shifts on the Growth of the College-High School Differential, 1973-95

	March CPS			ORG CPS		
	Industry Composition		**Industry Effect****	**Industry Composition**		**Industry Effect****
Gender/ Year	**Varies***	**Fixed***		**Varies***	**Fixed***	
	(1)	(2)	(3)	(4)	(5)	(6)
Men						
1973	n.a.	n.a.		32.5%	35.9%	
1979	26.6%	30.1%		27.3	30.5	
1989	40.9	41.7		41.8	42.4	
1995***	44.0	44.4		44.1	44.4	
Change						
1979-89	14.3	11.6	19.0%	14.5	11.9	17.6%
1989-95***	3.1	2.7	13.6	2.3	1.9	16.9
1979-95***	17.4	14.3	18.1	16.8	13.9	17.5
Women						
1973	n.a.	n.a.		43.0%	39.6%	
1979	32.6%	31.2%		30.8	28.6	
1989	49.3	44.9		46.0	40.8	
1995***	50.3	45.6		51.8	46.0	
Change						
1979-89	16.7	13.7	17.9%	15.2	12.2	19.6%
1989-95***	1.0	0.7	37.9	5.8	5.2	11.7
1979-95***	17.7	14.4	19.1	21.0	17.4	17.4

*   Estimated with controls for experience as a quartic, marital status, race, and four regions. Estimates are presented that do ("Fixed") and do not ("Varies") control for industry composition.

**   The difference in the growth of the differential when industry composition held "constant" or "fixed" as a share of the total growth in the differential (e.g., ((1)-(2))/(1)).

*** Data in March CPS are for 1994.

of employment on the growth of the college-high school wage premium. This analysis suggests that the employment shift to low-wage industries can account for roughly 20% of the growth of education premiums over the 1979-95 period. The analysis uses two different wage data sets (the March and the ORG CPS) to determine the growth of the college-high school wage premium when one does and does not control for industry shifts—labeled respectively "industry composition fixed" and "industry composition varies." Comparing the growth of the education premium in columns 1 versus 2 and 4 versus 5 provides information on the impact of changes in the industry composition of employment, or "industry shifts." Among men, for instance, the college-high school wage premium grew 17.4 percentage points from 1979 to 1995 (using the March CPS data, column 1), but would have grown 14.3 percentage points had industry composition not changed. Therefore, 3.1 percentage points (17.4 less 14.3) of the 17.4-percentage-point growth, equivalent to 18.1% of the total growth, in the college/high school differential can be accounted for by industry shifts.

Trade and Wages

The process of "globalization" in the 1980s and 1990s has been an important factor both in slowing the growth rate of average wages and in reducing the wage levels of workers with less than a college degree. The increase in international trade and investment flows affects wages through several channels. First, increases in imports of finished manufactured goods, especially from countries where workers earn only a fraction of what U.S. workers earn, reduces manufacturing employment in the United States. While increases in exports create employment opportunities for some domestic workers, imports mean job losses for many others. Large, chronic trade deficits over the last 15 years suggest that the jobs lost to import competition have outnumbered the jobs gained from increasing exports. Given that export industries tend to be less labor intensive than import-competing industries, even growth in "balanced trade" (where exports and imports both increase by the same dollar amount) would lead to a decline in manufacturing jobs.

Second, imports of intermediate manufactured goods (used as inputs in the production of final goods) also help to lower domestic manufacturing employment, especially for production workers and others with less than a college education. The expansion of export "platforms" in low-wage countries has induced many U.S. manufacturing firms to "outsource" part of their production processes to low-wage countries. Since firms generally find it most profitable to outsource the most labor-intensive processes, the increase in outsourcing has hit non-college-educated production workers hardest.

Third, low wages and greater world capacity for producing manufactured goods can lower the prices of many international goods. Since workers' pay is tied to the value of the goods they produce, lower prices internationally can lead to a reduction in the earnings of U.S. workers, even if imports themselves do not increase.

Fourth, in many cases the mere threat of direct foreign competition or of the relocation of part or all of a production facility can lead workers to grant wage concessions to their employers.

Fifth, the very large increases in international investment flows (in percentage terms the increases are much larger than for international trade) have meant reduced investment in the domestic manufacturing base and significant growth in the foreign manufacturing capacity capable of competing directly with U.S.-based manufacturers.

Finally, the effects of globalization go beyond those workers exposed directly to foreign competition. As trade drives workers out of manufacturing and into lower-paying service jobs, not only do their own wages fall, but the new supply of workers to the service sector (from displaced workers plus young workers not able to find manufacturing jobs) also helps to lower the wages of those already employed in service jobs.

This section briefly examines the role of international trade and investment in recent changes in the U.S. wage structure. Since even the preceding list of channels through which "globalization" affects wages is not complete, this analysis may well *understate* the impact of globalization on wages in the 1980s and 1990s. This topic is a relatively new area of inquiry in empirical labor economics and international trade; as befits a new area of investigation, there is considerable controversy and confusion.

Table 3.31 highlights the scope of the increase in foreign manufactured imports. The first column describes the rise in the share of imported final manufactured goods in the total consumption of final manufactured goods. In 1972, imports were about 5% of domestic consumption; by 1990, the share had more than doubled to almost 11%, with the fastest growth occurring between 1979 and 1987. The second column shows a similar increase in the share of imported manufactured inputs in total inputs to manufacturing, which rose from 5.3% in 1972 to 11.6% in 1990. Again, the largest increase took place between 1979 and 1987, with an annual growth rate of 0.43%—four times higher than between 1972 and 1979 (0.11%).

TABLE 3.31

Final and Intermediate Manufacturing Imports, 1972-90

Year	Final Goods/Total Final Consumption	Imported Inputs/ Total Inputs
1972	5.0%	5.3%
1979	6.7	7.7
1987	10.5	11.5
1990	10.7	11.6
Annual Percentage Change		
1972-79	0.3%	0.1%
1979-87	0.4	0.4
1987-90	0.3	0.4

Source: Feenstra and Hanson (1996).

The next two tables show estimates of the impact of this increase in manu-factured imports on manufacturing employment. As mentioned earlier, we ex-pect that imports will disproportionately displace low- and middle-wage work-ers, who compete most directly with low-wage workers in developing countries. The results in both tables generally confirm these expectations.

Table 3.32 ranks manufacturing industries into ten groups based on the overall industry skill level in 1979. The last column shows the estimated effect of trade (total exports minus total imports, or "net exports") on employment for indus-tries in each of the skill categories, under the assumption that the industry had the same net export share in 1989 as in 1979. (This does not mean that exports and imports were held at their 1979 level, only that industry exports and imports represented the same share of industry output in 1989 as they did in 1979.) By these calculations, the increase in imports between 1978 and 1990 reduced manu-facturing employment by 5.9% over the same period. As expected, production workers (a category that includes roughly 70% of manufacturing employment, corresponding roughly to the less-skilled workforce) bore the brunt of the em-ployment losses, with trade reducing production-worker employment during the 1980s by 7.2%, compared to a smaller 2.1% drop for nonproduction workers (white-collar and other workers who are not production workers). Moreover, the

TABLE 3.32

Impact of Foreign Trade on Manufacturing Employment, 1978-90

Industry Skill Decile	Change in Employment Due to Trade with:		
	Developing Countries	Developed Countries	All
Highest	0.2%	12.2%	12.3%
2	-0.9	0.9	0.0
3	-2.8	-1.7	-4.4
4	-2.3	2.9	0.5
5	-2.0	-1.6	-3.6
6	-5.5	-2.4	-7.9
7	-5.2	-1.4	-6.6
8	-2.6	-2.1	-4.7
9	-3.4	-6.7	-10.1
Lowest	-23.5	-3.6	-27.1
All Manufacturing	-5.7%	-0.2%	-5.9%
Production Workers	-6.2	-1.0	-7.2
Nonproduction Workers	-4.3	2.2	-2.1

Source: Sachs and Shatz (1994).

rise in trade with low-wage, developing countries was responsible for almost all (5.7 percentage points) of trade's contribution to the decline in overall manufacturing employment.

Table 3.33 displays results from a different approach to estimating the impact of trade on manufacturing employment. Here, the experiences of different developed countries with import competition and manufacturing employment are used to gauge the impact of trade on the long-term trend in manufacturing employment. The table indicates that in the United States manufacturing employment as a share of total employment fell by 8.17 percentage points between 1970 and 1990. Trade with developing countries was responsible for about 2.7 percentage points, or about one-third, of the long-term decline in manufacturing's employment share in the United States. The table shows trade with developing

TABLE 3.33

Trade with Low-Wage Countries and Change in Manufacturing Employment Share for G-7 Countries, 1970-90

Country	Actual Deindustrialization	Change in Manufacturing Imports** from Low-Wage Countries	Net Impact*** of Trade with Low-Wage Countries	Share of Deindustrialization* Due to Trade with Low-Wage Countries
Canada	-5.89	1.38	-2.02	34.4%
France	-5.76	1.34	-1.76	30.5
Germany	-6.70	1.96	-2.60	38.8
Italy	-3.86	-0.90	-1.18	30.6
Japan	-3.96	0.87	-1.35	34.0
United Kingdom	-14.05	1.44	-2.46	17.5
United States	**-8.17**	**2.09**	**-2.73**	**33.4**

*   Change in the manufacturing share of employment.
** Change in the share of GDP.
*** Impact net of changes in exports to low-wage countries (not shown here).

Source: Saeger (1995).

countries accounting for a similar proportion of the fall in manufacturing employment over the 1970-90 period in the other G-7 countries. The only exception is the United Kingdom, which experienced a moderate increase in trade with developing countries but suffered an enormous drop in manufacturing employment (about 14%).

Both tables suggest that trade, particularly with low-wage developing countries, accelerated the long-term decline in manufacturing employment. The data also suggest that the fall in employment opportunities was especially severe for generally non-college-educated production workers. Since production workers in manufacturing on average earn substantially more than workers with similar skills in nonmanufacturing jobs, these trade-induced job losses contributed directly to the deterioration in the wage structure. Since millions of trade-displaced workers sought jobs in nonmanufacturing sectors, trade also worked to depress wages outside manufacturing.

As discussed earlier, international trade can also affect U.S. wages through the prices of internationally traded manufactured goods without any change in the quantity of exports or imports. The expansion of manufacturing capacity in low-wage countries since the 1970s has significantly increased the supply of less-skill-intensive manufactured goods, inducing a reduction in the U.S. price of these goods. Since workers' earnings reflect changes in the prices of the goods they produce, a lower price for less-skill-intensive goods drives down the wages of less-skilled workers. **Table 3.34** presents results from some simple calculations designed to estimate the effect of trade-induced price changes on U.S. wages. It

TABLE 3.34

Effect of Changes in Prices* of Internationally Traded Manufactured Goods on Wage Inequality

Industry Price Changes	1959-69	1969-79	1979-89
College-Weighted	12.9%	159.5%	61.4%
Noncollege-Weighted	15.1	142.8	58.5
Difference	-2.2	16.7	2.9
Nonproduction-Weighted	16.1%	137.0%	62.0%
Production-Weighted	16.2	137.5	56.6
Difference	-0.1	-0.5	5.4
Labor Share in Value-Added			70.0%
Implied Decline in Wages**			
Noncollege			4.1%
Production			7.7
Actual Change in Relative Wages			
Noncollege			13.9%
Nonproduction-Production			7.7
Share of Change in Relative Wages Caused by Change in Relative Prices			
College-Noncollege			29.8%
Nonproduction-Production			110.2

* Change in value-added producer price indexes over the period.
** Assuming no change in the real wage of nonproduction and college workers.
*** Change between 1979 and 1989 in regression-based college-noncollege wage differential, controlling for workers' experience and region of residence.

Source: Authors' analysis of Schmitt and Mishel (1996).

examines whether prices grew more slowly in the manufacturing industries most reliant on non-college-educated or unskilled and semi-skilled workers—the industries most affected by low-wage imports. Two measures of "skill intensity" are shown. The first panel shows that between 1979 and 1989 the price of college-worker-intensive industries increased by 2.9% relative to noncollege-worker-intensive industries. The second panel shows that the price of nonproduction-intensive industries rose by 5.4% relative to production-worker-intensive industries over the same period.

These relative price changes require wages of noncollege-educated and production workers to fall. The size of the wage declines depend on the importance of labor costs in overall manufacturing costs. If labor were a small share of total manufacturing costs, say 10%, then a 1% decline in the relative prices of less-skill-intensive goods would require a large fall (10%) in the less-skilled workers' wage in order to leave the overall industry costs unchanged (a 10% fall in something that is 10% of total costs represents a 1% saving on overall costs). If labor were a large share of total manufacturing costs, or value-added (say, 100%), then a 1% decline in the relative prices of less-skill-intensive industries would require a much smaller (1%) decline in the costs of less-skilled labor (a 1% fall in the costs of something that is 100% of total costs represents a 1% savings on overall costs). Since labor costs are, on average, 70% of total manufacturing costs, then a 1% fall in the relative less-skill-intensive industry price requires about a 1.4% fall in the wage of the relatively less-skilled worker. If we assume that the average real wage for college-educated and nonproduction workers was unchanged between 1979 and 1989 (as is generally the case), then the 2.9% fall in the relative prices in noncollege-educated-intensive industries should have lowered the noncollege wage by 4.1% over the period. The 5.4% relative fall in production-worker-intensive prices should have lowered production-worker wages by 7.7%. Since the wages of noncollege-educated relative to college-educated workers actually fell 14% over the period, trade appears to have contributed about 30% of the decline in the college-noncollege wage over the 1979-89 period. By this measure, trade was entirely responsible for the 7.7% fall in production-worker wages relative to nonproduction workers.

The preceding tables document the rise in intermediate and final manufactured imports and the decline in prices of less-skill-intensive, internationally traded manufactured goods. These channels have contributed to the long-term decline in manufacturing employment and directly and indirectly to the deterioration in the U.S. wage structure. Little concrete evidence is available on the other channels discussed at the beginning of this section—the "threat effect" of imports and plant relocation on U.S. manufacturing wages, and the reality of large-scale international investment flows. Nevertheless, these effects are likely to be as large or larger than those that are more readily quantifiable.

Another aspect of globalization is immigration. After six decades of decline in the percentage of immigrants in the total population of the United States, the immigrant share began to grow in the 1970s (**Table 3.35**). Holding all else constant, a rise in immigration increases the available labor supply in the United States and thus tends to reduce wages. **Table 3.36** shows that a large share of recent immigrants have less than the equivalent of a high school education (although immigrants, at least until 1990, also were more likely than natives to have a college degree). The table presents data only for legal immigrants; the skill mix would probably be even more heavily skewed toward those with less than a high school degree if undocumented immigrants were also included. These numbers suggest that immigrants compete disproportionately with less-skilled U.S. workers and therefore may have contributed to lower wages for those without a high school degree since the end of the 1970s.

TABLE 3.35

Legal Immigrant Flow to the United States, 1881-1990

Decade	Number (000s)	As Percentage of Change in Population	Foreign-Born as Share of Population*
1881-1890	5,246.6	41.0%	14.7%
1891-1900	3,687.6	28.3	13.6
1901-1910	8,795.4	53.9	14.6
1911-1920	5,735.8	40.8	13.2
1921-1930	4,107.2	24.6	11.6
1931-1940	528.4	5.9	8.8
1941-1950	1,350.0	5.3	6.9
1951-1960	2,515.5	8.7	5.4
1961-1970	3,321.7	13.7	4.7
1971-1980	4,493.3	20.7	6.2
1981-1990	7,338.1	33.1	7.9

* At end of decade.

Source: Borjas (1994).

TABLE 3.36

Educational Attainment of Immigrant and Native Men, 1970-90

	Less Than High School		College-Educated	
Year	Native	Immigrants	Native	Immigrants
1970	39.6%	48.2%	15.4%	18.9%
1980	23.1	37.4	22.9	25.3
1990	14.8	36.9	26.6	26.6

Source: Authors' analysis of Borjas (1994).

The Union Dimension

The percentage of the workforce represented by unions fell rapidly in the 1980s after having been stable in the 1970s, as shown in **Figure 3O**. This falling rate of unionization has lowered wages, not only because some workers no longer receive the higher union wage but also because there is less pressure on non-union employers to raise wages. There are also reasons to believe that there has been a weakening of union bargaining power, a qualitative shift beyond the quantitative decline. This erosion of bargaining power is partially related to a harsher economic context for unions because of trade pressures, the shift to services, and ongoing technological change. However, analysts have also pointed to other factors, such as employer militancy and changes in the application and administration of labor law, that have helped to weaken unions.

Table 3.37 shows the union wage premium—the degree to which union wages exceed nonunion wages—by type of pay (benefits or wages) for all workers and for blue-collar workers. The union premium is larger for total compensation (37.8%) than for wages alone (25.0%), reflecting the fact that unionized workers are provided insurance and pension benefits that are more than double those of nonunion workers. For blue-collar workers, the union premium in insurance and benefits is even larger: union blue-collar workers receive 148.9% and 322.6% more in health and pensions than do their nonunion counterparts.

Table 3.38, using a different data source and methodology (and year), pre-

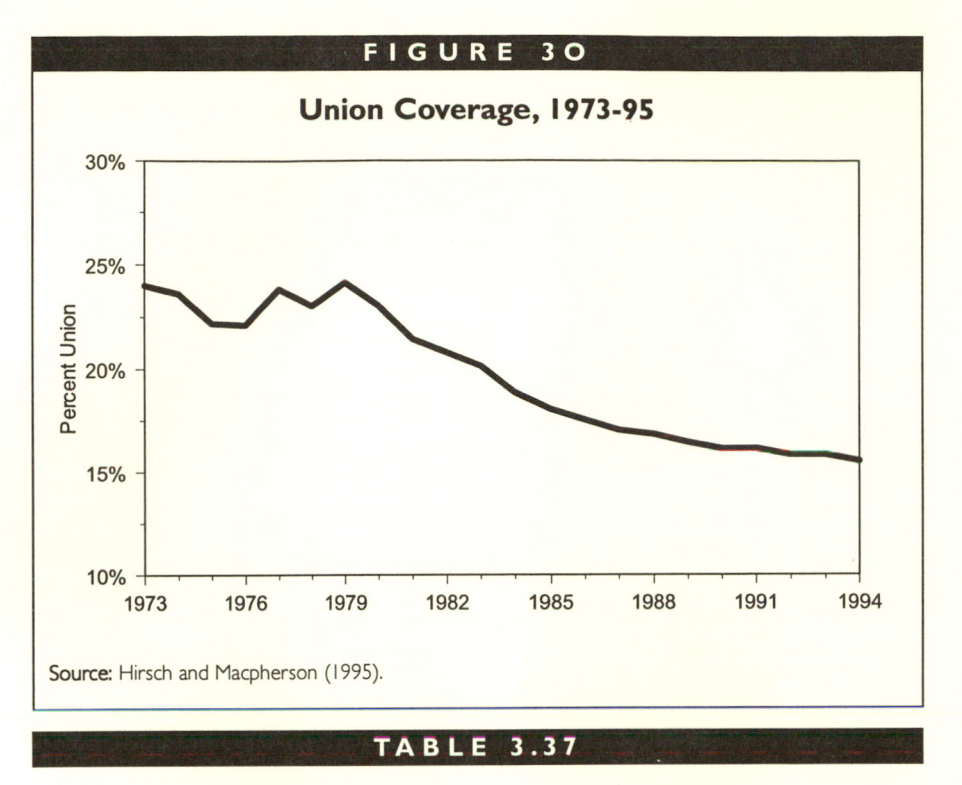

FIGURE 30

Union Coverage, 1973-95

Source: Hirsch and Macpherson (1995).

TABLE 3.37

Union Wage and Benefit Premium, 1995
(1995 Dollars)

	Wages	Insurance	Pension	Compensation
All Workers				
Union	$16.69	$2.24	$1.15	$22.40
Nonunion	13.35	0.98	0.42	16.26
Union Premium				
Dollars	$3.34	$1.26	$0.73	$6.14
Percent	25.0%	128.6%	173.8%	37.8%
Blue Collar				
Union	$16.81	$2.34	$1.31	$23.07
Nonunion	11.21	0.94	0.31	14.14
Union Premium				
Dollars	$5.60	$1.40	$1.00	$8.93
Percent	50.0%	148.9%	322.6%	63.2%

Source: Authors' analysis of BLS data.

TABLE 3.38

Union Wage Premium by Demographic Group, 1991

Group	Percent Union	Union Premium	
		Dollars	Percent
Total	18.2%	$1.71	19.8%
Men	21.3	1.56	18.2
Women	14.8	1.79	20.4
Whites	17.4%	$1.75	20.0%
Men	20.6	1.59	17.9
Women	13.8	1.87	20.9
Blacks	24.4%	$1.49	18.1%
Men	27.7	1.54	19.0
Women	21.2	1.46	17.0
Hispanics	17.7%	$1.77	21.8%
Men	18.6	1.80	21.9
Women	16.2	1.65	20.1

* Union member or covered by collective-bargaining agreement.
** Union wage advantage controlling for experience, education, region, industry, occupation, and marital status.

Source: Authors' analysis.

---

sents another set of estimates of the union wage premium. Specifically, the union wage premium is computed so as to reflect differences in hourly wages between union and nonunion workers who are otherwise comparable in experience, education, region, industry, occupation, and marital status. This methodology yields a lower but still sizable union premium of 19.8% overall—18.2% for men and 20.4% for women. The differences in union wage premiums across demographic groups are relatively small, ranging from 17% to 22%. Hispanic union members tend to reap the greatest wage advantage from unionism, although the black workforce benefits the most, since its rate of unionization, 24.4%, is the highest.

The effect of the erosion of unionization on the wages of a segment of the workforce depends on the degree to which deunionization has taken place and the size of the union wage premium among that segment of the workforce. **Table 3.39**

TABLE 3.39

Effect of Deunionization on Male Occupation and Education Differentials, 1978-88

A. EFFECTS OF UNION DECLINE ON WAGES*

		Percent Union			Effect of
Group	Union Wage Premium**	1978	1988	Change 1978-88	Union Decline on Wages
By Occupation					
White Collar	1%	18%	13%	-5	-0.1%
Blue Collar	26	47	33	-14	-3.6
Difference					3.5
By Education					
College	-2%	17%	14%	-3	0.1%
High School	16	42	30	-12	-1.4
Difference					1.5

B. CONTRIBUTION OF DEUNIONIZATION TO HIGHER WAGE DIFFERENTIALS*

	(1) Change in Wage Differential 1978-88*	(2) Union Decline Effect on Wage Differential	(3) Higher Differential Explained by Union Decline
White Collar/Blue Collar	7%	3.5%	50%
College/High School	6	1.5	25

* Differentials and change in differentials computed in natural log percentage points.
** Controlling for workforce characteristics.

Source: Freeman (1991).

shows both the degree to which unionization declined and the union wage premium by occupation and education level. These data, which are for men only (the underlying study did not include women), are used to calculate the effect of deunionization over the 1978-88 period on the wages of particular groups and how deunionization affected occupation and education wage differentials—the contribution of deunionization to the growth of between-group inequality.

Union representation fell dramatically among blue-collar and high-school-educated workers from 1978 to 1988. Among the high-school-graduate workforce, 12% fewer were unionized in 1988 than in 1978, more than a 25% shrink-age in the unionization rate. Because unionized high school graduates earned 16% more than equivalent nonunion workers, the loss of unionization lowered the average high school graduate's wage by 1.4%. The net effect of deunion-ization was to increase the college/high school wage differential by 1.5 percent-age points.

Deunionization had a larger negative effect on blue-collar wages—lowering them 3.6%—and thus a larger effect on the occupational than the educational wage differential. Less unionization can account for 25% and 50% respectively of the higher educational and occupational wage differentials in 1988.

Table 3.40 examines the effect of lower unionization on workers at various wage levels and allows us to analyze the impact of deunionization on overall wage inequality, not only on between-group inequality. The data show that unions have their largest effect on the wages of lower-wage workers, raising the wages of union members in the lowest and second-lowest fifths by 27.9% and 16.2% respectively. Because workers in the bottom three-fifths have higher unioniza-tion rates and higher union wage premiums, the effect of unions on average wages

TABLE 3.40

Effect of Unions on Wages, by Wage Fifth, 1973-87

	Lowest Fifth	Second Fifth	Middle Fifth	Fourth Fifth	Top Fifth	Average
Percent Union						
1973	39.9%	43.7%	38.3%	33.5%	12.5%	33.7%
1987	23.5	30.3	33.1	24.7	17.7	26.4
Change, 1973-87	-15.4	-13.4	-5.2	-8.8	7.2	-7.3
Effect of Union on:						
Union Wage, 1987	27.9%	16.2%	18.0%	0.9%	10.5%	15.9%
Average Wage, 1987	6.6	4.9	6.0	2.1	2.1	4.2
Wage Effect of:						
Deunionization						
1973-87	-4.3%	-2.2%	-0.9%	-0.1%	0.8%	-1.1%

Source: Card (1991).

for these groups is largest—increasing the average wage from 4.9% to 6.6%.

Unionization declined more among low-wage than high-wage workers from 1973 to 1987, with unionization actually increasing among the top fifth. The wage impact of changes in unionization was to increase the wage gap between high- and low-wage workers. For instance, an increase in union representation lifted the wages of the top-fifth by 0.8%, but deunionization lowered the wages in the bottom fifth by 4.3%, creating a roughly 5-percentage-point divergence between high- and low-wage earners.

The data in **Table 3.41** report the results of three studies of the effect of the drop in unionization on overall male wage inequality. These data show that there was sizable growth in wage inequality between the 1970s and the late 1980s. Remarkably, all three studies found that lower unionization can account for the same proportion of overall higher wage inequality—21%—even though they employ radically different methodologies. Unfortunately, these studies do not examine women's wages. Another study, discussed below (Table 3.47), shows deunionization playing a smaller role among women than men.

TABLE 3.41

Effect of Deunionization on Male Wage Inequality

Item	Wage Inequality		
	1973-87*	1978-88**	1979-88***
Early Year	.227	.235	n.a.
Later Year	.284	.269	n.a.
Change in Inequality	.057	.034	.066
Change Due to Lower Unionization	.012	.007	.014
Deunionization Contribution to Total Rise in Inequality	21%	21%	21%

*   Change in variance of log earnings among men age 25-64.
** Change in variance of log earnings among men age 25-65.
*** Change in standard deviation of log earnings among men age 25-65.

Sources: Card (1991); Dinardo, Fortin, and Lemieux (1994); Freeman (1991).

An Eroded Minimum Wage

The real value of the minimum wage has fallen considerably since its high point in the late 1960s (**Figure 3P**). The decline was particularly steep and steady between 1979 and 1989, when inflation whittled down the real minimum wage (in 1995 dollars) from $5.97 to $4.12, a fall of 31.1% (**Table 3.42**). Despite the legislated increases in the minimum wage in 1990 and 1991, its value of $4.25 in 1995 was $1.72, or 28.8%, less than in 1979. In fact, the minimum wage's purchasing power in 1995 ($4.25) was 23.7% less than the value of the minimum wage 28 years earlier, in 1967.

The U.S. Congress voted to increase the minimum wage to $5.15 in 1997. This is a modest increase that will not restore the value of the minimum wage to anywhere near its value of 20 to 30 years ago. Table 3.42 shows what the value of the minimum wage will be in 2000 (using projected rates of inflation). Even with the increase, the minimum wage will be 26.7% below its 1979 level in the year 2000.

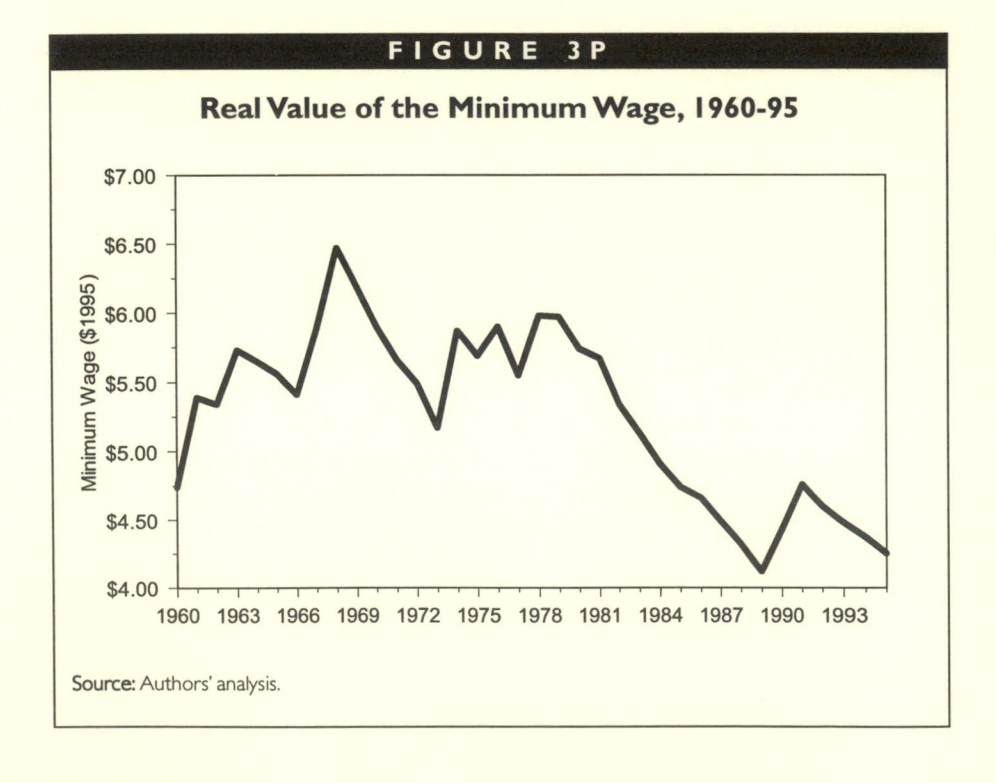

FIGURE 3P

Real Value of the Minimum Wage, 1960-95

Source: Authors' analysis.

TABLE 3.42

Value of the Minimum Wage, 1967-2000

Year	Current $	1995$
1967	$1.40	$5.88
1973	1.60	5.17
1979	2.90	5.97
1989	3.35	4.12
1990	3.80	4.43
1991	4.25	4.76
1995	4.25	4.25
2000*	5.15	4.38
Period Averages		
1960s		$5.64
1970s		5.72
1980s		4.91
1990-95		4.48
Percent Change		
1967-95		-27.7%
1979-89		-31.1
1979-95		-28.8
1979-2000		-26.7

* Minimum wage will increase to $5.15 in 1997.

Source: Authors' analysis.

It has been argued that the minimum wage primarily affects teenagers and others with no family responsibilities. **Table 3.43** examines the demographic composition of the workforce that would benefit from the proposed new minimum wage. In fact, only 25.6% of the 12,260,000 minimum-wage workers in 1993 were teenagers, suggesting that many minimum-wage workers have economic responsibilities. Although the majority work part-time (less than 35 hours weekly), 47.2% in 1993 worked full-time. While minorities are disproportionately represented among minimum-wage workers, in 1993 more than two-thirds

TABLE 3.43

Characteristics of Minimum-Wage and Other Wage Earners, 1993

Characteristic	Workers Affected by New Minimum* ($4.25-$5.14)	Other Low-Wage Workers ($5.15-$6.14)	Workers Above Minimum Wage ($6.15+)	All Workers
Average Wage	$4.46	$5.71	$13.73	$11.66
Employment (000)	12,260	8,933	80,320	104,681
Share of Total	11.7%	8.5%	76.7%	100.0%
Demographics				
Male	42.1%	42.5%	55.2%	52.1%
Female	57.9	57.5	44.8	47.9
White	68.2%	70.0%	80.0%	77.6%
Male	27.3	27.8	44.2	40.3
Female	40.9	42.2	35.8	37.3
Black	15.0	14.6	9.9	11.0
Male	6.3	6.4	5.0	5.3
Female	8.7	8.2	4.9	5.7
Hispanic	13.8	12.1	6.8	8.1
Male	7.3	6.9	4.2	4.8
Female	6.5	5.2	2.6	3.3
Total	100.0%	100.0%	100.0%	100.0%
Teens (16-19)	25.6	9.7	1.0	5.1
Work Hours				
Full-Time (35+)	47.2%	67.6%	89.1%	81.2%
Part-Time				
20-34 hours	33.3	22.7	7.8	12.8
1-19 hours	19.4	9.6	3.1	6.0
Total	100.0%	100.0%	100.0%	100.0%
Avg. Weekly Hours	30.0 hrs.	35.1 hrs.	40.3 hrs.	38.5 hrs.
Industry				
Manufacturing	9.8%	14.3%	20.0%	17.9%
Retail Trade	44.3	31.1	10.5	17.0

* Minimum wage will increase to $5.15 in 1997.
** Numbers presented do not sum to 100 because some ethnic minorities are excluded.

Source: Mishel, Bernstein, and Rasell (1995).

were white. These workers also tend to be women (57.9% of the total). Table 3.43 also shows that minimum wage and "other" low-wage workers are heavily concentrated in the retail trade industry but are underrepresented in manufacturing industries.

An analysis of just those earning between the old and the new minimum wage would be too narrow, however, since a higher minimum wage affects workers who earn more than but close to the minimum—they receive increases when the minimum wage rises. For these reasons, **Table 3.44** also presents the demographic breakdown of those workers who, in 1993, earned within a dollar of the new minimum-wage level ($5.15-$6.14), a group labeled "other low-wage workers." This more broadly defined minimum-wage workforce includes an additional 8,933,000 workers, or an additional 8.5% of the total workforce. Thus, any significant change in the minimum wage would affect a substantial group, amounting to nearly 20% of the workforce. The demographic breakdown of "other low-wage workers" is more inclusive of full-time and adult workers but has a similar gender and racial distribution as the group of directly affected minimum-wage earners.

Table 3.44 examines the extent to which a minimum-wage increase will affect wage differentials (i.e., the magnitude of the wage gap between highly paid workers and low-wage workers, or between more-educated and less-educated workers) and will reverse the growth in wage inequality since 1979. Two levels of a new minimum-wage increase are considered—the most recent increase to $5.15 and the level needed to restore the minimum to the purchasing power it had in 1979, or $5.97 (in 1995 dollars). More specifically, the analysis examines the impact of the minimum wage in terms of the growth of the wage gaps between high-wage (the 90th-percentile wage) and middle-wage (the 50th-percentile wage) earners and low-wage earners (at the 10th percentile). The wage gap between those with a college education and both high school graduates and those without a high school degree is also considered.

It is important to realize that the pay level of 10th-percentile earners relative to what was earned in 1979 has been essentially determined by the decline in the value of the minimum wage. In 1979, for instance, the wage earned by the 10th-percentile woman worker was $5.82, almost exactly the value of the minimum (note that not all workers are covered by the minimum wage). In contrast, the 10th-percentile women's wage in 1993 of $4.94 was roughly one dollar below the minimum wage's inflation-adjusted value in 1979. Clearly, many low-wage women in 1993 were earning wages that would have been illegal in 1979. It should not be surprising, therefore, to find that the growth of the 50/10 wage

TABLE 3.44

Impact of New Minimum Wage
on Key Wage Differentials, 1993

(1995 Dollars)

	Actual Increase in Differential, 1979-93*	Decline in Differential Due to Minimum-Wage Increase*	
		Increase to $5.15, Direct Impact**	Restore 1979 Value ($5.97), Direct Impact**
Women			
90/10	34.6%pts.	13.5% pts.	22.9% pts.
50/10	21.7	13.5	22.9
College/High School	16.9	0.7	1.7
College/Less Than High School	26.7	3.2	6.2
Men			
90/10	24.9% pts.	3.0% pts.	12.4% pts.
50/10	7.8	2.9	12.4
College/High School	15.6	0.3	0.7
College/Less Than High School	26.6	1.5	3.2

*   Differentials measured in logs of nominal dollar ratios.
** Direct impact is raising the wage of those between the old and the new minimum to the new minimum (either $5.15 or $5.97).

Source: Mishel, Bernstein, and Rasell (1995).

gap (in the context of only moderate wage growth at the 50th percentile) among women has been totally determined by a fall in the minimum wage (22.9 of the 21.7 percentage-point change). The reduction in the minimum wage also had a substantial impact on the wage gap between college-educated women and those with less than a high school degree (6.2 of the 26.7 percentage-point change).

The minimum wage's decline had a lesser impact on low-wage men because low-wage men in 1979 were earning significantly above the minimum ($6.71 versus $5.97) and were earning $5.44 in 1993. It appears that the wage floor matters much more to working women. The 50/10 differential fell much less among men than women over the 1979-93 period (7.8 versus 21.7), but there would have been no growth at all in the 50/10 wage gap among men had there not been a reduction in the minimum wage.

If the 1997 increase in the minimum wage to $5.15 had taken affect in 1993, there would have been a significant closing of the 50/10 wage differentials among men and women, but not by nearly as much as if the 1979 minimum had been restored.

Because there is substantial evidence (with some controversy, of course) that a moderately higher minimum wage does not significantly lower employment (or reduce it at all), there has been an increased focus on who benefits from a higher minimum wage. In other words, because a higher minimum may not have much of an effect on efficiency or output, the merit of such a policy will depend greatly on its fairness or, in other words, who benefits.

Table 3.45 categorizes families by their annual income and locates where minimum-wage earners fall in the income distribution of working families. These data show that minimum-wage earners are concentrated in the bottom segments of the income distribution: 39.6% are in the poorest fifth of families (those with annual incomes less than $22,000 in 1993). Moreover, 71.3% of minimum-wage earners are in families with below-average incomes. A higher minimum wage will also benefit many working families in the middle class, since 32.8% of minimum-wage earners are in families with annual incomes ranging from $22,000 to $48,937.

The data in Table 3.45 also show that minimum-wage earners provide a non-trivial share of their families' economic resources. For instance, workers who will be affected by the latest increase to $5.15 provide nearly half (48.6%) of their family's total earnings and 37.2% of their family's annual income. That minimum-wage earners provide an important component of their family's economic well-being is not surprising since they work, on average, 40 weeks during a year, with about half (52.4%) working the full year.

Table 3.46 presents a further breakdown of minimum-wage earners to assess how many are teens in upper-income families. As we have seen, teens make up only a small proportion—25.4%—of all minimum-wage earners, and many of them come from families with modest incomes. In fact, only 11.7% of minimum-wage earners are teens in families with above-average incomes (those above $47,507). In contrast, 57.6% of minimum-wage earners are adults in families with below-average incomes.

Figure 3Q presents the "bottom line" computation of which families benefit from a higher minimum wage. This is done by calculating the potential annual gain to each worker based on the amount of his or her wage increase (i.e.,

TABLE 3.45

Distribution of Minimum-Wage and Other Earners by Family Income Fifth, 1993

(1993 Dollars)

Characteristic	Income Range	Workers Affected by Increase to $5.15	Workers Above Minimum Wage
Income Fifth*			
Bottom Fifth	Less than $22,000	39.6%	16.9%
Second Fifth	$22,001-34-265	18.0	19.3
Middle Fifth	$34,266-48,937	14.8	20.5
Fourth Fifth	$48,938-68,390	14.6	20.5
Upper Fifth	$68,391 and Above	13.1	22.8
Total		100.0%	100.0%
Percent Below:			
Median Family Income		56.1%	46.2%
Average Family Income		71.3	54.7
Work Time			
Weeks Worked		40.0 wks	48.6 wks
Percent Working Full Year		52.4%	81.9%
Earner's Share of Family:			
Annual Earnings		48.6%	67.9%
Annual Income**		37.2	60.7

* Sample limited to working families (i.e., families with at least one earner).
** Includes earnings plus government assistance, interest, dividends, etc.

Source: Mishel, Bernstein, and Rasell (1995).

---

based on the distance to the new minimum) and annual hours worked. Given this information, it is possible to calculate the share of the aggregate wage gain generated from the higher minimum wage that accrues to each family income fifth. As shown in Figure 3Q, 40.9% of the gains generated by a higher minimum wage would be received by the poorest 20% of families; 61.1% of the gains would be received by the poorest 40% of families. In all, 76% of the benefits of a higher minimum wage would go to families with below-average incomes (not shown).

TABLE 3.46

Distribution of Minimum-Wage Earners by Age and Income Fifth, 1993

Family Income Fifth*	Age 16-19	Age 20 or Above	Total
Bottom Fifth	5.4%	34.2%	39.6%
Second Fifth	3.8	14.1	18.0
Middle Fifth	4.6	10.2	14.8
Fourth Fifth	5.5	9.1	14.6
Upper Fifth	6.1	7.0	13.1
Total	25.4%	74.6%	100.0%
Percent:			
Above Median Family Income	13.8%	21.1%	34.9%
Above Average Family Income	11.7	17.0	28.7
Below Median Family Income	11.6	53.5	65.1
Below Average Family Income	13.7	57.6	71.3

* Sample limited to working families (i.e., families with at least one earner).

Source: Mishel, Bernstein, and Rasell (1995).

FIGURE 3Q

Distribution of Minimum-Wage Gains and Income Shares, by Fifth, 1993

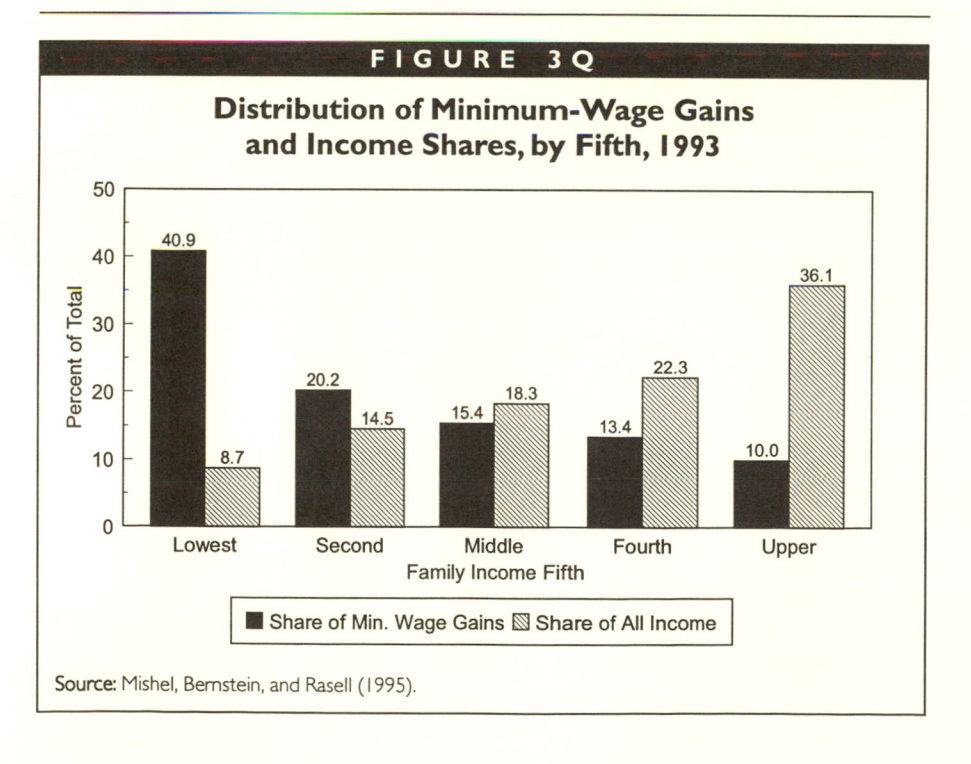

Source: Mishel, Bernstein, and Rasell (1995).

The minimum wage generates the most help to those with the least income and the least help to those with the most income. For instance, as Figure 3Q also shows, the poorest fifth of working families had 8.7% of all income in 1993 but will receive roughly 40% of the gains from the higher minimum wage. In contrast, the best-off families received 36.1% of all income in 1993 but will obtain only 10% of the benefits of the higher minimum wage.

Summarizing the Role of Labor-Market Institutions

The analysis in **Table 3.47**, which examines the impact of changes in labor-market institutions on wage differentials, adds several new dimensions to our discussion. First, it looks at the effect of specific factors on different dimensions of the overall wage structure—the 90/50 and 50/10 differentials. The analysis, therefore, permits a more refined discussion that allows some factors to affect the bottom of the wage structure while other factors might affect the top. Second, the analysis covers several subperiods (1973-79, 1979-88, 1988-92), so one can observe how a factor's impact can shift over time.

Over the 1973-79 period there was a growth in the minimum wage and stability of union representation. The result of the strong minimum wage was a sizable lowering of the 50/10 differential among women (4.6 percentage points) and a slight lowering of the wage gap at the bottom among men (0.3 percentage points). Changes in unionism in this period were equalizing among men but disequalizing among women.

The results for the 1979-88 period make clear that deunionization was an important factor in the growth of male wage inequality at the top, contributing 4.0 of the 11.9-percentage-point growth in the 90/50 differential. The reduction of the minimum wage over the 1979-88 period, on the other hand, generated 15.0 of the 24.3-percentage-point growth in the 50/10 differential among women and a large part (5.0) of the 7.6-percentage-point growth in the male 50/10 differential. Thus, a lower minimum wage was a major factor in lowering the wages of low-wage men and women relative to the median. Deunionization, in contrast, primarily allowed high-wage men to fare better than middle-wage men.

In the 1988-92 period, a modest rise in the minimum wage tightened the wage structure at the bottom, and continued deunionization helped to widen the male wage structure at the top.

Looking at the 1979-92 period as a whole, deunionization was a major fac-

TABLE 3.47

The Impact of Labor-Market Institutions on Wage Differentials, 1973-92

Period	Men 90/10	90/50	50/10	Women 90/10	90/50	50/10
1973-79						
Total Change	-0.4	-1.8	1.5	-1.7	-1.6	-0.1
Minimum Wage	-0.2	0.1	-0.3	-4.4	0.3	-4.6
Unions	-0.9	-1.0	0.2	0.7	0.1	-0.5
1979-88						
Total Change	19.5	11.9	7.6	32.8	8.5	24.3
Minimum Wage	4.9	0.0	5.0	14.8	-0.2	15.0
Unions	2.1	4.0	-1.9	0.4	1.4	-1.0
1988-92						
Total Change	2.0	2.5	-0.5	1.9	3.7	-1.9
Minimum Wage	-0.1	0.0	-0.1	-0.4	-0.1	-0.3
Unions	0.9	1.0	-0.1	0.2	0.2	0.0
Contribution to Growing Wage Inequality **1979-92**						
Total	100%	100%	100%	100%	100%	100%
Minimum Wage	22	0	69	42	-2	66
Unions	14	35	-28	2	13	-5

Source: Fortin and Lemieux (1996).

tor driving wage inequality at the top of the wage structure, responsible for 5 of the 14.4-percentage-point rise of the 90/50 differential (contributing 35% of the total growth). The erosion of the minimum wage, on the other hand, was the major factor generating women's wage inequality (contributing 66% of the growth), which primarily occurred at the bottom, and the wage gap at the bottom for men (contributing 69% of the growth). Together, the shifts in labor-market institutions—deunionization and a lower minimum wage—over the 1979-92 period can explain 36% and 44% of the growth of overall wage inequality respectively (the 90/10 differential) among men and women.

Technology's Impact

Technological change can affect the wage structure by displacing some types of workers and by increasing demand for others. Given the seemingly rapid diffusion of microelectronic technologies in recent years, many analysts have considered technological change as a major factor in the recent increase in wage inequality. Unfortunately, because it is difficult to measure the extent of technological change and its overall character (whether it is generally de-skilling or up-skilling and by how much), it is difficult to identify the role of technological change on recent wage trends. More than a few analysts, in fact, have simply assumed that whatever portion of wage inequality is unexplained can be considered to be the consequence of technological change. This type of analysis, however, only puts a name to our ignorance.

It is easy to understand why people might consider technology to be a major factor explaining recent wage and employment trends. We are often told that the pace of change in the workplace is accelerating, and there is a widespread visibility of automation and robotics; computers and microelectronics provide a visible dimension evident in workplaces, such as offices, not usually affected by technology. The economic intuition goes beyond this; research has shown (see Table 3.30, for instance) that the most recent wage inequality and the employment shift to more-educated workers has occurred within industries and has not been caused primarily by shifts across industries (i.e., more service jobs, fewer manufacturing jobs). Research has also shown that technological change has traditionally been associated with an increased demand for more-educated or "skilled" workers. This pattern of change suggests an increase in "skill-biased technological change" driving large changes within industries.

Because wages have risen the most for groups whose supply expanded the fastest (e.g., college graduates), most economists have concluded that nonsupply factors (i.e., shifts in demand or institutional factors) are the driving force behind growing wage inequality. They reason that those groups with the relatively fastest growth in supply would be expected to see their wages depressed relative to other groups unless there were other factors working very strongly in their favor, such as a rapid expansion in demand. Rapid technological change favoring more-educated groups could logically explain demand-side shifts leading to wider wage differences.

There are many reasons to be skeptical of a technology-led increase in demand for "skill" as an explanation for growing wage inequality. First, note that there has been little or no growth in multifactor productivity (a commonly used proxy for technological change) for decades, nor has there been any greater growth in labor productivity in recent years. However, the technology explanation assumes that there was a large technology-led transformation of the workplace that substantially decreased the need for "unskilled" workers and thereby led to a large shift in wage differentials. It is implausible that there has been a technology shock that has transformed workplaces but has not boosted productivity growth.

Second, the experience since the mid- to late 1980s does not accord with a technology explanation, whose imagery is of computer-driven technology bidding up the wages of "more-skilled" and "more-educated" workers, leaving behind a small group of "unskilled" workers with inadequate skills. The facts are hard to reconcile with the notion that technological change grew as fast or faster in the 1990s than in earlier periods. If technology were adverse for "unskilled" or "less-educated" workers, then we would expect a continued expansion of the wage differential between middle-wage and low-wage workers (the 50/10 differential). Yet, the 50/10 differential has been stable or declining among both men and women since 1986 or 1987. Instead, we are seeing the top earners pulling away from nearly all other earners. Therefore, there seem to be factors driving a wedge between the top 10% and everyone else, rather than a single factor aiding the vast majority but leaving a small group of unskilled workers behind. Further confirmation of the breadth of those left behind is that wages have been stable or in decline for the bottom 80% of men and the bottom 70% of women over the 1989-95 period, with wages falling for the entire non-college-educated workforce (roughly 75% of the workforce). Of course, even high-wage, white-collar, or college-graduate men have failed to see real wage growth in 10 years.

The flattening of the growth of education differentials in the late 1980s and 1990s among men also does not easily fit a technology story. Since the wages of college-graduate men are not being "bid up" relative to others at the same pace as in the early and mid-1980s, one can only conclude that there has been a deceleration of the relative demand for education (given that the supply of college workers did not accelerate). This would not be the case if technology was being introduced into workplaces at the same or a faster pace in the late 1980s or in the 1990s. Moreover, the late 1980s to mid-1990s period has been one of continued growth of wage inequality as the top pulls away from the middle and bottom; since this growing gap is not being driven by wider education differentials (the primary mechanism by which technology leads to greater wage inequality), it is hard to believe that technology is playing a major role. As shown earlier, only a small portion of the growth of wage inequality in the 1990s can be attributed to a change in the "returns to skill."

Third, there is no evidence that the growth of wage inequality over the entire 1973-95 period has been primarily driven by changes in the economic return to education or experience, the most easily measured dimensions of skill. Rather, wage inequality has been largely driven by the growth of within-group wage inequality—the growing gap among workers with similar education and experience. The growth of within-group inequality may be related to technological change if it is interpreted as a reflection of growing economic returns to worker skills that are not easily measured (motivation, aptitudes for math, etc). However, there are no signs that the growth of within-group wage inequality has been fastest in those industries where the use of technology grew the most (as discussed below). It is also unclear why the economic returns for measurable skills (e.g., education) and unmeasured skills (e.g., motivation) should not grow in tandem. In fact, between-group and within-group inequality have not moved together in the various subperiods since 1973.

Finally, the notion that technology has been "bidding up" the wages of the "skilled" relative to the "unskilled" does not accord with the basic facts presented earlier. Or, it holds true in a "relative" but not an "absolute" sense. The wages of skilled men, defined as white-collar, college-educated, or 90th-percentile workers, have been flat or declining since the mid-1980s. As described in Chapter 4, white-collar men have increasingly become displaced and beset by employment problems. High-wage women have continued to see their wages grow, but it does not seem likely that technology is primarily affecting skilled women but not skilled men.

The rhetoric in the discussion of technology's role in growing wage inequality presumes that we have entered a new era of technological change, signified by the computer revolution. In this scenario, either the rate of introduction of new technologies or the types of technologies being introduced is creating a new situation in today's workplace, along with an enhanced demand for cognitive skills. Some analysts have explicitly talked in terms of a "technology shock." This widely expressed view assumes an *acceleration* of technology's impact on relative demand, suggesting that one test of the technology hypothesis is whether technology had a greater impact on skill demand in the 1980s or 1990s than in the 1970s or earlier periods.

That a technology explanation requires an acceleration of technology's impact on workplace skills is implicit in the conventional demand-and-supply framework used to explain wage differentials. As discussed earlier, most analysts have concluded that the growth of wage inequality since 1979 must be primarily explained by demand-side factors (or non-supply-side factors, including institutional shifts) rather than supply-side factors (i.e., fewer college graduates). This is why there has been such a focus on trade, industry shifts, and technological change, all factors that could explain shifts in "relative demand." However, it would not make sense to be seeking the source of relative-demand shifts in the 1980s and 1990s if demand trends were essentially the same over the last few decades. Similarly, demand-side shifts seem relevant to explaining a wage inequality originating in the 1980s only if there were something new and different about recent demand trends. In fact, if the relative demand for skill grew at the same pace over the last three decades—at a smooth, secular, or historic rate—then the only factors that could be different in the 1980s and explain growing wage inequality are those affecting the supply of "skills," a context with no possible special role for trade, technology, or other factors shaping relative demand.

Commonly accepted evaluations of wage trends also suggest that there was a demand-side acceleration in the 1980s. One can potentially find a demand-side acceleration through an examination of either between-group or within-group wage-inequality trends. That is, one can find demand-side acceleration in the "relative demand for education" or the demand for skills as reflected in within-group wage inequality. **Table 3.48** presents the possible combinations of trends, with an evaluation of each demand trend as either "accelerated" or "historic," the latter meaning a smooth, constant, or secular growth. The point is that in three of the four scenarios there is an implicit acceptance of demand-side acceleration. In the remaining scenario, number four, the demands for skill or education grew at the "historic" rate, leaving supply-side factors as the force driving wage inequality. Thus, technology, a demand-side factor, can only be a cause of growing wage inequality if one of the first three scenarios holds and technology is the source of the acceleration. Again, a technology explanation makes sense only if there is a greater growth in the demand for skills in the 1980s and 1990s than in earlier periods and if these demand-side changes can be attributed to technological change. This motivates our efforts to test for an acceleration of technology's impact on the use of "more-educated" and "higher-paid" workers.

It is also useful to distinguish between the role of technology in the growth of wage inequality and the issue of "skill complementarity," the concept that there is a positive relationship between capital (e.g., computers) and worker skill. The existence of skill complementarity is one of the main explanations of the growing need for workers with more education and skills—as investment or capital per worker has grown, the need for more skills has grown commensurately. The explanation of growing wage inequality, on the other hand, requires an analysis

TABLE 3.48

Possible Empirical Scenarios and Demand Acceleration

| | Growth in 1980s Relative to 1970s | | |
Scenario	Relative Demand for Education	Within-Group Wage Inequality	Was There Demand Side Acceleration?
1.	Accelerated	Accelerated	Yes
2.	Normal	Accelerated	Yes
3.	Accelerated	Normal	Yes
4.	Normal	Normal	No

Source: Mishel and Bernstein (1996).

that separates out the *growth* of the relative supply and demand for education/ skill. To show that relative demand for skill is accelerating (as is necessary, as argued above), it is not enough to simply cite the existence of skill complementarities, since such complementarities have long been associated with the need for greater skills and education. That is, technological change has been a force for increasing employers' demand for "more-skilled" and "more-educated" workers for a long time. The issue regarding wage inequality is whether technological change has increased "demand for skill" faster than the "supply of skill" has been growing.

We do not question that technological change and capital accumulation have been historically associated with the need for greater skills and education. Technology and investment have been major forces driving the long-term growth of demands for skill.

But, is there reason to believe that technology's impact accelerated in the 1980s or 1990s? Technological change is inherently difficult to quantify. The approach taken here is to examine the "impact of technological change," a concept with two components. The first is a set of "technology indicators," such as equipment accumulation and R&D, that are closely correlated with or accompany the introduction of new technology in the workplace. The second component is the relationship, or "complementarity," between technology and the need for more skill or education. Technology will have a greater impact the faster the introduction of new technologies, proxied by "technology indicators," and the more that skills are required by the new technologies, as reflected in estimated "complementarities."

Table 3.49 presents some indicators of technological change. Two measures of productivity growth are presented, since technology is considered to be a major factor behind productivity growth. Neither the measure of labor productivity (changes in output per hour worked) nor that for multifactor productivity (the growth in output after netting out the contribution of more hours, more capital, and a higher-quality workforce) grew faster in the 1980s or 1990s than in the 1970s.

Capital accumulation, or increased investment per worker, is often considered to be the main mechanism through which technology is brought into the workplace—as employers upgrade their equipment or build new facilities, they frequently incorporate technological advances and new work systems. Yet the growth of equipment per worker was actually slower in the 1980s than in the

TABLE 3.49

Technology Indicators, 1973-94

| | Annual Growth | | |
	1973-79	1979-89	1989-94
R&D			
Total R&D Capital Stock/Worker	-0.01%	0.85%	n.a.
Share of Scientists/Engineers*	0.64	0.44	0.81%
Investment**			
Equipment per Worker	3.57%	2.53%	0.48%
Computer Equipment per Worker	24.05	25.71	12.06
Productivity***			
Labor	1.0%	1.0%	1.1%
Multifactor	0.3	0.0	0.1

*   In private sector. Annualized percentage-point change.
**   Per private-sector FTE.
*** Private nonfarm business sector. The last period is 1989-93.

Source: Mishel and Bernstein (1996).

1970s, suggesting a possible deceleration of technological change. Equipment accumulation slowed nearly to a halt (0.48% per year) in the 1990s. However, there was an acceleration in investment per worker in computerized equipment in the 1980s, but a slowdown in the 1990s. If computerized equipment has a greater effect on the employment structure than other types of equipment (i.e., stronger complementarities), then a shift in the composition of equipment toward computerization could potentially have created a technology shock in the 1980s. Whether investment trends have led to an accelerated technology impact depends, therefore, on whether computerized equipment had a larger impact than other types of equipment investment in the 1980s or 1990s.

Last, aggregate research and development (R&D) activity grew faster in the 1980s than in the 1970s in one measure (R&D capital stock per worker). The trend in the growth in the share of scientists and engineers in total employment slowed in the 1980s but accelerated in the 1990s. Thus, R&D trends, like those for investment, present a mix of evidence, some pointing to a possible acceleration and some to deceleration. Whether technological change had a greater impact on the demand for skills in the 1980s and 1990s relative to the 1970s will thus depend heavily on whether there was a shift in "complementarities," the second component.

Table 3.50 presents quantitative estimates of the impact of technological change on the rate at which there were within-industry shifts toward the use of more-educated workers (i.e., the effect of technology on relative demand within industries). These estimates combine the effect of changes in both components of "technology's impact"—changes in the rate of introduction of new technology and changes in the relationship of new technology to skill requirements. The study from which these data are drawn determined that computerized equipment had no different effect than other types of equipment. Thus, a changing composition of capital investment (proportionately more computers but less of other equipment) did not create a 1980s or 1990s technology shock. The study, therefore, estimated the effect of R&D activity and equipment accumulation on educational upgrading in each period, allowing the per-dollar impact (the complementarity) to vary in each decade. The estimated "impact of technology" reflects new investment, R&D innovations, and any associated technical, work organization, or work-process changes. Estimates are also presented that allow for a possible impact of the shift toward more computerized equipment.

Specifically, Table 3.50 presents the estimated impact of technology on the growth in the shares of workers with particular levels of education in three periods, 1973-79, 1979-89, and 1989-94. Estimates are also presented in the differences in technology's impact across time periods. The critical issue to be addressed is whether technology's impact was greater in the 1980s or 1990s than in the 1970s.

The data in Table 3.50 suggest that technology did not have a greater impact in more recent years. This can be seen in the results for the share of workers with a high school degree in the first column. Technology's impact has been to reduce the share of male workers with a high school degree in each time period, but more strongly so in the 1970s than in the later periods. Over the 10 years from 1979 to 1989, technology led to a 1.21-percentage-point (.121 per year) shrinkage in the share of high school workers employed within industries. This technology impact was significantly lower than that found for the 1973-79 period (a 0.378-percentage-point shrinkage per year). Technology's impact on male high school graduates not only did not accelerate in the 1980s, but actually decelerated. Comparable results are seen for the impact of technology on the use of male college graduates: technology is associated with increased male "college or more" employment in each period, but more so in the 1970s than in later periods. For men, there is no evidence of an "acceleration" of technology's impact and some evidence for deceleration.

There is some support for an acceleration of technological change among women. Technology's impact on the employment of high school graduates was negative in the 1980s and 1990s but positive in the 1970s. Similarly, the impact on the use of women with a "college degree or more" grew in each period. Nevertheless, the shift in technology's impact between the 1970s and later periods generally does not pass a statistical test for significance (see the last two panels). Moreover, the size of the acceleration was small at best. In the case of high school "equivalents," for instance, the acceleration between the 1970s and 1980s implies a demand shift away from them, amounting to about half of a percentage point less over a 10-year period.

These estimates of technology's impact address the issue of the acceleration of demand for education and thus relate to the growth of education wage differentials. As previously discussed, however, changes in education differentials can account for just a third of the growth of overall wage inequality, the other portion being the growth of within-group inequality. The results in **Table 3.51** relate to the broadest measure of technology's impact—its effect on the use of workers with high, middle, or low wages (divided into five different categories). These estimates incorporate the impact of technology on both education differentials and within-group inequality.

The results for men run counter to the notion that technology was more ad-

TABLE 3.50

Technology Impact on Annual Growth in Education Shares, 1973-94

| | Technology Impact* | | | |
| | Men | | Women | |
Dependent Variable	Without Computers	With Computers	Without Computers	With Computers
% Less Than High School				
1. 1973-79	0.097	-0.066	-0.182	-0.443
2. 1979-89	-0.015	0.055	0.040	0.071
3. 1989-94	0.131**	-0.055	0.029	0.488
4. 80s Less 70s	-0.112	0.121	0.022***	0.514
5. 90s Less 70s	0.035	0.011	0.211***	-0.045
6. 90s Less 80s	0.147***	-0.109	-0.011	-0.559
% High School				
1. 1973-79	-0.378**	-0.291	0.117	0.507
2. 1979-89	-0.121**	-0.599***	-0.216***	-0.264
3. 1989-94	-0.163**	0.298	-0.014	0.512
4. 80s Less 70s	0.257***	-0.308	-0.333***	-0.770
5. 90s Less 70s	0.214***	0.589**	-0.131	0.006
6. 90s Less 80s	-0.043	0.897**	0.202	0.776
% Some College				
1. 1973-79	0.039	0.180	0.020	-0.014
2. 1979-89	0.010	0.392	0.090	0.387
3. 1989-94	-0.092**	0.202	-0.155**	0.177
4. 80s Less 70s	-0.029	0.212	0.070	0.401
5. 90s Less 70s	-0.132	0.021	-0.175***	-0.163
6. 90s Less 80s	-0.103***	-0.191	-0.245**	-0.564
% College Only				
1. 1973-79	0.142	-0.005	0.143**	0.082
2. 1979-89	0.069***	0.088	0.097***	0.059
3. 1989-94	0.044	-0.407**	0.048	-0.123
4. 80s Less 70s	-0.073	0.092	-0.046	-0.023
5. 90s Less 70s	-0.099	-0.403***	-0.095	-0.205
6. 90s Less 80s	-0.026	-0.495***	0.049	-0.181
% College or More				
1. 1973-79	0.241**	0.177	0.045	-0.050
2. 1979-89	0.126**	0.152	0.086	-0.194
3. 1989-94	0.125**	-0.444**	0.140***	0.154
4. 80s Less 70s	-0.116	-0.024	0.041	-0.144
5. 90s Less 80s	-0.117	-0.621**	0.095	0.203
6. 90s Less 80s	-0.001	-0.597***	0.054	0.348

TABLE 3.50 *(cont.)*

Technology Impact on Annual Growth in Education Shares, 1973-94

| | Technology Impact* | | | |
| | Men | | Women | |
Dependent Variable	Without Computers	With Computers	Without Computers	With Computers
% High School Equivalent				
1. 1973-79	-0.254**	-0.239***	-0.061	0.030
2. 1979-89	-0.130**	-0.275	-0.114***	0.079
3. 1989-94	-0.091**	0.371**	-0.091**	-0.133
4. 80s Less 70s	0.124	-0.035	-0.054	0.049
5. 90s Less 70s	0.162	0.610**	-0.030	-0.163
6. 90s Less 80s	0.039	0.645**	0.024	0.212

* The impact of technology indicators on the annual rate of growth of educational upgrading within industries. Technology represented by the impact of R&D and equipment accumulation per worker in all estimates. Computer accumulation added for the second specification.

** Significantly different from zero at 5% level of confidence.

*** Significantly different from zero at 10% level of confidence.

Source: Mishel and Bernstein (1996).

---

verse for low-wage workers in recent years and more favorable for high-wage workers. In fact, technological change was less favorable for men in the upper half of the wage distribution (the top three groups) in the 1980s and 1990s than in the 1970s. There was an especially large, and statistically significant, decline in technology's impact on the usage of "high-wage" men. For instance, technology led to a 0.481-percentage-point growth (per year) in the use of high-wage men in the 1970s, but only a 0.109 growth in the 1979-89 period, a deceleration that led to a 3.72-percentage-point (-.372 times 10) reduction in the employment of high-wage men by 1989 relative to the trend for the 1970s. Overall, the results for men do not support the conventional story—technology shifts being favorable for high-wage groups but unfavorable for the bottom 75%. Rather, technology became more favorable to the bottom half and less favorable to the top half.

TABLE 3.51

Technology Impact on Annual Change in Wage Quantities, 1973-94

| | Technology Impact* | | | |
| | Men | | Women | |
Dependent Variable	Without Computers	With Computers	Without Computers	With Computers
Low Wage				
1. 1973-79	-0.123	-0.066	0.283**	0.101**
2. 1979-89	-0.026	0.503	-0.006	0.621***
3. 1989-94	-0.126**	0.429	-0.034	0.071**
4. 80s Less 70s	0.097	0.569	-0.289***	0.520
5. 90s Less 70s	-0.003	0.495	-0.317**	-0.029
6. 90s Less 80s	0.101	-0.073	-0.028	-0.550
Low-Middle Wage				
1. 1973-79	-0.684	-0.734**	-0.412**	-0.354
2. 1979-89	-0.060	-0.472	0.008	-0.169
3. 1989-94	0.023	0.151	-0.003	-0.200
4. 80s Less 70s	0.624**	0.262	0.403**	0.186
5. 90s Less 70s	0.708**	0.885	0.408**	0.154
6. 90s Less 80s	0.084	0.623	0.005	-0.031
Upper-Middle Wage				
1. 1973-79	0.027	0.228	-0.411**	-0.717***
2. 1979-89	-0.163**	-0.046	-0.133	0.013
3. 1989-94	-0.004	-0.536	0.062	0.372
4. 80s Less 70s	-0.189	-0.274	0.278**	0.730***
5. 90s Less 70s	-0.031	-0.764**	0.472**	1.088**
6. 90s Less 80s	0.159**	-0.490	0.194	.358
High Wage				
1. 1973-79	0.481**	0.259	0.209**	0.652**
2. 1979-89	0.109***	0.016	-0.023	-0.053
3. 1989-94	0.096	0.127	-0.031	-0.037
4. 80s Less 70s	-0.372**	-0.242	-0.232***	-0.706**
5. 90s Less 70s	-0.384**	-0.132	-0.240**	-0.689**
6. 90s Less 80s	-0.012	0.111	-0.008	0.017

TABLE 3.51 *(cont.)*

Technology Impact on Annual Change in Wage Quantities, 1973-94

| | Technology Impact* | | | |
| | Men | | Women | |
Dependent Variable	Without Computers	With Computers	Without Computers	With Computers
Very High Wage				
1. 1973-79	0.300**	0.312**	0.330**	0.319
2. 1979-89	0.140**	-0.001	0.170**	-0.412
3. 1989-94	0.011	-0.171	0.007	-0.206
4. 80s Less 70s	-0.160***	-0.313	-0.159	-0.730***
5. 90s Less 80s	-0.289**	-0.484**	-0.323**	-0.525
6. 90s Less 80s	-0.129**	-0.171	-0.164	.206

* The impact of technology indicators on the annual rate of growth of education upgrading within industries. Technology represented by the impact of R&D and equipment accumulation per worker in all estimates. Computer accumulation added for the second specification.

** Significantly different from zero at 5% level of confidence.

*** Significantly different from zero at 10% level of confidence.

Source: Mishel and Bernstein (1996).

Among women, technology shifted against the highest wage groups (the "high" and "very-high" groups) and the low-wage group but favored the employment of middle-wage women. The "strengthening of the middle" phenomenon among women again contradicts the story that technology has been helping the "skilled" relative to the "unskilled," unless one's view of the "unskilled" includes only the lowest-wage women (about 20% of the total).

These estimates of technology's impact on the use of more-educated or higher-wage workers do not support a technology explanation for growing wage inequality. The primary mechanism by which technology is thought to affect wage inequality is increasing the demand for "more-educated" workers (i.e., college graduates) and thereby bidding up their wages as demand exceeds supply. Our estimates, however, suggest there was no technology-led acceleration of demand for educated workers (or a quantitatively trivial acceleration in the case of women) in the 1980s or 1990s that could have led to increased education wage differentials. Further, when looking at the increased use of high-wage workers (presumably "high-skilled"), we find that technology was less favorable to the increased utilization of high-wage men or women after 1979. Among women, technology may have played a role in creating wage inequality at the bottom, since technology had an adverse impact on very low-wage women. However, technology was a force for compressing rather than expanding the wage gap between the top and the middle among women. Among men, technology's impact was equalizing at both the top and the bottom of the distribution after 1979 and, therefore, technological change is not a plausible explanation for the widening of the male wage structure.

Executive Pay Soars

Another cause of greater wage inequality has been the enormous pay increases received by top executives and the spillover effects of these increases. These large pay raises go far beyond those received by other white-collar workers.

The 1980s and 1990s have been prosperous times for top U.S. executives. In stark contrast to the declining real wages of typical workers, the total pay (salaries, bonuses, and benefits) of the chief executive officers (CEOs) of major U.S. companies grew 5.7% annually from 1978 to 1989, a total growth of 83.2% **(Table 3.52)**.

In the 1989-95 period, CEO total pay grew 5.4% annually. CEO salaries were stable: the pay raises were the result of large increases in bonuses, stock options, and other forms of compensation. Between 1978 and 1995, the total pay of the average CEO at a major U.S. company grew 152%, from $1,736,000 to $4,367,000 (in 1995 dollars).

The increased divergence between the growth of CEO pay and an average worker's pay is captured in the growth of the ratio of CEO to worker pay, shown in Table 3.52. In 1978, U.S. CEOs in major companies earned 60.2 times more than an average worker; this ratio grew to 172.5 by 1995. This contrasts even more sharply with the 39.5 ratio prevailing in 1965 (See **Figure 3R**).

U.S. executives are not only paid far better than U.S. workers, they also earn substantially more than CEOs in other advanced countries. **Table 3.53** presents an index of CEO pay, with U.S. compensation set to 100 (any index value less than 100 implies that that country's CEOs earn less than U.S. CEOs). The index shows that U.S. CEOs earn double the average of the 13 other advanced coun-

TABLE 3.52

Growth of CEO Pay in Major U.S. Companies, 1965-95

(1995 Dollars)

Year	CEO Pay		Ratio of CEO to Worker Pay	
	Total* ($000)	Salary ($000)	Total	Salary
1965	$971	$615	39.5	27.8
1968	1,209	558	48.3	24.8
1973	1,269	655	44.8	26.9
1978	1,736	695	60.2	29.1
1989	3,180	998	122.0	46.7
1995	4,367	991	172.5	48.2
Annual Growth				
1965-73	3.4%	0.8%		
1973-78	6.5	1.2		
1978-89	5.7	3.3		
1989-95	5.4	-0.1		

* Includes salaries, bonuses, value of restricted stock, stock options at time of grant, plus other long-term payouts.

Source: *Wall Street Journal* and Pearl Meyer & Partners Inc.

FIGURE 3R

Ratio of CEO to Average Worker Pay, 1965-95

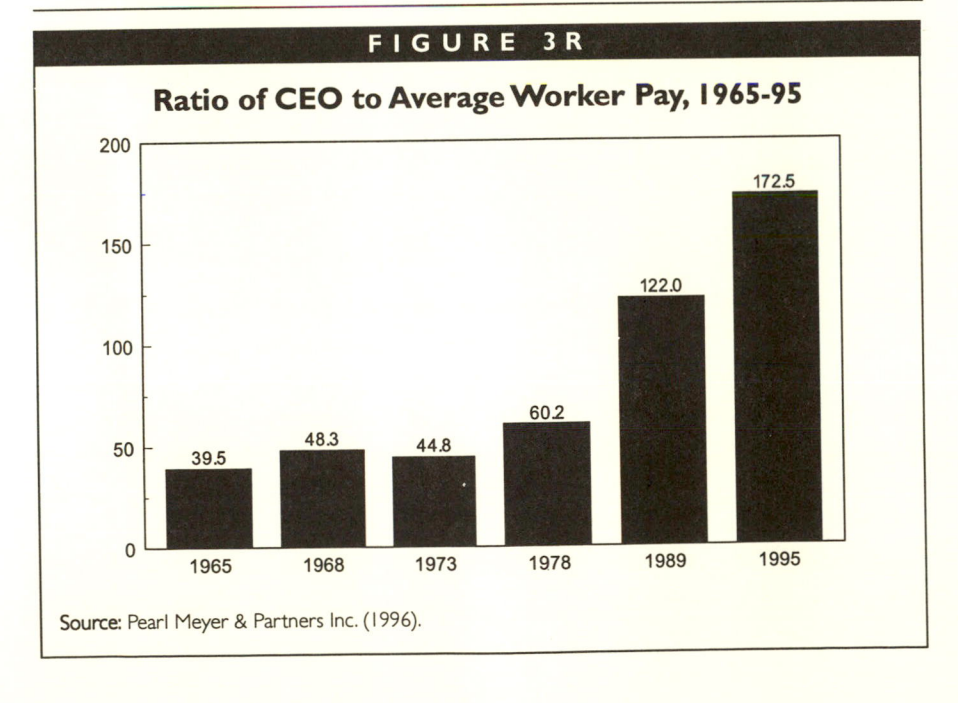

Source: Pearl Meyer & Partners Inc. (1996).

TABLE 3.53

CEO Pay in Advanced Countries, 1994

Country	CEO Compensation ($000)	U.S. Pay Relative to Foreign Pay U.S.=100		Ratio of CEO to Worker Pay
		CEO	Worker	
Australia	$377.3	40.7	79.7	13.8
Belgium	554.7	59.8	134.3	12.1
Canada	399.3	43.0	91.7	12.7
France	600.1	64.7	99.6	17.6
Germany	512.7	55.2	159.7	9.4
Italy	421.8	45.5	94.5	13.1
Japan	558.5	60.2	125.3	13.0
Netherlands	458.0	49.4	122.3	11.0
New Zealand	163.0	17.6	52.2	9.1
Spain	415.9	44.8	67.0	18.2
Sweden	297.6	32.1	110.0	7.9
Switzerland	572.4	61.7	145.2	11.5
United Kingdom	483.8	52.1	79.6	17.8
United States	927.9	100.0	100.0	27.1
Non-U.S. Average	$447.3	48.2	104.7	12.9

Source: Towers Perrin (1995) and BLS.

tries for which there are comparable data (see the non-U.S. average of 48.2). In fact, there is no country listed whose CEOs are paid even as much as two-thirds that of U.S. CEOs. This international pattern does not hold true for the pay of manufacturing workers, for whom an index is also presented in Table 3.53. Workers in other advanced countries earn, on average, more than that of U.S. workers (the non-U.S. average index value of 104.7), with workers in 10 of the 13 countries earning at least 90% of what U.S. workers earn. Not surprisingly, the ratio of CEO to worker pay is far larger in the United States than in other countries, 27.1 versus 12.9.

Race, Academic Achievement, and Wages

Another dimension of wage inequality that has expanded since 1979 is the gap between black and white workers. The growth in the racial wage gap is surprising since there has been a substantial increase in the academic achievement of black workers, both in absolute terms and relative to white workers.

Table 3.54 examines the educational attainment (years of schooling or degree attained) of both white and black workers by gender. The analysis is limited to 25- to 34-year-olds in order to focus on the achievements of new workers (presuming that this age group has attained most of the schooling it will ever attain). In the early 1970s, there were large differences in educational attainment

---

TABLE 3.54

Changes in Educational Attainment
Among 25- to 34-Year-Olds by Race and Gender, 1973-95

Race/ Gender	Share of Employed with:				
	Less Than High School	High School	Some College	College or More	Total
White Men					
1973-74*	16.4%	39.1%	19.6%	24.9%	100.0%
1995	6.7	34.1	28.2	31.1	100.0
1973-95	-9.7	-5.1	8.5	6.2	
Black Men					
1973-74*	32.0%	43.7%	15.3%	9.0%	100.0%
1995	7.8	43.3	31.7	17.2	100.0
1973-95	-24.2	-0.4	16.4	8.2	
White Women					
1973-74*	14.0%	47.0%	16.5%	22.5%	100.0%
1995	4.3	30.5	31.8	33.5	100.0
1973-95	-9.7	-16.6	15.3	11.0	
Black Women					
1973-74*	27.6%	43.5%	15.7%	13.2%	100.0%
1995	6.5	35.3	39.0	19.2	100.0
1973-95	-21.1	-8.2	23.3	6.0	

* Average for 1973 and 1974.

Source: Authors' analysis, update of Bernstein (1995).

---

between young whites and blacks. For instance, nearly a third (32%) of black men had not attained a high school degree, compared to only 16% of white men. Meanwhile, a fourth (24.9%) of white men had a four-year college education or more, but only 9% of black men were in this education group. There was a similarly large education gap between white and black women workers in the early 1970s.

The educational attainment of young workers, both black and white, was far higher in 1995 than in the 1973-74 period. The growth of schooling was so great among blacks that the racial education gap narrowed substantially. By 1995, only a small percentage of any race/gender group had not achieved at least a high school education. There was a larger growth among black men than white men of those with a college or "some college" education, though the college education gap (31.1% versus 17.2%) is still sizable. Among women, there was a stronger shift toward a college education among whites than blacks, but nearly 60% of young black women in 1995 had at least "some college."

The academic catch-up of blacks took place in test scores as well as in years of schooling. **Table 3.55** presents test scores of white and black students (17-year-olds) from the mid-1970s to 1990 by geographic area and in different subjects. White test scores remained stable over the period in every subject and geographic area. In contrast, black students were testing significantly higher in mathematics and reading and somewhat higher in science. This improvement in black test scores took place among urban (i.e., metro area) as well as nonurban blacks. The growth in black test scores closed roughly 40% of the racial test score gap in math and reading over this period. The data discussed so far, therefore, indicate that both the quantity (educational attainment) and quality (test scores) of young black workers' education improved substantially over the last two decades and improved relative to whites.

Given this catch-up and improvement in black academic achievement, it might have been expected that the racial wage gap would have closed somewhat. As **Table 3.56** shows, however, wages for blacks have fallen relative to whites since 1979 and especially over the 1979-89 period. Among young men, for instance, black wages were 83.7% that of white wages in 1979, but fell to 75.5% in 1989 before rising to 77.5% in 1995. Among young women, black wages were nearly comparable to white wages in 1979 (a 95.3% ratio) but had fallen to just 83.9% of white wages by 1995.

The overall racial wage gap has not closed because the racial wage gaps within each education group have been expanding. For instance, black male college graduates earned 92.8% of that of whites in 1973, but only 87.1% as much in 1995. Among women college graduates, there was racial parity in 1979

TABLE 3.55

National Assessment of Educational Progress (NAEP) Scores by Race, 17-Year-Olds

	All Areas				Metro Areas Only			
	White	Black	Difference (White-) Black)	Share of Gap Closed	White	Black	Difference (White-) Black)	Share of Gap Closed
Reading								
1975	293.0	240.6	52.4		293.6	240.0	53.6	
1980	292.8	243.1	49.7		294.6	244.4	50.2	
1988	294.7	274.4	20.3		297.2	278.9	18.3	
1990	296.6	267.3	29.3		299.3	267.9	31.4	
Change								
1975-90	3.6	26.7	-23.1	0.44	5.7	27.9	-22.2	0.41
Mathematics								
1978	305.9	268.4	37.5		307.6	269.3	38.3	
1982	303.7	271.8	31.9		306.0	273.2	32.8	
1986	307.5	278.6	28.9		309.4	279.6	29.8	
1990	309.5	288.5	21.0		311.2	287.3	23.9	
Change								
1978-90	3.6	20.1	-16.5	0.44	3.6	18.0	-14.4	0.38
Science								
1977	297.7	240.2	57.5		298.6	242.0	56.6	
1982	293.1	234.7	58.4		294.3	236.4	57.9	
1986	297.5	252.8	44.7		297.9	253.3	44.6	
1990	300.9	253.0	47.9		302.3	253.3	49.0	
Change								
1977-90	3.2	12.8	-6.9	0.17	3.7	11.3	-7.6	0.13

Source: Greenberg's analysis of NAEP data.

but a substantial gap in 1995 (blacks earned only 87.3% as much as whites). There was a significant growth in nearly every educational group's racial wage gap after 1979, especially among women.

These data suggest that racial disparities in wages still remain and have even grown over the last 16 years. Moreover, the last 20 years' experience also suggests that greater academic achievement for minorities does not necessarily lead to either higher real wages or a lessening of racial inequalities.

TABLE 3.56

Change in Hourly Wages Among
25- to 34-Year-Olds by Race and Gender, 1973-95
(1995 Dollars)

Race/ Gender	Hourly Wage				
	Less Than High School	High School	Some College	College or More	Total
Men					
White Men					
1973*	$12.79	$14.87	$15.65	$17.70	$15.57
1979	12.65	14.59	15.31	17.11	15.48
1989	10.48	12.31	13.95	17.59	14.16
1995	9.39	11.23	12.35	16.35	13.25
Black Men					
1973*	$10.18	$13.11	$12.99	$16.78	$12.52
1979	10.32	12.52	13.79	15.87	12.96
1989	8.21	9.98	11.38	13.64	10.70
1995	7.79	9.08	10.18	14.24	10.27
Black/White Ratio					
1973*	79.6%	88.1%	83.0%	94.8%	80.4%
1979	81.6	85.8	90.1	92.8	83.7
1989	78.3	81.1	81.6	77.6	75.5
1995	82.9	80.9	82.4	87.1	77.5
Women					
White Women					
1973*	$7.71	$9.40	$11.36	$13.33	$10.56
1979	8.06	9.54	11.01	12.56	10.75
1989	7.09	9.20	11.27	14.31	11.30
1995	6.84	8.68	10.24	14.32	11.19
Black Women					
1973*	$7.58	$9.09	$11.31	$16.23	$10.09
1979	8.01	9.58	10.85	12.75	10.24
1989	6.35	8.07	10.22	13.23	9.62
1995	6.19	7.79	9.59	12.50	9.38
Black/White Ratio					
1973*	98.3%	96.6%	99.6%	121.8%	95.5%
1979	99.3	100.4	98.5	101.5	95.3
1989	89.6	87.7	90.8	92.5	85.1
1995	90.4	89.7	93.6	87.3	83.9

* Average of 1973 and 1974.

Source: Authors' analysis, update of Bernstein (1995).

What Does the Future Hold?

This section examines future trends in wages and job quality by analyzing the projected trends of the key forces that will shape the wage structure—demand (skill requirements), labor-supply factors (education, age, immigration), and various institutional factors. We do not attempt to predict wages in the future, but our assessment of wage trends over the current business cycle and the forces at work over the next decade lead us to believe that wage inequality will continue to grow, although perhaps not as quickly as it has over the last 15 years. Unless there is a sizable improvement in productivity growth, as some optimists predict, it is reasonable to expect that real wages will continue to decline, as they have, for most men and many women. It seems unlikely that there will be significant improvements in wages in the late 1990s for those groups whose wages have suffered in recent years. That is, we do not expect to see any reversal of the wage trends described in this chapter over the next 10 years.

The first dimension of change we consider are shifts in demand for skills. The greater the increase in employer demand for workers with more skill and education, the greater is the economy's ability to shift people into better-paying jobs (although there is not necessarily a one-to-one relationship between skill and pay).

Some analyses in the late 1980s contended that there would be an explosive growth in the demand for skill in the 1990s. In fact, an analysis of recent trends and future projections suggests that the jobs of the future will not be markedly different from the jobs available today. Future jobs will have somewhat greater educational and skill requirements, primarily the need for basic literacy and numeracy, but the job structure will not shift markedly toward higher-paying jobs. Most important, the skill and education requirements of jobs are expected to grow more slowly than they did in the 1970s, 1980s, and early 1990s. Despite the widely held assumption that higher-paying white-collar jobs are the wave of the future, there is little evidence that the deterioration of job quality and wages that took place in the 1980s and 1990s will be reversed in the late-1990s, unless current trends change dramatically.

This view of future jobs is based on an analysis of labor-market trends anticipated by the Bureau of Labor Statistics (BLS) in its employment projections to the year 2005. The data in **Table 3.57** allow us to assess the effect of occupational upgrading (e.g., the rising importance of white-collar professional/technical jobs) on education requirements. Specifically, the data show the effect of changes in the distribution of employment among occupations on the education levels required and the pay received on jobs over the last two decades as well as

TABLE 3.57

Demand Shifts: Changes in Pay and Education Requirements, 1973-2005*

Job Characteristic	1973-79	1979-89	1989-95	BLS Projections 1994-2005
Pay		(Annual Growth)		
Hourly Compensation	1.6%	2.3%	1.4%	0.7%
Hourly Wages	2.0	2.9	1.8	0.9
Education Requirements				
Years of Schooling	0.9%	1.4%	0.9%	0.6%
Shares of Employment Requiring:		(Percentage-Point Change per Decade)		
Less Than High School	-1.57	-1.33	-0.57	-0.39
High School**	-1.03	-1.51	-1.69	-0.96
Associate College	0.33	0.26	0.05	0.07
College (4 yr.)	1.21	1.69	1.25	0.70
Advanced Degree	0.73	0.99	0.95	0.61

* Based on a shift-share analysis using the shares of employment by occupation and the 1995 education distributions of 13 occupation groups and their relative pay structure over the 1979-93 period.

** Includes those with "some college" but no degree beyond high school.

Source: Authors' analysis.

the expected shifts implicit in BLS employment projections.

The analysis shows that job education requirements have been increasing since 1973 and are projected to increase over the late 1990s and into the next century. Rather than the skills explosion projected by some analysts, however, future growth in education requirements will be historically modest. For instance, the new distribution of jobs across occupations in 2005 will require a worker's average years of schooling to grow at a 0.6% (10-year) rate over the 1994-2005 period, slower than in any period since 1973. Thus, occupation shifts are not expected to generate a large growth in the demand for education. This can also be seen in the analysis of the effects of occupation shifts on the need for workers at various education levels. For instance, projected changes in the occupational composition of employment imply an extra growth of 0.7% of the workforce needing a college degree every 10 years, a slower upward growth than that generated by the actual employment shifts in the 1970s, 1980s, or early 1990s. This analysis corroborates one of our conclusions drawn from the recent declines in the pay of white-collar and college-educated workers and the flattening of education premiums among men—the expansion of demand for "more-skilled" and "more-educated" workers is slowing down. The ultimate conclusion to be drawn from these analyses is that demand shifts in the future will not be a powerful force for improving overall job quality and pay, absent some change in government policies and employer strategies.

Table 3.58 presents data on future labor-supply trends that affect the wage structure. One major factor is how fast the supply of more-educated workers, or college graduates, will expand. If the supply outpaces the demand for college graduates, then the college premium will fall, creating a tendency toward less wage inequality. The data in Table 3.58 show that college enrollment rates are expected to rise by 2005, presumably in response to the increased economic returns to having a college degree. This suggests that the supply of college-educated workers may expand (as it has over the entire postwar period).

It is important to note, however, that the rate of college enrollment will be growing at a time when the college-age population is growing slowly—about 0.8% per year—from 25.8 million in 1993 to 28.3 million in 2005. The labor force is expected to grow somewhat faster, by 1.1% per year, in this same period, so there has to be a greater enrollment rate to keep the number of new college graduates growing as fast as the labor force. That is, the offsetting demographic trend (a slow growth in the college-age population) will blunt the rise in the number of college graduates entering the labor force as college enrollment rates grow. As Table 3.58 shows, the number of bachelor's degrees awarded annually is expected to rise by at most 14% (i.e., from 533,000 to a range of 528,000 to 606,000) for men between 1993 and 2005. The growth in the numbers completing college is less than the expected growth rate of the labor force, as seen in the trend of degrees awarded as a share of employment. Thus, new entrants will not be driving up the relative supply of "educated workers." In fact, as Table 3.58 shows, the amount of new college degrees relative to the size of the labor force is expected to be stable over the 1993-2005 period (down slightly for men, stable for women). The fact that the workforce retiring over the next decade is relatively highly educated also means that the process of replacing the retiring cohort with the entering cohort will raise the relative supply of college graduates less than it has over the past few decades (when retirees were educated in the 1920s and 1930s and had relatively low education levels). Overall, then, the sup-

TABLE 3.58

Future Labor Supply Trends

Characteristic	1979	1989	1993	2005
College Education				
a. College Enrollment Rate				
Men	n.a.	n.a.	22.4%	24.4%
Women	n.a.	n.a.	24.5	26.7
b. College-Age Population (000)				
18-24 Years	30,048	27,379	25,789	28,268
c. Bachelor's Degrees Awarded (000)				
Men	477	483	533	528-606
Women	444	535	632	655-818
d. Degrees Awarded				
as Share of Employment				
Men	0.90%	0.79%	0.86%	0.73-0.84%
Women	1.08	1.01	1.16	0.99-1.24

	1979	1988	2001	
Immigrant Share of Labor Force				
Men	7.0%	9.9%	13.3-14.8%	
Women	6.8	8.6	10.9-13.4	

	1980	1990	1994	2005
Labor Force Age (Median)	34.6	36.6	37.6	40.6

Source: Authors' analysis.

ply of college graduates is not likely to be a strong force for restoring a lesser college wage premium. The historical and expected trend in bachelor's degrees awarded as a share of employment are shown in **Figure 3S**.

Immigration trends imply a further growth of immigrants as a share of the labor force. If future immigrants are proportionately less educated, in accordance with recent trends, then future immigration will also serve to depress low-end wages and be a force for a further widening of wage inequality.

The workforce is expected to have a significantly higher age in 2005 than in recent years. The move by the youngest of the baby boomers into their forties and fifties should put upward pressure on average wages (wage trajectories are

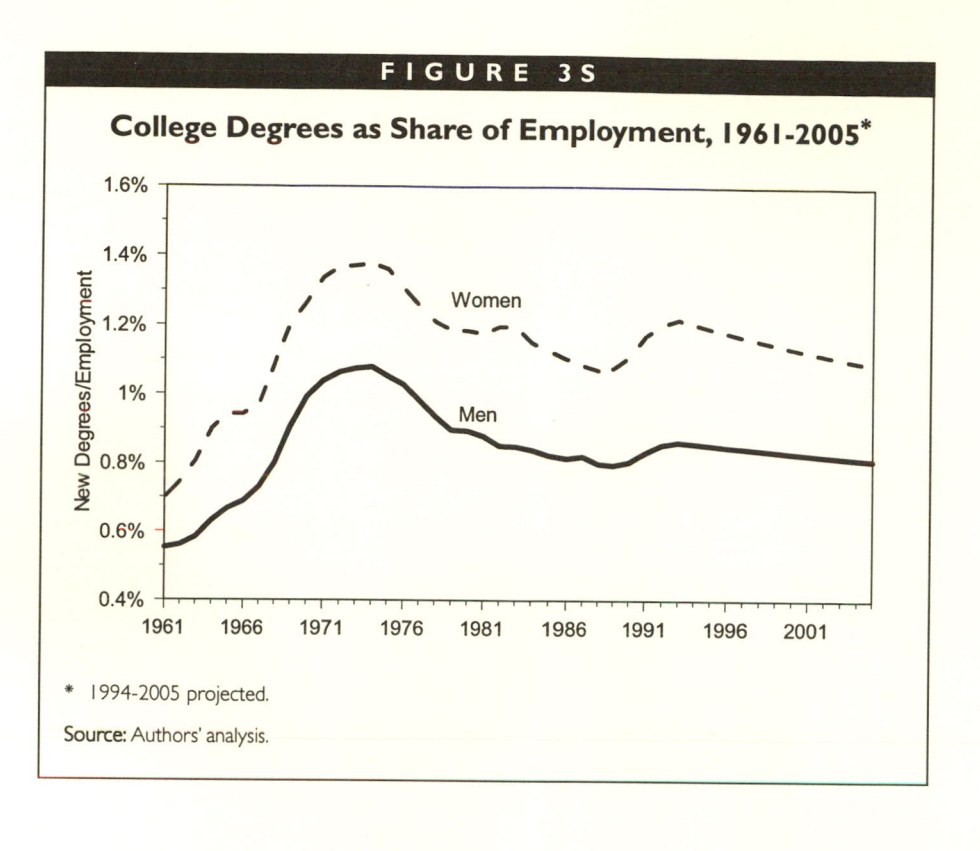

FIGURE 3S

College Degrees as Share of Employment, 1961-2005*

* 1994-2005 projected.

Source: Authors' analysis.

relatively rapid for these age groups) and may serve to narrow the wage gap between younger and older workers. How powerful a force this will be is uncertain. Note that the age of the workforce grew considerably over the 1980-90 period (from 34.6 to 36.6 years), when experience differentials actually widened.

Table 3.59 examines additional trends that will affect the wage structure. The expected expansion of international trade's role in the economy (indicated by the share of exports and imports in GDP) and the continued shrinkage of employment in goods production will act to depress wages for the non-college-educated workforce, as they have in recent years. If union coverage rates stabilize and grow (in response to a renewed union effort at organizing), some of the pressure for greater inequality may lessen or reverse itself. Likewise, if the minimum wage rises modestly in the late 1990s, as we expect, then there will be less pressure for wage inequality at the bottom to grow, especially among women. This mix of trends suggests some continuation of the growth of wage inequality, but perhaps not as quickly as in the recent past.

TABLE 3.59

Future Trade and Institutional Factors

	1979	1989	1994	2005
Trade Share of GDP*	15.7%	22.8%	26.7%	34.0-38.4%
Goods Production				
Share of Employment	29.6%	23.4%	21.1%	17.4-18.0%
Minimum Wage ($1995)	$5.97	$4.12	$4.37	modest up
Union Coverage	27.0%	18.6%	17.4%	modest up

* The share of exports plus imports in GDP.

Source: Authors' analysis.

The most optimistic trend is the possibility of higher productivity growth in the future. To the extent that higher productivity leads to higher average-wage growth (they are closely related but, as we have shown, less so than in the past), wages can be expected to grow more for every type of worker. Put another way, a productivity-related acceleration of average-wage growth can partially offset any further growth of wage inequality. However, it is uncertain whether a faster pace of productivity can be counted on in the future. Most analysts do not anticipate higher productivity growth.

How might a higher productivity trajectory affect wage growth? First, not all of the productivity pickup will translate into higher compensation, according to recent experience, because of the "leakage" of a shift toward unearned or capital income and the "terms of trade" effect discussed earlier (consumer prices increasing faster than output prices). Ignoring this leakage, however, what could be expected? In the 1979-95 period the structure of wage growth produced median wages falling 1% annually for men and growing 0.3% annually for women (and actually falling from 1989 to 1995). If male wage inequality grows at nearly the same pace in the future as it did in the 1980s and early 1990s (which is our guess), then the productivity pickup may allow the median male wage to hold steady (i.e., no real wage growth) rather than continue its 1% decline each year. That is, unless male wage inequality trends slow down, even with a 1% productivity acceleration there will be no reversal of the wage declines suffered during the 1979-95 period by the typical, or median, male worker. This is especially the case if any "leakage" between productivity growth and pay growth occurs.

With wage inequality among women growing strongly and median wages faltering, an acceleration of productivity could generate median wage growth for women of about 1% per year.

To conclude, the forces that drove wage inequality in the past can be expected to have a similar, although possibly lesser, effect in the future. And if productivity growth persists in its recent (1980s and 1990s) trajectory, then wages will continue to deteriorate for most men, rise modestly only among high-wage women, and stagnate at the median.

However, a minority view holds that a productivity acceleration may occur in the 1990s. If so, the median male wage may achieve stagnation but the median women's wage would grow by about 1.0% per year. Any slowing in the growth of wage inequality would imply faster growth of the median hourly wage.

Conclusion

There have been dramatic changes in the wage structure over the last 16 years. The real hourly wages of most workers have fallen, and the group experiencing the greatest wage decline has been non-college-educated workers, especially new entrants to the labor force. Given that three-fourths of the workforce has not earned a four-year college degree, the continuing deterioration of the wages of high school graduates (whose wages fell somewhat less than those of high school dropouts but somewhat more than those of workers with "some college") means that the vast majority of men and many women are working at far lower wages than their counterparts did a generation earlier. More recently (i.e., since the mid-1980s), wages have been falling or stagnant among college graduates and white-collar workers, especially men.

The wage trends of the 1989-95 period mirror those of the 1980s in that wage inequality at the top of the wage scale has continued to grow and median male wages have continued their 1% annual decline. The difference between the 1980s and 1990s is that there is a broader decline of wages among women, including a decline at the median, and there has been no growth in inequality at the bottom—wages at the median and the 10th percentile are falling in tandem.

Given that the economic forces driving falling wages and increased wage inequality (i.e., deunionization, employment shifts to low-wage service industries, trade liberalization, a faltering minimum wage) are likely to persist in the future suggests that there are probably hard times ahead for those groups that have already experienced the labor-market difficulties of recent years.

CHAPTER 4

JOBS
Growing Employment Instability

JOB GROWTH OVER THE LAST TWO BUSINESS CYCLES (FROM 1979 THROUGH 1989, and the incomplete cycle from 1989 to the present) has been substantially lower than in the rest of the postwar period. Despite slower job growth, the unemployment rate, which stood below 6% in mid-1996, has been lower on average since 1989 than during any business cycle since the 1960s. Nevertheless, considerable underemployment, which includes the unemployed, involuntary part-time workers, and "marginally attached" workers, persists.

Recent discussions on jobs have focused not so much on the creation of new jobs as on raising the quality of existing jobs. Concern with job quality reflects widespread anxiety over stagnant and declining wages (detailed in the previous chapter) and the perception that jobs in the 1980s and 1990s have become less secure and less stable. In this chapter, we present evidence that the anxiety many workers feel about their job situations is justified. Job stability, especially for men, declined in the 1980s and 1990s. The share of men in long-term jobs—those that allow workers to acquire specific skills and knowledge of a particular firm and consequently increase their earnings substantially—has also fallen. Job loss in the 1991-93 recovery period was as high as it was in the depths of the 1981-83 recession, the deepest in the postwar period. Job-loss rates, while still higher for blue-collar workers, have increased greatly among white-collar workers, probably reflecting the trend toward "corporate downsizing." Economic circumstances have also forced many workers into part-time and contingent work situations or into multiple jobs or reluctant self-employment.

Most of these developments have placed significant financial and time burdens on workers. Wage growth is slower for workers who change jobs frequently. Many who lose their jobs are reemployed at lower wages and with fewer or no benefits. Since health and other benefits are generally tied to employment, job instability, job loss, and marginal employment often lead workers and their families to lose health insurance coverage.

This chapter first examines developments in unemployment and underemployment. It then briefly analyzes job creation in the last two decades. Finally, the chapter reviews the evidence on various aspects of job quality: job stability, part-time work, multiple jobholding, contingent work, and self-employment.

Unemployment and Underemployment

Table 4.1 gives a broad overview of unemployment rates by gender and race during the various peak years in the business cycles since World War II and for 1995, the most recent year for which data are available. The economy is at its strongest in peak years, and therefore unemployment is at its lowest. In 1989, the most recent cyclical peak year, unemployment in every category was less than or roughly equal to that in 1979, the prior cyclical peak. Relative to 1973 and earlier peak years, however, 1989 unemployment rates were generally above average. The early-1990s recession caused unemployment to rise to as high as 7.7% in mid-1992. By mid-1996 unemployment was 5.3%, slightly above the previous cyclical peak. (A change implemented in 1994 in the underlying survey used to estimate the unemployment rate, however, cautions against strong comparisons between 1994 or 1995 and earlier years. Government statisticians believe that the new, more accurate survey shows a slightly higher unemployment rate in any given economic situation than the earlier versions of the survey.)

As has been the case over the postwar period, unemployment among minority workers continues to be about double that of white workers. The unemployment rate for black workers, at 10.4% in 1995, was still higher than the overall unemployment rate in any postwar *recession* (see Table 4.4 below). Over the period 1947-79, women workers had an unemployment rate substantially higher than the rate for males. Since 1979, however, in line with the generally more favorable wage growth that they have experienced compared to men, women have seen their unemployment rate converge on and then fall below the male rate.

TABLE 4.1

Unemployment Rates
(Peak Years and 1995)

	Total	Male	Female	White	Black	Hispanic
1947	3.9%	4.0%	3.7%	n.a.	n.a.	n.a.
1967	3.8	3.1	5.2	3.4%	n.a.	n.a.
1973*	4.9	4.2	6.0	4.3	9.4%	7.7%
1979	5.8	5.1	6.8	5.1	12.3	8.3
1989	5.3	5.2	5.4	4.5	11.4	8.0
1995*	5.6	5.6	5.6	4.9	10.4	9.3
Annual Averages						
1947-67	4.7%	4.5%	5.0%	n.a.	n.a.	n.a.
1967-73	4.6	4.0	5.7	4.1	n.a.	n.a.
1973-79	6.5	5.8	7.5	5.8	12.5	9.5
1979-89	7.1	7.0	7.3	6.2	14.7	10.3
1989-95*	6.2	6.4	6.0	5.4	12.0	9.7

* Changes to the Current Population Survey in 1994 mean that data for 1994 and 1995 are not directly comparable with earlier years.

Source: Authors' analysis.

Table 4.2 presents data on "underemployment," a broader measure of the lack of employment success in the labor market. This alternative measure includes unemployed workers as well as (1) those working part time but who want to work full time ("involuntary" part-timers); (2) those who want to work but have been discouraged by their lack of success ("discouraged" workers); and (3) others who are neither working nor seeking work at the moment but who indicate that they want and are available to work and have looked for a job in the last 12 months. (The second and third categories together are described as "marginally attached" workers.) At 10.1%, the 1995 underemployment rate (see Table 4.2 and **Figure 4A**) was substantially higher than the 5.6% unemployment rate, primarily because of the almost 4.5 million involuntary part-time workers. Discouraged and other marginally attached workers added another 1.6 million to the number underemployed.

TABLE 4.2

Rates of Underemployment, 1995

Category	1995 (000)
Civilian Labor Force	132,304
Unemployed	7,404
Discouraged*	410
Other Marginally Attached*	1,182
Involuntary Part-Time	4,473
Total Underemployed**	13,469
Rate of Underemployment	10.1%
Unemployment Rate	5.6

* Marginally attached workers are persons who currently are neither working nor looking for work, but who indicate that they want and are available for a job and have looked for work in the last 12 months. Discouraged workers are the subset of the marginally attached who have given a job-market-related reason for not currently looking for a job.

** Total underemployed workers divided by the sum of the labor force plus discouraged and other marginally attached workers.

Source: Authors' analysis.

FIGURE 4A

Underemployment, 1995

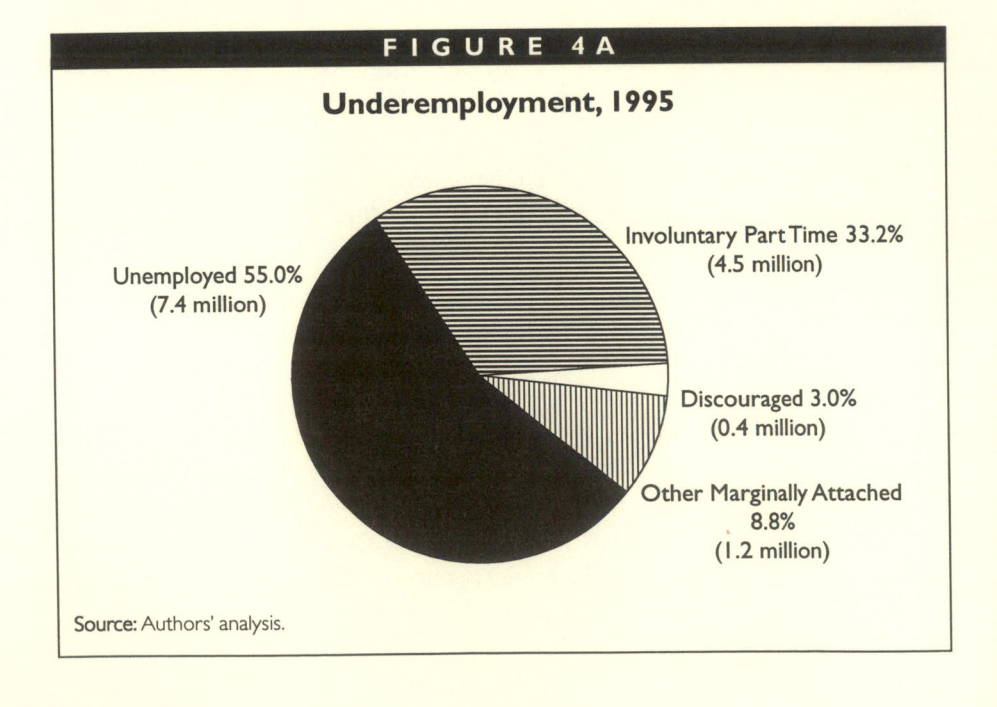

Involuntary Part Time 33.2%
(4.5 million)

Unemployed 55.0%
(7.4 million)

Discouraged 3.0%
(0.4 million)

Other Marginally Attached
8.8%
(1.2 million)

Source: Authors' analysis.

Unemployment and the Earnings Distribution

A slowing of the economy and the associated rise in unemployment disproportionately affects the bottom 60% of families. This effect can be seen in **Table
4.3**, which displays the effect of a 1% increase in unemployment on the number
of weeks unemployed and employed in a year and on annual earnings for families in each income group (estimated over the 1967-91 period). The last column
shows the effect of a 1% rise in the unemployment rate on the "average" family;
among all persons, an extra 0.46 weeks of unemployment means 0.62 fewer
weeks of work and $457 (1991 dollars), or 1.7%, less in annual earnings. (Weeks
worked in a year falls by a greater amount than weeks spent unemployed as a
consequence of people withdrawing from the labor force.)

The disparate impact of unemployment among different income groups is
most apparent for weeks unemployed among household heads: an overall 1%

TABLE 4.3

Effect of 1% Higher Unemployment Rate on Weeks Unemployed and Employed and on Annual Earnings, 1967-91

	Lowest Fifth	Second Fifth	Middle Fifth	Fourth Fifth	Highest Fifth	All
Weeks Unemployed						
Household Head	0.49	0.33	0.23	0.15	0.06	0.25
Other Adults	0.13	0.16	0.22	0.27	0.25	0.21
All Persons	0.63	0.50	0.45	0.42	0.31	0.46
Weeks Employed						
All Persons	-0.51	-0.89	-0.61	-0.57	-0.46	-0.62
Annual Earnings ($1991)						
Household Head	-$75	-$334	-$292	-$278	-$435	-$288
Other Adults	-5	-29	-89	-232	-488	-169
All Persons	-80	-362	-381	-511	-924	-457
Annual Earnings (%)						
All Persons	-3.7%	-3.7%	-1.8%	-1.4%	-1.4%	-1.7%

Source: Blank and Card (1993).

increase in unemployment leads to a half a week (0.49) more unemployment among household heads in the lowest-income group, but it barely affects households in the highest fifth.

The total impact of unemployment on families depends not just on the effect on the head of household but also on the effect on other earners in the family. Since low-income households tend to have fewer earners, the impact of rising unemployment on "other adult workers" is not as great as it is for upper-income groups, where two-earner families are more prevalent. Thus, the effect of higher unemployment on "all persons" is not as unequal as for household heads. Nevertheless, unemployment more adversely affects middle- and low-income families relative to the best-off families.

Finally, Table 4.3 shows the earnings lost to each income group as unemployment grows. Although better-off families lose more money than middle- or lower-income families, on a percentage basis the reduction in earnings is disproportionately greater in lower-income families.

Moreover, being unemployed was a bigger financial hardship in the 1980s and 1990s than it was in the 1970s. As **Table 4.4** shows, in 1989 and 1994 fewer than 40% of the unemployed received unemployment compensation, a substantial drop from the financial protection available in the 1975 and 1976 recession years, when 76% and 67% respectively of the unemployed received unemployment insurance payments. Legislation passed in late 1991, which extended unemployment compensation to the long-term unemployed, temporarily increased the coverage level to 51% in 1992. Because of changes in the laws and in the administration of unemployment insurance at both the federal and state levels, unemployment insurance has provided a weaker safety net in the 1990s than in the 1970s.

Job Growth Slows Since the 1970s

Table 4.5 looks at employment growth over the last three business cycles (1973-79, 1979-89, and the period since 1989) relative to the earlier postwar period. The table presents four measures of employment growth: nonfarm payroll employment (from a national survey of business establishments), civilian employment (from a national survey of households), total hours worked, and full-time equivalent employment (which combines part time and full time according to practices in each industry). The trend is unmistakable: each measure of employ-

TABLE 4.4

Proportion of the Unemployed Who Receive Some Unemployment Insurance Payment

Peak and Trough Years	Percent of Unemployed Receiving Benefits	Unemployment Rate
1960	54%	5.5%
1967	43	3.8
1970	51	4.9
1973	41	4.9
1974	50	5.6
1975	76	8.5
1976	67	7.7
1979	42	5.8
1982	45	9.7
1989	33	5.3
1992	51	7.4
1994	36	6.1

Source: Center for Budget and Policy Priorities (1995).

TABLE 4.5

Employment Growth, 1947-95

Period	Measures of Employment				Working-Age Population	Labor-Force Participation Rate**
	Nonfarm Payroll	Civilian Employment	Hours of Work	Full-Time Equivalent Employment		
(Annual Rates of Growth)						
1947-67	2.0%	1.3%	n.a.	n.a.	1.2%	0.07
1967-73	2.6	2.3	1.6%	1.9%	2.1	0.20
1973-79	2.6	2.5	1.8	2.4	1.9	0.48
1979-89	1.9	1.7	1.6	1.7	1.2	0.28
1989-95*	1.3	1.0	0.8	1.1	1.1	0.02

* Data for hours of work and full-time equivalent employment are for 1989-94.
** Average annual percentage-point change.

Source: Authors' analysis.

ment grew far more slowly in the still-incomplete business cycle between 1989 and 1995 than during the full business cycle from 1979 to 1989, when job growth rates, in turn, were much lower than for the 1973-79 period. The rate at which civilian employment rose from 1989 to 1995 (1.0% annually), for example, was about 70% slower than between 1979 and 1989. The 1.7% annual rate for the 1979-89 period, in turn, was more than 30% slower than the 2.5% annual employment-creation rate prevailing between 1973 and 1979.

The last two columns of Table 4.5 show two reasons why unemployment was able to fall in the 1980s and 1990s despite much slower growth in job creation. First, in the last two decades, the working-age population has grown more slowly than it did in the 1967-79 period. As a result, there were fewer potential new young workers to be absorbed into the economy in 1995 and 1989 than in 1979. For example, in 1995, there were 32.4 million 16- to 24-year-olds, a smaller number than the 37.0 million in 1979 or even the 33.5 million in 1973. The slow growth in the size of the potential labor force is reflected in the slower growth of the working-age population in Table 4.5.

Second, the long-term rise in the proportion of the working-age population seeking work (the labor-force participation rate) also decelerated in the 1980s and approached zero growth in the first half of the 1990s. As Table 4.5 shows, the annual percentage-point increase in the labor-force participation rate in the 10 years between 1979 and 1989 (0.28) and in the 6 years between 1989 and 1995 (0.02) was substantially less than in the 6 years between 1973 and 1979 (0.48), primarily reflecting a slowdown in the growth of women's labor-force participation and a decline in participation among men 55 years old and older.

These two trends—the smaller number of potential young workers and slower labor-force participation growth—have meant slower growth in the number of people seeking work. Thus, the lower unemployment of the later part of the 1980s and the first half of the 1990s has not been due to superior job creation. Despite the slower growth rate of new jobs, unemployment was reduced primarily because of the slow growth of new workers seeking employment.

The evidence on the number of jobs created in the 1980s and 1990s, however, tells us nothing about the changing characteristics of new and existing jobs. In Chapter 3, we saw that the hourly wages for most men and many women have been declining over the last 15 years. In the remainder of this chapter, we look at other aspects of job quality: job security, full- and part-time status, multiple jobholding, contingent work, and self-employment.

Declining Job Stability

The widespread anxiety expressed about living standards has often been linked to the feeling that job security and long-term employment prospects have declined considerably in the 1980s and 1990s. **Table 4.6** reports the results of an analysis of employment stability for a large group of men whose job situations were tracked yearly over the 1970s and 1980s. (Women were also interviewed, but the sample was too small to produce reliable estimates.) In each year, the survey noted the occupation, industry, and specific employer of each member of the sample. At the end of the two decades, the men were sorted into groups according to "strong," "medium," or "weak" attachment to their occupation, industry, and employer in each of the two decades. Those with strong occupation and industry stability were in the same broad occupation or industry category in 8 or more out of 10 years. Strong employer stability was defined as having at most 1 year in 10 in which the worker's employer changed. Medium occupation and industry stability required

TABLE 4.6

Employment Stability for Men, 1970s vs. 1980s

	Percent of All Workers		Percentage-Point Change
	1970s	1980s	
Occupational Attachment			
Strong	68%	68%	0
Medium	28	27	-1
Weak	4	5	1
Industry Attachment			
Strong	63%	59%	-4
Medium	29	31	2
Weak	8	10	2
Employer Attachment			
Strong	67%	52%	-15
Medium	21	24	3
Weak	12	24	12

Source: Authors' analysis based on Rose (1995).

being in the same broad category in 5 to 7 years out of 10. Workers who changed employers in only 2 or 3 of the 10 years were classified as having medium employer stability. Weak occupation and industry stability meant fewer than 5 years in the same category, while those with weak employer stability had four or more employers.

The last column of Table 4.6 shows the change in job stability between the 1970s and 1980s. Occupational stability changed little: the share of workers with strong attachment to their occupations was unchanged across the two decades. Industry attachment changed slightly more. Those with strong ties fell by 4 percentage points, with increases of 2 percentage points for both those with medium and weak stability. Employer stability, however, appears to have eroded significantly between the 1970s and the 1980s. The share of workers with the same employer for eight years in each decade fell 15 percentage points, from 67% to 52%. At the same time, workers with weak ties to their employers increased by 12 percentage points.

As job instability increased, so too did its costs to workers. **Table 4.7** looks at earnings growth by workers' level of job stability in both of the decades. During the 1970s, those with strong occupation, industry, and employer stability experienced, on average, about a 25% increase in their inflation-adjusted earnings. Over the same period, those with weak occupation and employer stability saw small declines in their real earnings, while those with weak industry ties managed a small increase. In the 1980s, strong job stability yielded even larger increases in average real earnings than in the 1970s, but weak stability had far worse consequences than in the earlier period. Workers with weak industry ties suffered an average 9.1% decline in real earnings; weak employer stability was associated with an average earnings drop of 13.2% (recall from the previous table that the share of workers with weak employer stability doubled between the 1970s and 1980s); and weak occupational stability led to an average 22.2% fall in annual earnings over the decade.

Table 4.8 displays additional evidence on job stability that is also consistent with the idea that job stability has declined since the 1970s. The table shows the share of workers, by age and gender, who were in their current jobs for 10 or more years at a given point in time between 1973 and 1993. The age breakdown is important because job tenure (the time a worker has spent with his or her current employer) depends heavily on workers' ages—few 25-year-olds can or will be with their current employer for 10 or more years. The gender breakdown allows an examination of the situation facing women, whose experience was ignored in the previous two tables because of data limitations. Finally, the inclu-

TABLE 4.7

Employment Stability and Earnings for Men, 1970s vs. 1980s

(1995 Dollars)

	1970s			1980s		
	Start*	End*	Change	Start*	End*	Change
Occupational Attachment						
Strong	$39,943	$49,170	23.1%	$41,819	$53,440	27.8%
Medium	32,635	37,752	15.7	31,928	31,588	-1.1
Weak	32,802	32,384	-1.3	27,499	21,401	-22.2
Industry Attachment						
Strong	$38,431	$48,125	25.2%	$40,533	$52,568	29.7%
Medium	37,425	42,548	13.7	37,424	40,008	6.9
Weak	32,166	33,669	4.7	30,134	27,377	-9.1
Employer Attachment						
Strong	$40,180	$50,029	24.5%	$42,189	$54,578	29.4%
Medium	35,343	41,033	16.1	38,172	46,822	22.7
Weak	27,282	26,344	-3.4	30,991	26,890	-13.2

* The starting and ending periods are three-year averages: for the 1970s, of 1967-69 and 1977-79; for the 1980s, of 1977-79 and 1987-89.

Source: Authors' analysis based on Rose (1995).

---

sion of data from 1993 will shed some light on the experience of the 1990s.

Between 1973 and 1979, the share of men age 45-54 and 55-64 with 10 or more years of job tenure increased by over 2 percentage points. Over the same period, women in the same age range saw a much smaller increase in their share of long-tenure employment. Between 1979 and 1993, however, circumstances changed considerably. Men age 35-64 experienced a steep decline in their share of long-tenure jobs; the decline was particularly sharp for those age 55-64 (down 5.5 percentage points, from 62.9% to 57.4% of all jobs held). Meanwhile, women at all age ranges enjoyed significant increases in the share with long-tenure employment. Women age 35-44 had the largest increase—up 8.1 percentage points, from 17.1% to 25.2% with long tenure. Older women also benefited from substantially higher long-term tenure, though the increases were smaller

TABLE 4.8

Share of Employed Workers
in Job for 10 Years or More, 1973-93

	Share of Employment with 10 or More Years of Tenure				Change	
	1973	1979	1987	1993	1973-79	1979-93
All Workers						
25-34	6.6%	5.7%	6.6%	7.4%	-0.9	1.7
35-44	28.8	28.4	28.2	30.0	-0.4	1.6
45-54	45.1	46.5	43.8	45.6	1.4	-0.9
55-64	54.6	56.1	53.6	53.8	1.5	-2.3
Men						
25-34	7.5%	6.6%	7.5%	8.4%	-0.9	1.8
35-44	35.6	36.3	34.5	34.1	0.7	-2.2
45-54	53.7	55.8	52.3	51.9	2.1	-3.9
55-64	60.3	62.9	59.0	57.4	2.6	-5.5
Women						
25-34	5.0%	4.3%	5.5%	6.2%	-0.7	1.9
35-44	17.3	17.1	20.5	25.2	-0.2	8.1
45-54	31.0	31.8	32.9	38.4	0.8	6.6
55-64	45.1	45.1	46.0	49.1	0.0	4.0

Source: Authors' analysis based on Farber (1995).

(up 6.6 percentage points for 45- to 54-year-olds and 4.0 percentage points for 55- to 64-year-olds). Note, however, that even after these gains, women in all ranges were still substantially less likely than men to be in their jobs for 10 or more years.

The combined figures for men and women (see the first panel of Table 4.8) mask the different experiences by gender. In particular, between 1979 and 1993, the data show a modest increase in long-tenure jobs for those under 44 and a modest decrease for those age 45 and older, leaving the impression that, on average, job tenure has changed little since the 1970s. On average this is true, but the preceding analysis makes clear that job tenure generally decreased significantly for men during the 1980s and 1990s relative to what it was in the 1970s. Meanwhile, job tenure increased significantly for women, probably reflecting the growing stability of women's labor-force attachment.

Displacement

Job tenure can decline because workers change jobs more frequently in order to take advantage of other opportunities, or it can fall because employers lay off or fire workers in greater numbers. The evidence on the poor wage growth prospects of those with weak job stability (see Table 4.7) argues that much of the increase in job instability was probably involuntary. This section focuses special attention on involuntary job loss.

Table 4.9 indicates that about 15% of men and just over 10% of women experience at least one involuntary job loss over a three-year period. The rate of job loss for both men and women rose slightly between 1981-83, when it was

TABLE 4.9

Rate of Job Loss,* by Gender and Reason, 1981-93

	1981-83	1989-91	1991-93	Change 1981-83 to 1991-93
Men				
All Reasons	14.5%	14.3%	15.0%	0.5
Plant Closing	4.7	4.7	4.0	-0.7
Slack Work	6.5	5.5	5.2	-1.3
Position Abolished	1.9	2.5	3.4	1.5
Other	1.9	2.5	3.4	1.5
Unemployment Rate	9.1	5.9	7.3	-1.8
Women				
All Reasons	10.8%	10.3%	11.4%	0.6
Plant Closing	4.0	4.1	3.4	-0.6
Slack Work	3.7	2.9	2.8	-0.9
Position Abolished	1.3	1.3	2.2	0.9
Other	1.9	1.9	3.0	1.1
Unemployment Rate	8.8	5.7	6.6	-2.3

* Share of labor force that reports having lost a job in the previous three years.

Source: Authors' analysis based on Farber (1996).

14.5% for men and 10.8% for women, and 1991-93, when it reached 15.0% for men and 11.4% for women. While the increase is small, it is still surprising that the job loss rate should be higher in the later period, which includes two years of economic recovery, than in the earlier period, which includes the deepest recession in the postwar period. This suggests that the structural rate of job loss (that is, the component of job loss that is independent of the rise and fall of the business cycle) accelerated in the 1990s. The table also displays important information about how the reasons for job loss have changed over time. Plant closings and "slack work" both declined between 1981-83 and 1991-93. At the same time, "position abolished," a term that may reflect the "downsizing" phenomenon, almost doubled for both men and women.

Table 4.10 examines differences in job loss by occupation. The first striking feature is the high rate of job loss for blue-collar workers ("craftsmen, operatives, and laborers") relative to workers in other professions. The job-loss rate for blue-collar workers over the 1981-83 period was 21.1%, almost three times higher than the next most heavily affected group ("sales and administration workers," with 8.2%). By 1991-93, the job-loss rate for blue collars had fallen 7.3 percentage points to 13.8%, but it still exceeded the rates for all other broad occupational categories. The second important pattern is the large increase between 1981-83 and 1991-93 in the job-loss rate for "managers" (a 2.5 percentage point rise, from 7.7% to 10.2%). Plant closings were responsible for a small portion (0.3 percentage points) of the increase, but abolished positions accounted for the lion's share—2.2 percentage points—of the total rise in job loss. Between the early 1980s and the early 1990s, then, job displacement went upscale, exposing a new group of workers to the types of job losses previously confined largely to blue-collar workers.

Workers who choose to leave their jobs generally do so because a new job offers them better pay or working conditions or because they prefer to leave the labor market temporarily (to study or raise children, for example) or permanently (to retire). Those workers who lose their jobs, however, generally end up worse off even after they are able to find a replacement job. **Table 4.11** reports the average real earnings loss (between the current job and the job lost) for workers who had lost a job in the previous three years but who had since found new employment. The numbers make plain that displaced workers, on average, are forced into lower-paying jobs. Workers who worked full time in the job they lost suffer about a 10% decline in real earnings even if they are able to secure another full-time job after their displacement. The figures for all workers—including those who managed only to find part-time work—show larger earnings

TABLE 4.10

Rate of Job Loss,*
by Occupation and Reason,** 1981-93

				Change
	1981-83	1989-91	1991-93	1981-83 to 1991-93
Managers				
All Reasons	7.7%	9.5%	10.2%	2.5
Plant Closing	3.7	4.6	4.0	0.3
Slack Work	2.2	2.5	2.2	0.0
Position Abolished	1.8	2.3	4.0	2.2
Professional, Technical Workers				
All Reasons	5.3%	5.6%	6.4%	1.1
Plant Closing	1.6	1.6	1.6	0.0
Slack Work	2.4	2.2	2.3	-0.1
Position Abolished	1.2	1.7	2.5	1.3
Sales and Administration Workers				
All Reasons	8.2%	9.2%	9.3%	1.1
Plant Closing	3.9	4.5	3.8	-0.1
Slack Work	3.0	2.9	3.0	0.0
Position Abolished	1.3	1.8	2.5	1.2
Service Workers				
All Reasons	6.2%	7.2%	7.1%	0.9
Plant Closing	3.0	3.7	3.0	0.0
Slack Work	2.4	2.7	2.7	0.3
Position Abolished	0.8	0.8	1.4	0.6
Craftsmen, Operatives, and Laborers				
All Reasons	21.1%	17.4%	13.8%	-7.3
Plant Closing	7.6	6.8	5.1	-2.5
Slack Work	12.0	9.4	7.0	-5.0
Position Abolished	1.5	1.2	1.6	0.1
Overall Unemployment Rate	9.0	5.8	7.0	-2.0

* Share of labor force that reports having lost a job in the previous three years.
** This table does not include an "other" category because the 1994 Displaced Workers Survey contains no information on the occupation of workers displaced for "other reasons."

Source: Authors' analysis based on Farber (1996).

TABLE 4.11

Post-Displacement Earnings Loss, 1981-93

Transition Type/ Displacement Reason	Real Earnings Loss*			Change
	1981-83	1989-91	1991-93	1981-83 to 1991-93
Full Time to Full Time Only				
All Reasons	-9.2%	-10.5%	-11.2%	-2.0
Plant Closing	-8.9	-9.0	-12.4	-3.5
Slack Work	-10.1	-11.9	-7.1	2.9
Position Abolished	-7.8	-12.0	-14.9	-7.1
All Job Changes				
All Reasons	-14.1%	-15.9%	-15.0%	-0.9
Plant Closing	-10.1	-12.8	-16.2	-6.2
Slack Work	-16.7	-18.4	-11.2	5.5
Position Abolished	-17.1	-19.3	-18.6	-1.5

* Percent difference between weekly earnings on current job relative to earnings on job from which displaced.

Source: Authors' analysis based on Farber (1996).

---

losses (about 15%). In 1991-93, earnings declines were particularly steep for those whose positions were abolished: weekly earnings for full-time workers fell 14.9% and for those working full or part time by 18.6%.

Wage declines are, of course, only one cost of job displacement. Another is the loss of employer-provided health benefits. **Table 4.12** indicates that about three-fourths of those displaced workers who were with their previous employer three years or more had health insurance coverage through their employer before they lost their jobs (see column 1). Of these, roughly 25-40% were without it up to three years later. In the early 1990s, however, loss of coverage appears to be below the rates of the early 1980s, possibly reflecting the greater share of white-collar workers among all displaced workers.

TABLE 4.12

Health Insurance Coverage After Job Loss, 1981-92

Year	Covered Before Job Loss	Share Previously Covered Who Lost Coverage
1981-82	81.2%	37.5%
1983-84	75.4	33.3
1985-86	76.5	28.4
1987-88	71.5	23.3
1989-90	75.9	27.3
1991-92	71.5	24.9

Source: Authors' analysis based on Gardener (1995).

Long-Term Growth in Part-Time Work

As we saw earlier, one important reason for the high level of underemployment in 1995 was the large number of workers who wanted full-time jobs but who were able only to find part-time work. This section examines the growth of part-time work more closely.

The expansion of part-time work is not necessarily a problem; many workers prefer a part-time schedule because it allows time to pursue education, leisure, or family responsibilities. Nevertheless, large numbers of part-timers would prefer to work full time. Part-timers generally have lower pay, less-skilled jobs, poor chances of promotion, less job security, inferior benefits (such as vacation, health insurance, and pension), and lower status overall within their places of employment.

Table 4.13 shows that the share of total employment made up by full-timers declined steadily from 1973 to 1993. At the same time, the share of jobs that are part time increased from 16.6% in 1973 to 18.1% in 1989 and to 18.8% in 1993. This increase in part-time work from 1973 to 1993 resulted almost entirely from the rise in *involuntary* part-time employment (**Figure 4B**), reflecting the more widespread use of part-timers by employers and not the preference of the workforce for shorter hours. In 1989, for instance, involuntary part-time workers made up 4.3% of the workforce, an increase of 0.5 percentage points over 1979 and 1.2 percentage points compared to 1973. By 1989, nearly one-fourth of all part-time workers were involuntary part-timers. Involuntary part-

TABLE 4.13

Nonagricultural Employment, by Full-Time and Part-Time Status, 1973-95

| | Percent Part Time | | | Percent | |
Year	Total	Involuntary	Voluntary	Full Time	Total
1973	16.6	3.1	13.5	83.4	100.0
1979	17.6	3.8	13.8	82.4	100.0
1989	18.1	4.3	13.8	81.9	100.0
1993	18.8	5.5	13.3	81.2	100.0
1995*	18.4	3.7	14.7	81.6	100.0

* Data for 1995 not directly comparable with earlier years because of survey changes.

Source: Authors' analysis.

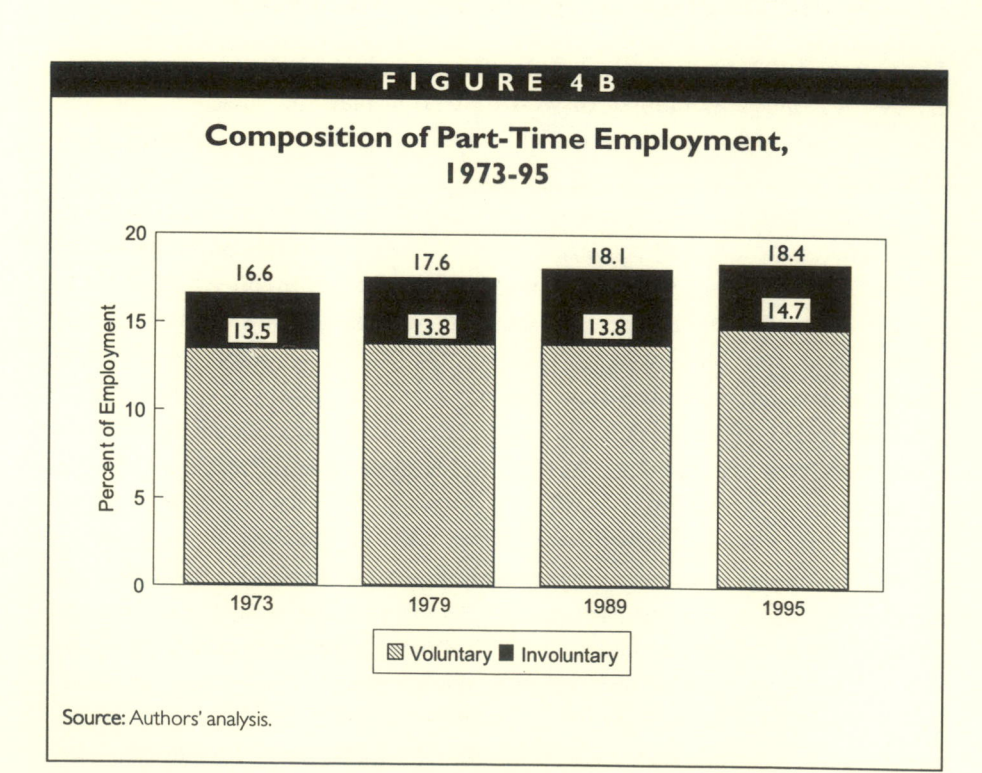

FIGURE 4B

Composition of Part-Time Employment, 1973-95

Source: Authors' analysis.

time work continued to grow during the downturn in the early 1990s, reaching 5.5% of total employment in 1993. But the overall rate of part-time employment has declined slightly since then, with the share of involuntary part-time employment falling by 1995 to below its level in 1979. (Again, changes to the Current Population Survey suggest caution in drawing strong conclusions when comparing these kind of data before and after 1994. In identical economic circumstances, the new survey appears to yield a higher number of part-time workers than older versions of the survey.)

A major problem associated with part-time employment is lower hourly pay received by part-time workers compared to equivalent full-time workers (**Table 4.14**). Women who work part time earn, on average, 23.1% less in wages per hour than those working full time. This wage differential is not due simply to the concentration of part-timers in low-wage occupations, since part-timers

TABLE 4.14

Wage Differences Between Part-Time and Full-Time Workers by Gender and Selected Occupations, 1995

	Percent of Part-Time Workers	Average Hourly Wage, 1995 (1995 Dollars)		Wage Difference	
		Part Time	Full Time	Dollars	Percent
Women					
All Workers	100.0%	$8.82	$11.48	-$2.66	-23.1%
Prof., Tech.	23.0	14.51	15.21	-0.70	-4.6
Sales	17.4	6.54	10.09	-3.56	-35.2
Admin.	22.9	8.48	10.23	-1.76	-17.2
Service	29.5	6.38	7.21	-0.83	-11.5
Laborers	2.0	6.57	7.74	-1.17	-15.2
Other	5.2	7.57	8.70	-1.13	-12.9
Men					
All Workers	100.0%	$8.71	$14.39	-$5.69	-39.5%
Prof., Tech.	16.4	16.04	20.39	-4.35	-21.4
Sales	12.0	7.15	15.22	-8.07	-53.0
Admin.	9.0	7.78	12.50	-4.73	-37.8
Service	25.4	6.35	9.98	-3.62	-36.3
Laborers	14.1	6.72	9.24	-2.53	-27.3
Other	23.1	8.48	11.85	-3.37	-28.4

Source: Authors' analysis.

are paid significantly less in each occupation. The part-time wage differential, at 39.5%, is even greater for men than for women, and again the pay differences hold across all occupations.

The gap between part-time and full-time workers is even greater for benefits (**Table 4.15**). In 1993 (the most recent data available), only 37% of part-time workers worked for firms that sponsored pension plans for their part-time workers, compared to 63% for full-time workers. Even where employers made pension plans available to part-timers, fewer than one-third (12% of the 37% of part-time workers eligible) were actually covered by the plans. The coverage rate for full-timers was much higher (50% of the 63% eligible). These differences in coverage reflect many factors, including the demographic differences between full-time and part-time workers. Nevertheless, they undoubtedly also reflect the less generous terms under which firms offer pension benefits to their part-time employees.

In the same year, fewer than half of part-time workers were in jobs with employer-sponsored health insurance, a benefit that was available to 80% of full-timers. Only 15% of part-time workers, compared to 67% of full-timers, were actually covered by employer plans. As with pension benefits, the lower coverage rates for part-timers reflect, in part, the higher employee costs of such

TABLE 4.15

Differences in Fringe Benefits for Full-Time and Part-Time Workers, 1993

Type of Benefit	Share of All:	
	Full Time	Part Time
Pension Plan		
Employer Sponsors	63.0%	37.0%
Employee Covered	50.0	12.0
Men	48.0	15.0
Women	51.0	8.0
Health Plan		
Employer Sponsors	80.0%	47.0%
Employee Covered	67.0	15.0
Employee Not Covered by Any Plan	15.0	26.0

Source: Authors' analysis of Department of Labor (1994).

plans for part-time workers. While some part-timers have private health insurance through a spouse or other relative, many do not. About one-fourth (26%) of all part-timers had no health insurance (other than Medicare or Medicaid), compared to 15% for full-time workers.

More Than One Job

The growth of part-time work, documented in the previous section, reflects growing underemployment and deteriorating pay and job opportunities. The growth of multiple jobholding—people working in at least two jobs—reflects over-employment due to the deterioration of real wages since 1979. In 1989, 7.2 million workers held at least two jobs (**Table 4.16**). The rate of multiple jobholding grew from 4.9% in 1979 to 6.2% in 1989, an increase of 1.3 percentage points (**Figure 4C**). Most of this growth occurred in the recovery years from

TABLE 4.16

Growth of Multiple Jobholding, All Workers, 1973-95

Year	Number of Multiple Jobholders (000)	Multiple-Jobholding Rate	Percent of Workforce Who Hold Multiple Jobs Because of:	
			Economic Hardship*	Other Reasons**
1973	4,262	5.1%	n.a.	n.a.
1979	4,724	4.9	1.8%	3.1%
1985	5,730	5.4	2.2	3.2
1989	7,225	6.2	2.8	3.4
1995	7,952	6.4	n.a.	n.a.
Change				
1973-79	462	-0.2	n.a.	n.a.
1979-85	1,006	0.5	0.4	0.1
1985-89	1,495	0.8	0.6	0.2
1989-95***	727	0.2	n.a.	n.a.

* To meet regular household expenses or pay off debts.
** Includes savings for the future, getting experience, helping a friend or relative, buying something special, enjoying the work, and so on.
*** Data for 1995 not strictly comparable with data for earlier years because of survey design changes.

Source: Authors' analysis.

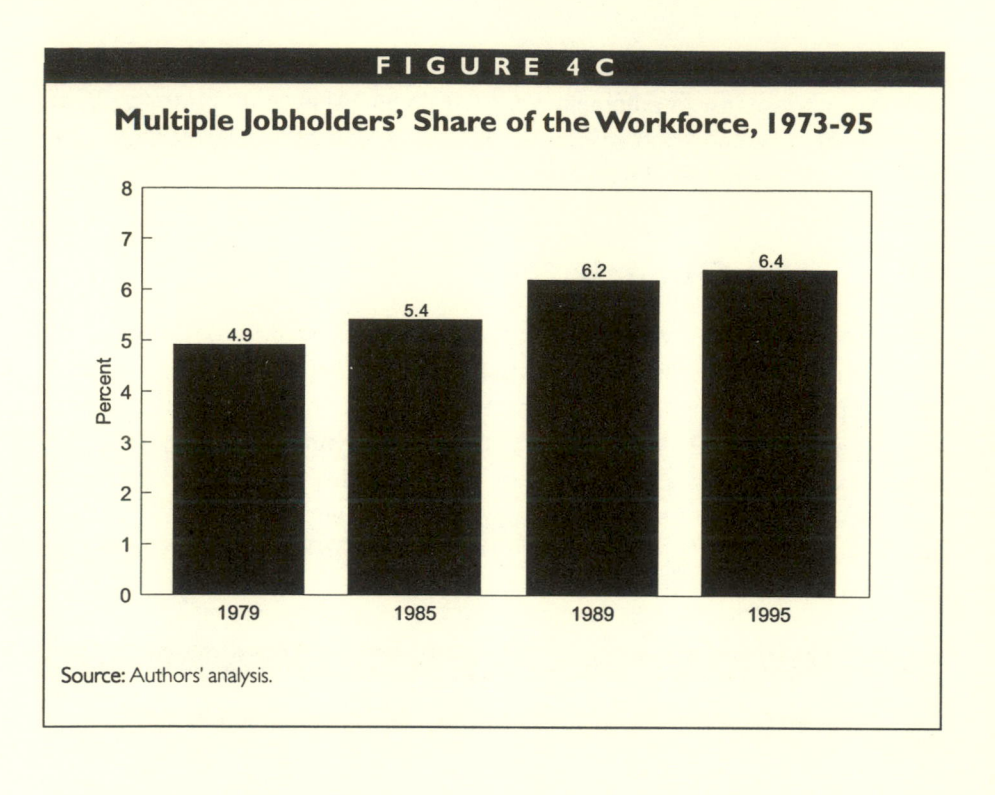

FIGURE 4C

Multiple Jobholders' Share of the Workforce, 1973-95

Source: Authors' analysis.

1985 to 1989, when an additional 1.5 million workers began working more than one job. Of these workers, about 1.2 million cited economic hardship as the reason for working more than one job. The multiple-jobholding rate held steady at 6.2% in the 1989-91 period (not shown in table), even as total employment declined, and it actually rose slightly, to 6.4%, by 1995.

An analysis of the reasons for multiple jobholding shows that the increase over the 1979 to 1989 period stems from deteriorating economic circumstances rather than enhanced opportunities. The growth of multiple jobholding occurred primarily among workers who worked at more than one job because of "economic hardship"—the need to meet regular expenses or to pay off debts. Multiple jobholding due to economic hardship increased by 1.0 percentage point from 1979 to 1989, accounting for more than three-fourths of the 1.3-percentage-point rise in multiple jobholding. This same pattern holds over the recovery years from 1985 to 1989, when increased economic hardship accounted for 0.6 percentage points of the 0.8-percentage-point rise in the multiple-jobholding rate. In contrast, between 1979 and 1989, the multiple-jobholding rate for "other reasons" rose only 0.3%, from 3.1% to 3.4%. Because data on the reasons people work multiple jobs are not available after 1991, it is difficult to speculate about what caused multiple jobholding to decline in the early-1990s downturn and rise slightly thereafter.

The multiple-jobholding rate among women rose rapidly between 1979 and 1989, from 3.5% to 5.9% (**Table 4.17**). Economic hardship explains roughly

TABLE 4.17

Growth of Multiple Jobholding by Gender, 1973-95

Year	Number of Multiple Jobholders (000)	Multiple-Jobholding Rate	Percent of Workforce Who Hold Multiple Jobs Because of:	
			Economic Hardship*	Other Reasons**
Women				
1973	869	2.7%	n.a.	n.a.
1979	1,407	3.5	1.5%	2.0%
1985	2,192	4.7	2.0	2.7
1989	3,109	5.9	2.9	3.0
1995	3,727	6.5	n.a.	n.a.
Change				
1973-79	538	0.8	n.a.	n.a.
1979-85	785	1.2	0.5	0.7
1985-89	917	1.2	0.9	0.3
1989-95***	618	0.6	n.a.	n.a.
Men				
1973	3,393	6.6%	n.a.	n.a.
1979	3,317	5.9	1.5%	2.0%
1985	3,537	5.9	2.0	2.7
1989	4,115	6.4	2.9	3.0
1995	4,225	6.3	n.a.	n.a.
Change				
1973-79	-76	-0.7	n.a.	n.a.
1979-85	220	0.0	0.5	0.7
1985-89	578	0.5	0.9	0.3
1989-95***	110	-0.1	n.a.	n.a.

* To meet regular household expenses or pay off debts.
** Includes savings for the future, getting experience, helping a friend or relative, buying something special, enjoying the work, and so on.
***Data for 1995 not strictly comparable with data for earlier years because of survey design changes.

Source: Authors' analysis.

60% of this increase (1.4 percentage points of the 2.4-percentage-point increase). Between 1985 and 1989, 75% of the rise in women's multiple jobholding was due to economic hardship. By 1989, a slightly larger proportion of women (2.9%) than men (2.6%) worked more than one job in order to meet regular expenses or to pay off debts. The multiple-jobholding rate for women increased by another 0.6 percentage point between 1989 and 1995, to 6.5%, a rate that exceeded that of men (6.3%).

Table 4.18 provides a demographic breakdown of those working more than one job for reasons of economic hardship. As Table 4.17 suggested, by 1989 nearly half of those workers in multiple jobs for reasons of economic hardship were women. In the same year, more than half of multiple jobholders were married (wives, 19.8%; husbands, 36.2%) and an additional fifth were widowed, divorced, or separated men or women. These data thus show that the hardship associated with and reflected by multiple jobholding is concentrated in working families and among adult workers.

TABLE 4.18

Distribution of Multiple Jobholders Experiencing Economic Hardship,* 1979-89

Gender/Marital Status	1979	1985	1989
Total, 16 Years and Over	100.0%	100.0%	100.0%
Women	33.7%	40.6%	48.2%
Married, Spouse Present	11.2	14.9	19.8
Other	22.5	25.7	28.5
Single	n.a.	10.8	13.1
Widowed, Divorced, or Separated	n.a.	14.9	15.5
Men	66.4%	59.3%	51.8%
Married, Spouse Present	54.9	42.8	36.2
Other	11.6	16.5	15.6
Single	n.a.	10.2	11.4
Widowed, Divorced, or Separated	n.a.	6.4	4.2

* Workers who report they have multiple jobs in order to meet regular household expenses or pay off debts.

Source: Authors' analysis.

Table 4.19 makes clear that the majority of those working multiple jobs do not combine two part-time jobs to create the equivalent of a full-time position: multiple jobholders, on average, work more than the standard 40-hour week, and the majority in 1995 worked at least 50 hours per week. More than 60% of the men and almost 40% of the women with more than one job worked at least 50 hours per week.

TABLE 4.19

Hours Worked by Multiple Jobholders, by Gender, 1995

| Gender | Average Weekly Hours | Percent of Multiple Jobholders Working: | | | | |
		0-39 Hours	40-49 Hours	50-69 Hours	70+ Hours	Total
All	48.2	24.6%	24.7%	39.5%	11.2%	100.0%
Men	52.5	16.1	22.6	45.3	16.0	100.0
Women	43.2	34.4	27.2	32.8	5.6	100.0

Source: Authors' analysis of unpublished BLS data.

The Contingent Workforce

A significant portion of people in today's workforce have become "contingent workers." Workers can be hired on a temporary or "contingent" basis in a variety of ways. Some firms put workers directly on their payrolls but assign them to an internal temporary-worker pool. Others hire on-call workers and day laborers. Employers also use temporary-help agencies and contracting firms to obtain workers on a temporary basis, sometimes for long periods. Some businesses hire independent contractors to perform work that would otherwise be done by employees. All these types of contingent workers are frequently denied health insurance and pension coverage and have little access to promotions and better jobs.

Data drawn from surveys of major companies suggest that the use of contingent labor is widespread and rising (**Table 4.20**). In 1986, 36% of the sur-

TABLE 4.20

The Use of Various Types of Contingent Labor

	Percent of Surveyed Firms That Use Contingent Labor, by Type of Labor		
Survey	Internal Temporary-Worker Pool	Temporary-Help Agencies	Independent Contracting
1986*	36%	77%	63%
1989**	49	97	78

* Survey of 47 major companies.
** Survey of 521 major companies.

Source: Carre (1992).

veyed firms had an internal temporary-worker pool; a later survey (not of the same firms) showed that 49% of firms use their own temporary-worker pool. The hiring of workers through temporary-help agencies is now nearly universal among large companies: in the 1989 survey, 97% of the firms used temporary-help agencies. Independent contracting is also widespread, with 78% of the firms using this method in 1989.

Unfortunately, these surveys do not have information on how many contingent workers these firms actually used, and little historical information is available. The only subgroup of contingent workers that is captured over time by government statistics is the workforce employed through temporary-help agencies, and these data are not available for the years before 1982. For a longer perspective, however, it is possible to examine the growth of the entire personnel-services industry, which consists primarily of workers hired through or working for temporary agencies (three-fourths of the total) but also includes people working in employment agencies (**Table 4.21** and **Figure 4D**). Employment in personnel services exploded over the 1982-89 recovery and again in the recovery after 1992. Industry employment rose by 947,000 from 1979 to 1989 and an additional 956,000 by 1995. As a result, the share of the workforce employed in the personnel-services industry more than tripled between 1979 (0.6%) and 1995 (2.1%). Women are more likely to be employed as temporary workers, partly because such work provides flexible hours but also because much temporary work is in occupations

TABLE 4.21

Growth in Employment in Personnel-Services Industry, 1973-95

Year	Number (000)			As Share of Total Employment		
	All	Men	Women	All	Men	Women
1973	247	119	128	0.3%	0.1%	0.2%
1979	508	210	298	0.6	0.3	0.3
1989	1,455	581	874	1.3	0.5	0.8
1995	2,411	1,080	1,330	2.1	0.9	1.1

Source: Authors' analysis.

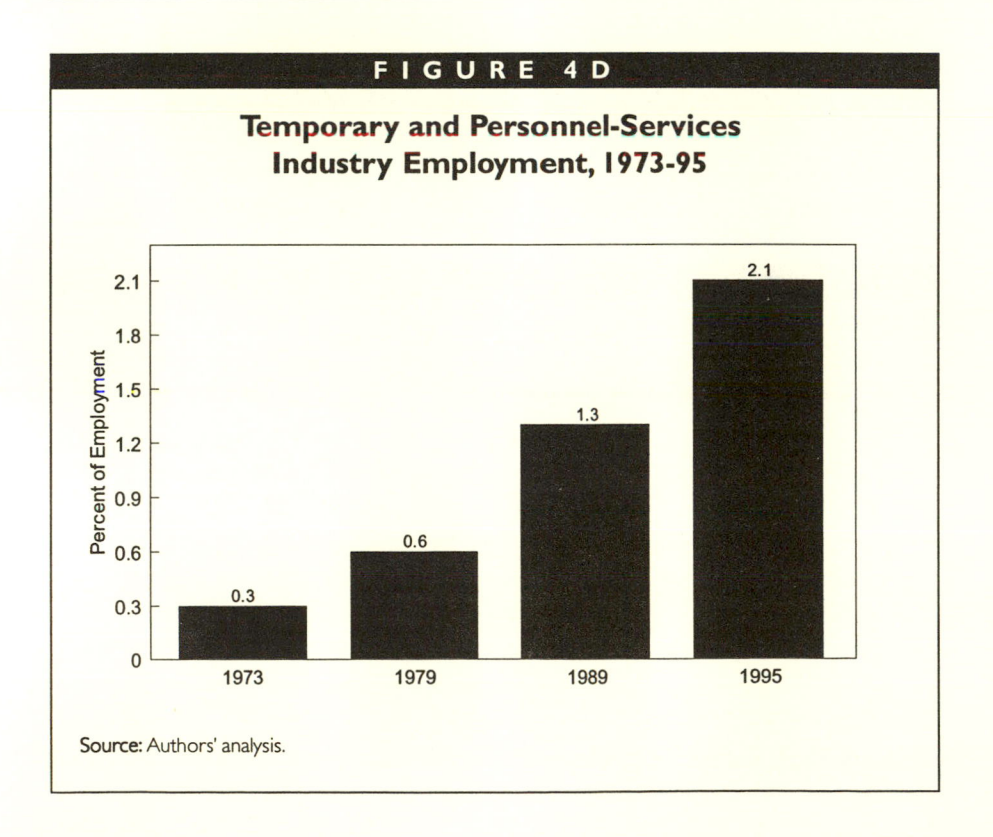

FIGURE 4D

Temporary and Personnel-Services Industry Employment, 1973-95

Source: Authors' analysis.

dominated by women, such as clerical work. In 1995, about 55% of personnel-services workers were women (1.3 million of 2.4 million), down from about 60% in 1979 and 1989 but higher than the 51% proportion in 1973.

The available information on temporary-help industry employment since 1982 is presented in **Table 4.22**. These data confirm that the growth in the overall personnel-services industry is due primarily to growth in temporary-help employment. An additional 0.7% of the workforce, or 994,000 more workers, was employed through temporary-help agencies in 1995 than in 1982 (the earliest year for which data exist), with almost all of the increase (90%) among women.

Contingent workers, however, are not limited to those employed through temporary-help agencies. A recent study by the Bureau of Labor Statistics (BLS) provides a much broader snapshot of the contingent and alternative workforce in 1995. The BLS labeled workers as "contingent" if workers did not expect their current jobs to last more than one additional year. The BLS separately counted a second (potentially overlapping) group of workers with "alternative" employment arrangements, including independent contractors, on-call workers, day laborers, temporary workers, and workers employed through contracting firms. **Table 4.23** reports the results of the BLS investigation. About 4.9% of all workers in 1995 thought that their jobs would not exist in a year's time. The number of workers with alternative employment arrangements was even higher. About 6.7% of all workers in 1995 were independent contractors on their cur-

TABLE 4.22

Growth in Employment in Temporary-Help Industry, 1982-95

Year	Number (000)			As Share of Total Employment		
	All	Men	Women	All	Men	Women
1982*	417	158	259	0.5%	0.2%	0.3%
1989	1,216	494	722	1.1	0.4	0.7
1995	1,411	254	1,157	1.2	0.2	1.0

* Earlier data not available.

Source: Authors' analysis.

TABLE 4.23

Elements of the Marginal Workforce, February 1995

Type of Worker	Number of Workers (000)	Percent of Total Employed
Contingent Workers		
Workers who do not expect their jobs to last more than one more year	6,034	4.9%
With Alternative Arrangements		
Independent contractors	8,309	6.7
On-call workers and day laborers	2,078	1.7
Workers paid by temporary-help agencies	1,181	1.0
Workers provided by contract firms	652	0.5
Total with Alternative Arrangements	12,220	9.9

Source: Authors' analysis of BLS (1995).

rent jobs; 1.7% were on-call or day laborers; 1.0% were temporary workers (note that this is below the esimate of temporary-agency employment, based on different BLS data, presented in Table 4.23); and 0.5% were employed through contracting firms. Together, the "alternative arrangement" workers represented about 9.9% of the total workforce in 1995.

Contingent workers and those in alternative employment arrangements generally earn substantially less than their noncontingent and traditionally employed counterparts. **Table 4.24** reports the median weekly earnings in 1995 for workers in the BLS employment categories. Contingent workers earn about $178 per week less than noncontingent workers. The difference in weekly earnings is larger for men ($202) than women ($148), but since men's earnings are on average higher than those of women's, the pay gap is about the same, in percentage terms, for both. Workers in alternative employment arrangements also fall far behind those who work in traditional employment arrangements.

As was the case for part-time workers, contingent workers and those with alternative employment arrangements generally have much lower access to health and other employer-provided benefits. **Table 4.25** reports the share of workers

TABLE 4.24

Median Usual Weekly Earnings of Contingent and Alternative Workers, February 1995

Type of Worker	All	Men	Women
Contingent Workers	$238	$297	$192
Noncontingent	416	499	340
Difference (Contingent-Noncontingent)	-178	-202	-148
With Alternative Arrangements	$253	$298	$203
With Traditional Arrangements	414	498	337
Difference (Alternative-Traditional)	-161	-200	-134

Source: Authors' analysis of unpublished BLS data.

TABLE 4.25

Health Insurance Coverage by Employment Status, February 1995

Type of Worker	Percent with Coverage Through: Employer	Other Source	Total
Contingent Workers			
Workers who do not expect their jobs to last more than one more year	20.4%	44.5%	64.9%
Noncontingent	53.9	28.3	82.2
With Alternative Arrangements			
Independent contractors	n.a.	72.6%	72.6%
On-call workers and day laborers	16.9%	46.6	63.5
Workers paid by temporary-help agencies	5.7	39.2	44.9
Workers provided by contract firms	42.5	27.4	69.9
With Traditional Arrangements	57.2	25.5	82.7

Source: Authors' analysis of BLS (1995).

in each of the employment categories in Table 4.23 with health insurance through their employer. While 53.9% of noncontingent workers have health insurance through their employers, only 20.4% of contingent workers have such coverage. Similarly, about 57% of workers with traditional employment relationships have employer-provided coverage, far more than those with any type of alternative arrangements. Only about 6% of temporary-help agency workers have employer-provided health coverage. On-call workers and day laborers (with 17% covered) and workers with contracting firms (43% covered) are better off, but still trail far behind traditionally employed workers.

The BLS study sheds important light on the state of contingent work, but it has two limitations. First, it contains no historical detail, so that it is impossible to know how these new measures of the contingent and alternative workforces have changed over time. If these new measures mirror developments in temporary-help-agency employment, then, as we saw above, they will have increased substantially since 1973. Second, the definitions of contingent employment may be overly narrow. Economists often consider other criteria when estimating the level of contingent employment, including low or variable earnings and hours worked, especially when such outcomes are involuntary. As we saw earlier (Table 4.13), about 20% of total part-time employment is involuntary—these part-time workers would like to work full time but cannot find full-time work. A broader definition of contingent workers would include these workers, raising the total share of contingent employment in 1995 from 4.9% to about 8.6%.

Self-Employment

A significant portion of total employment consists of self-employed workers, those whose primary job is working in their own business, farm, craft, or profession. Individual independent contracting, discussed in the previous section, is another form of self-employment.

In 1995, the self-employed accounted for 7.9% of total employment, up from 7.1% in 1979 (**Table 4.26**). Over the 1973-95 period, the greatest growth in self-employment was among women workers—1.6 percentage points of total employment, compared to a 1.0-percentage-point increase for men.

Much self-employment is disguised underemployment, as can be seen from the fact that self-employed workers earn far less than those on regular payrolls (**Table 4.27**). Self-employed women, for example, earn only 63% as much as female wage and salary workers, despite the fact that self-employed women

TABLE 4.26

Growth of Self-Employment, 1948-95

Year	Self-Employment as Share of Total Employment* Among:		
	All	**Men**	**Women**
1948	12.1%	n.a.	n.a.
1967	7.3	8.8%	4.4%
1973	6.7	8.2	4.9
1979	7.1	8.8	5.8
1989	7.5	9.0	6.0
1995**	7.9	9.2	6.5

* Nonagricultural industries.
** Not directly comparable with data for earlier years because of a redesign of Current Population Survey.

Source: Authors' analysis.

TABLE 4.27

Wages and Benefits, Self-Employed versus Wage and Salary Employment, 1990

Pay/Benefit	Men	Women
Ratio of Hourly Wage		
Self-Employed/Wage and Salary	98%	63%
Average Years of Schooling		
Wage and Salary	13.0 yrs.	13.0 yrs.
Self-Employed	13.6	13.3
Percent with Job-Related Health Care Coverage		
Wage and Salary	79%	72%
Self-Employed	38	16

* Comparisons are of full-time, full-year workers.

Source: Devine (1994).

have more education (13.3 versus 13.0 years). The wage differences between self-employed men and male wage and salary workers is slight (98%), but self-employed men are on average even better educated than their wage and salary worker counterparts (13.6 versus 13.0 years).

Table 4.27 also demonstrates that self-employed workers have fewer benefits than are provided to wage and salary workers. The most visible and important benefit—health coverage—was provided to roughly three-fourths of wage and salary workers that worked full time and full year in 1990, but to only 38% of self-employed men and 16% of self-employed women. Although economists have not conducted a comprehensive analysis (including adequate controls for differences in human capital and other job-quality factors) that would determine the degree to which self-employment pays less than wage and salary employment, the pay and benefits information in Table 4.27 argues that for many workers self-employment is another form of underemployment.

Conclusion

Unemployment and underemployment continue to impose severe economic hardships on a large portion of the population. Job creation has slowed considerably since the late 1970s, dimming prospects for the millions of workers currently unable to find work or seeking full-time work but who have been forced to settle for part-time employment. Even more worrying is the trend toward declining job stability, which undermines the economic security of many American workers. For men, job stability declined in the 1980s, and the availability of long-term jobs continued to decline into the 1990s. The rise in long-term employment opportunities for women is encouraging, but women continue to trail men in their rates of long-term employment.

Job loss was as common in the 1991-93 recovery as it had been in the 1981-83 recession, with white-collar layoffs accounting for a significant share of the increase. Since the average job loser's new job pays about 15% less than his or her old job, the sustained high level of job displacement has profound implications for American living standards. The supply of jobs has become increasingly more contingent, with many workers in jobs with low and variable pay and hours and few prospects for greater job security or advancement. A rising share of workers have had to respond to declining wage levels and job security by working more than one job, often requiring 50 or more hours of work a week to make ends meet.

Slow job growth, high underemployment, declining job security, and the growth in contingent work arrangements have contributed to the deteriorating wage structure discussed in Chapter 3. These factors have also led a substantial number of workers and their families to lose medical coverage and pension benefits for their retirement.

CHAPTER 5

WEALTH
More for the Wealthy, Financial Decline and Insecurity for the Majority

STAGNANT INCOMES AND FALLING WAGES ARE ONLY PART OF THE DECLINE IN the well-being of working Americans. A family's standard of living, as well as its ability to cope with financial emergencies, are affected by its wealth. For example, financial assets such as money in a bank account or stocks and bonds can help a family make ends meet during periods of illness or unemployment. Tangible assets such as a home or a car can directly affect a family's quality of life and the ease with which it meets its needs for housing and transportation. Families also need to accumulate wealth for their future needs, such as retirement income or college expenses and tuition for children.

The distribution of wealth is even more concentrated at the top than is the distribution of income, and it has become more uneven since 1983, despite a slight reversal in the early 1990s. For instance, over the 1983-89 recovery, the distribution of wealth became significantly more concentrated. In fact, the vast majority of the accumulated household wealth over the 1983-89 period accrued to the very richest families, while wealth among the bottom 40% of families actually fell. The consequence of this increased wealth inequality is a larger gap in overall financial security between the rich on the one hand and the middle class and the poor on the other.

In the early 1990s, there was a slight lessening of inequality, which primarily took the form of a redistribution among the top 10%. Unfortunately, nearly all groups saw the value of their wealth decline from 1989 to 1992 (although the bottom 40% saw their indebtness decline).

While the most recent data on the distribution of wealth are for 1992, aggregate wealth data are available up to 1994. These data show that between 1989 and 1994 overall wealth per adult has actually declined and the value of tangible assets (the most widely held type of asset) has dropped nearly 2% each year. In contrast, the value of financial assets (mostly held by the wealthy) grew, although at only a 0.4% annual rate. Other measures also show a decline in the wealth owned by middle-class families. These trends suggest an increase in economic insecurity in the early 1990s. The positive news is that lower interest rates have somewhat lessened the burden of household debt, which has remained high by historical standards.

The stock market boom of the 1980s and 1990s has not enriched working families for the single reason that working families do not own much stock. In fact, less than a third of households own more than $2,000 in stock, and two-thirds of the value of stock is owned by the best-off 10% of households. This concentrated ownership of stock is as evident in pension and savings plans (where stock is held "indirectly") as in the direct ownership of stock or stock mutual fund shares. Thus, there is no basis for believing that the wage or income "squeeze" on working families has been offset in any way by benefits derived from a booming stock market. The conditions that have created stock market growth have not generated widely shared income or wealth growth.

Aggregate Household Wealth: Financial Assets Boomed, Tangibles Failed to Grow

We have seen in earlier chapters that income growth in recent years was slow by historical standards, increasingly unequal, and, for many, characterized by more work at lower wages. Has there been a similar trend regarding wealth creation and distribution? In this section we examine the change in the overall growth of wealth. Trends in wealth inequality are examined in the next section.

A basic measure of aggregate wealth is *household net worth*, which is the total assets of all households minus their debts. **Table 5.1** and **Figure 5A** trace the growth of household net worth (per adult) over the postwar period between cyclical peak years and to 1994. Household net worth per adult declined slightly, at a rate of 0.1% per year, from 1989 to 1994. This follows a period of modest wealth growth of 1.9% per year between 1979 and 1989, somewhat better than the 1.7% rate of 1973-79 but well under the 3.2% annual growth rate of 1949-67. Thus, the disappointing decline of household wealth over the current business cycle follows the period of the 1980s, where both wealth and income grew slowly, at least by historical standards.

TABLE 5.1

Growth of Household Wealth, 1949-94

Type of Wealth	Annual Growth of Real Household Net Worth per Adult				
	1949-67	1967-73	1973-79	1979-89	1989-94
Total Net Worth*	3.2%	0.9%	1.7%	1.9%	-0.1%
Net Tangible Assets**	2.8	4.3	4.2	0.2	-1.8
Net Financial Assets***	3.3	-0.5	0.4	2.9	0.4

* Includes all households, personal trusts, and nonprofit organizations.
** Consumer durables, housing, and land assets less home mortgages.
*** Financial assets less nonmortgage debt.

Source: Authors' analysis of Federal Reserve Board and other data.

FIGURE 5A

Growth of Household Wealth per Adult, 1949-94

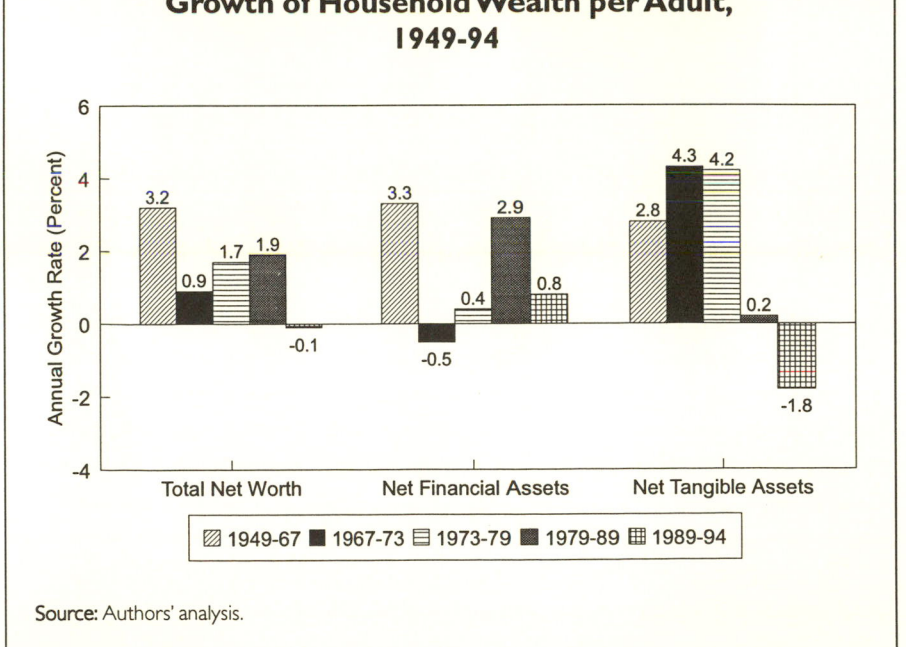

Source: Authors' analysis.

Not all household assets grew at the same rate. Table 5.1 distinguishes between "tangible assets"—the consumer durables (cars, refrigerators, and so on) and housing, which are the most widely held form of wealth—and "financial assets," which are owned mostly by the wealthy (as discussed below). Although financial assets grew slowly (0.4% annually) in the 1989-94 period, this occurred at a time when overall net worth was declining. Financial assets did absolutely and relatively better in the 1979-89 period, achieving growth of 2.9% per year at a rate close to the 3.3% growth rate of 1949-67. The rapid growth in financial assets in the 1980s contrasts starkly with the modest 0.4% annual growth of 1973-79 and the 0.5% decline between 1967 and 1973.

In contrast, the value per adult of tangible assets, such as housing and land, automobiles, appliances, and so on, grew just 0.2% a year in the 1979-89 period and *fell* over the 1989-94 period. This disappointing growth of tangible assets since 1979 is especially impressive because there had been strong tangible asset growth throughout the 1950s, 1960s, and 1970s. Since tangible assets are distributed more evenly than financial assets, their stagnation indicates that the bulk of the population was unable to accumulate possessions in the post-1979 period. The pattern of wealth growth shown in Table 5.1—higher growth of financial than tangible assets—thus previews the growing wealth inequality detailed in the next section.

Wealth Inequality Exceeds Income Gap

The distribution of wealth is considerably less equal than the distribution of income. The concentration of wealth among very high-income households is dramatic. **Table 5.2** and **Figure 5B** reveal that in 1989 the top 1% of families earned 16.4% of total income, yet owned 38.9% of total net worth (the value of one's assets minus one's debts) and a remarkable 48.1% of net financial assets. (These income data are from a different source than that used in Chapters 1 and 2.) For a typical family net worth reflects the value of its house, car, other consumer goods, and bank accounts, less the amount owed on its mortgages and credit cards. Net financial assets are financial assets minus debts. For the same family, this would be the bank account balance minus mortgage and credit card debts. The value of pension plans is not included in this analysis.

In contrast, the bottom 90% of households received 59.7% of all income but held just 27.6% of total net worth and just 16.2% of net financial assets. Many of the families at the bottom of the income distribution have no assets to fall

TABLE 5.2

Distribution of Income and Wealth, 1989

Wealth Class	Distribution of:		
	Net Worth	Net Financial Assets	Household Income
All	100.0%	100.0%	100.0%
Top 1%	38.9	48.1	16.4
Next 9%	33.4	35.6	23.7
Bottom 90%	27.6	16.2	59.7

Source: Analysis of Wolff (1994).

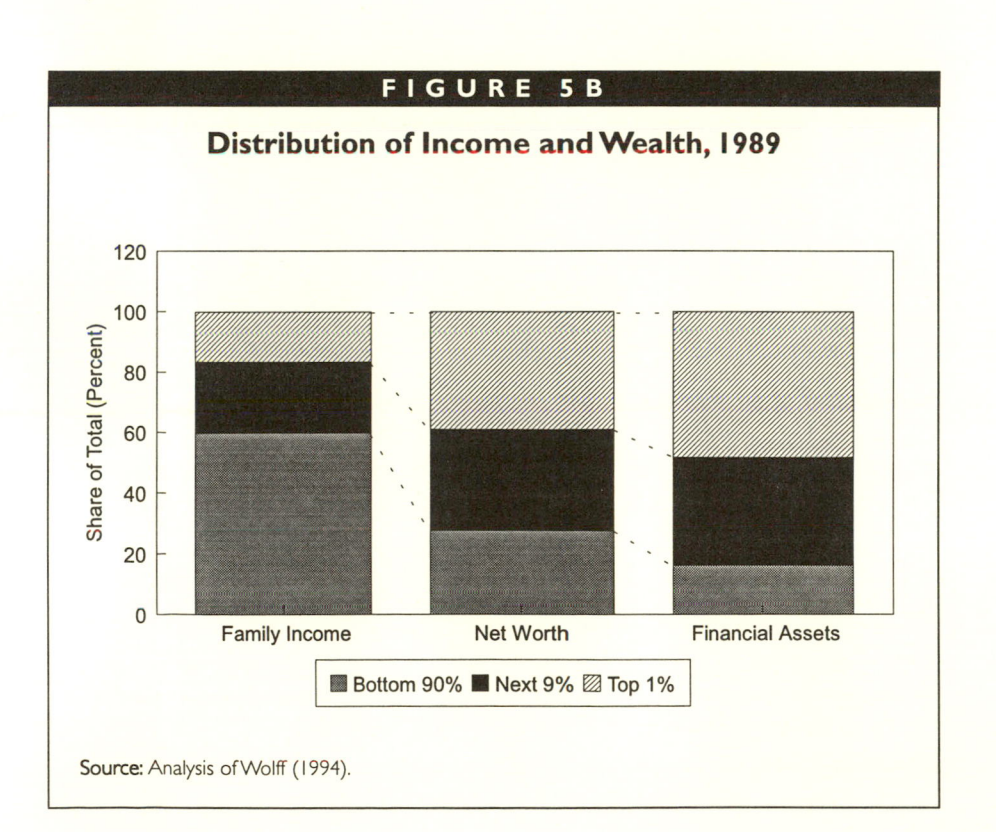

FIGURE 5B

Distribution of Income and Wealth, 1989

Source: Analysis of Wolff (1994).

back on. In 1983 (the latest year for which data are available), 20% of families had a zero or negative net worth, and 54% had zero or negative net financial assets. Though most of the latter are not poor, their lack of financial assets indicates that more than half of American families are living from paycheck to paycheck, with little or nothing in the bank in case of job loss or another serious financial emergency.

The concentration of financial assets at the top implies that American businesses are owned and financed primarily by the richest families. In 1992, for example, the wealthiest top 1% owned 49.6% of all corporate stocks, while the bottom 90% owned only 13.6% (**Table 5.3**). The top 1% also owned 62.4% of

TABLE 5.3

Percent of Total Assets
Held by Wealth Class, 1992

Asset Type	Top 1%	Next 9%	Bottom 90%	Total	Share of Top 10% 1989	Share of Top 10% 1992
A. Assets Held Primarily by the Wealthy						
Stocks	49.6%	36.7%	13.6%	100.0%	89.4%	86.4%
Bonds	62.4	28.9	8.7	100.0	88.7	91.3
Trusts	52.9	35.1	12.0	100.0	89.1	88.0
Business Equity	61.6	29.5	8.9	100.0	90.1	91.1
Non-Home Real Estate	45.9	37.1	17.0	100.0	80.1	83.0
Total for Group	54.4	33.3	12.3	100.0	87.1	87.7
B. Assets and Liabilities Held Primarily by the Nonwealthy						
Principal Residence	9.0%	27.1%	63.9%	100.0%	33.8%	36.1%
Deposits*	22.4	37.3	40.3	100.0	60.4	59.7
Life Insurance	10.0	35.1	54.9	100.0	44.7	45.1
Pension Accounts**	16.4	45.9	37.7	100.0	52.9	62.3
Total for Group	12.9	32.3	54.8	100.0	42.7	45.2
Total Debt	13.8%	23.8%	62.5%	100.0%	30.1%	37.5%

*   Includes demand deposits, savings, time deposits, money-market funds, and certificates of deposit.
** IRAs, Keogh plans, 401(k) plans, the accumulated value of defined contribution pension plans, and other retirement accounts.

Source: Wolff (1996).

bonds and 61.6% of private business equity (ownership of firms that do not sell stock to the public), while the bottom 90% owned only 8.7% of bonds and 8.9% of business equity. Overall, Table 5.3 shows that the types of wealth that generate income, such as bonds, businesses, stocks, and other financial assets, tend to be held almost exclusively by the richest 10%, with the majority held by the top 1%, of families. This concentrated ownership at the top was evident in 1989 as much as in 1992.

The types of wealth held by the bottom 90% of families are primarily homes and life insurance. Nonwealthy families also own "deposits" (primarily cash in checking, savings, and money-market accounts), which are used to meet regular expenses. The bottom 90% of families also owe 62.5% of all debt, consisting primarily of mortgages on their homes.

Growing Wealth Inequality

As we shall see, there was a dramatic growth in wealth inequality during the late 1980s. It is important to note, however, that the long-term trend prior to the 1980s was toward a lesser concentration of wealth. **Table 5.4** shows the share of total wealth (both excluding and including retirement wealth) over the 1922-81 period for years in which data are available. In general, wealth was more concentrated in the 1920s and 1930s than in any period after World War II. The concentration of wealth (excluding retirement wealth) held by the wealthiest 1% remained fairly steady over the 1940s, 1950s, and 1960s, ranging from a low of 25.7% in 1949 to a high of 31.9% in 1965, with no discernible trend up or down. The data for 1976 and 1981, however, suggest that wealth became less concentrated during the 1970s.

Surveys by the Federal Reserve Board in 1962, 1983, 1989, and 1992 allow a direct examination of changes in the distribution of wealth. Between 1962 and 1983 there were only minor changes (**Table 5.5**). For instance, the percentage of total wealth held by each fifth of families remained comparable between 1962 and 1983, with a modest redistribution to the bottom 40% and to the upper 5%. Between 1983 and 1989, however, there was a major upward redistribution of wealth. In 1989, the richest 1% of families owned 39.0% of household net worth, up 5.2 percentage points from the 33.8% share in 1983. This group's share of wealth grew by 0.4 percentage points (from 33.4% to 33.8%) over the entire 21-year period between 1962 and 1983, then grew 13 times as much as that in just six years between 1983 and 1989. No group other than the richest 1% increased

TABLE 5.4

Share of Total Household Wealth Held
by Richest 1% of Individuals, 1922-81

Year	Excluding Retirement Wealth	Including Retirement Wealth
1922	38.3%	37.9%
1929	37.2	36.7
1933	28.9	28.2
1939	38.1	33.4
1945	28.9	22.4
1949	25.7	20.5
1953	28.1	21.6
1958	27.0	20.7
1962	30.1	22.5
1965	31.9	23.4
1969	29.0	21.0
1972	28.6	20.5
1976	18.9	13.8
1981	23.6	n.a.

Source: Wolff (1992a).

its share of wealth between 1983 and 1989, and the share of wealth that the top 1% *gained*—5.2 percentage points—was more than the *total* wealth held by the bottom 60% of families in 1989.

Most startling is the erosion of the wealth shares of the bottom 40% of families. The poorest fifth of families had more debt than assets in 1983 and fell further in debt by 1989. The second fifth saw its share of wealth reduced by a third, shrinking from a negligible 1.2% in 1983 to just 0.8% in 1989.

We have several clues as to why this spectacular redistribution occurred. As shown in Chapter 1, there was a redistribution of family income during this same period. Given that the incomes of the well-off grew rapidly, it could be expected that their accumulation of wealth would also grow. In 1989, the upper fifth had an additional 4.2% of total family income relative to 1983, while the bottom 60% of families had a lower share. These shifts parallel the trends in wealth. This wealth accumulation, in turn, helped to fuel the income growth of

TABLE 5.5

Changes in the Distribution of Wealth, 1962-92

Wealth Class	Share of Wealth*				Change		
	1962	1983	1989	1992	1983-89	1989-92	1983-92
Top Fifth	81.0%	81.3%	84.6%	83.8%	3.3	-0.8	2.5
Top 1%	33.4	33.8	39.0	37.2	5.2	-1.8	3.4
Next 4%	21.2	22.3	21.9	22.8	-0.4	0.9	0.5
Next 5%	12.4	12.1	11.5	11.8	-0.6	0.3	-0.3
Next 10%	14.0	13.1	12.2	12.0	-0.9	-0.2	-1.1
Bottom Four-Fifths	19.1%	18.7%	15.5%	16.3%	-3.2	0.8	-2.4
Fourth	13.4	12.6	11.5	11.5	-1.1	0.0	-1.1
Middle	5.4	5.2	4.6	4.4	-0.6	-0.2	-0.8
Second	1.0	1.2	0.8	0.9	-0.4	0.1	-0.3
Lowest	-0.7	-0.3	-1.4	-0.5	-1.1	0.9	-0.2
Total	100.0%	100.0%	100.0%	100.0%			

* Wealth defined as net worth, equal to a household's assets less its debt.

Source: Wolff (1996).

the best-off families through greater interest income and capital gains.

The growth of income shares at the top (not shown), however, was somewhat less than what occurred for wealth. That income and wealth concentration should generally move together is not surprising. Neither should it be surprising that there were differences in the extent of the growth between the two.

Despite the slight lessening of wealth inequality between 1989 and 1992, the concentration of wealth was still far greater in 1992 than in 1983 (**Figure 5C**). And most of the decline in the wealth share of the top 1% translated into the 1.2-percentage-point gain for the rest of the top 10% (the "next 4%" and "next 5%"). There was in addition, however, a lessening of the indebtedness, or negative wealth, of the poorest fifth.

Table 5.6 shows another dimension of growing wealth inequality by presenting the pattern of wealth growth for the various wealth classes over the 1962-92 period. First, consider the pattern over the 1983-89 economic expansion. The bottom 40% of families not only saw their *share* of wealth decline, as shown above, but also experienced significant losses in the *value* of their wealth.

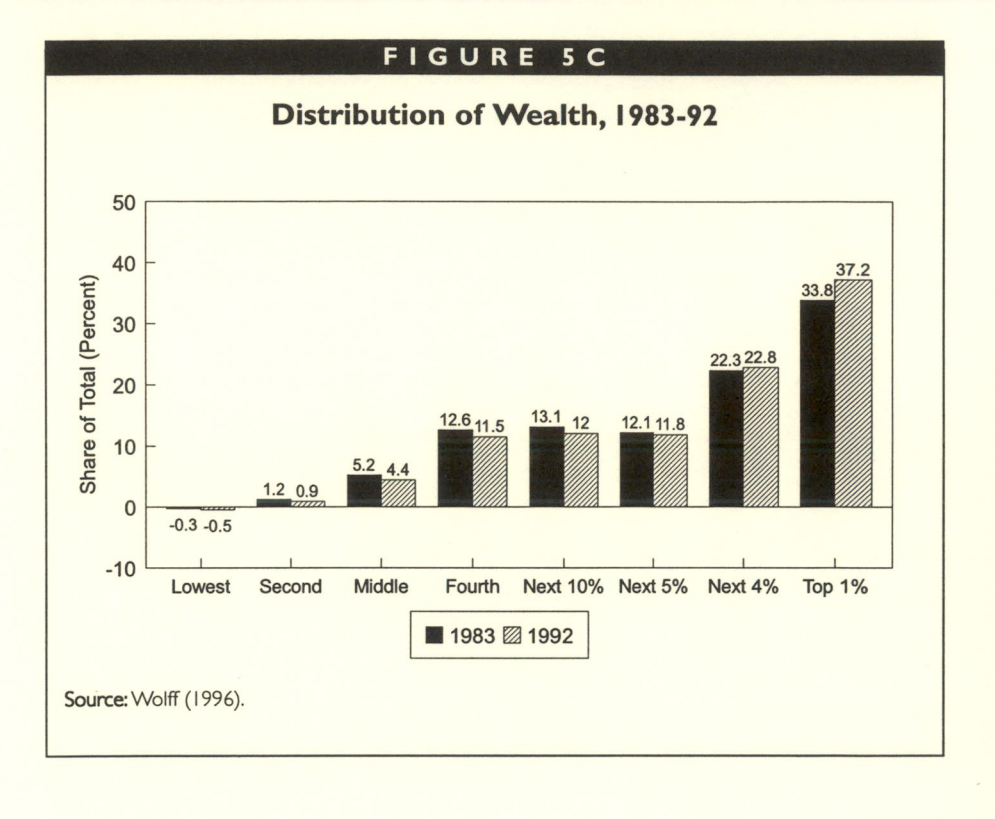

FIGURE 5C

Distribution of Wealth, 1983-92

Source: Wolff (1996).

For instance, the bottom 40% saw their modest wealth holdings (in 1992 dollars) of $4,000 in 1983 reduced to $1,400 by 1989, despite six years of economic expansion.

In the 1983-89 period, only the upper 1% experienced faster-than-average growth in wealth. This group's holdings rose 42% in the six years after 1983, for an annual growth rate of 6%. These wealthy families had achieved an average net worth of $8.7 million by 1989, an increase of $2.6 million per family. In contrast, the median family's wealth grew by $3,800, or 8.1%.

The slight reversal of wealth inequality over the 1989-92 period occurred as the average family's wealth fell by 5.1% and wealth declined for each wealth class, except the bottom 40% (who gained, on average, $600 per family). Despite this wealth setback for the wealthiest groups, wealth holdings in 1992 were greater than in 1983 for the upper 40% and especially for the top 1%, whose wealth was 28.3% greater. In contrast, the bottom 60% of families lost ground, as reflected in the 8.1% decline in median wealth over the 1983-92 period.

The data in **Table 5.7** are taken from a different set of surveys (from the

TABLE 5.6

Change in Wealth by Wealth Class, 1962-92
(1992 Dollars)

Wealth Class	Wealth *(000)				Percent Change		
	1962	1983	1989	1992	1983-89	1989-92	1983-92
Top Fifth	$505.8	$744.1	$950.8	$893.6	27.8%	-6.0%	20.1%
Top 1%	4,176.2	6,176.0	8,772.0	7,925.0	42.0	-9.7	28.3
Next 4%	n.a.	1,022.0	1,228.0	1,218.0	20.2	-0.8	19.2
Next 5%	n.a.	444.3	516.1	503.9	16.2	-2.4	13.4
Next 10%	174.2	239.9	275.2	255.8	14.7	-7.0	6.6
Bottom Four-Fifths	$29.4	$42.7	$45.7	$43.2	7.1%	-5.5%	1.2%
Fourth	83.7	115.0	129.0	122.2	12.2	-5.3	6.3
Middle	33.9	47.8	51.1	46.7	7.1	-8.6	-2.2
Bottom 40%	0.6	4.0	1.4	2.0	-65.2	44.8	-49.7
Average	$124.5	$183.0	$224.8	$213.3	22.9%	-5.1%	16.6%
Median	33.4	47.0	50.8	43.2	8.1	-15.0	-8.1

*   Wealth defined as net worth, equal to a household's assets less its debt.
** Change calculated from underlying unrounded data.

Source: Wolff (1996).

TABLE 5.7

Change in Wealth by Income Class, 1984-93
(1995 Dollars)

Income Class	Median Net Worth				Percent Change			
	1984	1988	1991	1993	1984-88	1988-91	1991-93	1984-93
Lowest	$6,609	$5,570	$5,845	$4,481	-15.7%	4.9%	-23.3%	-32.2%
Second	27,373	25,371	21,474	21,336	-7.3	-15.4	-0.6	-22.1
Middle	37,951	36,128	32,292	32,471	-4.8	-10.6	0.6	-14.4
Fourth	64,344	59,585	55,056	52,734	-7.4	-7.6	-4.2	-18.0
Top	126,778	143,988	137,816	125,502	13.6	-4.3	-8.9	-1.0
Average	47,681	46,058	40,979	39,642	-3.4	-11.0	-3.3	-16.9

Source: Authors' analysis of U.S. Bureau of the Census data.

Census Bureau) and confirm the pattern of unequal wealth growth over the late 1980s that was shown in previous tables. Unfortunately, these surveys do not have large enough samples to allow an analysis of the wealthiest 1% or 5% of families, where, as we have seen, most of the wealth is held. These data also rank families by income rather than wealth, and they measure changes in wealth for each income group by changes in the median wealth of the group. They show that only the top 20% of families saw their wealth increase in the 1984-88 period; the rest had less wealth in 1988 than in 1984. The startling truth is that, during the 1980s recovery, the vast majority of families lost wealth as the economy grew, unemployment fell, and family income rose. Between 1988 and 1993, however, there was a broad-based erosion of household net worth, with every income fifth experiencing a sizable loss of wealth of at least 10%.

Looking over the entire 1984-93 period, one does not see broad-based wealth accumulation but widespread wealth erosion, with wealth declining from 14% to 22% among the middle three-fifths. Only the best-off 20% were able to maintain, roughly, the value of their wealth.

Table 5.8 utilizes the same Census data to examine the change in (median) wealth by age group and income group. The top panel, for instance, combines all income groups and shows the change in wealth of each age group over the 1984-93 period. Except for the most senior group, each age group had less wealth in 1993 than it did in 1984, with a significant loss of wealth for each group. Note, however, that the same people or households were not in the same age group in both 1984 and 1993, since those age 35-44 in 1984 were mostly in the 45-54 group in 1993. If one views these data through "cohorts," then one sees that the wealth of those age 35-44 in 1984 grew from $51,780 to $60,913 by the time they reached 45-54 years old. This is a positive accumulation of wealth over a household's prime working years, as would be expected. Nevertheless, the group age 45-54 accumulated less wealth than the similar age cohort had achieved in 1984 ($60,913 versus $82,894).

The remaining panels of Table 5.8 show that within each of the middle three income fifths there was a consistent pattern of decline in wealth by age group over the 1984-93 period. This analysis reinforces the idea that the post-1984 period was one of declining wealth and that this decline occurred among households of nearly all income and age groups (although these data cannot trace what happened among the best-off 1% or 5% of families).

TABLE 5.8

Change in Median Household Wealth by Age and Income Fifth, 1984-93
(1995 Dollars)

Income Fifth	Median Wealth by Age Group				
	Under 35	35-44	45-54	55-64	65+
All Incomes					
1984	$8,272	$51,870	$82,894	$107,891	$88,374
1993	6,102	30,799	60,913	96,482	91,043
1984-93	-2,170	-21,072	-21,981	-11,409	2,669
Second					
1984	3,494	13,386	27,106	75,093	95,091
1993	2,992	5,001	16,373	60,195	85,402
1984-93	-502	-8,385	-10,733	-14,898	-9,689
Middle					
1984	10,439	35,321	55,910	99,842	141,705
1993	7,375	18,262	39,458	91,129	146,129
1984-93	-3,063	-17,060	-16,452	-8,713	4,424
Fourth					
1984	21,385	62,347	83,710	130,862	251,049
1993	16,740	43,091	65,422	128,963	210,492
1984-93	-4,645	-19,257	-18,288	-1,899	-40,557

Source: Authors' analysis of U.S. Bureau of the Census data.

Who Gains from the Stock Market Boom?

As **Figure 5D** shows, the stock market has steadily, and rapidly, risen in value over the 1980s and 1990s. This continuous gain in the stock market, however, has been accompanied by income stagnation and widespread real wage declines. It seems likely, then, that the conditions for stock market growth do not also necessarily lead to widespread income and wage growth. However, if stock market gains are widely shared, then it may be the case that families experiencing income or wage problems are benefiting from the stock market boom. This would be the case if many families owned stock directly or owned it indirectly through

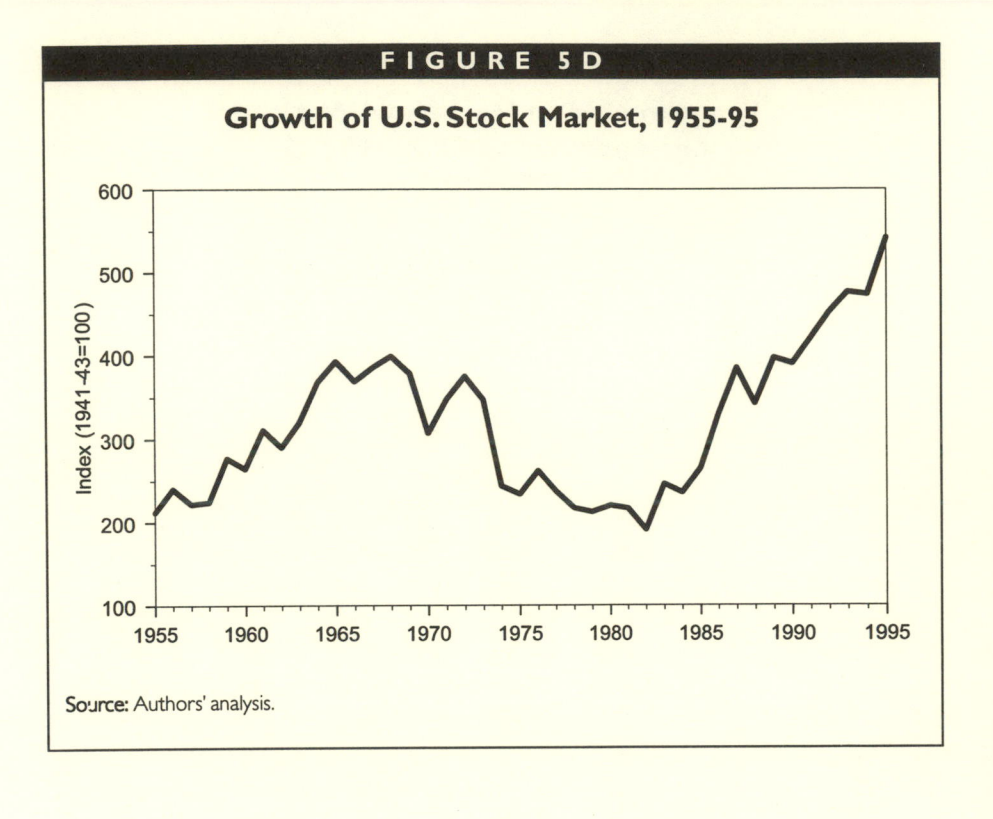

FIGURE 5D

Growth of U.S. Stock Market, 1955-95

Source: Authors' analysis.

their pension funds or savings plans. This possibility raises the question, how widespread is the ownership of stocks? We have already seen (Table 5.3) that the value of stock directly held by families is highly concentrated (roughly 87% of stock was owned by the richest 10% of families). This section examines the concentration of stock ownership held directly or indirectly.

Table 5.9 presents the available information on the extent of direct and indirect holdings of stock among U.S. households. The top panel shows that the share of households directly holding publicly traded stock has been relatively stable over the last three decades, ranging from 17.2% in 1963 to 16.9% in 1992 (with a somewhat larger 19.1% share in 1989). When ownership of stock through mutual funds is included, there is a persistent, but small, upward trend in the share of households owning stock. Looking at the broadest measure of stock ownership, including stock in IRA or Keogh accounts, 401(k) plans, or any defined-contribution pension plans, the data show that 36.8% of households owned some stock, up from 33.2% in 1983.

Thus, there is some support for the notion that stock ownership has become more widespread. But the breadth of ownership is hardly widespread, since the 36.8% of households that own stock are clearly a minority. Moreover, if one examines the share of households with more than $2,000 worth of stock, as the second panel of Table 5.9 shows, then one finds that only 28.9% of households have more than a minimal ownership of stock. These data do not support the notion that pension fund or mutual fund managers have a primarily "middle-class constituency" or that the gains of the stock market are widely shared, since any significant stock gain goes to, at most, 29% of households. Also, recall that Table 5.3 showed that 49.6% of stocks were owned by the wealthiest 1% of households, compared to only 10.6% of stock owned by the least wealthy 90% in 1992. Finally, whatever gains the middle class made from the recent stock market boom were not enough to allow these households to accumulate wealth: the total wealth of the median household (the median of the middle-fifth) actually

TABLE 5.9

Stock Ownership, 1962, 1983, and 1992

Investment Form and Household Category	Share of All Households with:		
	1962	1983	1992
Any Stock Holdings			
Publicly Traded	17.2%	19.1%	16.9%
Plus Mutual Fund	19.0	20.1	20.9
Plus IRA/Keogh Account	—	23.5	29.0
Plus 401(k) Plan	—	27.7	32.3
Plus All Defined Contribution Plan	—	33.2	36.8
Stock Holdings $2,000*			
Publicly Traded	12.6%	13.7%	12.5%
Plus Mutual Fund	14.3	14.6	16.2
Plus IRA/Keogh Accounts	—	17.1	22.7
Plus 401(k) Plan	—	20.0	25.5
Plus All Defined Contribution Plan	—	24.6	28.9

* In 1992 dollars.

Source: Poterba and Samwick (1996), revised.

fell 14.4% over the 1984-93 period in the Census data series (Table 5.7) and fell 8.1% over the 1983-92 period in the Federal Reserve Board surveys (Table 5.6).

The data in **Table 5.10** and **Figure 5E** provide greater detail on the concentration of the value of stocks, including direct and indirect holdings. These data describe the distribution of stock across income groups, both the share of each income group that owns any stock ("percent who own") and the share of the total value of stock owned by each income group ("percent of stock owned"). Three categories of stock are analyzed: (1) "publicly traded" stock directly held by households; (2) "stock in pension plans," including 401(k) and defined-contribution (the employers puts in a fixed amount or share of salary each year) plans; and (3) all stock, whether held directly or indirectly (such as through a pension or savings plan).

Several results emerge from Table 5.10. It is no surprise that households with higher incomes are more likely to own stock. For instance, 64.7% of households with incomes over $250,000 in 1992 held some publicly traded stock, while only 18.2% of households with incomes in the $25,000-$50,000 range held this type of stock. Even in the broadest measure of stock ownership, less than half (45.2%) of households in the $25,000-$50,000 income group held any stock, compared to 89.7% for the best-off group.

A second conclusion is that stock ownership, no matter how defined, is highly concentrated. The three highest income groups, which make up 10.5% of all households, controlled 73.2% of publicly traded stock, 58.8% of pension-plan stock, and 66.4% of all stock. In contrast, the three lowest income groups (these with less than $50,000 of income), which make up 76.4% of all households, owned 16.7% of public traded stock, 17.3% of pension stock, and 19.2% of all stock. *This means that about 20% of the gains in the stock market accrue to the bottom three-fourths of households, while 66% of the gains accrue to the best-off 10%.*

Third, pension assets, as reflected by stock ownership, are highly concentrated even though they are more evenly distributed than many other types of assets, including all stock. The main difference between stock holdings in pension plans and other stock holdings is that pension assets are more evenly distributed *among the top fifth of households.* That is, while the highest income group controls 24.1% of all stock, it controls only 11.2% of stock in pension plans. Nevertheless, the bottom three-fourths of households (with less than $50,000 of income) own 17.4% of the stock in pension plans, a lower share than their holding of all stock. Another analysis of the distribution of pension assets, using a broader definition of assets (not just stock) and pensions, also shows that

TABLE 5.10

Concentration of Stock Ownership, 1992

Income Level (000)	Share of Households	Percent Who Own	Percent of Stock Owned	
			Shares	Cumulative
Publicly Traded Stock				
Over 250	0.8%	64.7%	31.5%	31.5%
100-250	4.7	48.8	27.0	58.6
75-100	5.0	44.3	14.7	73.2
50-75	13.2	26.7	10.1	83.3
25-50	29.4	18.2	12.5	95.8
15-25	19.4	8.4	2.8	98.6
Under 15	27.6	5.0	1.4	100.0
Total	100.0		100.0	
Stock in Pension Plans*				
Over 250	0.8%	36.0%	11.2%	11.2%
100-250	4.7	42.7	30.0	41.2
75-100	5.0	34.9	17.6	58.8
50-75	13.2	34.8	23.9	82.7
25-50	29.4	19.2	15.5	98.2
15-25	19.4	6.4	1.2	99.3
Under 15	27.6	1.3	0.7	100.0
Total	100.0		100.0	
All Stock**				
Over 250	0.8%	89.7%	24.1%	24.1%
100-250	4.7	77.6	27.0	51.1
75-100	5.0	71.8	15.3	66.4
50-75	13.2	64.9	14.4	80.8
25-50	29.4	45.2	14.6	95.4
15-25	19.4	22.7	3.2	98.6
Under 15	27.6	9.7	1.4	100.0
Total	100.0		100.0	

* All defined contribution stock plans including 401(k) plans.
** All stock directly or indirectly held in mutual funds, IRA or Keogh plans and defined contribution pension plans.

Source: Poterba and Samwick (1995), revised.

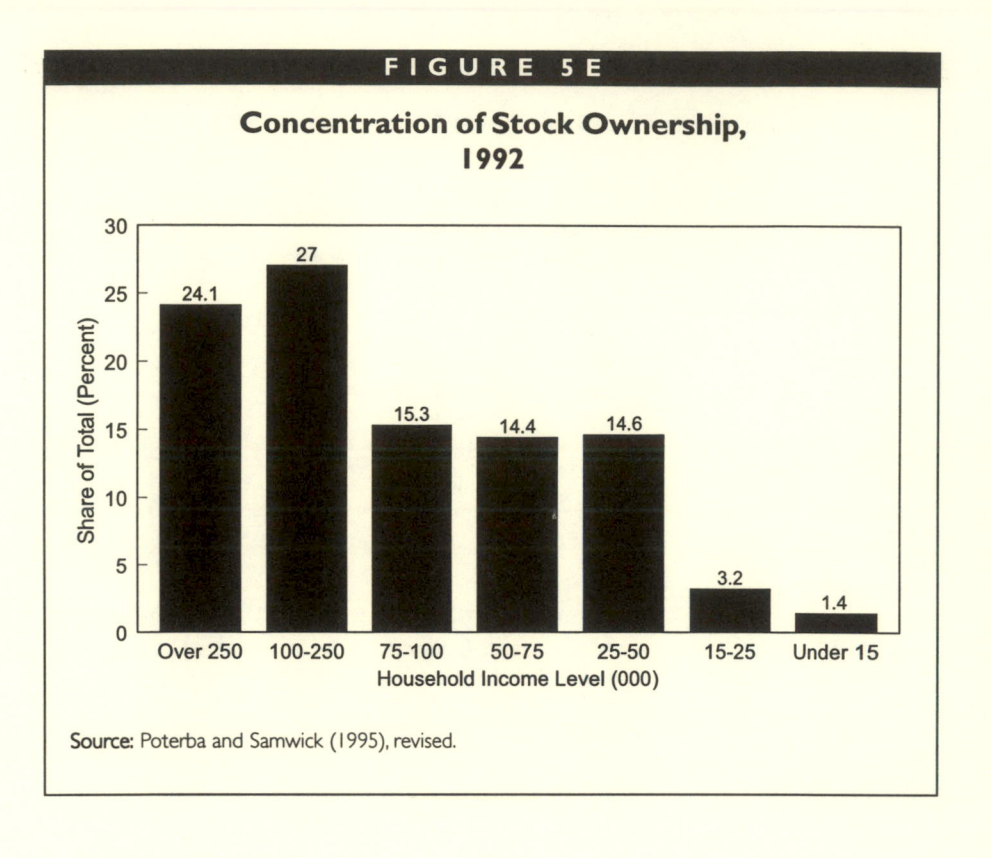

FIGURE 5E

Concentration of Stock Ownership, 1992

Source: Poterba and Samwick (1995), revised.

pension assets are highly concentrated, with the top 10% owning 62.3% of all the value of pension accounts (Table 5.3).

Table 5.11 uses the Census data to provide another view of the extent of stock ownership. In both 1984 and 1993, roughly 20% of households owned stocks directly or through a mutual fund. Not surprisingly, stock ownership is more prevalent in the highest-income fifth—about 44%—than in lower-income groups. Less than a fifth of households in the middle-income group owned any stock directly or in mutual funds. Stocks held in IRA and Keogh plans are distributed similarly. Unfortunately, this information source does not provide data on the shares of households owning stock through any vehicle, such as directly or through mutual funds or IRAs, so a direct comparison cannot be made with the data in Table 5.10. The data do show, however, that those owning stock had a higher value of stock, especially in IRAs and Keogh plans, in 1993 than in 1984, regardless of income level.

TABLE 5.11

Ownership of Stock and IRA/Keogh Accounts, 1984-93

| | Percent of Households Owning: | | | | Median Value of Holdings ($1995) | | | |
| | Stock or Mutual Fund | | IRA or Keogh | | Stock or Mutual Fund | | IRA or Keogh | |
Income Fifth	1984	1993	1984	1993	1984	1993	1984	1993
Lowest	5.0%	4.4%	3.4%	5.4%	$3,983	$3,480	$6,136	$10,547
Second	11.1	11.6	8.4	14.0	6,120	5,185	6,213	11,601
Middle	16.1	18.1	15.0	20.5	3,491	4,904	6,109	10,019
Fourth	24.5	26.0	25.0	28.3	3,735	6,223	6,526	12,445
Top	43.4	44.3	45.8	47.1	7,861	10,538	9,038	16,980
All	20.0%	20.9%	19.5%	23.1%	$5,701	$7,341	$7,060	$13,695

Source: Authors' analysis of U.S. Bureau of the Census data.

Soaring Debt

Household debt has skyrocketed in recent years. Two measures of the total debt burdens of households—debt as a percent of assets and as a percent of personal income—have each grown steadily since at least 1973 (**Table 5.12**). These higher levels of debt have left families more vulnerable whenever the economy weakens. Household debt leapt from 64.0% of personal income in 1979 to 83.9% in 1994, and from 13.5% of household assets in 1979 to 16.9% in 1994.

These measures of debt burden do not reflect changes in debt-service payments as interest rates change. Such fluctuations can make paying down any debt either more or less difficult. For instance, when interest rates fall, the burden of paying off new debt is lessened. The estimates of debt-service payments presented in the last three columns of Table 5.12 take changes in interest rates and repayment schedules (i.e., more 30-year versus fewer 15-year mortgages) into account. These data also show a sizable growth in the debt burden over the period between 1979 and 1989, because of a greater burden of home mortgages. Between 1989 and 1995, however, the overall debt burden fell, from 17.3% to 16.5%, but it was still higher than in the late 1970s.

TABLE 5.12

Household Debt Burden, 1949-95

Year	Debt as Percent of:		Debt Service as Percent of Disposable Income:		
	Personal Income	Assets*	Total Debt	Consumer Debt	Mortgage
1949	29.7%	6.3%	n.a.	n.a.	n.a.
1967	60.4	12.2	15.7%	11.8%	3.9%
1973	58.6	13.1	15.5	11.5	4.0
1979	64.0	13.5	15.6	10.7	4.9
1989	77.9	15.5	17.3	10.7	6.7
1994/1995**	83.9	16.9	16.5	10.7	5.8

* Financial assets (including pension funds and insurance), real estate, and consumer durables.
** Data for first two columns are for 1994.

Source: Authors' analysis.

Conclusion

An examination of changes in the level and distribution of household wealth helps complete the picture of the typical family's economic status. An accumulation of wealth is needed to weather emergencies (health problems, job loss, and so on), to finance retirement, and to pay for large expenditures, such as a child's college expenses or a house downpayment. The available evidence indicates that middle-income families have less wealth now than in 1989 or in 1983. The stock market boom neither enriched these families directly via their stock holdings or indirectly via their pension or savings plans.

In contrast, the richest households were able to significantly increase (by 28%) their wealth since 1983, despite a setback in the early 1990s. Two-thirds of the benefits of the stock market boom accrue to the highest-income 10% of households.

CHAPTER 6

POVERTY
High Rates Persist
Despite Overall Growth

THE PREVIOUS CHAPTERS HAVE DOCUMENTED THE WINNERS AND LOSERS IN the highly uneven growth periods of the 1980s and 1990s. This chapter focuses on the experience of the poorest members of society, those persons and families whose economic situations are the most precarious.

The evidence presented below reveals that the recent debate over poverty in America has become misguided. The conventional wisdom typically defines the problem in terms of the supposedly counterproductive behavior of poor people themselves, implying that, with more effort, the poor could lift themselves up by their bootstraps. The implication is that, because of bad choices about family structure and lack of work effort, the poor have failed to be lifted by the rising economic tide.

Recent trends in family structure and low-wage labor markets, however, contradict this analysis. For example, when we analyze the perceived problem of female-headed family formation, or the question of whether welfare programs have created incentives that increase poverty, or explore the issue of whether the poor choose not to work, we find that the data do not support these explanations for the high and intractable poverty rates throughout the economic expansions of the 1980s and 1990s.

Some critics take another tack, arguing that poverty is mismeasured and that the economic condition of the poor has improved more than the official statistics show. However, our analysis of both the government's official measurement and a series of more conceptually satisfying ways to measure poverty reveals that the general finding of the disconnection between economic growth and poverty is valid no matter how poverty is measured.

In fact, the problems analyzed in previous chapters—the heightened inequality of the income distribution, lessened progressivity of the tax system (with the notable exception of the recently expanded earned income tax credit), and, in particular, falling wages—all conspired to keep poverty rates historically high throughout the 1980s and into the 1990s. Moreover, the "safety net" (the social provision of assistance to those in poverty) grew less effective at providing relief to the poor.

Background: The Failure of Economic Growth

The failed relationship between poverty and economic growth that began in the 1980s is portrayed graphically in **Figure 6A**. The dotted line in the figure represents a statistical model of the poverty rate over time, based on economic variables historically correlated with poverty rates: unemployment, inflation, income, and government transfers. The bold line is actual poverty rates. From 1983-94, the dotted line represents forecasted values, based on the pre-1983

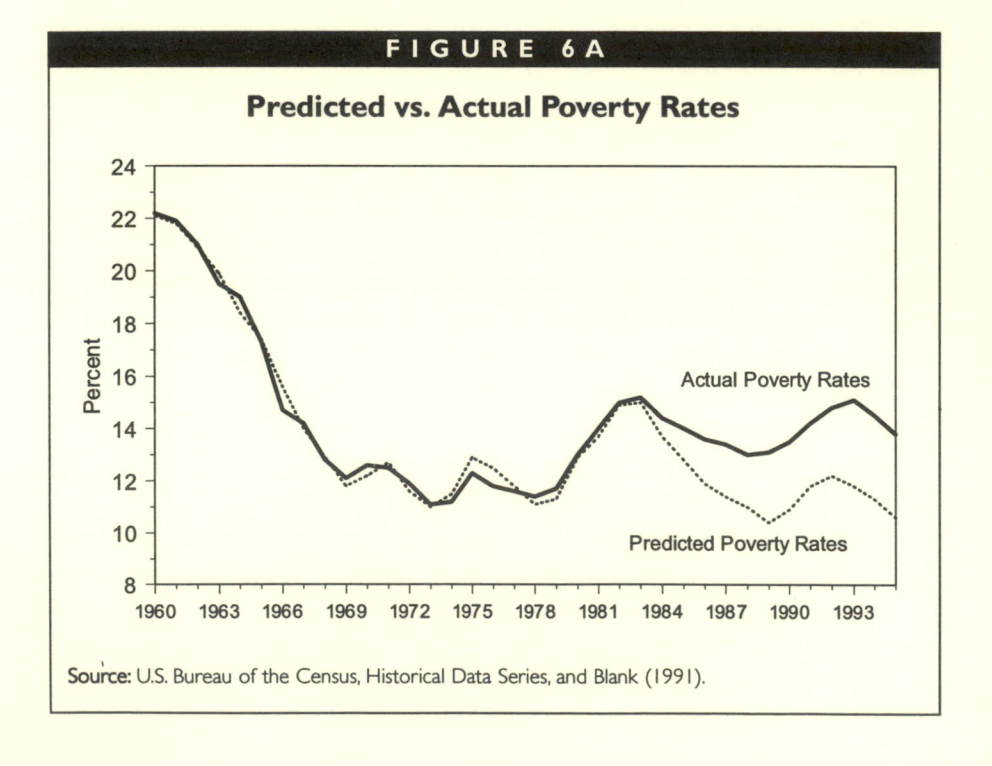

FIGURE 6A

Predicted vs. Actual Poverty Rates

Source: U.S. Bureau of the Census, Historical Data Series, and Blank (1991).

relationships between poverty and the economic factors noted above.

What is particularly notable about Figure 6A is the divergence of forecasted and actual values that began in the 1980s. The model tracks poverty extremely well up until 1983 (the beginning of the 1980s expansion), when the model incorrectly forecasts a much steeper fall in poverty rates than actually occurred. In other words, a major shift in the relationship between economic growth and poverty occurred in the 1980s such that the economic recovery in that decade failed to reduce poverty as much as occurred in earlier periods of growth (such as the 1960s or 1970s).

For the years shown in **Table 6.1**, the predicted poverty rates never diverge more than 0.4 percentage points from the actual rates until after 1983. These findings tell us that, based on the way economic growth has affected poverty in

TABLE 6.1

Percent and Number of Persons in Poverty, 1960-95, Actual and Predicted Values

Year	Actual Poverty Rates	Predicted Poverty Rates*	Change	Number in Poverty (000)
1960	22.2%	22.1%	-0.1	39,851
1967	14.2	14.0	-0.2	27,769
1973	11.1	11.0	-0.1	22,973
1979	11.7	11.3	-0.4	26,072
1983	15.2	15.0	-0.2	35,303
1989	13.1	10.4	-2.7	32,415
1995	13.8	10.6	-3.2	36,425
Averages over Peak Cycles				
1960-67	18.7%	18.8%	0.0	
1967-73	12.5	12.3	-0.1	
1973-79	11.6	11.7	0.1	
1979-89	13.7	12.6	-1.0	
1989-95	14.1	11.3	-2.8	

* Poverty rates as predicted by a set of economic variables over the 1959-83 period.

Source: Authors' analysis of U.S. Bureau of the Census, Historical Data Series, and Blank (1991).

the past, the rates should have fallen by 4.6 percentage points between 1983 and 1989, from 15.0% to 10.4%. However, the actual rates fell only 2.1 points over this period, from 15.2% to 13.1%. Given the size of the population in 1989, this means that over 6 million more persons were poor in that year than would have been the case had poverty rates continued to respond to economic growth as they had in the past. In the most recent period, 1989-95, the model captures the "turning point" in the trend due to the recession, but it continues to forecast lower poverty rates. The causes of this divergence between the predicted and actual poverty rates are unique to the growth period of the 1980s and 1990s and will be examined throughout the chapter.

Measuring the Extent of Poverty

Table 6.1 also shows actual poverty rates at peaks in the business cycle since 1960 and for 1995, the last year for which data are available. Poverty was exceptionally high in 1960, but began falling in the 1960s in response to economic growth and more generous government transfers; it dropped from 22.2% in 1960 to 14.2% in 1967. Poverty rates continued to fall during the early 1970s, hitting a low of 11.1% in 1973, before climbing again. On average, poverty rates were higher throughout expansions of the 1980s and 1990s, at 13.7% and 14.1%, than over the growth periods from 1967 onward, when they ranged from 12.5% (1967-73) to 11.6% (1973-79).

While the rates in Table 6.1 are the most commonly cited measures of poverty, there are a variety of ways to measure it. The rates presented so far are based on a comparison of each family's pre-tax, post-cash transfer (e.g., unemployment insurance, Social Security, and public assistance payments) income against the official Census poverty thresholds, adjusted for family size and price changes. Thus, a family of four with cash income below $15,569 in 1995 was categorized as poor by the Census Bureau (the poverty threshold for a family of three that year was $12,158). While there exist a number of potentially important conceptual problems with this definition of poverty (e.g., it ignores the value of noncash benefits such as food and medical care, and it has never been updated to reflect new consumption patterns), the official poverty measures have a long history and are a widely used measure of economic deprivation. Some alternative measurements are presented below, but the poverty trends they expose are similar.

Alternative Measurements of Poverty

A common criticism of the official poverty lines is that they no longer reflect even minimal levels of consumption and thus understate the extent of poverty. The original consumption data were collected in 1955, when it was assumed that poor families spent one-third of their income on food (thus assuming that families could purchase all other necessities for twice what they spent on food). The poverty lines were then constructed by multiplying the Department of Agriculture's minimum food budgets for different-sized families by three. Patterns of consumption, however, have changed since 1955. For example, the proportion of income spent on food has shifted over time, with the average family spending a smaller proportion of the family budget on this necessity and, in turn, a larger proportion on other necessities. Therefore, if the poverty lines were recalculated today, they would be higher (as would poverty rates), since the food budget would be multiplied by a number larger than three.

A panel of poverty experts examined these issues and released a study in 1995 under the aegis of the National Research Council (NRC). The panel found that changes in consumption, work patterns, taxes, and government benefits all suggested the need for an updated measure of poverty. Their alternative measure incorporates these factors. It reflects contemporary consumption patterns, adds the cash value of food stamps and housing benefits, and subtracts out-of-pocket medical, child-care, and work-related expenses.

Table 6.2 shows that this alternative measure has the effect of raising poverty rates by 3.6 percentage points in 1992 (the year on which the panel focused). In fact, poverty rates are higher for every group except those receiving cash benefits, who benefit under the alternative measure from the cash value of near-cash benefits such as food stamps. There is a marked increase in poverty rates among Hispanics (due in part to their high housing expenditures relative to other racial groups) and the uninsured (due to their out-of-pocket payments for health care). Thus, this more comprehensive measure of poverty would have increased the number of poor persons in 1992 by about 9 million persons.

Table 6.3 reveals how the NRC's alternative measure affects the distribution of poor persons in 1992. The largest shift is among persons receiving cash benefits (down 11.3 points) and those persons in families with one or more workers (up 10.5 points). These shifts reflect the fact that most recipients of cash benefits also receive in-kind benefits and that the alternative measure includes expenses associated with work (which lowers the income of families with workers). Despite these shifts, however, the previous table (Table 6.2) shows that persons in families without workers have significantly higher pov-

TABLE 6.2

1992 Poverty Rates
Under Official and Alternative Measures

	Official	Alternative*	Percentage-Point Change
Total	14.5%	18.1%	3.6
Age			
Children Under 18	21.9	26.4	4.5
Adults 65 and Over	12.9	14.6	1.7
Race/Ethnicity			
White	11.6	15.3	3.7
Black	33.2	35.6	2.4
Hispanic (any race)	29.4	41.0	11.6
Receiving Cash Benefits**	59.4	53.4	-6.0
One or More Workers	9.1	13.7	4.6
No Health Insurance	32.0	44.9	12.9

* Alternative measure updates consumption requirements, includes cash value of near-cash benefits, and subtracts medical and work-related expenses.
** AFDC or SSI (i.e., means-tested benefits).

Source: National Research Council (1995).

erty rates than families with at least one worker.

Table 6.4 further explores the issue of noncash benefits by isolating the effects of including the market value of food and housing benefits in recipients' income. Medical benefits are omitted for two reasons: they are not a common part of everyday consumption, like food and housing, and their inclusion would have the perverse effect of making the ill appear less poor. Although the inclusion of food and housing benefits lowers the absolute rates in each period, the increase in poverty over both the 1980s and 1990s (bottom panel) is slightly *greater* using the broader measure. This suggests that the poverty-reducing effects of these noncash transfers lessened over time, and the last column (percent of poverty reduced) shows this to be the case.

As noted above, the official poverty lines are indexed for inflation. However, some analysts claim that the price index used to adjust the poverty lines overstated inflation in the 1970s and early 1980s and thereby overestimated real

T A B L E   6 . 3

Demographic Characteristics of Poor Persons Under Alternative Definitions, 1992

Demographics	Official	Alternative*	Change
Age			
Children Under 18	39.7%	38.4	-1.4
Adults 65 and Over	10.9	9.8	-1.0
Race/Ethnicity			
White	66.9	70.7	3.8
Black	28.6	24.6	-4.0
Receiving Cash Benefits**	40.6	29.2	-11.3
One or More Workers	50.9	61.4	10.5
No Health Insurance	30.2	34.0	3.8

*   Alternative measure updates consumption requirements, includes cash value of near-cash benefits, and subtracts medical and work-related expenses.

** AFDC or SSI (i.e., means-tested benefits).

Source: National Research Council (1995).

T A B L E   6 . 4

Poverty Rates When (Nonmedical) Noncash Benefits Are Included

Year	Current Definition	Plus Market Value of Food and Housing Benefits	Change	Percent of Poverty Reduced
1979	11.7%	9.6%	2.1%	17.9%
1989	12.8	11.2	1.6	12.5
1994	14.5	12.7	1.8	12.4
Percentage-Point Change				
1979-89	1.1	1.6		
1989-94	1.7	1.5		

Source: 1979 and 1989: *Green Book* (1993,1320); 1994: unpublished Census data.

poverty rates. **Figure 6B** tracks poverty rates, 1968-94, using an alternative price index, the CPI-U-X1, which is considered a more conservative measure of inflation (see the Methodology section for a discussion of the differences in these deflators). As would be expected, the more conservative price index leads to lower measured poverty rates. However, Figure 6B shows that, regardless of the price index chosen to adjust the poverty lines for price changes, there has been a rise in poverty since 1979 despite overall income growth.

Another important indicator of poverty is *relative* economic well-being. A conceptual shortcoming of the absolute poverty lines used in the above tables is that they are adjusted only for inflation; they do not reflect overall income growth. The poverty lines are fixed levels of income that represent a particular standard of living (level of consumption) at a point in time. However, as average income grows over time and standards of living rise, the economic "distance" between the officially poor and the rest of society expands. While the earliest poverty lines were in fact close to 50% of the median family income for a given family size, they have fallen to about 35%.

Table 6.5 presents a measure of poverty that adjusts for economic growth

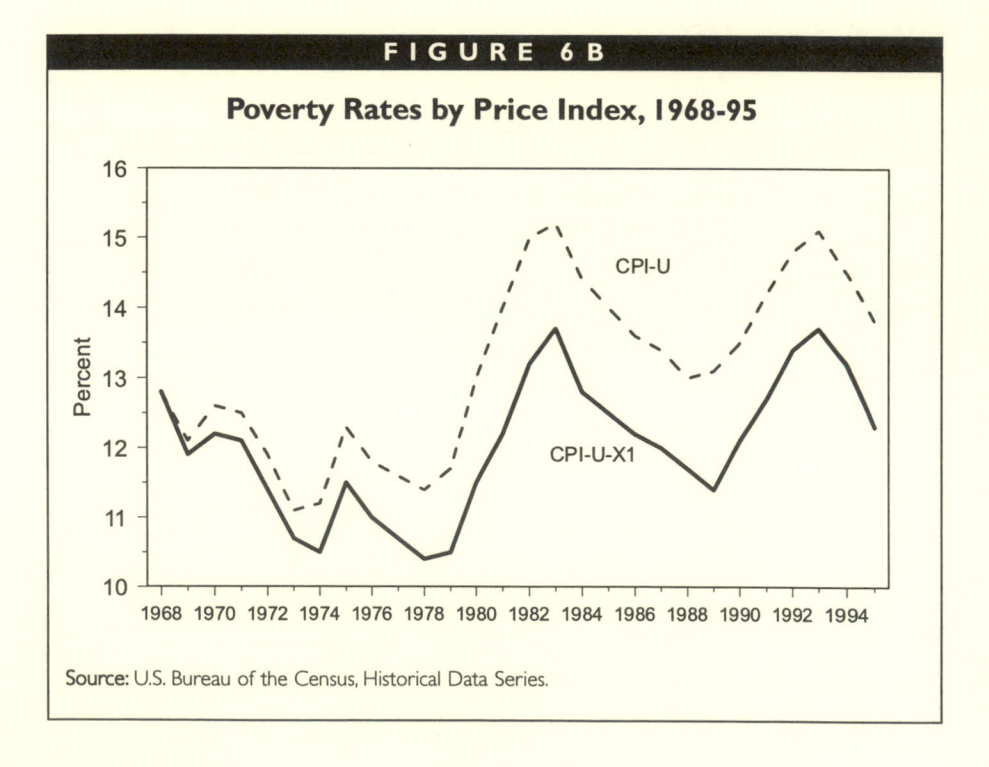

FIGURE 6B

Poverty Rates by Price Index, 1968-95

Source: U.S. Bureau of the Census, Historical Data Series.

TABLE 6.5

Percent of Persons with Low Relative Income, 1969-95, by Race, Adjusted for Family Size

	Relative-Income Poverty Rates				Percentage-Point Difference, Relative-Income Rate and Official Rate
	Less Than 1/4 of the Median	1/4 to 1/2 of the Median	Less Than 1/2 of the Median	Official Rate	
All					
1969	5.5%	12.4%	17.9%	12.1%	5.8
1979	6.7	13.3	20.0	11.7	8.3
1989	8.3	13.7	22.0	13.1	8.9
1995	8.6	13.6	22.2	13.8	8.4
Whites					
1969	4.3	10.4	14.7	9.5	5.2
1979	5.0	11.7	16.7	9.0	7.7
1989	6.3	12.5	18.8	10.2	8.6
1995	6.6	12.5	19.1	11.2	7.9
Blacks					
1969	15.3	27.3	42.6	32.2	10.4
1979	18.8	25.3	44.1	31.0	13.1
1989	21.8	22.1	43.9	30.8	13.1
1995	20.0	20.7	40.7	29.3	11.4
Hispanics					
(Any Race)					
1969	NA	NA	NA	NA	NA
1979	11.6	22.6	34.2	21.8	12.4
1989	16.3	23.8	40.1	26.3	13.8
1995	18.6	24.6	43.2	30.3	12.9

NA: Data not available.

Source: U.S. Bureau of the Census (1991) and unpublished data.

by measuring poverty *relative* to the median family income (which changes yearly), by race. As would be expected (since median family income grew faster than prices throughout the 1980s), the poverty rates at one-half the median are substantially higher than the absolute rates in Table 6.1. For example, whereas 13.8% of the population was poor according to the official, or absolute, poverty measure in 1994, 22.2% of all persons were in families with incomes below one-half of the median family income. Of these, the relatively poorest group (with incomes less than one-quarter of the median) grew the fastest since 1979. And, once again, the trend of worsening poverty over the last two decades is evident.

As we will see throughout the chapter, poverty rates for minorities—relative or absolute—are higher than those of whites. The relative poverty rates for blacks and Hispanics (Hispanics in these data can be of any race) are notably higher than those of whites. In addition, the gap between relative and absolute rates (last column of Table 6.5) is higher for minorities, suggesting that they are, in general, farther below the absolute poverty line than whites. In 1995, relative poverty rates for blacks were 40.7% (11.4 points above the absolute rate), and blacks were equally divided between zero to one-quarter of the median and one-quarter to one-half. Relative poverty rates for whites in that year were half those of blacks (19.1%, 7.9 points above the absolute rate) and fell disproportionately in the one-quarter to one-half category. (Note, however, that black poverty rates fell in the 1989-95 period, while those of whites rose.)

Figure 6C, which shows relative child poverty rates in an international context, reveals the high degree of relative deprivation of U.S. children compared to children from other industrialized countries. This measure, which includes the value of near-cash transfers (see Table 6.4), shows that more than one-fifth of U.S. children were relatively poor in 1991, while other similar economies had much lower rates. Child poverty in Canada was 13.5%, in the United Kingdom it was 9.9%, and in Germany and France it was below 7%. The Scandinavian countries had almost no relative child poverty.

The Poor Get Poorer

The depth of poverty at a point in time is another useful gauge of how the poor are faring. As **Table 6.6** shows, there has not only been a growth in poverty; the poor have also become poorer. This is evident in measures of the so-called "poverty gap," or the distance in the aggregate or average dollar amounts of a person or family from the poverty line. For instance, in 1995 the average poor family had an income $6,038 below the poverty line (in 1995 dollars). The

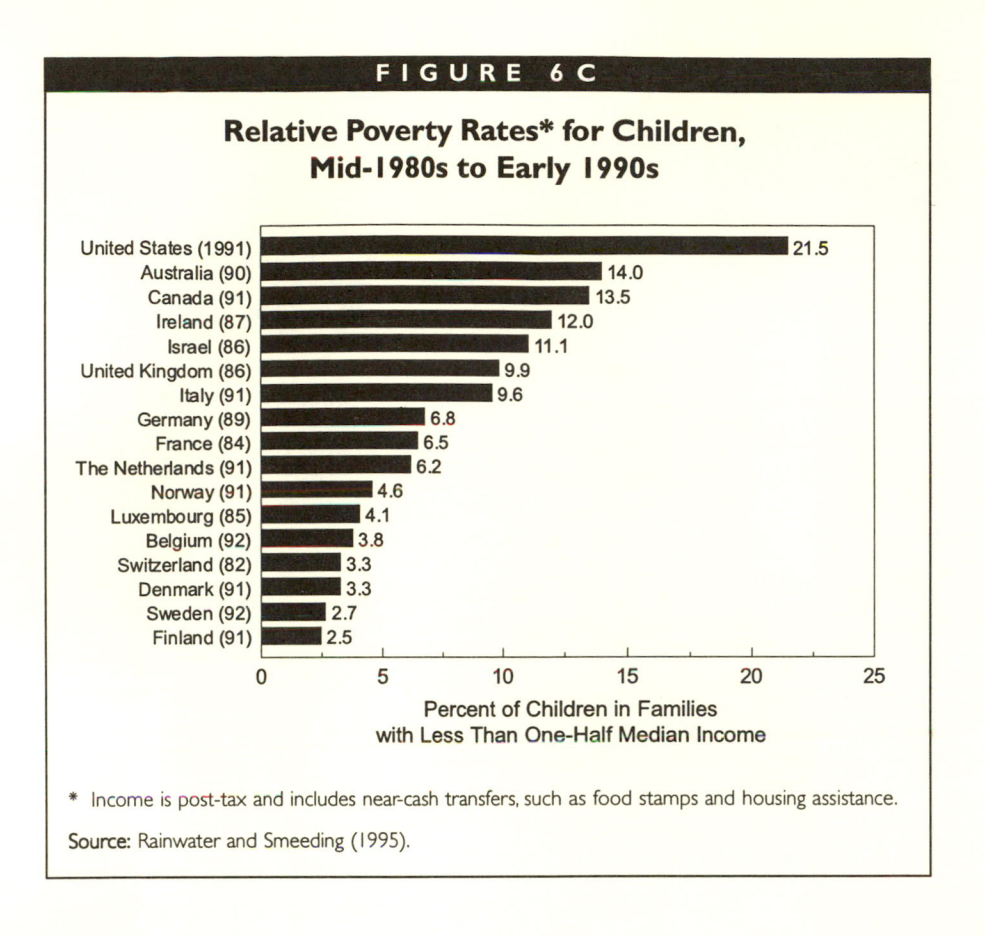

FIGURE 6 C

Relative Poverty Rates* for Children, Mid-1980s to Early 1990s

Country	Percent
United States (1991)	21.5
Australia (90)	14.0
Canada (91)	13.5
Ireland (87)	12.0
Israel (86)	11.1
United Kingdom (86)	9.9
Italy (91)	9.6
Germany (89)	6.8
France (84)	6.5
The Netherlands (91)	6.2
Norway (91)	4.6
Luxembourg (85)	4.1
Belgium (92)	3.8
Switzerland (82)	3.3
Denmark (91)	3.3
Sweden (92)	2.7
Finland (91)	2.5

Percent of Children in Families
with Less Than One-Half Median Income

* Income is post-tax and includes near-cash transfers, such as food stamps and housing assistance.

Source: Rainwater and Smeeding (1995).

aggregate family poverty gap, which was over $45 billion in 1995, is the sum of every poor family's income deficit.

Looking again at trends, the aggregate family poverty gap actually shrank by 2.6% a year between 1967 and 1973. Since poverty rates also fell over this period, the trend led to a smaller share of families who were less poor. In the ensuing periods, however, the aggregate gap for families grew around 3% per year, with a slight acceleration during the 1980s. Note that the mean gap grew at a steady rate in the 1970s and 1980s, suggesting that increases in the aggregate gap were due to a combination of increasing poverty rates and increasing population. Between 1989 and 1995, the annual growth in both the aggregate and mean family gaps decelerated significantly, to 0.9% and -0.2% respectively. However, there was an increase in the growth rate of the aggregate poverty gap of persons not in families (their mean gap grew slightly faster than

TABLE 6.6

Poverty Gap: Aggregate and Mean, 1967-95
($1995)

Year	Families		Persons Not in Families	
	Aggregate Poverty Gap (Millions)	Mean Poverty Gap	Aggregate Poverty Gap (Millions)	Mean Poverty Gap
1967	$30,597	$5,398	$16,612	$3,322
1973	26,104	5,406	14,950	3,200
1979	30,914	5,660	18,009	3,136
1983	48,633	6,158	22,500	2,674
1989	43,103	6,107	23,582	3,486
1995	45,478	6,038	31,025	3,762
Annual Growth Rates				
1967-73	-2.6%	0.0%	-1.7%	-0.6%
1973-79	2.9	0.8	3.2	-0.3
1979-89	3.4	0.8	2.7	1.1
1989-95	0.9	-0.2	4.7	1.3

Source: Authors' analysis of Center for Budget and Policy Priorities (1996).

over the 1980s). As shown below, this results from an increase in this group's poverty rate as well as its population share.

Table 6.7 and **Figure 6D** show another measure of the depth of poverty: the percentage of the poor below 50% of the poverty line, which in 1995 meant a pre-tax income of $7,785 for a family of four. In 1979, slightly less than one-third (30.2%) of the poor were in "deep poverty." By 1983, this proportion had approached two-fifths (38.5%), where it essentially held throughout the decade. As expected, the share of deeply poor persons expanded in the recession that began in 1990, but it did not fall in the recovery and reached 38.1% in 1995. Thus, not only have poverty rates failed to fall in the context of recent economic expansions (as Figure 6A and Table 6.1 show), but more of the poor have fallen into deep poverty.

TABLE 6.7

Poor Persons Below 50% of Poverty Level

Year	Percent of All Poor	Number of Persons (000)
1975	29.9%	7,733
1979	30.2	8,340
1983	38.5	13,590
1989	38.0	11,983
1995	38.1	13,892

Source: Center for Budget and Policy Priorities (1996).

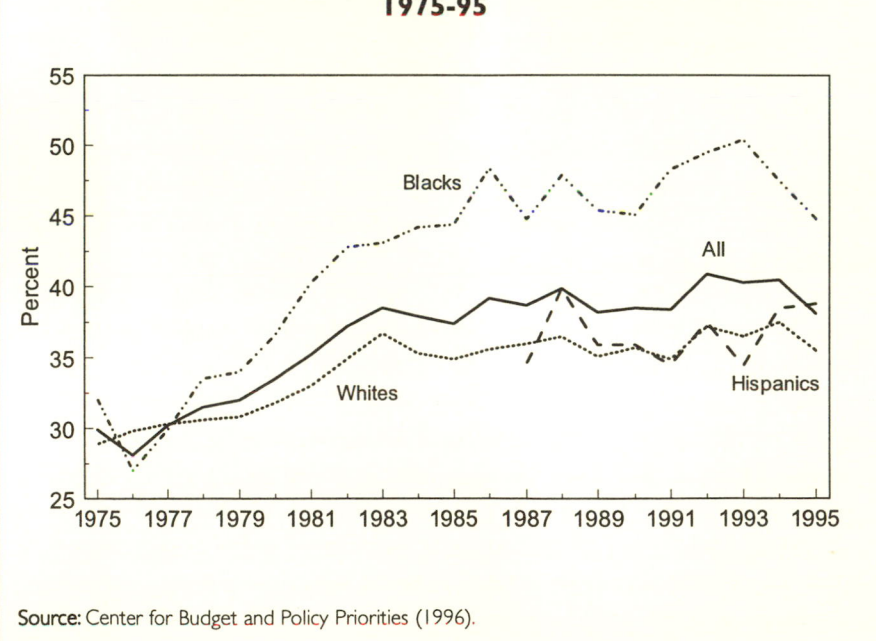

FIGURE 6D

Percent of Poor Persons Below 50% of Poverty Level, 1975-95

Source: Center for Budget and Policy Priorities (1996).

Poverty Spells: The Length of Time Spent in Poverty

All of the measures of poverty examined thus far have been "point-in-time" measures. That is, they compare those in poverty (using different definitions) at one point in time to those in poverty at a different point. This approach fails to answer important questions about the dynamics of poverty. How much mobility exists in the population of poor persons? Are most poor persons in poverty for a short or a long period? What personal characteristics are associated with those experiencing short versus long spells of poverty?

Researchers have analyzed these questions and found a good deal of turn-over in the poverty population; chronic poverty is the exception, not the rule. As the next table shows, most "poverty spells"—continuous periods in which income is below the poverty line—are relatively short, although a small group does suffer long-term poverty. Also, since persons who are poor at one point in time may well be poor again at a later point, a full accounting of poverty spells calls for an examination of multiple spells.

Table 6.8 portrays these dynamics by race. The numbers in the first half of the table can be interpreted as answering the following question: "Of those persons just beginning a poverty spell, what percentage will leave poverty after a certain number of years?" The table shows the distribution of poverty spells of persons over the 1969-88 period (the most recent data available) and finds that the majority of poverty spells lasted for just one (52.5%) or two (17.2%) years. Only a minority of spells (17.1%) lasted for five or more years.

The second half of the table examines multiple spells over the period. Thus, if someone is poor for one year in the beginning of the period and one year later in the period, this would be tabulated as two one-year spells in the first panel of the table and one two-year spell in the second. As might be expected, the second panel shows less mobility (i.e., a greater share of spells of longer duration than in the first panel). For example, the "single-spell" method finds that 78% of the spells lasted three or fewer years; the "multiple-spell" method finds 56% of spells in this category.

Poverty spells among blacks tend to be of longer duration than those of whites. As the single-spell panel shows, twice the share of blacks experience spells of five or more years relative to whites (26.3% vs. 13.3%). The multiple-spell tabulations reveal that over half of black spells (53.4%) last five or more years. Nevertheless, the largest single share of poverty spells under either definition, and for either race, is for spells lasting one year or less.

More recent research on poverty spells among children (**Table 6.9**) shows that among those who turned 18 between 1988 and 1990 (born 1970-72), 65%

TABLE 6.8

Distribution of Poverty Spells for Persons Entering Poverty and for Multiple Spells, 1969-88

Spell Length (Years)	Percent of Persons Entering Poverty Completing Spells			Including Multiple Spells Over a 10-Year Period		
	All	**Black**	**White**	**All**	**Black**	**White**
1	52.5%	41.8%	57.0%	29.5%	17.7%	33.8%
2	17.2	18.5	16.6	14.7	10.8	16.0
3	8.2	8.0	8.2	11.7	10.5	12.2
4	5.0	5.4	4.9	9.3	7.5	10.0
5	3.2	3.9	3.0	6.2	6.8	5.9
6	2.2	2.9	1.9	7.3	9.4	6.5
7	1.8	2.9	1.3	5.5	7.4	4.8
8	1.2	1.4	1.2	5.0	8.1	3.9
9	1.0	1.2	0.9	5.7	10.7	3.9
10 or More	7.7	14.0	5.0	5.2	11.0	3.9
Total	100.0	100.0	100.0	100.0	100.0	100.0
Spells of Five or More Years	17.1	26.3	13.3	34.9	53.4	28.9

Source: Stevens (1995).

TABLE 6.9

Percent of Children in Poverty by Number of Years of Childhood Poverty

	18 Years Old in 1988-90		
	All Children	**Black**	**Nonblack**
Never Poor	65%	28%	73%
Ever Poor	35	72	27
1-5 yrs	21	26	20
6-10 yrs.	6	19	4
11-16 yrs.	7	22	4
17 yrs.	1	6	*

* Less than 1%.

Source: U.S. Department of Health and Human Services (1996).

were never poor during their childhoods. Among the 35% who did experience poverty over this period, the majority of spells (21% out of 35%) were 1 to 5 years. Note, however, that blacks and nonblacks (mostly whites) have precisely opposite experiences: 73% of nonblack children were never poor during childhood; the comparable number for blacks is 28%. Black children also faced longer spells: 28% were poor for 7 out of their 17 years of childhood. For white children, the comparable number is 4%.

The high rates of turnover in the poverty population implied by Table 6.8 suggest that, for most persons entering poverty, being poor is a temporary condition. In fact, other research into poverty dynamics over the 1970s found that as much as one-quarter of the U.S. population was poor at some point within a 10-year period, usually for a short time. Also, as shown in Chapter 1 (Table 1.20), the probability of falling out of the middle class to low-income status rose in the 1980s. Such findings are at odds with the popular notion that the majority of the poor are chronically impoverished and exhibit long-term dependency on government assistance (research on "welfare spells," presented next, shows similar findings). Furthermore, as shown in the following table, the events that most commonly cause a poverty spell are phenomena common to most working persons (e.g., job or earnings' loss, childbirth). Most persons experiencing such events will be poor for a relatively short time.

The events that cause a poverty spell to begin are given in **Table 6.10**. This table covers two periods, 1970-79 and 1980-87, the most recent years for which data are available. As noted, the most common event to lead to a poverty spell is the loss of earnings, and the share of poverty spells induced by this event has grown over time, from 37.1% in 1970-79 to 41.1% in 1980-87. Otherwise, spells are generally related to demographic events, such as the formation of a new family (child became family head) or the birth of a child into poverty.

The notion of dependency is often raised in debates over welfare or government assistance to the poorest families with children. There is a popular but incorrect notion that these families, the vast majority of which are headed by females, are excessively dependent on public assistance. **Table 6.11** challenges this notion. Column 1 shows the total percent of income (TPI) from welfare that went to women age 15 to 44 in two time periods, 1974-80 and 1981-87. For all women, the share of total income from welfare was only 2.7% in the first seven-year period and slightly less in the later period. While a slightly larger share of women were ever on welfare in the later period (13.2% versus 11.6%), their share of income from welfare and the average number of years on welfare actually fell in the 1980s, contrary to the popular impression of increased

TABLE 6.10

Events Leading to Poverty Spells, 1970-87

Primary Reason for Spell Beginning	Percent of Beginnings	
	1970-79	1980-87
Decrease in Head's Earnings	37.1%	41.1%
Decrease in Unearned Income	15.3	13.0
Born into Poverty	8.1	10.2
Decrease in Others' Earnings	9.7	10.2
Child Becomes Head of Family or Wife	10.7	9.7
Decrease in Wife's Earnings	4.8	5.1
Wife Becomes Female Head	4.2	4.2
Child of Male Head Becomes Child of Female Head	5.2	3.7
Addition of New Family Member	4.8	2.8

Source: Stevens (1993).

welfare dependency. The decline in the share of income from welfare among those "ever on" is evident in each age group, particularly among women 35-44, for whom it fell by half. The slight fall in the average number of years of welfare was driven by reduced time on welfare by older women.

Having examined a variety of alternative measures of poverty, we have seen that some measures—the inclusion of in-kind benefits and the alternate price index—make the official measure appear to overstate poverty. Other measures—consumption adjustments and relative measures—make the official measure appear to understate poverty. Furthermore, changes in the poverty gap, the incidence of deep poverty, and poverty dynamics are beyond the scope of the official measure. However, none of these alternative measures changes the fundamental finding regarding a structural shift toward higher poverty rates than economic growth would have predicted. Given the wide use of the official measure and the fact that it adequately captures poverty trends, we will use it throughout the rest of this chapter, except where noted.

TABLE 6.11

Trends in Welfare Dependency
Among Women, Age 15-44, 1974-87

Age at Start of Period	All Women		Women Ever on Welfare	
	TPI*	Percent Ever On	TPI*	Number of Years On
Ages 15-44				
1974-80	2.7%	11.6%	23.3%	3.3
1981-87	2.5	13.2	18.9	3.2
Ages 15-24				
1974-80	3.3	15.1	21.9	3.1
1981-87	4.0	18.7	21.4	3.3
Ages 25-34				
1974-80	2.3	9.6	24.0	3.5
1981-87	2.1	11.0	19.1	3.3
Ages 35-44				
1974-80	2.3	8.6	26.7	3.5
1981-87	1.2	9.3	12.9	2.9

*TPI: Total Percent of income from either AFDC or General Assistance.

Source: Gottschalk and Moffitt (1994).

The Poverty Status
of Different Demographic Groups

Certain demographic groups are more vulnerable to poverty than others. Members of minority groups, families headed by an unmarried female, and children are at the highest risk of poverty. The poverty problem of the elderly, though historically significant, has been lessened to a degree by government transfers (particularly Social Security and Medicare).

Table 6.12 shows the official poverty rate for different racial and ethnic categories. While both white and black poverty rates fell from 1959 to 1973, there remains a wide differential between them. In all cases, black and Hispanic

TABLE 6.12

Persons in Poverty, by Race/Ethnicity, 1959-95

Year	White	Black	Hispanic
1959	18.1%	55.1%	NA
1967	11.0	39.3	NA
1973	8.4	31.4	21.9
1979	9.0	31.0	21.8
1989	10.2	30.8	26.3
1995	11.2	29.3	30.3

Source: U.S. Bureau of the Census, Historical Data Series.

poverty is more extensive than that of whites. The black poverty rate has been about three times that of whites since 1979, while the Hispanic rate has climbed from 21.9% in 1973 to 30.3% in 1995.

Table 6.13 has poverty rates for children by race/ethnicity. Child poverty grew in all racial categories between 1979 and 1989 and again for white and Hispanic (but not black) children from 1989 to 1995. Young Hispanic children (under six) experienced the steepest annual growth rates in poverty over the 1980s, gaining 0.96 percentage point per year; poverty rates in the 1990s grew at a slightly slower annual rate for all Hispanic children.

By 1995, more than one out of every five children was poor (20.8%). For children under six years old, the rate was even higher, reaching 23.7%. Black children have the highest poverty rates; in 1989, half of all black children under six were poor. These rates for blacks have fallen only slightly since then.

Table 6.14 shows poverty rates for families with children, sorted by the education level of the family head, from 1973 to 1992 (these are the most recent data of this type available). As expected, as the education level of the family head rises, the likelihood that the family is poor falls. Among families headed by a person with less than a high school degree, poverty has risen sharply since 1973, from 21.3% to 43.9%. There was also sizable growth in poverty among families headed by a high school graduate or someone with 1-3 years of college. For example, by the end of the period, close to one-fifth of these families headed by a high school graduate were poor. Thus, being poor is not limited to those without an education sufficient to enter the "mainstream economy."

TABLE 6.13

Percent of Children in Poverty, by Race, 1979-95

| | Total | Children Under 18 | | |
		White	Black	Hispanic
1979	16.4%	11.8%	41.2%	28.0%
1989	20.1	15.1	43.8	36.2
1995	20.8	16.2	41.9	40.0
Percentage-Point Change (Annualized)				
1979-89	0.37	0.33	0.26	0.82
1989-95	0.12	0.18	-0.32	0.63

| | Total | Children Under 6 | | |
		White	Black	Hispanic
1979	18.1%	13.3%	43.6%	29.2%
1989	22.5	16.9	49.8	38.8
1995	23.7	18.2	48.9	42.4
Percentage-Point Change (Annualized)				
1979-89	0.44	0.36	0.62	0.96
1989-95	0.20	0.22	-0.15	0.60

Source: Center for Budget and Policy Priorities (1996).

During the downturn and recovery from 1989 to 1992, poverty grew about the same amount among those families headed by a high school graduate as among families headed by those not completing high school. In prior periods, poverty grew more slowly for families headed by high school graduates (35.3% of families with children in 1993) than for those headed by high school dropouts.

As the previous tables have shown, certain demographic characteristics (e.g., gender, race, education level, marital status) significantly affect the probability of poverty. In particular, women family heads with less than a high school degree have historically had poverty rates well above average. **Table 6.15** presents these poverty rates by race. Because of data limitations, we focus on women age 25 and

TABLE 6.14

Poverty Rates of Families with Children, by Education Level of Family Head, 1973-92

| | 1973 | 1979 | 1989 | 1992 | Percentage-Point Change | | |
					1973-79	1979-89	1989-92
Less Than High School	21.3%	26.5%	39.0%	43.9%	5.2	12.5	4.9
High School	7.6	10.3	15.3	19.3	2.7	5.0	4.0
Some College	5.5	6.7	9.0	12.0	1.2	2.3	3.0
College or More	1.8	2.5	2.7	2.9	0.7	0.2	0.2
All	10.6	12.1	15.0	17.3	1.5	2.9	2.3

Source: Sum, Fogg, and Fogg (1994).

TABLE 6.15

High-Risk Factors for Poverty, Females 25 and over, 1994

	White	Black	Hispanic
All	10.7%	27.4%	26.8%
(1) Single Heads of Households	25.9	42.9	48.8
(2) Less Than a High-School Degree	26.5	47.2	40.3
(1) and (2)	44.6	59.6	61.7
(1) and (2) with Children	63.3	73.0	71.2
Addendum			
Single Heads of Housholds with Children, 18-21	80.1	78.0	NA

* Hispanics can be of any race.

Source: U.S. Bureau of the Census, unpublished tables.

over, but since young women are at higher risk, we include them in the analysis as an addendum.

The first line of Table 6.15 shows that race is an important determinant of female poverty status, with black women almost three times as likely to be poor than white women. Single women who head households are significantly more likely to be poor than the average female: about one-quarter of the single white women who headed households in 1994 were poor; for blacks, the poverty rate was 42.9%. Having less than a high school degree led to similarly high rates of poverty. Note, however, that the poverty rate of all black females was slightly higher than that for white high school dropouts, underscoring the dominant effect of race as a poverty determinant.

Combining these demographic characteristics greatly increases the likelihood of being poor. About three-fifths of the black and Hispanic females who were both single heads of households and less than high school educated were poor in 1994. When children are added to the picture, the poverty rates go up to 73.0% and 71.2%. Youth is associated with even higher poverty rates. For white and black females age 18-21 with children (across education levels), only 20% were nonpoor in 1994. For women in this highest-risk category, race makes almost no difference.

Whether these risk factors—families headed by a single person, low levels of education, race—have led to higher poverty rates depends on (1) the extent to which we have, over time, shifted to more vulnerable categories of family type, race, etc., and (2) the change in poverty rates within each category. We address these issues below.

Family Structure and Poverty

Family structure has historically been an important determinant of poverty status, as certain family types are more vulnerable to poverty than others. However, the important questions regarding family structure and poverty are as follows: to what extent are poverty rates and family structure changes *causally* related? To what degree are the high and intractable poverty rates documented above driven by individuals' choices to form vulnerable family types? What is the relative contribution to poverty trends of shifts in demographic factors—including family type, race, and education levels—as opposed to shifts in economic trends, such as wage decline?

Table 6.16 takes a first look at these questions by showing the percentage

TABLE 6.16

Changing Family Structure and Poverty, 1959-95

Year	Percent of Persons in:				Poverty Rate of Persons in:			
	Female-Headed Families	Married-Couple and Male-Headed Families	Not Living in Families	Total	Female-Headed Families	Married-Couple and Male-Headed Families	Not Living in Families	All Persons
1959	8.0	85.9	6.1	100.0	49.4	18.2	46.1	22.4
1967	9.1	84.2	6.7	100.0	38.8	9.6	38.1	14.2
1973	10.5	80.7	8.8	100.0	37.5	6.0	25.6	11.1
1979	12.1	76.2	11.7	100.0	34.9	6.4	21.9	11.7
1989	13.5	72.3	14.3	100.0	36.4	7.5	19.3	13.1
1995	14.8	70.3	15.0	100.0	36.5	7.5	20.9	13.8
Percentage-Point Changes								
1967-73	1.4	-3.5	2.1	0.0	-1.3	-3.6	-12.5	-3.1
1973-79	1.6	-4.5	2.9	0.0	-2.6	0.4	-3.7	0.6
1979-89	1.4	-3.9	2.5	0.0	1.5	1.1	-2.6	1.4
1989-95	1.3	-2.0	0.7	0.0	0.1	0.0	1.6	0.7

Source: U.S. Bureau of the Census, various years.

of persons in female-headed families, married couple and male-headed families, and not in families (i.e., single persons) from 1959 to 1994. The table also shows the poverty rates for each group in each time period, along with percentage-point changes over time.

Persons in female-headed families and persons not in families are more likely to be poor than persons in married-couple or male-headed families. In 1995, 36.5% of persons in families headed by a woman were poor. For persons not in families in 1995, the poverty rate (20.9%) was also substantially higher than the rate for all persons. Those in married-couple and male-headed families are the least likely to be poor; their poverty rates have stayed below 10% since 1967.

The distribution of family types has shifted toward family structures more vulnerable to poverty for many decades. For instance, the percentage of persons in married-couple and male-headed families, which have the lowest poverty rates, has consistently fallen, from 85.9% in 1959 to 70.3% in 1995. Conversely, there has been a consistent expansion of female-headed families and an even faster growth of singles.

Turning to the poverty trends of these different groups, all family types saw their poverty rates fall between 1967 and 1979, with single persons showing the largest drop (16.2 points). This trend then reversed, and between 1979 and 1989 the poverty rate grew comparably for persons in female-headed families (1.5 points) and in married-couple families (1.1 points), while falling more slowly for individuals. Between 1989 and 1995, poverty grew at a faster rate for individuals not living in families.

What does Table 6.16 reveal about the relationship between demographic shifts and changes in poverty rates? The *prima facie* evidence is mixed. On the one hand, it is clear that there has been a compositional shift to families more vulnerable to poverty. However, when the demographic shifts were occurring most rapidly, in the 1967-79 period, the overall poverty rates declined from 14.2% to 11.7% and poverty fell among persons in female-headed families and among singles. Conversely, when demographic forces slowed over the 1980s, the poverty trend reversed. Moreover, poverty also grew among the family type least vulnerable to poverty: persons in married-couple families. Thus, while demographic shifts to family types with higher poverty rates have played a role in the high poverty rates of the 1980s, the extent of that role is unclear. It is to this issue we now turn.

Quantifying the Role of Demographics

One way to investigate the effect of demographic change on poverty rates is to assume that poverty rates are influenced by the changes in demographics, such as changes in the distribution of families by marital status and race of the family head, and changes in economic factors, like lower wages and benefits. Also influencing poverty rates is the distribution of family levels by the education level of the family head (see Table 6.14).

Each of these factors would be expected to help explain changes in poverty throughout our period of interest, 1973-95. For example, the shift to more vulnerable family types continuing throughout the period (though relatively slower in the 1980s than the 1970s) should be poverty inducing, while higher education levels across all family types should lower family poverty rates. Equally important are the effects of wage trends and other economic factors on the poverty rates of particular family types with a certain education level (i.e., "within-group" shifts). **Table 6.17** quantifies these separate factors for persons in the family groups shown in the previous table for the period 1973-95; **Table 6.18** does so for families with children for the period 1973-92.

TABLE 6.17

Changes in Family Structure and Poverty, 1973-95
(Annualized)

Period	Change in Poverty Rate	Predicted Change Due to Family Structure*	Change Due to Other Factors**
1973-79	0.11	0.16	-0.06
1979-89	0.14	0.07	0.06
1989-95	0.12	0.08	0.04

* Effect on overall poverty rate of changes in proportions of persons in female-headed families, married-couple and male-headed families, and individuals not in families.

** Effect on overall poverty rate of changes in poverty rates within these three main demographic groups.

Source: Authors' analysis of U.S. Bureau of the Census, various years.

TABLE 6.18

Changes in Demographic Structure and Poverty
for Families with Children, 1973-92

(Annualized Change Rates)

		Change Due to Demographics		
Period	**Change in Poverty Rate**	**Family Type***	**Education****	**Change Due to Other Factors****
1973-79	0.25	0.29	-0.18	0.14
1979-92	0.40	0.21	-0.19	0.38

* Increase in poverty due exclusively to shifts toward types more vulnerable to poverty (including racial composition).
** Fall in poverty due to educational upgrading of family head.
*** Change in family poverty rates due to poverty rate changes within demographic groups defined by race, education level, and marital status of family head.

Source: Authors' analysis of Sum, Fogg, and Fogg (1994).

Column 1 of Table 6.17 shows the change in the poverty rates over the three periods of interest. Column 2 shows how poverty rates would have been expected to grow given only the shift to more vulnerable families that occurred throughout these periods (i.e., the poverty rates of each group are held constant in the "base" year while only family structure is allowed to change). Conversely, column 3 shows how poverty rates would have changed had family structure remained constant while poverty rates within each group were allowed to follow their actual trend.

Over the first period, 1973-79, poverty grew at a rate of 0.11 points per year, and this growth was driven exclusively by the shift to female-headed and single-person families. In fact, if family structure had not changed, poverty would have fallen 0.06 points per year (column 3). In the next period, 1979-89, the growth in poverty was due equally to family structure and other factors. In the most recent period, poverty was again driven by family-structure changes, though these changes played a lesser role than in the 1970s. While the shift to more vulnerable family structure has played a clear role in the increase in poverty over the last 30 years, its role has generally diminished. This suggests that family-structure explanations for recent poverty trends have been overemphasized and, conversely, the growth of poverty driven by wage decline has been underappreciated.

Table 6.18 shows a similar pattern for families with children over two periods, 1973-79 and 1979-92. Here, the impact of demographic change on family poverty rates is broken down into two parts: that due to shifts to more vulnerable family types (in this table, racial shifts are included in this component) and that due to the change in the educational status of the family head (as would be expected, these work in opposite directions). Column 2 shows that, while demographic shifts (i.e., the shift toward fewer white, married-couple families) were important in both periods, their relative importance was greater in the earlier period, when they led to a 0.29-percentage-point-per-year increase in poverty rates of families with children. During this period, higher educational attainment among family heads lowered poverty rates by 0.18 points per year, while other factors contributed to a 0.14-point rise per year.

Between 1979 and 1992, however, the major factor driving the increase in poverty rates were factors other than demographics, primarily the types of negative wage trends discussed in Chapter 3. In this later period, the shift toward more vulnerable family types placed slightly less upward pressure on poverty rates; it caused poverty to rise 0.21 percentage points per year. Educational upgrading continued to reduce poverty, as it did between 1973 and 1979. But other factors caused poverty rates to grow at 0.38 points per year, almost three times the rates of the prior period.

The calculations in both of these tables reveal that, while the shift to more poverty-prone family types has continued to create upward pressure on poverty rates, that pressure has lessened (i.e., it has become responsible for a smaller share of the increase) throughout the 1980s and early 1990s. The shift over time to minority and female-headed families has added to poverty rates, yet such shifts fail to explain the high poverty rates of the 1980s, particularly when their higher education levels over time are taken into account. Moreover, the most important factor in rising poverty appears to be the failure of economic forces to lessen poverty in recent years as they did in earlier periods.

The Poverty of Female-Headed Families

Female-headed families, identified above as particularly vulnerable to poverty, are stereotypically thought to consist mostly of black women who have had children out of wedlock. The next few tables demonstrate that mother-only family poverty is not exclusively a minority problem, nor are most single mothers never-married women.

Table 6.19 examines the trend in poverty rates of female-headed families by race and Hispanic origin. Overall, their poverty rates have changed little since 1973. Furthermore, while minority female-headed families have the highest poverty rates, their rates declined between 1979 and 1989 (and again for blacks in 1995), while those for whites rose. By 1995, 32.4% of female-headed families were poor.

When the population of female-headed families is examined as a whole, it is clear that white families constitute the largest share (**Table 6.20**). In 1995, white families accounted for 54.2% of the total; black families accounted for 41.9% (but given their smaller share of the total population, blacks are disproportionately poor). The bottom part of Table 6.20 shows the share of the total increase in the number of poor female-headed families by race. While blacks accounted for the largest share of the increase between 1973 and 1979 (57.5%), whites were responsible for the largest share from 1979 to 1989 (57.6%) and from 1989 to 1995 (65.1%).

The fact that both poverty rates and the proportion who are poor fell for black female-headed families and rose for whites over the 1980s and 1990s

---

TABLE 6.19

Poverty Rates for Female-Headed Families

Year	All	White	Black	Hispanic
1973	32.2%	24.6%	52.8%	51.4%
1979	30.4	22.3	49.4	49.2
1989	32.6	25.8	46.7	48.0
1995	32.4	26.6	45.1	49.4

Source: U.S. Bureau of the Census, various years.

TABLE 6.20

Poor Female-Headed Families, by Race, 1973-95

Year	White	Black	Other	Total	Number (000)
1973	54.3%	44.4%	1.3%	100.0%	2,193
1979	51.0	46.7	2.3	100.0	2,645
1989	52.8	43.4	3.8	100.0	3,575
1995	54.2	41.9	3.8	100.0	4,057
Share of Total Increase					
1973-79	35.4%	57.5%	7.1%	100.0%	452
1979-89	57.6	34.3	8.1	100.0	930
1989-95	65.1	30.7	4.1	100.0	482

Source: Authors' analysis of Center for Budget and Policy Priorities (1996).

belies the notion that minority behavior is responsible for the increase in female-headed poverty. **Table 6.21** reveals that the largest quantitative factor driving the poverty rates of female-headed families in the 1980s and 1990s has been growing poverty rates of white, not black, female heads of households. This table presents a similar analysis to those in Tables 6.17 and 6.18; the increase in poverty among female heads of households is broken down into that which derived from the shift in the population to more poverty-prone racial groups (i.e., blacks) and that which derived from an increase in poverty rates within these racial groups. (Because of data limitations, Hispanics are included in all three racial categories; the "other" category accounts for a small share of the population, never more than 4%.)

The table shows that in the 1973-79 period poverty for female-headed families fell 0.30 points per year, as poverty rates fell for both whites and blacks. However, the increasing share of black female-headed families over this period was a countervailing factor that increased poverty by 0.14 points per year. As the last row of the table shows, these two factors essentially "canceled out" for blacks, and their total contribution (the sum of the race and within-race

TABLE 6.21

Poverty Rates in Female-Headed Families: Contributions to Growth, 1973-95

(Annualized)

	1973-79	1979-89	1989-95
Total Change	-0.30	0.22	-0.03
Race*	0.08	0.07	0.02
White	-0.06	-0.07	-0.03
Black	0.14	0.08	-0.02
Other	0.00	0.05	0.7
Within Race**	-0.37	0.17	-0.04
White	-0.27	0.24	0.11
Black	-0.15	-0.08	-0.10
Other	0.05	0.00	-0.05
Total Contribution to Poverty Rates***			
White Effect	-0.33	0.18	0.08
Black Effect	-0.01	0.00	-0.12

* The change in poverty rates for female-headed families due to changes in the racial composition of female-headed families. Hispanics can be in any racial group.

** The change in poverty rates for female-headed families due to changes in poverty rates within each racial category.

*** The sum of race and within-race effects for the two racial groups.

Source: Authors' analysis of U.S. Bureau of the Census, Historical Data Series.

---

effects) was to lower poverty rates by 0.01 points per year.

In the 1980s and 1990s (i.e., 1989-95), however, the largest factor driving the increase in poverty among female-headed families was the growing poverty rates of whites (a reversal in trend), which accounted for more than the full change in both periods. Black poverty rates continued to decline and led to 0.08- (1980s) and 0.10- (1990s) point annual decreases in poverty rates for female-headed families. In the most recent period, a small decrease in the black share of the population led to a slight decrease in poverty (0.02 points per year), but the increase of the poverty rates of white female-headed families led to a growth of 0.11 points per year. As the last two rows of the table show, the total black contribution was zero in the 1980s and a negative factor (0.12 per year) in the 1990s, while the total white contribution was 0.18 points per year in the 1980s and 0.08 points in the 1990s.

The stereotypical female head of a family is thought to have never been married and to have had a number of out-of-wedlock births. In fact, as **Table 6.22** shows, families headed by divorced women made up the largest share of female-headed families in 1994 (36.1%), followed by those made up of never-married females, representing just over one-quarter. While never-married mothers have consistently been the fastest-growing group, their annual rate of growth has slowed in each period, from 8.3% in 1973-79 to 6.0% in 1989-94.

A great deal of controversy exists regarding the rise of out-of-wedlock births documented in the previous table. Conventional thinking suggests that a precipitous rise in female-headed families led by never-married mothers, particularly among blacks, has become a major poverty problem. This perception has grown out of the fact that the ratio of expected unmarried to total lifetime births (this way of measuring birth trends is explained below) grew significantly, from 23.5% to 68.7% for blacks, between 1960 and 1993 (**Table 6.23**). However, the data show that while out-of-wedlock births have become more

TABLE 6.22

Marital Status of Female Heads of Household, 1973-94

Year	Married, Husband Absent	Widowed	Divorced	Never Married	Total	Number (000)
1973	23.9%	37.7%	25.9%	12.6%	100.0%	6,535
1979	21.0	29.8	33.0	16.2	100.0	8,220
1989	17.1	23.9	36.4	22.6	100.0	10,890
1994	17.8	19.5	36.1	26.6	100.0	12,406
Annual Growth Rates						
1973-79	1.7%	-0.1%	8.2%	8.3%	3.9%	
1979-89	0.8	0.6	3.9	6.3	2.9	
1989-94	3.5	-1.4	2.5	6.0	2.6	

Source: Authors' analysis of U.S. Bureau of the Census.

TABLE 6.23

Expected Lifetime Births, by Marital Status and Race, 1960-93

	1960	1970	1980	1990	1993	Change 1960-93
Unmarried Births						
White	0.08	0.14%	0.20	0.41	0.47	0.39
Black	1.07	1.17	1.22	1.65	1.70	0.63
Married Births						
White	3.45	2.25	1.57	1.60	1.52	-1.94
Black	3.47	1.93	0.96	0.83	0.78	-2.70
Total						
White	3.53	2.39	1.77	2.00	1.98	-1.55
Black	4.54	3.10	2.18	2.48	2.48	-2.06
Unmarried Births as Percent of Total Births						
White	2.3%	5.7%	11.2%	20.4%	23.6%	21.3%
Black	23.5	37.6	56.1	66.5	68.7	45.1
Unmarried Births as Percent of Total Births *(Married Births Fixed at 1960 Level)*						
White	2.3%	3.8%	5.5%	10.6%	11.9%	9.6%
Black	23.5	25.1	26.0	32.2	32.9	9.4

Source: Jencks (1991) updated by authors.

common for both blacks and whites, they have *not* increased dramatically. Rather, the rise in the ratio of unmarried to total births, particularly among blacks, is being driven less by an increase in out-of-wedlock births than by a decrease in married births.

Table 6.23 and **Figure 6E** present the relevant data. The table and figure use the concept of expected lifetime births, that is, the number of in- and out-of-wedlock children a woman could expect to have throughout her life. (Expected lifetime births are another name for age-weighted fertility rates in a given year. Thus, this concept assumes that age-specific fertility rates in a given year con-

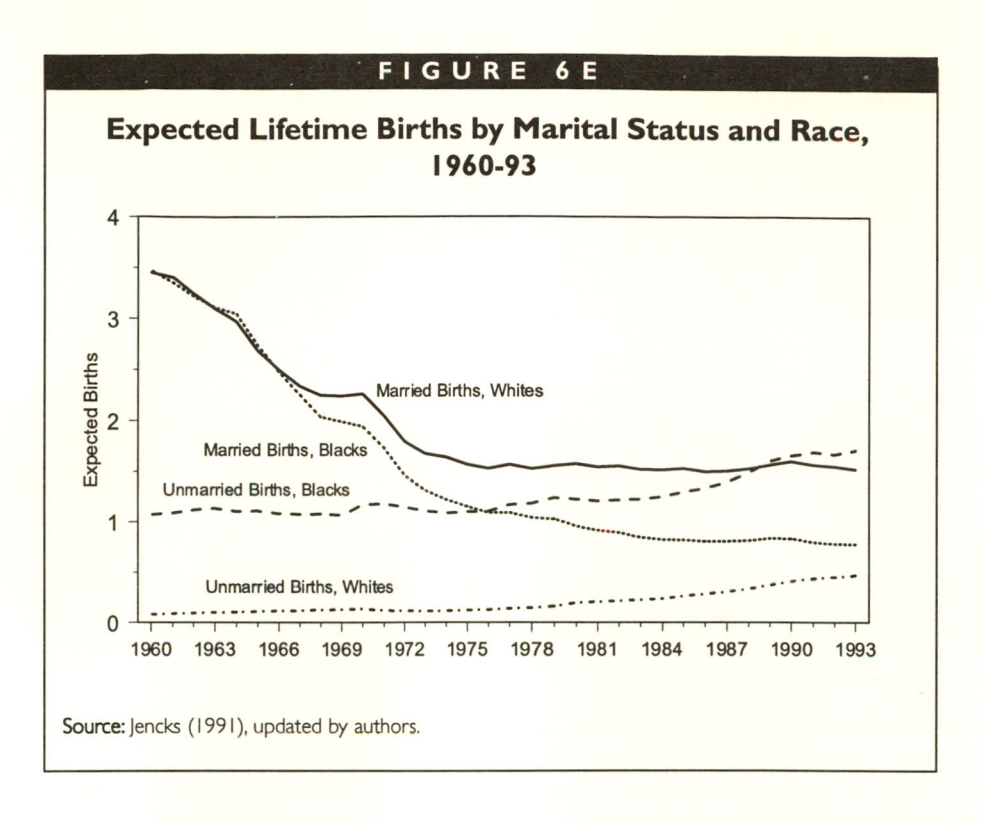

FIGURE 6E

Expected Lifetime Births by Marital Status and Race, 1960-93

Source: Jencks (1991), updated by authors.

tinue to hold.) For example, based on prevailing fertility rates at the time, married white women in 1960 would have been expected to have an average of 3.45 children over their lifetimes.

The trend lines in Figure 6E show that while blacks have a higher level of expected unmarried births than whites, both groups show a slight upward trend over the 1980s (which appears to have flattened in the early 1990s for blacks). While a rise in the number of unmarried births among blacks—1.07 in 1960 to 1.70 in 1993—is not a trivial development, it alone would have been unlikely to generate the controversy surrounding this issue. The significant trend is the steep drop in the expected births to married woman of both races. For married white women, the average dropped from 3.45 children in 1960 to 1.52 children in 1993. The expected child-bearing behavior of black women changed even more dramatically, falling from 3.47 to 0.78 over the same period. The ensuing rise in the ratio of unmarried births to all births, then, has been driven to a greater degree by the falling birth rates of married women than by the rising birth rates of unmarried women.

The numbers in the bottom rows of Table 6.23 answer this question: what would the proportion of unmarried-to-married births be if married birth rates had not fallen? Under these circumstances, the share of black children born out of wedlock would have risen to 32.9%, not 68.7%, and the percentage-point increase for white and black women would have been about the same: 9.6 points vs. 9.4 points. These percentage-point changes also suggest that four-fifths of the increase in unmarried births as a percent of all births for blacks is explained by falling married birth rates (1-(9.4/45.1)).

In sum, changes in family structure cannot be held accountable for the failure of economic growth to reduce poverty rates in the 1980s and early 1990s. Although a demographic shift to family types more vulnerable to poverty has contributed to high poverty rates over time, this shift played a greater poverty-inducing role in earlier periods. As Tables 6.17 and 6.18 show, demographics (marital status and education) had a larger impact on the poverty rates of the 1970s than on those of the 1980s or 1990s. The poverty of female-headed families, while high relative to overall poverty, rose only slightly over the 1980s (Table 6.19). In addition, the largest quantitative factor driving the poverty of female heads of households has been the increase in the poverty rates of white female-headed families. Finally, Tables 6.22 and 6.23 (and Figure 6E) show that the controversy surrounding out-of-wedlock births is overstated. Never-married mothers still make up a minority of female family heads, and the rise in the ratio of out-of-wedlock births to married births for blacks is being driven by a dramatic fall in the latter rather than a substantial rise in the former.

The Changing Effects of Taxes and Transfers

Chapter 2 made the point that the decreased progressivity of the tax system over the 1980s favored the wealthy and hurt the poor. In tandem with this development, government transfers became less generous over the decade, particularly in the early Reagan years. Since the official poverty statistics are calculated prior to tax payments (or receipts) and exclude the value of in-kind benefits, they shed little light on the effects of policy changes in these areas. Therefore, in this section we use a more inclusive measure of poverty than the official rate—one that includes four separate income definitions.

Table 6.24 examines the effect of taxes and benefits on poverty rates for all persons, all elderly persons, and for family types with children for the years 1979, 1989, and 1995. Column 1 shows the poverty rates generated by the

TABLE 6.24

Poverty-Reducing Effects of Taxes and Transfers, 1979-95

	Before Taxes and Transfers (1)	After Taxes (2)	Plus Non-Means Tested Transfers (Including Medicare)* (3)	Plus Means Tested Transfers (Including Medicaid)* (4)	Reduction in Poverty Due to Taxes and Transfers (5=1-4)	Reduction Effectiveness Rate (6=5/1)
All Persons						
1979	19.5	19.3	12.4	8.9	10.6	54%
1989	20.0	20.3	13.5	10.4	9.6	48%
1995	21.9	21.0	13.7	10.3	11.6	53%
Persons 65 and Over						
1979	54.2	54.1	15.4	12.3	41.9	77%
1989	47.6	48.1	11.4	8.6	39.0	82%
1995	49.9	50.2	10.3	10.7	39.2	79%
Persons in Female-Headed Families with Children Under 18						
1979	53.4	52.3	47.3	28.1	25.3	47%
1989	51.4	51.1	47.0	34.9	16.5	32%
1995	51.7	47.5	44.3	30.5	21.2	41%
Persons in Married-Couple Families with Children Under 18						
1979	9.4	9.1	7.3	5.2	4.2	45%
1989	10.3	10.5	9.0	6.6	3.7	36%
1995	10.2	9.1	7.5	5.3	4.9	48%

* Includes fungible value of Medicare and Medicaid benefits; see table note.

Source: Authors' analysis of U.S. Bureau of the Census, P-60, No. 182-RD and No. 189.

market; these rates represent the degree of poverty that would exist in the absence of any government intervention. Moving left to right, the table introduces different transfers and taxes and shows how poverty would be affected by each. In column 2, for example, the poverty rate for all persons fell slightly in 1979 after taxes, from 19.5% to 19.3%. The addition of non-means-tested benefits, including Medicare, lowered the rate to 12.4% in that year (column 3). Column 5 totals the effects of government tax and transfer policies, showing, for example, that in 1979 they reduced market-generated poverty by 10.6 points. The final column, "reduction effectiveness rate," is the previous column divided by column 1: it represents the share of market poverty reduced by government tax and transfer policy.

Market outcomes were steadily worse for all persons in each year, meaning that the tax and transfer system would have had to "work harder" to keep poverty from rising. In fact, as seen in column 4, for all persons, poverty rates *after* taxes and transfers were higher in each year in the table. Thus, despite the fact that taxes and transfers lowered market-induced poverty rates for all persons by more percentage points in 1995 than in 1979 (11.6 versus 10.6), poverty rates for all persons were higher at the end of the period because of the failure of taxes and transfers to compensate for lower market outcomes. This combination of higher market-induced poverty and less extensive reduction led to a decrease in the reduction effectiveness rate from 54% to 53%.

Table 6.24 also shows the importance of transfers for persons over 65, for whom poverty is reduced the most. Note that market outcomes (column 1) became less poverty inducing over the 1980s (but not in the 1990s) and that the reduction effectiveness of transfers increased over the 1980s, but not the 1990s, for the elderly.

Taxes and transfers were significantly less effective than they were for the elderly at reducing the poverty of persons in single-parent families with children in the period 1979-89. Over this period, market outcomes actually reduced their poverty by 2.0 percentage points, but a fall in benefits led to a post-tax and transfer poverty rate in 1989 that was 6.8 points higher than that of 1979 (column 4). Nor did this group of persons benefit from the most recent expansion in 1989-94: their pre-tax, pre-transfer poverty rates grew slightly. The effectiveness of taxes and transfers grew, however, so that their after tax/ transfer poverty rate was 4.4 points lower in 1995 than in 1989 and the reduction effectiveness rate grew by 9 percentage points (column 6).

Persons in married-couple families have also experienced increasing poverty rates since 1979. Over the 1980s, each category of taxes and transfers led to higher poverty rates; by 1989, the reduction effectiveness rate had fallen by 9 points. Again, this pattern reversed in 1989-95, and poverty among persons in these families fell from 10.2% to 5.3%, generating a reduction effectiveness rate (48%) slightly higher than that of 1979 (45%).

Government Benefits and Family Structure: Is There a Welfare Trap?

The previous sections examined the roles of family structure and benefit changes on poverty rates. This section looks at the interaction between these two issues and examines a question that has often been raised in the debate over government provision to the poor: to what extent have welfare programs caused poverty by creating incentives that heighten the probability that a family will be poor? Specifically, have welfare programs been the primary cause of the increased proportion of female-headed families?

The argument regarding family structure has been developed as follows. Since the most valuable benefit package is available to single-headed families with children, there is an incentive to form such families, either by delaying or avoiding marriage, dissolving existing unions, or having children out of wedlock. In fact, the evidence shows that the proportion of families with children headed by females has grown over time, as has the benefit sum, at least up to the mid-1970s. (The benefit sum includes the value of Aid to Families with Dependent Children [AFDC], Food Stamps, and Medicaid; see **Figure 6F**, bottom panel.) Critics of the system of social provision have suggested that there is a causal relationship between these two phenomena: family structure has been altered by the provision of benefits to female-headed families with children.

Yet, as Figure 6F demonstrates, this correlation between benefits and family structure holds up only to the early 1970s. Beginning around 1972 the benefit sum began to fall, due primarily to the declining real value of AFDC benefits. Yet none of the demographic indicators, which have generally risen consistently over time, follow the plunging benefit sum. If growing benefits led to increased formation of single-headed families, then falling benefits should have led to a decrease in the formation of these family types. The only series in the figure that reverses direction is the divorce rate, the one rate in the figure that is least relevant to the low-income population. While white female headship and nonwhite out-of-wedlock birth rates appear to decelerate slightly by the end

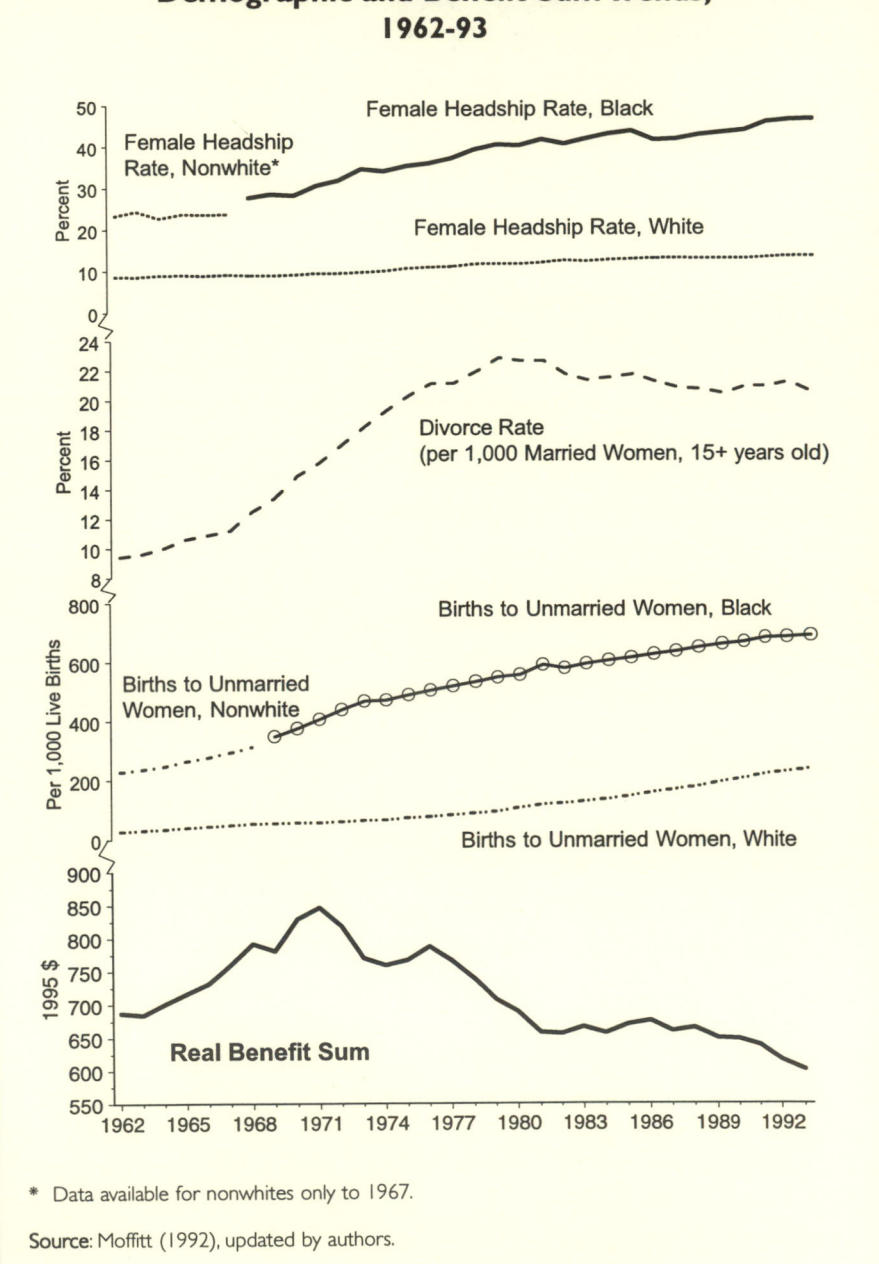

FIGURE 6F

Demographic and Benefit Sum Trends, 1962-93

* Data available for nonwhites only to 1967.

Source: Moffitt (1992), updated by authors.

of the period covered, the white out-of-wedlock birth rate does not appear to attenuate at all. The apparent independence of these demographic indicators and the benefit sum challenges the overly simplistic story that welfare causes the rising proportion of female-headed families.

Further evidence against the "welfare is the problem" argument comes from an analysis of AFDC participation rates, that is, the proportion of the demographi-cally eligible population (female-headed families with children) participating in the program. If single-mother families were forming specifically to take advan-tage of the eligibility for welfare, we would expect to see a greater proportion of female-headed families participating in AFDC over time (i.e., rising participa-tion rates). In fact, as **Table 6.25** and **Figure 6G** show, participation rates fell consistently through the mid-1970s and actually appeared to bottom out in 1989. Even in the deep recession of the early 1980s, participation rates continued their downward trend. The trend appears to have reversed in 1990, for reasons that are as yet unclear. Nevertheless, by the end of the period, participation rates remained 13 points below their peak at the start of this data series.

How are generally lower participation rates to be explained in the context of the growing proportion of female-headed families with children? The trends strongly suggest that female-headed families are forming for reasons other than to ensure AFDC eligibility. The decision to form a family of a particular struc-ture is most likely to be based on a wide variety of factors, reflecting not only economic factors but also social influences, such as society's changing mores regarding single-parent families and divorce.

TABLE 6.25

AFDC Participation Rates
Among Female Heads of Families with Children, 1976-92

1976	62%
1979	53
1983	46
1989	43
1992	49

Source: Wells and Sandefur (1996).

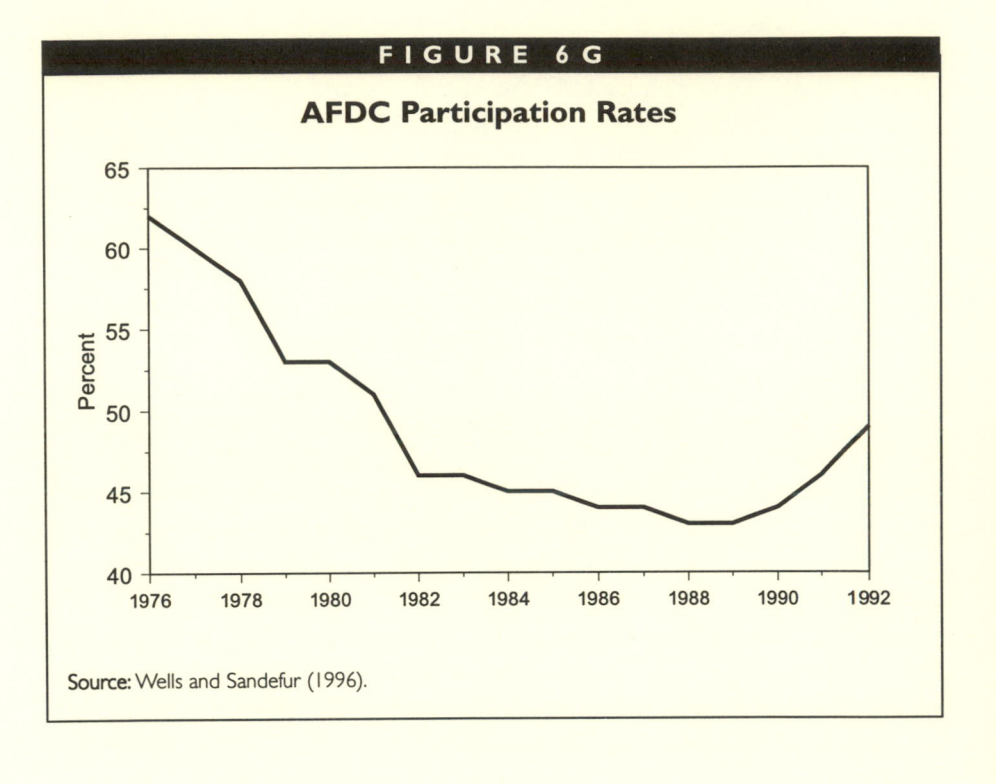

FIGURE 6G

AFDC Participation Rates

Source: Wells and Sandefur (1996).

Recent research that tracked mothers on AFDC throughout the 1980s provides more insight into the decline in participation rates. With the use of longitudinal data (tracking the same individuals over two-year periods in the 1980s), researchers were able to uncover much less welfare dependency (and more labor-force activity) among welfare users than was commonly thought to be the case. **Figure 6H** shows that 43% of mothers who used welfare over a two-year period also worked while they were on the rolls (combiners) or cycled between welfare and work. Another 30% sought work unsuccessfully or worked few hours (fewer than 100 hours per year). Thus, a minority (27%) fit the "dependency" label and, of these, 7% were disabled.

Finally, the question of family structure and welfare has been extensively examined by economists who, in modeling the family-formation process, have estimated the impact of a wide variety of variables, including welfare benefits, thought to play a role in family-structure decisions. A detailed discussion of this econometric work is beyond the scope of this text. However, the findings of this literature can be summarized as follows:

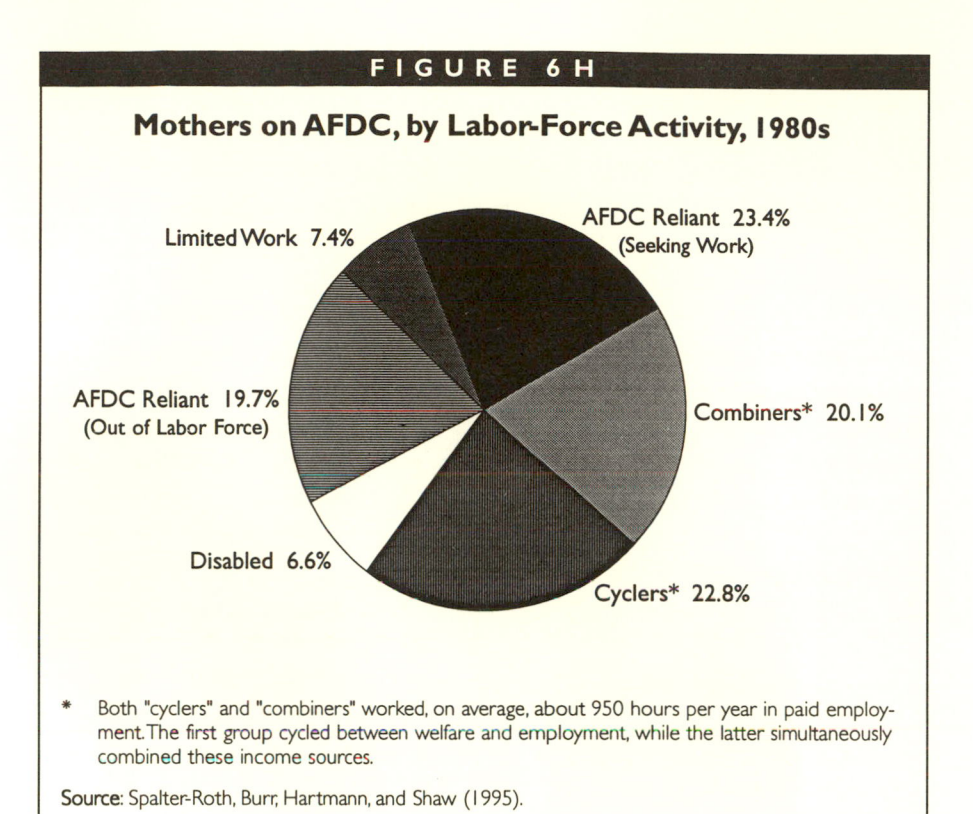

FIGURE 6H

Mothers on AFDC, by Labor-Force Activity, 1980s

AFDC Reliant 23.4%
(Seeking Work)

Limited Work 7.4%

AFDC Reliant 19.7%
(Out of Labor Force)

Combiners* 20.1%

Disabled 6.6%

Cyclers* 22.8%

* Both "cyclers" and "combiners" worked, on average, about 950 hours per year in paid employment. The first group cycled between welfare and employment, while the latter simultaneously combined these income sources.

Source: Spalter-Roth, Burr, Hartmann, and Shaw (1995).

• the value of the benefit package has a small effect on family structure;

• this small effect is most apparent in lower rates of remarriage and decisions by female-headed families to live independently (i.e., to form their own households instead of living with a relative);

• over the period covered in Figure 6G, the increase in the benefit sum led to a 9-14% increase in the prevalence of female-headed families with children. This is by no means a trivial effect, but it suggests that cutting or eliminating welfare will not drastically alter the picture.

Having examined the effect of the changes in taxes and transfers over the 1980s and the impact of benefits on family structure, we now turn to an explanation of the high poverty rates over the decade.

Explaining the High Poverty Rates of the 1980s

Over the 1980s, the tax system grew less progressive (see also Chapter 2), and government benefits grew less effective at reducing poverty (Table 6.24). However, when these findings are considered in the context of the relatively long economic expansion of 1983-89, another question is suggested: why were the poor unable to "cash in" on the economic growth that prevailed throughout most of the decade? That is, given the expansion, why didn't those at the bottom of the income distribution (at least those with some connection to the labor market) respond to less generous transfers and more regressive taxes by turning to the labor market? In the following section, we argue that such a reaction did in fact occur, but the wages of low-income workers declined significantly (see Chapter 3), keeping poverty rates high throughout the decade.

Falling Wages and Poverty in the 1980s

The problem of declining wages has already been discussed in Chapter 3. The relevant part of that presentation in the context of this chapter is the expansion of low-wage employment and the declining wages of low-wage workers. The following tables specifically examine earnings trends as they affect the poor.

We begin with an analysis of prime-age workers (25-54 years old) with year-round, full-time attachment to the labor force, yet with low earnings. These are persons who spent at least 50 weeks of the year at work or looking for work (i.e., in the labor force) and worked full time or were part time involuntarily. However, their annual earnings were not high enough to reach the poverty line for a family of four, which in 1994 was $13,828 (this threshold is based on the CPI-U-X1).

Figure 6I charts the share of these workers, by gender, for the period 1974-95. The trend shows an increased proportion earning poverty-level wages. This is particularly the case for men, whose share has grown by 6.8 percentage points since 1974. Although the proportion of male low-wage workers grew over the full period, the figure shows that the steepest growth was post-1979, when poverty was least responsive to overall economic growth. Interestingly, women saw their share fall between 1974 (the earliest year this type of data is available) and 1979 (with a continued slight decline 1979-89), but it has climbed since; by 1994, over one-quarter of prime-age female workers (8.4 million) earned poverty-level wages.

Figure 6J focuses on low-earners (again, with full labor-force attachment) in families with children; female-headed families are shown separately. Note

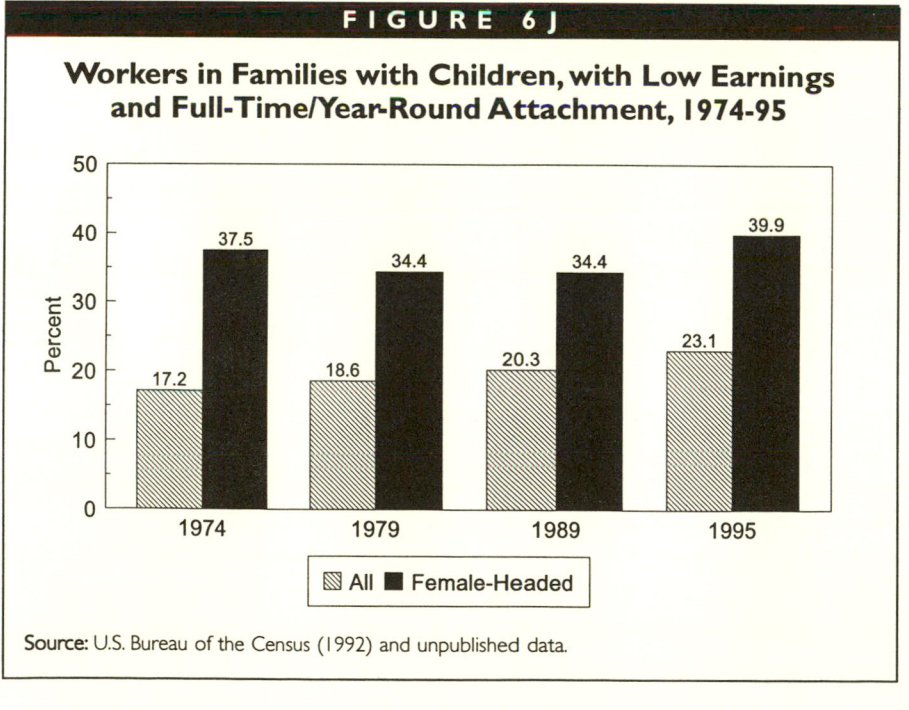

FIGURE 6I

Prime-Age Workers with Low Earnings and Full-Time/Year-Round Attachment, 1974-95

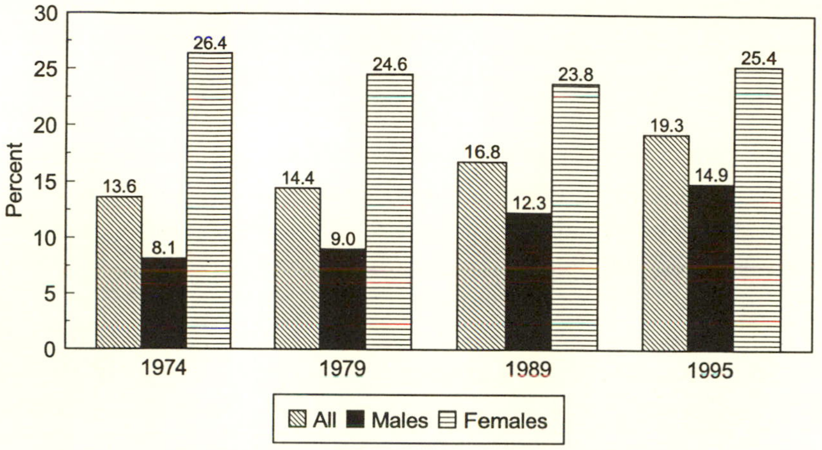

Legend: ▨ All ■ Males ⊟ Females

Source: U.S. Bureau of the Census (1992) and unpublished data.

FIGURE 6J

Workers in Families with Children, with Low Earnings and Full-Time/Year-Round Attachment, 1974-95

Legend: ▨ All ■ Female-Headed

Source: U.S. Bureau of the Census (1992) and unpublished data.

that this group of workers is worse off than those shown in the previous figure (compare the levels in the bars marked "All"), suggesting that families with children have a lower standard of living than the population of all prime-age workers. Families with children that are headed by a female have particularly high levels; in 1995, two-fifths of fully attached workers in these families earned poverty-level wages. Here, too, the pre-1979 trend was toward higher earnings.

Since the above figures focus only on those "fully attached" to the labor force, they show the combined effects of falling wages and fewer hours worked, or underemployment. **Table 6.26** examines the structure of hourly wages; it asks the question: given the structure of wage rates at a point in time, what percentage of workers fails to earn an hourly wage that would lift a family of four out of poverty, given full-time, full-year work?

The data in Table 6.26 show that rising wage rates in the 1973-79 period were poverty reducing, since the share of workers earning poverty-level wages fell in every category (except white males, which grew slightly). Interestingly, these positive shifts took place exclusively for the lowest earners, those earning up to 75% of the poverty line. However, between 1979 and 1989, this trend reversed, and the share of very low earners grew sharply while the share earning just below the poverty-level wage grew slightly or fell. For example, the share of black men earning very low wages (less than 75% of the poverty line) grew by 10.7 percentage points in the 1979-89 period; for Hispanic men, the increase was 13.9 points. These changes led to a dramatic rise in the share of males earning poverty-level wages. The proportion of females who were very low earners also grew between 1979 and 1989, but the share earning between 75% and 100% of the poverty line fell, and by the end of the period the share earning poverty-level wages was little changed.

Over the most recent period, 1989-94, the share of poverty-level earners grew among men (primarily whites and Hispanics) and Hispanic women. Again, in each case, the increase was driven primarily by the growth of the lowest-earning category. Note that by the end of the 22-year period covered in the table, the share of poverty-level-wage earners grew by 8 points for white men, 9 points for black men, and 19.5 points for Hispanic men. Women fared better over the full period, but the share of lowest earners (below 75% of poverty) grew sharply for each racial/ethnic group after 1979.

While Table 6.26 shows the proportion of low-wage workers, **Table 6.27** examines percentage changes in hourly wage levels of the poorest male and female workers (those in the bottom four-tenths of the hourly earnings distribution). For low-wage men between 1973 and 1979, there were small negative

TABLE 6.26

Share of Workers Earning Poverty-Level Wages*

Males	1973	1979	1989	1995
White				
Below 75% Poverty	3.1%	2.0%	7.4%	8.2%
To Below 100%	7.6	9.4	10.2	10.6
Total: Less Than Poverty	10.7	11.4	17.6	18.7
Black				
Below 75% Poverty	7.4	4.3	15.0	15.2
To Below 100%	17.4	19.1	18.2	18.6
Total: Less Than Poverty	24.8	23.4	33.2	33.8
Hispanic				
Below 75% Poverty	8.8	3.5	17.4	23.1
To Below 100%	16.2	19.8	21.6	21.4
Total: Less Than Poverty	25.0	23.3	39.0	44.5

Females	1973	1979	1989	1995
White				
Below 75% Poverty	12.5%	6.3%	16.9%	16.6%
To Below 100%	24.5	29.2	17.8	17.3
Total: Less Than Poverty	37.1	35.6	34.7	33.9
Black				
Below 75% Poverty	23.3	8.5	23.1	23.1
To Below 100%	27.3	34.3	20.5	20.5
Total: Less Than Poverty	50.7	42.8	43.6	43.7
Hispanic				
Below 75% Poverty	17.8	8.2	26.0	30.7
To Below 100%	32.6	41.0	24.9	22.7
Total: Less Than Poverty	50.4	49.1	50.9	53.5

* The poverty-level wage is the hourly wage rate needed to lift a family of four above the poverty line. It was $7.28 in 1994.

Source: Authors' analysis.

TABLE 6.27

Wage Trends Relevant
to the Poor and Near-Poor, 1973-95

	Lowest Tenth	2nd Tenth	3rd Tenth	4th Tenth
Men				
1973-79	-1.3%	-2.3%	-0.3%	1.2%
1979-89	-12.7	-13.9	-12.1	-10.6
1989-95	-6.4	-5.5	-8.5	-7.1
Women				
1973-79	21.3%	5.9%	2.3%	2.0%
1979-89	-18.2	-7.0	-0.9	2.1
1989-95	1.6	-1.6	-0.7	-0.5

Source: Authors' analysis.

changes in the bottom three-tenths and a slight gain (1.2%) in the fourth. For low-wage women, 1973-79 was a period of strong growth (21.3%) in the lowest tenth. This pattern of gains or small losses reversed, however, between 1979 and 1989 as all groups, except women at the fourth tenth, experienced falling wages. Men in particular (and the lowest-earning women) experienced the steepest losses. Those in the bottom three deciles saw a decrease of 12.7%, 13.9%, and 12.1% in their hourly wages. Thus, wage loss was greatest for the lowest earners, further evidence of a shifting down of the earnings distribution. Between 1989 and 1995, wage rates continued to fall for most low-wage workers, with similar declines for men in the bottom four deciles and small decreases for women. A notable exception is the 1.6% increase for women in the lowest decile, presumably due to the 1990-91 increase in the minimum wage, which is particularly relevant to the lowest-wage female workers.

The next few tables extend this analysis by examining the work effort of poor and low-wage workers. As Figures 6I and 6J have shown, full-time attachment to the labor force does not prevent low earnings. The following tables demonstrate that low-wage workers generally increased their work effort over the 1980s (and for some groups over the 1990s as well), yet they remain economically disadvantaged.

Table 6.28 examines the work experience of the prime-age poor (25-54) in 1979, 1989, and 1994. The absolute number of poor workers has grown over time, but the proportions of the employable poor (those not ill, disabled, or going to school) who worked have remained markedly constant, hovering around 50%. Over the same period, among those who worked, an increasing share have worked full time. One rate that does grow over the period is the percent of the prime-age poor unable to find work, which grew from 3.7% to 5.1%. In tandem with the increase in the not-employable category in 1994 (due mostly to an increase in the number of ill or disabled persons), there has been a decline in the percent of the employable poor who neither sought nor found work, which stood at 25.6% in 1994. Putting these results in the context of the last few tables suggests that low-wage workers are faced with both falling wages and diminishing employment opportunities.

Table 6.29 looks at average annual hours of work among low-income families within different family types: female-headed families with children, married

---

TABLE 6.28

Work Experience of the Poor, 1979-94

	1979	1989	1994
Number of Poor (000) Age 25-54	7,659*	9,674	12,312
Percent Not Employable	17.6%	18.4%	24.4%
Ill or Disabled	11.7	11.6	16.6
Going to School	5.5	6.3	6.8
Retired	0.4	0.4	0.9
Employable Poor Aged 25-54	82.4%	81.6%	75.6%
Unable to Find Work	3.7	4.9	5.1
Percent Who Worked	53.4	53.1	51.1
Year-Round, Full-Time	13.9	14.7	16.2
Part-Time or Part-Year	39.5	38.4	34.9
Percent of Employable Prime-Age Poor Who Neither Sought Nor Found Work	30.8%	29.0%	25.6%

* Includes persons 22-54.

Source: U.S. Bureau of the Census, various years.

TABLE 6.29

Annual Average Hours Worked by Family Type in Bottom Two-Fifths,* 1979-94

	1979	1989	1994	Annualized Rates of Change		
				1979-89	1989-94	1979-94
All Families**						
Lowest Fifth	999	1,096	1,064	0.9%	-0.6%	0.4%
Second Fifth	2,107	2,243	2,099	0.6	-1.3	0.0
Female-Headed Families with Children						
Lowest Fifth	302	316	339	0.5%	1.4%	0.8%
Second Fifth	739	753	824	0.2	1.8	0.7
Married-Couple Families with Children						
Lowest Fifth	2,186	2,395	2,296	0.9%	-0.8%	0.3%
Second Fifth	2,943	3,268	3,344	1.1	0.5	0.9
Unrelated Individuals (Nonelderly)						
Lowest Fifth	649	759	671	1.6%	-2.4%	0.2%
Second Fifth	1,387	1,603	1,572	1.5	-0.4	0.8

* Fifths are defined separately for each family type. Related subfamilies are included with primary families.

** Excludes one-person families.

Source: Authors' analysis.

couples, and unrelated individuals. Whereas the previous table included only the poor, Table 6.29 examines work effort by those in the bottom two-fifths (or quintiles) of the income distribution, which include both the poor and near-poor.

The average hours of work in Table 6.29 represent the pooled work effort of the family. The table shows that average annual hours of work grew for all family types between 1979 and 1989. However, even in light of extra work effort, the wage decline documented above constrained these families from realizing any economic gains. In the 1980s, members of these families were running faster, yet losing ground.

The largest growth in percentage terms over the 1980s was for unrelated individuals. Those at the bottom of the income distribution increased their average hours of work at an annual rate of 1.6% over the decade; those individuals in the second quintile increased their average hours by 1.5%. Married couples with children have by far the most hours of work; in each year these families supplied an average of well over 2,000 hours of labor. By 1989, the average married-couple family with children in the second quintile worked 3,268 hours, 11.0% more hours than in 1979. Mother-only families with children in the bottom quintile show a relatively small number of hours of work, but their hours worked grew slightly (0.5% per year) over the 1980s.

Hours fell for most low-income families in the 1990s, with the exception of the female-headed families and married couples (with children) in the second quintile. The cause of this decline is as yet undetermined, but it may reflect the fact that 1994 was still relatively early in an economic expansion that was slow to accelerate. Nevertheless, with one exception, each family type had a higher level of hours worked in 1994 than in 1979. There is no evidence in these tables to support the claim that the poor missed the rising economic tide because of lack of effort on their part.

An important policy change that has served to mitigate to some degree the impact of the negative wage trends on poverty is the expansion of the earned income tax credit (EITC) under Clinton's budget package, OBRA93. The EITC is a wage subsidy for families with children (the expanded program now contains a smaller subsidy for childless low-wage workers), targeted at low earners (the poverty-reducing effects of the current EITC are incorporated in Table 6.24, column 5). **Figure 6K** shows the level of the refundable credit (i.e., earners need not have a positive tax liability to receive the credit) as a function of earnings, both before and after the OBRA93 expansion for families with one and two children. (The results are for the fully phased-in EITC, which occurs in 1996.)

The figure reveals that OBRA93, by 1996, significantly expands the credit. For working families with one child, the maximum credit increases by $202 (1994 dollars); for those with two or more children, it increases by $1,372. The steeper slopes of the OBRA93 EITC schedule show that the credit increases at a faster rate under the expanded program as earnings rise. For example, a full-time/full-year male worker at the 20th percentile of the male wage distribution with two children would receive a $972 increase in the EITC under OBRA93. Thus, some of the poverty-inducing effects of wage decline will likely be offset when OBRA93 is fully phased in.

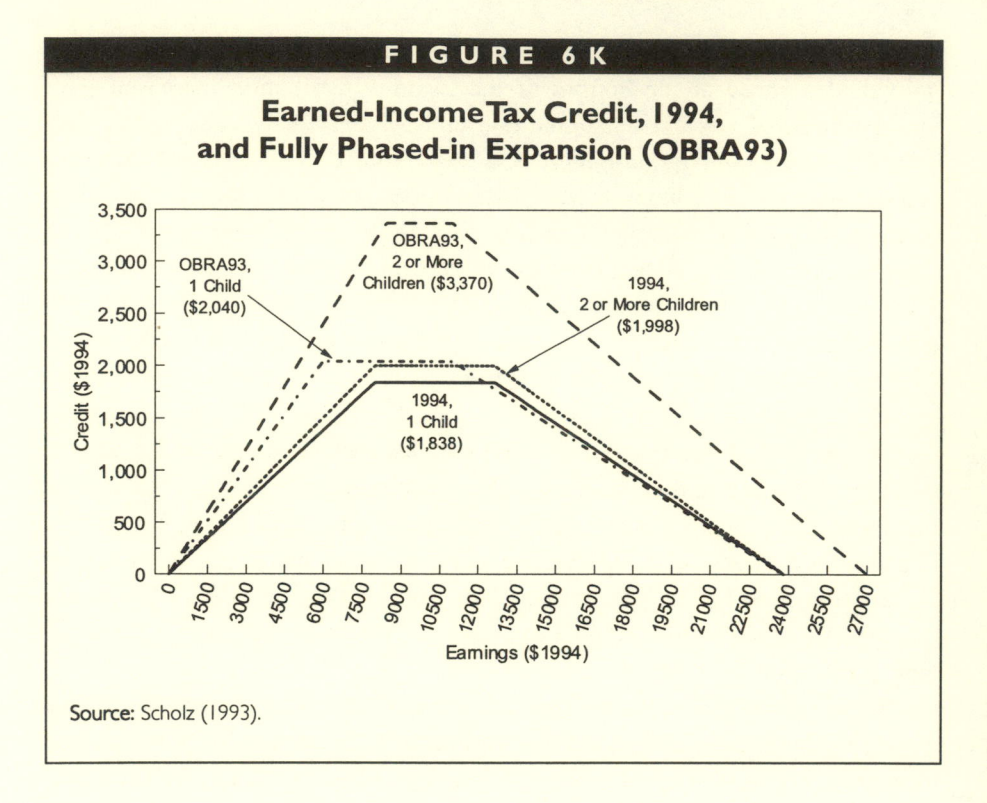

FIGURE 6 K

Earned-Income Tax Credit, 1994, and Fully Phased-in Expansion (OBRA93)

Source: Scholz (1993).

Conclusion

This chapter began with the observation that, based on the movement of the economic variables usually correlated with poverty rates, poverty should have fallen after 1983. Yet a wide array of evidence shows that this expectation did not materialize. Poverty rates stayed high throughout the decade, whether measured by the official thresholds or by alternative, more encompassing measures. Furthermore, demographic explanations (the increase of family types unresponsive to economic growth), while possibly relevant in earlier decades, are insufficient to explain the stubbornly high rates. Neither is lack of work effort a sufficient explanation, since the work effort of the poor and near-poor generally increased over the 1980s and remained higher than its 1979 level by 1994.

The conclusion we are left with is that two simultaneous effects occurred that kept poverty rates high over the decade: (1) the wages of those at the bottom of the income distribution fell precipitously, and (2) the system of tax and transfers designed to ameliorate poverty was less effective than in the past. In other words, the primary distribution of market income was such that more families (as well as unrelated individuals) were unable to achieve incomes above the poverty level through the wages they earned during the 1980s and early 1990s. This development necessarily puts additional pressure on the secondary distribution—taxes and transfers—to close a wider poverty gap. While the expanded EITC will partly counteract the trend in market income, the extent of wage erosion will eventually place an unacceptably high burden on taxpayers. In this regard, strengthening wage growth at the bottom of the wage scale is perhaps the most important direct way to reconnect poverty reduction and economic growth.

CHAPTER 7

REGIONAL ANALYSIS
Uneven Job Growth,
Consistent Wage Losses

MOST OF THE ANALYSIS UP TO THIS POINT HAS LOOKED AT THE NATION AS a whole. In this chapter, we examine trends in income, wages, employment, and poverty among regions, divisions (i.e., groups of states within regions), and states. We find that the trends in states and regions mirror those at the national level: the benefits of employment growth and falling unemployment have failed for the most part to translate into wage gains.

In general, over the 1980s most workers in the Northeast did notably better on each indicator (e.g., median wages and incomes rose and poverty and unemployment fell) than did workers in the other regions. However, despite low unemployment, low-wage workers in some northeastern states (e.g., New York and Pennsylvania) lost ground. States in the West, particularly California, experienced relatively flat growth rates in terms of employment and median incomes, and wages for workers at the median and below declined.

During the 1990s, these trends in the Northeast and California have reversed. Between 1989 and 1995, incomes and employment contracted and poverty grew the most in these states. By the end of the period, indicators in these geographic areas stood well below their 1989 peak levels. Wage growth at the median was flat or negative in most areas of the country over this period; even average earnings, which include all workers from the poorest to the most wealthy and which typically expand in a recovery, did not increase between 1989 and 1994.

Due to the limited nature of these regional data, some of these series are presented for time periods that differ from tables in the other chapters. Also, due to lack of sufficient data in some states, it is not possible to accurately show every variable for each state; consequently, in some cases the data are "aggregated up" to the level of division or region.

Median Family Income Declines in Most States

As discussed in Chapter 1, the income of the median family (the family at the midpoint of the family-income distribution) is a key indicator of the economic well-being of the typical family. **Figure 7A** and **Table 7.1** show that, in every region, the income of the median family rose more quickly prior to 1973 than after. While the trends were similar in most regions, the level of the median family's income has been consistently lower in the South. (From 1973 onward this difference has remained roughly constant, at about 10%.)

To some extent, the deregulation of financial markets in the 1980s favored the Northeast, where this sector is most heavily concentrated, and led to a no-

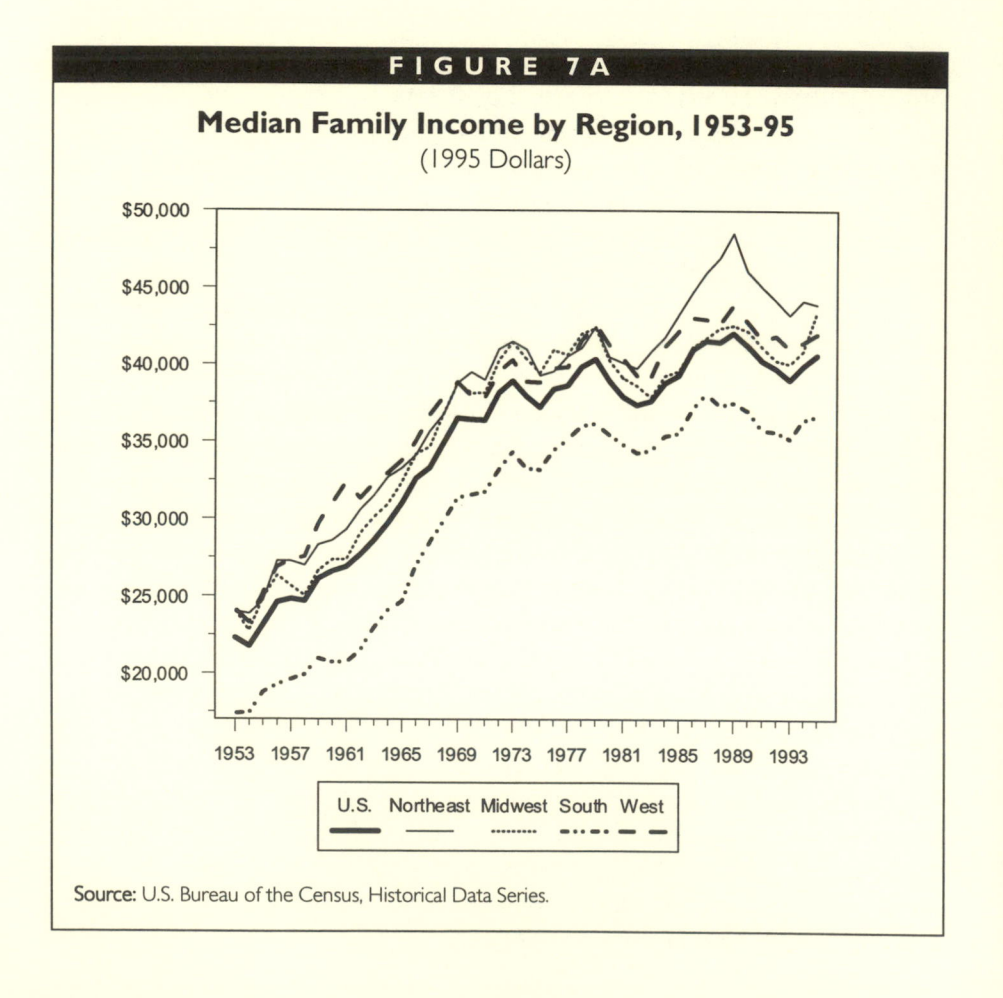

FIGURE 7A

Median Family Income by Region, 1953-95
(1995 Dollars)

U.S.   Northeast   Midwest   South   West

Source: U.S. Bureau of the Census, Historical Data Series.

TABLE 7.1

Median Family Income by Region
(1995 Dollars)

Year	U.S.	Northeast	Midwest	South	West
1953	$22,292	$24,042	$24,090	$17,384	$24,169
1973	38,910	41,490	41,429	34,313	40,263
1979	40,339	42,470	42,365	36,144	42,608
1989	42,049	48,527	42,540	37,484	43,874
1995	40,611	43,909	43,470	36,628	41,967
Annual Growth Rates					
1953-73	2.8%	2.8%	2.7%	3.5%	2.6%
1973-79	0.6	0.4	0.4	0.9	0.9
1979-89	0.4	1.3	0.0	0.4	0.3
1989-95	-0.6	-1.7	0.4	-0.4	-0.7

Source: U.S. Bureau of the Census, Historical Data Series.

table deviation from the national trend in this area in the mid- to late 1980s. As the annual changes in Table 7.1 show, while the income of the median family in the other regions was growing at historically moderate rates, the income of families in the Northeast was growing more than three times as fast in the 1980s.

However, the median family in the Northeast lost ground the fastest in the recession of the early 1990s. As noted in Chapter 3, the fact that white-collar workers were uncharacteristically vulnerable in that recession is probably to blame for the sharp northeastern decline. Thus, in 1995, the last year of available data, the median family in the Northeast was $4,618 dollars below its 1989 peak, representing a larger gap than that of any of the other regions.

Table 7.2 shows the trend in the median family income for four-person families by state, 1974-94. (This series of data—the only state-level series on median incomes by state produced by the Census—is available only for these years.) By controlling for family size, the data in this table address the argument by some analysts that, since family size has declined over time, income trends overstate recent income problems.

Income growth for the median four-person family was fairly uniform across

TABLE 7.2

Median Income for Four-Person Families, by State
(1995 Dollars)

	1974	1979	1989	1994	Annual Growth Rates		
					1974-79	1979-89	1989-94
NORTHEAST							
New England							
Maine	$36,858	$37,223	$47,116	$43,856	0.2%	2.4%	-1.4%
New Hampshire	41,069	45,998	58,973	52,950	2.3	2.5	-2.1
Vermont	38,599	39,776	49,649	47,633	0.6	2.2	-0.8
Massachusetts	45,896	48,986	63,663	60,358	1.3	2.7	-1.1
Rhode Island	42,296	44,558	53,190	53,174	1.0	1.8	-0.0
Connecticut	48,380	50,271	65,523	63,867	0.8	2.7	-0.5
Mid-Atlantic							
New York	44,542	43,418	53,700	52,408	-0.5	2.1	-0.5
New Jersey	49,117	50,745	65,420	62,417	0.7	2.6	-0.9
Pennsylvania	42,546	45,955	49,658	50,512	1.6	0.8	0.3
MIDWEST							
East North Central							
Ohio	44,402	46,396	50,967	48,176	0.9	0.9	-1.1
Indiana	42,513	46,573	46,950	48,550	1.8	0.1	0.7
Illinois	48,010	49,973	52,368	53,423	0.8	0.5	0.4
Michigan	47,494	50,296	52,633	52,797	1.2	0.5	0.1
Wisconsin	45,215	48,434	49,846	50,370	1.4	0.3	0.2
West North Central							
Minnesota	46,372	50,269	52,068	53,470	1.6	0.4	0.5
Iowa	42,199	46,476	45,150	46,339	1.9	-0.3	0.5
Missouri	40,434	43,854	47,291	45,521	1.6	0.8	-0.8
North Dakota	44,061	40,201	42,778	43,419	-1.8	0.6	0.3
South Dakota	37,657	39,560	40,348	44,182	1.0	0.2	1.8
Nebraska	39,242	42,732	46,583	46,786	1.7	0.9	0.1
Kansas	42,270	47,055	46,627	45,668	2.2	-0.1	-0.4
SOUTH							
South Atlantic							
Delaware	44,725	43,628	52,590	56,609	-0.5	1.9	1.5
Maryland	48,891	50,840	61,630	59,593	0.8	1.9	-0.7
District of Columbia	44,319	43,887	49,867	53,489	-0.2	1.3	1.4
Virginia	44,428	47,318	55,417	50,855	1.3	1.6	-1.7
West Virginia	36,908	38,874	39,097	39,444	1.0	0.1	0.2
North Carolina	38,711	40,464	46,787	45,845	0.9	1.5	-0.4
South Carolina	38,335	41,506	44,384	44,790	1.6	0.7	0.2
Georgia	40,129	44,439	49,185	46,371	2.1	1.0	-1.2
Florida	43,424	42,748	45,965	44,603	-0.3	0.7	-0.6

(continued)

TABLE 7.2 *(cont.)*

Median Income for Four-Person Families, by State
(1995 Dollars)

| | 1974 | 1979 | 1989 | 1994 | Annual Growth Rates | | |
					1974-79	1979-89	1989-94
SOUTH							
East South Central							
Kentucky	$36,746	$39,414	$42,266	$39,060	1.4%	0.7%	-1.6%
Tennessee	37,551	40,030	42,871	43,326	1.3	0.7	0.2
Alabama	37,601	38,333	42,930	42,913	0.4	1.1	-0.0
Mississippi	33,951	36,395	39,698	38,052	1.4	0.9	-0.8
West South Central							
Arkansas	34,914	38,086	39,148	37,545	1.8	0.3	-0.8
Louisiana	36,999	41,531	42,286	40,860	2.3	0.2	-0.7
Oklahoma	37,131	42,944	42,365	39,886	3.0	-0.1	-1.2
Texas	40,887	48,224	42,989	43,776	3.4	-1.1	0.4
WEST							
Mountain							
Montana	40,188	41,294	41,642	40,330	0.5	0.1	-0.6
Idaho	41,330	42,073	41,336	42,376	0.4	-0.2	0.5
Wyoming	43,556	46,694	43,778	49,320	1.4	-0.6	2.4
Colorado	45,893	51,956	49,487	50,184	2.5	-0.5	0.3
New Mexico	35,657	43,315	38,292	38,223	4.0	-1.2	-0.0
Arizona	44,722	47,368	47,130	42,778	1.2	-0.1	-1.9
Utah	41,119	43,764	44,936	46,143	1.3	0.3	0.5
Nevada	45,095	52,428	48,838	49,287	3.1	-0.7	0.2
Pacific							
Washington	45,224	50,271	51,285	50,319	2.1	0.2	-0.4
Oregon	44,084	49,491	47,592	45,691	2.3	-0.4	-0.8
California	46,780	51,711	52,619	50,137	2.0	0.2	-1.0
Alaska	56,873	63,919	59,499	55,073	2.4	-0.7	-1.5
Hawaii	50,122	50,626	55,292	58,607	0.2	0.9	1.2
U.S. TOTAL	43,303	46,122	50,099	48,344	1.3	0.8	-0.7

Source: U.S. Bureau of the Census, Historical Data Series.

states in the 1970s, although some of the energy-rich states in the Southwest appear to have benefited from the rise in energy prices. Growth was both slower and less uniform in the 1980s: a number of northeastern states experienced faster-than-average income growth, while some of the southwestern states saw their fortunes reverse as the growth in energy prices tapered off.

By 1994, the median four-person family in most states was below its 1989 level. As noted, the recession of the early 1990s led to significant losses for states in the Northeast. Large losses relative to the national average of -0.7% also befell the median four-person family in many of the southern states, such as Virginia (-1.7%), Kentucky (-1.6%), and Georgia (-1.2%).

Rising Inequality in Income and Earnings

An examination of relative incomes provides another perspective on regional family-income trends. In this analysis, the share of families with incomes within certain multiples of the median is calculated for each period. **Table 7.3** shows the percent of persons by division in the three relative income groups. Note that, with few exceptions, the middle class grew smaller in every period. In all three periods—the 1970s, '80s, and '90s—the shifts went in both directions. Nationally, the low and the high relative-income groups grew while the middle class was squeezed.

Once again, there are notable differences between divisions. In 1989, for example, New England had the smallest share of low-income persons (13.8%), while the East South Central had more than twice that share (31.4%).

As the final three columns illustrate, the rate of shifts from the middle to the upper and lower groups accelerated in the 1980s, particularly in the Northeast and the South Central regions. While shifts in the Northeast were exclusively upward, most other divisions experienced an expansion in the share of families with low relative incomes. In the West South Central division, for example, the share of families with middle incomes fell by 5.0 percentage points, and most of this drop was accounted for by a 4.2-point expansion in the number of low-income families.

Over the 1990s, this pattern shifted somewhat, and the southern and Mountain states increased their shares of families with high relative incomes. Conversely, the share of middle- and high-income families fell by 3.7 percentage points in New England in the 1990s.

As discussed throughout this book, wage trends are primarily responsible for income trends. **Table 7.4** shifts the focus from relative income trends to absolute wage trends. In this analysis, the structure of earnings in each region is examined by comparing a worker's annual earnings to the poverty line for a family of four. Workers are placed in categories determined by the ratio of their earnings to the poverty line. Those whose earnings are below the poverty level are placed in the first category. (Note that these persons are not necessarily poor by the official definition of poverty, because they may have access to other sources of income, including the income of other family members, or they may live in families with fewer than four people.) The highest earners have earnings' ratios four or more times the poverty line.

From 1973 to 1979, each region cut its share of workers earning poverty-level wages by more than half, with the largest decrease—24.3 percentage points—occurring in the South, where the levels of low earners was (and remains) the highest. Between 1979 and 1989, however, this pattern shifted, with the share of low earners expanding in each region. In the West, for example, the share of poverty-level workers grew by 3.1 percentage points. In the 1990s, the downward shift continued and even accelerated. Nationally, 2.6% of earners fell from the top two groups to the bottom two groups. In the West, this same pattern occurred for 3.4% of earners.

The 1970s saw a large shift from the low and low-middle categories to the two highest groups, with most workers shifting to the upper-middle group (2 to 4 times the poverty level). Shifts in the 1980s were more mixed. There was significant upward movement in the Northeast, where over 4% of the workforce went from the lower-middle to the highest category. The upward shift in the other regions, however, occurred at a much slower rate than in the previous decade. Finally, in the 1990s, the downward shift in the wage structure was pervasive. Between 1989 and 1995, the top share of earners either grew slightly (the Midwest) or fell.

Taken together, Tables 7.4 and 7.5 show evidence of an increase in inequality in the 1980s and 1990s. The following section provides a state-level analysis of more specific data: wages and other key labor-market indicators.

TABLE 7.3

Percent of Persons in Families with Low, Middle, and High Relative Incomes,* 1973-95, by Division

	1973	1979	1989	1995	Percentage-Point Changes		
					1973-79	1979-89	1989-95
NORTHEAST							
New England							
Low	14.8%	15.4%	13.8%	17.5%	0.6	-1.6	3.7
Middle	72.2	71.4	63.5	62.8	-0.8	-7.9	-0.7
High	13.0	13.2	22.7	19.7	0.2	9.5	-3.0
Total	100.0	100.0	100.0	100.0			
Mid-Atlantic							
Low	15.7	19.3	18.8	20.6	3.6	-0.5	1.8
Middle	71.6	68.7	62.6	60.9	-2.9	-6.1	-1.7
High	12.8	12.1	18.6	18.5	-0.7	6.5	-0.1
Total	100.0	100.0	100.0	100.0			
MIDWEST							
East North Central							
Low	14.5	16.7	19.9	18.3	2.2	3.2	-1.6
Middle	73.7	70.2	66.4	64.6	-3.5	-3.8	-1.8
High	11.9	13.1	13.7	17.1	1.2	0.6	3.4
Total	100.0	100.0	100.0	100.0			
West North Central							
Low	18.2	17.8	20.7	18.7	-0.4	2.9	-2.0
Middle	71.4	72.0	68.0	67.6	0.6	-4.0	-0.4
High	10.4	10.2	11.3	13.7	-0.2	1.1	2.4
Total	100.0	100.0	100.0	100.0			
SOUTH							
South Atlantic							
Low	21.2	22.5	22.9	22.7	1.3	0.4	-0.2
Middle	68.0	66.9	62.9	61.9	-1.1	-4.0	-1.0
High	10.7	10.6	14.2	15.4	-0.1	3.6	1.2
Total	100.0	100.0	100.0	100.0			
East South Central							
Low	29.5	27.5	31.4	27.1	-2.0	3.9	-4.3
Middle	63.3	65.7	60.8	62.4	2.4	-4.9	1.6
High	7.2	6.8	7.8	10.5	-0.4	1.0	2.7
Total	100.0	100.0	100.0	100.0			

(continued)

TABLE 7.3 (cont.)

Percent of Persons in Families with Low, Middle, and High Relative Incomes,* 1973-95, by Division

					Percentage-Point Changes		
	1973	1979	1989	1995	1973-79	1979-89	1989-95
SOUTH							
West South Central							
Low	27.7	25.4	29.6	27.7	-2.3	4.2	-1.9
Middle	63.2	64.1	59.1	60.3	0.9	-5.0	1.2
High	9.2	10.6	11.3	12.0	1.4	0.7	0.7
Total	100.0	100.0	100.0	100.0			
WEST							
Mountain							
Low	20.4	18.4	23.0	22.8	-2.0	4.6	-0.2
Middle	68.6	69.2	65.4	63.7	0.6	-3.8	-1.7
High	11.1	12.4	11.7	13.5	1.3	-0.7	1.8
Total	100.0	100.0	100.0	100.0			
Pacific							
Low	17.9	18.9	21.1	23.9	1.0	2.2	2.8
Middle	68.4	66.0	61.7	57.9	-2.4	-4.3	-3.8
High	13.7	15.2	17.2	18.2	1.5	2.0	1.0
Total	100.0	100.0	100.0	100.0			
U.S.							
Low	19.0	20.1	22.1	22.2	1.1	2.0	0.1
Middle	69.5	68.0	63.3	62.0	-1.5	-4.7	-1.4
High	11.5	11.9	14.7	15.9	0.4	2.8	1.2
Total	100.0	100.0	100.0	100.0			

* "Low" refers to persons in families with income less than one-half the median. "Middle" is from one-half to two times the median, and "high" is twice the median and above.

Source: Unpublished tabulations provided by Jack McNeil.

TABLE 7.4

Earnings Ratios* by Region, Year-Round, Full-Time Workers, 16 Years and Older, 1973-95

| | 1973 | 1979 | 1989 | 1995 | Percentage-Point Changes | | |
					1973-79	1979-89	1989-95
NORTHEAST							
Low	26.5%	9.6%	9.8%	12.4%	-16.9	0.2	2.6
Low-Middle	50.1	38.1	33.6	34.6	-12.0	-4.5	1.0
Upper-Middle	20.4	42.0	42.0	39.4	21.6	0.0	-2.6
High	3.0	10.2	14.6	13.6	7.2	4.4	-1.0
Total	100.0	100.0	100.0	100.0			
MIDWEST							
Low	27.5	11.0	13.9	14.6	-16.5	2.9	0.7
Low-Middle	49.6	35.1	37.3	36.9	-14.5	2.2	-0.4
Upper-Middle	20.5	43.5	38.5	37.4	23.0	-5.0	-1.1
High	2.4	10.4	10.3	11.0	8.0	-0.1	0.7
Total	100.0	100.0	100.0	100.0			
SOUTH							
Low	39.8	15.5	17.3	19.1	-24.3	1.8	1.8
Low-Middle	43.4	41.4	39.0	39.7	-2.0	-2.4	0.7
Upper-Middle	14.1	34.3	33.5	31.8	20.2	-0.8	-1.7
High	2.8	8.8	10.3	9.5	6.0	1.5	-0.8
Total	100.0	100.0	100.0	100.0			
WEST							
Low	25.2	10.5	13.6	16.2	-14.7	3.1	2.6
Low-Middle	49.4	33.9	33.4	34.2	-15.5	-0.5	0.8
Upper-Middle	22.0	42.8	39.5	36.2	20.8	-3.3	-3.3
High	3.4	12.8	13.6	13.5	9.4	0.8	-0.1
Total	100.0	100.0	100.0	100.0			
U.S.							
Low	30.7	12.1	14.1	16.1	-18.6	2.0	2.0
Low-Middle	47.7	37.6	36.3	36.9	-10.1	-1.3	0.6
Upper-Middle	18.8	40.0	37.7	35.5	21.2	-2.3	-2.2
High	2.9	10.3	11.9	11.1	7.4	1.6	-0.4
Total	100.0	100.0	100.0	100.0			

* The categories refer to the following earnings ratios: Low= 1.00; Low-Middle= 1-2; Upper-Middle=2-4; High=4+.

Source: Unpublished tabulations provided by Jack McNeil.

Job Growth, but Falling Median Wages

In this section, we examine employment, unemployment, average wages, and median wages, as well as analyze trends in the low-wage labor market. Two important findings emerge: (1) growth over the various periods examined was uneven, with a good deal of variation among the states, and (2) those states with strong job growth or low unemployment did not necessarily experience wage growth. Even the relatively low unemployment rates that prevailed in some states in the 1980s were insufficient to generate wage growth for middle- and low-wage workers (although wage trends were more adverse in areas with high unemployment).

Table 7.5 shows nonfarm payroll employment by state, 1973-95, along with annual rates of employment growth for various periods. While employment grew by about 40 million jobs over the full period, growth was uneven by region and time period. Over the 1970s (the fastest period of job growth in the period covered), the Mountain and Pacific states in the West experienced particularly strong growth rates. For example, employment growth in the relatively large Pacific states of California (4.0%) and Washington (5.4%) was notably faster than the average national growth rate (2.6%). At the same time, employment growth in some of the large eastern states, like New York (0.1%), New Jersey (1.6%), and Massachusetts (1.8%), was below average.

During the 1980s employment growth slowed in the West and in the "rust belt" states of the Midwest. Growth in Michigan and Illinois slowed to less than 1%; in Wisconsin, employment grew at about two-thirds the national rate. Growth accelerated, however, in New York and New Jersey as the service sector expanded in those states. A number of southern states also experienced above-average employment growth, but (as we show below) most did not experience corresponding wage growth.

The nation added 8.7 million jobs between 1989 and 1995 as employment grew by 1.3% per year. Most of this growth occurred at the end of the period, as the national economy expanded out of the recession of 1990-91. Employment growth was negative in only a few states; these tended to be in the Northeast, where the recession was most keenly felt. In the West, job growth in California slowed to a crawl, with fewer than 200,000 jobs created over the six years. Conversely, some of the Mountain states, such as Idaho, Utah, and Nevada, enjoyed relatively fast growth. Several states with large workforces experienced job losses, including New York, New Jersey, and Massachusetts.

State unemployment rates for 1979-95 are shown in **Table 7.6**. As noted

357

TABLE 7.5

Nonfarm Payroll Employment, by State, 1973-95
(in Thousands)

	1973	1979	1989	1995	Annual Growth Rates		
					1973-79	1979-89	1989-95
NORTHEAST	19,150	20,407	23,644	23,054	1.1%	1.5%	-0.4%
New England	4,752	5,394	6,569	6,329	2.1	2.0	-0.6
Maine	355	416	542	542	2.7	2.7	-0.0
New Hampshire	298	379	529	539	4.1	3.4	0.3
Vermont	161	198	262	270	3.5	2.8	0.5
Massachusetts	2,334	2,604	3,109	2,974	1.8	1.8	-0.7
Rhode Island	366	400	462	441	1.5	1.4	-0.8
Connecticut	1,239	1,398	1,666	1,564	2.0	1.8	-1.0
Mid-Atlantic	14,398	15,013	17,075	16,725	0.7	1.3	-0.3
New York	7,132	7,179	8,247	7,871	0.1	1.4	-0.8
New Jersey	2,760	3,027	3,690	3,606	1.6	2.0	-0.4
Pennsylvania	4,507	4,806	5,139	5,248	1.1	0.7	0.4
MIDWEST	21,408	24,172	26,580	29,332	2.0	1.0	1.7
East North Central	15,553	17,198	18,669	20,418	1.7	0.8	1.5
Ohio	4,113	4,485	4,817	5,232	1.5	0.7	1.4
Indiana	2,028	2,236	2,479	2,781	1.6	1.0	1.9
Illinois	4,467	4,880	5,214	5,599	1.5	0.7	1.2
Michigan	3,284	3,637	3,922	4,252	1.7	0.8	1.4
Wisconsin	1,661	1,960	2,236	2,555	2.8	1.3	2.2
West North Central	5,856	6,973	7,911	8,914	3.0	1.3	2.0
Minnesota	1,436	1,767	2,087	2,374	3.5	1.7	2.2
Iowa	961	1,132	1,200	1,357	2.8	0.6	2.1
Missouri	1,771	2,011	2,315	2,521	2.1	1.4	1.4
North Dakota	184	244	260	302	4.8	0.6	2.5
South Dakota	199	241	276	344	3.3	1.3	3.7
Nebraska	541	631	708	815	2.6	1.2	2.4
Kansas	763	947	1,064	1,201	3.7	1.2	2.0
SOUTH	23,365	28,571	35,989	40,675	3.4	2.3	2.1
South Atlantic	12,183	14,392	19,433	21,466	2.8	3.0	1.7
Delaware	239	257	345	366	1.2	3.0	1.0
Maryland	1,472	1,691	2,155	2,181	2.3	2.5	0.2
District of Columbia	574	613	681	643	1.1	1.1	-0.9
Virginia	1,753	2,115	2,862	3,068	3.2	3.1	1.2
West Virginia	562	659	615	688	2.7	-0.7	1.9
North Carolina	2,018	2,373	3,074	3,455	2.7	2.6	2.0
South Carolina	984	1,176	1,500	1,648	3.0	2.5	1.6
Georgia	1,803	2,128	2,941	3,417	2.8	3.3	2.5
Florida	2,779	3,381	5,261	6,000	3.3	4.5	2.2

(continued)

TABLE 7.5 (cont.)

Nonfarm Payroll Employment, by State, 1973-95
(in Thousands)

	1973	1979	1989	1995	Annual Growth Rates 1973-79	1979-89	1989-95
SOUTH (cont.)							
East South Central	4,398	5,223	6,121	7,024	2.9%	1.6%	2.3%
Kentucky	1,039	1,245	1,433	1,643	3.1	1.4	2.3
Tennessee	1,531	1,777	2,167	2,503	2.5	2.0	2.4
Alabama	1,136	1,362	1,601	1,803	3.1	1.6	2.0
Mississippi	693	638	919	1,075	3.2	0.9	2.6
West South Central	6,784	8,957	10,436	12,184	4.7	1.5	2.6
Arkansas	615	749	893	1,069	3.4	1.8	3.0
Louisiana	1,176	1,517	1,539	1,775	4.3	0.1	2.4
Oklahoma	852	1,088	1,164	1,314	4.2	0.7	2.0
Texas	4,142	5,602	6,840	8,027	5.2	2.0	2.7
WEST	13,286	17,276	21,845	24,051	4.5	2.4	1.6
Mountain	3,258	4,414	5,621	7,057	5.2	2.4	3.9
Montana	224	284	291	351	4.0	0.3	3.2
Idaho	252	338	366	477	5.0	0.8	4.5
Wyoming	126	201	193	220	8.1	-0.4	2.2
Colorado	936	1,218	1,482	1,839	4.5	2.0	3.7
New Mexico	346	461	562	690	4.9	2.0	3.5
Arizona	715	980	1,455	1,783	5.4	4.0	3.5
Utah	415	548	691	908	4.8	2.3	4.7
Nevada	245	384	581	789	7.8	4.2	5.2
Pacific	10,028	12,863	16,224	16,994	4.2	2.3	0.8
Washington	1,152	1,581	2,047	2,349	5.4	2.6	2.3
Oregon	816	1,056	1,206	1,417	4.4	1.3	2.7
California	7,622	9,665	12,239	12,434	4.0	2.4	0.3
Alaska	110	167	227	262	7.2	3.1	2.4
Hawaii	328	394	506	533	3.1	2.5	0.9
U.S. TOTAL	76,790	89,823	107,895	116,609	2.6	1.9	1.3

Note: Regional sums do not add to U.S. totals due to: (1) separate estimation techniques by states, and (2) different timing in benchmarking procedures between the state and national estimates.

Source: Authors' analysis of BLS data; the national number for 1995 is projected.

TABLE 7.6

Unemployment Rates, by State, 1979-95

	1979	1989	1993	1994*	1995*	1979-89	1989-93	1994-95*
NORTHEAST	6.6%	4.5%	7.3%	6.5%	6.0%	-2.1	2.8	-0.5
New England	5.5	3.8	6.8	5.9	5.4	-1.7	3.0	-0.5
Maine	7.2	4.1	7.9	7.4	5.7	-3.1	3.8	-1.7
New Hampshire	3.1	3.5	6.6	4.6	4.0	0.4	3.1	-0.6
Vermont	5.3	3.7	5.4	4.7	4.2	-1.6	1.7	-0.5
Massachusetts	5.5	4.0	6.9	6.0	5.4	-1.5	2.9	-0.6
Rhode Island	6.7	4.1	7.7	7.1	7.0	-2.6	3.6	-0.1
Connecticut	5.1	3.7	6.2	5.6	5.5	-1.4	2.5	-0.1
Mid-Atlantic	7.0	4.7	7.5	6.7	6.2	-2.3	2.8	-0.5
New York	7.1	5.1	7.7	6.9	6.3	-2.0	2.6	-0.6
New Jersey	6.9	4.1	7.4	6.8	6.4	-2.8	3.3	-0.4
Pennsylvania	6.9	4.5	7.0	6.2	5.9	-2.4	2.5	-0.3
MIDWEST	5.5	5.4	6.1	5.1	4.6	-0.1	0.7	-0.5
East North Central	6.1	5.7	6.5	5.5	4.8	-0.4	0.8	-0.7
Ohio	5.9	5.5	6.5	5.5	4.8	-0.4	1.0	-0.7
Indiana	6.4	4.7	5.3	4.9	4.7	-1.7	0.6	-0.2
Illinois	5.5	6.0	7.4	5.7	5.2	0.5	1.4	-0.5
Michigan	7.8	7.1	7.0	5.9	5.3	-0.7	-0.1	-0.6
Wisconsin	4.5	4.4	4.7	4.7	3.7	-0.1	0.3	-1.0
West North Central	4.0	4.5	5.0	4.2	3.9	0.5	0.5	-0.3
Minnesota	4.2	4.3	5.1	4.0	3.7	0.1	0.8	-0.3
Iowa	4.1	4.3	4.0	3.7	3.5	0.2	-0.3	-0.2
Missouri	4.5	5.5	6.4	4.9	4.8	1.0	0.9	-0.1
North Dakota	3.7	4.3	4.3	3.9	3.3	0.6	0.0	-0.6
South Dakota	3.6	4.2	3.5	3.3	2.9	0.6	-0.7	-0.4
Nebraska	3.1	3.1	2.6	2.9	2.6	0.0	-0.5	-0.3
Kansas	3.3	4.0	5.0	5.3	4.4	0.7	1.0	-0.9
SOUTH	5.4	5.7	6.6	5.9	5.4	0.3	0.9	-0.5
South Atlantic	5.5	4.8	6.3	5.7	5.1	-0.7	1.5	-0.6
Delaware	8.2	3.5	5.3	4.9	4.3	-4.7	1.8	-0.6
Maryland	5.9	3.7	6.2	5.1	5.1	-2.2	2.5	0.0
District of Columbia	7.3	5.0	8.5	8.2	8.9	-2.3	3.5	0.7
Virginia	4.7	3.9	5.0	4.9	4.5	-0.8	1.1	-0.4
West Virginia	6.7	8.6	10.8	8.9	7.9	1.9	2.2	-1.0
North Carolina	4.8	3.5	4.9	4.4	4.3	-1.3	1.4	-0.1
South Carolina	5.1	4.7	7.5	6.3	5.1	-0.4	2.8	-1.2
Georgia	5.1	5.5	5.8	5.2	4.9	0.4	0.3	-0.3
Florida	6.0	5.6	7.0	6.6	5.5	-0.4	1.4	-1.1

(continued)

TABLE 7.6 (cont.)

Unemployment Rates, by State, 1979-95

	1979	1989	1993	1994*	1995*	1979-89	1989-93	1994-95*
SOUTH (cont.)								
East South Central	6.1%	6.3%	6.5%	5.5%	5.7%	0.2	0.2	0.2
Kentucky	5.6	6.2	6.2	5.4	6.3	0.6	0.0	0.9
Tennessee	5.8	5.1	5.7	4.8	5.2	-0.7	0.6	0.4
Alabama	7.1	7.0	7.5	6.0	5.4	-0.1	0.5	-0.6
Mississippi	5.8	7.8	6.3	6.6	6.1	2.0	-1.5	-0.5
West South Central	4.7	6.8	7.0	6.5	5.9	2.1	0.2	-0.6
Arkansas	6.2	7.2	6.2	5.3	4.9	1.0	-1.0	-0.4
Louisiana	6.7	7.9	7.4	8.0	6.9	1.2	-0.5	-1.1
Oklahoma	3.4	5.6	6.0	5.8	4.7	2.2	0.4	-1.1
Texas	4.2	6.7	7.0	6.4	6.0	2.5	0.3	-0.4
WEST	6.0	5.3	8.1	7.2	6.7	-0.7	2.8	-0.5
Mountain	5.0	5.5	5.9	5.3	4.9			-0.4
Montana	5.1	5.9	6.0	5.1	5.9	0.8	0.1	0.8
Idaho	5.6	5.1	6.1	5.6	5.4	-0.5	1.0	-0.2
Wyoming	3.1	6.3	5.4	5.3	4.8	3.2	-0.9	-0.5
Colorado	4.8	5.8	5.2	4.2	4.2	1.0	-0.6	0.0
New Mexico	6.6	6.7	7.5	6.3	6.3	0.1	0.8	0.0
Arizona	5.0	5.2	6.2	6.4	5.1	0.2	1.0	-1.3
Utah	4.3	4.6	3.9	3.7	3.6	0.3	-0.7	-0.1
Nevada	5.0	5.0	7.2	6.2	5.4	0.0	2.2	-0.8
Pacific	6.4	5.2	8.8	8.0	7.3	-1.2	3.6	-0.7
Washington	6.8	6.2	7.5	6.4	6.4	-0.6	1.3	0.0
Oregon	6.8	5.7	7.2	5.4	4.8	-1.1	1.5	-0.6
California	6.2	5.1	9.2	8.6	7.8	-1.1	4.1	-0.8
Alaska	9.3	6.7	7.6	7.8	7.3	-2.6	0.9	-0.5
Hawaii	6.4	2.6	4.2	6.1	5.9	-3.8	1.6	-0.2
U.S. TOTAL	**5.8**	**5.3**	**6.8**	**6.1**	**5.6**	**-0.5**	**1.5**	**-0.5**

* Unemployment rates for 1994 and beyond are not directly comparable to those from earlier years, due to changes in BLS survey methodology.

Source: BLS.

in Chapter 4, in 1994 the Bureau of Labor Statistics redesigned the survey from which these data are drawn, and thus data from 1994 are not strictly comparable to earlier years (the change in the survey is considered to generate higher unemployment rates). Given the survey change, we cannot compare trends over the full period; we include levels and trends for 1994 and 1995, however, in order to provide up-to-date levels of unemployment.

Unemployment rates fell in most states over the 1980s, particularly in the Northeast region and in the South Atlantic and Pacific states. In many of these states unemployment rates—after reaching postwar highs in the early and mid-1980s (see Chapter 4)—fell to very low levels by historical standards (less than 4.0% in some states) by 1989. Other than states in the West South Central area, the increases that occurred were relatively small. Thus, state labor markets were generally "tighter" in 1989 than in 1979. As we show below, however, this tightening was not associated with higher wage growth.

With the recession in the early 1990s unemployment rose. By 1993, most states remained well above their unemployment rate in the peak year of 1989. The northeastern states, including the large mid-Atlantic states, were particularly hard hit. For example, by 1993 New Jersey remained 3.3 percentage points above its 1989 level. California suffered as well: its unemployment rate was 4.1 percentage points higher in 1993 than in 1989. These rates all fell in 1994 and 1995 (note, however, that the survey changed in those years) as the recovery took hold.

The wage data in **Table 7.7**, average weekly earnings by state, are a broad measure of earnings, reflecting the effects of both changes in hours worked and changes in hourly wage rates. Trends in average earnings also combine the trends of very highly paid workers with those of low-wage workers. In this regard, weekly earnings trends are not representative of the typical worker's labor-market experience. These data are included, however, because they are frequently cited in the national debate about wages and because they lead to some revealing comparisons with the more representative hourly wage trends presented below.

Between 1979 and 1989, the familiar pattern is repeated: strong growth in the Northeast contrasted with declines in many southern and midwestern states. Average weekly earnings in the northeastern states were relatively high (e.g., Connecticut's earnings level was 20% above that of the nation). In fact, the Northeast and California were the driving forces behind the national growth rate of 2.8%. For example, average earnings grew about 20% over the decade in Massachusetts and Connecticut and fell 6.2% in Michigan and 8.2% in Louisiana. Weekly wages in most western states also declined over this period, but average earnings in California were up 6.3%.

By 1994, despite the recovery from the early-1990s' recession, national average weekly earnings remained at their 1989 level. The strong growth rates in the Northeast and California decelerated, and although earnings rose (or fell more slowly) in most of the southern states, they did not move enough to lift the national average. It is unusual to see stagnant *average* wage growth over a recovery.

Looking at levels and growth rates of median hourly wages by state (**Table 7.8**) allows us to track the wage trends of middle-wage workers. Similarly, we can track the wages of low-wage workers (**Table 7.9**) by looking at wage levels at the 20th percentile (80% of the workforce earns a higher wage than these workers). Note that, while the wage percentile tables in Chapter 3 separated males and females, here they are combined. This practice generates larger sample sizes to allow for state-level analysis, while still capturing the broad trends.

Comparing the 1980s' trends in Table 7.8 with the weekly totals in Table 7.7 reveals that median hourly wages, for the most part, grew more slowly than average weekly wages. In other words, when the average weekly earnings were falling in a state, the median tended to fall even faster; when the average grew in a state, the median generally grew less. For example, average weekly earnings grew 6.3% in California from 1979 to 1989, while the median was flat. In the 1989-95 period, California's weekly wage was stagnant, and the median dropped 7.9%. This is the characteristic pattern of wage growth in a period of increasing inequality.

Table 7.8 reveals that, while the median hourly wage declined 2.4% at the national level during the 1980s, there was a great deal of variation among the states. Wages fell in most southern states and in every western and midwestern state over the 1980s, with particularly sharp declines in the Mountain states. In Utah, for example, the median wage was 19 cents higher than the national level in 1979, but by 1989, after falling 10.4%, it was 56 cents below.

Only 16 states—dispersed across the nation—saw their median hourly wage rise between 1989 and 1995. Median wage growth slowed, and became negative, in most of the northeastern states, but in many southern states the decline of the 1980s slowed or even reversed (e.g., Mississippi, Tennessee). By the end of the period, the median worker in most states earned a lower hourly rate in 1995 than in 1979.

The pattern of wage growth for low-wage workers (Table 7.9) is slightly different from that of median workers—workers lower down the wage scale

TABLE 7.7

Average Weekly Earnings, by State, 1979-94
(1995 Dollars)

	1979	1989	1994	Percent Changes 1979-89	Percent Changes 1989-94
NORTHEAST					
New England					
Maine	$416	$454	$443	9.1%	-2.4%
New Hampshire	449	509	505	13.5	-0.8
Vermont	432	461	454	6.6	-1.5
Massachusetts	500	596	614	19.2	2.9
Rhode Island	453	499	503	10.2	0.8
Connecticut	538	650	669	20.9	2.9
Mid-Atlantic					
New York	568	645	661	13.5	2.5
New Jersey	552	633	661	14.7	4.5
Pennsylvania	523	527	533	0.8	1.1
MIDWEST					
East North Central					
Ohio	554	520	517	-6.2	-0.5
Indiana	531	495	493	-6.9	-0.4
Illinois	575	572	576	-0.4	0.6
Michigan	624	585	584	-6.2	-0.2
Wisconsin	503	478	481	-5.0	0.7
West North Central					
Minnesota	505	524	523	3.8	-0.2
Iowa	478	435	439	-8.9	0.8
Missouri	498	494	487	-0.9	-1.4
North Dakota	443	400	393	-9.6	-1.7
South Dakota	404	374	381	-7.4	1.9
Nebraska	443	418	425	-5.6	1.7
Kansas	472	460	453	-2.4	-1.6
SOUTH					
South Atlantic					
Delaware	544	550	553	1.1	0.5
Maryland	503	555	562	10.4	1.3
District of Columbia	678	759	809	12.0	6.6
Virginia	480	517	515	7.8	-0.5
West Virginia	525	468	454	-10.9	-2.9
North Carolina	435	457	464	5.1	1.5
South Carolina	432	444	445	2.7	0.0
Georgia	467	498	500	6.5	0.5
Florida	455	474	473	4.2	-0.3

(continued)

TABLE 7.7 (cont.)

Average Weekly Earnings, by State, 1979-94
(1995 Dollars)

	1979	1989	1994	Percent Changes	
				1979-89	1989-94
SOUTH (cont.)					
East South Central					
Kentucky	$486	$449	$450	-7.6%	0.2%
Tennessee	459	466	477	1.4	2.3
Alabama	470	463	467	-1.4	0.8
Mississippi	412	403	403	-2.2	0.0
West South Central					
Arkansas	422	412	413	-2.5	0.4
Louisiana	509	467	458	-8.2	-1.8
Oklahoma	488	462	441	-5.4	-4.5
Texas	519	514	513	-1.0	-0.1
WEST					
Mountain					
Montana	461	407	400	-11.8	-1.8
Idaho	461	429	434	-7.0	1.2
Wyoming	550	455	436	-17.3	-4.0
Colorado	511	519	517	1.5	-0.2
New Mexico	470	441	442	-6.0	0.2
Arizona	494	492	480	-0.5	-2.4
Utah	484	458	451	-5.4	-1.4
Nevada	511	504	508	-1.3	0.8
Pacific					
Washington	568	511	521	-10.1	2.0
Oregon	521	480	490	-7.9	2.1
California	554	589	591	6.3	0.3
Alaska	830	702	646	-15.4	-8.0
Hawaii	488	511	529	4.7	3.5
U.S. TOTAL	**519**	**533**	**533**	**2.8**	**-0.1**

Source: BLS census of establishments covered by unemployment insurance.

TABLE 7.8

Median Hourly Wages, All Workers, by State, 1979-95
(1995 Dollars)

	1979	1989	1995	Percent Changes 1979-89	Percent Changes 1989-95
NORTHEAST					
New England					
Maine	$8.87	$9.82	$9.21	10.7%	-6.2%
New Hampshire	10.09	11.51	10.84	14.1	-5.8
Vermont	9.47	10.11	10.08	6.8	-0.3
Massachusetts	10.63	12.42	11.94	16.8	-3.8
Rhode Island	10.20	10.73	10.96	5.2	2.1
Connecticut	11.31	12.95	13.12	14.4	1.3
Mid-Atlantic					
New York	11.36	12.14	11.55	6.8	-4.9
New Jersey	11.65	12.85	12.75	10.3	-0.8
Pennsylvania	11.30	10.59	10.33	-6.3	-2.4
MIDWEST					
East North Central					
Ohio	11.82	10.65	10.09	-9.9	-5.2
Indiana	10.78	9.63	9.59	-10.7	-0.4
Illinois	12.19	11.35	11.06	-6.9	-2.5
Michigan	12.69	11.24	10.98	-11.4	-2.3
Wisconsin	11.38	10.08	10.17	-11.4	0.9
West North Central					
Minnesota	11.34	10.82	10.76	-4.6	-0.5
Iowa	10.61	9.40	9.17	-11.4	-2.4
Missouri	10.56	9.50	9.71	-10.0	2.2
North Dakota	9.91	8.43	8.22	-15.0	-2.5
South Dakota	8.73	8.03	8.49	-8.1	5.7
Nebraska	9.96	8.82	8.95	-11.5	1.5
Kansas	10.38	9.99	9.09	-3.7	-9.0
SOUTH					
South Atlantic					
Delaware	11.11	10.94	10.58	-1.5	-3.3
Maryland	11.96	12.02	12.03	0.5	0.1
District of Columbia	12.40	11.37	11.86	-8.3	4.3
Virginia	10.52	11.15	10.35	6.0	-7.2
West Virginia	11.63	8.88	9.12	-23.6	2.6
North Carolina	9.06	9.24	9.32	2.1	0.8
South Carolina	8.76	9.21	9.07	5.1	-1.5
Georgia	9.76	9.94	9.62	1.9	-3.2
Florida	9.24	9.58	9.26	3.7	-3.3

(continued)

TABLE 7.8 (cont.)

Median Hourly Wages, All Workers, by State, 1979-95
(1995 Dollars)

	1979	1989	1995	Percent Changes 1979-89	1989-95
East South Central					
Kentucky	$10.52	$9.49	$9.33	-9.8%	-1.7%
Tennessee	9.60	8.84	9.07	-7.9	2.5
Alabama	9.96	9.10	8.55	-8.6	-6.0
Mississippi	8.42	7.77	8.24	-7.7	6.1
West South Central					
Arkansas	8.52	8.14	8.41	-4.4	3.3
Louisiana	10.26	8.86	8.80	-13.7	-0.6
Oklahoma	10.70	9.49	8.99	-11.3	-5.2
Texas	10.31	9.52	9.16	-7.7	-3.8
WEST					
Mountain					
Montana	10.84	9.00	8.91	-17.0	-1.1
Idaho	10.40	8.85	9.22	-14.9	4.2
Wyoming	12.24	9.90	9.34	-19.1	-5.7
Colorado	11.67	10.67	10.91	-8.6	2.3
New Mexico	10.44	8.78	9.02	-15.9	2.8
Arizona	10.59	10.35	9.53	-2.3	-7.9
Utah	11.06	9.91	9.41	-10.4	-5.0
Nevada	10.92	10.80	9.98	-1.1	-7.6
Pacific					
Washington	12.72	11.72	10.90	-7.9	-7.0
Oregon	12.08	11.28	10.57	-6.6	-6.3
California	12.13	12.11	11.16	-0.2	-7.9
Alaska	17.25	13.78	13.10	-20.2	-4.9
Hawaii	10.95	11.33	10.59	3.5	-6.5
U.S.TOTAL	**10.88**	**10.61**	**10.13**	**-2.4**	**-4.5**

Source: Authors' analysis of BLS data.

367

TABLE 7.9

Low Hourly Wages, All Workers, by State, 1979-95
(1995 Dollars)

	1979	1989	1995	Percent Changes 1979-89	Percent Changes 1989-95
NORTHEAST					
New England					
Maine	$6.46	$6.89	$6.21	6.6%	-9.8%
New Hampshire	6.96	7.70	7.08	10.6	-8.0
Vermont	6.41	7.02	6.67	9.5	-5.0
Massachusetts	7.15	8.23	7.47	15.1	-9.3
Rhode Island	6.96	7.19	6.61	3.3	-8.1
Connecticut	7.47	8.52	7.69	14.1	-9.8
Mid-Atlantic					
New York	7.24	7.16	6.76	-1.1	-5.7
New Jersey	7.28	7.90	7.43	8.5	-6.0
Pennsylvania	7.26	6.58	6.40	-9.4	-2.7
MIDWEST					
East North Central					
Ohio	7.23	6.34	6.27	-12.3	-1.0
Indiana	6.95	6.03	6.24	-13.3	3.5
Illinois	7.72	6.67	6.36	-13.6	-4.6
Michigan	7.73	6.39	6.34	-17.4	-0.8
Wisconsin	7.18	6.15	6.40	-14.4	4.2
West North Central					
Minnesota	7.19	6.75	6.56	-6.0	-2.8
Iowa	6.82	5.81	6.01	-14.8	3.5
Missouri	6.74	5.87	6.04	-12.9	2.9
North Dakota	6.45	5.37	5.31	-16.7	-1.2
South Dakota	6.25	5.22	5.70	-16.5	9.2
Nebraska	6.63	5.74	5.94	-13.5	3.5
Kansas	6.94	6.06	6.07	-12.6	0.0
SOUTH					
South Atlantic					
Delaware	7.34	6.93	6.34	-5.6	-8.5
Maryland	7.44	7.37	7.22	-1.0	-1.9
District of Columbia	8.13	7.21	7.13	-11.4	-1.0
Virginia	6.67	6.74	6.34	1.1	-6.0
West Virginia	6.84	5.06	5.25	-26.0	3.7
North Carolina	6.45	6.14	6.23	-4.8	1.5
South Carolina	6.33	5.91	5.90	-6.6	-0.2
Georgia	6.54	6.22	6.05	-5.0	-2.7
Florida	6.40	6.22	5.93	-2.9	-4.6

(continued)

T A B L E   7.9 (cont.)

Low Hourly Wages, All Workers, by State, 1979-95
(1995 Dollars)

	1979	1989	1995	Percent Changes 1979-89	1989-95
SOUTH (cont.)					
East South Central					
Kentucky	$6.66	$5.50	$5.46	-17.5%	-0.7%
Tennessee	6.50	5.77	6.01	-11.2	4.2
Alabama	6.38	5.66	5.39	-11.4	-4.7
Mississippi	6.15	4.89	5.28	-11.9	7.9
West South Central					
Arkansas	6.30	5.34	5.38	-15.2	0.7
Louisiana	6.51	5.31	5.11	-18.4	-3.8
Oklahoma	6.89	5.88	5.40	-14.6	-8.2
Texas	6.58	5.65	5.49	-14.0	-2.8
WEST					
Mountain					
Montana	6.64	5.47	5.56	-17.6	1.5
Idaho	6.66	5.43	5.88	-18.3	8.2
Wyoming	7.39	5.69	5.45	-23.0	-4.3
Colorado	7.16	6.28	6.55	-12.3	4.3
New Mexico	6.53	5.37	5.75	-17.7	7.0
Arizona	6.90	6.28	5.98	-9.0	-4.8
Utah	6.98	6.21	6.06	-11.0	-2.4
Nevada	7.23	6.88	6.40	-4.9	-7.1
Pacific					
Washington	8.02	6.88	7.13	-14.1	3.5
Oregon	7.73	6.75	6.71	-12.7	-0.6
California	7.61	6.88	6.35	-9.5	-7.8
Alaska	10.82	8.61	8.29	-20.5	-3.8
Hawaii	6.65	7.11	7.29	6.9	2.6
U.S. TOTAL	**6.96**	**6.37**	**6.19**	**-8.5**	**-2.8**

Source: Authors' analysis of BLS data.

were even more susceptible to falling wages. For example, while the median worker in New York experienced a 6.8% increase in the 1979-89 period, the wage at the 20th percentile in that state fell by 1.1%. In Kentucky, the median wage fell 9.8%, while the 20th percentile wage fell 17.5%.

This pattern changed slightly in the most recent period, 1989-95, when the national 20th-percentile wage fell slightly less than the national median, -2.8% vs. -4.5%. This difference is in part due to the 1990-91 increase in the minimum wage, which can have a "ripple" effect in areas with low wage levels. Thus, while Arkansas' median wage grew slightly (0.7%), the low wage in that state increased by 3.3%. In Montana, the median wage grew slightly in the early 1990s, while the low wage grew 1.5%.

Another perspective on low wages by state is provided in **Table 7.10**, which shows the percent and numbers of minimum-wage workers by state in 1994. Here (as in Chapter 3), minimum-wage workers are defined as persons earning an hourly wage rate between $4.25 and $5.15. This range is chosen because it includes workers at the current minimum of $4.25 and those workers who would be affected by a legislated increase (proposed at the time of this writing) in the national minimum.

As the table shows, close to 12 million workers, representing 11.0% of the workforce, were in the affected range in 1994. Nine states had over 15% of their workforce in the affected range, with the highest shares in some of the southern states. (Close to a fifth of the Louisiana workforce were minimum-wage workers in 1994.) In the continental United States, the lowest share of minimum-wage workers was in New Jersey (which had a state minimum above the federal level in 1994) and other northeastern states.

Poverty Rates Vary Greatly by Region and Area

Figure 7B shows the trend in the percent of people who are poor—the poverty rate—by region for the period 1969-94.

Given that median family incomes are lower in the South, it is not surprising that southern poverty rates are consistently above those of the nation. The trends in the bottom panel of **Table 7.11** reveal, however, that the South has done well relative to the other regions. In the 1970s, poverty fell there (as it did in the West), while in the Northeast it grew at three times the national rate, and in the Midwest it expanded at just below twice the national rate.

In the 1980s, poverty declined only in the Northeast, again reflecting that region's more favorable growth in median income as well as its low unemployment rates during the 1980s' expansion. In contrast, in the Midwest and the West poverty rates grew 2.2 and 2.4 percentage points. Thus, the expansion of the 1980s did little to lower poverty rates. By 1989, six years of uninterrupted growth led to lower poverty rates only in the Northeast.

Poverty rates grew in each part of the country over the 1990-91 recession, and they did not begin to respond to the recovery until 1994 (**Table 7.12**). The Northeast and the West experienced the largest increases in their poverty rates in the 1989-94 period—2.9 and 2.8 points respectively. Since the West had the biggest increase over the 1980s, by the end of the period poverty rates there were 50% above their 1973 levels. As Table 7.12 shows, this increase was fully accounted for by the states in the Pacific area. California, by dint of its large population, dominates this group.

Table 7.13 presents recent results for poverty rates of persons by state. (These data are not available for earlier years.) Following the practice of the Census, this table merges two years together to generate more accurate estimates of state-level poverty rates.

The highest poverty rates are found in the District of Columbia and the southern states. In Louisiana and Mississippi, for example, between a fifth and a quarter of persons were poor over the period. Conversely, many northeastern states have less than 10% of their populations in poverty. Few states experienced poverty declines over this period. Notable increases occurred in California (1.8 percentage points), along with some of the southern states.

The Census data also allow an analysis of the New York and Los Angeles areas. They reveal a greater increase in poverty in Los Angeles over the 1991-94 period—2.3 percentage points—than in the state overall (1.8 points).

Figure 7C and **Table 7.14** shift the geographical focus on poverty from regions and states to residence. Census data allow for the comparison of poverty rates in metropolitan and nonmetropolitan (or rural) areas. Within metropolitan areas, poverty rates in central cities can be compared with those in surrounding areas. The last column in the table compares city and rural poverty rates.

As shown in the figure, rural poverty rates fell by more than half over the 1960s and 1970s. Poverty in urban areas, after falling in the 1960s, began to increase at a rate above the national average. As the last column of Table 7.14 shows, the urban poverty rate was about half that of rural areas in 1959, but by the end of the period urban poverty rates were 4.9 points above rural rates. The suburbs have consistently been the area with the lowest rates of poverty, although the increase in suburban poverty was significant in the most recent pe-

TABLE 7.10

Workers at or Near the Minimum Wage ($4.25-$5.14)

	Percent at or Near Minimum	Number at or Near Minimum	Total Workforce
NORTHEAST	8.0%	1,682,757	20,972,878
New England	7.0	399,731	5,687,449
Maine	10.6	48,687	458,273
New Hampshire	7.8	39,958	511,753
Vermont	7.5	18,189	241,558
Massachusetts	6.4	168,035	2,627,191
Rhode Island	9.2	37,704	408,758
Connecticut	6.1	87,158	1,439,916
Mid-Atlantic	8.4	1,283,026	15,285,428
New York	8.7	614,715	7,068,130
New Jersey	5.2	173,441	3,348,923
Pennsylvania	10.2	494,870	4,868,376
MIDWEST	10.9	2,894,740	26,461,866
East North Central	10.7	1,993,104	18,629,359
Ohio	10.7	500,596	4,684,163
Indiana	12.4	315,718	2,547,137
Illinois	10.8	545,647	5,042,948
Michigan	10.5	420,386	4,012,846
Wisconsin	9.0	210,757	2,342,266
West North Central	11.5	901,636	7,832,506
Minnesota	9.2	192,018	2,096,493
Iowa	10.9	131,759	1,212,250
Missouri	11.9	262,483	2,208,150
North Dakota	18.2	46,574	256,552
South Dakota	14.5	40,899	281,344
Nebraska	13.1	94,150	718,211
Kansas	12.6	133,752	1,059,508
SOUTH	13.1	4,916,502	37,409,000
South Atlantic	11.0	2,146,677	19,532,008
Delaware	9.5	31,341	330,946
Maryland	5.7	131,265	2,313,451
District of Columbia	7.8	20,292	259,418
Virginia	9.8	280,233	2,863,031
West Virginia	16.3	103,752	638,043
North Carolina	11.3	345,913	3,053,341
South Carolina	12.8	196,066	1,537,776
Georgia	11.9	361,887	3,048,241
Florida	12.3	675,928	5,487,763

(continued)

TABLE 7.10 *(cont.)*

Workers at or Near the Minimum Wage ($4.25-$5.14)

	Percent at or Near Minimum	Number at or Near Minimum	Total Workforce
SOUTH			
East South Central	15.0%	959,038	6,414,353
Kentucky	14.6	216,866	1,482,340
Tennessee	12.7	280,727	2,211,843
Alabama	16.9	285,250	1,685,378
Mississippi	17.0	176,194	1,034,793
West South Central	15.8	1,810,787	11,462,639
Arkansas	16.4	158,238	965,807
Louisiana	19.9	313,605	1,573,058
Oklahoma	17.0	210,881	1,240,985
Texas	14.7	1,128,064	7,682,789
WEST	10.3	2,329,253	22,587,300
Mountain	11.8	737,935	6,261,570
Montana	16.3	52,057	318,486
Idaho	13.9	62,524	450,302
Wyoming	16.8	32,310	192,655
Colorado	8.9	145,651	1,640,033
New Mexico	13.2	79,495	600,549
Arizona	12.6	200,320	1,585,686
Utah	12.8	104,305	817,055
Nevada	9.3	61,273	656,804
Pacific	9.7	1,591,317	16,325,729
Washington	7.2	157,979	2,201,188
Oregon	7.0	88,685	1,275,129
California	10.9	1,317,125	12,127,105
Alaska	4.0	9,649	242,062
Hawaii	3.7	17,880	480,246
U.S. TOTAL	**11.0**	**11,818,160**	**107,431,043**

Source: Authors' analysis of BLS data.

Note: Sample includes both hourly and salaried workers. U.S. totals differ slightly from state totals due to rounding.

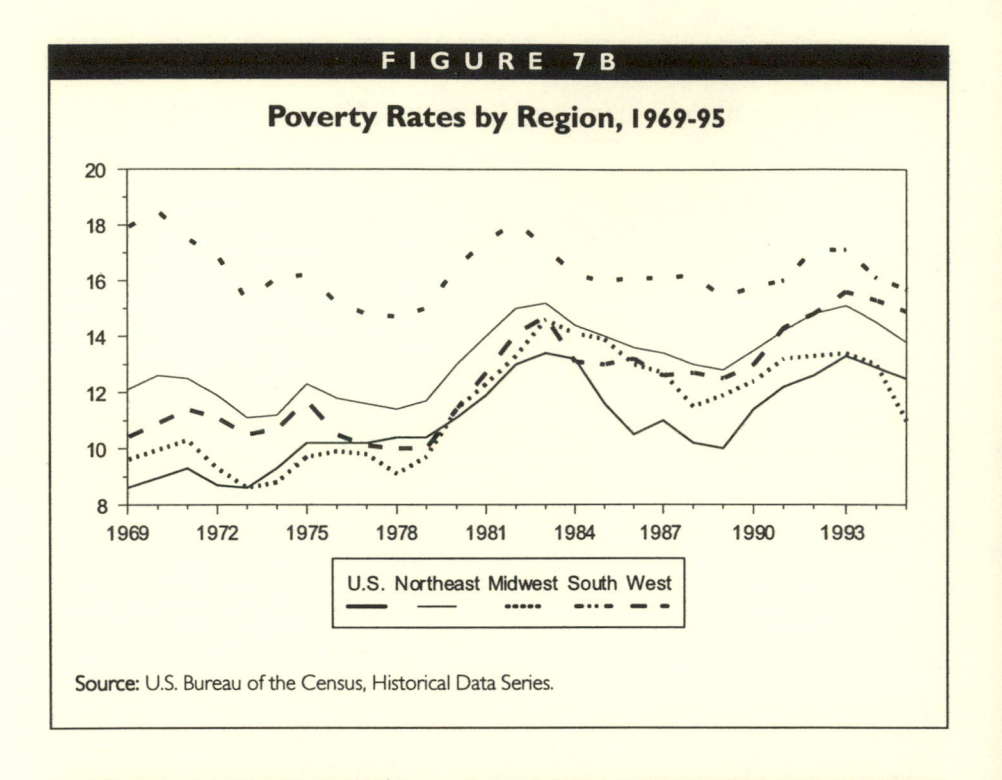

FIGURE 7B

Poverty Rates by Region, 1969-95

U.S. Northeast Midwest South West

Source: U.S. Bureau of the Census, Historical Data Series.

TABLE 7.11

Percent of Persons in Poverty, by Region

Year	U.S.	Northeast	Midwest	South	West
1973	11.1%	8.6%	8.6%	15.3%	10.5%
1979	11.7	10.4	9.7	15.0	10.0
1989*	12.8	10.0	11.9	15.4	12.5
1995	13.8	12.5	11.0	15.7	14.9
Percentage-Point Changes					
1973-79	0.6	1.8	1.1	-0.3	-0.4
1979-89	1.1	-0.4	2.2	0.4	2.4
1989-95	1.0	2.5	-0.9	0.3	2.4

* Unlike Chapter 6, 1989 rates by region are unrevised.

Source: U.S. Bureau of the Census, Historical Tables.

TABLE 7.12

Recent Poverty Rates by Division, 1989-94

Division	1989*	1990	1991	1992	1993	1994	Percentage-Point Change 1989-94
New England	7.2%	9.2%	10.4%	10.5%	10.5%	9.7%	2.5%
Mid-Atlantic	11.0	12.2	12.8	13.4	14.2	14.0	3.0
East North Central	11.9	12.7	13.5	13.3	13.6	13.0	1.1
West North Central	11.7	11.9	12.6	13.1	12.9	12.9	1.2
South Atlantic	12.7	13.7	14.2	15.2	14.9	13.7	1.0
East South Central	18.6	19.1	18.6	19.0	20.0	16.8	-1.8
West South Central	17.8	17.4	17.6	19.2	19.3	19.5	1.7
Mountain	13.1	13.6	13.9	14.0	12.9	12.6	-0.5
Pacific	12.3	12.8	14.5	15.1	16.5	16.3	4.0
U.S.	12.8	13.5	14.2	14.8	15.1	14.5	1.7

* Unlike Chapter 6, 1989 rates by region are unrevised.

Source: U.S. Bureau of the Census, P-60s, various years.

riod—it grew by 1.1 points between 1989 and 1995. The largest increase over the 1990s occurred in the cities, however, where poverty rates grew by 2.5 percentage points. This increase left urban poverty close to its highest historical levels and 2.3 percentage points above its level in 1959.

Table 7.15 decomposes, or breaks down, the changes in poverty over various time periods into (1) those that occurred due to population shifts (for example, from rural to suburban areas), and (2) those that occurred within regions. The changes in the table are annualized so that comparisons across periods of different length are analogous. In each period, the population shifted to areas with lower poverty rates, and after 1973 this shift occurred at a constant rate of -0.04 percentage points per year (meaning that population shifts lowered poverty rates by 0.4 percentage points over 10 years). The main factor behind this decrease was the shift from rural to suburban areas. From 1973 on, however, poverty rates within the different areas grew (as shown in Table 7.14), and in each period this factor outweighed the poverty-reducing effects of the population shifts.

TABLE 7.13

Two-Year Averaged Poverty Rates, by State, 1991-94

	1991-92	1992-93	1993-94
NORTHEAST			
New England			
Maine	13.9%	14.5%	12.4%
New Hampshire	8.0	9.3	8.8
Vermont	11.6	10.3	8.8
Massachusetts	10.8	10.5	10.2
Rhode Island	11.6	11.8	10.8
Connecticut	9.4	9.2	9.7
Mid-Atlantic			
New York	15.7	16.1	16.7
New Jersey	10.1	10.6	10.1
Pennsylvania	11.5	12.6	12.9
MIDWEST			
East North Central			
Ohio	13.0	12.8	13.6
Indiana	13.8	12.0	13.0
Illinois	14.7	14.6	13.0
Michigan	13.9	14.5	14.8
Wisconsin	10.4	11.8	10.8
West North Central			
Minnesota	13.1	12.3	11.7
Iowa	10.6	10.9	10.5
Missouri	15.3	15.9	15.9
North Dakota	13.4	11.7	10.8
South Dakota	14.7	14.7	14.4
Nebraska	10.2	10.5	9.6
Kansas	11.8	12.1	14.0
SOUTH			
South Atlantic			
Delaware	7.7	9.0	9.3
Maryland	10.5	10.8	10.2
Washington, DC	19.5	23.4	23.8
Virginia	9.8	9.6	10.2
West Virginia	20.1	22.3	20.4
North Carolina	15.2	15.1	14.3
South Carolina	17.7	18.9	16.3
Georgia	17.4	15.6	13.8
Florida	15.7	16.7	16.4

(continued)

Two-Year Averaged Poverty Rates, by State, 1991-94

	1991-92	1992-93	1993-94
SOUTH (cont.)			
East South Central			
Kentucky	19.3%	20.1%	19.5%
Tennessee	16.3	18.3	17.1
Alabama	18.2	17.4	16.9
Mississippi	24.2	24.7	22.3
West South Central			
Arkansas	17.4	18.8	17.7
Louisiana	21.9	25.5	26.1
Oklahoma	17.9	19.3	18.3
Texas	18.1	17.9	18.3
WEST			
Mountain			
Montana	14.7	14.4	13.2
Idaho	14.6	14.2	12.6
Wyoming	10.1	11.8	11.3
Colorado	10.7	10.4	9.5
New Mexico	22.3	19.5	19.3
Arizona	15.6	15.6	15.7
Utah	11.2	10.1	9.4
Nevada	13.2	12.3	10.5
Pacific			
Washington	10.4	11.7	11.9
Oregon	12.5	11.6	11.8
California	16.3	17.3	18.1
Alaska	11.1	9.7	9.7
Hawaii	9.5	9.6	8.4
Los Angeles	17.6	19.0	19.9
New York City	15.1	15.3	15.2

Source: U.S. Bureau of the Census, P-60s, various years.

FIGURE 7C

Poverty Rates by Metro/Nonmetro Area, 1959-94

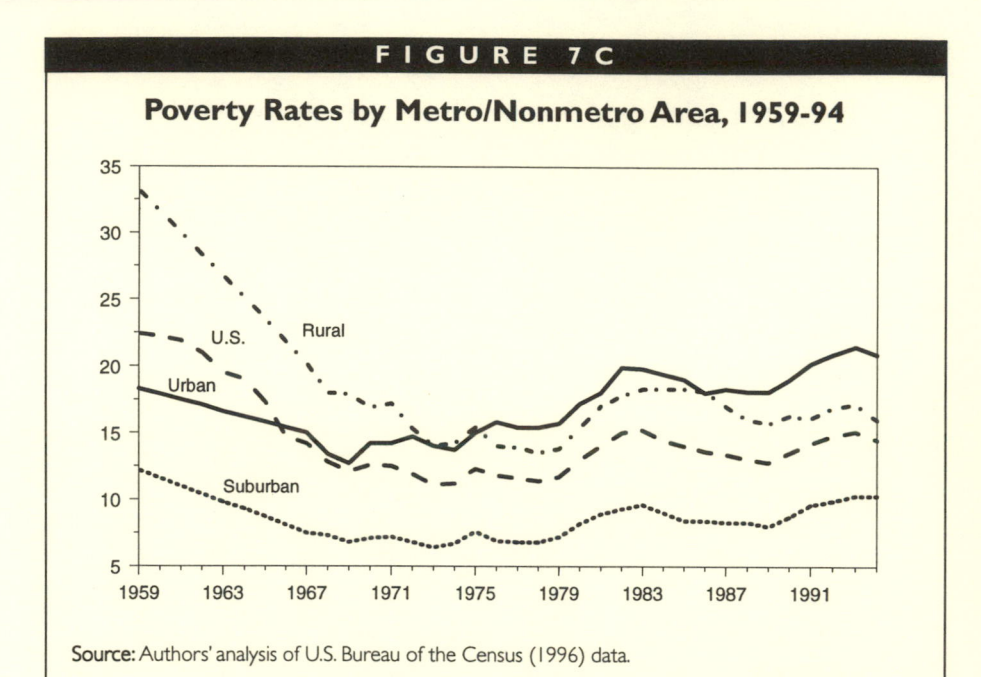

Source: Authors' analysis of U.S. Bureau of the Census (1996) data.

TABLE 7.14

Poverty Rates by Metro/Nonmetro Areas

Year	City	Suburbs	Rural	U.S.	City/Rural Difference
1959	18.3	12.2	33.2	22.4	-14.9
1973	14.0	6.4	14.0	11.1	0.0
1979	15.7	7.2	13.8	11.7	1.9
1989*	18.1	8.0	15.7	12.8	2.4
1995	20.6	9.1	15.6	13.8	5.0
Percentage-Point Changes					
1959-73	-4.3	-5.8	-19.2	-11.3	-14.9
1973-79	1.7	0.8	-0.2	0.6	1.9
1979-89	2.4	0.8	1.9	1.1	0.5
1989-95	2.5	1.1	-0.1	1.0	2.6

* Unlike Chapter 6, 1989 rates by region are unrevised.

Source: U.S. Bureau of the Census, Historical Tables.

TABLE 7.15

Change in Poverty Rates by Metro/Nonmetro Areas Due to Population and Within-Residence Shifts
(Annualized)

Year	Change in Poverty Rates	Due to Changes in:		
		Population*	Poverty Rates**	Interaction***
1959-73	-0.78	-0.09	-0.73	0.05
1973-89	0.11	-0.04	0.14	0.00
1979-94	0.19	-0.04	0.23	0.00
1973-94	0.16	-0.04	0.20	0.01

* Refers to the change in the overall poverty rate due to population shifts between the three types of areas shown in the previous table.

** Refers to the change in the overall poverty rate due to changes in poverty rates within each of the three areas.

*** Refers to the interaction between the variables in columns 2 and 3.

Source: Authors' analysis of U.S. Bureau of the Census, Historical Data Series.

Conclusion

The data from individual regions and states show a high degree of variation, but two general points emerge: (1) workers in regions and states with strong employment growth and low unemployment did not necessarily escape wage stagnation and decline, and (2) while the states of the Northeast and California did relatively well during the expansion of the 1980s, they suffered relatively more in terms of income, wages, employment, and poverty in the 1990s.

CHAPTER 8

INTERNATIONAL COMPARISONS
The United States Is Falling Behind in Productivity and Wage Growth

IN THIS CHAPTER WE EXAMINE HOW AMERICAN WORKERS AND THEIR FAMILIES have fared in comparison to their foreign counterparts. While Americans still rank highest in the world in per capita income as measured by relative purchasing power, on many indicators of economic well-being the United States is falling behind. Compared to other countries, U.S. productivity growth has been relatively stagnant. Likewise, wage growth (which is related to productivity) has been flat or negative here but strong in other countries. Though the U.S. economy seems to have had a faster rate of job growth than other countries since the late 1970s, this employment growth is less impressive when population growth is taken into account. In addition, our commitment to measures that protect the labor market, such as unemployment compensation, wage subsidies, and training, is much less than that of our competitors.

These trends have led to high levels of U.S. income inequality and poverty relative to other industrialized countries. U.S. wage inequality, discussed at length in Chapter 3, is particularly high when viewed in an international context. Poverty in the United States is both higher and more persistent than in other countries. Furthermore, the U.S. tax and transfer system has become *less* effective at poverty reduction since the beginning of the 1980s, while the systems of other countries have grown *more* effective.

Incomes and Productivity: Sluggish Growth in the United States

One widely accepted measure of living standards is per capita gross domestic product, the total value of goods and services produced in the domestic economy per member of the population. Growth of per capita GDP is considered an essential component of rising living standards. (However, this aggregate measure takes no account of distribution, an issue addressed below.) Such growth comes from two sources: greater output per worker (i.e., higher productivity) and employment of a greater proportion of the adult population. In general, if productivity growth is strong and wages rise accordingly, families can live better without sending more workers into the workforce; if it is weak, living standards can rise only if more people work (or those working put in longer hours). Therefore, it is useful to decompose, or break down, GDP growth into these two factors. **Table 8.1** does this in examining GDP growth over two periods—1979-89 and 1989-94—for the seven major industrialized countries as well as for three others (Australia, the Netherlands, and Sweden) for which comparable data are available. The weighted averages (with population shares as the weights) in this and subsequent tables omit the United States in order to provide a more direct comparison between trends in this country and those of others.

Column 1 of Table 8.1 shows the annual growth rates of real per capita GDP for the two periods. Although GDP per person in the United States rose over the 1980s, it grew at a below-average pace (1.6% vs. 2.4%), meaning other countries' per capita incomes were rising faster than ours. At 1.6%, the growth rate for the United States was below the growth rates sustained by Australia (1.8%), Canada (1.8%), Germany (1.9%), Italy (2.4%), Sweden (1.8%), and the United Kingdom (2.2%) and was less than half that of Japan (3.4%).

As noted above, it is important to determine whether per capita growth of GDP is generated through higher productivity or through "more work," that is, an increase in the proportion of the population in the workforce. The U.S. rate of growth attributable to more workers (0.5%) is well above the eight-country average annual rate of -0.1%. Conversely, the U.S. percentage of growth attributable to higher productivity (1.1%) is well below the average of 2.6%. Thus, the United States had less income growth than other countries, and a greater proportion of that growth came from more work rather than higher productivity.

The second panel shows the same data for the 1989-94 period. The significant variation in the timing of national business cycles over this period complicates the comparisons (for example, the U.S. downturn occurred in 1990-91, while the downturn came later in Japan and most European countries). Never-

TABLE 8.1

Per Capita GDP Growth, 1979-94, Broken Down into Growth of Employment and Productivity

| | Per Capita GDP Annual Growth Rate | Due to: | |
		More Employment	Higher Productivity
1979-89			
Australia	1.8%	0.4%	1.4%
Canada	1.8	0.6	1.2
France	1.6	-0.6	2.3
Germany	1.9	n.a.	n.a.
Italy	2.4	-0.5	2.9
Japan	3.4	-0.1	3.5
Netherlands	1.3	0.1	1.2
Sweden	1.8	0.1	1.7
United Kingdom	2.2	-0.0	2.3
United States	**1.6**	**0.5**	**1.1**
Average*	2.4%	-0.1%	2.6%
1989-94			
Australia	0.9%	-0.8%	1.7%
Canada	-0.2	-1.3	1.0
France	0.6	-0.7	1.3
Germany	1.3	n.a.	n.a.
Italy	0.8	-0.5	1.3
Japan	1.8	0.2	1.6
Netherlands**	1.5	0.6	0.9
Sweden	-1.0	-2.8	1.8
United Kingdom	0.4	-0.8	1.2
United States	**1.1**	**-0.2**	**1.2**
Average*	n.a.	n.a.	n.a.

*   Weighted by 1990 population, excludes the U.S.; averages of columns 2 and 3 may not sum to average for column 1 because of missing data for Germany.
** Decomposition uses 1993 employment-to-population rate.

Source: Authors' analysis of OECD and BLS data.

theless, the data reveal a trend similar to that of the 1980s. Between 1989 and 1994, all countries except the Netherlands had slower annual growth rates of GDP per capita than they did during the 1980s, with two countries (Canada and Sweden) experiencing declines in their per capita GDP. U.S. productivity accelerated over this period, while the contraction of its economy led to sharply declining rates of employment to population growth. Even so, U.S. productivity growth, at 1.2%, remained below the non-U.S. weighted average of 1.4%.

Table 8.1 emphasized the importance of worker productivity (GDP per worker) to the U.S. standard of living. **Table 8.2** presents the average annual growth rate of this measure for various periods between 1960 and 1994. (These data use a different source than earlier tables, which accounts for some slight differences.) The growth rates for the United States are relatively low—the lowest in two periods, and the second lowest for the cumulative period. U.S. productivity growth was at its highest between 1960 and 1967, when it grew at an annual rate of 2.7%. Since then, productivity growth has decelerated precipitously.

The rates of productivity growth for other countries have also slowed over the period, though all but that of the Netherlands remain higher than that of the

TABLE 8.2

Productivity Growth Rates, 1960-94

Country	1960-67	1967-73	1973-79	1979-89	1989-94*	Cumulative 1960-94**
Australia	n.a.	2.8%	1.8%	0.9%	1.6%	1.7%
Canada	2.4	2.6	1.3	1.2	-0.2	1.5
West Germany	3.9	4.3	2.9	1.1	2.1	2.7
France	4.4	4.2	2.4	1.9	1.2	2.8
Italy	6.3	5.1	2.7	2.0	1.9	3.5
Japan	8.1	8.0	2.9	2.8	1.0	4.5
Netherlands	n.a.	n.a.	1.7	0.6	0.5	0.9
Sweden	4.1	2.9	0.5	1.2	2.3	2.1
United Kingdom	2.3	3.4	1.3	1.9	1.4	2.0
United States	**2.7**	**0.9**	**-0.1**	**0.8**	**1.2**	**1.1**

*   Netherlands: 1989-93; Germany: 1989-92.
** Australia: 1967-94; Netherlands: 1973-93; Germany: 1960-92.

Source: Authors' analysis of OECD and BLS data.

United States (**Figure 8A**). Japan's productivity fell from an average annual rate of 8.1% between 1960 and 1967 to 1.0% over the most recent period. Similarly, West Germany's rate fell from 4.3% in the 1967-73 period to 2.1% in the most recent. However, even in the context of this general slowdown, the majority of the other countries still had faster productivity growth rates than those of the United States from 1973 to 1994.

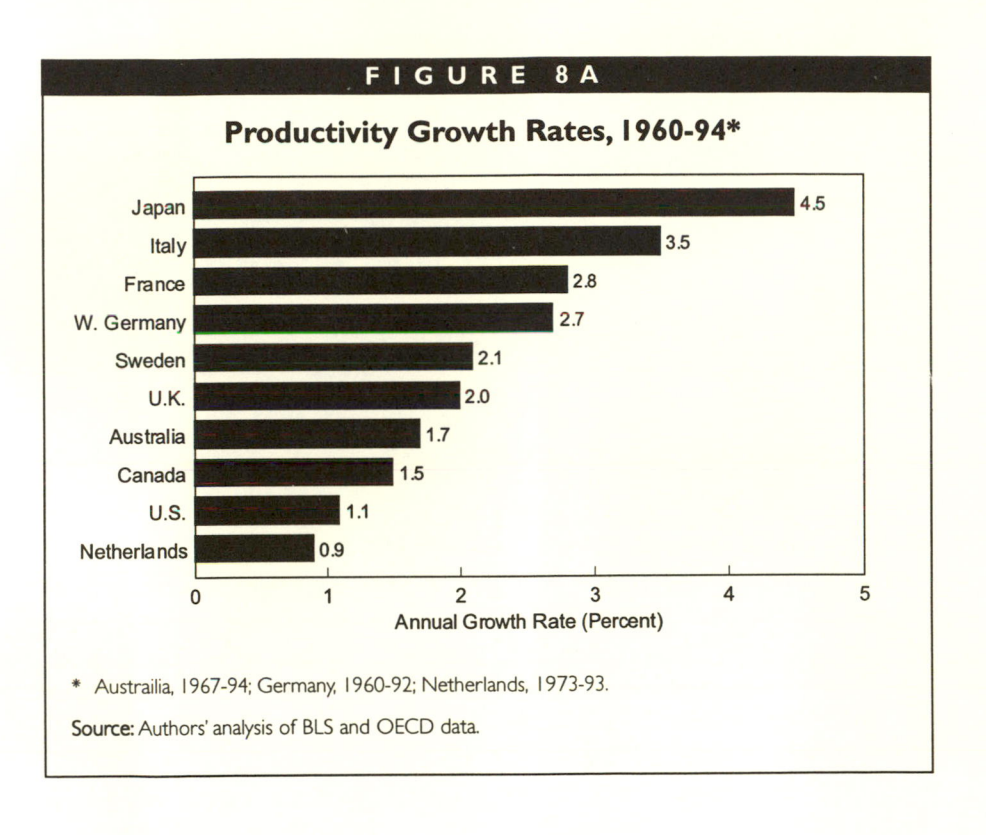

FIGURE 8A

Productivity Growth Rates, 1960-94*

* Austrailia, 1967-94; Germany, 1960-92; Netherlands, 1973-93.

Source: Authors' analysis of BLS and OECD data.

Compensation: U.S. Growth Flat or Negative

Given that wage growth is in part dependent on productivity growth, we would expect to see U.S. wages reflect the relatively stagnant growth of productivity presented above. In fact, **Table 8.3** reveals that compensation growth per employee in the U.S. business sector (excluding public employment) has been far below that of the other industrialized countries shown. Real compensation (wages plus fringe benefits) grew at an average annual rate of 0.26% over the 1980s,

TABLE 8.3

Annual Rate of Real Compensation Growth per Employee, Business Sector, 1979-95

Country	1979-89	1989-95
Canada	0.34%	0.10%
France	0.98	0.89
Germany	1.13	-0.24
Italy	1.30	0.62
Japan	1.31	0.55
United Kingdom	1.98	0.56
United States	**0.26**	**0.22**
Average*	1.27%	0.44%

* Weighted by 1989 employment; excludes United States.

Source: Authors' analysis of OECD and BLS data.

while compensation elsewhere grew between 0.34% (Canada) and 1.98% (United Kingdom). Since 1989, compensation growth has been slower in every country. The average rate of compensation growth per employee for the countries in the table fell to 0.44% per year, with large declines in Canada, Germany, Italy, Japan, and the United Kingdom. The relative drop in the United States was smaller, but compensation growth rates in the United States between 1989 and 1995 were only half the average rate.

The most extensive data of this sort is for the manufacturing sector. As with the business sector (of which manufacturing is a component), **Table 8.4** and **Figure 8B** show that the U.S. annual growth rate for hourly manufacturing compensation is well behind that of most comparable nations.

Between 1979 and 1989, real hourly manufacturing compensation in the United States grew at an average annual rate of 0.4%, compared with the non-U.S. weighted average of 1.8%. Only Canada and Denmark had lower rates. Meanwhile, compensation in West Germany grew at an average rate of 2.4% a year, six times the U.S. growth rate. Furthermore, what little growth U.S. manufacturing wages experienced benefited only supervisors and managers. Production workers saw their compensation fall at a rate of 0.6% a year. Since nonpro-

TABLE 8.4

Hourly Manufacturing Compensation Growth, 1979-94

Country	1979-89		1989-94	
	All Employees	Production Workers	All Employees	Production Workers
Canada	0.2%	0.1%	0.7%	1.4%
Belgium	1.1	1.0	2.1	1.8
Denmark*	0.1	-0.1	1.5	2.0
France	1.9	1.9	1.4	0.8
West Germany	2.4	1.9	2.4	n.a.
Italy	1.0	1.6	1.8	0.4
Japan	1.8	1.4	2.8	2.7
Netherlands	0.8	0.5	0.8	0.7
Norway	1.0	0.9	1.0	0.4
Sweden	0.9	0.8	-0.8	-0.8
United Kingdom	2.7	1.7	2.6	1.9
United States	**0.4**	**-0.6**	**0.3**	**-0.0**
Average**	1.8%	1.5%	2.2%	1.8%

*   Change in third column is for 1989-93.
** Weighted by 1990 employment; excludes the United States.

Source: Authors' analysis of BLS and OECD data.

duction workers have relatively higher compensation, this pattern contributes to the (within-manufacturing) growth in wage inequality documented in Chapter 3. The United States and Denmark were the only countries whose production workers experienced wage loss during this period.

Between 1989 and 1994, compensation generally grew faster than in the 1980s (average growth accelerated by 0.4%, from 1.8% to 2.2%), but U.S. manufacturing employees experienced lower than average growth, and compensation growth was flat for production workers. Compensation grew for production workers in all other countries in the table, except Sweden (-0.8%), although growth rates were lower than in the earlier period for Belgium, France, Italy, and Norway. Danish workers, however, gained back all the ground lost (and more) over the 1980s.

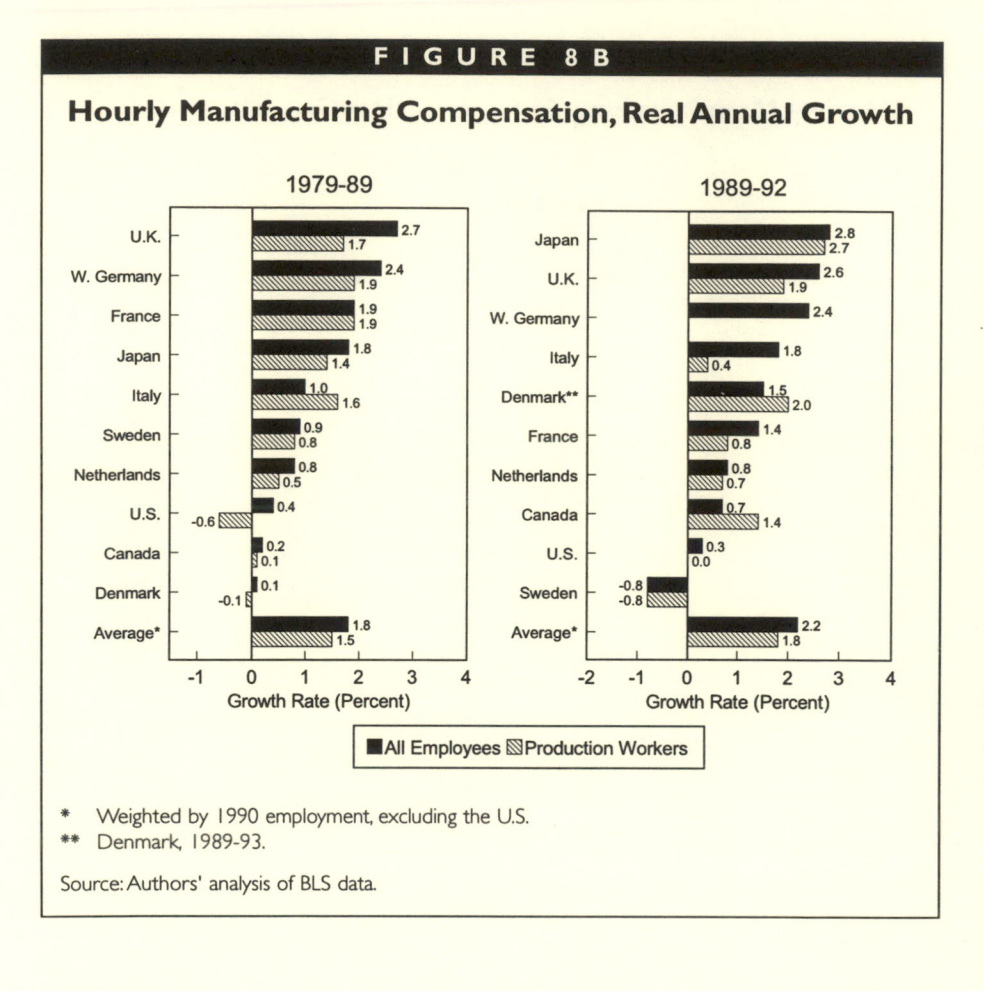

FIGURE 8 B

Hourly Manufacturing Compensation, Real Annual Growth

* Weighted by 1990 employment, excluding the U.S.
** Denmark, 1989-93.

Source: Authors' analysis of BLS data.

Whereas Table 8.4 examined the growth rates of manufacturing compensation, the next two tables compare the levels of compensation for production workers in manufacturing, indexed to the United States. In order to make such comparisons, wages were first converted from their national currency into dollars through the use of two different exchange-rate series: purchasing-power-parity exchange rates (PPPs) and market exchange rates. PPPs are currency values intended to measure the cost of buying the same "basket" of goods and services in all countries. Market exchange rates represent the value of the dollar relative to other currencies in world financial markets. While both exchange-rate measures have their drawbacks, the PPPs are commonly considered an indicator of the relative price of consumption and, therefore, a measure of relative living standards. Market exchange rates reflect the relative value of American goods, services (including labor), and assets in international markets. Thus, they reflect the relative costs to an employer of buying U.S. labor.

When PPPs are used to adjust for currency differences, as in **Table 8.5**, U.S. compensation consistently ranks among the highest for all countries. Given the findings in Table 8.4 regarding the falling compensation of U.S. production workers, however, it is not surprising that production workers in three countries—Germany, Canada, and the Netherlands—surpassed the United States by 1994 (**Figure 8C**, panel 1, shows the PPP-adjusted compensation). West Germany provided production workers with the highest compensation—119 (in 1992), compared to 100 for the United States (in 1994). The Netherlands (104) and Canada (101) slightly outperformed the United States, while Italy was close behind at 99. Other countries were farther back: Sweden (86), France (83), United Kingdom (80), Japan (71). As the average hourly compensation index indicates, most countries gained on the United States throughout the 1980s (recall that

TABLE 8.5

Hourly Compensation of Production Workers in Manufacturing, 1979-94

(Using Purchasing-Power-Parity Exchange Rates)

Country	1979	1989	1994
Canada	83	92	101
Denmark	73	78	87
France	67	84	83
West Germany	n.a.	n.a.	n.a.
Italy	88	100	99
Japan	49	61	71
Netherlands	88	101	104
Sweden	79	88	86
United Kingdom	63	76	80
United States	**100**	**100**	**100**
Average*	62	75	81

* Weighted by 1989 hours; excludes the United States and West Germany.

Source: Authors' analysis of BLS and OECD data.

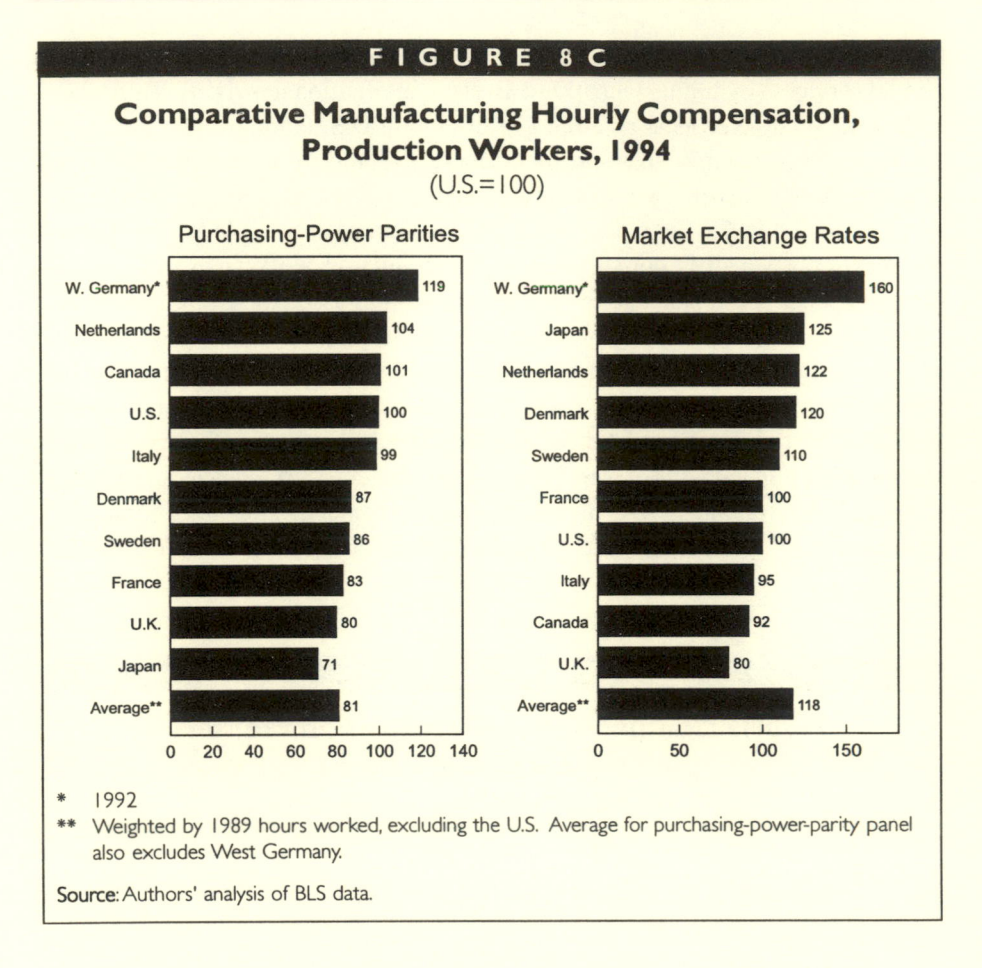

FIGURE 8C

Comparative Manufacturing Hourly Compensation, Production Workers, 1994
(U.S.=100)

Purchasing-Power Parities

W. Germany*	119
Netherlands	104
Canada	101
U.S.	100
Italy	99
Denmark	87
Sweden	86
France	83
U.K.	80
Japan	71
Average**	81

0 20 40 60 80 100 120 140

Market Exchange Rates

W. Germany*	160
Japan	125
Netherlands	122
Denmark	120
Sweden	110
France	100
U.S.	100
Italy	95
Canada	92
U.K.	80
Average**	118

0 50 100 150

* 1992

** Weighted by 1989 hours worked, excluding the U.S. Average for purchasing-power-parity panel also excludes West Germany.

Source: Authors' analysis of BLS data.

these averages exclude the United States). The average level of compensation in manufacturing grew from 62% of the U.S. level in 1979 to 81% in 1994. (The level and growth rates would have been higher with West Germany included; West Germany was excluded because the latest comparable figures are for 1992.)

While average U.S. manufacturing compensation is among the highest in PPP-adjusted terms, this measure paints a very incomplete picture of relative wage levels, since the manufacturing share of employment is relatively small (about 16% in the United States in 1993) and falling in most OECD countries. The second problem with the average measure is that it fails to capture the large growth in wage dispersion that has developed in most OECD countries (a topic discussed in detail below). **Figure 8D** addresses these shortcomings by showing the PPP-adjusted male wage at the 10th percentile, indexed to the United States, for Japan and Europe at the end of the 1980s. The figure shows that, despite U.S. dominance in average manufacturing compensation, low-wage male workers earn less (i.e., have lower purchasing power) than their counterparts in Japan and Europe, where workers at the 10th percentile make 106% and 144% of the U.S. wage.

Looking at manufacturing compensation in terms of market exchange rates (**Table 8.6** and Figure 8C, panel 2), the story changes significantly: American workers are no longer near the front of the pack. Since 1979, production workers in *most* countries have received higher hourly compensation than U.S. workers. The average hourly compensation for nonmanagerial (i.e., production) workers in other countries was 81% that of the United States in 1979, rising to 96% of the U.S. level in 1989. By 1994, compensation in these other countries was 118% that of the United States. In that year, production workers in West Germany were earning 160% of U.S. production workers' earnings. Japan, which paid its production workers 60% of the U.S. level in 1979, paid the same workers 25% more than the United States by 1994. In fact, production workers in all

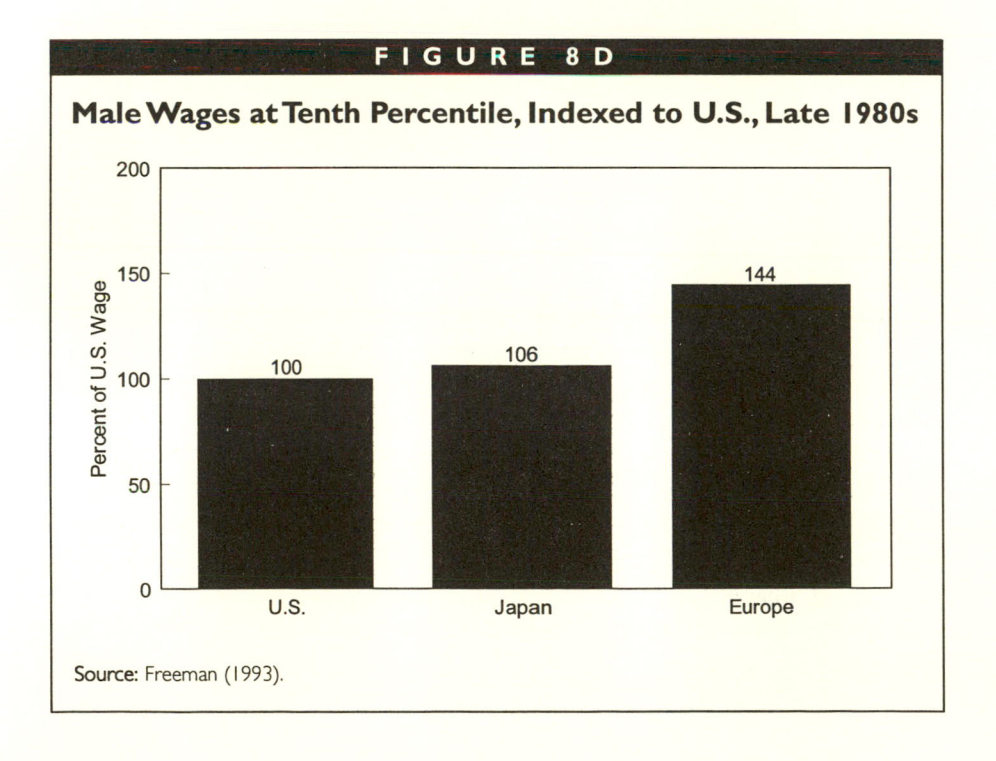

FIGURE 8D

Male Wages at Tenth Percentile, Indexed to U.S., Late 1980s

Source: Freeman (1993).

TABLE 8.6

Hourly Compensation of Production Workers
in Manufacturing, 1979-94

(Using Market Exchange Rates, U.S.=100)

Country	1979	1989	1994
Canada	87	103	92
Denmark	116	101	120
France	85	88	100
West Germany	125	124	160
Italy	78	101	95
Japan	60	87	125
Netherlands	126	105	122
Sweden	125	122	110
United Kingdom	63	74	80
United States	**100**	**100**	**100**
Average*	81	96	118

* Weighted by 1989 hours; excludes the United States.

Source: Authors' analysis of BLS data.

but Canada, Italy, and the United Kingdom had wage levels above those of the United States.

As market exchange rates reflect the relative attractiveness of U.S. products and labor in international markets, the comparisons in this table further underscore the charge that, among the industrialized countries, the United States is becoming a low-wage country (see Chapter 3).

These wage data make two important points regarding the economic position of the United States in international markets. First, the United States has had to let the market value of the dollar decline in order to offset its competitive decline. This tactic has caused the earnings of U.S. workers to fall relative to workers of other countries. Second, these data suggest that the trade imbalances the United States has with many of these countries cannot be blamed on an overpaid U.S. workforce.

Income Inequality

In discussions of America's relative prosperity, much is often made of its high per capita income. **Table 8.7** shows per capita income adjusted by purchasing-power-parity exchange rates, indexed to the United States. Indeed, per capita income in the United States remains the highest in the industrialized world, although its lead has been steadily eroding. (The average in other countries has risen from 66% of the U.S. level in 1973 to 77% in 1994.) However, a per capita income comparison contrasts only the "average" person in each country. Since the economies in each country generate different degrees of income inequality, this average measure obscures how the typical or median person's income compares across countries.

To make such comparisons, we need to examine evidence on how wages and income are distributed throughout each economy and how that distribution

TABLE 8.7

Per Capita Income Adjusted for Purchasing Power, 1973-92
(U.S. = 100)

Country	1973	1979	1989	1994
Australia	71	71	73	72
Canada	76	83	86	80
Denmark	72	73	75	80
France	73	77	78	75
Germany	64	69	71	77
Italy	61	68	73	73
Japan	60	65	77	81
Netherlands	70	73	71	73
Norway	62	74	79	86
Sweden	75	76	77	68
Switzerland	102	94	96	93
United Kingdom	67	68	72	69
United States	**100**	**100**	**100**	**100**
Average*	66	70	75	77

* Weighted by 1989 population; excludes United States.

Source: Authors' analysis of OECD data.

has shifted over time. **Table 8.8** presents a measure of the after-tax, after-transfer (including public cash transfers, such as welfare and unemployment benefits, retirement payments, and, in some countries, family allowances) income distributions of nine industrialized countries. The numbers in the tables represent percentages of the median personal income at the 10th, 90th, and 95th percentiles, adjusted for family size. For example, in Australia in 1985, persons in families at the 10th decile had family-size-adjusted income that was 46.5% of the median Australian income in that year; those at the 90th percentile had incomes 186.5% of the median. The last column shows the ratio of earnings of the 90th percentile to those of the 10th percentile. Countries with higher ratios have higher levels of income dispersion.

These data show the United States to have much greater levels of income inequality than comparable developed countries. U.S. families at the 10th percentile have incomes only 34.7% of the median. In all the other countries in the table, the 10th-percentile family receives at least 45% of the median family's income; in France, West Germany, the United Kingdom, Sweden, and the Neth-

TABLE 8.8

Family Income Distribution: Percent of the Median, Mid-1980s*

| | Percentiles | | | Distance |
Country	10th	90th	95th	Ratio 90/10
Australia (1985)	46.5	186.5	218.5	4.01
Canada (1987)	45.8	184.2	218.0	4.02
France (1984)	55.4	192.8	233.5	3.48
West Germany (1984)	56.9	170.8	201.7	3.00
Italy (1986)	48.9	197.9	233.8	4.05
Netherlands (1987)	61.5	175.0	206.4	2.85
Sweden (1987)	55.6	151.5	170.4	2.72
United Kingdom (1986)	51.1	194.1	232.1	3.80
United States (1986)	**34.7**	**206.1**	**247.3**	**5.94**

* Figures in columns 1-3 are family income, in percentage terms, relative to the median family in each country. Adjusted for family size.

Source: Atkinson, Rainwater, and Smeeding (1995).

erlands, the 10th percentile makes at least half the median. The United States is also alone at the other end of the income scale. U.S. families at the 90th and 95th deciles are further above the median than those in the same relative position in any other country. This income dispersion shows up graphically in the ratios of the 90th- to the 10th-percentile family in the final column (and in **Figure 8E**).

Table 8.9 extends the above analysis by examining the trends in the income distribution over the 1980s. (Unfortunately, trend data are not available for each country.) The numbers in this table represent the difference between the percents of the median for each decile shown in the years given. Thus, between 1979 and 1986, families at the 10th decile in the United States fell 3.4 percentage points farther below the median, while the incomes of those at the 95th percentile grew 25.4 points above the median. Only wealthy families in the United Kingdom saw a similar, though smaller, increase in their relative position. (Note, however, that poor families in the United Kingdom held their relative position.) The last column shows that, in countries other than the United States, the relative distance from the median was either unchanged or grew sightly over the period.

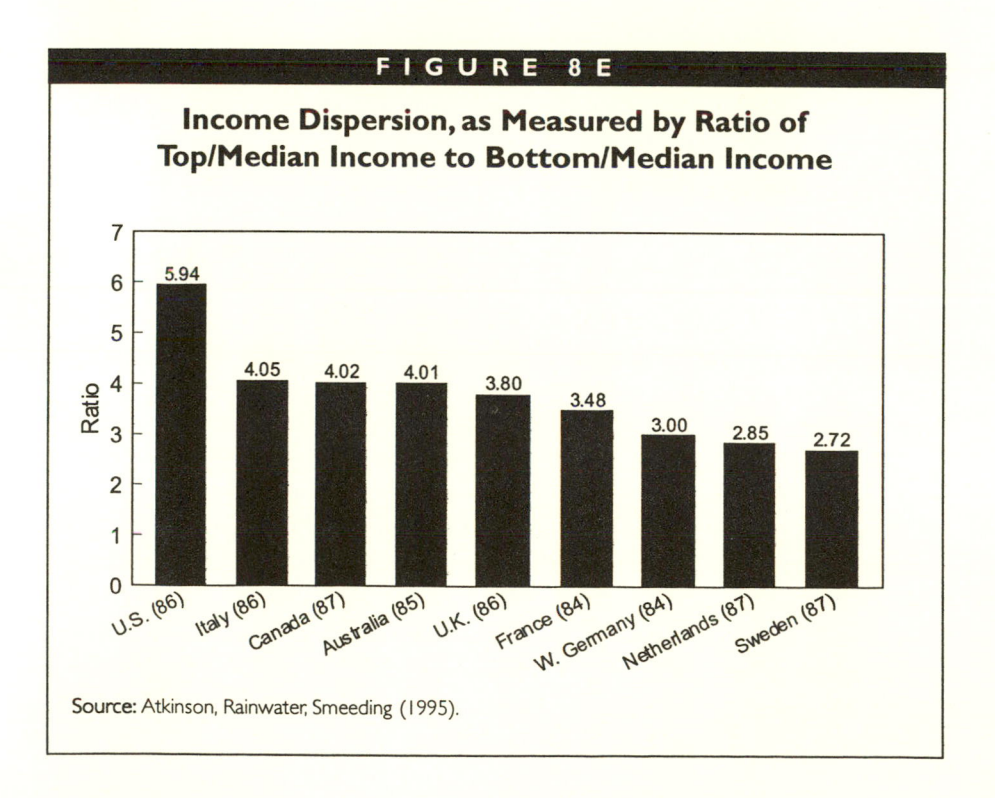

FIGURE 8 E

Income Dispersion, as Measured by Ratio of Top/Median Income to Bottom/Median Income

Source: Atkinson, Rainwater, Smeeding (1995).

TABLE 8.9

Income Distribution: Changes During the 1980s in Percent of the Median

Country	Change in Distance from Median			Change in 90/10 Ratio
	10th	90th	95th	
Australia (1981-85)	0.5	0.2	2.1	-0.04
Belgium (1985-88)	-0.8	0.7	3.6	0.05
Canada (1981-87)	0.9	1.5	6.5	-0.05
France (1979-84)	1.8	6.3	1.2	0.00
Netherlands (1983-87)	-3.3	-1.1	-1.7	0.00
Norway (1979-86)	-1.7	4.1	5.4	0.16
Sweden (1981-87)	-5.9	0.6	3.4	0.27
United Kingdom (1979-86)	0.2	14.4	23.2	0.26
United States (1979-86)	**-3.4**	**18.5**	**25.4**	**1.01**

Source: Authors' analysis of Atkinson, Rainwater, and Smeeding (1995).

Wage Inequality

As in the United States, the most important source of income in the other industrialized countries is earnings from the labor market. Thus, we would expect to see wage distribution patterns that are generating these income distribution patterns. **Figures 8F** and **8G** provide a time series of wage percentile trends for male and female workers in six countries. While these data are not strictly comparable, they present a reliable picture of the trends in the different countries.

The United States and the United Kingdom show the largest increases in both male and female wage inequality over the 1980s. However, the nature of U.S. wage inequality is singular in that it is generated by falling wages at the median (for males) and at the 10th percentile (for both males and females). In the United Kingdom wages rose, but at rates much more favorable to higher earners. Conversely, the other countries show either less consistent patterns of growth in wage inequality (e.g., Canada, where only low wages plummeted), or a decrease (e.g., France, among females up to 1986, Sweden, and Germany, where the 10th percentile grew faster than the 90th).

FIGURE 8 F

Wage Percentiles for Men, in Selected Industrialized Countries, 1980s

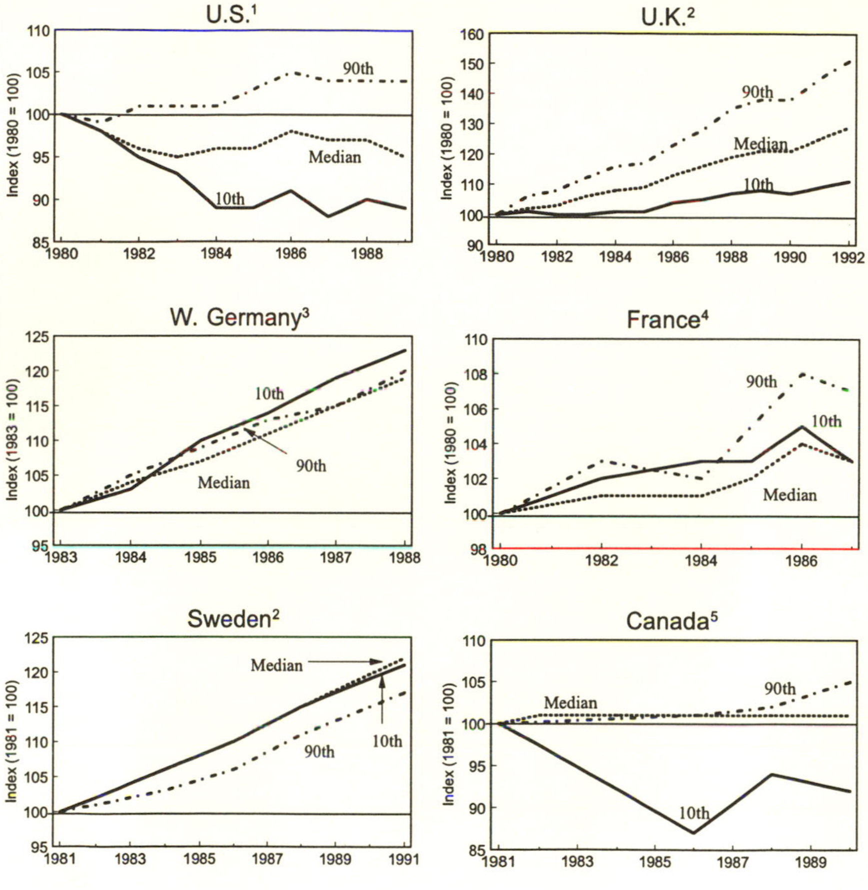

U.S.[1]

U.K.[2]

W. Germany[3]

France[4]

Sweden[2]

Canada[5]

1 Gross hourly earnings of wage and salary workers.
2 Gross hourly earnings.
3 Gross monthly earnings plus benefits.
4 Gross annual earnings of full-time workers.
5 Gross annual earnings of full-time year-round workers.

Source: OECD (1993).

FIGURE 8G

Wage Percentiles for Women, in Selected Industrialized Countries, 1980s

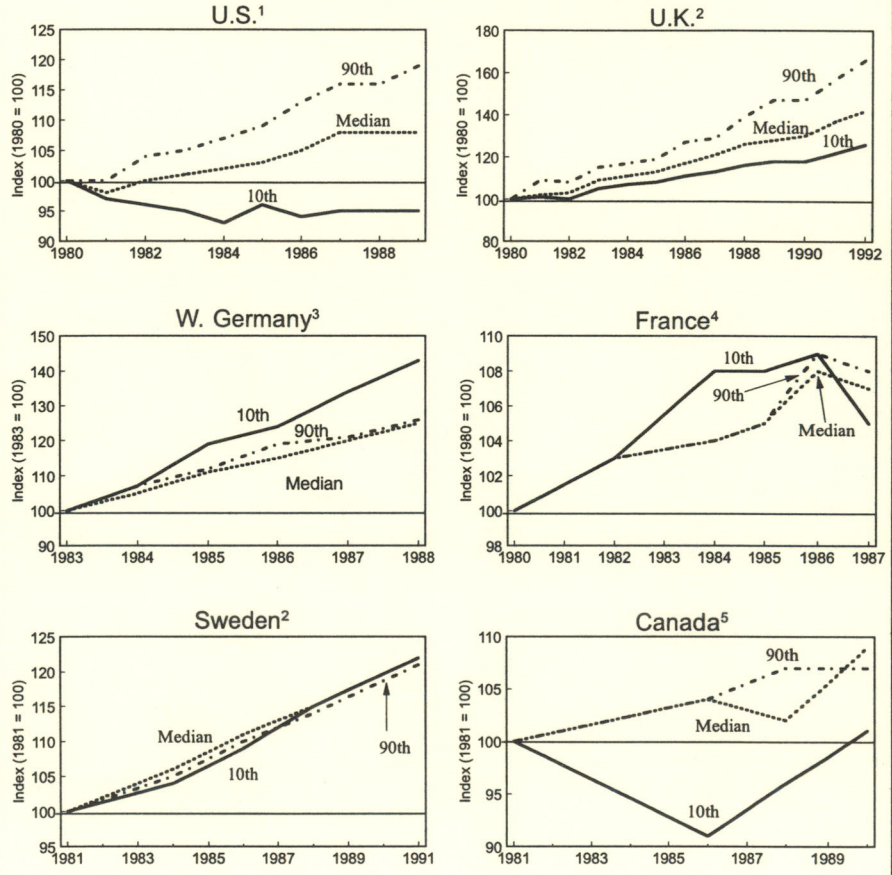

1   Gross hourly earnings of wage and salary workers.
2   Gross hourly earnings.
3   Gross monthly earnings plus benefits.
4   Gross annual earnings of full-time workers.
5   Gross annual earnings of full-time year-round workers.

Source: OECD (1993).

Table 8.10 presents more up-to-date information on the relative inequality of the distribution of wages for male and female workers together for 10 industrialized countries. The table measures inequality as the difference in earnings between high-wage workers (those making more than 90% of the total workforce) and the typical or median worker and, separately, as the difference in earnings between the median worker and a low-wage worker (who makes more than just 10% of the workforce). In the early 1980s, the United States was among the most unequal of the 10 countries. The ratio of earnings of the 90th-percentile worker to those of the 50th-percentile worker (the "90/50") was 1.96, well above the figure in most of the rest of the countries (only France, at 1.94, was close). At the same time, U.S. inequality was less pronounced at the bottom: the "50/10" ratio was 1.78 in the early 1980s, well below Canada (2.24) and Italy (1.96). During the course of the 1980s, both measures of inequality grew rapidly in Canada, the United Kingdom, and the United States, while inequality was unchanged or fell in the rest of the countries for which data are presented.

As discussed in Chapter 3, between the late 1980s and the mid-1990s the rise in wage inequality continued in the United States, with high-wage workers pulling away from the median workers (though the gap between median workers and low-wage earners narrowed somewhat). Australia followed a similar pattern, with widening dispersion at the top and some narrowing at the bottom. After experiencing sharp declines in earnings inequality in the 1980s, Italy suffered large increases in inequality both at the top and the bottom of the wage distribution. Inequality also grew in the United Kingdom, but at a rate well below the pace of the 1980s. In the remainder of the countries inequality changed little or fell. By the middle of the 1990s, the wage distribution in the United States, which began the 1980s more unequal than the rest of the countries in the table, had grown even more so. These developments occurred at a time when most of the rest of the economies experienced little or no growth in inequality or, in some cases, even managed to reduce overall wage inequality.

As has been documented in Chapter 3, an important dimension in the growth in wage inequality is the growth of educational differentials—for example, the rise in the "premium" paid to college-educated over high school-educated workers. **Table 8.11** puts this phenomenon in an international context by showing the change in comparable educational differentials over the 1980s as given by the ratio of the mean or median college-equivalent wage to the high school-equivalent wage. As suggested by the trends in the prior figure, the United States and the United Kingdom show the largest increase, by 0.09 and 0.07 points respectively. Growth of differentials in other countries was either slight (Sweden, Canada) or negative (Netherlands, West Germany).

T A B L E   8.10

Earnings Inequality,* 1979-95

| Country** | Early 1980s | | Late 1980s | | Mid-1990s | | Annual Point Change × 100 | | | |
| | | | | | | | Early '80s to Late '80s | | Late '80s to Mid '90s | |
	50/10	90/50	50/10	90/50	50/10	90/50	50/10	90/50	50/10	90/50
Australia	1.64	1.67	1.69	1.70	1.65	1.77	0.50	0.30	-0.67	1.17
Canada	2.24	1.79	2.39	1.86	2.28	1.84	1.50	0.70	-1.83	-0.33
France	1.67	1.94	1.65	1.99	1.65	1.99	-0.20	0.50	0.00	0.00
Germany	1.65	1.63	1.50	1.64	1.44	1.61	-1.50	0.10	-1.00	-0.50
Italy	1.96	1.50	1.50	1.44	1.75	1.60	-4.60	-0.60	4.17	2.67
Japan	1.71	1.76	1.70	1.86	1.63	1.85	-0.10	1.00	-1.17	-0.17
Netherlands	n.a.	n.a.	1.57	1.66	1.56	1.66	15.70	16.60	-0.17	0.00
Sweden	1.30	1.57	1.35	1.57	1.34	1.59	0.50	0.00	-0.17	0.33
United Kingdom	1.69	1.65	1.79	1.83	1.81	1.87	1.00	1.80	0.33	0.67
United States*	**1.78**	**1.96**	**2.07**	**2.10**	**2.00**	**2.21**	**2.90**	**1.40**	**-1.17**	**1.83**

*   Measured as the ratio of the earnings of the 90th-percentile worker to those of the 50th-percentile earner ("90/50") and of the 50th-percentile worker to those of the 10th-percentile earner ("90/10").

** Australia, United Kingdom, United States: 1979, 1989, 1995; Canada: 1981, 1988, 1994; Japan, France: 1979, 1989, 1994; Germany: 1983, 1989, 1994; Italy: 1979,1989, 1993; Netherlands: 1989, 1994; Sweden: 1980, 1989, 1993.

*** Based on CPS data.

Source: Authors' analysis of OECD and CPS data.

TABLE 8.11

International Educational Differentials for Males During the 1980s

Country	Ratios of Mean or Median College-Equivalent Wage to High School-Equivalent Wage*		
	1979 or Early 1980s	Mid- to Late 1980s	Average 5-Year Change
Canada	1.40	1.42	0.02
West Germany	2.00	1.94	-0.06
Japan	1.26	1.26	0.00
Netherlands	1.50	1.22	-0.04
Sweden	1.16	1.19	0.03
United Kingdom	1.53	1.65	0.07
United States	**1.37**	**1.51**	**0.09**

* All figures except the Netherlands and Germany control for changes in age composition of educational groups.

Sources: OECD (1993) and Abraham and Houseman (1994).

Poverty

Another important measure of income inequality is the extent of poverty. Chapter 6 presented an analysis of the problem of poverty in the United States. In this section, we introduce an international perspective and examine both the extent of poverty in other countries and the response. We find that American poverty rates are the highest and that its system of social protection is the weakest.

The next three tables examine poverty rates in the late 1970s and the mid-1980s, the years for which data are available. The poverty lines used are 40% of median income in each country, a relative definition of poverty that produces a poverty threshold close to the official U.S. poverty lines of the mid-1980s. Since levels of income and wealth vary significantly among countries, a relative threshold is essential to international comparisons. Like the official U.S. definition, these rates take cash transfers into account and are adjusted for family size but, unlike the U.S. definition, also account for taxes and the value of food stamps.

Table 8.12 shows the poverty rates from eight industrialized countries for all persons, all adults (age 18-64), and children (17 and under). The U.S. rates are by

TABLE 8.12

Poverty Rates* in the Mid-1980s

Country	All Persons	All Adults (18-64)	All Children (17 or Under)
Australia	6.7%	6.2%	9.0%
Canada	7.0	7.0	9.3
France	4.5	5.2	4.6
West Germany	2.8	2.6	2.8
Netherlands	3.4	3.9	3.8
Sweden	4.3	6.6	1.6
United Kingdom	5.2	5.3	7.4
United States	**13.3**	**10.5**	**20.4**
Average	5.9	5.9	7.4
Ratio of U.S. to Average	2.3	1.8	2.8

* Poverty defined as earnings less than 40% of median income, adjusted for family size.

Source: Smeeding (1992).

far the highest for each category. In the category for all persons, 13.3% of all Americans were poor in 1986, nearly twice the percentage as in the next highest country (Canada with 7.0%) and 2.3 times the average level of 5.9%. (As discussed in Chapter 6, relative poverty rates in the United States increased between 1989 and 1994 (see Table 6.5)). American child poverty is particularly high. At 20.4%, the U.S. child poverty rate in the mid-1980s was almost three times the average rate of 7.4% for the other countries in the table. (As Chapter 6 also noted, child poverty in the United States grew to 21.8% by 1994 (see Table 6.13)).

Table 8.13 examines the impact of the tax and transfer systems of the various countries for the same categories as in the previous table. The "Pre" columns give the poverty rates generated by the market prior to the introduction of taxes and transfers. Thus, these percentages represent the degree of poverty that would exist with no government intervention.

The extent of market-generated poverty in these eight industrialized countries is alarming: on average, over one-fifth of all persons were poor prior to government intervention. In France, the United Kingdom, and Sweden, that proportion rises to over one-fourth. To some degree, these high overall rates are driven by exceptionally high poverty rates of elderly persons (not shown), but the rates for adults and particularly children are also high. By this measure, the

TABLE 8.13

The Impact of Taxes and Transfers on International Poverty Rates, Mid-1980s

Country	All Persons			Adults (18-64)			Children (17 or Under)		
	Pre*	Post*	Point Change	Pre*	Post*	Point Change	Pre*	Post*	Point Change
Australia	19.1%	6.7%	-12.4	12.9%	6.1%	-6.8	16.4%	9.0%	-7.4
Canada	17.1	7.0	-10.1	11.5	7.0	-4.5	15.7	9.3	-6.4
France	26.4	4.5	-21.9	17.6	5.2	-12.4	21.1	4.6	-16.5
West Germany	21.6	2.8	-18.8	9.8	2.6	-7.2	8.4	2.8	-5.6
Netherlands	21.5	3.4	-18.1	17.4	3.9	-13.5	14.1	3.8	-10.3
Sweden	25.9	4.3	-21.0	13.4	6.6	-6.8	7.9	1.6	-6.3
United Kingdom	27.7	5.2	-22.5	18.1	5.3	-12.8	27.9	7.4	-20.5
United States	**19.9**	**13.3**	**-6.6**	**12.8**	**10.5**	**-2.3**	**22.3**	**20.4**	**-1.9**
Average	22.4%	5.9%	-16.5	14.2%	5.9%	-8.3	16.7%	7.4%	-9.3

* "Pre" refers to pre-tax, pre-transfer income; "post" refers to post-tax, post-transfer income.

Source: Smeeding (1992).

U.S. rates are relatively low (with the notable exception of child poverty). The U.S. pre-tax and pre-transfer poverty rate for all persons, 19.9%, is below the average rate of 22.4%; only Canada and Australia have lower rates.

However, the post-tax, post-transfer column tells a different story. Here, the U.S. rates are the *highest in all cases*. Thus, while market outcomes in this country, which leave one-fifth of all persons impoverished, generate relatively less poverty than most other countries, the U.S. system of taxes and transfers is much less effective in reducing poverty than that of any other country.

The effect of taxes and transfers is shown in the point-change columns of Table 8.13. For example, in the United Kingdom, the market economy of the mid-1980s left 27.7% of all persons poor. However, after taxes and benefits, the U.K. poverty rate fell to 5.2%, a drop of 22.5 percentage points. By this measure of poverty reduction, the United States is an extreme laggard. For all persons, the U.S. redistribution system lowered poverty by only 6.6 points, well below the average reduction of 16.5 points. For adults, poverty was reduced by a lesser amount, 2.3 points. (Note, however, that all countries show less poverty reduction for adults.) For U.S. children, poverty barely fell at all (1.9 points), a result in stark contrast to the child-poverty reduction of the other countries. (**Figure 8H** shows

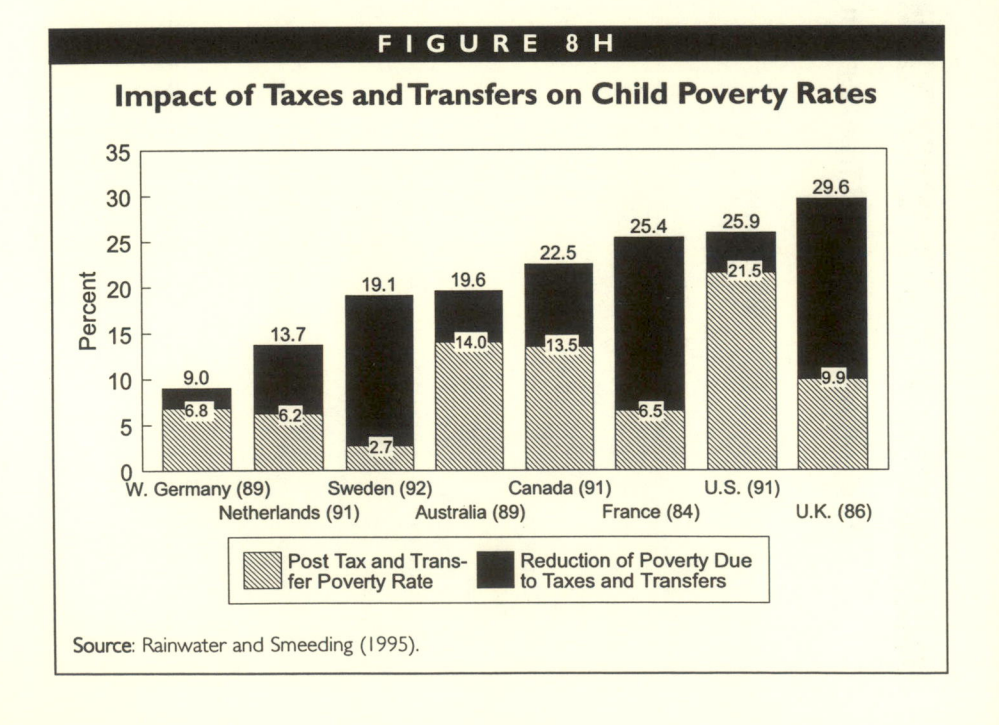

FIGURE 8H

Impact of Taxes and Transfers on Child Poverty Rates

Legend:
- Post Tax and Transfer Poverty Rate
- Reduction of Poverty Due to Taxes and Transfers

Source: Rainwater and Smeeding (1995).

similar, more up-to-date data for children only.)

Table 8.14, which looks at changes between two periods (see the table for a description of the time periods), compares the United States to the average of the other countries in the study. (The United Kingdom is omitted due to lack of data for the earlier year.) The table shows that poverty worsened over the 1980s in all countries for each category, both in pre- and post-transfer terms. However, comparing the United States and the average of the other countries shows that,

TABLE 8.14

Effectiveness of Tax and Transfer System, Early to Mid-1980s

	United States			Average of Other Nations*		
	1979	1986	Point Change	Period 1	Period 2	Point Change
All Persons						
Pre**	18.5%	19.9%	1.4	20.6%	21.6%	1.0
Post**	10.8	13.3	2.5	5.7	6.0	0.3
Point Change	-7.7	-6.6	1.1	-14.9	-15.6	-0.7
Percentage of Poverty Reduced	41.6%	33.2%		72.3%	72.2%	
Adults (18-64)						
Pre**	11.2%	12.8%	1.6	12.6%	13.6%	1.0
Post**	8.3	10.5	2.2	5.6	6.0	0.4
Point Change	-2.9	-2.3	0.6	-7.0	-7.6	-0.6
Percentage of Poverty Reduced	25.9%	18.0%		55.6%	55.9%	
Children (17 or Under)						
Pre**	19.0%	22.3%	3.3	13.7%	15.1%	1.4
Post**	14.7	20.4	5.7	6.5	7.4	0.9
Point Change	-4.3	-1.9	2.4	-7.2	-7.7	-0.5
Percentage of Poverty Reduced	22.6%	8.5%		52.6%	51.0%	

*   Average of Australia, Canada, France, West Germany, Netherlands, and Sweden. Period 1 is either 1979 or 1981, except for the Netherlands (1983). Period 2 is either 1986 or 1987, except for France and Germany (1984).

**   "Pre" refers to pre-tax, pre-transfer income; "post" refers to post-tax, post-transfer income.

Source: Smeeding (1992).

not only is poverty reduction less effective in the United States, as shown in the previous table, it has become even *less* effective over time. An encompassing measure of this trend is shown as the percentage of poverty reduced. If we consider pre-tax and pre-transfer poverty to be the total amount of poverty that the redistributive system can effect, then the percentage of poverty reduced is the ratio of the point change to the poverty induced by the market, expressed as a percent. The table shows a smaller (and falling) *percentage* reduction of pre-tax and pre-transfer poverty in the United States than in other countries. For all Americans in 1979, 41.6% of the pre-transfer poor were lifted out of poverty by taxes and transfers; in 1986, this percentage fell to 33.2%. In the other nations, the percentage of poverty reduced was both much higher than in the United States and essentially the same in both periods. For example, in the average foreign nation, child poverty was reduced 52.6% in Period 1 and 51.0% in Period 2. In the United States, child poverty was reduced by 22.6% in 1979 and an even smaller 8.5% in 1986.

Comparing Economic Mobility Among Countries

In Chapter 6, we noted that poverty is a dynamic, rather than a static, phenomenon. Research on the length of time spent poor has found a great deal of transition into and out of poverty. **Table 8.15** and **Figure 8I**, which present the results of an international study of the economic mobility of poor families with children in the mid-1980s, enable a comparison of U.S. economic mobility to that of other countries. (As above, we apply a relative definition of poverty; however, in this analysis, the poverty lines are set at 50% of median income—the previous tables used 40%. Again, income is post-tax and post-transfer, with adjustments for family size.)

The first column of Table 8.15 gives the poverty rates for families with children in the countries in this study. Once again, the U.S. rates are the highest; this is particularly the case for black families, whose poverty rate was 49.3%. However, it is the second and third columns in which we are most interested; in column 2 (labeled "Transition Rate") we find the percent of poor families in year 1 who escaped poverty by year 2, and in column 3 we find the percent of families who were poor for three consecutive years.

The horizontal axis of Figure 8I is the percent of families who were poor in year 1 of the study (column 1, Table 8.15). The vertical axis is the percentage of poor families who escaped poverty by year 2. Thus, as the data points in the

TABLE 8.15

Poverty Rates and Transitions out of Poverty for Families with Children, Mid-1980s

Country	Poverty Rate*	Transition Rate**	Percent of Families Poor in All 3 Years of a 3-Year Period
Canada	17.0%	12.0%	11.9%
France-Lorraine	4.0	27.5	1.6
West Germany			
All	7.8	25.6	1.5
German	6.7	26.9	1.4
Immigrants	18.0	20.0	4.0
Ireland	11.0	25.2	n.a.
Luxembourg***	4.4	26.0	0.4
Netherlands	2.7	44.4	0.4
Sweden	2.7	36.8	n.a.
United States			
All	20.3	13.8	14.4
White	15.3	17.0	9.5
Black	49.3	7.7	41.5

* Percent of families with income below 50% of that country's median income in year 1.
** Percent of families who were poor in year 1 who had more than 60% of median income in year 2.
*** Transition rate for Luxembourg based on 10-30 cases.

Source: Duncan et al. (1991).

figure move out to the lower right (higher poverty rates in year 1, a lower probability of escape by year 2), the economic situation worsens.

Most of the countries in Figure 8I show relatively low poverty rates and relatively high "escape" rates. France-Lorraine, for example, has a family poverty rate of 4% in year 1, and 27.5% of the poor in that year had escaped poverty by the next year (Table 8.15). However, the U.S. position in the figure reveals high poverty and low mobility. The U.S. overall poverty rate (20.3%) is the highest in the table, and the escape rate of 13.8% is the second lowest. The situation for U.S. blacks is particularly severe. As noted above, the poverty rate

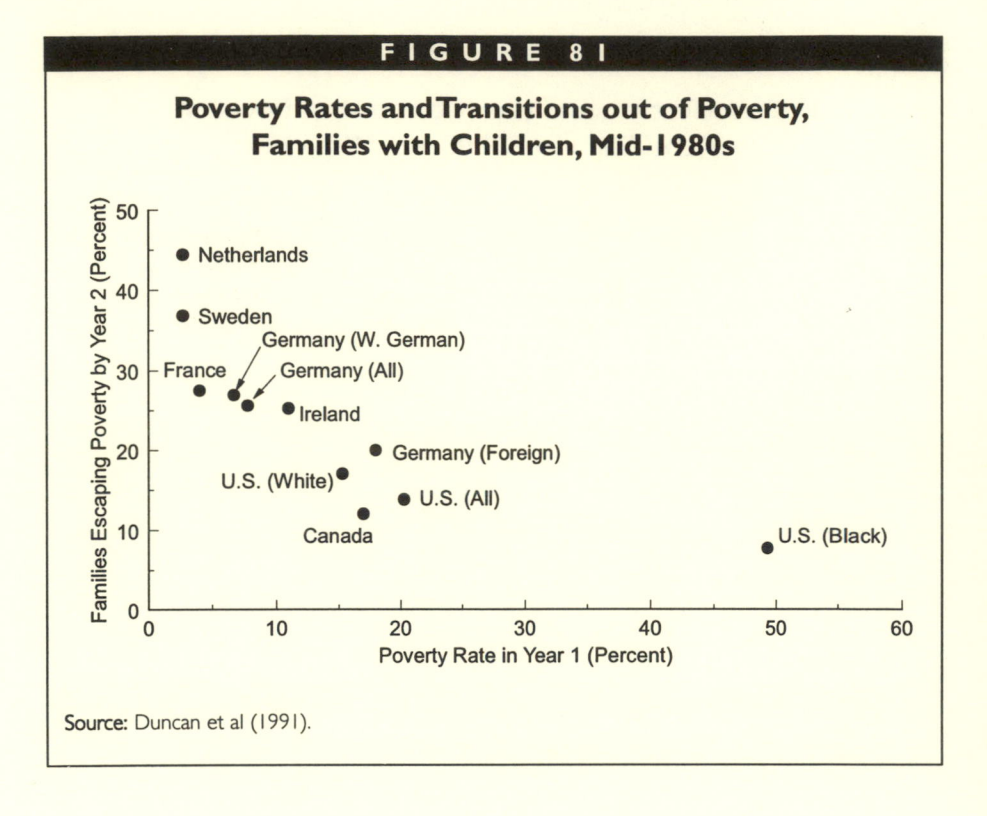

FIGURE 81

Poverty Rates and Transitions out of Poverty, Families with Children, Mid-1980s

Source: Duncan et al (1991).

for black families is 49.3%, the highest in the table. Blacks also have the lowest probability of escaping poverty; only 9.5% of the poor in year 1 were nonpoor in year 2 (see also Table 6.9). Only the Canadian poor are less likely than the U.S. poor to leave poverty. In fact, even foreigners within Germany, who have higher poverty rates than U.S. whites, have higher escape rates than the U.S. poor.

Column 3 of Table 8.15 shows further evidence of low economic mobility in the United States compared to the other countries in the table. The probability of a poor family with children remaining poor for the full length of the three-year period of the study was highest in the United States, at 14.4%. While the rate for Canada was slightly lower (11.9%), the other countries in the study had much lower persistent poverty rates than the United States. Black families were most likely to experience persistent poverty; 41.5% were poor for the full period.

Job Growth and the Public Commitment to Job Training and Unemployment Compensation

We have already shown (Chapter 4) that most of the net job growth over the 1980s was in low-paying service industries. Since we do not have comparable data on job growth by sector, we are unable to make international comparisons of the quality of the jobs created. In terms of aggregate job growth from an international perspective, we find U.S. job growth to be relatively strong, but not in orders of magnitude above its competitors. Furthermore, the public commitment in the United States to important labor market institutions lags behind that of its competitors.

Table 8.16 shows that, from 1979 to 1989, millions more jobs were created in the United States than in other countries (column 1). This is to be expected, however, since the United States is by far the largest country. A better indicator is the *rate* of job creation relative to employment, and by this measure the United

TABLE 8.16

Jobs Created in 10 Countries, 1979-94

Country	Total Created 1979-89 (000)	New Jobs as Percent of 1979 Employment	Total Created 1989-94 (000)	New Jobs as Percent of 1989 Employment
Australia	1,617	26.5%	193	2.4%
Canada	2,091	20.1	806	6.1
France	460	2.2	-40	-0.2
West Germany	1,120	4.3	700	2.5
Italy	840	4.2	-880	-4.4
Japan	6,460	12.0	3,360	5.3
Netherlands*	720	13.5	380	5.9
Sweden	364	8.7	-546	-13.7
United Kingdom	1,410	5.7	-760	-3.0
United States*	**18,518**	**18.7**	**1,964**	**1.6**

* Figures in columns 3 and 4 refer to 1993. U.S. data for 1994 are not directly comparable with earlier years because of changes in underlying survey.

Source: Authors' analysis of BLS data.

States ranks third out of 10. Column 2 of Table 8.16 shows that U.S. employment in 1989 was 18.7% greater than in 1979, compared to increases of 26.5% in Australia and 20.1% in Canada over the same period.

Between 1989 and 1994, job growth was tempered by the 1990-91 recession in this country and similar, generally later, downturns in some of the other industrialized nations. (Note the net decrease in jobs in four countries.) Among the countries with positive growth, U.S. employment grew the least relative to its 1989 level.

Another reason that simple job counts are misleading is that they do not take into account population growth, a factor that limits both the number of jobs created and the rate of job growth. Some countries (e.g., West Germany) have had very little population growth, while most others have grown at a much slower rate than the United States. Without population growth the only way in which additional job growth can be achieved is by raising the percentage of the population employed, which is always a slow process. On the other hand, countries with fast-growing populations have the possibility of creating substantial growth in employment.

To address this issue, **Table 8.17** breaks down the growth in employment into growth of population and growth of the employment/population ratio. Between 1979 and 1989, the U.S. annual employment growth rate (1.7%) turns out to be due more to population growth (1.2%) than to a rising employment/population ratio (0.5%). By this more appropriate standard—the employment/population ratio—the United States has still done well in creating employment, but not orders of magnitude better than the others. And, as shown above, this was accompanied by sharply rising wage inequality.

Between 1989 and 1994, job growth decelerated in the United States and in many other countries due to cyclical factors. The job growth that did occur in the United States came exclusively from population growth—the share of the population employed actually shrank over this period.

Workers in the United States have also been putting in more hours than workers in most other countries, in part to compensate for falling wages. **Table 8.18** shows the hours worked per employee in manufacturing (the only data of this type available), once again indexed to the United States. While two countries (Japan and the United Kingdom) had average hours of work in 1970 that exceeded U.S. hours, by 1995 only Japan had more hours of work per average manufacturing employee. The falling weighted average (weighted by each country's hours per employee, exclusive of the United States), from 1 percentage point above the U.S. level in 1979 to 8 percentage points below in 1995, shows the increase in U.S. manufacturing labor supply relative to other countries.

TABLE 8.17

Contributions to Employment Growth, 1979-94

Country	Employment Growth Rate	Breakdown of Employment Growth into Sum of:	
		Population Growth Rate	Employment/ Population Ratio Growth Rate
1979-89			
Australia	2.4%	2.0%	0.4%
Canada	1.8	1.3	0.6
France	0.2	0.9	-0.7
West Germany	0.4	0.6	-0.2
Italy	0.4	0.9	-0.5
Japan	1.1	1.2	-0.1
Netherlands	1.3	1.2	0.1
Sweden	0.8	0.6	0.3
United Kingdom	0.6	0.6	-0.0
United States	**1.7**	**1.2**	**0.5**
*Average**	0.8%	1.0%	-0.2%
1989-94			
Australia	0.5%	1.4%	-0.9%
Canada	1.3	2.4	-1.2
France	-0.0	0.7	-0.7
West Germany**	0.7	1.0	-0.3
Italy	-0.9	-0.4	-0.5
Japan	1.1	0.9	0.2
Netherlands**	1.2	0.6	0.7
Sweden	-2.5	0.6	-3.1
United Kingdom	-0.6	0.3	-0.8
United States	**1.0**	**1.1**	**-0.1**
*Average**	0.3%	0.7%	-0.4%

* Weighted by working-age population in 1989; excludes United States.
** Figures are for 1989-93.

Source: Authors' analysis of BLS data.

TABLE 8.18

Hours Worked per Employee in Manufacturing, Compared to United States, 1970-95

(U.S. = 100)

Country	1970	1979	1989	1995*
Canada	100	98	95	96
Denmark	96	86	82	80
France	98	90	83	81
West Germany	99	91	82	76
Italy	100	92	95	94
Japan	119	114	111	101
Netherlands	98	88	83	82
Sweden	91	80	76	83
United Kingdom	105	101	96	93
United States	**100**	**100**	**100**	**100**
Average**	107	101	97	92

* Denmark 1993; Netherlands 1994.
** Weighted by 1989 hours; excludes the United States.

Source: Authors' analysis of BLS data.

In addition, American workers had less generous vacation benefits than did European workers (**Table 8.19**). The majority of European workers receive four or five weeks of paid vacation, mandated by law; American workers typically get slightly over two weeks. (Yet American workers' lesser vacation time only partially explains the extra hours of work.)

Another way in which European countries are more generous to their workers is in the provision of publicly provided job training, job creation, and subsidies. Such programs are vital in an economy experiencing a shift from manufacturing to services and a reduction in the size of the armed forces. However, among countries listed in **Table 8.20**, only Japan, which has much lower rates of job displacement than the United States, devoted less of its national resources to these programs than did the United States. In 1994-95, the U.S. government spent only 0.11% of GDP on job training and much less (0.01%) on subsidies.

As Chapter 4 points out, unemployment rates provide only a broad measure

TABLE 8.19

Legally Mandated Paid Vacation in European Countries

Country	Number of Weeks
Austria	5
Belgium	4
Finland	5
France	5
Greece	4
West Germany	3
Iceland	5*
Ireland	3
Luxembourg	5
Malta	4
Netherlands	4
Norway	4*
Portugal	30 Days
Spain	30 Days
Sweden	5
Switzerland	4
United States**	**16.1 Days**

* Iceland has four weeks and 4 days; Norway, 4 weeks and 1 day.
** Estimated average (not legally mandated).

Source: Leete-Guy and Schor (1992).

---

of labor-force supply and demand; they fail to capture the underemployed and discouraged workers. A general sense of the performance of the U.S. labor market from an international perspective is given in **Table 8.21**. In 1979, U.S. unemployment, at 5.8%, was above the average of 4.9% for the major industrialized countries. By 1989, unemployment had fallen in the United States to 5.2%; among the seven major countries, only Japan's rate was lower. Among the smaller countries, the Scandinavian countries had lower unemployment rates than the United States. By 1994, the negative business cycle increased unemployment in most countries, particularly in Finland, Spain, and Sweden, where unemployment grew to historic highs.

TABLE 8.20

Public Spending on Training and Placement, Direct Job Creation, and Subsidies, as Percent of GDP

Country	Training and Placement	Direct Job Creation and Subsidies	Total
Australia (1994-95)	0.26	0.25	0.51
Canada (1995-96)	0.33	0.04	0.37
France (1994)	0.74	0.27	1.01
Germany (1995)	0.57	0.54	1.11
Italy (1994)	3.50	0.30	3.80
Japan (1994-95)	0.03	0.05	0.08
Netherlands (1995)	0.25	0.64	0.89
Sweden (1994-95)	1.11	1.62	2.73
United Kingdom (1994-95)	0.26	0.05	0.31
United States (1994-95)	**0.11**	**0.01**	**0.12**

Source: Authors' analysis of OECD data.

TABLE 8.21

Unemployment Rates in OECD Countries, 1973-95

Country	1973	1979	1989	1995
Canada	5.5%	7.4%	7.5%	9.5%
France	2.7	5.8	9.4	11.6
Germany*	0.8	3.2	5.6	8.2
Italy	6.2	7.6	10.9	12.2
Japan	1.3	2.1	2.3	3.1
United Kingdom	3.0	5.0	7.2	8.7
United States	**4.8**	**5.8**	**5.2**	**5.5**
Major Seven Countries	3.4%	4.9%	5.7%	6.8%
Smaller Countries				
Australia	2.3%	6.2%	6.1%	8.5%
Belgium	2.7	8.2	8.0	9.4
Finland	2.3	5.9	3.4	17.1
Netherlands	2.2	5.4	8.3	6.5
Norway	1.5	2.0	4.9	4.9
Spain	2.5	8.4	16.9	22.7
Sweden	2.5	2.1	1.6	9.2
Total OECD	3.3%	5.1%	6.2%	7.5%

* Figures for 1973-89 refer to West Germany only.

Source: OECD (1994, 1996).

As is the case with training and subsidies, most other countries are also more generous than the United States in the provision of unemployment compensation. **Table 8.22** shows that in 1994-95 the United States spent only 0.35% of GDP on compensating those out of work. Japan, which spent the same share on unemployment compensation, was the only other country listed that spent less than 1% of GDP on unemployment compensation. However, this figure does not take the level of unemployment into account. That is, a country might devote very few resources to unemployment compensation because of low unemployment. Therefore, column 2 gives the unemployment rates for the various countries (measured for the relevant time period), and column 3 provides the ratio of compensation to unemployment, a measure of relative generosity given the country's unemployment rate. The United States spent 0.06% of GDP per 1% of unemployment in 1994-95, the lowest expenditure rate among the countries in the table.

TABLE 8.22

Unemployment and Unemployment Compensation

Country	Percent of GDP Spent on Unemployment Compensation	Unemployment Rate*	Percent of GDP per Percent of Unemployment
Australia (1994-95)	1.64%	9.1%	0.18
Canada (1995-96)	1.31	9.5	0.14
France (1994)	1.57	12.3	0.13
Germany (1995)	2.08	8.2	0.25
Japan (1994-95)	0.35	3.0	0.12
Netherlands (1995)	3.06	6.5	0.47
Sweden (1994-95)	2.52	9.5	0.27
United Kingdom (1994-95)	1.41	9.2	0.15
United States (1994-95)	**0.35**	**5.8**	**0.06**

* Standardized unemployment rate. Where spending data span two calendar years, unemployment rates are the average for two corresponding calendar years, except Canada, where figure is for 1995.

Source: Authors' analysis of OECD (1996).

Conclusion

Compared to other industrialized countries, the United States is falling behind on many important economic indicators. Comparatively sluggish productivity growth is limiting U.S. wage growth at a time when most other countries are experiencing rising wages. (For an explanation of additional factors causing wage decline, see Chapter 3.) This development, in tandem with the diminished effectiveness of the U.S. tax and transfer system, has left the United States with both the highest (and most persistent) poverty rates and most unequal income distribution among the industrialized countries examined in this chapter. Furthermore, these trends have begun to seriously undermine the U.S. standard of living, once considered the highest in the world.

APPENDIX A
The Family Income Data Series

BY JARED BERNSTEIN AND EDITH RASELL

THE PRIMARY SOURCE OF DATA FOR THE ANALYSIS OF MARRIED-COUPLE incomes in this report is the March Current Population Survey (MCPS). This nationally representative survey is used to provide annual estimates of poverty and various important income measures presented throughout this book (primarily in Chapters 1, 6, and 7). The MCPS has the advantage of being large enough to generate reliable estimates for different subgroups within the population, and it is reasonably consistent over time. It is widely considered to be the best source of cross-sectional microdata for economic/demographic analysis in the nation.

Nevertheless, there are some known problems with the income data from the survey. First, various components of income are underreported, and one important component—realized capital gains and losses—is missing (though recent years include an imputation by the Census Bureau). In addition, for reasons of confidentiality, high income amounts are capped. This means that if someone reports an income amount that exceeds the cap, the income level shown in the data set is equal to the value of the cap. For example, in 1979 the cap on earnings was $50,000. Any respondent who reported earnings greater than $50,000 would be shown in the data set to have earnings equal to $50,000. Thus, it is impossible to know from the data set the amount by which the respondent's actual earnings exceeded the cap.

Regarding trends, underreporting and capped incomes would not be a problem if their effect were constant over time (levels, of course, would be biased downward). However, there is evidence that the assumption of constancy is un-

Edith Rasell is an economist at the Economic Policy Institute.

warranted. First, a larger share of incomes are capped over time, and second, the omission of capital gains created a larger bias over the 1980s; other data sources showed this income component to grow substantially in that period. Since we are interested in comprehensively measuring the increase in income inequality over the 1980s, and since capital gains are heavily concentrated among the wealthy (see Table 1.14), we judged the omission of capital gains from the MCPS to be a significant source of bias.

To correct for these problems in the MCPS, we created the Family Income Data Series, or FIDS. This data series is based on the MCPS, with added information from two additional data sources: (1) the Internal Revenue Service's Statistics of Income Database (SOI), from which we drew heavily, and the administrative records of the Aid to Families with Dependent Children (AFDC) program, which were used to correct for the underreporting of welfare benefits.

We will first list the adjustments made to the microdata in the MCPS and then briefly discuss the methods we used to make the adjustments:

The following adjustments were made using the SOI:

- values for capped income components, including earnings (wage and salary, self-employment, and farm), interest, dividends, and rental income were imputed;

- underreporting of interest, dividends, and AFDC payments was corrected for;

- realized capital gains were added.

We used AFDC administrative totals to correct for underreporting among those who received this transfer.

Appending SOI Values to the MCPS for 1979 and 1989

The SOI is a reliable source of information on income components reported to the IRS (it is a sample of tax returns, with representative weights, and not responses from a survey). It has several drawbacks: it is limited to tax filers, data are reported by tax filing units, and there are few demographic variables. These factors limit the SOI's utility as a stand-alone database for the type of analysis in Chapter 1 and led us (and others who have engaged in similar exercises, including the Census Bureau and the Congressional Budget Office (CBO)) to append necessary values to cases in the MCPS.

To ensure that we were matching SOI-generated values with appropriate MCPS records, we created filing units in the MCPS. We followed the same rules as the Census Bureau, as described in Series P-60, No. 182-RD, Appendix C. Next, we created cells in both data sets using the following variables:

- three types of filing units: single filers, married (filing jointly), and single heads of households;

- presence of a member in the filing unit over 65 years of age;

- various ranges of adjusted gross income (AGI).

While AGI is a variable in the SOI, it is not available in the MCPS. Thus, we used filing unit income as a proxy on the MCPS side.

Since the income data from the SOI are not capped, the SOI serves as a useful source for estimating average values above the capped levels in the MCPS. Averages for the relevant variables were calculated by cells as defined above. These averages were appended to the relevant records among the MCPS filing unit.

There are two types of underreporting: (1) failing to report any income actually received, and (2) reporting less than actually received. For type (2), we scaled up the reported level by using scalars derived from the SOI. For type (1), we first predicted receipt using a logit model, and then assigned an average amount using a cell-based matching procedure. We used similar scalars to correct for underreporting among both filing units and non-filers.

As noted, realized capital gains are not reported in the MCPS, but they are in the SOI. Instead of matching cell-based averages, we used a "hot-deck" technique and matched actual SOI donor records to MCPS records (capital gains and losses were modeled separately). To do this, we divided both databases into deciles by AGI and calculated the share of units in each decile that had either gains or losses. We then randomly chose records, by decile, on the MCPS side to receive values from the SOI, until the appropriate (weighted) share of records was reached. (This process was not entirely random because a higher probability of receipt was assigned to those MCPS cases with larger weights.)

Appending the 1994 MCPS

As this book went to press, SOI microdata for 1994 were not yet available. We did, however, have access to a set of unpublished tables with aggregated information from the 1994 SOI.

In order to adjust the capped values on the MCPS, we "aged" the replacement values from 1989 (described above) by applying the 1989-94 growth rates for the respective variable just below the top-code on the MCPS. For example, if nominal wage and salary income for a specific cell at the 98th percentile grew 2% from 1989 to 1994, we assigned the value 1.02*1989 SOI Wage and Salary Imputation to that cell for 1994. We followed this general procedure for all capped variables in the 1994 MCPS.

Because too few filing units in the MCPS reported dividend income, we selected additional filing units and assigned them dividend income. (There was no need to assign additional MCPS filing units to receive interest income since there were similar numbers of recipients in both the SOI and MCPS.) We used a logit model, estimated from 1989 SOI data, to predict the probability of receipt for each MCPS filing unit that reported no dividend income. From the published SOI data we knew the total number of filing units with dividend income by income range. We then assigned receipt to the appropriate weighted number of MCPS records in each income range, beginning with those with the greatest probability of receipt as predicted in the logit. The amount of income assigned was the average amount reported in the SOI, calculated for three different income ranges.

We also corrected underreported amounts of interest and dividend income. (The correction of underreported AFDC income was similar to the process for other years described above.) We determined the aggregate amounts of interest and dividend income reported in the MCPS and SOI. The sum of newly assigned dividend income was subtracted from both SOI and MCPS dividend totals, since there was no underreporting of these amounts. We then multiplied reported interest and dividends in the MCPS by the ratio of the SOI total to the MCPS total.

Comparing Our Results to CBO's

Since the CBO has published extensive results of its own version of this exercise, we can compare results. There are some important differences, however, between CBO's data and our own. While our analysis of the 1980s uses the years 1979 and 1989 (business cycle peaks), CBO uses 1980 and 1989, for reasons having to do with tax analysis. Thus, our only common year is 1989. Also, CBO includes employer contributions for federal social insurance and federal corporate income taxes in family income. Finally, CBO data are reported using an income-to-needs concept, i.e., family income is scaled using the poverty line for the relevant family size.

The table compares the outcomes for the common year, 1989. Small differences are apparent between the two data sets for all but the top 1%, with FIDS levels higher in the bottom 60% and notably lower in the top 1%. This difference among the highest-income families may stem from CBO's assignment of corporate income taxes back to families who pay them. Since this assignment is in part based on capital holdings, it is likely that this would account for CBO's higher levels among the top 1%.

TABLE APP-I

Comparing CBO and FIDS, 1989, Average Adjusted Incomes* for All Families

Income Group	Average Income Levels		
	CBO	FIDS	% Difference
Bottom Fifth	7,416	7,594	2.4
Second Fifth	17,800	18,161	2.0
Middle Fifth	28,884	29,201	1.1
Fourth Fifth	42,346	41,495	-2.0
81-90%	58,244	56,985	-2.2
91-95%	77,521	74,071	-4.5
96-99%	116,696	119,250	2.2
Top 1%	494,758	400,096	-19.1

Income Group	Average Income/Poverty Line		
	CBO	FIDS	% Difference
Bottom Fifth	0.89	0.94	5.6
Second Fifth	2.10	2.16	2.9
Middle Fifth	3.35	3.38	0.9
Fourth Fifth	4.94	4.91	-0.6
81-90%	7.02	6.94	-1.1
91-95%	9.37	9.21	-1.7
96-99%	14.50	14.59	0.6
Top 1%	59.89	49.88	-16.7

* Adjusted incomes represent income-to-poverty ratios.

Source: Authors' analysis (FIDS) and U.S. House of Representatives 1991 (CBO).

APPENDIX B
Wage Analysis Computations

BY DAVID E. WEBSTER

THIS APPENDIX PROVIDES BACKGROUND INFORMATION ON OUR ANALYSIS OF wage data from the Current Population Survey (CPS), which is prepared by the Bureau of the Census for the Bureau of Labor Statistics. Specifically, for 1979 and beyond, we analyze computer tapes provided by BLS that contain a full year's data on the outgoing rotation groups (ORG) in the CPS. (For years prior to 1979, we use the CPS May files; our use of these files is discussed below.) We believe that the CPS ORG files allow for a more timely, up-to-date, and accurate analysis of wage trends than the traditionally used March CPS files (which, for 1995, will not be available until the end of 1996), while still keeping within the familiar labor-force definitions and concepts employed by the CPS.

The ORG files provide data on those CPS respondents in either the fourth or eighth month of the CPS (i.e., in groups four or eight, out of a total of eight groups). Therefore, in any given month the ORG file represents a quarter of the CPS sample. For a given year, the ORG file is equivalent to three months of CPSs (1/4th of 12). For our analysis, we use the full-year ORG samples, whose sizes ranged from 160,802 in 1979 to 183,038 in 1991.

Changes in annual or weekly earnings can result from changes in hourly earnings or from more working time (either more hours per week or weeks per year). Our analysis is centered around the hourly wage, which represents the pure price of labor (exclusive of benefits), because we are interested in changing pay levels for the workforce and its subgroups. We do this to be able to clearly distinguish changes in earnings resulting from more (or less) work rather

David E. Webster is a research analyst at the Economic Policy Institute.

than more (or less) pay. Our wage analysis, therefore, does not take into account that weekly or annual earnings may have changed because of longer working hours or lesser or greater opportunities for employment. An exception to this is Table 3.1, where we present annual hours, earnings, and hourly weighted wages from the March CPS.

In our view, the ORG files provide a better source of data for wage analysis than the traditionally used March CPS files. In order to calculate hourly wages from the March CPS, analysts must make calculations using three retrospective variables: the annual earnings, weeks worked, and usual weekly hours worked in the year prior to the survey. Limiting the March sample to full-time, full-year workers is increasingly unsatisfactory, since they represent only two-thirds of wage earners and because there can be a significant variation of hours worked in this group over time and year by year. In contrast, respondents in the ORG are asked a set of questions about hours worked, weekly wages, and (for workers paid by the hour) hourly wages in the week prior to the survey. In this regard, the data from the ORG are likely to be more reliable than data from the March CPS. The ORG files are also more current and have a much larger sample size.

Our subsample includes all wage and salary workers with valid wage and hour data, whether paid weekly or by the hour. Specifically, in order to be included in our subsample, respondents had to meet the following criteria:

- age 18-64;

- employed in the public or private sector (self-employed were excluded);

- hours worked within the valid range in the survey (0-99 per week, or hours vary—see discussion below); and

- either hourly or weekly wages within the valid survey range (top-coding discussed below).

For those who met these criteria, an hourly wage was calculated in the following manner. If a valid hourly wage was reported, that wage was used throughout our analysis. For salaried workers (those who only report a weekly wage), the hourly wage was their weekly wage divided by their hours worked. Outliers, i.e., persons with hourly wages below 50 cents or above $100, in 1989 CPI-U-X1 adjusted dollars, were removed from the analysis. The yearly dollar values of the cutoffs move with inflation, starting at 19 cents and $38.07 in 1973, moving through 50 cents and $100 in 1989, and increasing to 62 cents and $122.90 in 1995. CPS weights were applied to make the sample nationally representative.

For tables that show wage percentiles, we "smooth" hourly wages to compensate for "wage clumps" in the wage distributions. This procedure, common to BLS wage quantile presentations, is explained in detail in Mishel and Bernstein (1993, 23).

For the survey years 1979-88, the weekly wage is top-coded at $999.00. Particularly for the later years, this truncation of the wage distribution creates a downward bias in the mean wage. In the analysis presented in this chapter, we dealt with the top-coding issue by imputing a new weekly wage for top-coded individuals. The imputed value is the Pareto imputed mean for the upper tail of the weekly earnings distribution, based on the distribution of weekly earnings up to the 80th percentile. This procedure was performed for men and women separately. A new hourly wage, equal to the new estimated value for weekly earnings, divided by that person's usual hours per week, was calculated. The imputed values for men and women ranged from a low of $1,370 in 1973 for men and $1,281 in 1981 for women to highs of $2,922 and $2721 in 1995 for men and women respectively.

As noted above, we extend our analysis back to 1973 by using the May CPS files, which typically have sample sizes of about 35,000 meeting our criteria. Given these relatively small samples, we pool the 1973 and 1974 May CPS for our wage analysis of education and experience by race.

Beginning in 1994, the CPS began allowing people to report that their usual hours worked per week vary. Hourly workers who reported that their hours varied but reported an hourly wage were assigned their reported wage. We estimated usual hours per week, however, for the remaining 5.4% 1994 and 5.7% in 1995. In order to include these persons in our wage analysis, we estimated their usual hours based upon persons with similar characteristics, using the 95% of persons with data on usual hours per week. An hourly wage was calculated by dividing weekly earnings by the estimate of hours.

Demographic variables are also used in the analysis. Education up to 1992 refers to years of school completed. Our race variable comprises four mutually exclusive categories:

- white, non-Hispanic;

- black, non-Hispanic;

- Hispanic, any race;

- all others.

Beginning in 1992, the CPS employed a new coding scheme for education, which is essentially the respondent's highest degree achieved. In order to create a consistent time series on wages, we developed a methodology to impute years of education completed given the categories on the 1992-95 files. Our imputation was facilitated by the 1990 February CPS, which contains both the old and new education coding. In order to impute years of education completed for 1992 and 1995, we regressed years of education on education categories (the new coding) plus a set of controls including age (and age-education interactions), region, urban status, five occupations, and the hourly wage. (Separate models were run for males and females.)

We employ these imputations in various tables in Chapter 3 where we present wage trends by education over time. While we are confident our imputations do a good job of representing the trend in wages by education level, we are less confident regarding predictions of educational attainment. Therefore, we do not use imputed years of education to estimate the shares of workers in different education categories to bridge the coding change.

APPENDIX C
The Measurement of Inflation

ALL OF THE ANALYSIS IN THIS BOOK RELIES ON THE CPI-U-X1, AN INFLATION index from the Bureau of Labor Statistics. The CPI-U-X1 measure differs from the regular CPI-U index only in the period between 1967 and 1983, and it does so to carry back in time the method with which housing costs have been measured since 1983. In other words, the CPI-U-X1 is a historically consistent series. For the 1947-67 period, the CPI-U-X1 series is constructed to parallel that of the CPI-U series. It shows *more* income and wage growth than the CPI-U.

In recent years some economists (Boskin et al. 1995; Lebow et al. 1996) have been critical of this measure, arguing that it overstates the true rate of increase in the cost of living by 0.5-2.0% annually. While there is some truth to the criticisms, many of the claims are exaggerated, and little effort has been devoted to examining the ways in which the CPI-U-X1 might *understate* inflation. Furthermore, the implications of a significant overstatement of inflation for past living standards are highly implausible.

If the inflation measure used in the analysis of this book shows too much inflation, then the American economic landscape may be far different than portrayed. Some matters, such as whether there has been a growth of income or wage *inequality*, would be unaffected. If the inflation in what high-income households purchase has been most mismeasured (i.e., the new-goods bias), then a corrected CPI might even suggest a greater growth in inequality. Nevertheless, the key trends that a "biased" inflation measure would affect are the amounts that family incomes, wages, or compensation have grown, with a lower mea-

---

Dean Baker is an economist at the Economic Policy Institute.

sured inflation indicating a faster growth in "real incomes." One cannot know whether, or by how much, there was a slowdown in income growth between the early postwar years and the post-1973 years unless one knows whether the "bias" was greater or less in the earlier period. Baker (1996b) argues that the BLS has regularly changed the measurement of inflation and that the new methods introduced have tended to lower measured inflation. The new methods, however, were never used to revise the historical series. This suggests that the earlier period has greater measurement errors than the recent period. If so, then any corrected CPI would show a *greater* slowdown in the income growth of the post-1973 period relative to the 1950s or 1960s.

For example, if current inflation is overstated by 1.0% annually, then the 0.4% growth in average wages over the last 15 years would be adjusted to instead show a 1.4% annual growth over this period. However, since this degree of bias would imply an inflation overstatement of around 2% in the 1960s, the 2.8% annual real wage growth of that era would be revised up to over 4.8%. Thus, a slowdown of 2.4 percentage points (2.8 less 0.4) would be revised to a 3.4 percentage-point slowdown (4.8 less 1.4).

There are four causes usually cited for the CPI-U-X1's overstatement of inflation: (1) the CPI-U-X1 does not measure the impact of switches by consumers to goods that rise less rapidly in price; (2) the CPI-U-X1 does not pick up the effect of consumers switching to discount stores; (3) the quality adjustments in the CPI-U-X1 are inadequate; and (4) the CPI-U-X1 does not pick up new goods when they first appear on the market.

The first bias is a legitimate concern, but most research on the topic has produced very low estimates of its size, usually about 0.2% annually. The second source of bias is almost certainly much smaller, as can be seen with some crude numbers. At most, only about 20% of the index consists of goods that can be sold at discount stores (food, appliances, apparel, etc.). The bias can only apply to the portion of these sales that *switches* in a given year to a discount store, and that amount is unlikely to exceed 2% of the total sales in this category. This means that 0.4% of the whole index (2% of 20%) might switch in a given year. If the quality-adjusted savings on these sales is 10%, then the resulting upward bias would be 0.04%. Many of the CPI's critics have pegged this bias at 0.2-0.4% annually, perhaps 10 times higher than the true measure.

The same sort of exaggerations characterize claims about the other biases in the CPI-U-X1. For example, the CPI-U-X1 already includes extensive adjustments for quality change. It is possible that it does not fully pick up improvements in quality, but some research has actually indicated that it overstates improvement in quality in certain cases (Gordon 1990). It has also done a far better job of picking up price declines in new products in recent years. Since 1980, new products have been rotated into the index over a five-year period. Prior to that year, new products could only be introduced when the whole survey was revised, or about every 15 years.

There are also reasons to believe that the CPI-U-X1 understates the true increase in the cost of living in certain types of spending. Increased spending on lawyers' fees because people are more worried about being sued will not show up in the CPI-U-X1, unless the hourly fee actually increases. Similarly, an increase in health insurance premiums occurring across the board because a small portion of the population is getting sicker will not appear as an increase in the cost of living. The decline in the quality of retailing and other services as customers "help themselves" has also not been captured in the CPI-U-X1. There are enough factors such as these, which have not generally been examined, that make it far too early to conclude that the CPI-U-X1 overstates the true increase in the cost of living. Such a conclusion should await research that examines a multitude of items in which the CPI-U-X1 might show either too little or too much inflation. The existing literature, in contrast, has only examined a few items, primarily ones where an upward bias is suspected.

Some of the implications of a large CPI-U-X1 bias suggest an implausible economic history. For instance, if the CPI-U-X1 overstates inflation, then income growth has to have been much more rapid over the last 30-40 years than is generally believed. This implies that the *level* of income in, say, 1960 was far lower than is generally believed. For instance, consider the new economic history implied by extrapolations based on a bias of 1.0%. From this 1.0% annual bias, one can derive a "low bias" and "high bias" scenario for the 1960-95 period. Baker (1996b) derives a "low bias" estimate of 1.7% in the 1960s and 1970s and 1.4% in the 1980s, and a "high bias" estimate of 2.5% in the 1960s, 2.3% in the 1970s, and 1.7% in the 1980s.

If one accepts the Census Bureau's current estimate of the poverty threshold in 1995 for a four-person family ($15,570), then the poverty line in 1960 (in 1960 dollars) was between $5,406 and $6,429, depending upon the use of the high or low CPI-U-X1 bias. This amount is close to the median household income in 1960 of $5,939, implying that nearly half of all households were poor in 1960. In the early 1960s, however, there was a belief that there were only pockets of urban and rural poverty (consisting of those "left behind" as overall incomes grew rapidly) and no sense of widespread poverty.

Similarly, one can take the Census Bureau's original poverty threshold and determine its current value using a revised inflation index. The high bias (a 1.9% per year average error) and the low bias (1.5%) in the CPI-U-X1 imply a poverty threshold only 56.2% or 65.2% as high as the current one. This means that the "true" poverty line in 1995 should be either $10,120 or $8,750. If so, then rather than a 14.5% poverty rate (of persons), as reported by the Census Bureau, there would be a poverty rate of 6.9% or 8.3%, with poverty significantly declining over the 1979-94 period. This result also seem implausible.

Last, if the CPI-U-X1 overstates inflation, then the overall economy—gross domestic product—has also grown much more than previously thought. This implies that productivity growth has been far better than previously believed (because there is more output growth for the same increase in employment or hours worked). A revised economic history could still show a significant slowdown in productivity growth in recent (post-1973) years relative to earlier years, but productivity would appear to be rising at double its current 1% annual growth. If so, then all of the current concerns about a "savings crisis" or the need to raise investment or, in fact, any worry about whether future generations will live better and be able to afford the retirement of baby boomers is widely misplaced.

TABLE NOTES

FREQUENTLY CITED SOURCES

The following abbreviations are used throughout the table notes.

ERP—President of the United States. Economic Report of the President, 1996.

P-60 Series—U.S. Department of Commerce, Bureau of the Census, Series P-60, various dates.

SCB—U.S. Department of Commerce, Survey of Current Business, monthly.

Employment and Earnings—U.S. Department of Labor, Employment and Earnings, monthly and historical supplements.

NIPA—U.S. Department of Commerce, National Income and Product Accounts, revisions as of spring 1996.

INTRODUCTION

A *Productivity Growth and Capital Accumulation.* The productivity data are from the regular Bureau of Labor Statistics (BLS) series for the nonfarm business sector. Multifactor productivity (output per unit of combined capital and labor inputs) growth is based on U.S. Department of Labor (1996a, Table 2). Labor productivity (output per hour) is from U.S. Department of Labor (1996b, Table 2) for the recent data and *ERP* (Table B-45, 332) for earlier years.

 The series on equipment accumulation per worker is presented in Mishel and Bernstein (1996b) and is based on the Bureau of Economic Analysis (BEA) gross capital stock series per full-time equivalent worker (for the private sector). The data have been adjusted to reflect the shift from a fixed-weight 1987-dollars basis to a chain-weighted basis. The capital services per hour series is the BLS series used in the calculation of multifactor productivity. This series differs from the capital stock series because it takes into account the rate of depreciation during the year, a difference which suggests more capital used per worker in recent years as we have shifted to equipment with faster economic depreciation (e.g., computers). These data were provided by Larry Rosenblum at BLS.

B *Hourly Compensation, Skill, and Education Growth.* Compensation is measured in real terms using the CPI-U-X1, but with health insurance costs deflated by the health care–specific index (except for 1994-95, where only the CPI-U-X1 is used because a health care breakout is not available for compensation). Average years of schooling in the private sector is based on the data described in Appendix B. All of those coded at 18 years of school (the topcode) were set at 18.5 years of schooling. The nonfarm business sector series on years of schooling and labor composition ("labor skill") is from the BLS multifactor productivity database as presented in Tables 8 and 28 of the U.S. Department of Labor (1993b). Larry Rosenblum of BLS provided the updates.

CHAPTER I

1.1   *Median Family Income.* Census Homepage, Historical Income Tables, Families, Table F2.

1.2   *Annual Growth of Median Family Income.* Yearly dollar change is annual average of total dollar change in period from sources listed in Table 1.1. Family size-adjusted income is average family income of the middle fifth adjusted for family size using the official poverty equivalence scale. Unpublished Census Bureau Family Income Table F-14.

1.3   *Median Family Income by Age of Householder.* Census Homepage, Historical Income Tables, Families, Table F8.

1.4   *Median Family Income by Race/Ethnic Group.* Census Homepage, Historical Income Tables, Families, Table F2.

1.5   *Median Family Income by Family Type.* Census Homepage, Historical Income Tables, Families, Table F4a.

1.6   *Shares of Family Income Going to Various Income Groups and to Top 5%.* Census Homepage, Historical Income Tables, Families, Table F1. Alternative data for 1994 provided by Census Bureau; these data impose the same topcode as 1989 data; however, they also reflect changes due to newly administered computerized collection techniques.

1.7   *Real Family Income Growth by Income Group.* Census Homepage, Historical Income Tables, Families, Table F1.

1.8   *Changes in Family Income by Family Type.* Authors' analysis of Family Income Data Series; see Appendix A. Unlike later tables, individuals living alone are excluded from this analysis. Related subfamilies are included with primary families; unrelated subfamilies are treated separately. Families with negative incomes are excluded. Each fifth has 20% of persons, not 20% of families.

1.9   *Income Growth by Fifth and Among Top Fifth.* Authors' analysis of Family Income Data Series; see Appendix A. Individuals living alone are included in this and following tables. Families with negative incomes are excluded. Each fifth has 20% of persons, not 20% of families.

1.10   *Sources of Income Growth of Top Fifth.* Authors' analysis of Family Income Data Series; see Appendix A. Families with negative incomes are excluded. Each fifth has 20% of persons, not 20% of families.

1.11   *Change in Family Income Shares.* See note to Table 1.10.

1.12   *Distribution of Real Consumption Expenditure.* U.S. Department of Labor (1995e), Tables 2-16 and 2-19. The equivalence scale used is derived from the official poverty scales.

1.13   *Source of Family Income for Each Family Income Group.* See note to Table 1.10.

1.14   *Shares of Market-Based Personal Income by Type.* From *NIPA*, Table 2.1. The earliest data available are for 1959.

1.15   *Shares of Income by Type and Sector.* Based on *NIPA*, Table 1.15. The "Corporate and Business" sector includes "corporate," "other private business," and "rest of world." The "government/nonprofit" sector includes the household, government enterprise, and government sectors, all of which generate no capital income.

1.16   *Profit Rates at Business Cycle Peaks.* Methodology is presented in Baker (1996); actual values are from unpublished tabulations.

1.17   *Growth in Household Income, Actual and Fixed Demographic Weights.* Census Homepage, Historical Income Tables, Families, Table F4b. Three family types are used in the fixed-weight analysis: married couple, single male head, and single female head. Single-headed families include at least one other person.

1.18   *Detailed Effects of Demographic Changes on Median Household Income.* *P-60*, No. 183, pp. 20-22. The analysis from which these numbers are taken is based on a standardization technique in which cases from the March Current Population Survey (CPS) are reweighted to reflect composition shifts in a number of factors over time. The factors used in the table reflect four age groups, three racial groups, three education categories, and three household types. The difference between the actual and the reweighted change in the median reflect the compositional shifts.

1.19   *Growth in Income Inequality as Measured by the Gini Ratio.* Authors' analysis of Karoly and Burtless (1995), Table 4, p. 397, and Burtless (1995), Table 2.

1.20   *Distribution of Persons, Households, and Families by Income Level.* *P-60*, No. 189, pp. B-2, B-8. Data for 1994, relative income, provided by John McNeil of the Census Bureau.

1.21   *Distribution of Prime-Age Adults by Relative Income Level.* Unpublished tabulations by John McNeil of the Census Bureau. Family incomes for different size families are made comparable using equivalence scales as in Ruggles (1990). Single individuals are treated as one-person families.

1.22   *Changes in Incomes of Married-Couple Families with Children.* Authors' analysis of Family Income Data Series; see Appendix A. Families with negative incomes are excluded. Each fifth has 20% of persons, not 20% of families. At least one member of each married couple is "prime-age," i.e., 25-54.

1.23   *Husbands' and Wives' Hours of Work.* See note to Table 1.22.

1.24   *Change in the Hourly Wages of Husbands and Wives.* See note to Table 1.22. Unlike other measures of average hourly wages in this book (see Chapter 3), these hourly wages are "hour-weighted," i.e., they are the ratio of total quintile earnings for either husbands or wives divided by total quintile hours. Since workers with more hours tend to be higher paid, this measure usually produces levels higher than those measures that are "person weighted."

1.25   *Role of Higher Wives' Earnings and Hours on Family Income Growth (Married Couples with Children)*. See notes to Tables 1.22 and 1.24.

1.26   *Effect of Wives' Earnings on Income Shares Among Married Couples with Children.* See note to Table 1.22.

1.27   *Changes in Income Inequality of Married-Couple Families with Children.* See note to Table 1.22. The methodology used is identical to that of Cancian et al. (1993, 218-19). As these authors point out, the decomposition of the squared CV is sensitive to the order in which components are changed. Our qualitative results, however, are the same when the order is changed.

1.28   *Changes in Family Hours Worked by Family Type.* Authors' analysis of March Demographic Files. Income fifths use Census income and are defined separately for each family type. Related subfamilies are included with the primary family in the household, both for income and hours calculations.

1.29   *Median Income by Male 10-Year Birth Cohorts.* Authors' analysis of unpublished tabulations by U.S. Bureau of the Census.

1.30   *Income Mobility.* Unpublished tabulations of the Panel Study of Income Dynamics by Peter Gottschalk. Family heads are less than 62 years of age over the full period. Quintiles are constructed such that 20% of persons, not 20% of families, are in each group. Quintile cutoffs are income-to-needs ratio, using the official poverty lines, so these rates are adjusted for family-size differences.

1.31   *Income Mobility over the 1970s and 1980s.* See note to Table 1.30.

CHAPTER 2

2.1   *Federal vs. State and Local Tax Burdens. NIPA,* Tables 1.1, 3.2, and 3.3. From a BEA diskette, released 1996.

2.2   *Tax Revenues in OECD Countries, as a Percent of GDP.* OECD (1995), Table 3, p. 73.

2.3   *Average After-Tax Family Income Growth.* Unpublished CBO tables, June 23, 26, 1995.

2.4   *Shares of After-Tax Income for All Families.* Unpublished CBO tables, June 23, 26, 1995.

2.5   *The Effects of Tax and Income Changes on After-Tax Income Shares.* Effective tax rates were applied to average before-tax incomes, and the resulting average after-tax incomes were multiplied by the number of families in each group to get total after-tax incomes per group. These group totals were converted to shares of the sum for all groups. Total income for all families necessarily excludes families with zero or negative incomes; in Table 2.4, however, such families were included. Figures for 1979 and 1989 are drawn from U.S. House of Representatives (1991, 67) and unpublished data supplied by Frank Sammartino of CBO. Figures for 1996, which are based on CBO income projections, are from unpublished CBO tables, June 23, 26, 1995.

2.6 *Effect of 1993 Tax Law on 1996 Tax Liabilities and Rates.* Pre- and post-OBRA93 effective tax rates are from unpublished data supplied by Frank Sammartino of CBO. Projected 1996 income from unpublished CBO tables, June 26, 1995.

2.7 *Effective Federal Tax Rates.* Data for 1977-89 from U.S. House of Representatives (1991, 73) and unpublished data supplied by Frank Sammartino of CBO. Data for 1992 and projections for 1996 from unpublished CBO tables, June 26, 1995.

2.8 *Estimated Effective Federal Tax Rates on 1996 Income Under Prevailing Tax Law.* Unpublished analysis supplied by Citizens for Tax Justice, March 1996.

2.9 *Effective Federal Tax Rate for a Family of Four with One Earner.* Department of Treasury (1995), Table 4.

2.10 *Effect of Federal Tax Changes on Family Tax Payments.* Effective federal tax rates from Table 2.8 have been applied to inflation-adjusted pre-tax income from unpublished CBO tables, June 26, 1995.

2.11 *Effective Tax Rates for Selected Federal Taxes.* Unpublished CBO tables, June 26, 1995.

2.12 *Changes in Effective Federal Taxes.* See note to Table 2.11.

2.13 *Taxed and Untaxed Corporate Profits.* NIPA, Tables 1.1 and 1.16. Taxes include federal, state, and local combined. Actual profits are taxed profits plus net interest (interest paid minus interest received) and the difference between the allowance for inventory investment and capital depreciation allowed in the tax code, on the one hand, and actual inventory investment and capital depreciation, on the other. The idea for this analysis is based on an unpublished paper by Thomas Karier. Only nonfinancial corporations are included because banks do not pay net interest—they *receive* net interest.

2.14 *Corporate Profits Tax Rates.* NIPA, Tables 1.1 and 1.16.

2.15 *Total State and Local Taxes in 1991 (Effective Rates) as Shares of Income for Families of Four.* Citizens for Tax Justice (1991, 18). Assumptions about the distribution of tax incidence (for example, half the property tax paid on rental units is allocated to owners and half to renters) are discussed in the study on pp. 70-72.

2.16 *Types of Federal vs. State and Local Taxes, as a Percent of Revenue at Each Level.* NIPA, Tables 3.2 and 3.3.

2.17 *Types of Taxes as a Percent of GDP.* NIPA, Tables 1.1, 3.2, and 3.3.

CHAPTER 3

3.1 *Trends in Average Wages and Average Hours.* The 1967-73 and 1973-79 trends are from unpublished tabulations provided by Kevin Murphy from an update of Murphy and Welch (1989). These data are based on the March CPS files. Hours of work were derived from differences between annual, weekly, and hourly wage trends. The Murphy and Welch data include self-employment as well as wage and salary workers. The trends from 1979 on are based on the authors' tabulations of March CPS files using a series on annual, weekly, and hourly wages for wage and salary workers. The Murphy data were bridged to the 1979 levels. Productivity data are from *ERP* (1996), Table B-45, p. 332, for the nonfarm business sector.

3.2 *Growth of Average Hourly Wages, Benefits, and Compensation.* These data are computed from *NIPA* data on hours worked and compensation, wages, other labor income, group health insurance, and social insurance for the public and private sectors. These data were inflation-adjusted by the *NIPA* Personal Consumption Expenditure (PCE, chain-weighted) index, with health adjusted by the PCE medical care index.

3.3 *Growth in Private-Sector Average Hourly Wages, Benefits, and Compensation.* Based on employment cost levels from the BLS Employment Cost Index series for March 1987 to March 1995 for private-sector workers (see 1995 data in U.S. Department of Labor (1995d). We categorize pay differently than BLS, putting all wage-related items (including paid leave) into the hourly wage. Benefits, in our definition, include only payroll taxes, pensions, insurance, and "other" benefits. It is important to use the current-weighted series rather than the fixed-weighted series because composition shifts have a large effect, as we show in Table 3.29. Employer costs for insurance are deflated by the medical care component of the CPI. All other pay is deflated by the CPI-U-X1 for "all items." Inflation is measured for the first quarter of each year.

3.4 *Production and Nonsupervisory Workers.* Data from 1959 to 1995 from ERP (1996), Table B-43, p. 330. Data for 1947, Supplement to *Employment and Earnings* (March 1985, 5).

3.5 *Changes in Hourly Wages by Occupation.* Based on analysis of CPS wage data described in Appendix B.

3.6 *Wages for All Workers by Wage Percentile.* Based on analysis of CPS wage data described in Appendix B.

3.7 *Wages for Male Workers by Wage Percentile.* Based on analysis of CPS wage data described in Appendix B.

3.8 *Wages for Female Workers by Wage Percentile.* Based on analysis of CPS wage data described in Appendix B.

3.9 *Changes in the Gender Wage Differential.* Based on data from Tables 3.7 and 3.8.

3.10 *Distribution of Total Employment by Wage Level.* Based on analysis of CPS wage data described in Appendix B. The poverty-level wage was defined as the four-person poverty threshold in 1994 divided by 2,080 hours and deflated by CPI-U-X1 to obtain levels for other years. We calculated more intervals than we show but aggregated for simplicity of presentation (no trends were lost).

3.11 *Distribution of White Employment by Wage Level.* See note to Table 3.10. These are non-Hispanic whites.

3.12 *Distribution of Black Employment by Wage Level.* See note to Table 3.10. These are non-Hispanic blacks.

3.13 *Distribution of Hispanic Employment by Wage Level.* See note to Table 3.10. Hispanics may be of any race.

3.14 *Growth of Specific Fringe Benefits.* Based on *NIPA* data described in note to Table 3.2.

3.15 *Change in Private-Sector Employer-Provided Health Insurance Coverage.* Based on tabulations of the Employee Benefit Supplements to the May 1979, May 1988, and April 1993 CPS provided by Dan Beller and Richard Hinz of the U.S. Department of Labor. The sample includes wage and salary workers age 18-64 in the private sector who worked at least 20 hours weekly and for at least 26 weeks.

3.16 *Change in Private-Sector Employer-Provided Pension Coverage.* See note to Table 3.15.

3.17 *Dimensions of Wage Inequality.* All of the data are based on analyses of the ORG CPS data described in Appendix B. The measures of total wage inequality are natural logs of wage ratios computed from Tables 3.6 and 3.7. The education and experience differentials are estimated from regressions of the log of hourly wages on education categorical variables (high school omitted), experience as a quartic, marital status, race and region (4). The college–high school premium is simply the coefficient on "college," a category representing 16 years of schooling. The experience differentials are the differences in the value of experience (calculated from the coefficients of the quartic specification) evaluated at 5, 15, and 30 years.

The changes in within-group wage inequality reflect the growth of the "residual wage" for wage earners at the 90th, 50th, and 10th percentiles. The "residual wage" was computed as the difference between the actual and predicted wage, with the predicted wage based on the model described above. The 90th, 50th, and 10th percentile worker was approximated by workers in the following percentile wage ranges: 85-94, 45-54, 5-14. The procedure forces the growth of within-group wage inequality to reflect the experiences of high-, middle-, and low-wage workers. Other procedures measure the growth of within-group wage inequality, but a high "residual" wage earner could be a low-, middle-, or high-wage earner.

3.18 *Change in Real Hourly Wage by Education.* Based on tabulations of CPS wage data described in Appendix B. The group with 17 years of schooling (college plus one) is omitted for simplicity of presentation. Since the CPS questions on educational attainment shifted in 1992, it was necessary to impute years of schooling in the data for 1992 and more recent years (see Appendix B for details). The procedure for estimating the college–high school wage premium is described in the note to Table 3.17. The shares of the workforce by education category are tabulated from the same data. We do not present 1995 data because we believe our imputations of years of schooling are not reliable for "quantity" trends.

3.19 *Change in Real Hourly Wage for Men by Education.* See note to Table 3.18.

3.20 *Change in Real Hourly Wage for Women by Education.* See note to Table 3.18.

3.21 *Educational Attainment of Workforce.* Based on analysis of CPS wage earners. The data are described in Appendix B.

3.22 *Hourly Wages by Education and Experience.* Based on analysis of CPS wage data described in Appendix B.

3.23 *Hourly Wages by Decile Within Education Groups.* Based on analysis of CPS wage data described in Appendix B.

3.24 *Decomposing the Change in Overall Wage Inequality Among Men.* All of the data are from the ORG CPS data sample described in Appendix B. The "overall" distribution in the first row of each panel is the raw wage data from the standard sample. The distribution for the "returns to skill" row in each panel is constructed in two stages. First, we fit a standard, human-capital regression equation (described in the note to Table 3.17) to the data for each year, saving the estimated coefficients from the regression and each individual's residual. Second, we calculated what each individual's wage would have been if he or she had the same characteristics (including residual wage) but the coefficients for education and experience from an earlier year. The figures in the "other" row of each panel are simply the difference between the changes in the overall and the returns-to-skill distribution.

3.25 *Decomposing the Change in Overall Wage Inequality Among Women.* See note to Table 3.24.

3.26 *Test Scores by Percentile.* Unpublished tabulations of microdata from the National Assessment of Educational Progress (NAEP), provided by Elizabeth Greenberg.

3.27 *Employment Growth by Sector.* Employment data from *Employment and Earnings* (March 1996), Table B-1, p. 51, and Table B-12, p. 72. Hourly compensation data from BLS Employment Cost Levels data for 1993. See note to Table 3.3.

3.28 *Changes in Employment Share by Sector.* Based on data in Table 3.27.

3.29 *Effect of Structural Employment Shifts on Pay Levels.* This comparison is based on two computations of pay levels in each of March 1989 and March 1995. One is the current weighted pay levels from the Employment Cost Index Levels data. See note to Table 3.3. The other is the fixed-weighted pay levels from the underlying unpublished data used to compute quarterly changes in hourly wages and compensation for the Employment Cost Index, which is based on 1980 Census weights in 1989 and 1990 Census weights in 1995. The major difference between the pay levels in these computations is the weighting scheme. Another difference arises because the data with current weights are based on an employer survey, while the Census data in 1980 and 1990 are based on a household survey; thus the difference in the weighted and unweighted pay levels also incorporates differences in how households and employers classify the workforce by occupation. Household data yield a larger share of executives, managers, and sales workers and a lesser share of administrative and service workers. We correct for this by calculating the effect of the difference between household (CPS) data and employer (OES) data on pay levels in 1990 and 1994 using a shift-share analysis of major occupations, excluding fishing and forestry. Pay levels are wage or compensation from the ECI for 1990. The CPS household employment data are from *Employment and Earnings* (January 1991), Table 21, p. 184, and *Employment and Earnings* (January 1995), Table 10, p. 174. The OES employer data are from Silvestri and Lukasiewic (1991), Table 1, p. 65, and Silvestri (1995), Table 1, p. 61. The shift-share analysis provides a "correction factor," reflecting the percent by which CPS-weighted occupation data leads to wages, benefits, and compensation exceeding that of OES data. The current-weight ECI is reduced by this "correction factor" and compared to the fixed-weight levels, the difference being the effect of shifts in employment composition.

3.30 *The Effect of Industry Shifts on the Growth of the College–High School Differential.* The industry shift effect is calculated from estimated college–high school wage differentials using the model described in the note to Table 3.17 ("industry composition varies") and a model that adds a set of industry controls (12), which gives "industry composition fixed." The difference in the growth of these estimates is the industry shift effect.

3.31 *Final and Intermediate Manufacturing Imports.* Feenstra and Hanson (1996), Table 1, p. 241.

3.32 *Impact of Foreign Trade on Manufacturing Employment.* Sachs and Shatz (1994), Table 13, p. 29.

3.33 *Trade with Low-Wage Countries and Change in Manufacturing Employment Share for G-7 Countries.* Saeger (1995), Table 7.

3.34 *Effect of Changes in Prices of Internationally Traded Manufactured Goods on Wage Inequality.* Schmitt and Mishel (1996), Table 9.

3.35 *Legal Immigrant Flow to the United States.* Borjas (1994), Table 1, p. 1668.

3.36 *Educational Attainment of Immigrant and Native Men.* Borjas (1994), Table 4, p. 1676.

3.37 *Union Wage and Benefit Premium.* Employment Cost Index pay level data in U.S. Department of Labor (1995d), Table 13.

3.38 *Union Wage Premium by Demographic Group.* Regression estimates of union wage differentials using CPS data for 1991. See Appendix B for description of the data. The data in the table are the coefficients on union membership in a model with controls for education, experience, experience squared, marital status, marital status, region, industry and occupation, and race/ethnicity and gender where appropriate. Percent union is percent of group "represented by unions" from Table 57 of *Employment and Earnings* (January 1992).

3.39 *Effect of Deunionization on Male Occupation and Education Differentials.* From Freeman (1991), Table 2.

3.40 *Effect of Unions on Wages, by Wage Fifth.* From Card (1991), Table 8. The effect of deunionization is the change in union coverage times the union wage premium.

3.41 *Effect of Deunionization on Male Wage Inequality.* From Card (1991), Table 9; Freeman (1991), Table 6; and Dinardo, Fortin, and Lemieux (1994), Table 4.

3.42 *Value of the Minimum Wage.* Historical values of minimum wage from Shapiro (1987, 19). Minimum wage in 2000 based on the CBO (August 1995) projection of inflation from 1995 to 2000 (3.4%, 3.4%, 3.3%, 3.2%, 3.2%).

3.43 *Characteristics of Minimum-Wage and Other Wage Earners.* Mishel, Bernstein, and Rasell (1995), Table 1.

3.44 *Impact of New Minimum Wage on Key Wage Differentials.* Mishel, Bernstein, and Rasell (1995), Table 3.

3.45 *Distribution of Minimum-Wage and Other Earners by Family Income Fifth.* Mishel, Bernstein, and Rasell (1995), Tables 5 and 6.

3.46　*Distribution of Minimum-Wage Earners by Age and Income Fifth.* Mishel, Bernstein, and Rasell (1995), Table 7.

3.47　*The Impact of Labor-Market Institutions on Wage Differentials.* Fortin and Lemieux (1996), Table 1.

3.48　*Possible Empirical Scenarios and Demand Acceleration.* This table appears in Mishel and Bernstein (1996b), Table 4.

3.49　*Technology Indicators.* This table appears in the longer unpublished version of Mishel and Bernstein (1996a), Table 6.

3.50　*Technology Impact on Annual Growth in Education Shares.* This table appears in the longer unpublished version of Mishel and Bernstein (1996a), Table 11.

3.51　*Technology Impact on Annual Change in Wage Quantities.* The results for men are from Mishel and Bernstein (1996a), Table 2. The results for women appear in the longer unpublished version of Mishel and Bernstein (1996a), Table 14.

3.52　*Growth of CEO Pay in Major U.S. Companies.* The data are from Pearl Meyer & Partners Inc., originally published in the April 11, 1996, *Wall Street Journal.* The compensation of the average worker was estimated using the annual salary data from Pearl Meyer & Partners Inc. and the compensation/wage ratio for the economy (see note to Table 3.2).

3.53　*CEO Pay in Advanced Countries.* Total CEO compensation in 1995 from Towers Perrin (1996). The ratio of CEO to production-worker pay based on BLS data on production-worker compensation in manufacturing in 1994 (provided by Jan Kmitch) with 2000 annual hours assumed.

3.54　*Changes in Educational Attainment Among 25- to 34-Year-Olds by Race and Gender.* Update of Bernstein (1995), Table A, using data described in Appendix B.

3.55　*National Assessment of Educational Progress (NAEP) Scores by Race, 17-Year-Olds.* Greenberg's analysis of NAEP data as presented in Bernstein (1995), Tables B, C, and D.

3.56　*Change in Hourly Wages Among 25- to 34-Year-Olds by Race and Gender.* Update of Bernstein (1995), Table F, using data described in Appendix B.

3.57　*Demand Shifts: Changes in Pay and Education Requirements.* Update of an analysis presented in Mishel and Teixeira (1991), Tables 2 and 7. It is based on a shift-share analysis of the employment distribution of 13 major occupations and the pay and education characteristics of these occupations. The education levels are from tabulations of the CPS data for 1995, as described in Appendix B. Wage levels are those prevailing over the 1979-93 period, and compensation is based on computing an occupation-specific compensation/wage ratio from ECI levels data and applying it to wages tabulated from the CPS.

3.58　*Future Labor Supply Trends.* Immigration was projected by extrapolating the 1980-88 trends in immigrant employment share of Borjas et al. (1991) to 1992. Data from Census *P-25* Series, No 1104, Table 1 were used to project the net immigrant (ages 16-64) increase to 2005 (13 times annual growth). The BLS projections of labor-force participation in 1998 were used to translate population growth into labor-force growth.

This estimate was reduced to account for the aging of the immigrant population beyond age 64, using Tables C-3 and C-4. The Census and BLS projections data for medium and high were matched.

Labor-force median age from Fullerton (1995), Table 12. Historical data on college degrees awarded are from Table 28, p. 61, of U.S. Department of Education (1996) and Table 2.28, p. 234, of U.S. Department of Education (1991). The projected college degrees awarded are the middle and high projections from Table 28, p. 61, of Department of Education (1996). Past employment is civilian employment (20 years or more) from Table B-32, p. 318, of *ERP* (1996), and future employment is from Fullerton (1995), Table 10, p. 39. The college enrollment rate is the average of those age 18-24 using the middle alternative projection for 2006 from Table A 1.3 of Department of Education (1996). The college-age population projection is the number of 18- to 24-year-olds from Day (1996), Table F. The ratio of imports and exports to GDP is from Saunders (1995), Table 2. Union coverage and minimum-wage trends are the authors' best judgment. The historical data on minimum-wage and union coverage are the same as in Table 4.2 and Figure 30.

3.59   *Future Trade and Institutional Factors.* Goods share of employment from Franklin (1995), Table 1. The trade share of GDP, or the ratio of imports and exports to GDP, from Saunders (1995), Table 2. Union coverage and minimum-wage trends are the authors' best judgment. The historical data on minimum-wage and union coverage are from Table 4.2 and Figure 30.

CHAPTER 4

4.1   *Unemployment Rates.* Data for years before 1995 are from U.S. Department of Labor (1988), Table A-24, pp. 404-61, and BLS website, May 8, 1996. Data for 1995 are from *Employment and Earnings*, January 1996, Tables 1-4, pp. 158-63.

4.2   *Rates of Underemployment.* Civilian labor force and unemployed from *Employment and Earnings* (January 1996), Table 1, p. 158. "Discouraged" workers are workers not in the labor force who wanted a job, had searched for work in the previous year, were available to work, but were not actively searching for work because of "discouragement over job prospects." "Other marginally attached" workers are in identical circumstances, but are not actively searching for work for reasons other than discouragement, including family responsibilities, school or training commitments, or ill health or disabilities. The source for both figures is *Employment and Earnings* (January 1996), Table 35, p. 202. "Involuntary part-time" workers cite "economic reasons" for working fewer than 35 hours per week (*Employment and Earnings*, January 1996, Table 20, p. 188).

4.3   *Effect of 1% Higher Unemployment Rate on Weeks Unemployed and Employed and on Annual Earnings.* Analysis of Tables 5 and 7 in Blank and Card (1993). These tables are slightly mismatched because the coefficients in Table 7 are for the 1973-91 period, while the means in Table 5 are for the 1967-91 period.

4.4 *Proportion of the Unemployed Who Receive Some Unemployment Insurance Payment.* Nichols and Shapiro (1995), Table 1, p. 7.

4.5 *Employment Growth.* Data for hours of work and full-time equivalent employment are from *NIPA,* Tables 6.5C and 6.9C. Nonfarm payroll, civilian employment, working-age population, and the labor-force participation rate are from *Employment and Earnings* (January 1996), Table 1, p. 158, and Table B-1, p. 46.

4.6 *Employment Stability for Men.* Rose (1995), Table 2, p.10.

4.7 *Employment Stability and Earnings for Men.* Rose (1995), Table 8, p. 11.

4.8 *Share of Employed Workers in Job for 10 Years or More.* Farber (1995), Table A6.

4.9 *Rate of Job Loss, by Gender and Reason.* Farber (1996), Appendix Table 1. Unemployment rates from *Employment and Earnings* (January 1996), Table 2, p. 159.

4.10 *Rate of Job Loss, by Occupation and Reason.* Farber (1996), Appendix Table 4. Unemployment rates from *Employment and Earnings* (January 1996), Table 1, p. 158.

4.11 *Post-Displacement Earnings Loss.* Farber (1996), Tables 16 and 17.

4.12 *Health Insurance Coverage After Job Loss.* Gardener (1995), Table 6, p. 52.

4.13 *Nonagricultural Employment, by Full-Time and Part-Time Status. Employment and Earnings* (January 1996), Table 21, p. 189.

4.14 *Wage Differences Between Part-Time and Full-Time Workers by Gender and Selected Occupations.* From analysis of CPS wage data as described in Appendix B.

4.15 *Differences in Fringe Benefits for Full-Time and Part-Time Workers.* Data are for private-sector wage and salary workers. Sponsorship refers to employers providing plans for some or all of their employees; coverage refers to worker participation in a plan. U.S. Department of Labor, Pension and Welfare Benefits Administration (1994), Tables A2, A3, and B1.

4.16 *Growth of Multiple Jobholding, All Workers.* All figures are from May of the given year. Data for 1973 and 1989 are from U.S. Department of Labor (1989); 1979 are from Sekscenski (1980); 1985 from Stinson (1986); and 1995 from *Employment and Earnings* (June 1995), Table A-35, p. 67.

4.17 *Growth of Multiple Jobholding, by Gender.* See note to Table 4.16.

4.18 *Distribution of Multiple Jobholders Experiencing Economic Hardship.* See note to Table 4.16.

4.19 *Hours Worked by Multiple Jobholders, by Gender.* Unpublished BLS Table 40, "Multiple jobholders by actual hours worked at all jobs during the reference week, class of worker, jobs, sex, race, Hispanic origin, and age, Annual Average 1995 (based on CPS)," supplied by John Stinson, BLS, May 13, 1996.

4.20 *The Use of Various Types of Contingent Labor.* The two surveys are a Conference Board survey conducted in 1989 and a Bureau of National Affairs survey conducted in 1986. For details see Carre (1992).

4.21 *Growth in Employment in Personnel-Services Industry.* Data for SIC 736, personnel supply services, from BLS website, May 13, 1996.

4.22   *Growth in Employment in Temporary-Help Industry.* Data for SIC 7363, help supply services, from BLS website, May 13, 1996.

4.23   *Elements of the Marginal Workforce.* The figure in row 1 of the table is from U.S. Department of Labor (1995b), Table A, p. 2, Estimate 3, and Table 1. The figures in rows 2 to 5 are from Table B, p. 3, and Table 5.

4.24   *Median Usual Weekly Earnings of Contingent and Alternative Workers.* Data are taken from unpublished BLS tables AE13, CE13.

4.25   *Health Insurance Coverage by Employment Status.* U.S. Department of Labor (1995b), Table 9.

4.26   *Growth of Self-Employment. Employment and Earnings* (January 1996), Table 15, p. 180.

4.27   *Wages and Benefits, Self-Employed versus Wage and Salary Employment.* Devine (1994), Tables 4, 9, and 11.

CHAPTER 5

5.1   *Growth of Household Wealth.* Assets and debts are year-end outstanding values from balance sheet data for households, personal trusts, and nonprofit organizations from Board of Governors (1995), pp. 20-25, for 1949-94. Nonprofit organizations, a small component judging from the breakout on tangible assets, were included because the Federal Reserve System does not give breakout for financial assets. Data were converted to real dollars using the CPI-U-X1 index. Growth rates in the table are assets net of debt per adult. Number of adults is from *ERP* (1996), Table B-30.

5.2   *Distribution of Income and Wealth.* From 1989 Survey of Consumer Finance (SCF) tabulations in Wolff (1994), Table 2. Net financial assets breakdown from telephone conversation with Wolff.

5.3   *Percent of Total Assets Held by Wealth Class.* 1989 SCF data from Wolff (1994), Table 12. 1992 SCF data from Wolff (1996), Table 6.

5.4   *Share of Total Household Wealth Held by Richest 1% of Individuals.* From Wolff (1992), Table 1.

5.5   *Changes in the Distribution of Wealth.* Data for 1983, 1989, and 1992 from Wolff (1996), Table 8. Data for 1962 from Wolff (1994), Tables 3 and 4.

5.6   *Change in Wealth by Wealth Class.* See note to Table 5.5.

5.7   *Change in Wealth by Income Class.* From Census Bureau Survey of Income and Program Participation (SIPP) data presented in Eargle (1990), Table B, p.3, and Eller and Fraser (1995), Table B, p. 5.

5.8   *Change in Median Household Wealth by Age and Income Fifth.* Eargle (1990), Tables E and F, pp. 6-7; Eller and Fraser (1995), Table D, p.7.

5.9   *Stock Ownership.* Update of Poterba and Samwick (1995), Table 7 using the new weights provided by the Federal Reserve Board since the original paper.

5.10   *Concentration of Stock Ownership*. Update of Poterba and Samwick (1995), Table 10. See note to Table 5.9.

5.11   *Ownership of Stock and IRA/Keogh Accounts*. Eargle (1990), Table C, p. 4, and Eller and Fraser (1995), Table C, p. 6.

5.12   *Household Debt Burden*. Asset and debt data from Federal Reserve Board balance sheet data (see note to Table 5.1). Personal income data from *ERP* (1996), Table B-25, p. 308. Debt service payment burdens from unpublished series prepared by the New York Federal Reserve Board.

CHAPTER 6

6.1   *Percent and Number of Persons in Poverty, Actual and Predicted Values*. Actual poverty rates are from Census Homepage, Historical Poverty Tables, Persons, Table 2. Predicted rates are based on poverty-rate model described in Blank (1991). Variables in the model include male unemployment, growth in the CPI, the ratio of the poverty line to mean household income, the ratio of transfers to GNP, and the poverty rate, lagged one year. Fitted values are used through 1983; forecasted values are used from 1984 forward. Poverty rates and levels for 1989 reflect revised demographic weights.

6.2   *1992 Poverty Rates Under Official and Alternative Measures*. Table 5-8, National Research Council (1995). Proposed measure "alternative 1" is used, which employs a scale economy factor of 0.75. This factor is used to construct equivalence scales for families of different sizes. The "alternative 2" scale factor, 0.65, leads to a higher overall poverty rate (19.0%) than alternative 1. Note also that NRC's official measure of poverty for 1992 does not reflect the Census update using revised demographic weights.

6.3   *Demographic Characteristics of Poor Persons Under Alternative Definitions*. Tables 5-6 and 5-8, National Research Council (1995). See note to Table 6.2.

6.4   *Poverty Rates When (Nonmedical) Noncash Benefits Are Included*. 1979 and 1989: U.S. House of Representatives (1993), p. 132; 1994: *P60*, No. 189, Table M.

6.5   *Percent of Persons with Low Relative Income, by Race, Adjusted for Family Size*. U.S. Bureau of the Census (1991) and unpublished data provided by Jack McNeil. Family incomes for different size families are made comparable using equivalence scales as in Ruggles (1990). Single individuals are treated as one-person families.

6.6   *Poverty Gap: Aggregate and Mean*. Center on Budget and Policy Priorities (1996, 41).

6.7   *Poor Persons Below 50% of Poverty Level*. Center on Budget and Policy Priorities (1996, 45).

6.8   *Distribution of Poverty Spells for Persons Entering Poverty and for Multiple Spells*. Stevens (1995), Table 2.

6.9   *Percent of Children in Poverty by Number of Years of Childhood Poverty*. U.S. Department of Health and Human Services (1996), Table ES 1.5, 1970-72 cohort. Based on analysis of the Panel Study of Income Dynamics by Greg Duncan.

6.10   *Events Leading to Poverty Spells.* Stevens (1993). Stevens' exit probabilities were converted to percent of persons completing spells using formula from Bane and Ellwood (1986, 10).

6.11   *Trends in Welfare Dependency Among Women, Age 15-44.* Gottschalk and Moffitt (1994, 39).

6.12   *Persons in Poverty, by Race/Ethnicity.* Census Homepage, Historical Poverty Tables, Persons, Table 3.

6.13   *Percent of Children in Poverty, by Race.* Center on Budget and Policy Priorities (1996, 21, 26).

6.14   *Poverty Rates of Families with Children, by Education Level of Family Head.* Sum, Fogg, and Fogg (1994, 58).

6.15   *High-Risk Factors for Poverty, Females 25 and Over.* Unpublished Census tabulation, 1994, Poverty Table 11, p. 70.

6.16   *Changing Family Structure and Poverty.* Census Homepage, Historical Poverty Tables, Persons, Table 2. Entries for 1989 reflect revised Census counts using updated demographic weights, provided by Census Income and Poverty Division.

6.17   *Changes in Family Structure and Poverty.* See note to Table 6.16. This conventional shift-share analysis assigns the increase in poverty rates to "between" and "within" factors. To the extent that either of these factors is endogenous to poverty changes, e.g., if increasing poverty rates *led* to family structure changes, this simple decomposition will fail to account for such behavioral changes. A small interaction effect between family structure and "other," which was never greater than 0.005, was divided evenly between these two categories. This procedure does not affect the results.

6.18   *Changes in Demographic Structure and Poverty for Families with Children.* Underlying data are from Sum, Fogg, and Fogg (1994, 64-65), and unpublished data provided by authors. This is a conventional shift share analysis with the effect of interactions divided evenly across between- and within-group changes. See note to Table 6.17 for technical points.

6.19   *Poverty Rates for Female-Headed Families.* Center on Budget and Policy Priorities (1996, 15).

6.20   *Poor Female-Headed Families, by Race.* Authors' analysis of Center on Budget and Policy Priorities (1996, 15).

6.21   *Poverty Rates in Female-Headed Families: Contributions to Growth.* Data from prior two sources. Hispanics could not be treated separately since they are combined by Census in each racial category. Thus, the "other" category represents all female-headed families headed by a woman who identified her race as neither white nor black.

6.22   *Marital Status of Female Heads of Households.* Women without dependents are not included. Data for 1973 and 1979 are for women age 14 and over, while 1989 and 1994 are restricted to women age 15 and over. 1973 numbers are from U.S. Department of Commerce, *P-20*, No. 255, pp. 25-26; 1979 data are from U.S. Department of Commerce, *P-20*, No. 349, pp. 31-32; 1989 data are from U.S. Department of Commerce, *P-20*, No. 445, p. 55; 1994 data are from U.S. Department of Commerce, *P-20*, No. 483, p. 93.

6.23 *Expected Lifetime Births, by Marital Status and Race.* Jencks (1991, 86). Updated using *Vital Statistics of the United States, Vol. 1* (1989), Tables 1-1, 1-9, and 1-76, and *Advance Report of Final Natality Statistics, 1990-93.* From 1980 forward, race is determined by race of mother; prior to 1980, race was determined by race of child.

6.24 *Poverty-Reducing Effects of Taxes and Transfers. P-60*, No. 182-RD and No. 189, p. 13.

6.25 *AFDC Participation Rates Among Female Heads of Families with Children.* Wells and Sandefur (1996), Table 1.

6.26 *Share of Workers Earning Poverty-Level Wages.* Based on analysis of CPS wage data as described in Appendix B. For wage cutoff levels, see Table 3.10.

6.27 *Wage Trends Relevant to the Poor and Near-Poor.* Based on analysis of CPS wage data as described in Appendix B.

6.28 *Work Experience of the Poor.* 1979: *P-60,* No. 130, p. 58; 1989: *P-60,* No. 168, p. 65; 1989: *P-60,* No. 185, p. 89; 1994: unpublished Census tabulation, Poverty Table 15, p. 52.

6.29 *Annual Average Hours Worked by Family Type in Bottom Two-Fifths.* Authors' analysis of various March Demographic Files. Income fifths use Census income and are defined separately for each family type. Related subfamilies are included with the primary family in the household, both for income and hours calculations.

CHAPTER 7

7.1 *Median Family Income by Region.* Census Homepage, Historical Income Tables, Families, Table F3.

7.2 *Median Income for Four-Person Families, by State.* Census Homepage, Historical Income Tables (no number), address: 4person.html.

7.3 *Percent of Persons in Families with Low, Middle, and High Relative Incomes, by Division.* Unpublished tabulations provided by Jack McNeil of the Census Bureau. Family incomes for different size families are made comparable using equivalence scales as in Ruggles (1990). Single individuals are treated as one-person families.

7.4 *Earnings Ratios by Region, Year-Round, Full-Time Workers, 16 Years and Older.* Unpublished tabulations provided by Jack McNeil of the Census Bureau. Low earnings are defined as annual earnings that fall below the official poverty level for a family of four, adjusted by the CPI-U-X1.

7.5 *Nonfarm Payroll Employment, by State.* BLS Homepage, Nonfarm Payroll Employment.

7.6 *Unemployment Rates, by State.* BLS Homepage, Statistics from the Household Survey, Unemployment by State.

7.7 *Average Weekly Earnings, by State.* Data from the BLS ES-202 Survey, Census of Establishments Covered by Unemployment Insurance, provided by the BLS.

7.8   *Median Hourly Wages, All Workers, by State.* Based on analysis of CPS wage data as described in Appendix B.

7.9   *Low Hourly Wages, All Workers, by State.* Based on analysis of CPS wage data as described in Appendix B.

7.10   *Workers at or Near the Minimum Wage ($4.25-$5.14).* Based on analysis of CPS wage data as described in Appendix B.

7.11   *Percent of Persons in Poverty, by Region.* Census Homepage, Historical Poverty Tables, Persons, Table 9.

7.12   *Recent Poverty Rates by Division. P-60,* various years: 1988: No. 168, p. 315; 1989: No. 168, p. 149; 1990: No. 175, p. 154; No. 181, p. 140; all other years provided by Census Bureau.

7.13   *Two-Year Averaged Poverty Rates, by State.* Census Homepage, Historical Poverty Tables, Persons, Table 19, and *P60,* No. 189, p. xix. Two-year averages are used to reduce statistical error induced by the small samples in some states.

7.14   *Poverty Rates by Metro/Nonmetro Areas.* Census Homepage, Historical Poverty Tables, Persons, Table 8.

7.15   *Change in Poverty Rates by Metro/Nonmetro Areas Due to Population and Within-Residence Shifts.* Census Homepage, Historical Poverty Tables, Persons, Table 8. This conventional shift-share analysis assigns the increase in poverty rates to "between" and "within" factors. To the extent that either of these factors is endogenous to poverty changes, e.g., if increasing poverty rates led to less inter-area mobility, this simple decomposition will fail to account for such behavioral changes.

CHAPTER 8

8.1   *Per Capita GDP Growth, Broken Down into Growth of Employment and Productivity.* GDP is gross domestic product, the total of all money received for goods and services produced in the economy in a single year. GDP per capita is commonly used when comparing living standards across countries or from one year to the next within the same country. GDP differs slightly from gross national product (GNP), which also includes net investment income from abroad. Real gross domestic product per head, at the price levels and exchange rates of 1990 (U.S. dollars), is taken from OECD (1996c), Table 20, p. 132. The employment-population ratio (approximating U.S. concepts) for 1979 comes from U.S. Department of Labor, *Monthly Labor Review,* January 1990, Table 49, p.125; for 1989 and 1994 from U.S. Department of Labor, *Monthly Labor Review,* April 1996, Table 47, p. 41. Averages are weighted by the 1990 population from individual country tables in the World Bank (1994). German data are not available since the GDP data from the OECD have been recalculated to include both former East and West Germany, while the consistent employment numbers from the Department of Labor refer only to West Germany.

8.2   *Productivity Growth Rates.* Productivity is defined here as GDP per worker in civilian employment. GDP data as in Table 8.1. Civilian employment (approximating U.S.

concepts) for 1960-89 are taken from U.S. Department of Labor (1994), Table 2, pp. 6-14; for 1994, U.S. Department of Labor, *Monthly Labor Review*, April 1996, Table 47, p. 41. West German figures, which end in 1992, use GDP from OECD (1994a) and employment data from U.S. Department of Labor, *Monthly Labor Review*, May 1994, p. 116.

8.3   *Annual Rate of Real Compensation Growth per Employee, Business Sector.* Nominal growth in compensation from OECD (1996a), Annex Table 12, p. A15, was deflated by changes in national consumer prices from OECD (1996a), Annex Table 16, p. A19, except for the United States, where the deflator was the CPI-U-X1. The average, which excludes the U.S., is weighted by 1989 employment from U.S. Department of Labor (1994), Table 2.

8.4   *Hourly Manufacturing Compensation Growth.* Hourly compensation in manufacturing in a national currency basis for all employees from U.S. Department of Labor (1996c), Table 7, p. 23, and hourly compensation costs in national currency for production workers in manufacturing from U.S. Department of Labor (1995a), Table 3, were deflated using national consumer price indexes derived from OECD (1996a), Annex Table 16, p. A19. Averages were weighted using 1990 manufacturing employment from OECD (1996b), p. 21. Data for West Germany for 1979-89 use OECD (1994a).

8.5   *Hourly Compensation of Production Workers in Manufacturing (Using Purchasing-Power-Parity Exchange Rates).* Hourly compensation costs in national currency for production workers in manufacturing from U.S. Department of Labor (1995a), Table 3, were converted to U.S. dollars using purchasing-power parities for GDP from OECD (1996c), Table 3, p. 158. Averages were weighted by total hours worked in manufacturing in 1989 from U.S. Department of Labor (1993a).

8.6   *Hourly Compensation of Production Workers in Manufacturing (Using Market Exchange Rates).* Hourly compensation costs in national currency for production workers in manufacturing from U.S. Department of Labor (1995a), Table 3, were converted to U.S. dollars using prevailing commercial market exchange rates from U.S. Department of Labor (1995a), Table 14. Averages were weighted by total hours worked in manufacturing in 1989 from U.S. Department of Labor (1993a).

8.7   *Per Capita Income Adjusted for Purchasing Power.* The indexed gross domestic product per head using current PPPs comes from OECD (1996c), Table 3, pp. 148-49. The averages are weighted by mid-year 1989 population from OECD (1996c), Table 1, pp. 158-59.

8.8   *Family Income Distribution: Percent of the Median.* Atkinson, Rainwater, and Smeeding (1995), Table 4.1, p. 40. Income is post-tax and post-cash-transfer.

8.9   *Income Distribution: Changes During the 1980s in Percent of the Median.* Atkinson, Rainwater, and Smeeding (1995), Table 4.5, p. 47. Income is post-tax and post-cash-transfer.

8.10   *Earnings Inequality.* OECD (1996d), Table 3.1, pp. 61-62.

8.11   *International Educational Differentials for Males During the 1980s.* Figures for West Germany are from Abraham and Houseman (1994), Table 2. Others are from OECD (1993, 171). All figures, except those for the Netherlands and West Germany, control for age or experience.

8.12　*Poverty Rates.* Smeeding (1992, 31). The poverty thresholds used are 40% of the median income in the relevant country, adjusted for family size. Income is post-tax and post-transfer and includes the value of food stamps.

8.13　*The Impact of Taxes and Transfers on International Poverty Rates.* Smeeding (1992, 33).

8.14　*Effectiveness of Tax and Transfer System.* Smeeding (1992, 34).

8.15　*Poverty Rates and Transitions out of Poverty for Families with Children.* Duncan et al. (1991), Table 1.

8.16　*Jobs Created in 10 Countries.* Civilian employment (approximating U.S. concepts) for 1960-89 taken from U.S. Department of Labor (1994), Table 2, pp. 6-14; for 1994, U.S. Department of Labor, *Monthly Labor Review*, April 1996, Table 47, p. 41.

8.17　*Contributions to Employment Growth.* Data for employment as in Table 8.15. Data on working-age population for 1960-89 from U.S. Department of Labor (1994), Table 1, p. 5, and for 1994 derived using the employment-population ratio and employment data from U.S. Department of Labor, *Monthly Labor Review*, April 1996, Table 47, p. 41. Employment-population ratio (employment as a percent of the working-age population) for 1960-89 from U.S. Department of Labor (1994), Table 5, pp. 19-21, and for 1994 from U.S. Department of Labor, *Monthly Labor Review*, Table 47, p. 41. The average, which excludes the United States, is weighted using civilian working-age population for 1989.

8.18　*Hours Worked per Employee in Manufacturing, Compared to the United States.* U.S. Department of Labor (1996c), Table 6, p. 22. Averages weighted using total hours worked in manufacturing in 1989 from U.S. Department of Labor (1993a).

8.19　*Legally Mandated Paid Vacation in European Countries.* Leete-Guy and Schor (1992, 19).

8.20　*Public Spending on Training and Placement, Direct Job Creation, and Subsidies, as Percent of GDP.* OECD (1996d), Table T, pp. 205-212. Column 1 is "Labour market training" plus "Youth measures" plus "Measures for the disabled—vocational rehabilitation"; column 2 is "Subsidized employment" plus "Measures for the disabled—work for the disabled."

8.21　*Unemployment Rates in OECD Countries.* Figures for 1973 from OECD (1994b), p. 203; for 1979-95, OECD (1996a), Appendix Table 22, p. A25. All rates are OECD standardized unemployment rates.

8.22　*Unemployment and Unemployment Compensation.* For expenditures on unemployment compensation, see notes to Table 8.19. For unemployment rates, see notes to Table 8.20.

FIGURE NOTES

CHAPTER 1

1A   *Median Family Income.* See note to Table 1.1.

1B   *Annual Growth of Median Family Income.* See note to Table 1.2.

1C   *Ratio of Family Income of Top 5% to Lowest 20%.* Ratios are of average incomes for families in each income group. Census Homepage, Historical Income Tables, Families, Table F1a.

1D   *Family Income, Average Annual Change.* Changes are for average incomes of each income group. Census Homepage, Historical Income Tables, Families, Table F1a.

1E   *Capital/Output Ratio.* Baker (1996), Table 3.

1F   *Corporate Profit Rates.* See note to Table 1.16.

1G   *Actual Average Income vs. Demographic-Constant Average Income.* See note to Table 1.17.

1H   *Working Wives' Contribution to Family Income.* Data for 1970-71 from Howard Hayghe (1993), Table 3; data for 1992 from communication with Mr. Hayghe.

1I   *Growth in Family Income by Wives' Higher Earnings.* See notes to Tables 1.22 and 1.24.

1J   *Median Family Income by Age of Householder.* See note to Table 1.3.

CHAPTER 2

2A   *Federal Tax Burden.* See note to Table 2.7.

2B   *Effective Federal Tax Rate for a Family of Four.* See note to Table 2.9.

2C   *Personal Income Tax Burden.* See note to Table 2.11.

2D   *Payroll Tax Burden.* See note to Table 2.11.

2E   *Corporate Tax Burden.* See note to Table 2.11.

2F   *Excise Tax Burden.* See note to Table 2.11.

2G   *Taxed and Untaxed Corporate Profits as a Percent of GDP.* See note to Table 2.13.

2H   *Corporate Profits Taxes.* See note to Table 2.14.

2I   *Total Tax Receipts as a Percent of GDP.* Update by original authors of Bajika and Steuerle (1991).

2J   *Federal Revenue Sources.* See note to Table 2.16.

2K   *State and Local Revenue Sources.* See note to Table 2.16.

CHAPTER 3

3A   *Growth of Hourly Wages and Compensation.* See note to Table 3.2.

3B   *Hourly Wage and Compensation Growth of Production/Nonsupervisory Workers.* See note to Table 3.4. Hourly compensation was estimated based on multiplying hourly wages by the ratio of compensation to wages for all workers in each year. The compensation/wage ratio is drawn from the *NIPA* data used in Table 3.2.

3C   *Hourly Wages for Men by Wage Percentile.* See note to Table 3.7.

3D   *Hourly Wages for Women by Wage Percentile.* See note to Table 3.8.

3E   *Share of Workers Earning Poverty-Level Wages.* See note to Table 3.10.

3F   *Share of Workers Earning Poverty-Level Wages, by Race/Ethnicity.* See note to Tables 3.11, 3.12, and 3.13.

3G   *Share of Workers in Pension Plans, by Type.* Tabulations of Form 5500 data provided by Dan Beller and Richard Hinz of the Department of Labor.

3H   *Men's Wage Inequality.* Based on ratios of wages by decile in Table 3.7.

3I   *Women's Wage Inequality.* Based on ratios of wages by decile in Table 3.8.

3J   *Productivity and Average and Median Compensation.* Average hourly productivity and compensation are for the nonfarm business sector and were provided by Larry Rosenblum at BLS. The median compensation of men and all workers is derived by multiplying the compensation/wage ratio (based on the *NIPA* data discussed in the note to Table 3.2) and the median wage series in Tables 3.6 and 3.7. All compensation series are deflated by the CPI-U-X1.

3K   *College–High School Wage Premium for Men.* Differentials estimated with controls for experience (as a quartic), region (4), marital status, and race/ethnicity, and education is specified as dummy variables for less than high school, some college, college, and advanced degree. Estimates were made on both the March and ORG CPS files. Sample selection is discussed in Appendix C. Originally presented in Mishel and Bernstein (1996).

3L   *College–High School Wage Premium for Women.* See note to Figure 3K.

3M   *Entry-Level Wages for Male and Female High School Graduates.* See note to Table 3.22.

3N   *Effect of Employment Shifts on Real Compensation Growth.* The "actual compensation" index is computed from the ECI data presented in Table 3.3. The "compensation fixed weight" index is based on the Employment Cost Index for the first quarter of every year. Both series were deflated by the CPI-U-X1.

3O   *Union Coverage.* Hirsch and Macpherson (1995), Table 1.

3P   *Real Value of the Minimum Wage.* See note to Table 3.42.

3Q   *Distribution of Minimum-Wage Gains and Income Shares, by Fifth.* Mishel, Bernstein, and Rasell (1995), Table 8.

3R   *Ratio of CEO to Average Worker Pay.* See note to Table 3.52.

3S   *College Degrees as Share of Employment.* See note to Table 3.58.

CHAPTER 4

4A   *Underemployment.* See note to Table 4.2.

4B   *Composition of Part-Time Employment.* See note to Table 4.13.

4C   *Multiple Jobholders' Share of the Workforce.* See note to Table 4.16.

4D   *Temporary and Personnel-Services Industry Employment.* See note to Table 4.21.

CHAPTER 5

5A   *Growth of Household Wealth per Adult.* See note to Table 5.1.

5B   *Distribution of Income and Wealth.* See note to Table 5.2.

5C   *Distribution of Wealth.* See note to Table 5.5.

5D   *Growth of U.S. Stock Market.* Standard and Poor's Composite Index from *ERP* (1996), Table B-91, p. 384, deflated by the CPI-UX-1.

5E   *Concentration of Stock Ownership.* See note to Table 5.10.

CHAPTER 6

6A   *Predicted vs. Actual Poverty Rates.* See note to Table 6.1.

6B   *Poverty Rates by Price Index.* Census Homepage, Historical Poverty Tables, Persons, Table 26.

6C   *Relative Poverty Rates for Children.* Rainwater and Smeeding (1995), Table 2.

6D   *Percent of Poor Persons Below 50% of Poverty Level.* See note to Table 6.7.

6E   *Expected Lifetime Births by Marital Status and Race.* See note to Table 6.23.

6F   *Demographic and Benefit Sum Trends.* Graph originally produced as Moffitt (1992), Figure 4. Updated using the following sources: Female headship rates: *P-20*, various years, Table 1; divorce rate and births to unmarried women: *Monthly Vital Statistics Report, Annual Summary of Births, Marriages, Divorces, and Deaths*, 1989-93 versions; benefit sum: Social Security Administration (1995), pp. 357, 360. Food Stamp monthly benefits per person were multiplied by the ratio of AFDC recipients per family and then deflated with the food component of the CPI-U. AFDC benefits were deflated by the CPI-U-X1.

6G   *AFDC Participation Rates.* See note to Table 6.25.

6H   *Mothers on AFDC, by Labor-Force Activity.* Spalter-Roth, Burr, Hartmann, and Shaw (1995), Figure 2.

6I   *Prime-Age Workers with Low Earnings and Full-Time/Year-Round Attachment.* Data for 1974-89 from *P-60*, No. 178, Table 3, p. 21. Data for 1994 provided by Jack McNeil of the Census Bureau.

6J   *Workers in Families with Children, with Low Earnings and Full-Time/Year-Round Attachment.* See note to Figure 6I.

6K   *Earned Income Tax Credit and Fully Phased-in Expansion (OBRA 93).* John Karl Scholz (1993).

CHAPTER 7

7A   *Median Family Income by Region.* See note to Table 7.1.

7B   *Poverty Rates by Region.* See note to Table 7.11.

7C   *Poverty Rates by Metro/Nonmetro Area.* See note to Table 7.14.

CHAPTER 8

8A   *Productivity Growth Rates.* See note to Table 8.2.

8B   *Hourly Manufacturing Compensation, Real Annual Growth.* See note to Table 8.3.

8C   *Comparative Manufacturing Hourly Compensation, Production Workers.* See notes to Tables 8.4 and 8.5.

8D   *Male Wages at Tenth Percentile, Indexed to U.S.* Freeman (1993), Exhibit 2B, p. 28.

8E   *Income Dispersion, as Measured by the Ratio of Top/Median Income to Bottom/Median Income.* See note to Table 8.8.

8F   *Wage Percentiles for Men, in Selected Industrialized Countries.* OECD (1993), Table 5.3, pp. 163-65.

8G   *Wage Percentiles for Women, in Selected Industrialized Countries.* See note for Figure 8F.

8H   *Impact of Taxes and Transfers on Child Poverty Rates.* Rainwater and Smeeding (1995), Appendix Table A-2.

8I   *Poverty Rates and Transitions out of Poverty, Families with Children.* See note to Table 8.15.

BIBLIOGRAPHY

Abraham, Katharine G., and Susan N. Houseman. 1994. "Earnings Inequality in Germany." Staff Working Paper No. 94-24. Washington, D.C.: W.E. Upjohn Institute for Employment Research.

Atkinson, Anthony, Lee Rainwater, and Timothy M. Smeeding. 1995. *Income Distribution in OECD Countries: Evidence from the Luxembourg Income Study.* Paris: Organization for Economic Cooperation and Development.

Bajika, Jon, and C. Eugene Steuerle. 1991. "Individual Income Taxation Since 1948." *National Tax Journal,* Vol. 44, No. 4, pp. 451-75.

Baker, Dean. 1996. "Trends in Corporate Profitability: Getting More for Less?" Technical Paper. Washington, D.C.: Economic Policy Institute.

Bane, Mary Jo, and David T. Ellwood. 1986. "Slipping into and out of Poverty: The Dynamics of Spells." *Journal of Human Resources*, Vol. 20, No. 1, pp. 1-23.

Bernstein, Jared. 1995. *Where's the Payoff?: The Gap Between Black Academic Progress and Economic Gains.* Washington, D.C.: Economic Policy Institute.

Blank, Rebecca M. 1991. "Why Were Poverty Rates So High in the 1980s?" National Bureau of Economic Research, Working Paper No. 3878. Cambridge, Mass.: NBER.

Blank, Rebecca M., and David Card. 1993. "Poverty, Income Distribution, and Growth: Are They Still Connected?" *Brookings Papers on Economic Activity*, No. 2. Washington, D.C.: Brookings Institution.

Bluestone, Barry M., Edith Rasell, and Lawrence Mishel. 1996. *Living Standards Chartbook.* Washington, D.C.: Economic Policy Institute, forthcoming.

Board of Governors, Federal Reserve System. 1995. *Balance Sheets for the U.S. Economy: 1945-1994.* Washington, D.C.: Federal Reserve System.

Borjas, George J. 1994. "The Economics of Immigration." *Journal of Economic Literature*, Vol. 32, No. 4, pp. 1667-1717.

Borjas, George J., Richard B. Freeman, and Lawrence F. Katz. 1991. "On the Labor Market Effects of Immigration and Trade." National Bureau of Economic Research. Working Paper No. 3761. Cambridge, Mass.: NBER.

Burtless, Gary. 1995. "Widening U.S. Income Inequality and the Growth in World Trade." Paper presented at the meeting of the Tokyo Club in Dresden, Germany, September 1995.

Cancian, Maria, Sheldon H. Danziger, and Peter Gottschalk. 1993. "Working Wives and Family Income Inequality Among Married Couples." In Sheldon H. Danziger and Peter Gottschalk, eds., *Uneven Tides: Rising Inequality in America.* New York, N.Y.: Russell Sage Foundation.

Card, David. 1991. "The Effect of Unions on the Distribution of Wages: Redistribution or Relabelling?" Working Paper No. 287. Princeton, N.J.: Department of Economics, Princeton University.

Carre, Francoise J. 1992. "Temporary Employment in the Eighties." In Virginia L. DuRivage, ed., *New Policies for the Part-Time and Contingent Workforce.* Economic Policy Institute Series. Armonk, N.Y.: M.E. Sharpe.

Center on Budget and Policy Priorities. 1996. *Poverty Tables.* Washington, D.C.: CBPP.

Citizens for Tax Justice. 1991. *A Far Cry from Fair.* Washington, D.C.: CTJ.

Congressional Budget Office. 1992. "Shares and Sources of Family Income: All Families, 1977, 1980, 1985, 1988, 1989." Unpublished.

Congressional Budget Office. 1995. *The Economic and Budget Outlook: An Update.* Washington, D.C.: CBO, August.

Day, Jennifer Cheeseman. 1996. *Population Projections of the United States by Age, Sex, Race, and Hispanic Origin: 1995 to 2050.* U.S. Bureau of the Census, Current Population Reports, P25-1130. Washington, D.C.: U.S. Government Printing Office.

Devine, Theresa J. 1994. "Characteristics of Self-Employed Women in the United States." *Monthly Labor Review*, Vol. 117, No. 3, pp. 20-34.

Dinardo, John, Nicole M. Fortin, and Thomas Lemieux. 1994. "Labor Market Institutions and the Distribution of Wages, 1973-1992: A Semiparametric Approach." Unpublished.

Dinardo, John, Nicole M. Fortin, and Thomas Lemieux. 1996. "Labor Market Institutions and Gender Differences in Wage Inequality." Paper presented at the Industrial Relations Research Association Meetings, San Francisco, January.

Duncan, Greg, et al. 1991. "Poverty and Social Assistance Dynamics in the United States, Canada and Europe." Paper presented at the Joint Center for Political and Economic Studies Conference of Poverty and Public Policy, Washington, D.C., September.

Eller, T.J., and Wallace Fraser. 1995. *Assets Ownership of Households: 1993.* U.S. Bureau of the Census, Current Population Reports, P70-47. Washington, D.C.: U.S. Government Printing Office.

Eargle, Judith. 1990. *Household Wealth and Asset Ownership: 1988.* U.S. Bureau of the Census, Current Population Reports, Series P-70, No. 22. Washington, D.C.: U.S. Government Printing Office.

Farber, Henry S. 1995. "Are Lifetime Jobs Disappearing? Job Duration in the United States: 1973-93." Working Paper No. 341, Princeton University Industrial Relations Section.

Farber, Henry S. 1996. "The Changing Face of Job Loss in the United States, 1981-1993." Working Paper No. 360, Princeton University Industrial Relations Section.

Feenstra, Robert C., and Gordon H. Hanson. 1996. "Globalization, Outsourcing, and Wage Inequality." *American Economics Association Papers and Proceedings*, Vol. 86, No. 2, pp. 240-5.

Franklin, James C. 1995. "Industry Output and Employment Projections to 2005." *Monthly Labor Review*, Vol. 118, No. 11, pp. 45-59.

Freeman, Richard B. 1991. "How Much Has De-unionization Contributed to the Rise in Male Earnings Inequality?" National Bureau of Economic Research, Working Paper No. 3826. Cambridge, Mass.: NBER.

Freeman, Richard B. 1993. *Is Globalization Impoverishing Low-Skill American Workers?* Washington, D.C.: Urban Institute.

Fullerton, Howard N., Jr. 1995. "The 2005 Labor Force: Growing, But Slowly." *Monthly Labor Review*, Vol. 118, No. 11, pp. 22-29.

Gardner, Jennifer M. 1995. "Worker Displacement: A Decade of Change." *Monthly Labor Review*, Vol. 118, No. 4, pp. 45-57.

Gottschalk, Peter. 1996. *Notes on "By Our Own Bootstraps: Economic Opportunity and the Dynamics of Income Distribution," by Cox and Alm.* Boston College. Unpublished manuscript.

Gottschalk, Peter, and Robert A. Moffitt. 1994. "Welfare Dependence: Concepts, Measures, and Trends." *The American Economic Review*, Vol. 84, No. 2, pp. 38-42.

Gottschalk, Peter, and Timothy M. Smedding. 1996. *Cross National Comparisons of Earnings and Income Inequality.* Unpublished.

Hayghe, Howard V. 1993. "Working Wives' Contributions to Family Incomes." *Monthly Labor Review*, Vol. 116, No. 8, pp. 39-43.

Hirsch, Barry T., and David A. Macpherson. 1995. *Union Membership and Earnings Data Book 1994: Compilations from the Current Population Survey.* Washington, D.C.: Bureau of National Affairs.

International Monetary Fund. Monthly. *International Financial Statistics.* Washington, D.C.: IMF.

Institute for Women's Policy Research. 1995. *Welfare That Works: The Working Lives of AFDC Recipients.* Washington, D.C.: IWPR.

Jencks, Christopher. 1991. "Is the American Underclass Growing?" In Christopher Jencks and Paul E. Peterson, eds., *The Urban Underclass.* Washington, D.C.: Brookings Institution.

Joint Economic Committee. 1992. *Families on a Treadmill: Work and Income in the 1980s.* Washington, D.C.: JEC.

Karoly, Lynn A., and Gary Burtless. 1995. "Demographic Change, Rising Earnings Inequality, and the Distribution of Personal Well-Being, 1959-89." *Demography*, Vol. 32, No. 3, pp. 379-405.

Krueger, Alan. 1996. "Labor Market Shifts and the Price Puzzle Revisited." Paper presented at the Industrial Relations Research Association Meetings, San Francisco, Calif., January.

Leete-Guy, Laura, and Juliet B. Schor. 1992. *The Great American Time Squeeze: Trends in Work and Leisure, 1969-1989*. Washington, D.C.: Economic Policy Institute.

Mishel, Lawrence, and Jared Bernstein. 1994. "Is the Technology Black Box Empty? An Empirical Examination of the Impact of Technology on Wage Inequality and the Employment Structure." Presented to the Labor Economics Workshop, Harvard University. Unpublished.

Mishel, Lawrence, and Jared Bernstein. 1996a. "Did Technology's Impact Accelerate in the 1980s?" Paper presented at the Industrial and Relations Research Association meetings, San Francisco, Calif., January.

Mishel, Lawrence, and Jared Bernstein. 1996b. "Technology and the Wage Structure: Has Technology's Impact Accelerated Since the 1920s?" Paper presented at the National Bureau of Economic Research Labor Studies Workshop, Cambridge, Mass., July.

Mishel, Lawrence, Jared Bernstein, and Edith Rasell. 1995. *Who Wins with a Higher Minimum Wage*. Briefing Paper. Washington, D.C.: Economic Policy Institute.

Mishel, Lawrence, and Ruy Teixeira. 1991. *The Myth of the Coming Labor Shortage: Jobs, Skills, and Incomes of America's Workforce 2000*. Washington, D.C.: Economic Policy Institute.

Moffit, Robert. 1992. "Incentive Effects of the U.S. Welfare System: A Review." *Journal of Economic Literature*, Vol. 30, No. 1, pp. 1-61.

Murphy, Kevin, and Finis Welch.1989. "Recent Trends in Real Wages: Evidence from Household Data." Paper prepared for the Health Care Financing Administration of the U.S. Department of Health and Human Services. Chicago, Ill.: University of Chicago.

National Research Council. 1995. *Measuring Poverty: A New Approach*. Washington, D.C.: National Research Council.

Nichols, Marion, and Isaac Shapiro. 1995. *Unemployment Insurance Protection in 1994*. Washington, D.C.: Center on Budget and Policy Priorities.

OECD. 1991. *Employment Outlook*. Paris: Organization for Economic Cooperation and Development.

OECD. 1993. *Employment Outlook*. Paris: OECD.

OECD. 1994a. *National Accounts, Main Aggregates Volume 1, 1960-92*. Paris: OECD.

OECD. 1994b. *Employment Outlook*. Paris: OECD.

OECD. 1995. *Revenue Statistics of OECD Member Countries, 1965-1993, 1995*. Paris: OECD.

OECD. 1996a. *Economic Outlook*, Paris: OECD.

OECD. 1996b. *Main Economic Indicators*. Paris: OECD.

OECD. 1996c. *National Accounts, Main Aggregates Volume 1, 1960-94*. Paris: OECD.

OECD. 1996d. *Employment Outlook*. Paris: OECD.

Poterba, James M., and Andrew A. Samwick. 1995. "Stock Ownership Patterns, Stock Market Fluctuations, and Consumption." *Brookings Papers on Economic Activity, 1995:2*. Washington, D.C.: Brookings Institution.

President of the United States. Annual. *Economic Report of the President.* Washington, D.C.: U.S. Government Printing Office.

Rainwater, Lee, and Timothy M. Smeeding. 1995. "Doing Poorly: The Real Income of American Children in a Comparative Perspective." Working Paper No. 127. Syracuse, N.Y.: Maxwell School of Citizenship and Public Affairs, Syracuse University.

Rose, Stephen J. 1995. "Declining Job Security and the Professionalization of Opportunity." Research Report No. 95-04. Washington, D.C.: National Commission for Employment Policy.

Ruggles, Patricia. 1990. *Drawing the Line: Alternative Poverty Measures and Their Implications for Public Policy.* Washington, D.C.: Urban Institute.

Sachs, Jeffrey D., and Howard J. Shatz. 1994. "Trade and Jobs in U.S. Manufacturing." *Brookings Papers on Economic Activity, 1994:1.* Washington, D.C.: Brookings Institution.

Saeger, Steven S. 1995. "Trade and Deindustrialization: Myth and Reality in the OECD." Harvard University. Unpublished.

Saunders, Norman C. 1995. "The U.S. Economy to 2005." *Monthly Labor Review*, Vol. 118, No. 11, pp. 10-28.

Schmitt, John, and Lawrence Mishel. 1996. "Did International Trade Lower Less-Skilled Wages During the 1980s? Standard Trade Theory and Evidence." Technical Paper. Washington, D.C.: Economic Policy Institute.

Scholz, John Karl. 1993. "Tax Policy and the Working Poor: The Earned Income Tax Credit." *Focus*, Vol. 15, No. 3, pp. 1-38.

Sekscenski, Edward S. 1980. "Women's Share of Moonlighting Nearly Doubles During 1969-79." *Monthly Labor Review*, Vol. 103, No. 5.

Shapiro, Isaac. 1987. *No Escape: The Minimum Wage and Poverty.* Washington, D.C.: Center on Budget and Policy Priorities.

Silvestri, George. 1995. "Occupational Employment to 2005." *Monthly Labor Review*, Vol. 118, No. 11.

Silvestri, George, and John Lukasiewicz. 1991. "Occupational Employment Projections." *Monthly Labor Review*, Vol. 114, No. 11.

Smeeding, Timothy M. 1992. "Why the U.S. Antipoverty System Doesn't Work Very Well." *Challenge*, January/February, pp. 30-35.

Social Security Administration, Office of Research and Statistics. 1995. *Annual Statistical Supplement, 1995.* Washington, D.C.: SSA.

Spalter-Roth, Roberta, Beverly Burr, Heidi Hartmann, and Lois Shaw. 1995. *Welfare That Works: The Working Lives of AFDC Recipients.* Washington, D.C.: Institute for Women's Policy Research.

Stevens, Ann Huff. 1993. *The Dynamics of Poverty Spells, 1970-1987: Updating Bane and Ellwood.* Ann Arbor, Mich.: University of Michigan.

Stevens, Ann Huff. 1995. "Climbing out of Poverty, Falling Back in: Measuring the Persistence of Poverty over Multiple Spells." National Bureau of Economic Research, Working Paper No. 5309. Cambridge, Mass.: NBER.

Stinson, John F., Jr. 1986. "Moonlighting by Women Jumped to Record Highs." *Monthly Labor Review*, Vol. 109, No. 11.

Sum, Andrew, Neal Fogg, and Neeta Fogg. 1994. *The Economic Well-Being of U.S. Families with Children: An Assessment of Recent Trends, an Exploration of Their Underlying Determinants, and Public Policy Implications.* Boston, Mass.: Northeastern University, Center for Labor Market Studies.

Towers, Perrin and Company. 1995. Worldwide Total Remuneration, 1995.

U.S. Department of Commerce, Bureau of the Census. Current Population Reports. Various dates. *Marital Status and Living Arrangements.* P-20 Series. Washington D.C.: U.S. Government Printing Office.

U.S. Department of Commerce, Bureau of the Census. Current Population Reports. Various dates. P-60 Series. Washington, D.C.: U.S. Government Printing Office.

U.S. Department of Commerce, Bureau of the Census. Current Population Reports. 1990. *Trends in Income, by Selected Characteristics: 1947 to 1988.* P60 Series, No. 167. Washington, D.C.: U.S. Government Printing Office.

U.S. Department of Commerce, Bureau of the Census. Current Population Reports. 1991. *Trends in Relative Income: 1964 to 1989.* P-60 Series, No. 177. Washington, D.C.: U.S. Government Printing Office.

U.S. Department of Commerce, Bureau of the Census. Current Population Reports. 1992. *Studies in the Distribution of Income.* Series P-60, No. 183. Washington, D.C.: U.S. Government Printing Office.

U.S. Department of Commerce, Bureau of the Census. Current Population Reports. 1995. *Household and Family Characteristics.* P20 Series. Washington, D.C.: U.S. Government Printing Office.

U.S. Department of Commerce, Bureau of the Census, Current Population Reports. 1996. *Income, Poverty, and Valuation of Noncash Benefits: 1994.* P60-189 Series. Washington, D.C.: U.S. Government Printing Office.

U.S. Department of Education, National Center for Education Statistics. 1991. *Digest of Education Statistics, 1991.* Washington, D.C.: U.S. Government Printing Office.

U.S. Department of Education, National Center for Education Statistics. 1996. *Projections of Education Statistics to 2006.* Washington, D.C.: U.S. Government Printing Office.

U.S. Department of Health and Human Services, Office of the Assistant Secretary for Planning and Evaluation. 1996. *Trends in the Well-Being of America's Children and Youth: 1996.* Washington, D.C.: U.S. Government Printing Office.

U.S. Department of Health and Human Services, Public Health Service, Centers for Disease Control and Prevention, National Center for Health Statistics. 1994. *Monthly Vital Statistics Report*, Vol. 43, No. 5, Supplement.

U.S. Department of Health and Human Services, Public Health Service, Centers for Disease Control and Prevention, National Center for Health Statistics. 1995. *Monthly Vital Statistics Report*, Vol. 44, No. 3, Supplement.

U.S. Department of Labor. Bureau of Labor Statistics. 1988. *Labor Force Statistics Derived from the Current Population Survey, 1948-87*. Washington, D.C.: U.S. Government Printing Office.

U.S. Department of Labor. Bureau of Labor Statistics. 1989. *Multiple Jobholding Reached Record High in May 1989*. No. 89-529. Washington, D.C.: U.S. Government Printing Office.

U.S. Department of Labor. Bureau of Labor Statistics. 1993a. *Underlying Data for Indexes of Ouput per Hour, Hourly Compensation, and Unit Labor Costs in Manufacturing, Twelve Industrial Countries 1950-92 and Labor Costs in Korea and Taiwan, 1970-92, 1993*. Washington, D.C.: U.S. Government Printing Office.

U.S. Department of Labor. Bureau of Labor Statistics. 1993b. *Labor Composition and U.S. Productivity Growth, 1948-90*. Washington, D.C.: U.S. Government Printing Office.

U.S. Department of Labor. Bureau of Labor Statistics. 1994. *Comparative Labor Force Statistics, Ten Countries 1959-93*. Washington, D.C.: U.S. Government Printing Office.

U.S. Department of Labor. Bureau of Labor Statistics. 1995a. *International Comparisons of Hourly Compensation Costs for Production Workers in Manufacturing 1975-94, Supplementary Tables for BLS Report 893 June 1995*. Washington, D.C.: U.S. Government Printing Office.

U.S. Department of Labor. Bureau of Labor Statistics. 1995b. *Contingent and Alternative Employment Arrangements, Report 900*. Washington, D.C.: U.S. Government Printing Office.

U.S. Department of Labor. 1995c. *Monthly Labor Review*. Washington, D.C.: Bureau of Labor Statistics.

U.S. Department of Labor. Bureau of Labor Statistics. 1995d. *International Comparisons of Manufacturing Productivity and Unit Labor Cost Trends, 1994*. Washington, D.C.: U.S. Government Printing Office.

U.S. Department of Labor. 1995e. *Report on the American Workforce*. Washington, D.C.: U.S. Government Printing Office.

U.S. Department of Labor. Bureau of Labor Statistics. 1996a. *Multifactor Productivity Trends, 1994: Private Business, Private Nonfarm Business, and Manufacturing*. Washington, D.C.: U.S. Government Printing Office.

U.S. Department of Labor. Bureau of Labor Statistics. 1996b. *Productivity and Costs: First Quarter 1996*. Washington, D.C.: U.S. Government Printing Office.

U.S. Department of Labor. Bureau of Labor Statistics. 1996c. *International Comparisons of Manufacturing Productivity and Unit Labor Cost Trends, 1995*. Washington, D.C.: U.S. Government Printing Office.

U.S. Department of Labor. Pension and Welfare Benefits Administration. 1994. *Pension and Health Benefits of American Workers: New Findings from the April 1993 Current Population Survey*. Washington, D.C.: U.S. Government Printing Office.

U.S. Department of the Treasury, Office of Tax Analysis. 1995. *Average and Marginal Federal Income, Social Security, and Medicare Tax Rates for Four-Person Families at the Same Relative Positions in the Income Distribution, 1955-95.* Washington, D.C.: U.S. Government Printing Office.

U.S. House of Representatives. 1993. *Green Book: Background Material and Data on Programs Within the Jurisdiction of the Committee on Ways and Means.* Washington, D.C.: U.S. Government Printing Office.

U.S. House of Representatives, Committee on Ways and Means, Subcommittee on Human Resources. 1991. *Background Material on Family Income and Benefit Changes.* Washington, D.C.: U.S. Government Printing Office.

Wells, Tom, and Gary Sandefur. 1996. "Trends in AFDC Participation, 1976-1992." Paper presented at the 1996 annual meeting of the Population Association of America, Madison, Wis., University of Wisconsin, May.

Wolff, Edward N. 1992. "Changing Inequality of Wealth." Paper presented at the American Economic Association Meetings, Boston, Mass., January.

Wolff, Edward N. 1993. *The Rich Get Increasingly Richer: Latest Data on Household Wealth During the 1980s.* Briefing Paper. Washington, D.C.: Economic Policy Institute.

Wolff, Edward N. 1994. "Trends in Household Wealth in the United States, 1962-1983 and 1983-1989." *Review of Income and Wealth,* Series 40, No. 2.

Wolff, Edward N. 1996. "Trends in Household Wealth During 1989-1992." Paper submitted to the Department of Labor. New York, N.Y.: New York University.

World Bank. 1994. *World Population Projections 1994-95.* Washington, D.C.: World Bank.

EPI Publications

BOOKS

RISKY BUSINESS:
Private Management of Public Schools
by Craig E. Richards, Rima Shore, &
Max B. Sawicky
0-944826-68-7 (paper) $19.95

RECLAIMING PROSPERITY:
A Blueprint for Progressive
Economic Reform
edited by Todd Schafer & Jeff Faux
Preface by Lester Thurow
1-56324-769-0 (paper) $19.95
1-56324-768-2 (cloth) $62.50

THE STATE OF WORKING AMERICA
1994-95
by Lawrence Mishel & Jared Bernstein
1-56324-533-7 (paper) $24.95
1-56324-532-9 (cloth) $55.00

TRADE POLICY AND GLOBAL GROWTH:
New Directions in
the International Economy
edited by Robert A. Blecker
1-56324-531-1 (paper) $22.95
1-56324-530-2 (cloth) $52.50

BEYOND THE TWIN DEFICITS:
A Trade Strategy for the 1990s
by Robert Blecker
1-56324-091-2 (paper) $22.95
1-56324-090-4 (cloth) $51.95

SCHOOL CHOICE:
Examining the Evidence
edited by Edith Rasell &
Richard Rothstein
0-944826-57-1 (paper) $17.95

TRANSFORMING THE U.S. FINANCIAL
SYSTEM: Equity and Efficiency
for the 21st Century
edited by Gary Dymski,
Gerald Epstein, & Robert Pollin
1-56324-269-9 (paper) $25.95
1-56324-268-0 (cloth) $62.95

BEWARE THE U.S. MODEL:
Jobs & Income in a Global Economy
edited by Lawrence Mishel &
John Schmitt
0-944826-58-X (paper) $24.95

THE NEW AMERICAN WORKPLACE:
Transforming Work Systems
in the United States
by Eileen Appelbaum & Rosemary Batt
0-87332-828-0 (paper) $18.95
0-87332-827-2 (cloth) $45.00

NEW POLICIES FOR THE PART-TIME
AND CONTINGENT WORKFORCE
edited by Virginia L. duRivage
1-56324-165-X (paper) $22.95
1-56324-164-1 (cloth) $51.95

UNIONS AND ECONOMIC
COMPETITIVENESS
edited by Lawrence Mishel &
Paula B. Voos
0-87332-828-0 (paper) $20.95
0-87332-827-2 (cloth) $46.95

STUDIES, BRIEFING PAPERS, & WORKING PAPERS

BACK TO INVESTMENT: A Proposal to Create a Capital Investment Fund
by Jeff Faux, Dean Baker, & Todd Schafer
February '94 (9 pages, $5)

JOBS AND THE ENVIRONMENT:
The Myth of a National Trade-Off
by Eban Goodstein
January '95 (44 pages, $12)

PAYING THE TOLL: Economic Deregulation of the Trucking Industry
by Michael Belzer
April '94 (84 pages, $12)

LOST IN FINDINGS: A Critique of the Interim Report of the Bipartisan Commission on Entitlements and Tax Reform
by Max Sawicky
November '94 (13 pages, $5)

PAYING FOR HEALTH CARE: Affordability and Equity in Health Care Reform
by Edith Rasell & Kainan Tang
February '95 (54 pages, $10)

LEAD-BASED PAINT ABATEMENT IN PRIVATE HOMES:
A Study of Policies and Costs
by Meg Koppel & Ross Koppel
August '94 (38 pages, $5)

TRADE & COMPETITIVENESS

JOBS ON THE WING: Trading Away the Future of the U.S. Aerospace Industry
by Randy Barber & Robert E. Scott
August '95 (96 pages, $12)

NEW PRIORITIES IN FINANCING LATIN AMERICAN DEVELOPMENT:
Balancing Worker Rights, Democracy, and Financial Reform
by Jerome Levinson
June '94 (64 pages, $12)

FALSE PROPHETS:
The Selling of NAFTA
by Thea Lee
July '95 (20 pages, $5)

POLITICS & PUBLIC OPINION

THE POLITICS OF THE HIGH-WAGE PATH:
The Challenge Facing Democrats
by Ruy Teixeira
November '94 (25 pages, $10)

ECONOMIC NATIONALISM AND THE FUTURE OF AMERICAN POLITICS
by Ruy Teixeira & Guy Molyneux
October '93 (40 pages, $12)

HOW TO ORDER

All orders for EPI publications should be addressed to:

EPI Publications
1660 L Street, NW, Suite 1200
Washington, D.C. 20036

Or call: (800) EPI-4844/(202) 331-5510 • Fax: (202) 775-0819.

EPI will send a complete catalog of all publications.
Discounts are available to libraries and bookstores and for quantity sales.

About EPI

THE ECONOMIC POLICY INSTITUTE was founded in 1986 to widen the debate about policies to achieve healthy economic growth, prosperity, and opportunity in the difficult new era America has entered.

Today, America's economy is threatened by stagnant growth and increasing inequality. Expanding global competition, changes in the nature of work, and rapid technological advances are altering economic reality. Yet many of our policies, attitudes, and institutions are based on assumptions that no longer reflect real world conditions.

Central to the Economic Policy Institute's search for solutions is the exploration of policies that encourage every segment of the American economy (business, labor, government, universities, voluntary organizations, etc.) to work cooperatively to raise productivity and living standards for all Americans. Such an undertaking involves a challenge to conventional views of market behavior and a revival of a cooperative relationship between the public and private sectors.

With the support of leaders from labor, business, and the foundation world, the Institute has sponsored research and public discussion of a wide variety of topics: trade and fiscal policies; trends in wages, incomes, and prices; the causes of the productivity slowdown; labor-market problems; rural and urban policies; inflation; state-level economic development strategies; comparative international economic performance; and studies of the overall health of the U.S. manufacturing sector and of specific key industries.

The Institute works with a growing network of innovative economists and other social science researchers in universities and research centers all over the country who are willing to go beyond the conventional wisdom in considering strategies for public policy.

Founding scholars of the Institute include Jeff Faux, EPI president; Lester Thurow, Sloan School of Management, MIT; Ray Marshall, former U.S. secretary of labor, professor at the LBJ School of Public Affairs, University of Texas; Barry Bluestone, University of Massachusetts-Boston; Robert Reich, U.S. secretary of labor; and Robert Kuttner, author, editor of *The American Prospect,* and columnist for *Business Week* and the Washington Post Writers Group.

For additional information about the Institute, contact EPI at 1660 L Street, NW, Suite 1200, Washington, DC 20036, (202) 775-8810.

About the Authors

LAWRENCE MISHEL is the research director of the Economic Policy Institute. He is the co-author of the previous versions of *The State of Working America,* as well as *The Myth of the Coming Labor Shortage* (with Ruy Teixeira) and *Manufacturing Numbers,* and the editor (with Paula Voos) of *Unions and Economic Competitiveness.* He holds a Ph.D. in economics from the University of Wisconsin, and his articles have appeared in a variety of academic and nonacademic journals. His areas of research are labor economics, wage and income distribution, industrial relations, productivity growth, and the economics of education. In some circles he is known as the coach of the red team in the Takoma Park Babe Ruth Baseball League.

JARED BERNSTEIN is a labor economist with the Economic Policy Institute. He is the co-author, with Lawrence Mishel, of two previous editions of *The State of Working America.* He specializes in the analysis of wage and income inequality, with an emphasis on low-wage labor markets and poverty, and his articles have appeared in popular and academic journals. Between 1995 and 1996, he held the post of deputy chief economist at the U.S. Department of Labor, where, among other topics, he worked on the initiative to raise the minimum wage. He rejoined EPI in February 1996. Mr. Bernstein holds a Ph.D. in social welfare from Columbia University.

JOHN SCHMITT is a labor economist with the Economic Policy Institute. His areas of research include wage inequality, unemployment, and economic development. His recent publications include "The Changing Structure of Male Earnings in Britain, 1974-88," in Richard Freeman and Lawrence Katz (eds.) *Differences and Changes in Wage Structures* (University of Chicago Press, 1995) and *Beware the U.S. Model: Jobs and Wages in a Deregulated Economy*, which he edited with Lawrence Mishel. Mr. Schmitt has an A.B. from the Woodrow Wilson School of Public and International Affairs at Princeton University and an M.Sc. and Ph.D. in economics from the London School of Economics.